Revolutionary Patriots

of

Prince George's County

Maryland

1775-1783

Henry C. Peden, Jr.

HERITAGE BOOKS
2006

HERITAGE BOOKS
AN IMPRINT OF HERITAGE BOOKS, INC.

Books, CDs, and more—Worldwide

For our listing of thousands of titles see our website at
www.HeritageBooks.com

Published 2006 by
HERITAGE BOOKS, INC.
Publishing Division
65 East Main Street
Westminster, Maryland 21157-5026

Copyright © 1997 Henry C. Peden, Jr.

All rights reserved. No part of this book may be reproduced or transmitted in any form or by any means, electronic or mechanical, including photocopying, recording or by any information storage and retrieval system without written permission from the author, except for the inclusion of brief quotations in a review.

International Standard Book Number: 978-1-58549-431-3

INTRODUCTION

This book has been compiled for the purpose of serving as a research tool for locating the men and women of Prince George's County, Maryland, who served in the military, rendered material aid to the army or navy, took the Oath of Allegiance and Fidelity, served in an office or on a committee at the town, county or state level, or in some fashion contributed and supported the fight for freedom by the American colonies from the rule of Great Britain during the Revolutionary War, 1775-1783.

It is hoped that this book, which is the ninth in a series on Revolutionary War patriots and soldiers in Maryland, will encourage and enable interested persons to become members of such patriotic organizations as The Sons of the American Revolution, The Daughters of the American Revolution, The Sons of the Revolution, and The Society of the Cincinnati.

Information for this book has been gleaned from many primary and secondary sources, which makes this book far more than just a listing of names and ranks. Most of the approximately 4,000 persons named herein have genealogical data included with their respective entries, such as places of residence and dates of birth, death, and marriage, names of wives, husbands, children and other relatives, plus physical descriptions, occupations, and information gleaned from military, pension, probate, and other court records, including the census of 1776.

Each entry in this book has been documented and a key to that documentation has been implemented within the text to enable the reader to review the cited source. A letter followed by a number is the code used for a source and the page within that source. For example, [Ref: D-555] indicates that the information can be found in Reference D, page 555, which is *Archives of Maryland, Volume 18*. Coded sources cited in this book are as follows:

A = *Archives of Maryland, Volume XI*. "Journal of the Maryland Convention, July 26, 1775 - August 14, 1775, and Journal and Correspondence of the Maryland Council of Safety, August 29, 1775 -July 6, 1776" (Baltimore: Maryland Historical Society, 1892)

B = *Archives of Maryland, Volume XII*. "Journal and Correspondence of the Maryland Council of Safety, July 7, 1776 - December 31, 1776" (Baltimore: Maryland Historical Society, 1893)

C = *Archives of Maryland, Volume XVI*. "Journal and Correspondence of the Council of Safety, January 1, 1777 - March 20, 1777" and "Journal and Correspondence of the State Council, March 20, 1777 - March 28, 1778" (Baltimore: Maryland Historical Society, 1897)

D = *Archives of Maryland, Volume XVIII*. "Muster Rolls and Other Records of Service of Maryland Troops in the American Revolution, 1775-1783" (Baltimore: Maryland Historical Society, 1900)

E = *Archives of Maryland, Volume XXI*. "Journal and Correspondence of the Council of Maryland, April 1, 1778 - October 26, 1779" (Baltimore: Maryland Historical Society, 1901)

F = *Archives of Maryland, Volume XLIII*. "Journal and Correspondence of the State Council of Maryland, 1779-1780" (Baltimore: Maryland Historical Society, 1924)

G = *Archives of Maryland, Volume XLV*. "Journal and Correspondence of the State Council of Maryland, 1780-1781" (Baltimore: Maryland Historical Society, 1927)

H = *Archives of Maryland, Volume XLVII*. "Journal and Correspondence of the State Council of Maryland, 1781" (Baltimore: Maryland Historical Society, 1930)

I = *Archives of Maryland, Vol. XLVIII*. "Journal and Correspondence of the State Council of Maryland, 1781-1784" (Baltimore: Maryland Historical Society, 1931)

J = "Some Little Known Data Regarding Maryland Signers of the Oath of Fidelity," by Richard B. Miller, *Maryland Genealogical Society Bulletin*, Volume 27, No. 1 (Winter, 1986), pp. 101-124

K = *Revolutionary War Military Collection, Manuscript MS.1814* (Baltimore: Maryland Historical Society, Manuscript Division)

L = *Maryland State Archives MdHR19970* (Original muster rolls of the Lower Battalion of Militia in Prince George's County, 1781-1782)

M = Clements, S. Eugene and Wright, F. Edward. *The Maryland Militia in the Revolutionary War* (Silver Spring, Maryland: Family Line Publications, 1987)

N = Hodges, Margaret. *Unpublished Revolutionary Records of Maryland, Volume 2* (Baltimore: Privately compiled circa 1941)

O = Brumbaugh, Gaius M. *Maryland Records: Colonial, Revolutionary, County and Church From Original Sources, Volume II* (Baltimore: Genealogical Publishing Compnay, Inc., 1985, reprint)

P = White, Virgil D. *Genealogical Abstracts of Revolutionary War Pension Files* (Waynesboro, Tennessee: The National Historical Publishing Company, 1990, 4 volumes)

Q = Papenfuse, Edward, et al. *An Inventory of Maryland State Papers, Volume I,* "The Era of the American Revolution, 1775-1789" (Annapolis: Hall of Records Commission, 1977)

R = Brumbaugh, Gaius M. *Maryland Records: Colonial, Revolutionary, County and Church From Original Sources, Volume I* (Baltimore: Genealogical Publishing Company, Inc., 1985, reprint)

S = *Maryland State Archives MdHR6636* (Original records and muster rolls of the Select Militia of Prince George's County in 1781)

T = *Maryland Pension Rolls of 1835: Report from the Secretary of War in Relation to the Pension Establishment of the United States* (Baltimore: Genealogical Publishing Company, Inc., 1968, reprint)

U = Papenfuse, Edward, et al. *A Biographical Dictionary of the Maryland Legislature, 1635-1789* (Baltimore: Johns Hopkins Press, 1979)

V = *National Genealogical Society Quarterly* (as cited herein)

W = *Maryland State Archives MdHR4648* (Original lists of signers of the Oath of Allegiance and Fidelity to the State of Maryland in 1778 in Prince George's County)

X = *DAR Patriot Index* (Washington, D. C.: National Society of the Daughters of the American Revolution, Centennial Edition, 1994)

Y = Sargent, Jean A., ed. *Stones and Bones: Cemetery Records of Prince George's County, Maryland* (Bowie, Maryland: Prince George's County Genealogical Society, Inc., 1988 reprint)

Z = *Maryland State Archives MdHR5781* (Original records of the Prince George's County Court, Liber EE, No. 2, 1777-1782)

ZA = Bowie, Effie Gwynn. *Across the Years in Prince George's County* (Baltimore: Genealogical Publishing Company, 1975 reprint)

ZB = Brown, Helen W. *Index to Marriage Licenses, Prince George's County, Maryland, 1777-1886* (Baltimore: Genealogical Publishing Company, 1973 reprint)

ZC = Brown, Helen W. *Prince George's County, Maryland, Indexes of Church Registers, Volume 1* - Protestant Episcopal Church - St. Paul's Parish and Prince George's Parish (Westminster, Maryland: Family Line Publications, 1988 reprint)

ZD = Brown, Helen W. *Prince George's County, Maryland, Indexes of Church Registers, Volume 2* - Protestant Episcopal Church - King George's Parish and Queen Anne's Parish (Westminster, Maryland: Family Line Publications, 1988 reprint)

ZE = *Index to the Probate Records of Prince George's County, Maryland, 1696-1900* (Bowie, Maryland: Compiled by the Records Committee, Prince George's County Genealogical Society, 1988)

With respect to two of the above mentioned references, the following must be pointed out. The Oaths of Fidelity in Brumbaugh's Volume II for the most part are photocopies of the originals, but there are some lists therein that are typewritten. These lists were compared with the originals at the Maryland State Archives and, unfortunately, the lists for the returns of Fielder Bowie, Thomas Gantt and Osborn Sprigg are replete with spelling errors (and some omissions). The mistakes have been corrected herein. Also, militia lists for Prince George's County are woefully lacking and only a couple of lists were published in Clements and Wright's book. Some additional lists of the militia in 1781 and 1782 were found in the Maryland State Archives and have been included herein.

It must be noted that it is not possible to know who all of the patriots were who served in or from Prince George's County during the entire Revolutionary War. This is especially true for those who joined the Maryland Line and served in the Continental Army. Due to the constant reorganization of the Maryland troops during the war, it is not easily determinable which soldier served from which county. It is apparent, however, that men from Prince George's County served in every regiment, especially the 1st, 2nd, 3rd, and 6th Maryland Continental Lines.

It should also be mentioned that soldiers who served in the Maryland Line under a captain from Prince George's County may not have themselves been from Prince George's County. Therefore, if it was not known if a soldier was from Prince George's County, it was thought best to err by inclusion rather than omission. Such may be the case if the soldier served under Capt. Horatio Clagett, Capt. Henry Hill, Capt. Patrick Sim, and Capt. Alexander Truman. These captains recruited soldiers in and around Prince George's County. Additional research may be necessary before drawing conclusions.

As may be the case in works such as this, it is possible that some patriots may have been inadvertently omitted. Therefore, one should check the many lists found in the *Archives of Maryland, Volume 18*, for perhaps even more names of soldiers from Prince George's County.

Henry C. Peden, Jr.
Bel Air, Maryland
March 1, 1997

Prince George's County

Dennis Griffith, *Map of the State of Maryland*, 1794

REVOLUTIONARY PATRIOTS OF
PRINCE GEORGE'S COUNTY, MARYLAND
1775-1783

ACTON, Burgis. See "Smallwood Acton," q.v.

ACTON, Henry (1732 -   ). Took the Oath of Allegiance before the Hon. Thomas Clagett in 1778 [Ref: O-265]. Henry Acton married Hester Smallwood [Ref: X-9].

ACTON, Henry Jr. (1755 - July 10, 1842). Private, Maryland Line, enrolled by Ensign Horatio Clagett on July 15, 1776 [Ref: R-15, D-35, which latter source mistakenly spelled the name "Aeton"]. He applied for and received a pension (S2337) in Belmont County, Ohio on Nov. 5, 1832, aged 77, stating he enlisted in the Maryland Line in Prince George's County [Ref: P-8, R-15, X-9]. "Henry Acton 3rd" took the Oath of Allegiance (made his "I" mark with an equidistant horizontal line through the middle) before the Hon. Thomas Clagett in 1778 [Ref: O-265].

ACTON, Nancy. See "Smallwood Acton," q.v.

ACTON, Smallwood (Sep. 14, 1758, Maryland - Mar. 25, 1844, Clark County, Kentucky). Private, enrolled by Ensign Horatio Clagett on July 15, 1776, for continental service, Maryland Line, for six months, serving under Capt. John Lowe. In August, 1777, he was drafted into the militia of Prince George's County and was later mustered into the Maryland Line. He joined Gen. Washington's Army a few days after the Battle of Brandywine and was wounded in the leg by a gunshot at the Battle of Germantown [Ref: D-35, which mistakenly listed his name as "Smallwood Aeton"]. He took the Oath of Allegiance (made his "X" mark) before the Hon. Thomas Clagett in 1778 [Ref: O-265, R-15]. Smallwood Acton applied for a pension on May 26, 1834, aged 75, in Clark County, Kentucky, stating he was born in Prince George's County, Maryland in 1758 and moved to Kentucky about 33 or 34 years ago. He married (1) Mary Wilson and (2) Nancy Cave on Dec. 16, 1823, by Rev. Josiah Cornelius, which was proven by a county court record provided by Burgis Acton and Pleasant Martin. Smallwood Acton died on Mar. 25, 1844 and his widow Nancy applied for pension (W26658) on Nov. 9, 1855, aged 81, through her agent James Flanagan, as she was not able to travel the eight miles to the Winchester Court House [Ref: P-8, X-9, and Annie Walker Burns' *Maryland Soldiers of the Revolutionary War Who Settled in Kentucky*, page 26].

ADAMS, Alexander (Feb. 18, 1760 -   ). Son of Benjamin and Sarah Adams, of Prince George's Parish in Prince George's County [Ref: ZD-109]. He enrolled as a private in the Upper District of Frederick County on July 22, 1776 [Ref: D-49].

ADAMS, Benjamin. See "Alexander Adams," q.v.

ADAMS, Elizabeth. See "George Naylor," q.v.

ADAMS, George. Took the Oath of Allegiance before the Hon. Osborn Sprigg in 1778 [Ref: O-308, W-4648 (Box 4, folder 29)]. Rendered service to the State on Sep. 5, 1781, when the Council of Maryland directed that he deliver money from the State Treasurer to the Commissaries of Prince George's and Montgomery Counties [Ref: G-602]. Sergeant, Militia, Capt. Jesse Hellen's Company; guarded Magruder's Warehouse in the spring of 1782 [Ref: L-19970 (Box 6, folder 21)]. George Adams married Mary Wright by license dated Jan. 21, 1783 [Ref: ZB-1]. One George Adams died by May 7, 1794 [Ref: ZE-1].

ADAMS, James (Nov. 2, 1741 - died after 1800). Private, 2nd Maryland Line, Capt. Patrick Sim's Company, 1776 [Ref: D-7]. Private, Capt. Hezekiah Wheeler's Company, 11th Militia Battalion, April, 1781 [Ref: L-19970 (Box 6, folder 21), R-3]. Took the Oath of Allegiance before the Hon. William Lyles, Jr. in 1778 [Ref: O-290, which spelled his name "Addams"]. James Adams married Jane Brinam [Ref: X-14].

ADAMS, John. Took the Oath of Allegiance before the Hon. Joshua Beall in 1778 [Ref: O-251]. Private, 1st Maryland Line, who was paid for his services "in cloathing" on Apr. 17, 1779 [Ref: E-351]. One John Adams died by Nov. 30, 1824 [Ref: ZE-1].

ADAMS, Joseph (1721-   ). Took the Oath of Allegiance (made his "X" mark) before the Hon. Thomas Clagett in 1778 [Ref: O-266, R-81].

ADAMS, Josephus. Private, Capt. Alexander H. Magruder's Militia Company, Lower Battalion; on duty guarding Magruder's Warehouse in the spring of 1782 [Ref: L-19970 (Box 6, folder 21)]. He married Elizabeth Watson by license dated Oct. 24, 1777 [Ref: ZB-1].

ADAMS, Luke. Took the Oath of Allegiance before the Hon. Thomas Gantt, Jr. in 1778 [Ref: O-305, W-4648 (Box 4, folder 15), and R-48, which spelled his name "Luke Addams"]. The records of the Council of Maryland on Aug. 22, 1781, include a letter from the County Lieutenant as follows: "This will be delivered to you by Luke Adams, one of the drafts from the last Class, he and another married man were drafted in the same Class, they drew for the chance of going, the lot fell on Adams who was marryed this Spring, has a crop on hand which he must loose if he goes out, which must be a great prejudice to him, though he has at present no children to maintain; He has been in the service and finding it prejuditial to his health imployed another man to take his place, he had been lately sick and now complains of a pain in his hip which he says renders him incapable of marching, he has been of some use to me, having imployed him to ride after some of those men who did not appear and particularly in taking one Nacey Smith a black fellow who deserted from Marlbro. He now goes up with one Wise who keept out of the way. If this shuld not be thought a sufficient excuse, and your Excellency and Honorables think proper to keep him in service, I could wish him to return again to assist in catching some of those men who keep out of the way, as he is well acquainted in the different parts of the county, and prety active when in health." [Ref: H-437].

ADAMS, Richard (1756-   ). Took the Oath of Allegiance before the Hon. Osborn Sprigg in 1778 [Ref: R-78, O-307, which latter source spelled his name "Richard Addams"].

ADAMS, Robert. Took the Oath of Allegiance before the Hon. Benjamin Hall in 1778 [Ref: O-275, which listed the name as "Robert Adam"].

ADAMS, Sarah. See "Alexander Adams," q.v.

ADAMS, Thomas Jr. Private, Militia, 1776 [Ref: M-207, A-325]. Took the Oath of Allegiance before the Hon. Joshua Beall in 1778 [Ref: O-251]. One Thomas Adams was aged 49 and another Thomas Adams was aged 24 in the 1776 census of Prince George's County [Ref: R-70].

ADAMS, Thomas Kelso. Took the Oath of Allegiance before the Hon. Joshua Beall in 1778 [Ref: O-251].

ADAMS, William. Lieutenant, 4th Maryland Line, Capt. Bowie's Company, Dec. 10, 1776 to Aug., 1778 (resigned). [Ref: D-80]. Took the Oath of Allegiance before the Hon. William Lyles, Jr. in 1778 [Ref: O-289, which spelled his name "William Addams"].

ADAMS, William. Private, Capt. Hezekiah Wheeler's Company, 11th Militia Battalion, April, 1781 [Ref: L-19970 (Box 6, folder 21)].

ADAMSON, Rebecca. See "Richard Beall," q.v.

ADDISON, Ann. See "Addison Murdock" and "John Murdock," q.v.

ADDISON, Elizabeth. See "Thomas Clagett," q.v.

ADDISON, John (1742 or 1751 - 1817). Took the Oath of Allegiance before the Hon. George Lee in 1778 [Ref: O-279]. Captain, Mar. 15, 1776 (resigned on Aug. 7, 1776). Lieutenant Colonel, Middle Battalion, May 1, 1778. Colonel, Nov. 13, 1779 [Ref: M-47, A-252, B-185, E-63, F-13, N-35, D-333]. John Addison married Mrs. Lucy (Belt) Watkins [Ref: X-21, R-43]. See "Thomas Walls," q.v.

ADDISON, Rebecca. See "Thomas Hanson," q.v.

ALBEE, John. "John Albee" took the Oath of Allegiance (made his "X" mark) before the Hon. James Mullikin in 1778 [Ref: O-296]. "John Albey" was a private in the 1st Maryland Line, 1780-1781, and a private in the 7th Maryland Line, 1783 [Ref: D-357, D-444, D-494]. "John Olbee" married Susannah Tarman by license dated June 30, 1786 [Ref: ZB-163].

ALDER, Elizabeth Latimore. See "George Alder," q.v.

ALDER, George (c1757, Maryland - Aug. 28, 1824, Loudoun County, Virginia). Private, Maryland Line. Took the Oath of Allegiance before the Hon. Thomas Clagett in 1778 [Ref: O-267]. He applied for pension on Apr. 25, 1818 in Jefferson County, Virginia (resident of Loudoun County, Virginia) stating that he had enlisted in the Maryland Line and married Lucy Ann Wynn (born Sep. 26, 1762) on Nov. 17, 1778. Their marriage license was dated Oct. 31, 1778 [Ref: ZB-2]. Lucy Ann Alder applied for and received a pension (W20580) on Oct. 26, 1839, in

Loudoun County, Virginia, stating George had died on Aug. 28, 1824. Her parents were John (died Oct. 13, 1782) and Sarah (died May 22, 1777) Wynn. George and Lucy's children were: James Alder (born Aug. 14, 1779), John Wynn Alder (born Sep. 20, 1781), James Latimore Alder (born May 16, 1783), Sary Roby Alder (born Jan. 23, 1785, died Aug. 23, 1802), George Hawkins Alder (born June 22, 1789), Elizabeth Latimore Alder (born Feb. 6, 1793), Mary Hawkins Alder (born Nov. 9, 1795), Nancy Hawkins Alder (born Oct. 28, 1800), Sary Roby Alder (born Mar. 2, 1804), and Marcus Alder (born Nov. --, 1807). Lucy Ann's sisters were also mentioned: Priscillah Ann Wynn (born Apr. 16, 1764) and Eleanor Ann Wynn (born Nov. 13, 1767). [Ref: P-24].

ALDER, George Hawkins. See "George Alder," q.v.

ALDER, James L. (Feb. 13, 1760 - died by Sep. 21, 1852). Private, Select Militia, Capt. Hezekiah Wheeler's Company, July 14, 1781 [Ref: S-6636 (Box 31, folder 5)]. He applied for and received pension S8022 in Prince George's County on Oct. 8, 1832, aged 72, stating he served in the Maryland Line. He was still living there in 1843 [Ref: P-24, T-50, but he is not listed in *Maryland Archives, Volume 18*]. One James Alder married Rebecca Atchison in Prince George's County by license dated Jan. 6, 1790 [Ref: ZB-2]. The estate of "James L. Allder" was probated on Sep. 21, 1852 in Prince George's County [Ref: ZE-2].

ALDER, James. See "George Alder," q.v.

ALDER, John. See "George Alder," q.v.

ALDER, Joanna. See "Philip Ryon," q.v.

ALDER, Marcus. See "George Alder," q.v.

ALDER, Mary. See "George Alder," q.v.

ALDER, Nancy. See "George Alder," q.v.

ALDER, Sary. See "George Alder," q.v.

ALDRIDGE, Jacob (1741-1815). Took the Oath of Allegiance before the Hon. James Beck in 1778 [Ref: O-255, R-49]. Private (drafted), in continental service, Maryland Line, 1781 [Ref: D-382]. The estate of one Jacob Aldridge was probated on Mar. 1, 1815 [Ref: ZE-2].

ALEXANDER, Mary. See "Electious Thompson," q.v.

ALEXANDER, Rachel. See "William Hayes," q.v.

ALLBRIGHT, William (1748, Germany -   ). Private, enlisted June 12, 1781, for 3 years in continental service, Maryland Line; on duty July 13, 1781 [Ref: D-382].

ALLBY, William. Took the Oath of Allegiance before the Hon. Osborn Sprigg in 1778 [Ref: O-307].

ALLCOCK, Martin. Private, 4th Maryland Line, Capt. Burgess' Company, from December, 1776 until reported missing on Aug. 16, 1780 (at the Battle of Camden). [Ref: D-80].

ALLEIN, William. Served on the Board of Patuxent Associators and signed a resolution at Nottingham on Apr. 21, 1781 relative to the defence of the rivers of Potomac and Patuxent and the completion of the fort at Drum Point [Ref: K-1814].

ALLEN, Ann. See "Haswell Magruder," q.v.

ALLEN, Austin. Rendered patriotic service by providing wheat for the military on Apr. 12, 1783 [Ref: Q-593]. Took the Oath of Allegiance before the Hon. David Craufurd in 1778 [Ref: O-272]. The estate of Austin Allen was probated in Prince George's County on Dec. 20, 1804 [Ref: ZE-3].

ALLEN, Barna. Private, 1st Maryland Line, enlisted on Dec. 10, 1776, and was taken prisoner on Aug. 16, 1780 at the Battle of Camden [Ref: D-78]. The estate of "Barna Allen (soldier)" was probated in Prince George's County on Mar. 4, 1793 [Ref: ZE-3].

ALLEN, Gilbert. Private, 5th Maryland Line, enlisted on Aug. 20, 1777, and was taken prisoner on Aug. 16, 1780 at the Battle of Camden [Ref: D-182]. The estate of "Gilbert Allen (soldier)" was probated in Prince George's County on Mar. 4, 1793 [Ref: ZE-3].

ALLEN, John. In the County Court in August, 1778, he took the Oath of Allegiance at the same time he took the oath to be a practicing attorney at law in Prince George's County [Ref: Z-94].

ALLEN, Joseph. Took the Oath of Allegiance before the Hon. Thomas Boyd in 1778 [Ref: O-261]. He was paid thirty shillings by the State Treasurer (for services rendered) on May 13, 1782, by order of the Council of Maryland [Ref: I-164]. Sergeant in the Northern Detachment, 3rd Maryland Line, Capt. Horatio Clagett's Company, 1782-1783 [Ref: D-465, D-501]. He rendered patriotic service by providing wheat for the military on Apr. 29, 1783 [Ref: Q-594]. The estate of "Joseph Allen (soldier)" was probated in Prince George's County on Mar. 6, 1793. There was another Joseph Allen who died testate by Nov. 10, 1800 [Ref: ZE-3]. Additional research may be necessary before drawing conclusions as to which one rendered patriotic service, i. e., took the oath in 1778, rendered services in 1782, and supplied wheat in 1783.

ALLEN, Susannah. See "John Downs Lanham," q.v.

ALLEN, William. Took the Oath of Allegiance before the Hon. James Mullikin in 1778 [Ref: O-296].

ALLISON, Barbery. See "James Allison" and "Thomas Allison," q.v.

ALLISON, Charles. See "Thomas Allison" and "James Allison," q.v.

ALLISON, James (Mar. 30, 1747 -   ). Son of Charles and Barbery Allison, of Prince George's Parish [Ref: ZD-109]. Lieutenant, 3rd Maryland Line, 1777-1778 [Ref: D-79].

ALLISON, Thomas (Oct. 17, 1745 -   ). Son of Charles and Barbery Allison, of Prince George's Parish [Ref: ZD-109]. Private, 1st Maryland Line, enlisted Dec. 10, 1776, and taken prisoner on Aug. 16, 1780, at the Battle of Camden [Ref: D-78, I-22].

ALLMAN, William. Private, Maryland Line; defective in July, 1780 [Ref: D-414].

ALLNUTT, Ernest C. Jr. See "Benjamin Wailes" and "Edward Lloyd Wailes" and "Levin C. Wailes" and "Samuel Perrie Wailes," q.v.
ALSEY, William. Private (substitute), Maryland Line, discharged on Dec. 3, 1781 [Ref: I-10].
AMBLER, Elizabeth. See "Thomas Peirce," q.v.
AMBLER, Joseph. "Joseph Ambler" was a private in Capt. Benjamin Wailes' Militia Company, Lower Battalion, and on duty guarding Magruder's Warehouse in the spring of 1782 [Ref: L-19970 (Box 6, folder 21)]. One "Josephus Amblen" married Elizabeth Pearce by license dated Oct. 16, 1787 [Ref: ZB-2].
AMBLER, Thomas. Took the Oath of Allegiance (made his "T" mark) before the Hon. Alexander Howard Magruder in 1778 [Ref: O-293].
AMIR, William. Took the Oath of Allegiance before the Hon. Christopher Lowndes in 1778 [Ref: O-287].
ANDERSON, John (1737, Scotland -   ). Private, enlisted June 9, 1781, for 3 years in continental service, Maryland Line; on duty July 13, 1781 [Ref: D-382].
ANDERSON, John. Private, 3rd Maryland Line, enlisted Feb. 25, 1777. Private, Capt. Horatio Clagett's Company, 1779 [Ref: D-295].
ANDERSON, William (1754-1810). Private, enrolled in the Flying Camp by Lieut. Benjamin Brooks on July 8, 1776; aged 22; nativity: Prince George's County; height 5' 10"; has own gun [Ref: D-36]. The estate of one William Anderson was probated in Prince George's County on Apr. 10, 1810 [Ref: ZE-3].
ARDERY, Mrs. William Breckenridge. See "Samuel Luckett," q.v.
ARMAND, Marquis de la Rouerie. See "Basil Lowe" and "Dennis Lowe," q.v.
ARMSTRONG, John 1st. Private, 2nd Maryland Line, Capt. Alexander Truman's Company, 1782 [Ref: D-440].
ARMSTRONG, John Jr. Private, enlisted Feb. 19, 1780, for 3 years or during war, in continental service, Maryland Line [Ref: D-333].
ARMSTRONG, John Sr. Private, enlisted Jan. 31, 1780, for 3 years or during war, in continental service, Maryland Line [Ref: D-333].
ARNOLD, Christopher (1726-1818). Took the Oath of Allegiance before the Hon. Osborn Sprigg in 1778 [Ref: O-307, R-83]. The estate of one Christopher Arnold was probated in Prince George's County on Feb. 27, 1818 [Ref: ZE-4].
ARVIN, Elias. Private, Capt. Richard Stonestreet's Militia Company, 11th Battalion, June, 1782 [Ref: L-19970 (Box 6, folder 21)].
ASHFORD, Ally. See "Hezekiah Speaks," q.v.
ASHFORD, Michael. See "Hezekiah Speaks," q.v.
ASHTON, John. Took the Oath of Allegiance before the Hon. Thomas Clagett in 1778 [Ref: O-267].
ATCHERSON, Mildred. See "Thomas Jenkins," q.v.

ATCHESON, Edward. Took the Oath of Allegiance in 1780 [Ref: J-104]. "Edward Atchinson" was a private (draft), continental service, Maryland Line, 1781 [Ref: D-382]. See "Edward Utcherson," q.v.

ATCHESON, James. Took the Oath of Allegiance in 1780 [Ref: J-104]. See "James Utcherson," q.v.

ATCHISON, Jeremiah (1758-   ). Private, enrolled in the Flying Camp by Capt. Robert Bowie on July 27, 1776; nativity: Prince George's County; height 5' 8"; has own gun [Ref: D-36].

ATCHISON, Rebecca. See "James L. Alder," q.v.

ATCHISON, William. Took the Oath of Allegiance (made his mark that resembled a large "O" with a small "v" connected to the top) before the Hon. Thomas Clagett in 1778 [Ref: O-269].

ATHEY, Ebenezer. Took the Oath of Allegiance (made his "X" mark) before the Hon. Thomas Clagett in 1778 [Ref: O-268]. Private, enrolled by Lt. William Duvall, Lower Battalion, on July 18, 1776, for continental service, Maryland Line [Ref: D-35, which spelled his name "Ebenezar Athy"]. Private, 1st Maryland Line, who was paid for his service "in cloathing" on Apr. 15, 1779 [Ref: E-347, which spelled his name "Ebenezer Athy"].

ATHEY, Ebesworth. Private, Capt. Hezekiah Wheeler's Company, 11th Militia Battalion, April, 1781 [Ref: L-19970 (Box 6, folder 21)].

ATHEY, Elijah (June 2, 1755, Maryland - December, 1838, Ohio). Son of Elijah and Mary Athey [Ref: ZC-2]. Private, Select Militia, Capt. Hezekiah Wheeler's Company, July 14, 1781 [Ref: S-6636 (Box 31, folder 5)]. Private, Capt. Hezekiah Wheeler's Company, 11th Militia Battalion, April, 1781 [Ref: L-19970 (Box 6, folder 21)]. Elijah Athey married Mary Jane Green [Ref: X-89].

ATHEY, Henry. Private, Capt. Hezekiah Wheeler's Company, 11th Militia Battalion, April, 1781 [Ref: L-19970 (Box 6, folder 21)].

ATHEY, Hezekiah (1738-   ). Took the Oath of Allegiance (made his "X" mark) before the Hon. Thomas Clagett in 1778 [Ref: O-268, R-58]. Private, Capt. Hezekiah Wheeler's Company, 11th Militia Battalion, April, 1781 [Ref: L-19970 (Box 6, folder 21)].

ATHEY, Mary. See "Elijah Athey," q.v.

ATHEY, Owen (1736-   ). Took the Oath of Allegiance before the Hon. William Berry in 1778 [Ref: O-259, R-82].

ATHEY, Wilson. Took the Oath of Allegiance before the Hon. Christopher Lowndes in 1778 [Ref: O-287, which spelled his name "Wilson Athy"].

ATKIN, Thomas. Took the Oath of Allegiance before the Hon. Osborn Sprigg in 1778 [Ref: O-306].

ATTWOOD, Anne. See "George Digges" and "William Digges," q.v.

ATWELL, John. Took the Oath of Allegiance before the Hon. Benjamin Hall in 1778 [Ref: O-274].

AUBER, John (1745, England -   ). Private (substitute), 1780, in continental service [Ref: D-338]. Drum Major, 2nd Maryland Line, Capt. Murdock's Company, Mar. 15, 1781 [Ref: D-366].
AUSTIN, Eleanor. See "Batson Naylor," q.v.
AUSTIN, Jonas. Took the Oath of Allegiance before the Hon. Truman Skinner in 1778 [Ref: O-297]. The estate of "Jonas Auston" was probated on Nov. 18, 1794 [Ref: ZE-4].
AUSTIN, Richard (Apr. 18, 1756, Maryland - died after Sep., 1832, Bedford County, Virginia). He applied for and received pension S6513 in Bedford County, Virginia on Sep. 24, 1832, aged 76, stating he was born in Prince George's County, Maryland and enlisted there and served in the Maryland Line. About 1788 he moved to Bedford County, Virginia [Ref: P-95].
AUSTIN, Sarah. See "Jacob Wheeler," q.v.
AVERY, Robert (1752, England -   ). Private (substitute), 1780, continental service, in the Maryland line [Ref: D-338].
AYERS, Frederick (died Aug. 16, 1780). Private, 6th Maryland Line, enlisted on May 19, 1778, and was killed at the Battle of Camden (South Carolina) on Aug. 16, 1780 [Ref: D-183]. The estate of "Frederick Ayers (soldier)" was probated in Prince George's County on Nov. 28, 1792 [Ref: ZE-4].
BADEN, Benjamin. Ensign, Capt. Alexander H. Magruder's Company, Lower Battalion, July 4, 1780 [Ref: M-49, F-210]. Took the Oath of Allegiance before the Hon. Fielder Bowie in 1778 [Ref: O-303, W-4648 (Box 4, folder 15)].
BADEN, Eliza. See "Robert Baden," q.v.
BADEN, Elizabeth. See "George Walls" and "John Marlow," q.v.
BADEN, Jeremiah. Private, enrolled by Capt. Alexander H. Magruder, 11th Battalion, on July 3, 1776, for continental service, Maryland Line [Ref: D-38]. Took the Oath of Allegiance before the Hon. Fielder Bowie in 1778 [Ref: O-303, W-4648 (Box 4, folder 15)]. Private, Select Militia, Capt. Hezekiah Wheeler's Company, July 14, 1781 [Ref: S-6636 (Box 31, folder 5)].
BADEN, John. Private, Capt. Alexander H. Magruder's Militia Company, Lower Battalion; on duty guarding Magruder's Warehouse in the spring of 1782 [Ref: L-19970 (Box 6, folder 21)]. One John Baden married Willimina M. Maulden by license dated Jan. 12, 1782 [Ref: ZB-7]. The estate of one "John Baden" was probated by Aug. 13, 1805, and the estate of "John T. Baden" was probated on Jan. 1, 1814 [Ref: ZE-5]. See "George Walls," q.v.
BADEN, John Sr. Took the Oath of Allegiance before the Hon. Fielder Bowie in 1778 [Ref: O-303, W-4648 (Box 4, folder 15)]. The estate of "John Baden, Sr." was probated on Oct. 25, 1824 [Ref: ZE-5].
BADEN, John, of Thomas. Took the Oath of Allegiance before the Hon. Fielder Bowie in 1778 [Ref: O-304, W-4648 (Box 4, folder 15)]. The

estate of "John Baden, of Thomas" was probated on June 11, 1805 [Ref: ZE-5].
BADEN, John T. See "John Baden," q.v.
BADEN, Martha. See "Joshua Naylor," q.v.
BADEN, Robert. Private, enrolled by Capt. Alexander H. Magruder, 11th Battalion, on July 3, 1776, for continental service, Maryland Line [Ref: D-38]. Second Lieutenant, Capt. Robert Bowie's Company, Lower Battalion, Sep. 1, 1777. First Lieutenant, May 1, 1778, 11th Battalion. First Lieutenant, Capt. John Beanes' Company, 11th Battalion, May 24, 1779 [Ref: M-49, C-356, E-62, E-414, N-33]. Took the Oath of Allegiance before the Hon. Fielder Bowie in 1778 [Ref: O-303, W-4648 (Box 4, folder 15)]. One "Robert Baden, Jr." married Frances Gover by license dated Nov. 10, 1779 [Ref: ZB-7]. The estate of "Robert Baden" was probated on Jan. 13, 1817 by Eliza Baden (inventory dated Apr. 2, 1817). [Ref: ZE-5].
BADEN, Thomas. Private, enrolled by Ensign Alexander Truman on July 3, 1776, continental service, Maryland Line [Ref: D-38]. Ensign, Capt. Alexander H. Magruder's Company, May 1, 1778, 11th (Lower) Battalion, and Second Lieutenant, July 3, 1780 [Ref: M-49, E-62, F-210, N-33]. The estate of one Thomas Baden was probated in Prince George's County on Dec. 6, 1825 [Ref: ZE-5].
BAGBY, Nancy Elizabeth. See "Alexander Truman," q.v.
BAGGERLY, Nancy. See "Nathan Walker," q.v.
BAILEY, Jemima. See "John Bailey" and "Robert Bailey," q.v.
BAILEY, John (Apr. 24, 1753 -   ). Son of John and Jemima "Baley" of Prince George's Parish [Ref: ZD-109]. Lieutenant, 3rd Maryland Line, 1777; resigned Nov. 18, 1779 [Ref: D-85]. See "Robert Bailey," q.v.
BAILEY, Robert (Dec. 26, 1751 -   ). Son of John and Jemima "Baley" of Prince George's Parish [Ref: ZD-109]. Private, 1st Maryland Line, enlisted June 2, 1777, and reportedly "deserted" on Aug. 3, 1780 [Ref: D-81].
BALDWIN, Catherine. See "Robert Simmons," q.v.
BALDWIN, James (Jan. 15, 1721/2 -   ). Son of James and Mary Baldwin, of Queen Anne's Parish [Ref: ZC-163]. Took the Oath of Allegiance before the Hon. James Beck in 1778 [Ref: O-254].
BALDWIN, John (May 1, 1717 - 1784). Son of James and Mary Baldwin, of Queen Anne's Parish [Ref: ZC-163]. Took the Oath of Allegiance before the Hon. James Beck in 1778 [Ref: O-253]. The estate of one John Baldwin was probated on Aug. 28, 1784 [Ref: ZE-5]. Another John Baldwin took the Oath of Allegiance before the Hon. Benjamin Hall in 1778 [Ref: O-274]. The estate of another John Baldwin was probated on Mar. 22, 1791 [Ref: ZE-5]. Additional research may be necessary before drawing conclusions on these two John Baldwins.
BALDWIN, Mary. See "James Baldwin" and "John Baldwin," q.v.

BALDWIN, Samuel (1758 - died after Apr. 1, 1851). Private in the Maryland Line until discharged on Dec. 3, 1781 [Ref: D-406, I-10]. He applied for and received a pension (S8044) in Anne Arundel County, Maryland on Mar. 4, 1834, aged 76, stating he had lived in Prince George's County at the time of his enlistment in the Maryland Line [Ref: P-133]. His first wife's name is not known, but his second wife was Nancy ----. [Ref: X-134].

BALDWIN, Thomas. Took the Oath of Allegiance before the Hon. Thomas Williams in 1778 [Ref: O-302]. The estate of one Thomas Baldwin was probated on Jan. 16, 1804 [Ref: ZE-6].

BALDWIN, Thomas Jr. Took the Oath of Allegiance (made his mark that looked like an "8" and "H" joined together side by side) before the Hon. James Beck in 1778 [Ref: O-253]. The estate of one Thomas Baldwin was probated on Jan. 16, 1804 and the estate of another Thomas Baldwin was probated on Nov. 2, 1847 [Ref: ZE-6]. Additional research may be necessary before drawing conclusions.

BALDWIN, Tyler. Took the Oath of Allegiance (made his "X" mark) before the Hon. James Beck in 1778 [Ref: O-253]. Tyler Baldwin married Tomsey Davidge [Ref: X-134, which source stated he was born circa 1755 and died in 1795]. However, the estate of one Tyler Baldwin was probated before Mar. 3, 1781, and the estate of another Tyler Baldwin was probated on Apr. 21, 1790 [Ref: ZE-6]. Additional research will be necessary before drawing conclusions.

BALDWIN, William J. Private, 6th Maryland Line, enlisted Feb. 5, 1778. Reported missing on Aug. 16, 1780 after the Battle of Camden (South Carolina), but returned to duty and was promoted to sergeant and subsequently to Sergeant Major on Feb. 5, 1779 [Ref: D-187]. The estate of a "William J. (or I.) Baldwin" was probated in Prince George's County on Mar. 22, 1794 [Ref: ZE-6].

BALEY, John. See "John Bailey," q.v.

BALL, Eleanor. See "Richard Ball," q.v.

BALL, Elizabeth. See "Francis Wheat," q.v.

BALL, James (1751, Prince George's County, Maryland - May 8, 1834, Allen County, Indiana). Private, enrolled by Lt. John M. Burgess, Lower Battalion, on July 20, 1776, for continental service, Maryland Line [Ref: D-35]. He applied for and received pension S32107 in Allen County, Indiana, on Oct. 10, 1832, aged 81, stating he was born in the lower part of Maryland and had enlisted in the Maryland Line at Frederickstown, Maryland; sergeant. He settled in Indiana in 1830. He married Rachel Hinton and mentioned a son (not named) who was a clergyman by 1832 [Ref: P-135, X-136].

BALL, Richard. Served on a Grand Jury in 1777 [Ref: Z-29]. Richard Ball married Eleanor --- [Ref: X-137, which source stated he was born circa 1725 and died on Feb. 21, 1807]. However, the estate of one Richard Ball was probated in Prince George's County on Oct. 16, 1775 (and

Richard Ball was the administrator) and the estate of another Richard Ball was probated on Feb. 17, 1792. There is no listing of a Richard Ball in Prince George's County probate records in 1807 [Ref: ZE-6]. Therefore, additional research will be necessary before drawing any conclusions.

BALLARD, John (1758, Montgomery County, Maryland -   ). "John Ballard" was a private who enlisted on Mar. 15, 1780, for 3 years or during war, in continental service, Maryland Line [Ref: D-333]. "John Ballett" married Joanna Gloyd by license dated Nov. 29, 1782, in Prince George's County [Ref: ZB-9].

BARKER, Abram. Private, 2nd Maryland Line, Capt. Murdock's Company, Mar. 15, 1781 [Ref: D-366].

BARKER, Susannah. See "Uriah Vermillion," q.v.

BARKLEY, Henry. Took the Oath of Allegiance before the Hon. William Berry in 1778 [Ref: O-259].

BARNES, Elizabeth. See "Henry Barnes," q.v.

BARNES, Henry (baptized Mar. 7, 1762, Maryland - died 1818, South Carolina). A son of Henry and Elizabeth Barnes [Ref: ZC-4], he married Ann Roby Lanham by license dated Feb. 3, 1790 [Ref: ZB-9]. Private, Maryland Line, 1782 [Ref: X-157, D-421, D-467].

BARNES, Henry (Jan. 18, 1753 - 1793). Son of Richard and Mary Barnes [Ref: ZC-4]. Took the Oath of Allegiance (made his "X" mark) before the Hon. Thomas Clagett in 1778 [Ref: O-266]. The estate of one Henry Barnes was probated in Prince George's County on Apr. 2, 1793 [Ref: ZE-7].

BARNES, Mary. See "James Wilson" and "Henry Barnes," q.v.

BARNES, Richard. See "Henry Barnes," q.v.

BARNETT, Isaac. Private, enrolled by Capt. Alexander H. Magruder, 11th Battalion, on July 9, 1776, for continental service, Maryland Line [Ref: D-38]. The estate of one Isaac Barnett was probated by July 19, 1777 (date inventory filed). [Ref: ZE-7].

BARNITT, Michael. Private, 2nd Maryland Line, Capt. Patrick Sim's Company, 1776 [Ref: D-8].

BARNFIELD, John. Took the Oath of Allegiance before the Hon. Benjamin Hall in 1778 [Ref: O-276].

BARREN, Mary. See "Daniel Barron," q.v.

BARRETT, Ann. See "William Mullikin, Jr.," q.v.

BARRON, Daniel. Private who enlisted in the Maryland Line from Charles County on July 8, 1776 [Ref: D-32]. The estate of one "Daniel Barren" was probated in Prince George's County by July 24, 1810 (date of inventory filed by Mary Barren). [Ref: ZE-7].

BARRON, Rebecca. See "Benjamin Burch," q.v.

BARTLY, Elizabeth. See "Zadock Riston," q.v.

BASSETT, Richard. Took the Oath of Allegiance before the Hon. Osborn Sprigg in 1778 [Ref: O-306].

BATT, Dorcas. See "William Turner," q.v.
BATT, Margaret. See "Moses Batt," q.v.
BATT, Moses. Took the Oath of Allegiance (made his "X" mark) before the Hon. James Beck in 1778 [Ref: O-253]. The estate of Moses Batt was probated by July 5, 1785 (date of inventory filed by Margaret Batt) in Prince George's County [Ref: ZE-8].
BATTERMAN, George. Private, 1st Maryland Line, who was paid for his services "in cloathing" on Apr. 17, 1779 [Ref: E-351].
BAXTER, John. Private, Northern Detachment, 3rd Maryland Line, Capt. Horatio Clagett's Company, 1783 [Ref: D-501].
BAXTER, Thomas. Private, Northern Detachment, 3rd Maryland Line, Capt. Horatio Clagett's Company, 1783; discharged Sep. 24, 1783 [Ref: D-502].
BAYNE, Amelia. See "Daniel Hurley," q.v.
BAYNE, Colmore. See "William Bayne" and "Colmore Beanes," q.v.
BAYNE, Ebsworth (1719 - died before Nov. 26, 1793). "Ebsworth Bean" was aged 57 in 1776 [Ref: R-68]. "Hebsworth Bayne" took the Oath of Allegiance before the Hon. George Lee in 1778 [Ref: O-279]. One "Ebsworth Bayne" (1767 - Feb. 4, 1846) and wife Mary (1775 - Aug. 31, 1831), among others, are buried in the Bayne Family Cemetery and Monument near Apple Grove Elementary School (2604 Kingsway Road), Oxon Hill, Prince George's County, Maryland [Ref: Y-555]. Ebsworth Bayne married Susannah ---- [Ref: X-192]. The estate of Ebsworth Bayne was probated on Nov. 26, 1793 [Ref: ZE-8, which mistakenly indexed his name as "Elsworth"].
BAYNE, Eleanor. See "William Bayne," q.v.
BAYNE, Elizabeth. See "William Bayne," q.v.
BAYNE, Josias. Private, enrolled by Capt. John H. Lowe on July 13, 1776, for continental service, Maryland Line [Ref: D-34]. "Josias Bean" was aged 33 and "Josiah Bayne" was aged 31 in 1776 [Ref: R-68, R-83].
BAYNE, Martha. See "William Bayne," q.v.
BAYNE, Mary. See "Ebsworth Bayne," q.v.
BAYNE, Prescella. See "John Masters," q.v.
BAYNE, Samuel Hawkins (1748-   ). Took the Oath of Allegiance before the Hon. George Lee in 1778 [Ref: O-279, R-9]. Captain, Middle Battalion, Sep. 1, 1777 [Ref: M-51, M-52, C-356, which listed his name as "Samuel Hawkins Bayne" and "Samuel Hawkins Baynes" and "Samuel H. Beanes"]. See "Thomas Bayne," q.v.
BAYNE, Susannah. See "Ebsworth Bayne," q.v.
BAYNE, Thomas (1728-c1792). Took the Oath of Allegiance before the Hon. Thomas Clagett in 1778 [Ref: O-265, R-9]. The estate of one Thomas Bayne was probated by Apr. 5, 1792 (date of account filed by Samuel H. Bayne). [Ref: ZE-8]. See "Thomas Bean," q.v.

BAYNE, Walter (Sep. 2, 1750 -   ). Private, enrolled by Capt. John H. Lowe on July 13, 1776, for continental service, Maryland Line [Ref: D-34, ZC-5].

BAYNE, William (1729-1826). Took the Oath of Allegiance before the Hon. George Lee in 1778 [Ref: O-279, R-44]. A monument was erected in the Bayne Cemetery in Apple Grove (at 2604 Kingsway Road) by his descendant Henrietta Dawson (Ayers) Sheppard (Mrs. Harper Donelson) who was Honorary Vice President General DAR, 1943-1960. William was a lieutenant in Capt. Samuel Hawkins Bayne's Company in the Lower Battalion of Militia in Prince George's County, which was called out during the alarm caused by Lord Dunmore's fleet coming up the Potomac River in July, 1776. He married Mary Fenley on Nov. 4, 1753, and they had these children: William Bayne, Rev. Colmore S. Bayne, Elizabeth Bayne, Martha Hawkins Bayne, and Eleanor Bayne [Ref: Y-556, Y-613, X-192, ZC-5]. The estate of "William Bayne, Jr." was probated on Jan. 17, 1826, and the estate of "William Bayne, Sr." was probated on Nov. 11, 1826 [Ref: ZE-8]. Additional research may be necessary before drawing conclusions. See "William Beanes" and "William Beans," q.v.

BAYNES, John (Mar. 23, 1726 - 1790). A son of Daniel and Mary Baynes, "John Baynes Sr." rendered civil service and married Mary Noble on Aug. 20, 1749 [Ref: X-192, R-38, ZC-6]. The estate of one "John Bayne" was probated on Aug. 9, 1790 [Ref: ZE-8].

BAYNES, John Jr. (1752-1813). "John Baynes, Jr." took the Oath of Allegiance in 1780 [Ref: J-105]. "John Baynes" married Catherine Beall by license dated Nov. 2, 1784 [Ref: ZB-11]. The estate of one "John Bayne" was probated on Feb. 9, 1813 [Ref: ZE-8].

BAYNES, Joseph Noble (1751-1805). Took the Oath of Allegiance in 1780 [Ref: J-105, R-38]. The estate of "Joseph N. Baynes" was probated on Feb. 23, 1805 [Ref: ZE-8].

BEALL, Aaron. Private, Select Militia, Upper Battalion, June 12, 1781 [Ref: S-6636 (Box 27, folder 82B)]. He participated in the capture of an enemy boat and crew on Apr. 17, 1781 [Ref: M-209].

BEALL, Agnes. See "Shadrach Beall," q.v.

BEALL, Ann. See "John Igleheart," q.v.

BEALL, Alexander Jr. Captain, Militia, 1776. He was elected to be the company captain over William Hamilton [Ref: M-207, A-325].

BEALL, Amelia. See "Joshua Beall" and "Rezin Beall," q.v.

BEALL, Andrew (1721-c1781). Took the Oath of Allegiance before the Hon. Christopher Lowndes in 1778 [Ref: O-283, R-21]. On Mar. 10, 1778, the Maryland Council "ordered that the Sheriff of Prince George's County pay to Andrew Beall two hundred and forty dollars on account of the Recruiting Service." [Ref: C-532]. Captain of a militia company in 1778 [Ref: C-554]. Served on a Grand Jury in 1777 [Ref: Z-23]. Andrew Beall, Sr. married Margaret Beall [Ref: X-195]. The estate of Andrew

Beall was probated on Aug. 20, 1781 [Ref: ZE-9]. See "Joseph Jenkins," q.v.

BEALL, Andrew Jr. "Andrew Beall, Jr." took the Oath of Allegiance before the Hon. James Beck in 1778 [Ref: O-254]. "Andrew Beall" married Mary Beall by license dated Nov. 9, 1782 [Ref: ZB-13]. The estate of one Andrew Beall was probated on Oct. 20, 1804, and the estate of another Andrew Beall was probated on Oct. 5, 1844, in Prince George's County [Ref: ZE-9].

BEALL, Ann. See "Thomas Wilson" and "Josias Beall," q.v.

BEALL, Anna. See "Josias Beall," q.v.

BEALL, Anney. See "Levin Covington Beall," q.v.

BEALL, Ariana. See "Basil Beall," q.v.

BEALL, Basil. Took the Oath of Allegiance before the Hon. David Craufurd in 1778 [Ref: O-271]. Served on a Grand Jury in 1778 [Ref: Z-52]. Reference X-195 lists three men with the name Basil Beall: (1) Basil Beall (1725-1818) married Harriet ----, was a lieutenant in Maryland, and died in Virginia; (2) Basil Beall (1754-1824) married Anne Jourdan, rendered patriotic service in Maryland, and died in Washington, DC; and (3) Basil Beall (1751-c1819) married Ariana ----, rendered civil service in Maryland and also died in Maryland [Ref: X-195]. There appears to be some confusion between the latter two men because both were listed as being born on Mar. 19th (one in 1751 and one in 1754). It is therefore possible that they were one and the same person. The estate of one Basil Beall was probated on Sep. 8, 1792 and the estate of another Basil Beall was probated on May 19, 1795, in Prince George's County, Maryland [Ref: ZE-9]. Additional research will be necessary before drawing conclusions.

BEALL, Benjamin. See "Josias Beall," q.v.

BEALL, Cassandra. See "Henry Hilleary, Sr.," q.v.

BEALL, Catherine. See "John Baynes, Jr.," q.v.

BEALL, Charity. See "Haswell Magruder," q.v.

BEALL, Charles (c1750 - December, 1789). Private, Maryland Line. Charles Beall married Tabitha Beall [Ref: X-195].

BEALL, Christopher (1753 - July 17, 1831). Private, Maryland Line, who was reported to be "a deserter from 2nd Maryland Regiment, June 15th, 1778" [Ref: D-328]. On June 22, 1778, the County Lieutenant was informed by the Maryland Council that "we have sent Mr. Gordon after him and request you to give him any necessary assistance." [Ref: E-146]. He apparently served faithfully thereafter because he applied for and received pension S34649 in Baltimore County on Apr. 24, 1819, aged 66, stating he had enlisted at Bladensburg in Prince George's County. In 1820 his wife (not named) was aged 61. He died in 1831 and his children received final payment on Feb. 2, 1839. In 1850 only two children survived him: Margaret Logan and James Beall [Ref: P-197]. One

Christopher Beall married Ann Brooke by license dated Jan. 11, 1780 [Ref: ZB-12].
BEALL, Clement (1734 - died after 1790). Private, Maryland Line. Also rendered patriotic and civil service. Clement Beall married Priscilla Perry [Ref: X-195].
BEALL, David. Took the Oath of Allegiance before the Hon. Thomas Williams in 1778 [Ref: O-302]. The estate of one David Beall was probated on Oct. 19, 1817 [Ref: ZE-9]. See "Josias Beall," q.v.
BEALL, Duke. Private, Select Militia, Upper Battalion, June 12, 1781 [Ref: S-6636 (Box 27, folder 82B)].
BEALL, Edward (Oct. 25, 1743 - Dec. 7, 1797). Rendered patriotic service. He married Rachel Edmonston [Ref: X-195].
BEALL, Eleanor. See "Joshua Beall," q.v.
BEALL, Elizabeth. See "Peter Brown" and "Joshua Beall," q.v.
BEALL, George. See "Levin Covington Beall" and "Thomas Beall, of George," q.v.
BEALL, George 3rd (1746-   ). First Lieutenant, Middle Battalion, Capt. William Berry's Company, May 1, 1778 [Ref: M-51, E-63, R-20, N-35]. Took the Oath of Allegiance before the Hon. Joshua Beall in 1778 [Ref: O-251]. Son of "Joshua Beall," q.v. [Ref: U-122].
BEALL, Harriet. See "Basil Beall" and "Jeremiah Igleheart," q.v.
BEALL, Isaac. See "William Dent Beall," q.v.
BEALL, James. See "Christopher Beall," q.v.
BEALL, James (1729-1804). Took the Oath of Allegiance before the Hon. Christopher Lowndes in 1778 [Ref: O-285, R-16]. James Beall married Mary Elizabeth Edmonson (or Edmonston). [Ref: X-196].
BEALL, James (1736-1806). Took the Oath of Allegiance before the Hon. Osborn Sprigg in 1778 [Ref: O-306]. This could be the "James Beall, of John" who was aged 40 in 1776 [Ref: R-52]. One James Beall married Ann Mitchell by license dated May 9, 1787 [Ref: ZB-12]. The estate of one James Beall was probated on May 15, 1806, and the estate of another James Beall was probated on Sep. 6, 1821, in Prince George's County [Ref: ZE-10].
BEALL, James Alexander. See "Josias Beall," q.v.
BEALL, Jeremiah (1725-1802). Took the Oath of Allegiance before the Hon. Christopher Lowndes in 1778 [Ref: O-288]. One Jeremiah Beall married Sabina Beall [Ref: X-196].
BEALL, Jeremiah (1759 - died after June 26, 1841, Virginia). He served in Maryland and married Delilah Gatrill [Ref: X-196, R-34].
BEALL, John (1729-1797). On July 15 and July 29, 1780, the Council of Maryland ordered the Collector of the Tax in Prince George's County to "pay to John Beall six thousand dollars to be expended in the Purchase of Horses, etc., under the Act to procure an Extra Supply of Provisions of the Bread kind, also Waggons and Horses for the use of the Continental Army to be Accounted for." He was appointed by the

Council of Maryland to be one of two Tobacco Inspectors at Bladensburg Warehouse on Aug. 30, 1780. Qualified as County Surveyor, took the oath of office on June 13, 1782, and resigned by Jan. 7, 1783. Elected Sheriff of Prince George's County on Oct. 31, 1782 [Ref: F-222, F-239, F-271, I-295, I-339, Q-522, R-28]. The estate of one John Beall, of Ninian (which also listed his name simply as John Beall) was probated on June 13, 1797, and the estate of another John Beall was probated on Dec. 17, 1800 (and listed again on Jan. 8, 1801). [Ref: DE-10, DE-11). Additional research will be necessary before drawing any conclusions. See "Josias Beall" and "John Beall," q.v.

BEALL, John. Private, Militia, 1776 [Ref: M-207, A-325]. Took the Oath of Allegiance before the Hon. Christopher Lowndes in 1778 [Ref: O-282]. See comment under the other "John Beall," q.v.

BEALL, John, of John. Took the Oath of Allegiance before the Hon. Christopher Lowndes in 1778 [Ref: O-286, R-52]. "John Beall, of John" was aged 41 in 1776 and "John Beall, Jr." was aged 48 in 1776 [Ref: R-52, R-73]. See comment under "John Beall," q.v.

BEALL, John 3rd. Took the Oath of Allegiance before the Hon. Christopher Lowndes in 1778 [Ref: O-283].

BEALL, John Bradley (Nov. 23, 1760 - 1846). Eldest son of Josias and Millicent Beall [Ref: ZC-6]. Private, Capt. Hezekiah Wheeler's Company, 11th Militia Battalion, April, 1781 [Ref: L-19970 (Box 6, folder 21)]. Sergeant, Select Militia, Capt. Hezekiah Wheeler's Company, July 14, 1781 [Ref: S-6636 (Box 31, folder 5)]. The estate of one "John B. Beall" was probated on Jan. 19, 1846, in Prince George's County [Ref: ZE-10].

BEALL, Joseph. Took the Oath of Allegiance before the Hon. Christopher Lowndes in 1778 [Ref: O-288].

BEALL, Joshua (1719-1796). Son of Capt. Charles Beall and Mary Wolstad, he married (1) Eleanor Smith and (2) Elizabeth Waring, widow of Basil, by license dated Feb. 3, 1787 [Ref: ZB-13]. His children were George Beall and Amelia Beall (who married Gen. Rezin Beall). Joshua was Captain of troops, 1756-1758, and Major and Colonel of militia, 25th Battalion, 1775-1776. Justice of the County Court, 1777-1778. Administered the Oath of Allegiance in 1778 [Ref: C-273, O-251, R-20, U-122, U-123, Z-90]. Delegate to the Maryland Convention in 1775-1776, and Speaker of the House of Delegates in 1780 [Ref: A-3, U-70, U-82]. Chairman of the Committee of Safety, 1776-1777 [Ref: C-115]. County Lieutenant, Nov. 29, 1777 to Apr. 8, 1781 [Ref: M-51, A-49, C-373, C-429, D-333, M-208, M-51, B-14]. Stored arms and ammunition at his home in July, 1780 [Ref: G-4]. The estate of Col. Joshua Beall was probated in January, 1796 [Ref: ZE-11].

BEALL, Josiah. Private, Select Militia, Upper Battalion, June 12, 1781 [Ref: S-6636 (Box 27, folder 82B)].

BEALL, Josias (1725-1803). Son of John Beall and Elizabeth Fendall, he married (1) Millicent Bradley and (2) Ann Boswell, and had these children: John Bradley Beall, Josias Fendall Beall, James Alexander Beall, Robert Augustus Beall, Benjamin Bradley Beall, David Fendall Beall, Ann Fendall Beall, Anna Beall, Ann Elizabeth Beall, and the eldest daughter (name not stated). Served in Lower House of the Legislature, 1758-1761, 1778-1779. Delegate to the Maryland Convention, 1775-1776. House of Delegates, 1779 and 1782 [Ref: A-5, U-70, U-80, U-86, U-123, U-124]. Took the Oath of Allegiance before the Hon. William Lyles, Jr. in 1778 [Ref: O-289, R-38], and served on a Grand Jury in 1778 [Ref: Z-52]. It should be noted that there appears to be some discrepancy as another source has listed Josias Beall (1725-1796) who married Priscilla Clarke as a colonel who rendered civil and patriotic service in Maryland [Ref: X-196]. The same source also listed a Josias Beall (1723-1803) who married Millicent Beall Bradley and rendered patriotic service in Maryland [Ref: X-196]. The estate of one Josias Beall was probated on Apr. 24, 1787 and the estate of another Josias Beall was probated on July 6, 1803 [Ref: DE-11]. Additional research may be necessary before drawing conclusions.

BEALL, Josias Jr. Took the Oath of Allegiance before the Hon. Thomas Williams in 1778 [Ref: O-302]. The estate of one Josias Beall was probated on Nov. 26, 1818, and the estate of another Josias Beall was probated on Oct. 14, 1823 [Ref: DE-11]. See comments under "Josias Beall," q.v., before drawing conclusions.

BEALL, Josias, of Benjamin. Served on Grand Jury, 1777 [Ref: Z-23].

BEALL, Josias Fendall. Private, Capt. Hezekiah Wheeler's Company, 11th Militia Battalion, April, 1781 [Ref: L-19970 (Box 6, folder 21)]. One Josias Fendall Beall married Ann Middleton Marlowe by license dated Jan. 18, 1804 [Ref: ZB-13]. The estate of one "Josias F. Beall" was probated on Nov. 25, 1816 [Ref: ZE-11].

BEALL, Lethea. See "Samuel White," q.v.

BEALL, Levin Covington (June 7, 1760 -   ). "Leaven (Leven) Beall" was a private in the militia in the Lower District of Frederick County [now Montgomery County] in July, 1776 [Ref: D-42]. "Leaven Coventon Beall" was born in Prince George's Parish in Prince George's County, a son of George and Anney Beall [Ref: ZD-109]. Additional research may be necessary before drawing conclusions.

BEALL, Lucy. See "Thomas Beall," q.v.

BEALL, Margaret. See "Andrew Beall," q.v.

BEALL, Mary. See "William Whitmore" and Andrew Beall, Jr.," q.v.

BEALL, Millicent. See "Josias Beall" and "John B. Beall," q.v.

BEALL, Nathan. Took the Oath of Allegiance before the Hon. Christopher Lowndes in 1778 [Ref: O-285]. The estate of Nathan Beall was probated on June 2, 1818 [Ref: ZE-11].

BEALL, Ninian (1751-c1784). Took the Oath of Allegiance before the Hon. James Beck in 1778 [Ref: O-254, R-28]. Ninian Beall married Ann Sissell [Ref: X-197, which stated he died circa 1784]. The estate of

"Ninian Beall, Sr." was probated on Aug. 29, 1780, the estate of "Ninian Beall, Jr." was probated on Sep. 22, 1781, and the estate of "Ninian Beall" was probated on May 15, 1784, in Prince George's County [Ref: DE-11]. Additional research will be necessary before drawing conclusions. See "Ninian Beall 3rd," q.v.

BEALL, Ninian 3rd. Took the Oath of Allegiance before the Hon. Christopher Lowndes in 1778 [Ref: O-285]. "Ninian Beall, Sr." was aged 80 and "Ninian Beall, Jr." was aged 53 in 1776 [Ref: R-29, R-36]. See comments under "Ninian Beall," q.v.

BEALL, Patrick (1735-1809/1810). Took the Oath of Allegiance before the Hon. George Lee in 1778 [Ref: O-279, R-44]. Patrick Beall married Elinor Goddard in March, 1756 [Ref: ZC-7]. The estate of Patrick Beall was probated on Jan. 9, 1810 [Ref: ZE-12].

BEALL, Priscilla. See "John Crow," q.v.

BEALL, Rezin (1723 - Oct. 14, 1809). Captain, 1st Independent Maryland Company, Jan. 2, 1776, and severely wounded engaging Lord Dunmore's fleet at St. George's Island, St. Mary's County, on July 16, 1776. Served as Brigadier General of the Flying Camp of Pennsylvania, Maryland and Delaware through Dec. 1, 1776 [Ref: Y-611, A-207, C-66]. Lieutenant Colonel, Middle Battalion, Prince George's County Militia, Mar. 10, 1778 [Ref: M-51, C-532]. Served on a Grand Jury in 1777 [Ref: Z-23]. Took the Oath of Allegiance before the Hon. Joshua Beall in 1778 [Ref: O-251, which spelled his name "Reason Beall"]. Rezin Beall married Amelia Beall, daughter of "Joshua Beall," q.v., and they are buried at St. John's Episcopal Cemetery in Beltsville, Maryland [Ref: Y-611]. Source X-197 states that Rezin Beall married (1) Amelia Beall and (2) Valinda Sheppard. The estate of Rezin Beall was probated on Oct. 24, 1809 [Ref: ZE-12].

BEALL, Richard (1735 - December, 1799). Captain, 25th Battalion, May 1, 1778 [Ref: M-51, E-62, R-72, N-34]. Served on a General Courts-Martial for the trial of Capt. Richard Bennett Hall, Lieut. Jeremiah Ryley, Lieut. Jonathan Wright, and Lieut. James Mullikin on Aug. 23, 1776, at Upper Marlboro [Ref: B-233]. Richard Beall married Rebecca Adamson [Ref: X-197]. The estate of Capt. Richard Beall was probated on Dec. 12, 1799 [Ref: ZE-12]. One Richard Beall also took the Oath of Allegiance before the Hon. Osborn Sprigg in 1778 [Ref: O-306, R-29]. Source X-197 lists a Richard Beall (1738 - Aug. 18, 1778) who married Sarah Brooke, served as an ensign, and rendered patriotic service in Maryland. Additional research may be necessary before drawing conclusions.

BEALL, Richard, of Ninian. Took the Oath of Allegiance before the Hon. Thomas Williams in 1778 [Ref: O-302].

BEALL, Robert. See "Josias Beall," q.v.

BEALL, Roger Brook (1734-1790). Took the Oath of Allegiance before the Hon. William Berry in 1778 [Ref: O-259]. "Roger Beall" was aged 42 in

1776 [Ref: R-66]. "Roger Brooke Beall" married Ruth Hamilton [Ref: X-197].

BEALL, Sabina. See "Jeremiah Beall," q.v.

BEALL, Sarah. See "Thomas Gantt, Jr." and "Samuel Hanson" and "Elisha Harrison," q.v.

BEALL, Shadrach (1745-1826). Took the Oath of Allegiance before the Hon. Christopher Lowndes in 1778 [Ref: O-286, R-49, which spelled his name "Shadrick"]. He married Agnes ---- [Ref: X-197]. The estate of Shadrach Beall was probated on Feb. 3, 1826 [Ref: DE-12].

BEALL, Tabitha. See "Charles Beall," q.v.

BEALL, Thomas (1742 - Nov. 16, 1823). First Lieutenant, Capt. Richardson's Company, 25th Battalion, May 1, 1778. Captain, 25th Battalion, May 24, 1779 [Ref: M-51, E-62, E-414, N-32, N-34]. Took the Oath of Allegiance before the Hon. Christopher Lowndes in 1778 [Ref: O-285, R-28]. He married Verlinda Beall [Ref: X-197]. This same source also listed a Thomas Beall (no birth date; died before 1818) who married Lucy Beall and served as a captain in Maryland, and also a Thomas Beall (Nov. 18, 1753 - died by Dec. 10, 1785), married Catherine Brown (by license dated Jan. 13, 1779) and rendered patriotic service [Ref: ZB-14, Z-197]. As there are other Thomas Bealls listed below, additional research will be necessary before drawing conclusions.

BEALL, Thomas. Private, Militia, 1776 [Ref: M-207, A-325]. Took the Oath of Allegiance before the Hon. James Beck in 1778 [Ref: O-256]. See "Capt. Thomas Beall," q.v.

BEALL, Thomas. Took the Oath of Allegiance before the Hon. James Beck in 1778 [Ref: O-254]. See "Capt. Thomas Beall," q.v.

BEALL, Thomas, of George (1735-1819). Born in Prince George's County, a son of Col. George Beall and Elizabeth Brooke, he married Nancy Orme by 1775 and held public office in Montgomery County when that county was created in 1776 [Ref: U-125].

BEALL, Thomas, of Thomas (1760/1761-   ). "A substitute to serve for nine months, June 15th, 1778," continental service, Maryland Line [Ref: D-328]. "Thomas Beall, Jr." was aged 16 in 1776 [Ref: R-53]. The records of the Council of Maryland on June 22, 1778, state that Thomas Beall, son of Thomas Beall, enlisted for nine months as a substitute for Thomas Duvall who had been drafted to serve nine months [Ref: E-146]. One Thomas Beall (born in July, 1761) applied for and received pension S45270 in Preble County, Ohio on June 28, 1818 [Ref: P-197].

BEALL, Verlinda. See "Thomas Beall," q.v.

BEALL, William. Private, Col. Rawlings' Regiment, Maryland Line. Enlisted on Feb. 8, 1779, for six months [Ref: D-90]. The estate of one "William Beall" was probated on Sep. 25, 1802, and the estate of one "William Thomas Beall" was probated on Apr. 4, 1810, in Prince George's County [Ref: ZE-12].

BEALL, William Dent (died Sep. 24, 1829). Second Lieutenant, Maryland Line, Capt. Robert Bowie's Company in 1776 [Ref: D-34]. First Lieutenant, Capt. Waring's Company, 25th Battalion, Mar. 18, 1776. Captain, 6th Maryland Line, involved in recruiting in March, 1780 [Ref: M-51, M-52, A-260, H-188, D-332, F-102, F-321]. Major, 2nd Maryland Line, Nov. 6, 1781, commissioned after the death of Major Dean [Ref: D-479]. Received bounty land warrant 229-400-2 in March, 1795 [Ref: P-197]. His pension commenced on July 25, 1828 and he died at Piscataway, Maryland in 1829. Isaac D. Beall was his administrator [Ref: V-1957 (Volume 45, No. 4, p. 192), and T-54, which latter source listed his name as "William D. Beale"]. William D. Beall married Sarah A. Brooke by license dated Aug. 30, 1786 [Ref: ZB-14]. The estate of "William D. Beall" was probated on Oct. 14, 1829 [Ref: ZE-12].

BEALL, Zephaniah. Ensign, Lower District, Frederick County Militia, 1776 [Ref: D-42]. He married Virlinda Fergusson by license dated Jan. 5, 1783, in Prince George's County [Ref: ZB-15].

BEAM, Ann. See "Henry Jones," q.v.

BEAM, John. Private, 3rd Maryland Line, enlisted Jan. 9, 1779; Capt. Horatio Clagett's Company, December, 1779 [Ref: D-295].

BEAN, Benjamin. Took the Oath of Allegiance before the Hon. Osborn Sprigg in 1778 [Ref: O-308, W-4648 (Box 4, folder 29)]. Benjamin Bean married Rebecca Evans by license dated Dec. 8, 1779 [Ref: ZB-15].

BEAN, Christopher Jr. Took the Oath of Allegiance before the Hon. Christopher Lowndes in 1778 [Ref: O-283]. "Christopher Beanes, Sr." was aged 70 in 1776 [Ref: R-27].

BEAN, Ebsworth. See "Hebsworth Bayne," q.v.

BEAN, George (1723, England - died before 1797, Maryland). Took the Oath of Allegiance before the Hon. George Lee in 1778 [Ref: O-279, R-67]. He married (1) Unknown, and (2) Ann ---- [Ref: X-199]. This may be the George Bean or Bayne who married Mary Gatton, daughter of Thomas Gatton and Elizabeth Waters, but this information has not yet been documented. See "Azariah Gatton," q.v.

BEAN, Henry (Oct. 24, 1753 - May 22, 1840). Private, enrolled by Capt. Alexander H. Magruder, 11th Battalion, on July 4, 1776, for continental service, Maryland Line [Ref: D-38]. "Henry H. Bean" married Amelia ---- and served as a private in the Maryland Line [Ref: X-199].

BEAN, John (1743-   ). Took the Oath of Allegiance (made his "X" mark) before the Hon. Alexander Howard Magruder in 1778 [Ref: O-293, R-68]. Private, enrolled by Ensign Alexander Truman on July 4, 1776, for continental service, Maryland Line [Ref: D-38]. Private, 3rd Maryland Line, wounded at the Battle of Camden on Apr. 25, 1781; register's report on Jan. 20, 1790 indicated he had been paid in full for his wounds [Ref: D-634, D-635, K-1814]. See "John Beanes," q.v.

BEAN, Josias. See "Josias Bayne" and "Josias Beanes," q.v.

BEAN, Thomas. Private, Militia, 1776 [Ref: M-207, A-325]. Private, enrolled by Capt. Alexander H. Magruder, 11th Battalion, on July 18, 1776, for continental service, Maryland Line [Ref: D-38]. Took the Oath of Allegiance before the Hon. Osborn Sprigg in 1778 [Ref: O-308, W-4648 (Box 4, folder 29)]. One Thomas Bean was born in Maryland in 1755, served in the Maryland Line, married Mary Gwynne, and died in Virginia after 1805 [Ref: X-200]. See "Thomas Bayne," q.v.

BEANES, Colmore. Took the Oath of Allegiance before the Hon. Thomas Clagett in 1778 [Ref: O-264]. Ensign, 11th Battalion, July 3, 1776 [Ref: M-52, A-544]. Ensign, Maryland Line, Capt. Robert Bowie's Company; resigned before July 6, 1776 [Ref: D-34, which spelled his name "Beans"]. Colonel Colmore Beanes married Millicent Tyler (daughter of "Robert Tyler," q.v.) by license dated Apr. 10, 1778 [Ref: U-846, ZB-15]. He was a physician and brother of Elizabeth Beanes who married "Luke Marbury," q.v. [Ref: U-573]. The estate of "Colmore Beans" was probated on Oct. 4, 1831 [Ref: ZE-13]. See "William Bayne," q.v.

BEANES, Easther. See "Thomas Pennifield," q.v.

BEANES, Elizabeth. See "Luke Marbury," q.v.

BEANES, Henrietta. See "Robert Bradley Tyler," q.v.

BEANES, John H. First Lieutenant, Militia, 1778 [Ref: N-36, which listed his name as "John Beanes"]. Captain, 11th Battalion, May 24, 1779, and Lower Battalion, June 12, 1781 (succeeded). [Ref: M-52, E-414, G-472]. Major, Militia, commissioned Jan. 18, 1781 [Ref: G-277, L-19970 (Box 6, folder 21), which latter source listed his name as "John H. Beane"]. One John H. Beanes married Henrietta Dyer by license dated Dec. 23, 1785, and a John H. Beanes married Harriett Clagett by license dated May 20, 1795 [Ref: ZB-15]. The estate of one John H. Beanes was probated on Mar. 20, 1811, and the estate of another John H. Beanes was probated on Mar. 13, 1837 [Ref: ZE-13]. Additional research may be necessary before drawing conclusions.

BEANES, Josias. Private (draft), continental service, Maryland Line, 1781 [Ref: D-382]. See "Josias Bean" and "Josias Bayne," q.v.

BEANES, Mary. See "Baruch Duckett" and "Jeremiah Cooke," q.v.

BEANES, Millicent. See "Robert Tyler" and "Colmore Beanes," q.v.

BEANES, Samuel Hawkins. Captain, Militia, Sep. 1, 1777 [Ref: N-35]. See "Samuel Hawkins Bayne," q.v.

BEANES, William (Jan. 24, 1749 - Oct. 12, 1828). Physician and Surgeon, Mar.ing Militia, Sep. 4, 1777 [Ref: M-52, C-362]. Justice of the County Court, 1777 [Ref: C-273]. "William Beanes, Jr." took the Oath of Allegiance before the Hon. Thomas Clagett in 1778 [Ref: O-264, R-39]. He married Sarah Hawkins (1750-1822) on Nov. 25, 1773. They are buried in the Beanes Family Cemetery located on Elm Street near the former high school in Upper Marlboro [Ref: Y-557, Y-613]. The estate of one "William Beanes" was probated on Oct. 10, 1801, the estate of one "William B. Beanes" was probated on Apr. 7, 1818, the estate of one

"William Beans" (also shown as "Dr. William Beanes") was probated on Oct. 15, 1828, and the estate of one "William Beans" was probated on July 17, 1838, all in Prince George's County [Ref: ZE-13]. Additional research may be necessary before drawing conclusions. See "Luke Marbury," q.v.

BEANS, John. Second Lieutenant, 2nd Maryland Line, Jan. 3, 1776 [Ref: D-7]. First Lieutenant, Middle Battalion, Capt. Samuel H. Beans' Company, May 1, 1778 [Ref: M-52, E-63]. See "John Bean," q.v.

BEANS, Joseph. Took the Oath of Allegiance before the Hon. Christopher Lowndes in 1778 [Ref: O-284]. Private, Maryland Line, discharged on Dec. 3, 1781 [Ref: I-10].

BEAVEN (BEAVIN), Ann. See "Henry Truman, Jr.," q.v.

BEAVEN, Charles. Private, Capt. Jesse Hellen's Militia Company; guarded Magruder's Warehouse in the spring of 1782 [Ref: L-19970 (Box 6, folder 21)]. One Charles Beaven married Sarah Sasscer by license dated Jan. 13, 1778, a Charles Beavin married Amy Sasscer by license dated Dec. 13, 1791, and a Charles Beavin married Catharine Long by license dated Mar. 28, 1793 [Ref: XB-16].

BEAVEN, Henrietta. See "William Cooke," q.v.

BEAVEN, Maryland [sic]. Private, enrolled by Capt. Alexander H. Magruder, 11th Battalion, on July 20, 1776, for continental service, Maryland Line [Ref: D-38].

BECK, ----. See "William Dunnington," q.v.

BECK, Anthony (Oct. 25, 1737 -   ). Son of James Beck and Sarah Duvall, of Queen Anne's Parish [Ref: ZC-164]. Took the Oath of Allegiance before the Hon. James Beck in 1778 [Ref: O-254, R-36].

BECK, James (Oct. 6, 1735 - 1785). Son of James Beck and Sarah Duvall, of Queen Anne's Parish, he married Rebekah Walker on June 23, 1761 [Ref: ZC-164]. Justice of the County Court, 1777-1778 [Ref: C-273, Z-90]. Administered the Oath of Allegiance in 1778 [Ref: O-256, R-54]. First Lieutenant, Militia, 1778 [Ref: N-34]. First Lieutenant, 25th Battalion, Capt. Richard Beall's Company, May 1, 1778 [Ref: M-52, E-78]. The estate of one James Beck was probated by Sep. 10, 1785 (date of inventory filed by Rebecca Beck). There was also an estate probated for another James Beck on Dec. 17, 1821 [Ref: ZE-14]. See "Anthony Beck," q.v.

BECK, John (Feb. 14, 1749 - 1797). Son of James Beck and Sarah Duvall, of Queen Anne's Parish [Ref: ZC-164]. Took the Oath of Allegiance before the Hon. Thomas Williams in 1778 [Ref: O-302]. John Beck married Sarah Hamilton by license dated Nov. 18, 1778 [Ref: ZB-16]. The estate of John Beck was probated on Feb. 28, 1797 [Ref: ZE-14].

BECK, Osborne (Aug. 17, 1744 - c1786). Son of James Beck and Sarah Duvall, of Queen Anne's Parish [Ref: ZC-164]. Private, 2nd Maryland Line, 1778; discharged Jan. 10, 1780 [Ref: D-83]. The estate of "Osborn

Beck" was probated by Sep. 23, 1786 (date an account was filed). [Ref: ZE-14].

BECK, Rebecca. See "James Beck," q.v.

BECK, Samuel Duvall (Jan. 7, 1733 - 1794 or 1806). Son of James Beck and Sarah Duvall, of Queen Anne's Parish, he married Susanna Tyler on Mar. 29, 1767 [Ref: ZC-164]. Took the Oath of Allegiance before the Hon. James Beck in 1778 [Ref: O-254]. The estate of one "Samuel Beck, Jr." was probated on Nov. 19, 1794, and the estate of "Samuel D. Beck, Jr." was probated on Dec. 9, 1806. An inventory of the estate of "Samuel D. Beck, Jr." was filed on Dec. 23, 1806, and an administrative account was filed on the estate of "Samuel D. Beck" on June 9, 1812. In all these cases (and others) an Andrew Hamilton was the executor or administrator [Ref: ZE-14]. Additional research may be necessary before drawing conclusions.

BECK, Sarah. See "Anthony Beck" and "James Beck" and "John Beck" and "Osborne Beck" and "Samuel Duvall Beck," q.v.

BECKETT, Benjamin. Took the Oath of Allegiance before the Hon. Benjamin Hall in 1778 [Ref: O-274].

BECKETT, Easter. See "Henry Clark, of Henry," q.v.

BECKETT, Humphrey. Private, 7th Maryland Line, 1778-1781 [Ref: D-189, D-354]. Humphrey Beckett married Mary Shreeves by license dated Feb. 22, 1786, in Prince George's County [Ref: ZB-16].

BECKETT, John. Two men with this name took the Oath of Allegiance in 1778: one made his "IB" mark (with the "I" having a horizontal line equidistant through the middle) before the Hon. Thomas Boyd and another signed his name before the Hon. Osborn Sprigg [Ref: O-262, O-308, W-4648 (Box 4, folder 29)]. One John Beckett married Mary Walker by license dated Sep. 29, 1778 [Ref: ZB-16].

BECKETT, Rebecca. See "Charles Duvall," q.v.

BEDDO, Absolum (c1754-1807). He rendered patriotic service, married Mary ----, and died in Maryland in 1807 [Ref: X-209].

BEDDO, Elizabeth. See "Thomas Beddo" and "Thomas Hooper," q.v.

BEDDO (BEDDER), James. "James Beddoe" took the Oath of Allegiance (made his "X" mark) which was recorded on a "return of Captain Tapley of the brig *Royal*" and subsequently filed in court by the Hon. Thomas Gantt, Jr. in 1778 [Ref: O-305, W-4648 (Box 4, folder 15)]. "James Bedder" was a private in the 7th Maryland Line who enlisted on Apr. 25, 1778 and was still in service in November, 1780 [Ref: D-189].

BEDDO, Levey. See "Thomas Beddo (Beddow)," q.v.

BEDDO, Mary. See "Absolum Beddo," q.v.

BEDDO, Micale. See "Thomas Beddo (Beddow)," q.v.

BEDDO, Richard. See "Thomas Beddo (Beddow)," q.v.

BEDDO, Sarah. See "Thomas Beddo (Beddow)," q.v.

BEDDO (BEDDOW), Thomas (Jan. 2, 1761, Prince George's County, Maryland - Nov. 10, 1851, Delaware County, Ohio). Private, Maryland

Line. Applied for pension in Delaware County, Ohio on Nov. 20, 1832, aged 71, stating he was born in Prince George's County and during the war lived near Nottingham, about 22 miles from N. Marlborough. After the war he moved to Albemarle County, Virginia near Port Republic about 11 miles from Charlottesville. In August, 1828, he moved to Rockingham County, Virginia, and in 1831 to Delaware County, Ohio. On Aug. 30, 1852, his widow Sarah, aged 93, applied for pension W5816 and stated they were married in 1777 and he died on Nov. 10, 1851, aged over 90. The pension file contains a sheet of births of their children too light to read; some of them appear to have been as follows: William Beddo (born 1780), Thomas Beddo (born 1787), Richard Beddo (born 1789), Elizabeth Beddo (born 179?), Micale Beddow and Fe??? Beddo [sic], twins (born 1794), and Levey Beddo (born 1797). [Ref: P-210, P-211, which advised readers to "use these with caution"].

BEDDO, William. See "Thomas Beddo (Beddow)," q.v.

BELL, John. Private, Maryland Line, 1780-1783. In March, 1834, at Indiana Township in Allegheny County, Pennsylvania, he verified that he had served in the Maryland Line with David Howe and John Clevidence [Ref: V-1947 (Volume 35, No. 2, p. 63)]. See "David Howe" and "John Cleverdence," q.v.

BELT, ----. See "Marsham Belt," q.v.

BELT, Ann. See "John Murdock," q.v.

BELT, Basil. Ensign, Militia, 1778 [Ref: N-34]. Select Militia, Upper Battalion, June 12, 1781 [Ref: S-6636 (Box 27, folder 82B)]. Took the Oath of Allegiance before the Hon. Benjamin Hall in 1778 [Ref: O-276]. See "Robert Orme," q.v.

BELT, Benjamin. Took the Oath of Allegiance before the Hon. James Beck in 1778 [Ref: O-253]. The estate of one Benjamin Belt was probated by Nov. 10, 1775 (date of inventory) and a Benjamin Belt was the administrator. The estate of "Benjamin Belt, Jr." was probated on May 10, 1814 [Ref: ZE-15]. See "James Mullikin," q.v.

BELT, Dryden Gorden. See "Robert Bradley Tyler," q.v.

BELT, Edward (Mar. 15, 1749 -   ). Son of Jeremiah and Mary Belt [Ref: ZC-164]. Took the Oath of Allegiance before the Hon. Thomas Williams in 1778 [Ref: O-302].

BELT, Ester. See "Tobias Belt," q.v.

BELT, Fielder or Fielding (Mar. 29, 1761 - 1801). "Fielding Belt" was a son of Jeremiah and Mary Belt, of Queen Anne's Parish [Ref: ZC-164]. "Fielder Belt" was a private in the Select Militia, Upper Battalion, on June 12, 1781 [Ref: S-6636 (Box 27, folder 82B)]. The estate of "Fielding Belt" was probated on Apr. 11, 1801. An inventory of the estate of "Fielder Belt" was recorded on July 8, 1801, and an inventory of the estate of "Fielding Belt" was also recorded on Apr. 7, 1802. In both cases, Beal (or Beall) Duvall was the administrator [Ref: ZE-15].

BELT, Horatio. Took the Oath of Allegiance before the Hon. David Craufurd in 1778 [Ref: O-271].
BELT, Humphrey. Lieutenant, Militia, Aug. 23, 1776. Captain, Middle (25th) Battalion, May 1, 1778 to May 24, 1779 (succeeded). [Ref: M-52, B-233, E-63, E-414, N-35]. County Court Justice, 1777 [Ref: C-273]. Served on a General Courts-Martial for the trial of Capt. Richard Bennett Hall, Lieut. Jeremiah Ryley, Lieut. Jonathan Wright, and Lieut. James Mullikin on July 25, 1776, and Aug. 23, 1776, at Upper Marlboro [Ref: A-553, B-233]. Took the Oath of Allegiance before the Hon. David Craufurd in 1778 [Ref: O-271]. Served on a Grand Jury in 1777 [Ref: Z-23]. "Humphrey Belt, Jr." married Elizabeth Tyler by license dated Feb. 4, 1792, and "Humphrey Belt, Sr." married Elizabeth Vincent by license dated Mar. 3, 1804 [Ref: ZB-17]. The estate of "Humphrey Belt, Sen." was probated on Sep. 20, 1813 [Ref: ZE-15].
BELT, Jeremiah. Took the Oath of Allegiance before the Hon. Thomas Williams in 1778 [Ref: O-302]. "Jeremiah Belt" was born on Mar. 4, 1724, and married Mary Sprigg on June 21, 1746, in Queen Anne's Parish [Ref: ZC-164]. "Jeremiah Belt, Jr." married Priscilla Gantt by license dated Mar. 4, 1778 [Ref: ZB-17]. The estate of one "Jerremiah Belt" was probated on Jan. 18, 1785 [Ref: ZE-15]. See "Edward Belt" and "Fielding Belt" and "James Belt" and "John Sprigg Belt," q.v.
BELT, John Sprigg (Sep. 18, 1752 -   ). Son of Jeremiah and Mary Belt, of Queen Anne's Parish in Prince George's County [Ref: ZC-164]. He served as a lieutenant in 1776 and a captain in the 4th Maryland Line in 1777 and retired Jan. 1, 1783 [Ref: D-38, D-40, D-88, D-353, D-362, D-378, D-435]. See Henry C. Peden, Jr.'s *Revolutionary Patriots of Anne Arundel County, 1775-1783*, page 12.
BELT, Joseph. Private, Select Militia, Upper Battalion, June 12, 1781 [Ref: S-6636 (Box 27, folder 82B)]. "Joseph Belt" married Rachel Brashears by license dated Jan. 12, 1791, and "Joseph Sprigg Belt" married Sarah Burgess by license dated Apr. 29, 1790 [Ref: ZB-17, ZB-18]. See "Tobias Belt," q.v.
BELT, Josiah. Ensign, Militia, 1779 [Ref: N-34]. Ensign, 25th Battalion, Capt. Joseph Jones' Company, May 24, 1779 [Ref: M-52, E-414]. Took the Oath of Allegiance before the Hon. Thomas Boyd in 1778 [Ref: O-262].
BELT, Josiah, of Osburn. Private, Select Militia, Upper Battalion, June 12, 1781 [Ref: S-6636 (Box 27, folder 82B)].
BELT, Josias. Second Lieutenant, Upper Battalion, Capt. Benjamin Harwood's Company, June 24, 1780 [Ref: M-52, F-203].
BELT, Leonard. Rendered patriotic service by providing wheat for the military on Aug. 5, 1780 [Ref: Q-307].
BELT, Lucy. See "Thomas Watkins," q.v.
BELT, Marsham (c1735, Maryland - died before Oct. 8, 1802 in Kentucky). Took the Oath of Allegiance before the Hon. Benjamin Hall

in 1778 [Ref: O-274]. Marsham Belt married Elizabeth Cross and these children are listed in the Queen Anne's Parish register: ---- *[sic]* Belt (daughter, born Jan. 6, 1764), Thomas Belt (born June 15, 1765), and Marsham Belt (born in July, 1767). [Ref: X-223, ZC-164, ZC-165].

BELT, Mary. See "Tobias Belt" and "Jeremiah Belt" and "Bennett Gwynn," q.v.

BELT, Middleton (1747 or 1756 - Jan. 15, 1807). Took the Oath of Allegiance before the Hon. James Beck in 1778 [Ref: R-50, which source stated he was aged 20 in 1776, and O-254, which listed his name as "Middle Belt"]. Middleton Belt married Mary Ann Dyer [Ref: X-223, which source stated he was born in 1747].

BELT, Osborne Sprigg. "Osburn Belt" took the Oath of Allegiance before the Hon. Thomas MacGill in 1778 [Ref: O-291]. "Osborne Sprigg Belt" married (1) Rachel Brashears, and (2) Dorothy Cissel, and rendered patriotic service [Ref: X-223, which source stated he died before Dec. 24, 1816]. It should be noted that the estate of "Osbourn Belt" was probated on Oct. 14, 1831 [Ref: ZE-15].

BELT, Priscilla. See "Thomas Belt," q.v.

BELT, Rachel. See "Osborn Sprigg" and "Cornelius Duvall," q.v.

BELT, Rebecca. See "Henry Hilleary, Sr.," q.v.

BELT, Thomas (born before 1740, Maryland - died after Feb. 21, 1810, North Carolina). Took the Oath of Allegiance before the Hon. Thomas Williams in 1778 [Ref: O-302]. Private, Maryland Line. He married Priscilla---- [Ref: X-223]. There was also a Thomas Belt who married Sarah Hodges by license dated July 25, 1787 [Ref: ZB-18]. The estate of one Thomas Belt was probated on Nov. 30, 1792 in Prince George's County, Maryland [Ref: ZE-16]. Additional research may be necessary before drawing conclusions. See "Marsham Belt," q.v.

BELT, Tobias (Aug. 20, 1720 - 1785). Took the Oath of Allegiance before the Hon. Osborn Sprigg in 1778 [Ref: O-306]. Tobias Belt, a son of Col. Joseph and Ester Belt, married Mary Gordon [Ref: X-223, ZC-164, ZC-165]. The estate of Tobias Belt was probated on May 17, 1785. and an administrative account filed by Mary Belt on Oct. 1, 1789, referred to him as captain [Ref: ZE-16].

BELT, Waring. Private, Militia, 1781; participated in capturing an enemy boat and crew on Apr. 17, 1781 [Ref: M-209]. Private, Select Militia, Upper Battalion, June 12, 1781 [Ref: S-6636 (Box 27, folder 82B), which spelled the name "Warring Belt"].

BENCE, George Sebastian (1755-1779). "George Sebastian Bence" was a private, county militia, 1776 [Ref: M-207, A-325]. Took the Oath of Allegiance before the Hon. William Berry in 1778 [Ref: O-258]. "George Bence" was aged 21 in 1776 [Ref: R-20]. A "George Bens" was the constable in Bladensburg Hundred in 1777 [Ref: Z-3]. The estate of one George Bence was probated on Aug. 25, 1779 [Ref: ZE-16].

BENHAM, Elizabeth. See "John Burch," q.v.

BENNETT, Joshua. Private, Maryland Line, discharged on Dec. 3, 1781 [Ref: I-10].
BENNETT, Richard. Captain, 25th Battalion, May 23, 1776 [Ref: M-52, A-440].
BENNETT, Thomas. Private, Militia, 1781; participated in capturing an enemy boat and crew on Apr. 17, 1781 [Ref: M-209]. Private, Select Militia, Upper Battalion, June 12, 1781 [Ref: S-6636 (Box 27, folder 82B)].
BENTLY, David. Private, enrolled by Capt. John H. Lowe on July 13, 1776, for continental service, Maryland Line [Ref: D-35].
BERK, William (1759-   ). Private, enrolled in the Flying Camp by Lieut. Benjamin Brooks on July 10, 1776; nativity: Prince George's County; height 5' 4" [Ref: D-36].
BERRY, Barbary. See "Zachariah Berry," q.v.
BERRY, Benjamin. Ensign, Militia, 1778 [Ref: N-35]. Ensign, Middle Battalion, Capt. William Berry's Company, May 1, 1778 [Ref: M-53, E-63]. "Benjamin Berry, Jr." was aged 35 in 1776 [Ref: R-22]. Took the Oath of Allegiance before the Hon. William Berry in 1778 [Ref: O-257]. Source X-239 listed two Benjamin Berry's in Maryland, but neither man was an ensign: one was Benjamin Berry (1739-1815) who rendered patriotic service and had a wife Deborah Eversfield, and the other was Benjamin Berry (c1755-c1804) who was a private in the Maryland Line and had a wife Chloe ---- [Ref: X-239, ZA-60]. Benjamin Berry, son of Samuel Berry, was born Feb. 21, 1756 [Ref: ZC-8]. The estate of one Benjamin Berry was probated on May 8, 1777, and the estate of another Benjamin Berry was probated on Dec. 24, 1827 [Ref: ZE-16, ZE-17]. Additional research may be necessary before drawing conclusions.
BERRY, Chloe. See "Benjamin Berry," q.v.
BERRY, Deborah. See "Thomas Hodges" and "Benjamin Berry," q.v.
BERRY, Eleanor. See "George Naylor," q.v.
BERRY, Elisha (1755-1813). Ensign, Middle Battalion, Capt. Charles Clagett's Company, Nov. 13, 1779 [Ref: M-53, F-13, N-35]. Took the Oath of Allegiance before the Hon. William Berry in 1778 [Ref: O-257]. Elisha married (1) Eleanor Eversfield, and (2) Mrs. Jane Ferguson (widow), and had a son by each marriage: William Berry (who moved to the West), and William Ferguson Berry [Ref: ZA-63]. The estate of one Elisha Berry was probated on Aug. 18, 1813 in Prince George's County [Ref: ZE-17].
BERRY, Elizabeth. See "Zachariah Berry," q.v.
BERRY, Isaac (1761, England -   ). Private (substitute), 1780, continental service, Maryland Line [Ref: D-338].
BERRY, Jeremiah. See "Zachariah Berry," q.v.
BERRY, John. Rendered patriotic service by providing wheat for the military on Aug. 4, 1780 [Ref: Q-306]. It should be noted that there

were two men with this name in Prince George's County in 1776: one was aged 40 and the other aged 24 [Ref: R-87, ZA-59].

BERRY, Philip. Took the Oath of Allegiance before the Hon. David Craufurd in 1778 [Ref: O-271]. The estate of one Philip Berry was probated by July 31, 1781 (date of inventory). [Ref: ZE-17].

BERRY, Priscilla. See "Zachariah Berry," q.v.

BERRY, Samuel. See "Benjamin Berry," q.v.

BERRY, Thomas. See "Thomas Owen Williams," q.v.

BERRY, Walter. See "Zachariah Berry," q.v.

BERRY, William (1742-1784). Justice of the County Court, 1777-1778 [Ref: Z-90, ZA-60, C-273]. Captain, Militia, Middle Battalion, on May 1, 1778 [Ref: M-53, E-63, N-35]. He administered the Oath of Allegiance in 1778 [Ref: O-259]. The estate of "Capt. William Berry" was probated by June 14, 1785 (date of inventory) and he may have been the William Berry whose estate was probated on Aug. 30, 1784 [Ref: ZE-17, ZE-18].

BERRY, William. Private, enrolled by Ensign Horatio Clagett on July 15, 1776, for continental service, Maryland Line [Ref: D-35, which spelled his name "William Berrey"]. The estate of "William Berry" was probated on Mar. 8, 1815 and the estate of "William E. Berry" was probated on May 2, 1805 [Ref: ZE-18]. Additional research may be necessry before drawing conclusions. See "Elisha Berry," q.v.

BERRY, William E. See. William Berry," q.v.

BERRY, William F. See "Elisha Berry," q.v.

BERRY, Zachariah (July 11, 1749 - Mar. 25 or 27, 1845). First Lieutenant, Middle Battalion, Capt. Clement Wheeler's Company, May 1, 1778, and Captain, June 24, 1780 [Ref: M-53, E-62, F-203, N-36, which latter source misspelled his name "Zacha. Bevy"]. Took the Oath of Allegiance before the Hon. William Berry in 1778 [Ref: O-257]. "Zachariah Berry (July 11, 1749 - Mar. 25, 1845) is buried with wife Elizabeth Owen Berry (Oct. 30, 1749 - Oct. 3, 1805) at "Concord"... Other sources state that he married Mary, daughter of Colonel Williams, of Georgetown, D.C." [Ref: Query from Irene Beall Unfug, 3872 Mud Pike, Christiansburg, Virginia 24073 in *Prince George's County Genealogical Society Bulletin*, Volume 25, No. 10 (June, 1994), page 195]. DAR *Patriot Index (Centennial Edition)* indicates he died on Mar. 27, 1845; *Stone and Bones* indicates it was on Mar. 25, 1845 [Ref: X-241, Y-558, Y-612]. Buried in the Berry Family Cemetery in Prince George's County (now in District Heights, 8000 Walker Mill Road) are: Zachariah Berry (Nov. 17, 1785 - Mar. 3, 1859); Priscilla Berry, wife of Zachariah (Feb. 14, 1801 - June 24, 1876); Jeremiah Berry (Apr. 16, 1779 - July 10, 1812); Walter Jack Berry (Apr. 4, 1805 - July 29, 1834); and, Barbary Berry (Jan. 23, 1778 - Mar. 22, 1793). [Ref: Y-558, ZA-60-61]. The estate of Zachariah Berry was probated on Apr. 2, 1845 [Ref: ZE-18].

BERRY, Zachariah. Private, 2nd Maryland Regiment, enlisted Mar. 6, 1782 for 3 years and sworn in Mar. 29, 1782 [Ref: D-417]. This or another Zachariah Berry was a private in Capt. Joseph Marbury's Company of Light Infantry who served at Fort Pitt in 1780 and may have been from Frederick or Montgomery County, Maryland [Ref: L-19970 (Box 6, folder 21)]. Additional research may be necessary before drawing conclusions.

BEVERLEY, Sarah. See "Joseph Digges," q.v.

BIDDEN, Richard. Took the Oath of Allegiance before the Hon. Osborn Sprigg in 1778 [Ref: O-307].

BIDDLE, John. Took the Oath of Allegiance before the Hon. James Beck in 1778 [Ref: O-255].

BIDDLE, Richard. Private, 2nd Maryland Line, Capt. Murdock's Company, Mar. 15, 1781 [Ref: D-366].

BIGGS, Benjamin (July 29, 1760 - May 5, 1819). Private, 7th Maryland Line, from Apr. 11, 1778 to Aug. 16, 1780, when he was reported missing at the Battle of Camden [Ref: D-189]. Benjamin Biggs married Elizabeth Ohler [Ref: X-252].

BIGGS, Henry (1725-   ). Took the Oath of Allegiance before the Hon. Osborn Sprigg in 1778 [Ref: O-307, R-69].

BIGGS, John (May 11, 1758 - Oct. 8, 1823). Corporal, Maryland Line, 3rd Maryland Line, 1781. He married Priscilla Wilson [Ref: D-396, Z-252]. There was also a John Biggs who married Susanna King by license dated Dec. 11, 1779 [Ref: ZB-21].

BIGGS, John. Took the Oath of Allegiance in 1780 [Ref: J-105]. Rendered patriotic service by providing wheat for the military on Sep. 23, 1780 [Ref: Q-320, which spelled his name "Bigg"]. The estate of one John Biggs was probated on Mar. 4, 1815, in Prince George's County [Ref: ZE-18].

BIGGS, Priscilla. See "Henry Boteler," q.v.

BILLOP, Henry. "Henry Billop" was a private in the Maryland Line, 1780-1781 [Ref: D-354]. "Harry Billip" was a private, 2nd Maryland Line, Capt. Alexander Truman's Company, 1782 [Ref: D-440].

BIRD, Francis (Feb. 21, 1731-   ). Son of Francis Bird and Jane Littleton [Ref: ZC-8]. Took the Oath of Allegiance (made his "B" mark) before the Hon. James Beck in 1778 [Ref: O-253].

BIRD, Jane. See "Francis Bird" and "Thomas Bird," q.v.

BIRD, Thomas. Two men with this name took the Oath of Allegiance in 1778: one before the Hon. James Beck [Ref: O-253], and another before the Hon. Osborn Sprigg [Ref: O-308, W-4648 (Box 4, folder 29)]. One was a private in the 3rd Maryland Line; prisoner of war, "exchanged from Charles Town" by Sep. 3, 1781, at which time he was paid 5 pounds specie on his account [Ref: D-616]. Reference X-259 lists two men in Maryland with the name of Thomas Bird who were soldiers in the war. One Thomas Bird married Jemima Wheeler by license dated Dec. 14, 1780 [Ref: ZB-21]. There was also a Thomas Bird, son of

Francis and Jane, who was born on Dec. 24, 1729 [Ref: ZC-8]. Additional research will be necessary before drawing conclusions.

BLACKLOCK, Edward. Private, 2nd Maryland Line, Capt. Patrick Sim's Company, 1776 [Ref: D-8]. The estate of one Edward Blacklock was probated on Sep. 3, 1793 [Ref: ZE-19].

BLACKLOCK, Nicholas. Third Sergeant, 1st Guard, Capt. Henry Hill's Militia Company, Lower Battalion; on duty at Nottingham on the Patuxent, Apr. 12, 1781 [Ref: L-19970 (Box 6, folder 21)]. Took the Oath of Allegiance before the Hon. Truman Skinner in 1778 [Ref: O-298]. One Nicholas Blacklock married Elizabeth Cawood (or Caywood) by license dated Nov. 24, 1786 [Ref: ZB-21]. See "Thomas Blacklock," q.v.

BLACKLOCK, Thomas Sr. (1716-1790). Took the Oath of Allegiance before the Hon. Truman Skinner in 1778 [Ref: O-297, R-39]. The estate of one Thomas Blacklock was probated on Mar. 16, 1790 and Nicholas Blacklock filed an account on Feb. 19, 1794 [Ref: ZE-19].

BLACKLOCK, Thomas. Ensign, 2nd Guard, Capt. Henry Hill's Militia Company, Lower Battalion; on duty at Nottingham on the Patuxent, Apr. 12, 1781 [Ref: L-19970 (Box 6, folder 21)]. Ensign, Lower Battalion, Capt. Henry Hill's Company, July 3, 1780 [Ref: M-53, F-210]. Took the Oath of Allegiance before the Hon. Truman Skinner in 1778 [Ref: O-297]. One Thomas Blacklock married Sarah Sansbury by license dated Jan. 30, 1783, and a Thomas Blacklock married Ann Wynn by license dated Nov. 22, 1783 [Ref: ZB-21].

BLANDFORD, Catherine. See "Charles Thomas Blandford," q.v.

BLANDFORD, Charles Thomas (c1758, Maryland - died before Dec. 7, 1812, Kentucky). He rendered patriotic service, and married Catherine ----- [Ref: X-279].

BLANFORD, Henrietta. See "Henry Miles," q.v.

BLANFORD, James. Private, 1st Guard, Capt. Henry Hill's Militia Company, Lower Battalion; on duty at Nottingham on the Patuxent, Apr. 12, 1781 [Ref: L-19970, which spelled his name "Blanfoard"].

BLANFORD, John. Took the Oath of Allegiance before the Hon. Truman Skinner in 1778 [Ref: O-298].

BLANFORD, Joseph. Private, Select Militia, Capt. Hezekiah Wheeler's Company, July 14, 1781 [Ref: S-6636 (Box 31, folder 5)]. Took the Oath of Allegiance before the Hon. Truman Skinner in 1778 [Ref: O-299].

BLANFORD, Mary. See "Thomas Edelen," q.v.

BLANFORD, Rebecca. See "William White," q.v.

BLANFORD, Richard. Took the Oath of Allegiance before the Hon. Truman Skinner in 1778 [Ref: O-299]. The estate of one "Richard Blandford" was probated on Nov. 13, 1779 [Ref: ZE-19].

BLANFORD, Richard. Private, 2nd Maryland Line; prisoner of war, "exchanged from Charles Town" by Oct. 11, 1781, at which time he was

paid five pounds specie on his account [Ref: D-617, which listed his name as "Rich. Blandford"].
BLANFORD, Susan. See "Francis Hamilton," q.v.
BLANFORD, Thomas. Private, 1st Guard, Capt. Henry Hill's Militia Company, Lower Battalion; on duty at Nottingham on the Patuxent, Apr. 12, 1781 [Ref: L-19970, which spelled his name "Blanfoard"]. Took the Oath of Allegiance before the Hon. Truman Skinner in 1778 [Ref: O-298]. Served on a Grand Jury in 1777 [Ref: Z-29].
BOARMAN, Joseph Jr. Took the Oath of Allegiance before the Hon. William Lyles, Jr. in 1778 [Ref: O-289]. Sergeant, 11th Militia Battalion, Capt. Hezekiah Wheeler's Company, April, 1781 [Ref: L-19970 (Box 6, folder 21)]. Corporal, Select Militia, Capt. Hezekiah Wheeler's Company, July 14, 1781 [Ref: S-6636 (Box 31, folder 5), which listed the name without the "Jr."]. The estate of one Joseph Boarman was probated on July 12, 1830 [Ref: ZE-19].
BOARMAN, Joseph Sr. (1732-1811). Took the Oath of Allegiance before the Hon. William Lyles, Jr. in 1778 [Ref: O-290, R-58]. The estate of one Joseph Boarman was probated on Sep. 9, 1811 [Ref: ZE-19]. See "Joseph Boarman, Jr.," q.v.
BOARMAN, Lucy. See "Giles Green Dyer," q.v.
BOARMAN, Raphael. Corporal, 11th Militia Battalion, Capt. Hezekiah Wheeler's Company, April, 1781 [Ref: L-19970 (Box 6, folder 21)]. Private, Select Militia, Capt. Hezekiah Wheeler's Company, July 14, 1781 [Ref: S-6636 (Box 31, folder 5)].
BOARMAN, Rebecca. See "George Edelen," q.v.
BOHAN, James. Private, Select Militia, Upper Battalion, June 12, 1781 [Ref: S-6636 (Box 27, folder 82B)].
BOLIN, Thomas P. Took the Oath of Allegiance before the Hon. George Lee in 1778 [Ref: O-279].
BOLTON, George (1741-   ). Took the Oath of Allegiance before the Hon. Benjamin Hall in 1778 [Ref: O-276, R-25, which spelled his name "George Boulton"].
BOMGARDNER, George. Private, 2nd Maryland Line, Capt. Alexander Truman's Company, 1782 [Ref: D-440].
BOND, Samuel (1747-1818). Took the Oath of Allegiance before the Hon. Thomas Clagett in 1778 [Ref: O-269, R-41]. The estate of one Samuel Bond (also listed as Samuel S. Bond) was probated on Aug. 31, 1818 [Ref: ZE-20].
BONIFANT, James. Took the Oath of Allegiance before the Hon. Thomas Clagett in 1778 [Ref: O-267, which spelled the name "Bonnifant"]. Served on a Grand Jury in 1778 [Ref: Z-52]. Rendered patriotic service by providing wheat for the military on May 10, 1783 [Ref: Q-599]. The estate of one James Bonifant (also spelled "Bonefant" and "Boniafant") was probated on Aug. 3, 1802 [Ref: ZE-20].

BONIFANT, Samuel (June 3, 1731, France - Jan. 6, 1810, Maryland). Took the Oath of Allegiance before the Hon. Christopher Lowndes in 1778 [Ref: O-285]. He married Sarah Townshend and was a private in the Maryland Line [Ref: X-302, but he is not listed in *Maryland Archives, Volume 18*].

BONIFIELD, John. Took the Oath of Allegiance before the Hon. William Berry in 1778 [Ref: O-259].

BOODY, John. Private, Northern Detachment, 3rd Maryland Line, Capt. Horatio Clagett's Company, 1783 [Ref: D-501].

BOONE, Alexis (Alextious). Ensign, 3rd Guard, Capt. Henry Hill's Militia Company, Lower Battalion; on duty at Nottingham on the Patuxent, Apr. 12, 1781 [Ref: L-19970, which spelled his name "Alexious Boon"]. Took the Oath of Allegiance before the Hon. Truman Skinner in 1778 [Ref: O-297]. Ensign, 11th Battalion, Capt. Robert Bowie's Company, May 1, 1778. Ensign, Capt. John Beanes' Company, 11th Battalion, May 24, 1779 [Ref: M-54, E-62, E-414, which spelled his name as "Alextious Boone" and "Alexius Boone"]. Ensign, Militia, 1778 [Ref: N-33, which also spelled his name as "Alextious Boone" and "Elexious Boone"]. "Electius Boone" married Mary Smith by license dated Jan. 8, 1779, and "Alectius Boone" married Anna Statia Martin by license dated Nov. 8, 1806 [Ref: ZB-22].

BOONE, Anne. See "James Haddock Waring," q.v.

BOONE, Charles. Took the Oath of Allegiance before the Hon. Truman Skinner in 1778 [Ref: O-297]. The estate of one Charles Boone was probated on Mar. 26, 1783 [Ref: ZE-20].

BOONE, Francis. Private, 1st Guard, Capt. Henry Hill's Militia Company, Lower Battalion; on duty at Nottingham on the Patuxent, Apr. 12, 1781 [Ref: L-19970 (Box 6, folder 21)]. Took the Oath of Allegiance before the Hon. Truman Skinner in 1778 [Ref: O-297]. Served as a Constable in Grubb Hundred in 1778 [Ref: Z-30].

BOONE, Henry. Private, 1st Guard, Capt. Henry Hill's Militia Company, Lower Battalion; on duty at Nottingham on the Patuxent, Apr. 12, 1781 [Ref: L-19970 (Box 6, folder 21)]. Took the Oath of Allegiance before the Hon. Truman Skinner in 1778 [Ref: O-297]. The estate of one Henry Boone was probated on Oct. 15, 1793 [Ref: ZE-20].

BOONE, Ignatious. Took the Oath of Allegiance before the Hon. Truman Skinner in 1778 [Ref: O-297]. One Ignatius Boone married Martha Boone by license dated Apr. 21, 1790, and Ignatius Boone married Eleanor Sansbury by license dated Jan. 14, 1796 [Ref: ZB-22]. The estate of one "Ignatius Boone" was probated by Oct. 25, 1824 (date inventory was taken) and the estate of "Ignatius Boone, of Nicholas" was probated on Oct. 16, 1815 [Ref: ZE-20]. Additional research may be necessary before drawing conclusions. See "Bennett Gwynn," q.v.

BOONE, John. Took the Oath of Allegiance before the Hon. Truman Skinner in 1778 [Ref: O-297]. On Mar. 14, 1780, "John Boone, of Prince

George's County, was appointed Ensign in the 1st Maryland Regiment" by the Council of Maryland [Ref: F-111, F-112]. This may be the Capt. John Boone (1736-c1800) who served in the Maryland Line and married Elizabeth Williams [Ref: X-305]. There was also a John Boone who married Ann Hardey by license dated Jan. 12, 1782 [Ref: ZB-22]. The estate of one "John Boone" was probated on Feb. 28, 1789, and the estate of "John Francis Boone" was probated on May 25, 1824 [Ref: ZE-20]. Additional research may be necessary before drawing conclusions.

BOONE, Martha. See "Ignatius Boone," q.v.

BOONE, Thomas. Private, 1st Guard, Capt. Henry Hill's Militia Company, Lower Battalion; on duty at Nottingham on the Patuxent, Apr. 12, 1781 [Ref: L-19970 (Box 6, folder 21)]. Took the Oath of Allegiance before the Hon. Truman Skinner in 1778 [Ref: O-298].

BOONE, Walter. Took the Oath of Allegiance before the Hon. Truman Skinner in 1778 [Ref: O-298]. Private, Select Militia, Capt. Hezekiah Wheeler's Company, July 14, 1781 [Ref: S-6636 (Box 31, folder 5)]. Private, Capt. Hezekiah Wheeler's Company, 11th Militia Battalion, April, 1781 [Ref: L-19970 (Box 6, folder 21), which sources spelled his name "Boon"]. Walter Boone married Mildred Edelen by license dated Oct. 9, 1783 [Ref: ZB-23].

BOSWELL, David (1751-   ). Took the Oath of Allegiance before the Hon. George Lee in 1778 [Ref: O-279, R-1].

BOSWELL, George (1749-c1779). Private, enrolled by Lt. William Duvall of the Lower Battalion of Militia on July 18, 1776, for continental service, Maryland Line [Ref: D-35, R-16]. George Boswell married Mary Ann ---- before 1777 [Ref: X-312].

BOSWELL, Jesse (1755, Maryland - Nov. 23, 1828, South Carolina). Sergeant, 2nd Maryland Line, 1782. He married (1) Elizabeth Carrington, and (2) Mary Kelough [Ref: D-445, X-312].

BOSWELL, John (1740 or 1750 - 1815). Private, Militia, 1776 [Ref: M-207, A-325, which spelled his name "Bozwell"]. Took the Oath of Allegiance before the Hon. Christopher Lowndes in 1778 [Ref: O-287, R-72, which latter source stated he was aged 36 in 1776]. He married Mary Robey and rendered patriotic service [Ref: X-312, which stated he was born on Mar. 10, 1750]. The estate of one John Boswell was probated on May 9, 1818 [Ref: ZE-21]. Additional research may be necessary before drawing conclusions. See "Josias Beall," q.v.

BOSWELL, John Baptist (1731-1807). Took the Oath of Allegiance before the Hon. William Lyles, Jr. in 1778 [Ref: O-290, R-56, which also listed his name as "John B. Boswell"]. The estate of John B. Boswell was probated on Oct. 7, 1807 [Ref: ZE-21].

BOSWELL, Mary Ann. See "George Boswell," q.v.

BOSWELL, Peter. Took the Oath of Allegiance before the Hon. William Lyles, Jr. in 1778 [Ref: O-289]. One Peter Boswell was aged 22 and

another was aged 21 in 1776 [Ref: R-16, R-74]. One Peter Boswell married Ann Findley by license dated May 4, 1783 [Ref: ZB-24].
BOSWELL, Samuel. Private, Maryland Line, 1780-1781 [Ref: D-354].
BOTELER, Charles. Took the Oath of Allegiance before the Hon. Fielder Bowie in 1778 [Ref: O-303, W-4648 (Box 4, folder 15)]. The estate of one Charles Boteler was probated on Jan. 26, 1792, in Prince George's County [Ref: ZE-21].
BOTELER, Charles Jr. Took the Oath of Allegiance before the Hon. Fielder Bowie in 1778 [Ref: O-303, W-4648 (Box 4, folder 15)]. One Charles Boteler married Sarah Robinson by license dated Jan. 22, 1785, a Charles Boteler married Harriott Brashears by license dated Jan. 25, 1799, and a Charles Boteler married Sarah Jones by license dated Feb. 21, 1806 [Ref: ZB-24]. Additional research may be necessary before drawing conclusions. The estate of Charles Boteler, Jr. was probated by Aug. 2, 1791 (date of an administrative account) in Prince George's County [Ref: ZE-21].
BOTELER, Edward (c1730 - before Aug. 31, 1818). First Sergeant, 3rd Guard, Capt. Henry Hill's Militia Company, Lower Battalion; on duty at Nottingham on the Patuxent, Apr. 12, 1781 [Ref: L-19970 (Box 6, folder 21)]. Took the Oath of Allegiance before the Hon. Fielder Bowie in 1778 [Ref: O-303, W-4648 (Box 4, folder 15)]. Edward Boteler married Elizabeth DeLashmutt [Ref: X-313]. There was also an Edward Boteler who married Elizabeth Saunders by license dated Jan. 31, 1781 [Ref: ZB-24].
BOTELER, Henry (Oct. 15, 1728 - 1797 or 1804). Took the Oath of Allegiance before the Hon. Fielder Bowie in 1778 [Ref: O-303, W-4648 (Box 4, folder 15)]. He was a captain in the Maryland Line and married Sallie Elsby [Ref: X-313]. There was also a "Henry Bottler" who married Priscilla Biggs by license dated Feb. 9, 1789 [Ref: ZB-25]. The estate of "Henry Boteler, Jr." was probated by Mar. 2, 1797 (date of inventory), and the estate of a "Henry Boteler" was probated on Jan. 19, 1804 [Ref: ZE-21]. Additional research may be necessary before drawing conclusions.
BOTELER, Lingan. Private, 2nd Guard, Capt. Henry Hill's Militia Company, Lower Battalion; on duty at Nottingham on the Patuxent, Apr. 12, 1781 [Ref: L-19970 (Box 6, folder 21)].
BOTELER, Thomas. Constable in Mattapony Hundred, 1777 [Ref: Z-3]. Served on a Grand Jury in 1778 [Ref: Z-52]. One Thomas Boteler married Ann Clarke by license dated May 24, 1784 [Ref: ZB-25]. The estate of one Thomas Boteler was probated by July 17, 1779 (date of inventory) in Prince George's County [Ref: ZE-21].
BOTELER, Walter. Private, Select Militia, Capt. Hezekiah Wheeler's Company, July 14, 1781 [Ref: S-6636 (Box 31, folder 5)]. Corporal, Capt. Jesse Hellen's Company; guarded Magruder's Warehouse in the spring of 1782 [Ref: L-19970 (Box 6, folder 21)].

BOUCHER, John Thomas (1746-   ). Took the Oath of Allegiance before the Hon. Christopher Lowndes in 1778 [Ref: O-284, R-24].
BOUGH, George. Private, 3rd Maryland Line, 1781 [Ref: D-392]. "George Bough (or Buck)" was a private in the German Regiment, 1780-1781 [Ref: D-190]. "George Bough" was a private in the 2nd Maryland Line, 1782-1783 [Ref: D-447]. The estate of one George Bough was probated on May 12, 1794 in Prince George's County [Ref: ZE-22].
BOURNE, Elsie. See "Zachariah Moore," q.v.
BOWIE, Allen Jr. (1737 - May 28, 1803). Born in Prince George's County, a son of John Bowie, Jr. and Elizabeth Pottinger, he married Ruth Cramphin (his stepsister) in 1766 and had these children: Thomas Bowie, Dr. John Bowie, Elizabeth (Bowie) Davis, Mary Bowie, Washington Bowie, Allen Bowie, Hannah Bowie, and Richard Bowie (the last three children died young). [Ref: ZA-668]. Allen held public offices in Montgomery County after that county was created in 1776 and also served as a captain in 1776, colonel in 1780, and took the Oath of Allegiance before the Hon. Fielder Bowie in 1778 in Prince George's County [Ref: U-149, U-150, O-303, W-4648 (Box 4, folder 15), X-322].
BOWIE, Allen Sr. (1719-1783). Son of John Bowie, Sr. (c1688-1759) and Mary Mullikin, he married (1) Mrs. Priscilla Finch (widow of Capt. William Finch, Jr.) in 1744 and they had a son Fielder Bowie (1745-1794). Priscilla died in 1747 and he married (2) Anne Fraser in 1748 and had these children: Susanna Fraser (Bowie) Eversfield, Priscilla (Bowie) Duckett, and Anne (Bowie) Brookes [Ref: ZA-643 to ZA-647, ZE-22]. Allen Bowie served as Justice of the Peace from 1752 to 1754 and was Inspector of Tobacco at Marlborough Warehouse in 1757. He was appointed by the Council of Maryland to be the Tobacco Inspector at Nottingham Warehouse on Aug. 30, 1780, and resigned some time in September, 1780 [Ref: F-302, F-271, U-150]. Source X-322 states he was born in 1709, while Source ZA-643 states he was born in 1719. See "John Smith Brookes," q.v.
BOWIE, Ann. See "William Bowie" and "Allen Bowie, Sr." and "John Smith Brookes," q.v.
BOWIE, Caroline. See "Robert Bowie," q.v.
BOWIE, Catherine. See "Benjamin Hall, of Francis," q.v.
BOWIE, Charles. See "William Bowie 3rd," q.v.
BOWIE, Daniel. See "Walter Bowie," q.v.
BOWIE, Eleanor. See "George Fraser Magruder," q.v.
BOWIE, Elizabeth. See "Fielder Bowie" and "Walter Bowie" and "William Bowie" and "William Sprigg Bowie" and "Robert Bowie" and "Allen Bowie, Jr.," q.v.
BOWIE, Eversfield. See "Fielder Bowie," q.v.
BOWIE, Fielder (1745 - Sep., 1794). Born near Nottingham in Prince George's County, son of Allen Bowie, Sr. and Priscilla Finch (widow of Capt. William Finch, Jr.), he married Elizabeth Clagett Eversfield,

daughter of Rev. John Eversfield, circa 1765 and had these children: Allen Bowie, Thomas Contee Bowie, Eversfield Bowie, John Fraser Bowie, Jr., Priscilla Bowie, and Elizabeth Susanna Howard [Ref: U-150, ZA-671 to ZA-673, ZE-22]. Captain, 11th Battalion, Militia, Feb. 20, 1776 [Ref: A-173, X-322]. Fielder served on a General Courts-Martial for the trial of Capt. Richard Bennett Hall, Lieut. Jeremiah Ryley, Lieut. Jonathan Wright, and Lieut. James Mullikin on July 25, 1776, at Upper Marlboro [Ref: A-553]. Justice of the County Court, 1777-1794 [Ref: C-273, U-151]. Administered the Oath of Allegiance in 1778 [Ref: O-303, W-4648 (Box 4, folder 15)]. Served on the Board of Patuxent Associators and signed a resolution at Nottingham on Apr. 21, 1781 relative to the defence of the rivers of Potomac and Patuxent and the completion of the fort at Drum Point [Ref: K-1814]. Maryland State Elector, 1786. Chief Justice, 1793-1794 [Ref: U-151, Z-90]. See "Allen Bowie, Sr.," q.v.

BOWIE, Hannah. See "Allen Bowie, Jr.," q.v.

BOWIE, James John. See "Robert Bowie," q.v.

BOWIE, John Fraser (Jan. 17, 1755 - May 18, 1815). Took the Oath of Allegiance before the Hon. Fielder Bowie in 1778 [Ref: O-303, W-4648 (Box 4, folder 15)]. Physician who served on the Board of Patuxent Associators and signed a resolution at Nottingham on Apr. 21, 1781 relative to the defence of the rivers of Potomac and Patuxent and the completion of the fort at Drum Point [Ref: K-1814]. He married Susan Anne Hawkins (had no children) and was a surgeon in the Continental Army [Ref: ZA-649]. John F. Bowie married Susanna A. Hawkins by license dated Apr. 23, 1784 [Ref: ZB-25, ZE-22]. See "Fielder Bowie" and "Allen Bowie, Jr." and "William Bowie," q.v.

BOWIE, John Fraser Jr. See "Fielder Bowie," q.v.

BOWIE, Juliet. See "Walter Bowie," q.v.

BOWIE, Margaret. See "Robert Bowie" and "William Bowie" and "Benjamin Brookes" and "Walter Bowie," q.v.

BOWIE, Mary. See "Allen Bowie, Sr." and "Allen Bowie, Jr." and "Robert Bowie" and "Isaac Duckett" and "William T. Wootton," q.v.

BOWIE, Osborn Sprigg (c1753/1755 - Mar. 31, 1806). A son of Capt. William Bowie, Osborn was referred to in his mother Margaret's will in 1802 as having been long absent from his country. "It is thought that he served in the Navy during the Revolutionary War." In 1794 he was referred to as Capt. Osborne S. Bowie and at one time served on the U. S. S. *Constellation* on or before 1800 [Ref: ZA-657, ZE-23].

BOWIE, Priscilla. See "Fielder Bowie" and "Allen Bowie," q.v.

BOWIE, Richard. See "Allen Bowie, Jr.," q.v.

BOWIE, Robert (Mar. 6, 1750 - Jan. 8, 1818). Son of William Bowie and Margaret Sprigg. He married Priscilla Mackall circa 1773 (eloped) and had children: James John Bowie (1785-1809, killed in a duel); Robert William Bowie (1787-1848); Robert H. Bowie (died young); Mary Mackall

(Bowie) (Wooton) Bowie (1776-1825); Elizabeth Margaret Waring (1780-1854); Margaret Anne Ghiselin (1783-1850); and Caroline Bowie (died young). [Ref: U-151, U-152, ZA-677 to ZA-681, ZE-23]. First Lieutenant, Militia, Mar., 1776; Captain, 1777; resigned Sep. 1, 1777 [Ref: A-246, D-34, N-33, X-322]. Took the Oath of Allegiance before the Hon. David Craufurd in 1778 [Ref: O-271]. Captain, 11th Battalion, from May 1, 1778 through May 24, 1779 (succeeded, but another source indicates he was a Captain in the Lower Battalion on June 12, 1781). Lieutenant, Horse Troops, Sep. 1, 1781 [Ref: M-55, E-62, E-414, G-472, G-596, H-407]. Collector of Horses for Prince George's County in 1781-1782 [Ref: G-520, I-208]. Served on the Board of Patuxent Associators and signed a resolution at Nottingham on Apr. 21, 1781 relative to the defence of the rivers of Potomac and Patuxent and the completion of the fort at Drum Point [Ref: K-1814]. Robert held many public offices, including: Lower House, 1785-1803; Governor of Maryland, 1803-1806; State Senator, 1806-1811; and, Governor, 1811-1812 [Ref: U-152]. Robert Bowie is probably buried in the family cemetery on "Mattaponi" estate, but no tombstone has been found [Ref: Y-614].
BOWIE, Robert William. See "Robert Bowie," q.v.
BOWIE, Susannah Fraser. See "Allen Bowie, Sr.," q.v.
BOWIE, Thomas. See "Fielder Bowie" and "Allen Bowie, Jr.," q.v.
BOWIE, Ursula. See "William Bowie 3rd," q.v.
BOWIE, Walter (1748 - Nov. 9, 1810). A son of William Bowie and Margaret Sprigg, he married Mary Brookes in 1771 and had children: William Bowie, Daniel Bowie, Walter Bowie, Jr., Margaret Duckett, Elizabeth Brooke, and Juliet Matilda Brookes [Ref: U-152, U-153, ZE-23]. Delegate to the Maryland Convention, 1775-1776, and House of Delegates, 1777-1779 and 1782-1783 [Ref: A-4, U-74, U-76, U-78, U-80, U-86, U-87]. First Lieutenant, 25th Battalion, Sep. 5, 1777, and First Lieutenant, Capt. Marsh Duvall's Company, 25th Battalion, May 1, 1778; resigned 1779 [Ref: M-55, C-363, E-62, N-34, X-322]. He held many public offices after the war, including Lower House (1784-1797), Senate (1801-1806), Associate Justice, First District (1791-1792), and U. S. Congress (1802-1805). [Ref: U-153]. He also signed the Declaration of Association of Freemen of Maryland in 1775 and in November, 1776 he was one of four delegates from Prince George's County at the convention which framed the first Constitution of the State of Maryland. He lived at his estate "Willow Grove" on Route 450 near Collington and is probably buried there, but no tombstone has been found [Ref: Y-560, Y-612, ZA-677].
BOWIE, Washington. See "Allen Bowie, Jr.," q.v.
BOWIE, William (1721 - Apr. 9, 1791). A son of John Bowie, Sr. and Mary Mullikin, he married Margaret Sprigg circa 1745 and had these children: Walter Bowie (1748-1810), Robert Bowie (c1750-1818), William Sprigg Bowie (1751-1809), Osborn Sprigg Bowie (died 1806), Elizabeth Smith,

Ann Chew, and Margaret Sprigg Brookes [Ref: U-153, U-154, ZA-655, ZE-23]. Captain in the militia by 1760. Delegate to the Maryland Convention, 1774-1775. Committee of Correspondence, 1774. Committee of Observation, 1775. Commissioner of Tax, 1777-1783. Committee to Raise Supplies for the Army, 1778. Judge of Court of Appeals for Tax Assessment, 1786 (declined). [Ref: A-3, U-70, U-151, U-153, U-154]. See "Robert Bowie" and "Walter Bowie" and "Osborn Sprigg Bowie," q.v.

BOWIE, William 2nd. First Lieutenant, Militia, 1778 [Ref: N-35, which listed his name as "Will Bowie 2"].

BOWIE, William 3rd (c1752 - Sep. 17, 1809). First Lieutenant, Middle Battalion, Capt. John Burgess' Company, on May 1, 1778 [Ref: M-55, E-63]. Took the Oath of Allegiance before the Hon. David Craufurd in 1778 [Ref: O-271]. Served on a Grand Jury in 1778 [Ref: Z-90]. Source X-323 states he was a lieutenant in the Maryland Line and "married (1) Ursula Burgess and (2) Ursula Burgess" *[sic]*. It must be noted that his dates of birth and death very closely match those of "William Sprigg Bowie," q.v., who was also a lieutenant. Source ZA-684 states that William Bowie 3rd was born early in 1753, married Ursula Burgess in 1777, and died intestate on Sep. 13, 1807, according to a Bible record. Ursula Bowie died testate in 1824 and mentioned sons William M. and Charles Bowie in her will [Ref: ZA-684, ZA-685, ZE-23].

BOWIE, William Sprigg (c1751-1809). A son of William Bowie and Margaret Sprigg, he married Elizabeth Brookes Sprigg (daughter of Benjamin Brookes and widow of John Clark Sprigg) by license dated Dec. 18, 1781 [Ref: U-154, ZA-682, ZA-683, ZB-26, ZE-24]. Second Lieutenant, Militia, May 1, 1776. First Lieutenant, 6th Maryland Line, Capt. Alexander Magruder's Company, 1776. Captain, 4th Maryland Line, Jan., 1777. A severe wound at the Battle of Germantown on Oct. 4, 1777, forced him to resign his commission on Dec. 15, 1777. Subsequently, his poor health kept him from making his mercantile business a success and in 1800 he petitioned the General Assembly as an insolvent debtor [Ref: D-34, D-88, M-55, U-153, U-154]. See "William Bowie 3rd," q.v.

BOWLING, John (1733-1791). Took the Oath of Allegiance before the Hon. William Lyles, Jr. in 1778 [Ref: O-289, R-86]. The estate of one John Bowling was probated on Oct. 11, 1791 [Ref: ZE-24].

BOWLING, Levinah. See "Charles Nevitt," q.v.

BOWLING, Walter. Private, Select Militia, Capt. Hezekiah Wheeler's Company, July 14, 1781 [Ref: S-6636 (Box 31, folder 5)]. Private, Capt. Hezekiah Wheeler's Company, 11th Militia Battalion, April, 1781 [Ref: L-19970 (Box 6, folder 21)]. The estate of Walter Bowling was probated on Sep. 13, 1815 [Ref: ZE-24].

BOWLING, William Lang (1748-1803). "William Lang Bowling" took the Oath of Allegiance before the Hon. Thomas Clagett in 1778 [Ref: O-265, R-86]. "William L. Bowling" enlisted in the Maryland Line on Mar. 12,

1781 [Ref: D-420, which listed his name as "William T. Bowling"]. "William Bowling" was a sergeant in the Maryland Line in 1782 [Ref: D-470]. The estate of one "William L. Bowling" was probated on June 7, 1803 [Ref: ZE-24].

BOYD, Abraham (1736-1800). Took the Oath of Allegiance before the Hon. Thomas Williams in 1778 [Ref: O-302, R-23]. Captain, Militia, 25th Battalion, May 23, 1776. Major, Mar. 10, 1778. Lieutenant Colonel, May 1, 1778 [Ref: M-55, A-440, C-532, E-63, N-33, D-333]. Served on a Grand Jury in 1777 [Ref: Z-29]. The estate of Abraham Boyd was probated by Dec. 18, 1800 (date of inventory). [Ref: ZE-24]. See "John Igleheart," q.v.

BOYD, Benjamin (1744-1822). Surgeon's Mate in the Maryland Line; pension commenced on June 24, 1818 [Ref: T-39]. Took the Oath of Allegiance before the Hon. Benjamin Hall in 1778 [Ref: O-275], and rendered patriotic service by providing wheat for the military on Sep. 2, 1780 [Ref: Q-314]. Source X-327 also lists a Benjamin Boyd (1734-1784) who married Eleanor Taylor and was a private in the Maryland Line. The estate of "Dr. Benjamin Boyd" was probated on June 18, 1822, and the estate of another "Benjamin Boyd" was probated on July 21, 1800, in Prince George's County [Ref: ZE-24]. Additional research may be necessary before drawing conclusions.

BOYD, Eleanor. See "Cephas Sheckell," q.v.

BOYD, Joseph. Two men with this name took the Oath of Allegiance before the Hon. Benjamin Hall in 1778 [Ref: O-275]. The estate of one Joseph Boyd was probated on June 27, 1799 [Ref: ZE-25].

BOYD, Thomas (Sep. 14, 1734 - 1797). "Thomas Boyd" served as a Justice of the County Court in 1777-1778 and also administered the Oath of Allegiance in 1778 [Ref: C-273, Z-90, O-262]. "Thomas Boyd, Jr." took the Oath of Allegiance before the Hon. Thomas Williams in 1778 [Ref: O-302]. He was an ensign in the militia in 1778 and a second lieutenant in the 25th Battalion, Capt. Josiah Shaw's Company, on May 24, 1779 [Ref: M-55, E-414, N-33, N-34]. "Thomas Boyd" married (1) Charity Duckett on Mar. 24, 1757, in Queen Anne's Parish, and (2) ---- Lansdale [Ref: X-328, ZC-165]. The estate of Thomas Boyd was probated on Mar. 7, 1797 [Ref: ZE-25]. See "Thomas Duckett Boyd," q.v.

BOYD, Thomas Duckett (Mar. 11, 1761, Maryland - July 21, 1820, Virginia). Son of Thomas Boyd and Charity Duckett. "Thomas Duckett Boyd" was a second lieutenant in the Maryland Line and married Mary Magruder and "Thomas Boyd, Jr." married Mary Magruder by license dated Oct. 12, 1788 [Ref: X-328]. Additional research will be necessary before drawing conclusions.

BOYD, William. See "John Igleheart," q.v.

BOYLE, Sarah. See "Thomas Hammond," q.v.

BRADFORD, Eleanor. See "Isaac Walker" and "Henry Bradford," q.v.

BRADFORD, Henry (1728-1782). Took the Oath of Allegiance before the Hon. Christopher Lowndes in 1778 [Ref: O-282, R-70]. The estate of Henry Bradford was probated by Aug. 8, 1782 (administrative account filed by Eleanor Bradford). [Ref: ZE-25].
BRADLEY, Elinor. See "Robert Tyler" and "Robert B. Tyler," q.v.
BRADLEY, Millicent. See "Josias Beall," q.v.
BRADLEY, Susanna. See "Daniel Jones," q.v.
BRADY, John. There were several men with this name who served in the Maryland Line [Ref: D-357, D-395, D-443, D-494, D-526, D-564]. The estate of one John Brady was probated on Feb. 20, 1784 in Prince George's County [Ref: ZE-25].
BRADY, Mary. See "John Worland, Sr.," q.v.
BRAMBLE, Andrew. Private, Northern Detachment, 3rd Maryland Line, Capt. Horatio Clagett's Company, 1783 [Ref: D-501].
BRAMLEY, Bartholomew. Took the Oath of Allegiance before the Hon. David Craufurd in 1778 [Ref: O-272].
BRANT, Eleanor. See "Clement Hill, Jr.," q.v.
BRANT, Margaret. See "Richard Tarman, Jr.," q.v.
BRASHEARS, Ann. See "Ignatius Brashears," q.v.
BRASHEARS, Archibald. See "Ignatius Brashears," q.v.
BRASHEARS, Benedict. Took the Oath of Allegiance before the Hon. James Beck in 1778 [Ref: O-255, which spelled the name "Benedick Brashear"]. The estate of Benedict Brashears was probated by Feb. 11, 1785 (date of inventory). [Ref: ZE-26].
BRASHEARS, Cassia. See "Charles Duvall," q.v.
BRASHEARS, Charles. Took the Oath of Allegiance before the Hon. Benjamin Hall in 1778 [Ref: O-276].
BRASHEARS, Dennis. See "Ignatius Brashears," q.v.
BRASHEARS, Dorcas. See "Ignatius Brashears," q.v.
BRASHEARS, Elisha. Took the Oath of Allegiance (made his mark) before the Hon. James Mullikin in 1778 [Ref: O-296]. The estate of Elisha Brashears was probated on Oct. 27, 1819 [Ref: ZE-26].
BRASHEARS, Elizabeth. See "Ignatius Brashears" and "Basil Brown" and "Moses Orme, Jr." and "Jeremiah Brashears," q.v.
BRASHEARS, Harriott. See "Charles Boteler, Jr.," q.v.
BRASHEARS, Humphrey. Took the Oath of Allegiance (made his mark) before the Hon. James Mullikin in 1778 [Ref: O-296]. The estate of Humphrey Brashears was probated on May 11, 1815 [Ref: ZE-26].
BRASHEARS, Ignatius (1734 - Oct. 6, 1807, Kentucky). Private, 2nd Maryland Line, Jan. 18, 1777; discharged Jan. 18, 1780 [Ref: D-84]. Ignatius "Nacy" Brashears married Pamelia Frances Edmonston (1736-1804) on Sep. 22, 1759 in Prince George's County and had these children, all born in Maryland: Mary Brashears (born Mar. 1, 1760); Elizabeth Brashears (born July 12, 1761); Ann Brashears (born Mar. 23, 1763 and married Basil Crow); Thomas Brashears (born Nov. 10, 1764);

Samuel Brashears (born Oct. 12, 1766); Ignatius Brashears (born Mar. 28, 1768, married Mary Orme who died in 1851; Ignatius married on Mar. 23, 1796, and died May 10, 1821; their daughter Nancy Brashear(s), born 1797, Kentucky, died 1875, Port Gibson, Mississippi, and married Capt. Benjamin Hughes, born 1789, Maryland and died 1842, Grand Gulf, Mississippi); Robert Brashears (born Aug. 30, 1769 and married Elizabeth Beall Harrison); Archibald Edmonston Brashears (born Nov. 2, 1771); Levi Brashears (born Nov. 14, 1773); Walter Brashears (born Feb. 11, 1776); Joseph Brashears (born Dec. 9, 1778); Dennis Brashears (born Aug. 13, 1780 and married Lucinda McDowell); and, Ruth Brashears (born Sep. 13, 1782). After the war Ignatius Brashears and family migrated to Bullitt County, Kentucky and he died at Shepardsville in 1807 [Ref: DAR Application No. 471136 of Mrs. Julia Foard Peterson Pallozzi, of Catonsville, Maryland, approved on Nov. 21, 1969, which spelled the name "Brashear"]. "Nacy Brashears" took the Oath of Allegiance before the Hon. Thomas Williams in 1778 [Ref: O-302]. Source X-348 indicates Ignatius Brashears was born on Apr. 10, 1734.

BRASHEARS, Ignatius (1753 - died after 1832). Private, Maryland Line. In December, 1817, the Treasurer of the Western Shore was directed to pay to Ignatius Brashears, of Prince George's County, an old soldier of the Maryland Line, during life, the half pay of a private, as further compensation for his services during the Revolutionary War [Ref: O-322, O-323]. He was pensioned in Prince George's County and paid in the District of Columbia in 1831 [Ref: T-50]. He also applied for and received pension S12279 in Prince George's County on Apr. 14, 1832, aged 79, stating he had been previously pensioned under the Act of Mar. 18, 1818. His sister, Dorcas Brashears, aged 76, lived with him [Ref: P-369].

BRASHEARS, Isaac. Took the Oath of Allegiance before the Hon. James Mullikin in 1778 [Ref: O-295].

BRASHEARS, Jeremiah (Nov. 15, 1731 - 1785). Son of Samuel and Elizabeth Brashears, of Queen Anne's Parish [Ref: ZC-166]. Served on a Grand Jury in 1777-1778 [Ref: Z-23, Z-52]. Took the Oath of Allegiance before the Hon. Thomas Williams in 1778 [Ref: O-302]. The estate of one "Jerremiah Brashears" was probated on May 15, 1785 [Ref: ZE-26].

BRASHEARS, Jeremiah (1751-   ). Private, Select Militia, Upper Battalion, June 12, 1781 [Ref: S-6636 (Box 27, folder 82B), R-52].

BRASHEARS, John. There were several men with this name: (1) Took the Oath of Allegiance before the Hon. William Lock Weems in 1778 [Ref: O-301, R-77]. (2) Took the Oath of Allegiance before the Hon. Osborn Sprigg in 1778 [Ref: O-307]. (3) Took the Oath of Allegiance before the Hon. Thomas Williams in 1778 [Ref: O-302]. (4) Private (substitute), Maryland Line, discharged on Dec. 3, 1781 [Ref: D-406, I-

10]. One John Brashears was aged 53 in 1776 and John P. Brashears was aged 24 in 1776 [Ref: R-77]. "John P. Brashears" married Ann Pumphry by license dated Dec. 9, 1778 and "Jonathan Brashears" married Mary Brown by license dated June 12, 1781 [Ref: ZB-28]. Additional research may be necessary before drawing conclusions. See "Samuel Brashears," q.v.

BRASHEARS, Joseph. Took the Oath of Allegiance before the Hon. Thomas Williams in 1778 [Ref: O-302]. One Joseph Brashears married Mary Cross by license dated Dec. 10, 1780 [Ref: ZB-28]. The estate of one Joseph Brashears was probated by Mar. 7, 1788 (date of account). [Ref: ZE-26]. See "Ignatius Brashears," q.v.

BRASHEARS, Joshua. Took the Oath of Allegiance before the Hon. James Mullikin in 1778 [Ref: O-295].

BRASHEARS, Levi. See "Ignatius Brashears," q.v.

BRASHEARS, Lucy. See "Joseph Cross," q.v.

BRASHEARS, Martha. See "James Hodges," q.v.

BRASHEARS, Mary. See "Ignatius Brashears" and "Levin Willcoxen," q.v.

BRASHEARS, Morris (Sep. 24, 1756 - died after 1832). Private, Maryland Line. He applied for and received a pension (S3083) in Roan County, Tennessee on Sep. 24, 1832, aged 76, stating he enlisted in Prince George's County, Maryland in 1776 [Ref: P-369]. Morris Brashears was a private in Capt. Edward Burgess' Company of Frederick County militia in August, 1776 [Ref: D-42].

BRASHEARS, Nacy. See "Ignatius Brashears," q.v.

BRASHEARS, Nancy. See "Ignatius Brashears," q.v.

BRASHEARS, Osburn. Private, Select Militia, Upper Battalion, June 12, 1781 [Ref: S-6636 (Box 27, folder 82B)]. One Osburn Brashears married Martha Oden by license dated June 1, 1785, and "...burn" Brashears married "Elanor Procter" by license dated Feb. 14, 1795 [Ref: ZB-28]. The estate of one "Osborn Brashears" was probated by Apr. 13, 1791 (date of account). [Ref: ZE-26].

BRASHEARS, Pamelia. See "Ignatius Brashears," q.v.

BRASHEARS, Priscilla. See "William Brashears," q.v.

BRASHEARS, Rachel. See "Joseph Belt" and "Osborne S. Belt," q.v.

BRASHEARS, Robert. See "Ignatius Brashears," q.v.

BRASHEARS, Ruth. See "Frederick Miles" and "Samuel Brashears" and "Ignatius Brashears," q.v.

BRASHEARS, Samuel (Sep. 20, 1739 - 1794). Son of John and Ruth Brashears, of Queen Anne's Parish [Ref: ZC-166]. Took the Oath of Allegiance before the Hon. Christopher Lowndes in 1778 [Ref: O-284, which spelled the name "Brashear"]. The estate of one Samuel Brashears was probated on Aug. 9, 1794 [Ref: ZE-27]. See "Ignatius Brashears" and "Jeremiah Brashears," q.v.

BRASHEARS, Samuel Jr. Private, Militia, 1776 [Ref: M-207, A-325].

BRASHEARS, Thomas. See "Ignatius Brashears," q.v.

BRASHEARS, Thomas Jr. Took the Oath of Allegiance before the Hon. James Mullikin in 1778 [Ref: O-296].
BRASHEARS, Thomas Sr. "Thomas Brashear, Sr." took the Oath of Allegiance before the Hon. James Beck in 1778 [Ref: O-255]. The estate of one "Thomas Brashears" was probated by Sep. 21, 1802 (date of account and inventory). [Ref: ZE-27].
BRASHEARS, Tobias (c1756, Maryland - December, 1807, Mississippi). Captain, Virginia Line. He married Martha Brookes [Ref: X-349]. *Ed. Note:* He is listed here only because of the family connection that he and his wife both had to Prince George's County, Maryland.
BRASHEARS, Walter. See "Ignatius Brashears," q.v.
BRASHEARS, Wilkinson. "Wilkason Brashear" took the Oath of Allegiance before the Hon. James Beck in 1778 [Ref: O-255]. "Wilkinson Brashears" married Hannah Brown by license dated Feb. 4, 1788 [Ref: ZB-28]. The estate of Wilkinson Brashears was probated by Feb. 10, 1807 (date of inventory). [Ref: ZE-27].
BRASHEARS, William. Private, Select Militia, Upper Battalion, June 12, 1781 [Ref: S-6636 (Box 27, folder 82B)]. William Brashears, son of William and Priscilla Brashears, of Queen Anne's Parish, was born on Mar. 14, 1734 [Ref: ZC-166].
BRASHEARS, Zadock (1756 - died before Aug. 7, 1781, Kentucky). Took the Oath of Allegiance (made his "|" mark) before the Hon. James Mullikin in 1778 [Ref: O-295]. Source X-329 states Zadock Brashears served as a soldier in Maryland and married Susanna Vaughan. This was probably the Zadock Brashears who enlisted in Anne Arundel County on July 25, 1776 [Ref: D-40]. Another Zadock Brashears married Elizabeth Drane by license dated Feb. 9, 1790, in Prince George's County [Ref: ZB-29].
BREEDEN, George Blunt. See "Thomas Gantt, Jr.," q.v.
BRENT, Catherine. See "George Digges," q.v.
BRENT, Eleanor. See "Clement Hill, Jr." and "Henry Waring," q.v.
BRIANT, Richard. Took the Oath of Allegiance before the Hon. David Craufurd in 1778 [Ref: O-271].
BRICE, Sarah. See "Richard Henderson," q.v.
BRIGHTWELL, Allen. Corporal in Capt. Benjamin Wailes' Militia Company, Lower Battalion; on duty guarding Magruder's Warehouse in the spring of 1782 [Ref: L-19970 (Box 6, folder 21)]. One Allen Brightwell married Jane Pearce by license dated Mar. 13, 1802 [Ref: ZB-29]. The estate of one Allen Brightwell was probated on July 14, 1819 [Ref: ZE-27].
BRIGHTWELL, John Lawson. Took the Oath of Allegiance which was recorded on a "return of Capt. Tapley of the brig *Royal*" and filed in court by the Hon. Thomas Gantt, Jr. in 1778 [Ref: O-305, W-4648 (Box 4, folder 15)]. One "John Lawson Brightwell" married Sophinia

Brightwell by license dated Feb. 15, 1802 [Ref: ZB-29]. The estate of "John L. Brightwell" was probated on Feb. 26, 1805 [Ref: ZE-27].

BRIGHTWELL, Richard. Took the Oath of Allegiance before the Hon. Alexander Howard Magruder in 1778 [Ref: O-293]. Constable in Prince Frederick Hundred, 1777-1778 [Ref: Z-3, Z-30]. One Richard Brightwell married Mary Purce (Peerce or Pearce?) by license dated May 3, 1785 [Ref: ZB-29]. The estate of one "Richard Brightwell" was probated on Mar. 22, 1802, and the estate of one "Richard L. Brightwell" was probated on May 20, 1801 [Ref: ZE-27, ZE-28]. Additional research may be necessary before drawing conclusions.

BRIGHTWELL, Sophinia. See "John Lawson Brightwell," q.v.

BRIGHTWELL, Theodore. Private, Militia, who was inducted into the Maryland Line, and discharged on Dec. 3, 1781 [Ref: D-406, I-10, which spelled his name "Thiodore Bridewell"]. Corporal, Capt. Alexander H. Magruder's Militia Company, Lower Battalion; on duty guarding Magruder's Warehouse in the spring of 1782 [Ref: L-19970 (Box 6, folder 21)].

BRINAM, Jane. See "James Adams," q.v.

BRISCOE, Philip. Private, 1st Maryland Line, enlisted June 3, 1778 and discharged Aprl 5, 1779; paid for his services "in cloathing" on Apr. 17, 1779 [Ref: D-82, E-351].

BRISCOE, Sarah. See "Alexander Truman," q.v.

BRITTAIN, John. Private, Capt. Alexander Truman's Company, who was stationed at Annapolis in 1781 and reported on "a list of men who have deserted since Mar. 1, 1781." [Ref: L-19970 (Box 7, folder 52)].

BROCKHILL, Richard. Private, 2nd Maryland Line, Capt. Alexander Truman's Company, 1782; reported "not heard of since Mar. muster, then sick at Annapolis." [Ref: D-440].

BRODIE, Daniel. Private (draft), continental service, Maryland Line, 1781 [Ref: D-382].

BRODIE, John. "John Brodie" took the Oath of Allegiance before the Hon. William Berry in 1778 [Ref: O-258]. The estate of one "John Brodia" was probated by May 27, 1790 (date of account). [Ref: ZE-28].

BROGDEN, John (of Anne Arundel County). Took the Oath of Allegiance before the Hon. Thomas Boyd in Prince George's County in 1778 [Ref: O-261].

BROOKE, Ann. See "Richard Brooke" and "Thomas Duckett" and "Christopher Beall," q.v.

BROOKE, Barbara. See "John Eversfield," q.v.

BROOKE, Eleanor. See "Basil Waring, Sr.," q.v.

BROOKE, Elizabeth. See "Thomas Beall, of George" and "Walter Bowie" and "Henry Brooke," q.v.

BROOKE, Frederick Thomas. See "Richard Brooke," q.v.

BROOKE, Henry (1730-1784). Rendered patriotic service by providing wheat for the military on Apr. 30, 1783 [Ref: Q-594]. Took the Oath of

Allegiance before the Hon. Truman Skinner in 1778 [Ref: O-297]. Henry Brooke is spoken of as "Captain" and in his will he referred to himself as "I, Henry Brooke, Mariner." Apparently, he was the commander of a ship prior to the revolution. He married Mary Carroll and had these children: Henry Brooke, Henry Maxwell Brooke, and Elizabeth Brooke [Ref: X-378, ZA-90]. The estate of "Capt. Henry Brook" was probated by Jan. 17, 1785 (date of inventory). [Ref: ZE-28].

BROOKE, Hetta. See "Henry Hill, Jr.," q.v.

BROOKE, James. See "Richard Brooke," q.v.

BROOKE, Jane. See "John Contee," q.v.

BROOKE, Margaret. Rendered patriotic service by providing wheat for the military on Apr. 30, 1783 [Ref: Q-594]. The estate of one Margaret Brooke was probated on Aug. 27, 1812 [Ref: ZE-29].

BROOKE, Mary. See "Joseph Sim" and "Henry Waring," q.v.

BROOKE, Millicent. See "Henry Waring," q.v.

BROOKE, Nicholas (born before Feb. 13, 1752 - died before Dec. 14, 1797). Second Lieutenant, 1st Guard, Capt. Henry Hill's Militia Company, Lower Battalion; on duty at Nottingham on the Patuxent, Apr. 12, 1781 [Ref: L-19970 (Box 6, folder 21)]. Took the Oath of Allegiance before the Hon. Truman Skinner in 1778 [Ref: O-298]. Rendered patriotic service by providing wheat for the military on May 10, 1783 [Ref: Q-599]. Second Lieutenant, Lower Battalion, Capt. Henry Hill's Company, July 3, 1780 [Ref: M-56, F-210, which spelled his name "Nicholas Brooks"]. Nicholas Brooke married ---- Hill [Ref: X-378]. The estate of one Nicholas Brooke was probated by Dec. 14, 1797 (date of inventory). [Ref: ZE-29].

BROOKE, Oswell. Private, 3rd Guard, Capt. Henry Hill's Militia Company, Lower Battalion; on duty at Nottingham on the Patuxent, Apr. 12, 1781 [Ref: L-19970 (Box 6, folder 21)]. The estate of one "Dr. Oswald Brooke" was probated on Oct. 21, 1800 [Ref: ZE-29].

BROOKE, Priscilla. See "Fielder Gantt" and "Thomas Gantt," q.v.

BROOKE, Rachel. See "Richard Brooke" and "Thomas Gantt," q.v.

BROOKE, Richard (June 2, 1716 - July 12, 1783). A son of Thomas Brooke and Lucy Smith, he married Rachel Gantt in 1767 and had a son Frederick Thomas Brooke and a daughter Sarah (Brooke) Harper [Ref: U-169, U-170, ZA-85, ZA-86, ZE-30]. Doctor Brooke was a Delegate to the Maryland Convention, 1774-1776 [Ref: A-4, U-70], and took the Oath of Allegiance before the Hon. Thomas Gantt, Jr. in 1778 [Ref: O-305, W-4648 (Box 4, folder 15)].

BROOKE, Richard (July 8, 1736 - May 2, 1788). A son of James Brooke and Deborah Snowden, he married Jane Lynn in 1758 and had a son Roger Brooke and a daughter Ann Dorsey. Born in Prince George's County, he attended the Maryland Convention in 1774 and 1775 as a representative of Frederick County, and was Commissioner of the Tax

in Montgomery County, 1777-1785. Richard Brooke was a major and later a colonel during the war [Ref: U-170, X-378].
BROOKE, Roger. See "Richard Brooke," q.v.
BROOKE, Sarah. See "Richard Beall" and "William D. Beall," q.v.
BROOKE, Thomas. See "Richard Brooke," q.v.
BROOKE, Walter. Private, Capt. Jesse Hellen's Militia Company, by May 23, 1782; guarded Magruder's Warehouse in the spring of 1782 [Ref: L-19970 (Box 6, folder 21), which spelled his name "Brook"].
BROOKES, Anne. See "Allen Bowie, Sr.," q.v.
BROOKES, Benjamin (Sep. 4, 1752 - Jan., 1800). Brother of "John Smith Brookes," q.v. First Lieutenant, 11th Battalion, Capt. Robert Bowie's Company, July 3, 1776 [Ref: M-56, A-244, D-34]. He was paid by order of the Council of Safety for services rendered "for collecting [enumerating] the number of souls in part of Prince George's County" on Sep. 9, 1776 [Ref: B-259]. County Coroner, 1776-1777 [Ref: C-273]. On Feb. 13, 1781, David Crawford recommended to the Governor that "Benjamin Brooks" be appointed vendue master [Ref: Q-361]. "Benjamin Brookes, Jr." was a major in the war and married Margaret Sprigg Bowie [Ref: X-379. Source ZA-647 states he died on Nov. 3, 1786, aged 62, and was a brother of Lieut. John Smith Brookes. There is a discrepancy since the dates of birth and death do not match, and Source ZA-648 states Major Benjamin Brookes, of the Revolutionary War, married Margaret Bowie in 1785, and Benjamin Brookes, Sr. died in 1787. This latter Benjamin was the father of Major Benjamin Brookes and Lieut. John Smith Brookes]. "Benjamin Brookes" married Sarah Johnson by license dated Nov. 7, 1782, and "Benjamin Brookes, Jr." married Margaret S. Bowie by license dated Dec. 24, 1785 [Ref: ZB-31]. The estate of one Benjamin Brookes was probated on Jan. 15, 1787, and the estate of another Benjamin Brookes was probated on Feb. 11, 1800 [Ref: ZE-30]. Additional research will be necessary before drawing conclusions. See "James Drane" and "William Sprigg Bowie," q.v.
BROOKES, Elizabeth Sprigg. See "William Sprigg Bowie," q.v.
BROOKES, Henry. Lieutenant who served on a General Courts-Martial for the trial of Capt. Richard Bennett Hall, Lieut. Jeremiah Ryley, Lieut. Jonathan Wright, and Lieut. James Mullikin on July 25, 1776, at Upper Marlboro [Ref: A-553]. Took the Oath of Allegiance before the Hon. Truman Skinner in 1778 [Ref: O-297]. The estate of one Henry Brookes was probated on Oct. 8, 1806 [Ref: ZE-30].
BROOKES, John Smith. First Lieutenant, Lower Battalion, Aug. 23, 1776 to at least Sep. 1, 1777 [Ref: M-56, C-356, B-233]. He served on a General Courts-Martial for the trial of Capt. Richard Bennett Hall, Lieut. Jeremiah Ryley, Lieut. Jonathan Wright, and Lieut. James Mullikin on July 25, 1776, and Aug. 23, 1776, at Upper Marlboro [Ref: A-553, B-233]. Captain, Middle Battalion, 1778-1780 [Ref: M-56, N-35, E-63, which spelled his name "John Smith Brooks"]. Commissary of

Purchases for Prince George's County, 1780-1783 [Ref: Q-410, Q-425, Q-594, Q-598, F-222, F-215, which latter source spelled his name "Jno. Smith Brooks"]. Captain, Middle Battalion, June 24, 1780 (succeeded). [Ref: M-56, which spelled his name "Jonathan S. Brooke," and F-203, which spelled his name "Jonathan Smith Brookes"]. Lieut. John Smith Brookes married Anne Bowie (1751-1782, daughter of Allen Bowie, Sr.) by license dated Oct. 31, 1780 [Ref: ZA-647, ZB-30, which latter source spelled his name "John Smith Brooke"]. Also, John Smith Brookes married Eleanor Harwood by license dated June 3, 1786 [Ref: ZB-31]. The estate of John Smith Brookes was probated on Feb. 30 *[sic]*, 1815 [Ref: ZE-30]. See "Benjamin Brookes," q.v.

BROOKES, Juliet M. See "Walter Bowie," q.v.

BROOKES, Margaret S. See "William Bowie," q.v.

BROOKES, Martha. See "Tobias Brashears," q.v.

BROOKES, Mary. See "Walter Bowie," q.v.

BROOKES, William. Took the Oath of Allegiance before the Hon. Joshua Beall in 1778 [Ref: O-251].

BROOKS, Leonard. Took the Oath of Allegiance before the Hon. Truman Skinner in 1778 [Ref: O-297]. The estate of one "Capt. Leonard Brookes" was probated in 1783 [Ref: ZE-30].

BROWN, Alice. See "Frederick Duvall" and "Lewis Duvall," q.v.

BROWN, Ann. See "Samuel Hutchinson" and "Basil Brown," q.v.

BROWN, Basil (Oct. 25, 1732, Maryland - Feb. 10, 1807, Pennsylvania). Son of Thomas and Ann Brown, of Queen Anne's Parish, Prince George's County, Maryland [Ref: ZC-166]. Private, 3rd Maryland Line, Capt. Horatio Clagett's Company, December, 1779 [Ref: D-296]. "Bazil Brown" was a private in the Maryland Line and married Elizabeth Brashears [Ref: X-387].

BROWN, Benjamin (1741-   ). Took the Oath of Allegiance before the Hon. Christopher Lowndes in 1778 [Ref: O-284, R-44].

BROWN, Catherine. See "Thomas Beall," q.v.

BROWN, Elisha. Took the Oath of Allegiance (made his "X" mark) before the Hon. Alexander Howard Magruder in 1778 [Ref: O-293].

BROWN, Elizabeth. See "John Hooper," q.v.

BROWN, George. Private, 3rd Maryland Line, enlisted Apr. 28, 1778. Private, Capt. Horatio Clagett's Company, 1779 [Ref: D-295]. The estate of "George Brown (soldier)" was probated on Sep. 8, 1792, in Prince George's County [Ref: ZE-31].

BROWN, Hannah. See "Wilkerson Brashears," q.v.

BROWN, James (Oct. 8, 1727-   ). Son of John and Mary Brown [Ref: ZD-110]. Took the Oath of Allegiance before the Hon. Christopher Lowndes in 1778 [Ref: O-286].

BROWN, James. There were several men with this name who served in the Maryland Line [Ref: D-61, D-67, D-85, D-88, D-185, D-275, D-340]. One James Brown was aged 26 in the 1776 census of Prince George's

County and may have served in the Maryland Line. Additional research will be necessary before drawing conclusions.

BROWN, John. There were several men with this name. The estate of one "John Brown (soldier)" was probated on Apr. 13, 1793 in Prince George's County [Ref: ZE-31]. One John Brown took the Oath of Allegiance before the Hon. Osborn Sprigg in 1778 [Ref: O-307]. One John Brown was a private in the 4th Maryland Regiment who enlisted on May 18, 1782 for 3 years and was sworn in May 23, 1782 [Ref: D-417]. One John Brown was born in 1748 and another John Brown, son of Peter and Mary Brown, was born on Dec. 19, 1754 [Ref: ZD-110, R-67]. Additional may be necessary before drawing conclusions. Also see the other John Browns cited below.

BROWN, John, planter (1720-   ). Took the Oath of Allegiance before the Hon. Christopher Lowndes in 1778 [Ref: O-285, R-28].

BROWN, John, shoemaker (Jan. 21, 1723/4-   ). Son of John and Mary Brown, of Queen Anne's Parish [Ref: ZC-166, R-28]. Took the Oath of Allegiance before the Hon. Christopher Lowndes in 1778 [Ref: O-283].

BROWN, John, of John (1745-   ). Took the Oath of Allegiance before the Hon. Christopher Lowndes in 1778 [Ref: O-282, R-28].

BROWN, John Jr. Took the Oath of Allegiance before the Hon. Fielder Bowie in 1778 [Ref: O-303, which listed the name as "John ----;" however, the original list at the Maryland State Archives (Box 4, folder 15) clearly shows the name to be "John Brown, Jr."]. Served on the Board of Patuxent Associators and signed a resolution at Nottingham on Apr. 21, 1781 relative to the defence of the rivers of Potomac and Patuxent and the completion of the fort at Drum Point [Ref: K-1814]. See "John Brown," q.v.

BROWN, Mary. See "John Brashears" and "John Brown" and "John White," q.v.

BROWN, Peter (c1750, Germany - 1823, Maryland). Sergeant, Capt. Barton Lucas' Company, 3rd Maryland Line, enlisted Jan. 20, 1776 [Ref: D-9, M-207]. Also took the Oath of Allegiance before the Hon. Christopher Lowndes in 1778 [Ref: O-286]. Peter married Susan ---- [Ref: X-398]. There was also a Peter Brown who married Elizabeth Beall by license dated May 11, 1781 [Ref: ZB-34]. The records of the Maryland Society, Sons of the American Revolution, indicate that Sgt. Peter Brown was one of the famous "Maryland 400" who fought at the Battle of Long Island on Aug. 27, 1776 and saved Gen. Washington's Army from being totally destroyed. It should be noted that another Peter Brown was a lieutenant in the 1st Maryland Line from Dec. 10, 1776 until July 10, 1777, when he resigned [Ref: D-80]. Therefore, additional research may be necessary before drawing conclusions. See "John Brown," q.v.

BROWN, Sarah. See "William Manley," q.v.

BROWN, Thomas. Private in the militia in 1776 [Ref: M-207, A-325]. One Thomas Brown married Sarah Taylor by license dated June 29, 1777, a Thomas Brown married Mary Lowe by license dated Nov. 9, 1778, and a Thomas Brown married Mary Ann Taylor by license dated June 4, 1802 [Ref: ZB-34]. Additional research may be necessary before drawing conclusions. See "Basil Brown," q.v.
BROWN, Thomas, of John (shoemaker). Took the Oath of Allegiance before the Hon. Christopher Lowndes in 1778 [Ref: O-284].
BROWN, William (1688 - after 1778). Took the Oath of Allegiance before the Hon. Christopher Lowndes in 1778 [Ref: O-284, R-27, which latter source gave his age as 78 in the 1776 census].
BROWN, William Jr. Private, Militia, 1776 [Ref: M-207, A-325]. Took the Oath of Allegiance before the Hon. James Beck in 1778 [Ref: O-253].
BROWN, William, of John. Took the Oath of Allegiance before the Hon. Christopher Lowndes in 1778 [Ref: O-284].
BROWN, Zachariah. Took the Oath of Allegiance before the Hon. William Berry in 1778 [Ref: O-258].
BROWN, Zephaniah. Took the Oath of Allegiance before the Hon. Christopher Lowndes in 1778 [Ref: O-288].
BROWNE, John. Private, Capt. Alexander Truman's Company, stationed at Annapolis in 1781 and was reported on "a list of men who have deserted since Mar. 1, 1781." [Ref: L-19970 (Box 7, folder 52)].
BRUCE, Sarah Magruder. See "Thomas Clagett," q.v.
BRUCE, William. Sergeant, 9th Company of Light Infantry, enlisted on Jan. 26, 1776 [Ref: D-18]. Lieutenant, 1st Maryland Line, Dec. 10, 1776, and Captain, Aug. 1, 1779 [Ref: D-80, D-364, D-381]. The estate of one William Bruce was probated by Oct. 3, 1801 (date of inventory), and the estate of one William Bruce was probated on June 22, 1813 [Ref: ZE-32].
BRUINGTON, Preistly. Private, Northern Detachment, 3rd Maryland Line, Capt. Horatio Clagett's Company, 1783 [Ref: D-501].
BRYAN, George. Recruited for the military before Aug. 28, 1780 when the County Lieutenant reported to the Council of Maryland that he (Bryan) had not reported and he "shall endeavour to apprehend him if to be found in the county." [Ref: G-63].
BRYAN, John. Took the Oath of Allegiance before the Hon. Benjamin Hall in 1778 [Ref: O-274].
BRYAN, Peter. Private, 6th Maryland Line, enlisted June 1, 1779 and reportedly "deserted" on June 5, 1779 [Ref: D-275]. Took the Oath of Allegiance in 1780 [Ref: J-106]. The estate of one Peter Bryan was probated on Apr. 9, 1794 [Ref: ZE-32].
BRYAN, Richard (1730-1813). Took the Oath of Allegiance (made his "R" mark) before the Hon. Thomas Clagett in 1778 [Ref: O-266, R-17]. The estate of one Richard Bryan was probated on Feb. 6, 1813 [Ref: ZE-32].

BRYAN, Simpkin (Limpkin?). Simpkin (or Limpkin?) Bryan took the Oath of Allegiance before the Hon. Benjamin Hall in 1778 [Ref: O-274]. The estate of a "Limkin Bryan" was probated on Feb. 27, 1821 [Ref: ZE-32].
BRYAN, Thomas (baptized Aug. 25, 1751 - 1822). Son of William Bryan and Diana Gutteridge [Ref: ZC-10]. Took the Oath of Allegiance in 1780 [Ref: J-106, R-81]. The estate of one Thomas Bryan was probated on Dec. 21, 1822 [Ref: ZE-32].
BRYCE, Mary. See "Gabriel Duvall," q.v.
BUCHAN, Margaret. See "Kidd Morsell," q.v.
BUCHAN, Robert (1717-   ). Took the Oath of Allegiance before the Hon. William Berry in 1778 [Ref: O-258, R-20].
BUCHANAN, Mary. See "Robert Pottenger," q.v.
BUCHANAN, Sophia. See "Richard Duckett, Jr.," q.v.
BUCKHAM, James. Private, Militia, 1781; participated in capturing an enemy boat and crew on Apr. 17, 1781 [Ref: M-208].
BUCKINGHAM, Richard. Took the Oath of Allegiance before the Hon. Osborn Sprigg in 1778 [Ref: O-308, which spelled his name "Richard Buckinham"].
BUCKLER, John. Took the Oath of Allegiance before the Hon. James Beck in 1778 [Ref: O-255].
BUKNELL, Esau. Private, 3rd Maryland Line, Capt. Horatio Clagett's Company, December, 1779 [Ref: D-296].
BULGER, Richard (1728-1795). Took the Oath of Allegiance before the Hon. Christopher Lowndes in 1778 [Ref: O-286, R-49]. The estate of Richard Bulger was probated on Oct. 21, 1795 [Ref: ZE-32].
BULL, Mary. See "Banks Webb," q.v.
BUMFORD, Joseph. Fifer, enrolled by Capt. Alexander H. Magruder, 11th Battalion, on July 12, 1776, for continental service, Maryland Line [Ref: D-38].
BURCH, Anastasia. See "Edward Burch," q.v.
BURCH, Benjamin (May 9, 1761 - May 5, 1832). Private, and later sergeant, 6th Maryland Line; taken prisoner of war; exchanged by Sep. 3, 1781, at which time he was paid 5 pounds specie on his account [Ref: D-616]. His widow Rebecca applied and received pension W23743 in Washington, DC on Dec. 3, 1836, stating Benjamin had died on May 5, 1832. They married in Prince George's County on Sep. 17, 1784, and their oldest child Mildred Rhodes verified this information, stating she (Mildred) was a widow and resident of Washington, DC, born on Aug. 14, 1785, and her sister Martha married George I. Cain and died in 1837. In 1854 Benjamin Burch's surviving children were: Verlinda Wiltberger (wife of Charles H. Wiltberger, late Register of Washington, DC); Mildred Rhodes (wife of William Rhodes); Susan Hewit (widow of William Hewit, also a late Register of Washington, DC); and Elizabeth Wilson (wife of George W. Wilson, of Washington, DC). Captain Benjamin Burch served in the Revolutionary War and the War of 1812.

He was Doorkeeper for the U. S. House of Representatives for 22 years [Ref: P-464]. Benjamin Burch married Rebecca Barron by license dated Sep. 6, 1784 [Ref: X-430, ZB-36].
BURCH, Benjamin. Private, 4th Maryland Regiment, enlisted Feb. 14, 1782 for 3 years; sworn in Feb. 25, 1782 [Ref: D-417]. He may have been the Benjamin Burch with wife Chloe who lived in Ohio County, Kentucky when he applied for pension on Sep. 27, 1828 and his widow subsequently received pension W4137 [Ref: P-464, which source informed readers that "the microfilm (M804, roll 408) was too light to read regarding her affidavit."]. There was also a Benjamin Burch who married Mary Townsend by license dated Feb. 22, 1784, in Prince George's County [Ref: ZB-36].
BURCH, Edward (born circa 1755 - died after 1790). Took the Oath of Allegiance before the Hon. Osborn Sprigg in 1778 [Ref: O-308, W-4648 (Box 4, folder 29), X-430]. "Edward Burch II, son of Edward and Anastasia Burch (married second to Alex MacDonald), married Ann Spink on Oct. 15, 1779 in Prince George's County, and he was supposedly a corporal in the Revolution per descendants, but cannot find proof." [Ref: Query from Ms. Sarah A. Cannon, P. O. Box 9218 VRS, Beaumont, Texas 77709 in *Prince George's County Genealogical Society Bulletin*, Volume 25, No. 8 (Apr., 1994), p. 150]. Actually, Edward Burch married Mary Spinks by license dated Oct. 15, 1779 [Ref: ZB-36].
BURCH, Elizabeth. See "John Burch," q.v.
BURCH, Francis. Private, 1st Maryland Line, enlisted Mar. 29, 1777 and discharged on Mar. 29, 1780 [Ref: D-82]. He married Penelope Vermillion by license dated Jan. 24, 1783 [Ref: ZB-36].
BURCH, James. Private, 2nd Maryland Line, Capt. Alexander Truman's Company, 1782 [Ref: D-440, which spelled his name "James Burck"].
BURCH, Jane. See "Andrew Hamilton," q.v.
BURCH, John (Jan. 18, 1759 - Mar. 1, 1834). Born in Prince George's County, he lived in Charles County and moved to Prince William County, Virginia circa 1778. He married Elizabeth Benham in 1779 and served in the Maryland and Virginia Lines during the war. He later moved to Fauquier County, on to Amherst County, Virginia, and finally to Barren County, Kentucky circa 1810. He died in 1834 and his widow received a pension (W5238) beginning in 1848 [Ref: X-430, and Annie Walker Burns' *Maryland Soldiers of the Revolutionary War Who Settled in Kentucky*, p. 6].
BURCH, Jonathan Jr. (1740-   ). Took the Oath of Allegiance before the Hon. Thomas Clagett in 1778 [Ref: O-268, R-74].
BURCH, Margaret. See "Thomas Humphrey," q.v.
BURCH, Martha. See "Benjamin Burch," q.v.
BURCH, Mildred. See "Benjamin Burch," q.v.
BURCH, Oliver (1748-   ). Took the Oath of Allegiance before the Hon. Thomas Clagett in 1778 [Ref: O-264, R-24]. Ensign, Middle Battalion,

Capt. Samuel H. Beans' Company, May 1, 1778 [Ref: M-58, E-63, N-36]. There was also another Oliver Burch (1713-1795) who rendered patriotic service during the war [Ref: X-430].

BURCH, Philip. Private, Capt. Hezekiah Wheeler's Company, 11th Militia Battalion, April, 1781 [Ref: L-19970 (Box 6, folder 21)]. Took the Oath of Allegiance before the Hon. William Lyles, Jr. in 1778 [Ref: O-290].

BURCH, Rebecca. See "Benjamin Burch," q.v.

BURCH, Richard. Private, Capt. Hezekiah Wheeler's Company, 11th Militia Battalion, April, 1781 [Ref: L-19970 (Box 6, folder 21)].

BURCH, Thomas. Took the Oath of Allegiance before the Hon. Osborn Sprigg in 1778 [Ref: O-307]. One Thomas Burch married Susanna Talburt by license dated July 26, 1780, and a Thomas Burch married Lenny Harvey by license dated Sep. 5, 1794 [Ref: ZB-36].

BURCH, Zachariah (1757, Maryland - Nov. 19, 1844, Missouri). Took the Oath of Allegiance before the Hon. William Lyles, Jr. in 1778 [Ref: O-290]. Private, 3rd Maryland Line, enlisted May 26, 1778; Capt. Horatio Clagett's Company, December, 1779 [Ref: D-296, which listed his name as "Zach. Burck (or Burch)"]. He was paid for services rendered on Apr. 22, 1782 [Ref: I-144]. Zachariah Burch married Mildred Robey [Ref: X-431].

BURGESS, Ann. See "James Haddock Smith," q.v.

BURGESS, Charles. Took the Oath of Allegiance before the Hon. Osborn Sprigg in 1778 [Ref: O-306]. Served on a Grand Jury in 1778 [Ref: Z-52]. The estate of one Charles Burgess was probated on Aug. 17, 1801 [Ref: ZE-33].

BURGESS, Edward. See "Morris Brashears," q.v.

BURGESS, Ezekiel. See "Ezekiel Burque," q.v.

BURGESS, John. Cadet, 2nd Maryland Line, Capt. Patrick Sim's Company, Jan., 1776 [Ref: D-7, which spelled it "Burgis"].

BURGESS, John Magruder. Ensign, Militia, Capt. John H. Lowe's Company, 1776. First Lieutenant, Lower Battalion, Capt. Belt's Company, Sep. 1, 1777. Captain, Middle Battalion, May 1, 1778. Major, Middle Battalion, Nov. 13, 1779 [Ref: D-34, M-58, C-356, E-63, F-13, N-35]. Took the Oath of Allegiance before the Hon. David Craufurd in 1778 [Ref: O-271]. One John M. Burgess married Eleanor Magruder by license dated Oct. 18, 1779, and a John M. Burgess married Elizabeth Coolidge (Cooledge) by license dated Feb. 26, 1794 [Ref: ZB-37]. The estate of one John M. Burgess was probated on Oct. 25, 1802 [Ref: ZE-33].

BURGESS, Josias (Mar. 27, 1760 -   ). Son of William and Mary "Burgys" of Prince George's Parish [Ref: ZD-110]. Private, 7th Maryland Line, enlisted on Apr. 20, 1778 and served to at least Nov., 1780 [Ref: D-189].

BURGESS, Mary. See "Josias Burgess," q.v.

BURGESS, Michael (1754 - died after 1795). Sergeant, later Ensign, 2nd Maryland Line, Capt. Patrick Sim's Company, by Feb., 1776 [Ref: D-7, which spelled his name "Michael Burgis"]. He married Sarah Warfield [Ref: X-435].

BURGESS, Mordecai. Second Lieutenant, Middle Battalion, Capt. Clement Wheeler's Company, May 1, 1778. First Lieutenant, Capt. Zachariah Berry's Company, June 24, 1780 [Ref: M-58, E-63, F-203, N-36]. Took the Oath of Allegiance before the Hon. Osborn Sprigg in 1778 [Ref: W-4648 (Box 4, folder 29), and O-306, which latter source misspelled his name as "Mordis"]. The estate of "Mordicai Burgess" was probated on Mar. 13, 1788 [Ref: ZE-34].

BURGESS, Rachel. See "Richard Thompson," q.v.

BURGESS, Richard. Private (volunteer), Militia; participated in capturing an enemy boat and crew on Apr. 17, 1781 [Ref: M-208]. Rendered patriotic service by providing wheat for the military on Apr. 30, 1783 [Ref: Q-594]. Took the Oath of Allegiance before the Hon. Osborn Sprigg in 1778 [Ref: O-307]. The estate of one Richard Burgess was probated on May 8, 1784 [Ref: ZE-34].

BURGESS, Richard Jr. Ensign, Middle Battalion, Capt. John Brooks' Company, May 1, 1778. Second Lieutenant, Capt. Samuel Hepburn's Company, June 24, 1780 [Ref: M-58, E-63, F-203, N-35]. Took the Oath of Allegiance before the Hon. David Craufurd in 1778 [Ref: O-271]. The estate of "Dr. Richard Burgess" was probated on Dec. 10, 1793 [Ref: ZE-34].

BURGESS, Sarah. See "Joseph Belt," q.v.

BURGESS, Ursula. See "William Bowie, 3rd," q.v.

BURGESS, Veach. Private, 2nd Maryland Line, Capt. Patrick Sim's Company, 1776 [Ref: D-8].

BURGESS, William. See "Josias Burgess," q.v.

BURK, James. The estate of "James Burk (soldier)" was probated on Mar. 4, 1793 in Prince George's County [Ref: ZE-34]. There were several men with this name in the Maryland Line [Ref: D-66, D-184, D-186, D-191, D-322, D-349, D-418, D-422, D-440, D-460, D-504]. Additional research may be necessary before drawing conclusions.

BURKHEAD, Nathaniel. Took the Oath of Allegiance before the Hon. James Beck in 1778 [Ref: O-254].

BURNES, David (Feb. 14, 1745/6 -   ). Son of James and Jemima Burnes [Ref: ZD-110]. Second Lieutenant, 25th Militia Battalion, Capt. John Weight's Company, May 1, 1778 [Ref: M-58, E-78, N-83, which latter source spelled the name "Burns"]. Took the Oath of Allegiance before the Hon. Christopher Lowndes in 1778 [Ref: O-286].

BURNES, James. Second Lieutenant, 11th Battalion, Capt. John Perry's Company, May 1, 1778 [Ref: M-58, E-62]. Second Lieutenant, Militia, 1778; reportedly "left the county" by May, 1779 [Ref: N-33]. Took the Oath of Allegiance before the Hon. William Berry in 1778 [Ref: O-259, which spelled the name "Burns"]. See "David Burnes," q.v.

BURNES, Jemima. See "David Burnes," q.v.

BURNES, John (Aug. 24, 1749 -   ). Took the Oath of Allegiance before the Hon. Christopher Lowndes in 1778 [Ref: O-287, ZD-110].
BURNES, Thomas (Aug. 27, 1747 -   ). Private, Maryland Line [Ref: ZD-119, D-185, D-275, which latter two sources spelled the name "Burns"].
BURNES, William (July 3, 1755 -   ). Private, enrolled by Ensign Alexander Truman on July 20, 1776, for continental service, Maryland Line [Ref: D-38, D-185, ZD-110].
BURNS, Annie W. See "Smallwood Acton" and "John Burch," q.v.
BURNS, Hugh. Private, 2nd Maryland Line, Capt. Murdock's Company, Mar. 15, 1781 [Ref: D-366].
BURNS, John. Took the Oath of Allegiance before the Hon. Alexander Howard Magruder in 1778 [Ref: O-293].
BURNS Luke. Private, Maryland Line, whose name appeared on "a list of invalids now in service at the garrison at Philadelphia on June 19, 1781." [Ref: D-623]. The estate of one Luke Burns was probated on Apr. 18, 1794 in Prince George's County [Ref: ZE-34].
BURQUE (BURGES?), Ezekiel (1746-   ). Took the Oath of Allegiance before the Hon. Benjamin Hall in 1778 [Ref: O-275, R-54, which latter source listed it as "Ezekiel Burque" in the 1776 census].
BURRELL, Alexander. Took the Oath of Allegiance before the Hon. James Mullikin in 1778 [Ref: O-296]. Alexander Burrell married Elenor Dent on Aug. 19, 1759 [Ref: ZC-11]. The estate of one Alexander Burrell was probated on June 26, 1784 [Ref: ZE-34].
BURRELL, Allen (1743, England -   ). Private, enlisted May 25, 1781, for 3 years in continental service, Maryland Line; sent to Annapolis; on duty July 13, 1781 [Ref: D-381]. An Allen Burrell married Susanna Wood by license dated Mar. 18, 1789 [Ref: ZB-37].
BURRELL, Sarah. See "John Denune," q.v.
BURROUGHS, Benjamin. Private, 2nd Maryland Line, Capt. Patrick Sim's Company, 1776 [Ref: D-8].
BURROUGHS, Charles. Private, 2nd Maryland Line, Capt. Patrick Sim's Company, 1776 [Ref: D-8].
BURROUGHS, George. See "Benjamin Wailes," q.v.
BURTON, Ann. See "Jeremiah Igleheart," q.v.
BURTON, Basil. See "Lewis Duvall," q.v.
BURTON, David. Private, enrolled by Capt. John H. Lowe on July 13, 1776, for continental service, Maryland Line [Ref: D-34, which spelled his name "Burtin"].
BURTON, Sarah. See "Jeremiah Igleheart," q.v.
BURTON, William. See "Jeremiah Igleheart," q.v.
BUSEY, Samuel (1745-   ). Private, enrolled in the Flying Camp by Capt. Robert Bowie on July 20, 1776; nativity: Prince George's County; height 5' 6"; has own gun [Ref: D-36]. One Samuel Busey married Sarah Roberts by license dated July 13, 1777 [Ref: ZB-38].

BUSEY, William. Took the Oath of Allegiance before the Hon. Fielder Bowie in 1778 [Ref: O-304, W-4648 (Box 4, folder 15)].
BUTLER, James. See "Thomas Butler," q.v.
BUTLER, Joyce. See "Thomas Butler," q.v.
BUTLER, Thomas (June 14, 1707 -   ). Son of James and Joyce Butler [Ref: ZC-12]. Took the Oath of Allegiance before the Hon. Osborn Sprigg in 1778 [Ref: O-308, W-4648 (Box 4, folder 29)].
BUTT, Aaron (Aron). Took the Oath of Allegiance before the Hon. Benjamin Hall in 1778 [Ref: O-274].
BUTT, Archibald. Took the Oath of Allegiance before the Hon. James Beck in 1778 [Ref: O-254]. He applied for and received pension S39252 in Greenbrier County, Virginia, on Nov. 23, 1819, aged 54 or 55, stating he enlisted at Georgetown in Prince George's County, Maryland, and served in the Maryland and North Carolina Lines. In 1820 he had a wife (not named) aged 49 and these children: Betsy Butt, aged 14; William Butt, aged 11; John Butt, aged 9; and Thomas Butt, aged 5 [Ref: P-501].
BUTT, Baruch. Took the Oath of Allegiance before the Hon. Thomas Williams in 1778 [Ref: O-302]. He applied for and received pension S39258 in Berkeley County, Virginia, on Apr. 28, 1818, aged 63, stating he enlisted in Prince George's County, Maryland. In 1820 he had a wife Dianna Butt, aged 60, and daughter Mary Butt, aged 13 [Ref: P-501, D-84, D-358, D-523]. See "Zachariah Butt," q.v.
BUTT, Betsy. See "Archibald Butt," q.v.
BUTT, Dianna. See "Baruch Butt," q.v.
BUTT, Dorcas. See "Dorcas Batt," q.v.
BUTT, Edward. Took the Oath of Allegiance before the Hon. Thomas Williams in 1778 [Ref: O-302]. The estate of one Edward Butt was probated on June 19, 1779 [Ref: ZE-35].
BUTT, Edward. Fifer, 2nd Maryland Line, enlisted Mar. 28, 1778; private, July 1, 1779; killed on Mar. 15, 1781 [Ref: P-501, D-84, D-523]. See "Zachariah Butt," q.v.
BUTT, John. See "Archibald Butt," q.v.
BUTT, Mary. See "Baruch Butt," q.v.
BUTT, Moses. See "Moses Batt," q.v.
BUTT, Thomas. Drummer, 2nd Maryland Line, enlisted Apr. 8, 1778, and still in service in November, 1780 [Ref: D-84]. Took the Oath of Allegiance before the Hon. James Beck in 1778 [Ref: O-254]. See "Archibald Butt" and"Zachariah Butt," q.v.
BUTT, William. See "Archibald Butt," q.v.
BUTT, Zachariah (July 10, 1759 - Aug. 16, 1780). Took the Oath of Allegiance before the Hon. Thomas Williams in 1778 [Ref: O-302]. Private, 2nd Maryland Line, from Mar. 28, 1778 until Aug. 16, 1780 when reported missing (at the Battle of Camden). [Ref: D-84, ZD-110]. Bounty land warrant (#1072-100) was filed by the heirs of Edward Butt indicating that Zachariah Butt served in the same company and he

(Zachariah) was killed on Aug. 16, 1780. He was older than Edward Butt, who was killed on Mar. 15, 1781, while serving as a fifer under Capt. Williams' Company in the 2nd Maryland Line. An heir, Thomas Butt, of Greenbrier County, Virginia (relationship not given) stated that Zachariah and Edward Butt were brothers. Barruck Butt, of Berkeley, Virginia, was a witness in the case, but no relationship was stated [Ref: P-501].

BYRNE, Michael. Private, Maryland Line; defective in August, 1780 [Ref: D-414].

BYZCH, James. Private, 2nd Maryland Line, Capt. Patrick Sim's Company, 1776 [Ref: D-8].

CAGE, Peter B. Private, Capt. Benjamin Wailes' Militia Company, Lower Battalion; on duty guarding Magruder's Warehouse in the spring of 1782 [Ref: L-19970 (Box 6, folder 21)]. Peter B. Cage married Mary Parker by license dated Jan. 20, 1783 [Ref: ZB-39].

CAGE, William. Private, Capt. Benjamin Wailes' Militia Company, Lower Battalion; on duty guarding Magruder's Warehouse in the spring of 1782 [Ref: L-19970 (Box 6, folder 21)]. William Cage married Mary Mahew (Mayhew) by license dated Dec. 18, 1777 [Ref: ZB-39].

CAGE, Wilson. Private, enrolled by Ensign Alexander Truman on July 8, 1776, for continental service, Maryland Line [Ref: D-38]. There was a William Wilson Cage who married Verlinda Mahew (Mayhew) by license dated Dec. 22, 1807 [Ref: ZB-39].

CAHOE, Robert. Took the Oath of Allegiance before the Hon. Christopher Lowndes in 1778 [Ref: O-285].

CAHOE, Thomas. Private, enrolled by Ensign Alexander Truman on July 4, 1776, for continental service, Maryland Line [Ref: D-38, which spelled his name "Thomas Cohoe"].

CAHOE, Thomas Jr. Fifer, 2nd Maryland Line, Capt. Alexander Truman's Company, 1782; waiter to Lieut. Lynn, 1782 [Ref: D-439].

CAHOE, Thomas Sr. Private, 2nd Maryland Line, Capt. Alexander Truman's Company, 1782 [Ref: D-440].

CAIN, Edward. Private, 2nd Maryland Line, Capt. Patrick Sim's Company, 1776 [Ref: D-8, which spelled the name "Caine"]. The estate of one Edward Cain was probated on May 15, 1794 [Ref: ZE-35]. See "Edward Kaine," q.v.

CAIN, Elizabeth. See "Robert Conn," q.v.

CAIN, George. See "Benjamin Burch," q.v.

CAIN, Martha. See "Benjamin Burch," q.v.

CAIN, Michael. Private, 4th Maryland Line, May 28, 1777 to May 28, 1780; "discharged for inability." [Ref: D-98]. The estate of one Michael Cain was probated on Apr. 14, 1807 [Ref: ZE-36].

CALLAHAN, Eleanor. See "John Newton," q.v.

CALLAHANE, Rosamond. See "Zachariah Prather," q.v.

CALLICO, Peter. "Peter Callico" was a private in Capt. Alexander H. Magruder's Militia Company, Lower Battalion; on duty guarding Magruder's Warehouse in the spring of 1782 [Ref: L-19970 (Box 6, folder 21)]. See "Peter Carrico," q.v.

CALLIHORN, John (1713-   ). "John Callihorn" took the Oath of Allegiance (made his "X" mark) before the Hon. Thomas Clagett in 1778 [Ref: O-268]. "John Calihorn" was aged 63 in the 1776 census of Prince George's County [Ref: R-75]. There was also a "John Callahane" who married Susanna Sherwood by license dated Feb. 21, 1778 [Ref: ZB-40].

CALVERT, Benedict. Took the Oath of Allegiance in 1781 [Ref: J-107]. The estate of one Benedict Calvert was probated on Feb. 18, 1788 [Ref: ZE-36].

CALVERT, Elizabeth. See "Charles Stewart," q.v.

CAMEL, Robert. Private, Capt. Alexander Truman's Company, stationed at Annapolis in 1781 and reported on "a list of men who have deserted since Mar. 1, 1781." [Ref: L-19970 (Box 7, folder 52)].

CAMPBELL, Allen. Private, Maryland Line, discharged on Dec. 3, 1781 [Ref: D-407, I-10].

CAMPBELL, Daniel. Private, Maryland Line, 1782 [Ref: D-424, D-474]. The estate of one Daniel Campbell was probated by Feb. 6, 1783 (date of inventory). [Ref: ZE-36].

CAMPBELL, George (1744, Ireland -   ). Private (recruit), 1780, continental service, Maryland Line [Ref: D-338].

CAMPBELL, James. Took the Oath of Allegiance before the Hon. Fielder Bowie in 1778. One James Campbell was aged 22 and another was aged 42 in 1776 [Ref: O-304, R-25, R-56].

CAMPBELL, John. Private, Capt. Jesse Hellen's Militia Company, before May 23, 1782; guarded Magruder's Warehouse in the spring of 1782 [Ref: L-19970 (Box 6, folder 21)]. The estate of one John Campbell was probated on Jan. 8, 1796 [Ref: ZE-36].

CAMPBELL, Robert. See "Robert Camel," q.v.

CAMPBELL, William. Took the Oath of Allegiance before the Hon. Osborn Sprigg in 1778 [Ref: O-308 and W-4648 (Box 4, folder 29), which listed his name as "Wm. Camble"].

CANBERRY, Stephen. Took the Oath of Allegiance before the Hon. Osborn Sprigg in 1778 [Ref: O-308, W-4648 (Box 4, folder 29)].

CANE, Mary. See "Smallwood Acton," q.v.

CANNON, Patrick. Private, 6th Maryland Line, enlisted Aug. 6, 1777 and reported missing on Aug. 16, 1780 (at the Battle of Camden). [Ref: D-194]. The estate of one Patrick Cannon was probated on Mar. 22, 1794 [Ref: ZE-36].

CANNON, Sarah A. See "Edward Burch," q.v.

CANTER, Thomas. Took the Oath of Allegiance (made his "T" mark) before the Hon. Alexander Howard Magruder in 1778 [Ref: O-293].

CANTON, Joseph. Took the Oath of Allegiance before the Hon. Christopher Lowndes in 1778 [Ref: O-283].
CANTWELL, Edward. Private, Maryland Line, enlisted Sep. 1, 1782 and discharged Sep. 24, 1783 [Ref: D-418, D-503]. The estate of "Edward Cantwell (soldier)" was probated on Apr. 13, 1793 in Prince George's County [Ref: ZE-36].
CARBURY (CARBY), Richard. "Richard Carbury" was a private in the 4th Maryland Line who enlisted on Janaury 29, 1776 [Ref: D-12]. "Richard Carby" took the Oath of Allegiance before the Hon. William Berry in 1778 [Ref: O-259]. See "Richard Kirby," q.v.
CARD, Benson (c1724, Maryland - June 4, 1833, North Carolina). Private in the Maryland Line. He married Nancy ---- [Ref: X-485, but he is not listed in *Archives of Maryland, Volume 18*].
CARD, James. Private (draft), continental service, 1781 [Ref: D-382]. Private, Capt. Benjamin Wailes' Militia Company, Lower Battalion; on duty guarding Magruder's Warehouse in the spring of 1782 [Ref: L-19970 (Box 6, folder 21)].
CARLETON, Joseph (1754-   ). Ensign, 25th Battalion, Capt. Waring's Company, Mar. 25, 1776. Second Lieutenant, June 9, 1777 [Ref: M-59, A-285]. Captain, May 1, 1778 through May 24, 1779 (resigned). [Ref: R-58, M-59, E-62, E-414, N-33, which spelled his name "Carlton"].
CARMAN, James. Private, 5th Maryland Line, enlisted Feb. 21, 1777 and was reported missing on Aug. 16, 1780 (at the Battle of Camden). [Ref: D-192]. The estate of one James Carman was probated on Mar. 22, 1794 [Ref: ZE-36].
CARMIN, Salithiel. Private, 2nd Maryland Line, Capt. Murdock's Company, Mar. 15, 1781 [Ref: D-366].
CARNEGIE, John. Took the Oath of Allegiance before the Hon. Joshua Beall in 1778 [Ref: O-251].
CARNEY, Patrick. Private, 6th Maryland Line, enlisted May 11, 1777 and was reported missing on Aug. 16, 1780 (at the Battle of Camden). [Ref: ZE-193]. The estate of one Patrick Carney was probated on Mar. 22, 1793 [Ref: ZE-36].
CARNS, Francis. Private, Maryland Line, 1780 [Ref: D-354, which spelled his name "Fras. Karns"].
CARNS, Peter (1749-1827). Took the Oath of Allegiance before the Hon. Christopher Lowndes in 1778 [Ref: O-283, R-72]. The estate of one Peter Carnes was probated on Sep. 17, 1827 [Ref: ZE-36].
CARNS (CARNES), Richard (1737-   ). Took the Oath of Allegiance before the Hon. Thomas Clagett in 1778 [Ref: O-267, R-18].
CARRICK, Ann. See "John Warfield," q.v.
CARRICK, Benjamin H. See "Benjamin H. Kerrick," q.v.
CARRICK, John. Took the Oath of Allegiance before the Hon. Benjamin Hall in 1778 [Ref: O-274]. The estate of one John Carrick was probated on Dec. 15, 1792 [Ref: ZE-37].

CARRICK, Mareen (c1750-1793). Took the Oath of Allegiance before the Hon. Benjamin Hall in 1778 [Ref: O-275]. First wife unknown; second wife was Elizabeth Jones [Ref: X-499]. The estate of Mareen Carrick was probated on Nov. 9, 1793 [Ref: ZE-37].
CARRICO, Martha. See "Elijah Ellis," q.v.
CARRICO, Peter (c1743-c1803). Private, Capt. Benjamin Wailes' Militia Company, Lower Battalion; on duty guarding Magruder's Warehouse in the spring of 1782 [Ref: L-19970 (Box 6, folder 21)]. He married Catharine ---- [Ref: X-499]. See "Peter Callico," q.v.
CARRINGTON, Elizabeth. See "John Boswell," q.v.
CARROLL, Charles, of Carrollton. See "John Rogers," q.v.
CARROLL, Daniel (July 22, 1730 - May, 1796). "Daniel Carroll, Jr., of Rock Creek, the Commissioner" married Eleanor Carroll. He was a member of the Continental Congress, 1780-1784, signed the Articles of Confederation, was a delegate to the Convention that framed the Federal Constitution, served in the First Congress of the United States from Mar. 4, 1789 to Mar. 3, 1791, and served as Commissioner from 1791 through 1795 [Ref: ZA-116, ZA-117].
CARROLL, Edmd. Private, 2nd Maryland Line, Capt. Patrick Sim's Company, 1776 [Ref: D-9].
CARROLL, Eleanor. See "Daniel Carroll," q.v.
CARROLL, John. There were several men with this name who served in the Maryland Line [Ref: D-91, D-93, D-191, D-193, D-323, D-331, D-352, D-435, D-454]. The estate of one John Carroll was probated on May 18, 1793 in Prince George's County [Ref: ZE-37].
CARROLL, Joseph (1756-1793). Took the Oath of Allegiance before the Hon. James Beck in 1778 [Ref: R-53, O-253, which spelled the name "Carrel"]. The estate of one Joseph Carroll was probated on May 18, 1793 in Prince George's County [Ref: ZE-37].
CARROLL, Mary. See "Henry Brooke" and "Notley Young" and "Patrick Sim," q.v.
CARSON, Mary. See "Thomas Lloyd," q.v.
CARTER, Edward. Private, Maryland Line, paid for services rendered on Apr. 22, 1782 [Ref: I-144].
CARTER, John. Private, 2nd Maryland Line, Capt. Murdock's Company, Mar. 15, 1781 [Ref: D-366].
CASANAVE, Ann. See "Notley Young," q.v.
CASEY, John (1741-   ). Took the Oath of Allegiance before the Hon. George Lee in 1778 [Ref: O-279, R-7]. Captain, Middle Militia Battalion, May 1, 1778 through May 24, 1779 (succeeded). [Ref: M-60, E-63, E-414, N-36, which spelled his name "Cassey"]. One John Casey married Philorlea Edgeworth by license dated Aug. 12, 1778 [Ref: ZB-43].
CASH, Richard. Took the Oath of Allegiance before the Hon. William Berry in 1778 [Ref: O-258].
CASTEEL, Susannah. See "Nathan Scarce," q.v.

CATER (CATO), William. "William Cater" took the Oath of Allegiance before the Hon. Truman Skinner in 1778 [Ref: O-298]. "William Cato" was aged 35 in 1776 [Ref: R-39]. One "William Cater" married Elizabeth Clubb by license dated Feb. 1, 1792 [Ref: ZB-43]. The estate of one "William Cato" was probated on Jan. 23, 1793 [Ref: ZE-38].
CATTERTON, John. Private, Capt. Jesse Hellen's Militia Company, before May 23, 1782; guarded Capt. Alexander H. Magruder's Warehouse in the spring of 1782 [Ref: L-19970 (Box 6, folder 21)].
CAVE, Elizabeth. See "Henry Lee," q.v.
CAVE, Mary. See "Caleb Thomas," q.v.
CAVE, Nancy. See "Smallwood Acton," q.v.
CAVE, Samuel. Took the Oath of Allegiance before the Hon. Alexander Howard Magruder in 1778 [Ref: O-293]. The estate of one Samuel Cave was probated on Jan. 5, 1802 [Ref: ZE-38].
CAVE, Thomas. Took the Oath of Allegiance (made his "T" mark) before the Hon. Alexander Howard Magruder in 1778 [Ref: O-293].
CAVE, Thomas Jr. Took the Oath of Allegiance (made his "X" mark) before the Hon. Alexander Howard Magruder in 1778 [Ref: O-293]. Private, Capt. Benjamin Wailes' Militia Company, Lower Battalion; on duty guarding Magruder's Warehouse in the spring of 1782 [Ref: L-19970 (Box 6, folder 21)]. One Thomas Cave married Elizabeth Peirce by license dated Nov. 18, 1786 [Ref: ZB-44]. The estate of one Thomas Cave was probated on Apr. 10, 1787 [Ref: ZE-38].
CAYWOOD, Benjamin (1712-1783). Took the Oath of Allegiance before the Hon. William Lyles, Jr. in 1778 [Ref: O-290, R-74, which listed his name as "Benjamin Caywood, Senr."]. The estate of one "Benjamin Cawood" was probated on Mar. 1 1783 [Ref: ZE-38].
CAYWOOD (CAWOOD), Elizabeth. See "Thomas Blacklock," q.v.
CAYWOOD, Moses. Private, Capt. Hezekiah Wheeler's Company, 11th Militia Battalion, April, 1781 [Ref: L-19970 (Box 6, folder 21), which spelled his name "Cawood"]. The estate of one Moses Cawood was probated on Oct. 21, 1795 and the estate of another Moses Cawood was probated on June 28, 1811 [Ref: ZE-38].
CAYWOOD, Thomas. Took the Oath of Allegiance before the Hon. William Lyles, Jr. in 1778 [Ref: O-290].
CECIL, James (1734-   ). Took the Oath of Allegiance before the Hon. Christopher Lowndes in 1778 [Ref: O-286, R-50].
CECIL, John (1721-1779). Took the Oath of Allegiance before the Hon. William Berry in 1778 [Ref: O-258, R-34, which spelled his name "Cissell"]. He married Mrs. ---- (Brightwell) Wilson [Ref: X-521]. The estate of one "John Cissel" was probated on Apr. 13, 1779 (date of inventory) by Susanna Cissel. [Ref: ZE-39].
CECIL, Joshua. See "Josua Sissill," q.v.
CECIL, Philip. See "Phillip Siscill," q.v.
CECIL, Susannah. See "Clement Wilson" and "John Cecil," q.v.

CECIL, Thomas (1726-1790). Took the Oath of Allegiance before the Hon. Christopher Lowndes in 1778 [Ref: O-283, R-73, which latter source spelled his name "Cisell"]. The estate of one Thomas Cecil was probated on Aug. 10, 1790 [Ref: ZE-38].
CHAMBERLAIN, Clement (1746-   ). Took the Oath of Allegiance before the Hon. Osborn Sprigg in 1778 [Ref: O-306, R-66].
CHANDLER, Margaret. See "John Rogers," q.v.
CHANNON, Thomas. Private, Northern Detachment, 3rd Maryland Line, Capt. Horatio Clagett's Company, 1783 [Ref: D-502].
CHAPMAN, Amelia. See "William Lock Weems," q.v.
CHAPMAN, John (1726-   ). Took the Oath of Allegiance (made his "X" mark) before the Hon. Thomas Clagett in 1778 [Ref: O-267, R-3]. If his age in the 1776 census of Prince George's County is in error, this may be the John Chapman (son of John) who was born on Jan. 3, 1716, in Queen Anne's Parish [Ref: ZC-169]. Additional research may be necessary before drawing conclusions.
CHAPMAN, William. Took the Oath of Allegiance before the Hon. Benjamin Hall in 1778 [Ref: O-276].
CHARLTON, Edward. Private, Capt. Benjamin Wailes' Militia Company, Lower Battalion; on duty guarding Magruder's Warehouse in the spring of 1782 [Ref: L-19970 (Box 6, folder 21)].
CHENEY, Greenberry. Took the Oath of Allegiance before the Hon. Benjamin Hall in 1778 [Ref: O-275, which spelled it "Cheny"].
CHENEY, John. Private, 1st Maryland Line, from Feb. 10, 1778 to Sep. 10, 1779, when discharged [Ref: D-91]. John Cheney married Elizabeth Ferrell by license dated Dec. 12, 1780 [Ref: ZB-45].
CHENEY, Margaret. See "Samuel Cheney," q.v.
CHENEY, Mordecai. Took the Oath of Allegiance before the Hon. Benjamin Hall in 1778 [Ref: O-275, which spelled it "Cheny"].
CHENEY, Samuel (1730 - died before July 24, 1806). Took the Oath of Allegiance before the Hon. James Beck in 1778 [Ref: O-252, R-51]. Samuel Cheney married Margaret ---- [Ref: X-551].
CHEW, Ann. See "William Bowie," q.v.
CHILD, Elizabeth. See "Thomas Webb, Jr.," q.v.
CHILLAM, John. Rendered patriotic service by providing wheat for the military on July 14, 1781 [Ref: Q-410].
CHINA, Hezekiah. Took the Oath of Allegiance before the Hon. Christopher Lowndes in 1778 [Ref: O-287].
CHUBB, Jonn. [sic] (1762, Maryland -   ). Private (substitute), 1780, in continental service, Maryland Line [Ref: D-338].
CHURCH, Jonathan Montgomery. Took the Oath of Allegiance before the Hon. Christopher Lowndes in 1778 [Ref: O-284].
CIDWELL, Hezekiah. See "Hezekiah Kidwell," q.v.
CISSIL, Philip. See "Philip Siscill," q.v.
CLAGETT, Agnes. See "Wiseman Clagett," q.v.

CLAGETT, Ann. See "Richard Clagett" and "John Clagett," q.v.
CLAGETT, Anna. See "Joseph White Clagett," q.v.
CLAGETT, Charles (1753-1833). Second Lieutenant, Middle Battalion, Capt. John M. Burgess' Company, May 1, 1778. Captain, Nov. 13, 1779 [Ref: M-62, E-63, E-414, N-35, which also spelled his name "Charles Claggett"]. Took the Oath of Allegiance before the Hon. David Craufurd in 1778 [Ref: O-271]. Appointed by the Council of Maryland to be the Tobacco Inspector at Upper Marlboro Warehouse on Aug. 30, 1780 [Ref: F-271]. Served on a Grand Jury in 1777 [Ref: Z-29]. Charles Clagett married Verlinda ---- [Ref: ZA-140]. The estate of "Charles Nicholas Clagett" was probated on Apr. 25, 1833 [Ref: ZE-40].
CLAGETT, Edward. Took the Oath of Allegiance before the Hon. Fielder Bowie in 1778 [Ref: O-304, W-4648 (Box 4, folder 15)]. The estate of one Edward Clagett was probated on Apr. 7, 1788 [Ref: ZE-40]. See "Richard Clagett," q.v.
CLAGETT, Eleanor. See "Joseph White Clagett" and "Charles Eversfield" and "Richard Clagett" and "Wiseman Clagett," q.v.
CLAGETT, Elizabeth. See "Thomas Clagett," q.v.
CLAGETT, Hannibal. See "Thomas Clagett," q.v.
CLAGETT, Harriett. See "John H. Beanes," q.v.
CLAGETT, Hector. See "Thomas Clagett," q.v.
CLAGETT, Henrietta. See "Luke Marbury," q.v.
CLAGETT, Horatio (Aug. 10, 1756, Maryland - Dec. 15, 1815, England). Son of John and Sarah Clagett, of Prince George's Parish [Ref: ZD-111]. Ensign, Maryland Line, Capt. John H. Lowe's Company, 1776 [Ref: D-34, R-1]. Captain, 3rd Maryland Line, commissioned on Oct. 10, 1777, and was paid for recruiting services on Apr. 24, 1778 [Ref: D-295, E-57]. Captain, 2nd Company, Northern Detachment, 3rd Maryland Line, 1783 [Ref: D-501, which spelled his name "Horatio Claggett"]. After the war Horatio removed to England where he married and accumulated a considerable fortune. His death notice appeared in the *National Intelligencer*, Washington, DC, Sep. 26, 1816 [Ref: ZA-126]. See "Richard Clagett" and "William Tuell," q.v.
CLAGETT, Isaac. Private, 1st Guard, Capt. Henry Hill's Militia Company, Lower Battalion; on duty at Nottingham on the Patuxent, Apr. 12, 1781 [Ref: L-19970 (Box 6, folder 21)].
CLAGETT, James. Took the Oath of Allegiance before the Hon. William Berry in 1778 [Ref: O-258].
CLAGETT, John. See "Horatio Clagett" and "Thomas Clagett" and "John Clagett" and "William Clagett," q.v.
CLAGETT, John. Private, Capt. Hezekiah Wheeler's Company, 11th Militia Battalion, April, 1781 [Ref: L-19970 (Box 6, folder 21)]. Private, Select Militia, Capt. Hezekiah Wheeler's Company, July 14, 1781 [Ref: S-6636 (Box 31, folder 5)]. One John Clagett, son of Thomas and Ann Clagett, was born on Dec. 7, 1744, and one John Clagett, son of John

and Sarah Clagett, was born on Oct. 23, 1752; both families of Prince George's Parish [Ref: ZD-111]. Additional research may be necessary before drawing conclusions.

CLAGETT, John (1713-1790). Son of Thomas Clagett (1677-1732). He married Sarah Magruder, daughter of Capt. Alexander H. Magruder [Ref: U-221, X-568]. Took the Oath of Allegiance before the Hon. David Craufurd in 1778 [Ref: O-271]. Rendered patriotic service by providing wheat for the military on Sep. 23, 1780 [Ref: Q-230].

CLAGETT, John, of Edward (c1753, Croome, Prince George's County - Apr. 25, 1781, Anne Arundel County). Private in the "3rd Regiment of Maryland Fencibles." He married Cassandra White and had three sons: Joseph White, Walter, and William [Ref: ZA-128, ZA-129].

CLAGETT, John Marshall. See "Richard Clagett," q.v.

CLAGETT, Joseph White (c1758-1828). A son of John Clagett and Cassandra White, he married Eleanor Digges and had these children: Susanna Maria Clagett, Anna H. P. Clagett, William Digges Clagett, and Eleanor Clagett [Ref: ZA-129]. Second Lieutenant, Middle Battalion, Capt. Humphrey Belt's Militia Company, on May 1, 1778, and Captain, May 24, 1779 [Ref: M-62, E-63, E-414, which sources spelled his name "Joseph White Clagget," and N-35, which spelled his name "Joseph W. Claggett"]. Took the Oath of Allegiance before the Hon. David Craufurd in 1778 [Ref: O-271, which listed his name as "Joseph W. Clagett"]. The estate of "Joseph White Clagett" was probated on May 11, 1830 [Ref: ZE-40]. See "John Clagett, of Edward," q.v.

CLAGETT, Judson Magruder. See "Thomas Clagett," q.v.

CLAGETT, Margaret. See "Thomas D. Marlow," q.v.

CLAGETT, Mary. See "Thomas Clagett" and "Thomas Duckett" and "John Eversfield," q.v.

CLAGETT, Nathaniel (Mar. 27, 1751 - 1809). Son of John and Sarah Clagett. Took the Oath of Allegiance before the Hon. Thomas Clagett in 1778 [Ref: O-268, ZA-126, ZD-111]. The estate of Nathaniel Clagett was probated on Feb. 1, 1809 [Ref: ZE-40].

CLAGETT, Rachel. See "Thomas Clagett," q.v.

CLAGETT, Richard (1736-1789). A son of Edward and Eleanor Clagett, he married (1) Ann Hutchinson Parker, and (2) Mary Marshall. By his first wife he had a son John Clagett (born 1765) and by his second wife he had Elizabeth Clagett (born Jan. --, 1766), Ann Clagett (born Dec. --, 1766), Eleanor Bowie Clagett (born 1768), Lieut. John Marshall Clagett, U.S.N. (1776-c1804), Capt. Horatio Clagett (1777-1844), and Capt. Thomas Dorsey Clagett (1784-1866). [Ref: ZA-134, ZA-135]. Took the Oath of Allegiance before the Hon. William Lyles, Jr. in 1778 [Ref: O-290, R-74]. Ensign, 11th Battalion, Capt. Hezekiah Wheeler's Company, May 24, 1779 [Ref: M-62, E-414, N-32]. Appointed by the Council of Maryland to be the Tobacco Inspector at Piscataway Warehouse on Aug. 30, 1780 [Ref: F-271]. Ensign, 11th Militia Battalion, Capt. Hezekiah

Wheeler's Company, in April, 1781 [Ref: L-19970 (Box 6, folder 21)]. There was also a Richard Clagett, son of John and Sarah Clagett, who was born on June 27, 1746 in Prince George's Parish [Ref: ZD-111]. Additional research may be necessary before drawing conclusions.

CLAGETT, Sarah. See "Horatio Clagett" and "Thomas Clagett" and "Richard Clagett" and "Wiseman Clagett" and "Thomas Ramsey Hodges" and "William Clagett," q.v.

CLAGETT, Thomas (Feb. 12, 1740/1 - Dec. 17, 1792). A son of John Clagett and Sarah Magruder, Thomas married Mary Meek Magruder in 1768 and had these children: Judson Magruder Clagett (1769-1800), Thomas Clagett (born 1773), Hector Clagett (born 1776 and died young), Hector Clagett (born 1780), Hannibal Clagett, Mary (McElderry) Duckett (1771-1816), Elizabeth Addison (born 1778), and Sarah Magruder Bruce (born 1780). [Ref: U-220, U-221, ZC-13, ZD-111, ZE-41]. Served as a County Court Justice, 1777-1792 [Ref: C-273]. Administered the Oath of Allegiance in 1778 [Ref: O-269]. On Mar. 25, 1778, the Maryland Council appointed him the Agent for Purchasing Provisions for the Army of the United States in Prince George's County. Stored arms and ammunition at Piscataway in July, 1780. Served as Subscription Officer in the Continental Loan Office, 1779, House of Delegates, 1780-1781, Orphans Court Justice, 1777-1782, and Chief Justice, 1791 [Ref: U-84, U-221, C-551, G-4, Z-90, ZA-124, ZA-125]. "Thomas Clagett, of Piscataway, merchant" is buried in the Clagett Cemetery at "Mount Lubentia" in Prince George's County [Ref: Y-563]. See "Thomas Duckett" and "John Clagett" and two other men named "Thomas Clagett," q.v.

CLAGETT, Thomas (1750-1790). A son of Thomas Clagett, planter, he married his cousin Sarah White in 1785 and had two children, Rachel Clagett (born 1788) and Thomas Clagett (born 1790). [Ref: ZA-141]. Captain, Middle Battalion (no dates given). [Ref: R-1, M-62, which spelled his name "Claggett," and Ref: X-568, U-221, which latter source cites an identification problem as there were at least two other Thomas Clagett's living in 1780]. Took the Oath of Allegiance before the Hon. David Craufurd in 1778 [Ref: O-271]. Thomas and Sarah are buried in the Clagett Family Cemetery located at "Weston" just off Route 301 near Upper Marlboro [Ref: Y-562, which also lists three other Thomas Clagett's who are buried there: Thomas Clagett (c1726-1774), Thomas Clagett, Jr. (1702-c1737), and Thomas Clagett (1677-1732). They apparently were Thomas' father, grandfather, and great-grandfather; also buried there are Thomas Claggett (1791-1873), Thomas Clagett VII (1840-1907), and Thomas Clagett (1872-1873)]. Additional research may be necessary before drawing conclusions.

CLAGETT, Thomas (c1726-1774/1790). Source U-221 states that "Thomas Clagett, Sr." was illiterate and died circa 1790. This source also cites an identification problem because there were at least two other Thomas

Clagett's living in 1780. However, Source ZA-140 states that Thomas Clagett was born circa 1726 and died in 1774, but the administration and distribution of his estate was not completed until Aug., 1794. Thomas Clagett (c1726-1774) married Mary White, who died in 1796 [Ref: ZA-140]. There was apparently yet another Thomas Clagett who took the Oath of Allegiance before the Hon. Osborn Sprigg [Ref: O-308, W-4648 (Box 4, folder 29)]. Additional research may be necessary before drawing conclusions.

CLAGETT, Thomas Dorsey. See "Richard Clagett," q.v.

CLAGETT, Verlinda. See "Charles Clagett," q.v.

CLAGETT, Walter. See "John Clagett, of Edward," q.v.

CLAGETT, William (July 25, 1748 - 1789). Son of John and Sarah Clagett [Ref: ZD-111]. Took the Oath of Allegiance before the Hon. Thomas Clagett in 1778 [Ref: O-264, R-74]. He served as "Purchaser of Cloathing" for Prince George's County in 1781 [Ref: G-462]. William Clagett married Harriet Sothoron [Ref: X-568]. The estate of one William Clagett was probated on June 29, 1789 [Ref: ZE-41]. See "John Clagett, of Edward," q.v.

CLAGETT, William Digges. See "Joseph White Clagett," q.v.

CLAGETT, Wiseman (1753-1785). Private, enrolled in the Flying Camp by Capt. Robert Bowie on July 17, 1776; nativity: Prince George's County; height 5' 9"; has own gun [Ref: D-36]. Took the Oath of Allegiance before the Hon. David Craufurd in 1778 [Ref: O-272]. Wiseman Clagett married his cousin Priscilla Bowie Lyles by license dated Jan. 16, 1779, and had daughters Sarah Ann Clagett, Agnes Clagett, and Eleanor Bowie Clagett (who married Col. Gassaway Watkins). [Ref: ZA-133, ZB-47]. The estate of Wiseman Clagett was probated by July 9, 1785 (date of inventory). [Ref: ZE-41].

CLAGETT, Zadock. See "William Murdock," q.v.

CLANCEY, Joseph. Fifer, Northern Detachment, 3rd Maryland Line, Capt. Horatio Clagett's Company, 1783 [Ref: D-501].

CLARIDGE, Levin (1755 - Nov. 11, 1811). Private, 3rd Maryland Regiment, enlisted May 21, 1782 for 3 years [Ref: D-417, which spelled his name "Leavin Calridge"]. First wife unknown; second wife was Catherine McDowell [Ref: X-571].

CLARK, Abraham (Dec. 8, 1731 - 1782 or 1794). Son of Abraham and Margaret Clark, of Queen Anne's Parish [Ref: ZC-16]. Took the Oath of Allegiance before the Hon. Benjamin Hall in 1778. Abraham Clark married Ann --- [Ref: O-274, X-571]. The estate of one Abraham Clark was probated by May 8, 1782 (date of inventory) and the estate of "Abraham Clark, of Henry" was probated on Sep. 27, 1794. The estate of "Abraham Clarke" was administered upon by Ann Clarke on May 19, 1783 [Ref: ZE-41. ZE-42]. Additional research may be necessary before drawing conclusions. See "Benjamin Clark" and "Christopher Parrot," q.v.

CLARK, Ann (Anne). See "Daniel Clark" and "Gabriel Clark" and "Benjamin Hall, of Francis" and "Joshua Clark," q.v.

CLARK, Benjamin (Mar. 25, 1730 -   ). Son of Abraham and Margaret Clark, of Queen Anne's Parish [Ref: ZC-169]. Took the Oath of Allegiance before the Hon. Benjamin Hall in 1778 [Ref: O-275].

CLARK, Charles. See "Osborn Sprigg," q.v.

CLARK, Daniel (Feb. 14, 1733 -1806). Son of William and Ann Clark, of Queen Anne's Parish [Ref: ZC-169]. Took the Oath of Allegiance before the Hon. David Craufurd in 1778 [Ref: O-271]. The estate of "Daniel Clarke" was probated on Mar. 18, 1806 [Ref: ZE-42].

CLARK, Elizabeth. See "Abraham Cox," q.v.

CLARK, Frederick. Took the Oath of Allegiance before the Hon. Thomas MacGill in 1778 [Ref: O-291]. The estate of Frederick Clark was probated on Nov. 2, 1799 [Ref: ZE-42, ZE-43, which source also spelled his name "Frederic Clarke"].

CLARK, Gabriel (Sep. 8, 1724 - 1792). Son of William and Ann Clark, of Queen Anne's Parish [Ref: ZC-169]. Took the Oath of Allegiance before the Hon. Thomas MacGill in 1778 [Ref: O-291]. The estate of Gabriel Clark was probated on May 19, 1792 [Ref: Z-42, Z-43, which source also spelled his name "Clarke"].

CLARK, Henry Sr. Took the Oath of Allegiance before the Hon. Benjamin Hall in 1778 [Ref: O-274]. "Henry Clark, son of Abram: and Margrett Clark," of Queen Anne's Parish, was born on Dec. 30, 1737 [Ref: ZC-169]. The estate of one Henry Clark was probated on Apr. 30, 1779 [Ref: ZE-42, ZE-43, which source also spelled his name "Clarke"].

CLARK, Henry, of Henry. "Henry Clark, of Henry" took the Oath of Allegiance before the Hon. Benjamin Hall in 1778 [Ref: O-274]. "Henry Clarke" married Easter Beckett by license dated Dec. 20, 1777 [Ref: ZB-48]. The estate of a "Henry Clark" was probated on Dec. 31, 1805 [Ref: ZE-42, ZE-43, which source also spelled his name "Henry Clarke"].

CLARK, Joshua. "Joshua Clark" was a first Lieutenant in the militia in 1778 and resigned in 1779 [Ref: N-35]. "Joshua Clark, Jr." took the Oath of Allegiance before the Hon. James Mullikin in 1778 [Ref: O-296, which spelled his name "Clarke]. One Joshua Clark, son of Joshua and Mary Clark, of Queen Anne's Parish, was born on Apr. 6, 174?, and another Joshua Clark, son of William and Ann Clark, of Queen Anne's Parish, was born on Nov. 3, 1720 [Ref: ZC-170]. The estate of one "Joshua Clark" was probated on June 26, 1781 and the estate of "Joshua Clarke Sr." was probated on June 1, 1796 [Ref: ZE-42, ZE-43, which source also spelled the name "Clark"]. Additional research may be necessary before drawing conclusions.

CLARK, Josiah. First Lieutenant, Middle Battalion, Capt. Humphrey Belt's Company, May 1, 1778 [Ref: M-62, E-63].

CLARK, Margaret. See "Abraham Clark" and Benjamin Clark" and "John Rogers," q.v.

CLARK, Mary. See "Joshua Clark," q.v.
CLARK, Patrick. Took the Oath of Allegiance before the Hon. Alexander Howard Magruder in 1778 [Ref: O-293].
CLARK, Thomas. See "Benjamin Wailes," q.v.
CLARK, William. Two men with this name took the Oath of Allegiance in 1778: one before the Hon. James Beck and one before the Hon. Benjamin Hall [Ref: O-253, O-274]. See "Daniel Clark" and "Gabriel Clark" and "Joshua Clark," q.v.
CLARKE, Abram. Took the Oath of Allegiance before the Hon. Thomas Williams in 1778 [Ref: O-302]. See "Christopher Parrot," q.v.
CLARKE, Ann. See "Thomas Boteler" and "William Mockbee," q.v.
CLARKE, Caleb. Ensign, Militia, Capt. Marsh M. Duvall's Company, June 9, 1777 [Ref: M-63]. Took the Oath of Allegiance before the Hon. Thomas Williams in 1778 [Ref: O-302]. Second Lieutenant, Upper Battalion, Capt. Duvall's Company, June 27, 1781 [Ref: H-320, which spelled his name "Calib Clark"]. Constable, Horsepen Hundred, 1777-1778 [Ref: Z-3, Z-30]. The estate of one Caleb Clarke was probated on Jan. 9, 1796 [Ref: ZE-42].
CLARKE, Henry A. Took the Oath of Allegiance before the Hon. Truman Skinner in 1778 [Ref: O-298]. Private, 1st Guard, Capt. Henry Hill's Militia Company, Lower Battalion; on duty at Nottingham on the Patuxent, Apr. 12, 1781 [Ref: L-19970 (Box 6, folder 21)]. See "Henry Clark, of Henry," q.v.
CLARKE, Joseph. Took the Oath of Allegiance before the Hon. Truman Skinner in 1778 [Ref: O-297]. Served on a Grand Jury in 1777 [Ref: Z-29].
CLARKE, Martha. See "Christopher Parrot," q.v.
CLARKE, Mary. See "Elisha Green," q.v.
CLARKE, Peter. Sergeant, 2nd Maryland Line, Capt. Patrick Sim's Company, 1776 [Ref: D-7].
CLARKE, Priscilla. See "Josias Beall," q.v.
CLARKE, Sarah. See "Christopher Hyatt," q.v.
CLARKE, Susannah. See "Edward Perry," q.v.
CLARKE, Tamar. Private, 1st Guard, Capt. Henry Hill's Militia Company, Lower Battalion; on duty at Nottingham on the Patuxent, Apr. 12, 1781 [Ref: L-19970 (Box 6, folder 21)].
CLARKE, Willicy. See "John Riley," q.v.
CLARKSON, Ann. See "Francis Clements Dyer," q.v.
CLARKSON, Edward (1760-   ). Private, Capt. Richard Stonestreet's Militia Company, 11th Battalion, June, 1782 [Ref: L-19970, R-14]. Private, Select Militia, Capt. Hezekiah Wheeler's Company, July 14, 1781 [Ref: S-6636 (Box 31, folder 5)]. Took the Oath of Allegiance before the Hon. Thomas Clagett in 1778 [Ref: O-266].
CLARKSON, Edward Sr. (1722-1785). Took the Oath of Allegiance (made his "EC" mark) before the Hon. Thomas Clagett in 1778 [Ref: O-265, R-

14]. The estate of one Edward Clarke was probated on Dec. 2, 1785 [Ref: ZE-43].

CLARKSON, Elizabeth. See "Thomas Clarkson," q.v.

CLARKSON, Henry (1757-   ). Took the Oath of Allegiance before the Hon. Thomas Clagett in 1778 [Ref: O-266, R-14]. Second Sergeant, Capt. Richard Stonestreet's Militia Company, 11th Battalion, June, 1782 [Ref: L-19970 (Box 6, folder 21)].

CLARKSON, Joseph. Took the Oath of Allegiance before the Hon. Thomas Clagett in 1778 [Ref: O-265]. One Joseph Clarkson was aged 27 and another was aged 26 in 1776 [Ref: R-81, R-83]. One Joseph Clarkson married Jane Eaglin by license dated Apr. 11, 1788 [Ref: ZB-49]. The estate of one Joseph Clarkson was probated on July 8, 1819 [Ref: ZE-44].

CLARKSON, Notley (1731-   ). Took the Oath of Allegiance before the Hon. Osborn Sprigg in 1778 [Ref: O-307, R-68, which latter source spelled his name "Notley Claxen"]. Rendered patriotic service by providing wheat for the military on Aug. 4, 1780 [Ref: Q-306].

CLARKSON, Richard. Ensign, Militia, 1778. Second Lieutenant, 1779 [Ref: N-36, which misspelled his name as "Richard Claxon" and as "Richard Carkoon"]. Ensign, Middle Battalion, Capt. John Casey's Company, May 1, 1778. Second Lieutenant, Capt. Edward Lanham's Company, May 24, 1779 [Ref: M-63, E-63, E-414, which spelled his name as "Claxon"]. Took the Oath of Allegiance before the Hon. Thomas Clagett in 1778 [Ref: O-268]. The estate of one Richard Clarkson was probated on Oct. 23, 1787 [Ref: ZE-444].

CLARKSON, Sarah. See "George Dyer," q.v.

CLARKSON, Thomas (Sep., 1714 - 1780). Son of William and Elizabeth Clarkson [Ref: ZC-13]. Took the Oath of Allegiance before the Hon. Thomas Clagett in 1778 [Ref: O-266]. Thomas Clarkson was aged 61 in the 1776 census of Prince George's County. Thomas Clarkson, Jr. was aged 28 in 1776 [Ref: R-39, R-77]. The estate of one Thomas Clarkson was probated on Dec. 16, 1780 [Ref: ZE-44].

CLARKSON, William. Private (draft), continental service, 1781 [Ref: D-382]. Took the Oath of Allegiance before the Hon. George Lee in 1778 [Ref: O-279]. See "Thomas Clarkson," q.v.

CLAUD, Ephana. See "John Grant," q.v.

CLAXEN, Notley. See "Notley Clarkson" q.v.

CLAXON, Richard. See "Richard Clarkson," q.v.

CLEAVER, Benjamin. Private, 2nd Maryland Line, Capt. Alexander Truman's Company, 1782 [Ref: D-440].

CLELAND, Janet. See "Richard Henderson," q.v.

CLEMENTS, Ann. See "John Clements," q.v.

CLEMENTS, Aquilla (1765, Maryland -   ). Private, enlisted May 14, 1781, for 3 years in continental service, Maryland Line; sent to Annapolis; on duty July 13, 1781 [Ref: D-381].

CLEMENTS, Charles. Private, 3rd Maryland Line, Capt. Horatio Clagett's Company, December, 1779 [Ref: D-296].
CLEMENTS, Henrietta. See "Walter Dyer" and "Giles Green Dyer" and "Francis Clements Dyer," q.v.
CLEMENTS, Henry (baptized Dec. 8, 1751 -   ). Son of John and Mary Clements [Ref: ZC-13]. He was drafted from Charles County on July 27, 1781, but "since enrolled himself a substitute in Prince George's County and joined the Army." [Ref: D-377].
CLEMENTS, James (1755, Maryland -   ). "James Clemons" was a private enrolled by Lt. John M. Burgess, Lower Battalion, on July 20, 1776, for continental service, Maryland Line [Ref: D-35]. "James Clements" was a private who enlisted May 25, 1781, for 3 years, continental service, Maryland Line; sent to Annapolis; on duty July 13, 1781 [Ref: D-381].
CLEMENTS, John (Mar. 7, 1753 -   ). Son of William and Ann Clements [Ref: ZC-13]. Private, enrolled by Ensign Horatio Clagett on July 15, 1776, continental service, Maryland Line [Ref: D-35]. See "Ralph Clements" and "Henry Clements," q.v.
CLEMENTS, Mark. Private, 3rd Maryland Line, 1779 [Ref: D-297].
CLEMENTS, Martha. See "John Grimes," q.v.
CLEMENTS, Mary. See "Ralph Clements" and "Henry Clements," q.v.
CLEMENTS, Ralph (Nov. 14, 1753 -   ). "Ralph Fisher" was a private who was enrolled by Ensign Horatio Clagett on July 15, 1776, for continental service, Maryland Line [Ref: D-35]. "Ralph Fisher Clements" was a son of John and Mary Clements [Ref: Z-13].
CLEMENTS, William. See "John Clements," q.v.
CLEMMENS, Catherine. See "Samuel Wright," q.v.
CLEVERDENCE, John. Private, Northern Detachment, 3rd Maryland Line, Capt. Horatio Clagett's Company, 1780-1783. In March, 1834, "John Clevidence" of Pine Township in Allegheny County, Pennsylvania, verified the service of David Howe, stating they served together in the Maryland Line and he first knew David Howe while on duty at North River, New Jersey in 1780. They served together for over three years and were discharged at Pittsburgh, Pennsylvania, by Capt. David Luckett [Ref: V-1947 (Vol. 35, No. 2, p. 63), D-502]. See "David Howe," q.v.
CLIFFORD, Jeremiah. Took the Oath of Allegiance before the Hon. George Lee in 1778 [Ref: O-279].
CLIFFORD, John (1733-1782). Took the Oath of Allegiance before the Hon. David Craufurd in 1778 [Ref: O-272, R-84]. The estate of one John Clifford was probated on Apr. 9, 1782 [Ref: ZE-45].
CLIMESLAUGHT, John. Private, Northern Detachment, 3rd Maryland Line, Capt. Horatio Clagett's Company, 1783 [Ref: D-502].
CLOWER, John Jr. Took the Oath of Allegiance before the Hon. Osborn Sprigg in 1778 [Ref: O-306].

CLUBB, Elizabeth. See "William Cater (Cato)," q.v.
CLUBB, Jane. See "Samuel Clubb," q.v.
CLUBB, Matthew (1716-   ). Took the Oath of Allegiance before the Hon. Fielder Bowie in 1778 [Ref: R-38, which spelled the name "Mathew Clubb," and O-304, which mistakenly listed the name as "Matthew C----, 41," yet, the original list at the Maryland State Archives (Box 4, folder 15) clearly shows the name as "Matthew Club. There is no "41" after his name; rather, his name continues the 40 names from the preceding page, thus making him number 41].
CLUBB, Matthew. Private (draft), Maryland Line, 1780, continental service [Ref: D-382, which spelled the name "Mathew Clubb"]. The records of the Council of Maryland include a letter from Joshua Beall, County Lieutenant of Prince George's County, dated Aug. 21, 1781, in regards to the Middle Battalion of militia, stating, in part, "At the time of drafting this Class the lot fell on Sam. Club (a son of Mathew Clubs a poor man who had been drafted in the last Class and been at considerable expence in procuring a substitute) and Walter Findley; on Findley's being drafted, several persons averred that he was then entered and on board a vessel at Alexandria that was to sail the next day as Mathew Club had no chance of keeping his son who was but a lad to help him to labour..." [Ref: H-433]. See "Nicholas Waters," q.v.
CLUBB, Philip. See "Samuel Clubb," q.v.
CLUBB, Rebeccah. See "John Mitchell," q.v.
CLUBB, Samuel. Took the Oath of Allegiance before the Hon. Osborn Sprigg in 1778 [Ref: O-308, W-4648 (Box 4, folder 29)]. "Samuel Clubb" was aged 28 and "Samuel Club" was aged 37 in 1776 [Ref: R-75, R-80]. "Sam. Club" was drafted in 1781 and his father Matthew Club petitioned for his release [Ref: H-433]. There was also a Samuel Clubb, son of Philip and Jane Clubb, who was born on Apr. 5, 1761, in Prince George's Parish [Ref: ZD-111]. Additional research may be necessary before drawing conclusions. See "Mathew Clubb," q.v.
CLUBB, Sarah. See "George Walls," q.v.
COE, Alexander Benson. See "Richard Coe," q.v.
COE, Elijah (1751, Maryland - died after 1809, Virginia). Private, enrolled in the Flying Camp by Capt. Robert Bowie on July 22, 1776; nativity: Maryland; height: 6'; has own gun [Ref: D-37]. Took the Oath of Allegiance before the Hon. Thomas Clagett in 1778 [Ref: O-266]. Elijah Coe married Ann Smallwood by license dated Oct. 23, 1779 [Ref: X-608, ZB-50].
COE, George C. See "Richard Coe," q.v.
COE, Hezekiah. Private, 1st Maryland Line; died Nov. 31 [sic], 1777 [Ref: D-91].
COE, John. See "Richard Coe," q.v.
COE, Marsilva. See "Bayne Smallwood," q.v.
COE, Mary. See "Richard Coe," q.v.

COE, Milburn. Corporal, 1st Maryland Line; discharged Dec. 27, 1779 [Ref: D-91]. Milburn Coe married Mary Tongue by license dated Jan. 8, 1783 [Ref: ZB-51].
COE, Richard (Dec. 7, 1753 - 1833). Son of John and Mary Coe [Ref: ZC-14]. Sergeant, 1st Maryland Line, 1779; Quartermaster, Feb. 22, 1779; discharged Dec. 27, 1779 [Ref: D-91]. On Feb. 20, 1830, the Treasurer of the Western Shore was directed to pay Richard Coe, of Prince George's County, an old soldier, half pay of a sergeant, quarterly, for his services during the Revolutionary War. On Feb. 10, 1832, the Register of the Land Office was directed to issue to Richard Coe, of Prince George's County, a soldier of the revolution, warrant and later patent for 50 acres in Allegany County, without compensation money. On Jan. 12, 1835, the Treasurer was directed to pay to Alexander Benson Coe $50.00, being the amount of one year's pension due to Mary Coe at the time of her death. On Mar. 2, 1844, the Treasurer was directed to pay to George C. Coe, son of the late Richard Coe, of Prince George's County, $30.00, if so much was due to said Richard Coe at the time of his death. [Ref: O-329]. He applied for pension (S12543) in Prince George's County in 1818, aged 64, and was paid in the District of Columbia. He reapplied in Washington, DC on July 9, 1832, aged 78, a resident of Piscataway in Prince George's County, Maryland [Ref: T-40, P-692].
COE, Samuel (1744-1828). Took the Oath of Allegiance before the Hon. Thomas Clagett in 1778 [Ref: O-266, R-86]. The estate of one Samuel Coe was probated on Apr. 15, 1828 [Ref: ZE-45].
COE, William. Took the Oath of Allegiance (made his "C" mark) before the Hon. Thomas Clagett in 1778 [Ref: O-268].
COEWN, Joseph. See "Joseph Crown," q.v.
COFFIELD, Owen. Private, 1st Maryland Line, under Col. Grayson; wounded at second Battle of Camden on Apr. 25, 1781; disability (invalid) pension commenced Nov. 15, 1783; resided near Upper Marlboro, Prince George's County, in 1790 [Ref: D-634, D-635, K-1814].
COFFIN, Daniel. The estate of "Daniel Coffin (soldier)" was probated on Mar. 15, 1793 [Ref: ZE-45]. This may be the "Daniel Coffee" who was a private in the 5th Maryland Line and who was reported missing on Aug. 16, 1780 (at the Battle of Camden). [Ref: D-192]. Additional research may be necessary before drawing conclusions.
COGHLAN, Dennis. Took the Oath of Allegiance before the Hon. David Craufurd in 1778 [Ref: O-271]. Dennis Coghlan married Rebecca Smith by license dated July 18, 1777 [Ref: ZB-51].
COLE, George. Private, 2nd Guard, Capt. Henry Hill's Militia Company, Lower Battalion; on duty at Nottingham on the Patuxent, Apr. 12, 1781 [Ref: L-19970 (Box 6, folder 21)]. Took the Oath of Allegiance before the Hon. Osborn Sprigg in 1778 [Ref: O-306, which mistakenly listed the name as "George Cove," but the original list (very light) at the Maryland

State Archives (Box 4, folder 29) listed the name as "George Coal"]. George Cole married Priscilla Hooker by license dated May 6, 1778 [Ref: ZB-51].

COLE, Jessey (1762, Maryland -   ). Private (substitute), 1780, continental service, Maryland Line [Ref: D-338].

COLE, Joseph (1720-1785). Took the Oath of Allegiance before the Hon. William Berry in 1778 [Ref: O-259, R-35]. The estate of one Joseph Cole was probated on Jan. 28, 1785 [Ref: ZE-45].

COLEMAN (COLMAN), Ann. See "Jonathan Jewell," q.v.

COLEMAN, Ishom. Private, Northern Detachment, 3rd Maryland Line, Capt. Horatio Clagett's Company, 1783 [Ref: D-502]. It is also interesting to note that there was an "Isham Coleman" (1758-1825) who served as a private in Virginia, married Ann Roper, and died in Georgia [Ref: X-623].

COLLARD, Elizabeth. See "Francis Kirby," q.v.

COLLARD, Samuel (1726-   ). Took the Oath of Allegiance before the Hon. William Berry in 1778 [Ref: O-259, R-70]. He married Agnes Ouchterloney [Ouchterlong?] on Oct. 31, 1762 [Ref: ZC-14].

COLLINGS, Elizabeth. See "Samuel Silk," q.v.

COLLINGS, James (1746-1794). Took the Oath of Allegiance before the Hon. Alexander Howard Magruder in 1778 [Ref: O-293, R-49, which spelled his name "Calling"]. The estate of one "James Collins" was probated on Mar. 22, 1794 [Ref: ZE-46].

COLLINGS, Sarah. See "Cephas Hoye," q.v.

COLTART, Antipas. Sergeant, 3rd Maryland Line, in Capt. Horatio Clagett's Company, 1779; enlisted Apr. 23, 1777, for 3 years [Ref: D-295].

COLTER, William. Private, Northern Detachment, 3rd Maryland Line, Capt. Horatio Clagett's Company, 1783 [Ref: D-502].

COMBS, Barbara. See "Jeremiah Magruder," q.v.

COMPTON, Henry. Private, Select Militia, Capt. Hezekiah Wheeler's Company, July 14, 1781 [Ref: S-6636 (Box 31, folder 5)]. The estate of one Henry Compton was probated on Mar. 11, 1815 [Ref: ZE-46].

COMPTON, Henry T. Private, Capt. Alexander H. Magruder's Militia Company, Lower Battalion; on duty guarding Magruder's Warehouse in the spring of 1782 [Ref: L-19970 (Box 6, folder 21)].

COMPTON, Thomas. Took the Oath of Allegiance before the Hon. Alexander Howard Magruder in 1778 [Ref: O-293].

CONLEY, Ann. See "Bryan Mayhew," q.v.

CONLEY, Henry (1759, Maryland -   ). Private (substitute), 1780, in continental service, Maryland Line [Ref: D-338].

CONN, George (1732-   ). Took the Oath of Allegiance before the Hon. Christopher Lowndes in 1778 [Ref: O-283, R-21].

CONN, Hugh. Private, 3rd Maryland Line, enlisted Jan. 22, 1776 [Ref: D-9]. The estate of one Hugh Conn was probated by Sep. 14, 1778 (date of inventory). [Ref: ZE-46].
CONN, James (1726-   ). Took the Oath of Allegiance before the Hon. Christopher Lowndes in 1778 [Ref: O-283, R-52].
CONN, John. Took the Oath of Allegiance before the Hon. Christopher Lowndes in 1778 [Ref: O-283]. John Conn and Peter Conn were both corporals in the Maryland Line, apparently from Frederick County, and served under Capt. John Kershner at Fort Frederick, guarding prisoners on June 27, 1778 [Ref: D-328]. Additional research may be necessary before drawing conclusions.
CONN, Mary. See "John Veech (Veitch)," q.v.
CONN, Peter. See "John Conn," q.v.
CONN, Robert (1740/1750, Ireland - 1798, Maryland). Private, later Corporal, 3rd Maryland Line, from Jan. 10, 1778 until June 1, 1779, when reportedly "deserted." He married Elizabeth Cain [Ref: D-95, X-642].
CONN, William (1750-   ). Private, Militia, 1776 [Ref: M-207, A-325, R-71].
CONN, William, of George. Took the Oath of Allegiance before the Hon. Christopher Lowndes in 1778 [Ref: O-286].
CONN, William, of James. Took the Oath of Allegiance before the Hon. Christopher Lowndes in 1778 [Ref: O-288].
CONNELLY, Benjamin, and others. See "John Connolly," q.v.
CONNER, Alexius. Sergeant, 2nd Maryland Line, Capt. Patrick Sim's Company, 1776 [Ref: D-7].
CONNER, John. Private, enrolled by Lt. William Duvall, Lower Battalion, July 18, 1776, for continental service. Private, 3rd Maryland Line, Capt. Horatio Clagett's Company, Dec.; reported "deserted" on Dec. 17, 1779. Private, Northern Detachment, 3rd Maryland Line, Capt. Horatio Clagett's Company, 1783 [Ref: D-35, D-296, D-502]. One John Conner married Eleanor W. Tracy by license dated Dec. 1, 1778 [Ref: ZB-51].
CONNER, Joseph. Took the Oath of Allegiance before the Hon. Christopher Lowndes in 1778 [Ref: O-284].
CONNER, Thomas. Private, 2nd Maryland Line, Capt. Patrick Sim's Company, 1776 [Ref: D-8]. One Thomas Conner married Elizabeth Hutchinson by license dated Feb. 13, 1781, and a Thomas Conner married Susannah Jones by license dated Mar. 31, 1804 [Ref: ZB-52].
CONNER, William (c1750 - died before Feb. 14, 1838). Private, Northern Detachment, 3rd Maryland Line, Capt. Horatio Clagett's Company, 1783 [Ref: D-501]. He married Elinor Wyvill [Ref: X-644].
CONNER, Zadock. Took the Oath of Allegiance before the Hon. Christopher Lowndes in 1778 [Ref: O-285].
CONNOLLY, Benjamin. See "John Connolly," q.v.
CONNOLLY, Francis. See "John Connolly," q.v.

CONNOLLY, Henry. Private, 2nd Maryland Line, Capt. Murdock's Company, Mar. 15, 1781 [Ref: D-366].

CONNOLLY, James. See "John Connolly," q.v.

CONNOLLY, John (1762/1763, Maryland - Apr., 1849, Boone County, Missouri). Private, Maryland Line, enlisted on June 5, 1781, for 3 years in continental service; sent to Annapolis; on furlough on July 13, 1781 [Ref: D-382, which spelled his name "Connely"]. "John Connolly of Prince George's County" was discharged from the Maryland Line in 1781 [Ref: D-407]. "John Connelly" applied for and received pension S16719 on Oct. 1, 1832, aged about 70, in Boone County, Missouri, stating he had enlisted at Piscataway, Prince George's County, Maryland on June 5, 1781, and served in the 3rd Maryland Line. He was at Yorktown and the surrender of Cornwallis, and also served in South Carolina with the 2nd Maryland Line. He returned home to Maryland in the winter of 1783 and guarded Hessian prisoners at Fredericktown and was there discharged. His brother "Benjamin Connolly" of Charles County, served for 5 years in the war and was killed at Gates' defeat in Camden, South Carolina, leaving no issue. In 1849 the children of "John Connelly" were Milley A. Searcy, Jemima White, Sarah Ann Martin, Benjamin Connelly, Sandford Connelly, John Connelly, James Connelly, and Francis Connelly [Ref: P-735, P-736, V-1945 (Vol. 33, No. 2, p. 60].

CONNOLLY, Mary. Rendered patriotic service (not specified) and was paid one pound, two shillings and five pence by the State Treasurer on Apr. 23, 1782 [Ref: I-149].

CONNOLLY, Sandford. See "John Connolly," q.v.

CONTEE, Alexander. The records of the Maryland Council on Sep. 3, 1778, state that "Alexander Contee a Native of this State who hath been absent therefrom in South & North Carolina for about 12 months last past & hath lately that is to say within 3 months last past returned into this State appeared before the Council & before them did take repeat and Subscribe the Oath of Fidelity & Support to this State." [Ref: E-192. E-193]. See "John Contee" and "Thomas Contee," q.v.

CONTEE, Alice. See "Benjamin Contee," q.v.

CONTEE, Anne. See "Dennis Magruder" and "John Contee," q.v.

CONTEE, Barbara. See "John Read Magruder," q.v.

CONTEE, Benjamin (1755 - Nov. 23, 1815). Second son of Thomas Contee and Sarah Fendall, he married Sarah Russell Lee in 1794 and had these children: Philip Ashton Lee Contee, Eleanor Contee, Edmund Henry Contee, and Alice Lee (Contee) Kent [Ref: U-232, ZA-234]. Benjamin was a merchant, minister (ordained in 1803) and lawyer, and served as a Second Lieutenant, Maryland Line, Capt. Alexander H. Magruder's Company, 1776 [Ref: D-34]. Took the Oath of Allegiance before the Hon. Truman Skinner in 1778 [Ref: O-298]. First Lieutenant, 11th Battalion, Capt. Alexander H. Magruder's Company, May 1, 1778; resigned by May, 1779 [Ref: M-64, E-62, N-33]. Delegate to the

Continental Congress, 1787-1788, and U. S. Congressman, 1789-1791. Declared insolvent "due to mishaps in trade" in 1799 [Ref: U-232].
CONTEE, Edmund Henry. See "Benjamin Contee," q.v.
CONTEE, Eleanor. See "Thomas Contee" and "Benjamin Contee" and "Michael Wallace," q.v.
CONTEE, Elizabeth. See "John Contee" and Richard Alexander Contee," q.v.
CONTEE, Jane. See "John Contee" and "Thomas Contee" and "John Read Magruder," q.v.
CONTEE, John (1722 - Jan. 2, 1796). The eldest son of Alexander Contee and Jane Brooke, he married Margaret Snowden circa 1744 and they had these children: Richard Alexander Contee (1753-1818), Elizabeth (Contee) Keith, Jane (Contee) Digges (?), Anne (Contee) Magruder, and Mary (Contee) Magruder [Ref: U-231, X-645, ZA-229]. John served as a County Court Justice, 1746-1766, a Justice of the Court of Oyer and Terminer, 1759-1766, a Delegate to the Maryland Convention, 1774-1775, Committee of Observation, 1775, House of Delegates, 1778, and Commissioner of Tax between 1779 and 1790 [Ref: A-3, U-70, U-78, U-230, U-231]. The estate of John Contee was probated on Jan. 12, 1796 [Ref: ZE-47].
CONTEE, John Jr. See "Richard Alexander Contee," q.v.
CONTEE, Mary. See "John Contee" and "Richard Alexander Contee" and "David Craufurd," q.v.
CONTEE, Philip Ashton. See "Benjamin Contee," q.v.
CONTEE, Richard Alexander (1753-1803). Son of "John Contee," q.v. Took the Oath of Allegiance before the Hon. David Craufurd in 1778 [Ref: O-271]. He married (1) Mary Craufurd (1768-1787, daughter of David Craufurd) by license dated June 16, 1785, and (2) Mrs. Elizabeth Gassaway (Rawlings) Sanders (daughter of Gassaway Rawlings). His children were Elizabeth S. (Contee) Magruder, Lieut. John Contee, Jr., and Richard Alexander Contee, Jr. [Ref: ZA-229]. He was placed on the Committee of Inspection for Patuxent District to watch the movement of the British ships in 1775 [Ref: ZA-233]. "Richard Contee" was an ensign in the Middle Battalion in Capt. John M. Burgess' Company on May 1, 1778, and resigned by Nov., 1779 [Ref: M-64, E-78, N-35, X-645, ZA-229, ZB-52]. "Richard Alexander Contee" was declared insane in 1799 [Ref: U-231]. The estate of "Richard A. Contee" was probated by Apr. 25, 1803 (date of inventory) by Elizabeth G. Contee [Ref: ZE-47].
CONTEE, Sarah. See "Thomas Contee," q.v.
CONTEE, Thomas (1729 - Jan., 1811). Fourth son of Alexander Contee and Jane Brooke, he married his cousin Sarah Fendall circa 1755 and had these children: Alexander Contee (c1755-1810), Rev. Benjamin Contee (1755-1815), Eleanor Lee (Contee) Wallace (1758-1787), Jane (Contee) Worthington and Sarah (Contee) Slater [Ref: U-213, U-232, Y-567, ZA-228, ZE-47]. Thomas held several positions during the

Revolutionary War: Delegate to Maryland Convention, 1775-1776. Maryland Senate, 1777-1779 [Ref: A-3, U-70, U-72, U-76, U-78, U-80, U-232]. Lieutenant Colonel, 11th Battalion, Jan. 31, 1776 [Ref: M-64]. Appointed to collect gold and silver in Prince George's County in February, 1776 [Ref: A-132]. Stored arms and ammunition at Nottingham in July, 1780 [Ref: G-4]. Served on the Board of Patuxent Associators and signed a resolution at Nottingham on Apr. 21, 1781 relative to the defence of the rivers of Potomac and Patuxent and the completion of the fort at Drum Point [Ref: K-1814]. He was also a signer of the Declaration of the Association of Freemen of Maryland in 1775 [Ref: ZA-229].

COOK, Benjamin. Applied for pension (R2248) in Baltimore, Maryland on Mar. 19, 1853, aged about 91, stating he was formerly of Prince George's County. On Aug. 5, 1853, he made an affidavit in Howard County, stating he had lived on remote farms in Anne Arundel County and could not read and write [Ref: P-743]. Although his pension was rejected, there was a Benjamin Cook who was a private in the 2nd Maryland Line on May 1, 1778 and corporal on Oct. 12, 1778. He did not appear on the rolls after Jan., 1779. They may or may not be the same person [Ref: D-83, D-94].

COOK, John (Sep. 7, 1756 -   ). Son of John and Sarah Cook [Ref: ZD-111]. Private in the county militia in 1776 [Ref: M-207, A-325]. Took the Oath of Allegiance before the Hon. Benjamin Hall in 1778 [Ref: O-274].

COOK, Joseph. Private, Militia, 1776 [Ref: M-207, A-325].

COOK, Mary. See "William Cooke," q.v.

COOK, Richard. Private, 3rd Maryland Line, enlisted on Jan. 8, 1779; served in Capt. Horatio Clagett's Company, December, 1779 [Ref: D-295].

COOK, Samuel. Took the Oath of Allegiance before the Hon. Benjamin Hall in 1778 [Ref: O-275].

COOK, Sarah. See "John Cook," q.v.

COOK, William. See "William Cooke," q.v.

COOKE, Jeremiah (1758-   ). Private, enrolled in the Flying Camp by Lieut. William D. Beall on July 29, 1776; nativity: Maryland; height: 5' 4"; black hair, brown complexion [Ref: D-37]. Jeremiah Cooke married Mary Beanes by license dated Dec. 14, 1785 [Ref: ZB-53].

COOKE, John. Took the Oath of Allegiance before the Hon. Osborn Sprigg in 1778 [Ref: O-307]. The estate of one John Cooke was probated in 1791 [Ref: ZE-47].

COOKE, Joseph (1749-1800). Took the Oath of Allegiance before the Hon. Osborn Sprigg in 1778 [Ref: O-307, R-33, which latter source spelled his name "Cook"]. The estate of one Joseph Cooke was probated on Aug. 5, 1800 [Ref: ZE-47].

COOKE, William. One William Cooke was a private in the 3rd Maryland Line until Dec. 7, 1778, when he was "discharged from the Invalids."

[Ref: D-97]. Another William Cooke was a private in the 6th Maryland Line from Jan. 8, 1777 until May 25, 1779, when he was reported "deserted." [Ref: D-195]. One William Cooke married Henrietta Beaven by license dated Aug. 28, 1777 [Ref: ZB-53]. "William Cook" was born on Oct. 6, 1734, son of William and Mary Cook, of Queen Anne's Parish [Ref: ZC-170]. Additional research may be necessary before drawing conclusions.
COOKSEY, Ann. See "Elijah Ellis," q.v.
COOLEY, Jane. See "Benjamin Earley," q.v.
COOLIDGE, Elizabeth. See "John Magruder Burgess," q.v.
COOLIDGE, Judson. Took the Oath of Allegiance before the Hon. David Craufurd in 1778 [Ref: O-271]. The estate of one Judson Coolidge was probated on Nov. 17, 1784 [Ref: ZE-48, which source also referred to him as "Capt."].
COOMES (COOMBES), Joseph (1740-   ). Took the Oath of Allegiance before the Hon. Christopher Lowndes in 1778 [Ref: R-63, O-286, which spelled the name "Coams"]. Joseph Coombes and Dorothy Sherkliff were married by license dated May 4, 1783, and Joseph Coombes and Mary Lyles were married by license dated Oct. 27, 1793 [Ref: ZB-54]. The estate of one "Joseph Cooms" was probated by Aug. 8, 1786 (date of inventory). [Ref: ZE-48].
COOPER, Ann. See "William Tong," q.v.
CORKER, John. Private, 5th Maryland Line, enlisted Jan. 15, 1777 and reported missing on Aug. 16, 1780 (at the Battle of Camden). [Ref: D-193]. The estate of one John Corker was probated on Mar. 22, 1794 in Prince George's County [Ref: ZE-48].
CORNELIUS, Josiah. See "Smallwood Acton," q.v.
CORNISH, Constant. Private, 2nd Maryland Line, May 20, 1778 until discharged on Apr. 3, 1779 [Ref: D-94].
CORNISH, John. Private, 2nd Maryland Line, Apr. 27, 1778 until some time in 1779 when reported dead [Ref: D-93].
CORNISH, Samuel William Abiordiguis(?). Took the Oath of Allegiance before the Hon. William Berry in 1778 [Ref: O-259].
COSTEN, Mrs. Robert Emory. See "Jacob Igleheart," q.v.
COURTS, Eleanor C. See "Richard Hanley Courts," q.v.
COURTS, John. Private, Northern Detachment, 3rd Maryland Line, Capt. Horatio Clagett's Company, 1783; "time expired on Apr. 16, 1783." [Ref: D-502].
COURTS, Richard Hanley (c1755-1809). On Feb. 16, 1820, the Treasurer of the Western Shore was directed to pay to Eleanor C. Courts, of Prince George's County, the half pay of a surgeon's mate, as a compensation for those meritorious services rendered by her deceased husband, Dr. Richard Hanley Courts, during the Revolutionary War [Ref: O-331]. Eleanor C. Courts, widow of Richard, applied for and received pension W8627 in Washington, DC on Nov. 14, 1838, aged 74,

stating they had married in the winter of 1783 or 1784 and Richard had died in 1809 [Ref: P-780].

COVE, George. See "George Cole," q.v.

COVINGTON, Levin. Captain, Militia, Sep. 19, 1776 [Ref: M-65, B-285, which listed his name as "L. Covington"]. Took the Oath of Allegiance before the Hon. Alexander Howard Magruder in 1778 [Ref: O-293]. The estate of one Levin Covington was probated on Mar. 26, 1783 (date of inventory). [Ref: ZE-48].

COX, Abraham (1751-   ). Took the Oath of Allegiance before the Hon. Osborn Sprigg in 1778 [Ref: O-306, R-3]. It is interesting to note that there was an Abraham Cox who was born in Maryland on Jan. 1, 1752, married Elizabeth Clark, served as a second lieutenant in Virginia, and died on Mar. 24, 1834 [Ref: X-686].

COX, Charles. Private, Capt. Hezekiah Wheeler's Company, 11th Militia Battalion, April, 1781 [Ref: L-19970 (Box 6, folder 21)].

COX, Eliza. See "Thomas Lansdale," q.v.

COX, Elizabeth. See "Samuel Luckett," q.v.

COX, Hugh. Took the Oath of Allegiance before the Hon. William Berry in 1778 [Ref: O-257].

COX, Jacob. Private, Capt. Hezekiah Wheeler's Company, 11th Militia Battalion, April, 1781 [Ref: L-19970 (Box 6, folder 21)].

COX, Josiah. Took the Oath of Allegiance before the Hon. Osborn Sprigg in 1778 [Ref: O-307].

COX, Milburn. Private, 2nd Maryland Line, Capt. Patrick Sim's Company, 1776 [Ref: D-7].

COX, Richard. Private, 2nd Maryland Line, Capt. Patrick Sim's Company, 1776 [Ref: D-8].

COX, Thomas. Private, Select Militia, Capt. Hezekiah Wheeler's Company, July 14, 1781 [Ref: S-6636 (Box 31, folder 5)]. Took the Oath of Allegiance before the Hon. Fielder Bowie in 1778 [Ref: O-303, W-4648 (Box 4, folder 15)].

COX, Walter. Cadet, 2nd Maryland Line, Capt. Patrick Sim's Company, 1776 [Ref: D-7].

COX, Walter Brooke. "Walter Brooke Cox" took the Oath of Allegiance before the Hon. David Craufurd in 1778 [Ref: O-271]. "Walter B. Cox" married Ann Hollyday by license dated Nov. 19, 1778 [Ref: ZB-55]. The estate of "Walter B. Cox" was probated on Apr. 14, 1801 [Ref: ZE-49].

CRABB, Ralph. Second Lieutenant, Militia, Capt. Thomas Richardson's Company, until June 9, 1777, when he was succeeded [Ref: M-65].

CRABB, Richard. First Lieutenant, 25th Battalion, Capt. Thomas Richardson's Company, Mar. 18, 1776 [Ref: M-65, A-260]. Involved in the hiring of wagons and horses for use of the military in 1778 [Ref: C-554, E-128].

CRACKALLS, Thomas. Rendered patriotic service (not specified) and was paid one pound and eight shillings by the State Treasurer on Jan. 7, 1783, by order of the Council of Maryland [Ref: I-339].
CRACKELS, William. Private, Capt. Jesse Hellen's Militia Company, before May 23, 1782; guarded Magruder's Warehouse in the spring of 1782 [Ref: L-19970 (Box 6, folder 21)].
CRAFFORD, Alexander. Took the Oath of Allegiance before the Hon. Christopher Lowndes in 1778 [Ref: O-283].
CRAFFORD, Bazell. See "Basil Craufurd," q.v.
CRAIG, Adam (1740- 1814). Took the Oath of Allegiance before the Hon. Christopher Lowndes in 1778 [Ref: O-282, R-69]. Ensign, Upper Battalion, Capt. William Moore's Company, June 24, 1780 [Ref: M-66, F-203, which spelled his name "Craige"]. Second Lieutenant, Capt. Samuel Sheckell's Company, June 27, 1781 [Ref: H-320]. The estate of one Adam Craig was probated on Apr. 14, 1814 [Ref: ZE-49].
CRAIG, John. There were several men with this name who served in the Maryland Line [Ref: D-96, D-98, D-99, D-341, D-354, D-415, D-489]. The estate of one John Craig was probated on May 17, 1793 in Prince George's County [Ref: ZE-49].
CRAIG, Michael. Corporal, 5th Maryland Line, enlisted Jan. 20, 1777 and reported missing on Aug. 16, 1780 (at the Battle of Camden). [Ref: D-191]. The estate of one Michael Craig was probated on Mar. 22, 1794 in Prince George's County [Ref: ZE-49].
CRAMPHIN, Damond. Took the Oath of Allegiance before the Hon. Fielder Bowie in 1778 [Ref: O-304, W-4648 (Box 4, folder 15)].
CRAMPHIN, Henry. See "Thomas Cramphin," q.v.
CRAMPHIN, Richard. Ensign, 25th Battalion, Capt. Josiah Shaw's Company, May 24, 1779. First Lieutenant, Upper Battalion, Capt. William Moore's Company, June 24, 1780 [Ref: M-66, E-414, F-203]. Select Militia, Upper Battalion, June 12, 1781 [Ref: S-6636 (Box 27, folder 82B)]. The estate of one Richard Cramphin was probated on Nov. 17, 1806 [Ref: ZE-49].
CRAMPHIN, Ruth. See "Allen Bowie, Jr." and "John Francis," q.v.
CRAMPHIN, Thomas, Sr. (1715-1783). Son of Henry Cramphin and Mary Jackson. Thomas' son Thomas (c1740-1831) was active in Montgomery County during the Revolutionary War. He was never married [Ref: U-242]. Thomas Cramphin took the Oath of Allegiance before the Hon. Christopher Lowndes in 1778 [Ref: O-282, R-73]. The estate of Thomas Cramphin was probated on Nov. 17, 1783 in Prince George's County [Ref: ZE-49].
CRAMPKIN, Ruth. See "John Francis," q.v.
CRAUFURD, Basil (1746-1790). Took the Oath of Allegiance before the Hon. Christopher Lowndes in 1778 [Ref: O-284, R-34, which spelled his name "Bazell Crafford"]. The estate of one "Basil Crauford" was probated on Mar. 24, 1790 [Ref: ZE-50]. See "Basil Crawford," q.v.

CRAUFURD, David (c1738-1801). A son of David and Mary Crawford [sic], he married Sarah Offutt by 1764 and had these children: David Craufurd, Nathaniel Craufurd, Mary (Craufurd) Contee, Sarah (Craufurd) Forrest, and Martha (Craufurd) Walker (1777-1796). [Ref: U-243, Y-567]. David held many civil and military positions: Court Justice, 1761-1789. Captain, by 1776. Delegate to the Maryland Convention, 1775-1776. Committee of Correspondence, 1774. Committee of Observation, 1775-1776. Appointed Collector of Cloathing for Prince George's County on Nov. 27, 1777. House of Delegates, 1777-1780. Subscription Officer, Continental Loan Office, 1777-1779. Associate Justice, First District Court, 1790-1791. Maryland Senate Elector, 1791 and 1796 [Ref: A-4, C-426, Z-90, U-70, U-76, U-82, U-84, U-243, Y-613, which latter source stated he died in May, 1801, and was buried at his home "Kingston Park" at Upper Marlboro]. Justice of the County Court, 1777 [Ref: C-273, which spelled his name "David Crawford"]. Administered the Oath of Allegiance in 1778 [Ref: O-270]. He served on the Board of Patuxent Associators and signed a resolution at Nottingham on Apr. 21, 1781 relative to the defence of the rivers of Potomac and Patuxent and the completion of the fort at Drum Point [Ref: K-1814]. Captain who served on a General Courts-Martial for the trial of Capt. Richard Bennett Hall, Lieut. Jeremiah Ryley, Lieut. Jonathan Wright, and Lieut. James Mullikin on July 25 and Aug. 23, 1776 at Upper Marlboro [Ref: A-553, B-233, which spelled his name "Crawford"]. The estate of David Craufurd was probated on June 15, 1801 [Ref: ZE-50]. See "Richard Alexander Contee" and "Osborn Sprigg," q.v.

CRAUFURD, Hugh. Private, Maryland Line, discharged on Dec. 3, 1781 [Ref: I-10, D-407]. "Heugh Crawford" was a private, Capt. Richard Stonestreet's Militia Company, 11th Battalion, by May 13 1782. He served in the Maryland Line as he was paid for services on that date by order of the Council of Maryland and then appeared on the militia roster in June, 1782 [Ref: I-163, L-19970 (Box 6, folder 21)].

CRAUFURD, James. Took the Oath of Allegiance before the Hon. Christopher Lowndes in 1778 [Ref: O-283]. The estate of "James Crauford" was probated by Feb. 1, 1786 (date of inventory). The estate of one "James Crawford" was probated on Sep. 11, 1799 and the estate of another "James Crawford" was probated on Apr. 11, 1815 [Ref: ZE-50]. Additional research may be necessary before drawing conclusions.

CRAUFURD, Margaret. See "Osborn Sprigg," q.v.

CRAUFURD, Mary. See "Richard Alexander Contee," q.v.

CRAUFURD, Nathaniel. See "David Craufurd," q.v.

CRAUFURD, Thomas. Took the Oath of Allegiance before the Hon. Christopher Lowndes in 1778 [Ref: O-286].

CRAWFORD, Alexander (1740-   ). Private, Militia, 1776 [Ref: M-207, A-325, R-69]. See "Alexander Crafford," q.v.

CRAWFORD, Basil (1743-   ). Private, Militia, 1776 [Ref: M-207, A-325, R-69, which latter source spelled his name "Bazell"]. Served on a Grand Jury in 1778 [Ref: Z-52]. See "Basil Craufurd," q.v.
CRAWFORD, David. See "David Craufurd," q.v.
CRAWFORD, Hugh. See "Heugh Craufurd," q.v.
CRAWFORD, Jacob. Lieutenant in Capt. Alexander Truman's Company, 2nd Maryland Line, 1782 [Ref: D-439].
CRAWFORD, Joseph. Private (substitute), Maryland Line, discharged on Dec. 3, 1781 [Ref: I-10].
CRAWFORD, Thomas (1737-1826). Private, Militia, 1776 [Ref: M-207, A-325, R-69]. Served on a Grand Jury in 1778 [Ref: Z-90]. The estate of one Thomas Crawford was probated on June 3, 1826 [Ref: ZE-50].
CRAYCROFT, Bladen. Took the Oath of Allegiance before the Hon. Alexander Howard Magruder in 1778 [Ref: O-293]. Corporal in Capt. Benjamin Wailes' Militia Company, Lower Battalion; on duty guarding Magruder's Warehouse in the spring of 1782 [Ref: L-19970 (Box 6, folder 21)]. The estate of Bladen Craycroft was probated on Dec. 29, 1814 [Ref: ZE-51].
CRAYCROFT, Elizabeth. See "Ignatius Digges" and "John Duvall," q.v.
CRAYCROFT, John Sly. "John Sly Cracraft" took the Oath of Allegiance before the Hon. James Beck in 1778 [Ref: O-254]. "John Crecraft" was aged 48 in 1776 [Ref: R-35].
CREEK, Lodaway. See "Samuel Luckett," q.v.
CREEK, Nancy. See "Samuel Luckett," q.v.
CRENSHAW, Pearl. See "Alexander Truman," q.v.
CRISPIN, Alexander. Private, 3rd Maryland Line, Capt. Horatio Clagett's Company, 1779 [Ref: D-295].
CROMPTON, Richard. Ensign, Militia, 1779 [Ref: N-34].
CROOK, Charles. Took the Oath of Allegiance (made his "X" mark) before the Hon. Alexander Howard Magruder in 1778 [Ref: O-293].
CROOK, Mary. See "John Taylor," q.v.
CROSS, Ann. See "Jeremiah Cross" and "Jacob Igleheart," q.v.
CROSS, Benjamin. Took the Oath of Allegiance before the Hon. Thomas Williams in 1778 [Ref: O-302].
CROSS, Eleanor. See "Jacob Simmons," q.v.
CROSS, Elizabeth. See "Marsham Belt," q.v.
CROSS, Fielder. See "Joseph Cross," q.v.
CROSS, George. Two men with this name took the Oath of Allegiance in 1778: one before the Hon. Thomas Williams and another before the Hon. Benjamin Hall [Ref: O-275, O-392]. The estate of one George Cross was probated on Nov. 1, 1783 [Ref: ZE-51].
CROSS, Jane. See "John Cross," q.v.
CROSS, Jeremiah. Two men with this name took the Oath of Allegiance in 1778: one before the Hon. Thomas Williams and another (made his "X" mark) before the Hon. James Mullikin [Ref: O-302, O-296]. One

Jeremiah Cross (or possibly both) rendered patriotic service by providing wheat for the military on Aug. 16, 1781 [Ref: Q-425]. One Jeremiah Cross married Ann ---- and they had a son Jeremiah who was born on Jan. 8, 1765 in Queen Ann Parish [Ref: ZC-171].

CROSS, John (Jan. 9, 1732/3 -   ). Son of Robert and Jane Cross [Ref: ZC-171]. Took the Oath of Allegiance before the Hon. Osborn Sprigg in 1778 [Ref: O-307].

CROSS, Joseph (c1755 - Sep. 16, 1830). Sergeant, 2nd Maryland Line, Feb. 11, 1777, and discharged Jan. 10, 1780 [Ref: D-93]. Lieutenant, Select Militia, Upper Battalion, Capt. Osborn Williams' Company, June 15, 1781 [Ref: M-66, G-475, S-6636 (Box 27, folder 82B)]. Took the Oath of Allegiance before the Hon. Thomas Williams in 1778 [Ref: O-302]. Joseph Cross applied for and received pension S46375 on July 5, 1828, stating he was a resident of Queen Anne's Parish in Prince George's County. Joseph died on Sep. 16, 1830 and Fielder Cross (relationship not stated) was his executor [Ref: T-54, P-824, V-1957 (Volume 45, No. 4, p. 193, ZE-51]. One Joseph Cross married Lucy Brashears by license dated May 20, 1783 [Ref: ZB-57]. See "Rignal Hilleary," q.v.

CROSS, Joseph, of Thomas. Private, Militia, 1781; participated in capturing an enemy boat and crew on Apr. 17, 1781 [Ref: M-208]. Ensign, 4th Maryland Line, 1782 [Ref: D-458].

CROSS, Mary. See "Joseph Brashears" and "Jacob Igleheart," q.v.

CROSS, Robert. See "John Cross," q.v.

CROSS, Thomas (Oct. 30, 1711 - Mar., 1793). A son of George and Elizabeth Cross, of Queen Anne's Parish, he married Sophia ---- [Ref: X-717, ZC-171]. Took the Oath of Allegiance before the Hon. Thomas Williams in 1778 [Ref: O-302]. The estate of Thomas Cross was probated on Mar. 23, 1793 [Ref: ZE-52].

CROSS, William. Three men by this name took the Oath of Allegiance in 1778: one before the Hon. Osborn Sprigg, one before the Hon. James Beck, and one before the Hon. William Berry [Ref: O-255, O-257, O-306].

CROW, Basil. See "Ignatius Brashears," q.v.

CROW, John. Second Lieutenant, Militia, 1779 [Ref: N-34]. Second Lieutenant, 25th Battalion, Capt. Thomas Beall's Company, May 24, 1779 [Ref: M-66, E-414]. Took the Oath of Allegiance before the Hon. James Beck in 1778 [Ref: O-255]. John Crow married Priscilla Beall by license dated Oct. 25, 1780 [Ref: ZB-58]. The estate of John Crow was probated on Oct. 16, 1810 [Ref: ZE-52].

CROW, Thomas. Took the Oath of Allegiance before the Hon. James Beck in 1778 [Ref: O-255]. There was a Thomas Crow who was a private aboard the ship *Defence* in September, 1776 [Ref: D-607]. The estate of one Thomas Crow was probated on Jan. 3, 1782 [Ref: ZE-52].

CROWD, Jeaneth [sic]. Private, 2nd Maryland Line, Capt. Murdock's Company, Mar. 15, 1781 [Ref: D-366].

CROWN, Elisha (1743-1780). Took the Oath of Allegiance before the Hon. Christopher Lowndes in 1778 [Ref: O-284, R-22]. The estate of one Elisha Crown was probated on Oct. 19, 1780 [Ref: ZE-52].

CROWN, Gerard. Took the Oath of Allegiance before the Hon. William Berry in 1778 [Ref: O-258].

CROWN, Joseph (1751-   ). "Joseph Coewn(?)" was a private who was enrolled in the Flying Camp by Lieut. William D. Beall on Aug. 9, 1776; nativity: Maryland; height: 5' 5"; brown hair and brown complexion [Ref: D-37]. Perhaps the name is "Crown," not "Coewn?" Additional research will be necessary before drawing conclusions.

CROWSON, Ezekiah. Fifer, 2nd Maryland Line, Capt. Murdock's Company, Mar. 15, 1781 [Ref: D-366].

CRUTCHLEY (CRUCKLY), Benjamin. Private, 4th Maryland Line, Jan., 1777 to Jan. 12, 1780, when discharged [Ref: D-98]. Private (substitute), Maryland Line, discharged on Dec. 3, 1781 [Ref: I-10].

CRUTCHLY, Delia. See "Samuel Popham," q.v.

CULVER, Henry. Rendered patriotic service by providing wheat for the military on Aug. 4, 1780 [Ref: Q-306].

CULVER, Susannah. See "Richard Jones," q.v.

CUNNINGHAM, Martha. See "Vachell Ijams," q.v.

CURCAURD, Mary J. See "Theodore Hodgkin," q.v.

CURR, John. Took the Oath of Allegiance before the Hon. Fielder Bowie in 1778 [Ref: O-304, W-4648 (Box 4, folder 15)].

CURTAIN, Edward. Took the Oath of Allegiance (made his "X" mark) before the Hon. Thomas Clagett in 1778 [Ref: O-269].

DACORNE, John (1748, France -   ). Private, enlisted Feb. 14, 1780, for 3 years or during war, in continental service, Maryland Line [Ref: D-333].

DALEY, Bryan. Took the Oath of Allegiance before the Hon. Christopher Lowndes in 1778 [Ref: O-283].

DALEY, Peter. Private, enrolled by Capt. Alexander H. Magruder, 11th Battalion, on July 23, 1776, for continental service, Maryland Line [Ref: D-38, which spelled his name "Peter Dayley"].

DALTON, Rachel. See "George Dyer," q.v.

DANFORD, William. Took the Oath of Allegiance before the Hon. Christopher Lowndes in 1778 [Ref: O-282].

DARCEY, Ann. See "Nathan Soper," q.v.

DARCEY, John. Took the Oath of Allegiance before the Hon. Osborn Sprigg in 1778 [Ref: O-307]. John Darcey married Rebecca Hardey by license dated Nov. 21, 1786 [Ref: ZB-59]. The estate of one John Darcey was probated by Mar. 24, 1795 (date of account) and the estate of another John Darcey was probated on Mar. 3, 1818 [Ref: ZE-53].

DARNALL, Henry. Took the Oath of Allegiance before the Hon. Thomas Clagett in 1778 [Ref: O-265].

DARNALL, Nicholas L. Took the Oath of Allegiance before the Hon. Benjamin Hall in 1778 [Ref: O-276].
DARNALL, Robert. Justice of the County Court, 1777 [Ref: C-273]. Took the Oath of Allegiance before the Hon. David Craufurd in 1778 [Ref: O-271]. The estate of one Robert Darnall was probated on May 21, 1803 Ref: ZE-53].
DARNALL, Susannah. See "Basil Waring, Sr." and "Marsham Waring" and "Henry Waring," q.v.
DARNALL, Thomas Jr. (c1760, Maryland - died after 1825, Kentucky). Private, Maryland troops. He married Elizabeth Robey [Ref: X-762].
DARNALL, Thomas Sr. (1735, Maryland - July 1, 1825, Kentucky). He married (1) Susanna Soper, and (2) Elizabeth Nicholas, and served as a private in the Virginia troops [Ref: X-762].
DAVID, Henry. Private, 2nd Maryland Line, Capt. Alexander Truman's Company, 1782; "not heard of since Mar. muster, then sick in Virginia." [Ref: D-440].
DAVIDGE, Tomsey. See "Tyler Baldwin," q.v.
DAVIDSON, George. Took the Oath of Allegiance before the Hon. David Craufurd in 1778 [Ref: O-272]. Private, 5th Maryland Line, enlisted July 6, 1778 and discharged Feb. 23, 1779 [Ref: D-102].
DAVIDSON, John. One John Davidson was a captain on Dec. 10, 1776 and then a major in the 5th Maryland Line on Jan. 1, 1781 [Ref: D-62, D-102, D-349, D-380]. The estate of one John Davidson was probated by Apr. 17, 1787 (date of account) in Prince George's County [Ref: ZE-53].
DAVIS, Ann. See "Christopher Parrott" and "John Talbott," q.v.
DAVIS, Barbary. See "Jesse Davis," q.v.
DAVIS, Caleb. Private (substitute), Maryland Line, 1780; discharged on Dec. 3, 1781 [Ref: D-382, D-407, I-10].
DAVIS, Charles. There were several men with this name who served in the Maryland Line in 1781 [Ref: D-398, D-422, D-471, D-533]. One Charles Burgess Davis, son of Charles Davis, was born on May 27, 1753 in Prince George's County, King George's Parish [Ref: ZC-16]. The estate of one Charles Davis was probated on Apr. 20, 1794 [Ref: ZE-54]. Additional research may be necessary before drawing conclusions.
DAVIS, Cornelius. Private (substitute), Maryland Line, discharged on Nov. 29, 1781 [Ref: D-407, I-6].
DAVIS, Deborah. See "Nathaniel Davis," q.v.
DAVIS, Edward. Private, 3rd Maryland Line, Capt. Horatio Clagett's Company, 1779 [Ref: D-295].
DAVIS, Elizabeth. See "Allen Bowie, Jr.," q.v.
DAVIS, Enus (Eneas). "Enus Davis" served as a private in the 1st Maryland Line from May 21, 1778 until Apr. 5, 1779, when he was discharged. "Eneas Davis" was paid for his services "in cloathing" on Apr. 17, 1779 [Ref: D-101, E-351].

DAVIS, Henry (1760, Prince George's County, Maryland - died after 1832, Christian County, Kentucky). He applied for and received a pension (S30981) in Christian County, Kentucky, on Feb. 28, 1832, aged 72, stating that he was born in Prince George's County, Maryland and lived in Caswell County, North Carolina at the time of his enlistment in the North Carolina Line. He later moved into Tennessee and then to Christian County, Kentucky [Ref: P-895].

DAVIS, Henry Culver (Nov. 9, 1750, Maryland - May 24, 1819, South Carolina). He served as a private in the Maryland troops, married Elizabeth ----, and died in South Carolina [Ref: X-773].

DAVIS, Jesse. Baptized on Dec. 1, 1751, Prince George's County, King George's Parish, son of John and Barbary Davis [Ref: ZC-16]. Private, Maryland Line, 1781 [Ref: D-407, D-602]. It appears that he was drafted from Charles County on July 27, 1781 [Ref: D-377].

DAVIS, John. Private, Capt. Jesse Hellen's Militia Company, before May 23, 1782; guarded Magruder's Warehouse in the spring of 1782 [Ref: L-19970 (Box 6, folder 21)]. "John Davies" was aged 30 in 1776 [Ref: R-25]. The estate of "John Davis (soldier)" was probated on Mar. 13, 1793 [Ref: ZE-54]. See "Jesse Davis," q.v.

DAVIS, Martha. See "Thomas Meeks," q.v.

DAVIS, Nathaniel. "Nathaniel Davis" took the Oath of Allegiance before the Hon. Osborn Sprigg in 1778 [Ref: O-308, W-4648 (Box 4, folder 29)]. "Nathan Davis" was born on July 17, 1734, a son of Samuel and Deborah Davis, of Queen Anne's Parish [Ref: ZC-171].

DAVIS, Naylor. Took the Oath of Allegiance before the Hon. Alexander Howard Magruder in 1778 [Ref: O-293]. The estate of Naylor Davis was probated on July 31, 1798 [Ref: ZE-54].

DAVIS, Richard. Took the Oath of Allegiance before the Hon. James Beck in 1778 [Ref: O-253].

DAVIS, Robert. Private, 6th Maryland Line, enlisted Apr. 28, 1778 and still in service on Nov. 1, 1780 [Ref: D-200]. The estate of "Robert Davis (soldier)" was probated on Mar. 13, 1793 [Ref: ZE-54].

DAVIS, Robert. Took the Oath of Allegiance before the Hon. Osborn Sprigg in 1778 [Ref: O-308, W-4648 (Box 4, folder 29)]. "Robert Davies" was aged 60 in 1776 [Ref: R-43].

DAVIS, Samuel (Jan. 30, 1735 -   ). Son of Samuel and Deborah Davis, of Queen Anne's Parish [Ref: ZC-171]. Took the Oath of Allegiance before the Hon. William Berry in 1778 [Ref: O-259]. See "Nathaniel Davis," q.v.

DAVIS, Thomas. Private, 4th Maryland Line, enlisted Mar. 7, 1777, and reported missing on Aug. 16, 1780 (at the Battle of Camden). [Ref: D-104]. The estate of "Thomas Davis (soldier)" was probated on Jan. 18, 1793 [Ref: ZE-54].

DAVIS, Sarah. See "Walter White," q.v.

DAVISON, John. Took the Oath of Allegiance before the Hon. Thomas Clagett in 1778 [Ref: O-267].
DAWS, Thomas. Private, 2nd Maryland Line, Capt. Patrick Sim's Company, 1776 [Ref: D-9].
DAWSON, George. There were several men with this name who served in the Maryland Line in 1781 [Ref: D-384, D-385, D-402]. One George Dawson, son of Nicholas and Sarah Dawson, was born on Mar. 10, 1750 in King George's Parish, Prince George's County [Ref: ZC-16]. Additional research may be necessary before drawing conclusions.
DAWSON, Nicholas. See "George Dawson," q.v.
DAWSON, Richard. Took the Oath of Allegiance before the Hon. William Lyles, Jr. in 1778 [Ref: O-290].
DAWSON, Sarah. See "George Dawson," q.v.
DAWSON, Thomas (1735-   ). Took the Oath of Allegiance before the Hon. George Lee in 1778 [Ref: O-279, R-76].
DAY, Amey. See "Leonard Fry," q.v.
DAY, John. Took the Oath of Allegiance before the Hon. Christopher Lowndes in 1778 [Ref: O-286].
DAY, Thomas. Took the Oath of Allegiance before the Hon. Christopher Lowndes in 1778 [Ref: O-286].
DAYMOND, George. Private, enrolled by Lt. William Duvall, Lower Battalion, on July 18, 1776, for continental service, Maryland Line [Ref: D-35].
DEACON, John (1759, England -   ). Private (substitute), 1780, continental service, Maryland Line [Ref: D-338].
DEAKINS, Deborah Mandit. See "Leonard M. Deakins," q.v.
DEAKINS, Leonard M. (Mar. 9, 1746 - June 28, 1824). Captain of a company recruited in George Town, Frederick County [sic], which served in Col. Griffith's Regiment of the Flying Camp in 1776. He and wife Deborah M. (died 1846) are buried in the Deakins Family Cemetery in the 6500 block of 41st Street and Tennyson Road, off Queen Chapel Road, in University Park, Prince George's County [Ref: Y-611, D-42, ZE-55]. Leonard M. Deakins married (1) Ruth Orme, and (2) Deborah Mandit [Mauduit?] Duke [Ref: X-800].
DEDERICK, Barnard. Took the Oath of Allegiance before the Hon. George Lee in 1778 [Ref: O-279].
DELASHMUTT, Elizabeth. See "Edward Boteler," q.v.
DELOZEAR, Daniel. See "Thomas Delozier," q.v.
DELOZIER, Edward (1723-   ). Took the Oath of Allegiance (made a mark that resembled a "3") before the Hon. Thomas Clagett in 1778 [Ref: O-268, R-57].
DELOZIER, Thomas (1740/1745 - Jan. 19, 1811). Soldier in the Maryland troops. He married Sarah Garner [Ref: X-811]. There was also a "Thomas Delozear" who was the son of Daniel. His birth is recorded in King George's Parish on June 2, 1724 [Ref: ZC-17].

DELOZIER, William. Private, 1st Maryland Line, from June 4, 1778 until discharged on Feb. 14, 1779. On Feb. 24, 1778, he was paid for his services "in cloathing." [Ref: D-101, E-308].
DEMENT, Anne. See "James Waters," q.v.
DEMENT, John. See "William Dement," q.v.
DEMENT, Sarah. See "William Dement," q.v.
DEMENT, William (Apr. 23, 1752 -   ). Baptized in King George's Parish on Apr. 26, 1752, a son of John and Sarah Dement [Ref: ZC-17, ZC-18, which also spelled the name "Diment"]. Private, Capt. Hezekiah Wheeler's Company, 11th Militia Battalion, April, 1781 [Ref: L-19970 (Box 6, folder 21), which spelled it "Demint"].
DENINSON, Samuel. Took the Oath of Allegiance before the Hon. William Berry in 1778 [Ref: O-258].
DENT, George. See "James Truman," q.v.
DENT, John. See "Thomas Dent," q.v.
DENT, Lucy. See "George Hardey" and "Thomas Hardey," q.v.
DENT, Richard (1748-1810). Took the Oath of Allegiance before the Hon. William Lyles, Jr. in 1778 [Ref: O-290, R-4]. Served on a Grand Jury in 1777 and 1778 [Ref: Z-29, Z-90]. Quartermaster, 1782 [Ref: Q-514]. The estate of one Richard Dent was probated on Jan. 15, 1810 [Ref: ZE-55].
DENT, Sarah. See "Thomas Dent," q.v.
DENT, Thomas (1735-1788). He was paid by order of the Council of Safety for services rendered "for enumerating inhabitants in part of Prince George's County" on Sep. 13, 1776 [Ref: B-269]. Took the Oath of Allegiance before the Hon. Thomas Clagett in 1778 [Ref: O-264, R-2]. Captain, 11th (Lower) Battalion, Aug. 1, 1777 to May 1, 1778 [Ref: M-69, C-356, E-62, N-32]. Served on a Grand Jury in 1777 and 1778 [Ref: Z-29, Z-52, Z-90].
DENT, Thomas. "Thomas Dent" was a private in the Select Militia, Capt. Hezekiah Wheeler's Company, July 14, 1781 [Ref: S-6636 (Box 31, folder 5)]. "Thomas Marshall Dent" was born Oct. 22, 1761, son of John and Sarah Dent, of King George's Parish [Ref: ZC-18].
DENT, Thomas Marshall. See "Thomas Dent" and "Alexander Howard Magruder," q.v.
DENT, Walter (1744, Maryland - died after 1820, Georgia). Private, Capt. Hezekiah Wheeler's Company, 11th Militia Battalion, April, 1781 [Ref: L-19970 (Box 6, folder 21), R-4]. He married Elizabeth Montgomery [Ref: X-819].
DENUNE, Elizabeth. See "Jacob Denune," q.v.
DENUNE, Jacob. "Jacob Denune" took the Oath of Allegiance before the Hon. Thomas MacGill in 1778 [Ref: O-291]. "Jacob Henry Denune" was born on Nov. 24, 174?, son of William Denune and Elizabeth Duvall, of Queen Anne's Parish [Ref: ZC-172].
DENUNE, John (1761, France - Nov. 28, 1838, Ohio). Fifer, 2nd Maryland Line, Capt. Alexander Truman's Company, 1782, and waiter

to Lieut. Rutledge in 1782 [Ref: D-439, which spelled his name "Denoone"]. John Denune married Sarah Burrell [Ref: X-820].

DENUNE, Mary. See "John Igleheart," q.v.

DENUNE, William. See "Jacob Denune," q.v.

DERSEY, Ann. See "Nathan Soper," q.v.

DEVAROU (DEVARON, DEVENER), Michael. Michael Devarou (or Devaron) was a private in Capt. Jesse Hellen's Militia Company, before May 23, 1782; guarded Magruder's Warehouse in the spring of 1782 [Ref: L-19970 (Box 6, folder 21)]. "Michael Devener" was paid for his services "in cloathing" on Feb. 24, 1779 [Ref: E-308].

DEVERICKS, James. "Jno. or James Devereaux" was a sergeant in the 2nd Maryland Line until discharged on Jan. 10, 1780 [Ref: D-101]. "Jas. Deverex" was a sergeant in the Maryland Line between Aug. 1, 1780 to at least Jan. 1, 1781 [Ref: D-353]. "James Devericks" was a private in 2nd Maryland Line, Capt. Alexander Truman's Company, 1782; promoted to sergeant on Oct. 1, 1782 [Ref: D-440].

DEW, John (1756-   ). Private, enrolled in the Flying Camp by Lieut. Benjamin Brooks on July 25, 1776; nativity: Prince George's County; height 5' 9"; has own gun [Ref: D-36].

DICK, Robert. Stored arms and ammunition at Bladensburg in July, 1780 [Ref: G-4]. The estate of one Robert Dick was probated on Mar. 20, 1793 [Ref: ZE-56].

DICKERSON, Thomas. Private, Northern Detachment, 3rd Maryland Line, Capt. Horatio Clagett's Company, 1783 [Ref: D-502].

DICKINSON, Mary. See "Elisha Lanham," q.v.

DIGGES, Anne. See "George Digges" and "William Digges" and "John Plummer," q.v.

DIGGES, Charles. See "William Digges," q.v.

DIGGES, Edward. Took the Oath of Allegiance before the Hon. David Craufurd in 1778 [Ref: O-271]. The estate of one Edward Digges was probated on Oct. 9, 1786 [Ref: ZE-56].

DIGGES, Edward Jr. Took the Oath of Allegiance before the Hon. George Lee in 1778 [Ref: O-279].

DIGGES, Eleanor. See "Joseph White Clagett," q.v.

DIGGES, Ellenor. See "Notley Young," q.v.

DIGGES, George (1743 - Nov. 18, 1792). A son of William Digges and Anne Attwood, he married Catherine Brent (c1773-1835) and they had two children, William Dudley Digges (1790-1830) and Anna Maria Livingston. He was elected to the Committee of Inspection in 1775, served in the Lower House between 1783 and 1788, and attended the Constitution Ratification Convention in 1788 [Ref: U-270, U-271, X-837]. He died at Warburton Manor and his estate was probated on Dec. 4, 1792 [Ref: ZA-259, ZA-260, ZE-56].

DIGGES, Henrietta Maria. See "Basil Waring, Sr.," q.v.

DIGGES, Ignatius. A well-to-do land owner, he married Elizabeth Parnham Craycroft and their only child Mary Digges (1745-1805) married "Thomas Sim Lee," q.v. [Ref: U-529]. He took the Oath of Allegiance before the Hon. David Craufurd in 1778 [Ref: O-272. Also see Source ZA-274 through ZA-283 for additional information on this Digges family of "Mellwood Park" in Prince George's County]. His estate was probated on Aug. 22, 1785 [Ref: ZE-57].
DIGGES, Jane. See "Notley Young" and "John Fitzgerald," q.v.
DIGGES, Joseph (c1750 - died after June 12, 1816). Physician and surgeon to the Maryland Mar.ing Militia on Sep. 4, 1777 [Ref: C-362]. Took the Oath of Allegiance before the Hon. David Craufurd in 1778 [Ref: O-271]. He was born in Virginia, served in Maryland during the war, married (1) Sarah Beverley and (2) Jane Tompkins, and died in Virginia [Ref: X-819].
DIGGES, Mary. See "Thomas Sim Lee" and "Ignatius Digges" and "Clement Hill, Sr.," q.v.
DIGGES, Thomas. Took the Oath of Allegiance before the Hon. David Craufurd in 1778 [Ref: O-272].
DIGGES, William (1713-1783). Son of Charles Digges and Susannah Maria Lowe. He married Anne Attwood. Took the Oath of Allegiance before the Hon. Thomas Clagett in 1778 [Ref: U-270, O-264, R-40]. His estate was probated on Apr. 14, 1783 [Ref: ZE-56]. See "George Digges," q.v.
DIGGES, William Jr. (1731-   ). Took the Oath of Allegiance before the Hon. Thomas Clagett in 1778 [Ref: O-264, R-55].
DIGGES, William 3rd. Took the Oath of Allegiance before the Hon. Thomas Clagett in 1778 [Ref: O-265].
DIGGES, William Dudley. See "George Digges," q.v.
DIXON, William. Private, Maryland Line; listed as a defective on July 5, 1780 [Ref: D-414].
DONAHY, Edward. Recruited for the military before Aug. 28, 1780 when the County Lieutenant reported to the Council of Maryland that he (Donahy) had not reported and he "shall endeavour to apprehend him if to be found in the county." [Ref: G-63].
DONALDSON, Benjamin. Took the Oath of Allegiance before the Hon. Benjamin Hall in 1778 [Ref: O-275].
DONALDSON, Richard. Took the Oath of Allegiance (made his "X" mark) before the Hon. James Beck in 1778 [Ref: O-253].
DONALDSON, Zachariah. Took the Oath of Allegiance before the Hon. Benjamin Hall in 1778 [Ref: O-275].
DONOUGHE, Mary. See "John Fearall," q.v.
DOPHEY, Ann. See "Bryan Mayhew," q.v.
DORSETT, Theodore. Took the Oath of Allegiance before the Hon. Fielder Bowie in 1778 [Ref: O-304, W-4648 (Box 4, folder 15)].

DORSETT, Thomas. Took the Oath of Allegiance before the Hon. Fielder Bowie in 1778 [Ref: O-304, W-4648 (Box 4, folder 15)]. Thomas Dorsett married Ann Selby by license dated Dec. 16, 1784 [Ref: ZB-65].
DORSETT, Thomas M. Private, Capt. Alexander H. Magruder's Militia Company, Lower Battalion; on duty guarding Magruder's Warehouse in the spring of 1782 [Ref: L-19970 (Box 6, folder 21)].
DORSETT, William Newman. Second Lieutenant, Militia, Mar. 16, 1776 [Ref: M-70, A-246, A-353]. Served on a Grand Jury in 1777 [Ref: Z-23]. Took the Oath of Allegiance before the Hon. Fielder Bowie in 1778 [Ref: O-304, W-4648 (Box 4, folder 15)]. His estate was probated on Februry 15, 1812 [Ref: ZE-58].
DORSEY, Ann. See "Richard Brooke" and "Nathan Soper," q.v.
DOUGALL, Jonas. Took the Oath of Allegiance before the Hon. Christopher Lowndes in 1778 [Ref: O-287].
DOUGHERTY, Edward. Private, 4th Maryland Line, enlisted on May 13, 1778; corporal, Aug. 1, 1779; sergeant, Jan. 1, 1780 [Ref: D-105]. The estate of "Edward Dougherty (soldier)" was probated on Mar. 21, 1793 [Ref: ZE-58].
DOUGHERTY, Elizabeth. See "Samuel Perrie Wailes," q.v.
DOUGLAS, Eleanor. See "Thomas H. Luckett," q.v.
DOVE, Elizabeth. See "John Hooper" and "Philip Russell," q.v.
DOVE, John (1756, England - died after 1789, Maryland). On Apr. 27, 1782, the Western Shore Treasurer paid "John Dove for the use of Moses Morelick twelve pounds, six shillings and eight pence" by order of the Council of Maryland under the Act for the Emission of Bills of Credit [Ref: I-149]. John Dove was a sergeant, and also a quartermaster, and married Dianah Wilmot [Ref: X-866].
DOVE, Mary Ann. See "John Hooper," q.v.
DOVE, Richard (born in 1744, Anne Arundel County, Maryland - died after 1833, Licking County, Ohio). Took the Oath of Allegiance before the Hon. Benjamin Hall in Prince George's County, Maryland in 1778 [Ref: O-274]. Applied for and received pension S17391 in Licking County, Ohio on Mar. 13, 1833, a resident of Eden Township, stating he lived in Prince George's County, Maryland at the time of his enlistment in the Maryland Line [Ref: P-1013].
DOWDON, Clementius. Born in Prince George's County on Jan. 11, 1762, he lived in Montgomery County at the time of his enlistment in the Maryland Line and applied for pension (S30995) in Bourbon County, Kentucky on Dec. 3, 1832, where he had lived for four years [Ref: P-1015]. He died after 1836 in Illinois [Ref: X-868].
DOWNES, Lucy. See "John Hallsall," q.v.
DOWNES, William. Private, 4th Maryland Line, enlisted on Aug. 19, 1777, and was reported missing on Aug. 16, 1780 (at the Battle of Camden). [Ref: ZE-58]. The estate of one William Downes was probated on Dec. 13, 1804 [Ref: ZE-58].

DOWNING, Butler Marlow. See "Butler Marlow," q.v.
DOWNING, Henry (1736-   ). Took the Oath of Allegiance before the Hon. Thomas Clagett in 1778 [Ref: O-266, R-43].
DOWNING, James (1726-   ). Took the Oath of Allegiance (made his "I" mark with an equidistant horizontal line through the middle) before the Hon. Thomas Clagett in 1778 [Ref: O-265, R-53]. He may be the James Downing who married Susanna ---- and had twin sons, James and John, born on Feb. 16, 1756 [Ref: ZC-19]. There was also a James Downing who was born in Scotland in 1760, served as a private in the Maryland Line, married Asenath Walters, and died in Virginia in 1832 [Ref: X-870]. Additional research may be necessary before drawing conclusions.
DOWNING, John. Private, enrolled by Capt. Alexander H. Magruder, 11th Battalion, on July 10, 1776, for continental service, Maryland Line [Ref: D-38]. See "James Downing," q.v.
DOWNING, Nathaniel. Private, 1st Maryland Line, Dec. 10, 1776; discharged Dec. 27, 1779 [Ref: D-100]. In December, 1817, the Treasurer of the Western Shore was directed to pay to Nathaniel Downing, of Prince George's County, an old soldier, half pay of a private, as a further remuneration to him for the services rendered his country in the Revolutionary War [Ref: O-337, O-338].
DOWNING, Samuel (c1755, Maryland - 1834, Kentucky). Private, 1st Maryland Line, Mar. 16, 1777, and discharged Mar. 16, 1780 [Ref: D-101]. Applied for and received pension S35899 in Barren County, Kentucky on Nov. 15, 1819, stating that he had no family [Ref: P-1018]. He married Priscilla Webb and apparently had children because someone joined the DAR based on his service [Ref: X-870].
DOWNING, Susanna. See "James Downing," q.v.
DOWNS, Ann. See "James Downs," q.v.
DOWNS, Benjamin (1714-1783). Took the Oath of Allegiance before the Hon. Christopher Lowndes in 1778 [Ref: R-62, O-285, which spelled his name "Down"]. The estate of one "Benjamin Downes" was probated on Mar. 26, 1783 [Ref: ZE-58].
DOWNS, Henry (1750-   ). Took the Oath of Allegiance before the Hon. Christopher Lowndes in 1778 [Ref: O-288, R-62].
DOWNS, James. "James Downes" was a private in the 1st Maryland Line on Apr. 8, 1777 [Ref: D-101]. "James Gordon Downs" was baptized in King George's Parish on Apr. 25, 1751, and was the son of William and Ann Downs [Ref: ZC-19].
DOWNS, William. See "James Downs" and "William Downes," q.v.
DOYALL, Thomas. Private, 4th Maryland Line, Capt. Bowie's Company, from Feb. 4, 1778 to at least Nov. 1, 1780 [Ref: D-104].
DRANE, Ann. See "Richard Lamar," q.v.
DRANE, Anthony (c1719-1798). Took the Oath of Allegiance before the Hon. Benjamin Hall in 1778 [Ref: X-875, O-276, which latter source spelled the name "Drain"]. One Anthony Drane married Ann Smith by

license dated Dec. 23, 1778. He was probably the son of James and Elizabeth Drane, of Queen Anne's Parish [Ref: ZB-67, ZC-172].
DRANE, Elizabeth. See "Zadock Brashears" and "Anthony Drane," q.v.
DRANE, James (1720-1787). Took the Oath of Allegiance before the Hon. Benjamin Hall in 1778 [Ref: O-276, which spelled the name "Drain"]. Appointed Coroner in Prince George's County on June 4, 1777, upon the resignation of Benjamin Brookes [Ref: C-273]. James Drane married Elizabeth Smith Piles [Ref: X-875]. His estate was probated on Oct. 6, 1787 [Ref: ZE-58]. See "James Mullikin" and "Anthony Drane," q.v.
DRANE, James Jr. (1755-1829). Second Lieutenant, Middle Battalion, Capt. Charles Clagett's Company, Nov. 13, 1779 [Ref: M-71, F-13, N-35]. Took the Oath of Allegiance before the Hon. Benjamin Hall in 1778 [Ref: O-276, which spelled the name "James Drain, Jr."]. "James Drane" married Priscilla Lamar by license dated Februry 18, 1789 [Ref: X-875, ZB-67]. See "James Mullikin," q.v.
DRANE, Thomas. Rendered patriotic service by providing wheat for the military on July 29, 1780 [Ref: Q-305]. One Thomas Drane married Martha Wells by license dated Feb. 4, 1786 [Ref: ZB-67].
DRANE, Walter (circa 1757, Maryland - died before Jan. 5, 1808, Georgia). Took the Oath of Allegiance before the Hon. Benjamin Hall in 1778 [Ref: O-276, which spelled the name "Walter Drain"]. He married Allitha Magruder and served in the Maryland troops [Ref: X-875, but is not listed in *Maryland Archives, Volume 18*].
DRIVER, John. Private, 3rd Maryland Line, Capt. Horatio Clagett's Company, 1779 [Ref: D-295].
DROWN, Thomas (1741 or 1751 -   ). Private, enrolled in the Flying Camp by Lt. William D. Beall on July 18, 1776; aged 25; nativity: England; height: 5' 7"; dark hair, fair complexion [Ref: D-37]. The census of 1776 listed Thomas Drown as being aged 35 [Ref: R-69].
DRUDGE, Thomas. Private, 3rd Maryland Line, 1780-1782 [Ref: D-430, D-104, which latter source spelled the name "Drudges"]. The estate of one Thomas Drudge was probated on Apr. 9, 1794 [Ref: ZE-58].
DUCE, Samuel. See "Samuel Duer," q.v.
DUCKER, Jeremiah. Rendered patriotic service by providing wheat for the military on Aug. 3, 1780 [Ref: Q-306].
DUCKER, John (Sep. 23, 1722 -   ). Son of William and Mary Ducker, of Queen Anne's Parish [Ref: ZC-172]. Took the Oath of Allegiance before the Hon. Christopher Lowndes in 1778 [Ref: O-288].
DUCKER, Mary. See "Jeremiah Ducker" and "William Ducker," q.v.
DUCKER, William (July 5, 1725 -   ). Son of William and Mary Ducker, of Queen Anne's Parish [Ref: ZC-172]. Took the Oath of Allegiance before the Hon. Christopher Lowndes in 1778 [Ref: O-288].
DUCKETT, Allen Bowie. See "Thomas Duckett," q.v.
DUCKETT, Ann. See "Samuel Duckett" and "Basil Waring 3rd," q.v.

DUCKETT, Baruch (1744 or 1745 - Oct. 2, 1810). A son of Richard Duckett, Jr. and Mary Nuthall, he married Mary Bowie Beanes by license dated Jan. 11, 1783, and their only child was Kitty Beanes Duckett (born Dec. 4, 1783). [Ref: ZA-707, ZA-708, ZB-67, ZE-59]. Baruch was an ensign, 25th Battalion, Capt. Basil Waring's Company, Jan. 3, 1776, and a second lieutenant from Mar. 25, 1776 through May 1, 1778 (recommended for first lieutenant on June 9, 1777). He is buried in the Bowie Family Cemetery west of Church Road near Routes 50 and 450 [Ref: M-72, A-285, E-63, N-34, Y-559].

DUCKETT, Charity. See "Thomas Boyd," q.v.

DUCKETT, Eleanor. See "Thomas Lyles," q.v.

DUCKETT, Isaac. Private, Militia. He participated in capturing an enemy boat and crew on Apr. 17, 1781 [Ref: M-208]. Took the Oath of Allegiance before the Hon. James Mullikin in 1778 [Ref: O-296]. "Dr. Isaac Duckett (1753-1823) married Mary Bowie." [Ref: ZA-652]. One Isaac Duckett married Margaret Bowie by license dated Jan. 24, 1792 [Ref: ZB-68]. The estate of one Isaac Duckett was probated on July 7, 1823 [Ref: ZE-59].

DUCKETT, J. Took the Oath of Allegiance before the Hon. Thomas Boyd in 1778 [Ref: O-262].

DUCKETT, Jacob (1750 - June 4, 1816). On Jan. 5, 1778, he was "appointed Commissary to Procure Supplies and Distribute them to the Quota of Troops of the American Army agreeable to the Resolves of the General Assembly 13th Dec. last." [Ref: C-454]. He took the Oath of Allegiance before the Hon. Thomas Boyd in 1778 [Ref: O-262]. He is buried in St. John's Churchyard at Broad Creek, Prince George's County [Ref: Y-614, ZE-59]. Source X-883 states Jacob Duckett was born Sep. 20, 1751, rendered patriotic service in Maryland, married "Mary Meeks (Clagett) McElderry" and died after 1801 in North Carolina [Ref: X-883, ZA-652]. There appears to have been two men named Jacob Duckett or perhaps a discrepancy in the records. One "Thomas Duckett," q.v., also married a "Mary Meek Clagett" (his second wife). Source ZB-68 states that Jacob Duckett married Mary McElderry by license dated May 4, 1799, in Prince George's County, Maryland. Additional research will be necessary before drawing conclusions.

DUCKETT, John (1726-1784). Took the Oath of Allegiance before the Hon. Thomas Clagett in 1778 [Ref: O-266]. He married Sarah Waring and rendered civil service [Ref: X-883, ZE-59].

DUCKETT, John Bowie. See "Thomas Duckett," q.v.

DUCKETT, Kitty Beanes. See "Baruch Duckett," q.v.

DUCKETT, Margaret. See "Walter Bowie," q.v.

DUCKETT, Mary. See "Thomas Clagett" and "John Duckett Wells" and "Jacob Wells" and "George Wells," q.v.

DUCKETT, Priscilla. See "Allen Bowie, Sr.," q.v.

DUCKETT, Rachel. See "Thomas Williams," q.v.

DUCKETT, Richard Jr. (Apr. 12, 1732 - between 1795 and 1803). Ensign, 25th Battalion, Capt. James Mullikin's Company, May 1, 1778. Second Lieutenant, Upper Battalion, June 24, 1780 [Ref: M-72, N-35, E-63, F-203]. Court Justice, 1777 [Ref: C-273]. On Jan. 13, 1780, the Council of Maryland ordered the Collector of the Tax for Prince George's County to "pay Richard Duckett, Junr., Two hundred Pounds to enable him to Carry into Execution the Act for the immediate supply of Flour and other Provisions for the Army to be Accounted for." [Ref: F-57, Q-259, Q-270]. He married (1) Martha Waring, and (2) Sophia Buchanan [Ref: X-883]. The estate of one Richard Duckett was probated on May 21, 1803 [Ref: ZE-59]. See "Thomas Duckett" and "Richard Duckett, Sr.," q.v.

DUCKETT, Richard Sr. (Feb. 21, 1704/5 - 1788). Took the Oath of Allegiance before the Hon. James Mullikin in 1778 [Ref: O-296]. He married (1) Mary Nuthall [Nutwell?], and (2) Elizabeth Williams on June 2, 1735 [Ref: X-883, ZC-172, which latter source stated that "Richard Duckett, Jr. married Mary Nutwell" on Nov. 13, 1729]. His estate was probated on Sep. 28, 1788 [Ref: ZE-59].

DUCKETT, Rignal. Took the Oath of Allegiance before the Hon. Thomas Williams in 1778 [Ref: O-302].

DUCKETT, Samuel (1751 - died after 1800). Samuel Duckett married Ann ----, and rendered patriotic service [Ref: X-883].

DUCKETT, Thomas (Mar. 26, 1744 - 1806). A son of Richard Duckett and Elizabeth Williams, of Queen Anne's Parish, Thomas married (1) Priscilla Fraser Bowie, and (2) Mary Meek Clagett, widow of Thomas Clagett and daughter of Enoch Magruder. His children were Allen Bowie Duckett, John Bowie Duckett, Dr. Richard Duckett, Anne Fraser Brooke, and Susannah Rawlings [Ref: U-283, ZA-652, ZA-708, ZC-173, ZE-60]. Thomas served as a First Lieutenant in the 25th Battalion, Capt. James Mullikin's Company, on May 1, 1778 [Ref: M-72, E-63, N-34]. County Sheriff, 1777-1779. Collector of Supplies for the Army, 1779. Served in House of Delegates, 1781-1783. Judge, Court of Appeals for Tax Assessment, 1786. County Court Justice, 1788-1792. Associate Justice, First District Court, 1793-1802. State Senator, 1801-1806 [Ref: U-84, U-86, U-87, U-283, Z-29]. There appears to have been two men named Thomas Duckett or perhaps there may be a discrepancy in the records. The above Thomas Duckett was born in 1744 and died in 1806. Another Thomas Duckett was also born in 1744 (Nov. 24) in Maryland and married Mary (Polly) Odell. He served in the South Carolina troops and died in South Carolina before Oct. 4, 1824 [Ref: X-883]. Additional research will be necessary before drawing conclusions. See "Jacob Duckett," q.v.

DUER, Samuel. Took the Oath of Allegiance before the Hon. Osborn Sprigg in 1778 [Ref: O-306, but the original list at the Maryland State

Archives (Box 4, folder 29) is very light and unclear. The name could have been "Samuel Duer" or perhaps even "Samuel Duce"].

DUFFEE, Francis. Sergeant, 2nd Maryland Line, 1782 [Ref: D-445].

DUFFEE, Terence (1731, Ireland -   ). Private, enlisted Feb. 23, 1781, for 3 years in the continental service, Maryland Line; "Pennsylvania, sent to Annapolis" *[sic]* and on duty July 13, 1781 [Ref: D-381]. Sergeant, 2nd Maryland Line, 1782 [Ref: D-445].

DUFFEE, Thomas. Sergeant, 4th Maryland Line, 1782 [Ref: D-458].

DUFFEY, John. Private, 4th Maryland Line, enlisted May 8, 1777 and reported missing on Aug. 16, 1780 (at the Battle of Camden). [Ref: D-202]. The estate of "John Duffey (soldier)" was probated on Mar. 15, 1793 in Prince George's County [Ref: ZE-60].

DUKE, Deborah Mandit. See "Leonard M. Deakins," q.v.

DULEY, Henry (1731-   ). Took the Oath of Allegiance before the Hon. William Berry in 1778 [Ref: O-258, R-27, which spelled the name "Henry Duly"].

DULEY, Jonathan. Private, Select Militia, Upper Battalion, June 12, 1781 [Ref: S-6636 (Box 27, folder 82B)].

DULY, William. "William Duly" took the Oath of Allegiance before the Hon. Christopher Lowndes in 1778 [Ref: O-288]. "William Duley" was a private in the 7th Maryland Regiment, having enlisted on Mar. 24, 1777; reported missing on Aug. 16, 1780 (at the Battle of Camden). [Ref: D-202]. The estate of "William Duley (soldier)" was probated on Jan. 18, 1793 in Prince George's County [Ref: ZE-60].

DUNKIN, Isaac. Private, Northern Detachment, 3rd Maryland Line, Capt. Horatio Clagett's Company, 1783; discharged Nov. 15, 1783 [Ref: D-501].

DUNN, John (1706-1790). Took the Oath of Allegiance (made his "I" mark with an equidistant horizontal line through the middle) before the Hon. Thomas Clagett in 1778 [Ref: O-266, R-58]. The estate of one John Dunn was probated on Jan. 26, 1790 [Ref: ZE-60].

DUNNING, Dennis. Drummer, Northern Detachment, 3rd Maryland Line, Capt. Horatio Clagett's Company, 1783 [Ref: D-501].

DUNNINGTON, William (Apr. 13, 1740 - 1802). Private, 3rd Maryland Line, Capt. Horatio Clagett's Company, December, 1779 [Ref: D-296]. He married ---- Beck [Ref: X-898].

DUPRE, John (1740, France -   ). Private, enlisted Feb. 14, 1780, for 3 years or during war, in continental service, Maryland Line [Ref: D-333].

DUROUGH, John. Private, 2nd Maryland Line, Capt. Alexander Truman's Company, 1782; "prisoner of war, Mar. 15, 1781." [Ref: D-440].

DUTTON, Thomas. Private, 1st Maryland Line, who was paid for his services "in cloathing" on Apr. 17, 1779 [Ref: E-351].

DUVALL, Alexander (Apr. 1, 1755 - June 7, 1840, Pennsylvania). Took the Oath of Allegiance before the Hon. Thomas Williams in 1778 [Ref: O-302]. He married Elizabeth Patterson [Ref: X-906].

DUVALL, Alexander (July 10, 1739 - 1802). Son of Mareen and Ruth Duvall [Ref: ZC-173]. Served on a Grand Jury in 1777 [Ref: Z-29]. The estate of one Alexander Duvall was probated on Oct. 25, 1802 [Ref: ZE-61].
DUVALL, Alice. See "Lewis Duvall," q.v.
DUVALL, Ann. See "John Duvall, Jr." and "Marsh M. Duvall," q.v.
DUVALL, Beall. See "Fielder or Fielding Belt," q.v.
DUVALL, Benjamin (Apr. 4, 1711 -   ). Son of Mareen Jr. and Elizabeth Duvall [Ref: ZC-173]. Took the Oath of Allegiance before the Hon. Benjamin Hall in 1778 [Ref: O-275, R-51, which latter source stated he was aged 63 in 1776]. See "Charles Duvall," q.v.
DUVALL, Benjamin (Sep. 30, 1717 -   ). Son of Mareen "ye younger" and Sarah Duvall [Ref: ZC-173]. Took the Oath of Allegiance before the Hon. Thomas Clagett in 1778 [Ref: O-268, R-9]. See "Gabriel Duvall," q.v.
DUVALL, Benjamin, of Benjamin. One Benjamin Duvall, son of Benjamin and Sophia Duvall, was born on May 29, 1719, and another Benjamin Duvall, son of Benjamin and Susannah Duvall, was born on Nov. 5, 174?, both in Queen Anne's Parish [Ref: ZC-173]. One "Benjamin Duvall, of Benjamin" took the Oath of Allegiance before the Hon. Thomas Williams in 1778 [Ref: O-302]. Additional research may be necessary before drawing conclusions.
DUVALL, Benjamin, of Elisha (1760 - Jan. 17, 1831). Private (substitute), Maryland Line, 1780-1781, who was paid for services rendered on Apr. 22, 1782 [Ref: D-382, I-144]. On Feb. 18, 1822, the Treasurer of the Western Shore was directed to pay to Benjamin Duvall, of Elisha, an old soldier, half pay of a private, as a further remuneration for the services rendered his country during the Revolutionary War. On Feb. 16, 1830, the Treasurer was directed to pay to Benjamin L. Gantt, for the use of Benjamin Duvall, Jr. of Prince George's County, executor of Benjamin Duvall, of Elisha, of said county, a revolutionary soldier who died Jan. 30, 1830, the amount of $33.22 due him at death as a pensioner [Ref: O-338, T-39]. He applied for and received pension S34768 in Prince George's County on Mar. 7, 1818, aged about 60. In 1822 he had a wife aged 68 and daughter aged 38 (not named). From the file "it appeared soldier was a son of Elisha Duvall" and "the soldier died on Jan. 17, 1831." [Ref: P-1057]. Benjamin Duvall was a private who was enrolled in the Flying Camp by Lieut. Benjamin Brooks on July 12, 1776 (aged 16; nativity: Prince George's County; height 5' 10 1/2"; has own gun). [Ref: D-36]. Discharged from the Maryland in 1781 [Ref: D-407]. Private, Select Militia, Upper Battalion, June 12, 1781 [Ref: S-6636 (Box 27, folder 82B)]. Benjamin Duvall married [Mrs.] Eleanor Higgins by license dated July 4, 1787 [Ref: X-906, ZB-69]. See "Jesse Duvall," q.v.
DUVALL, Benjamin Jr. See "Benjamin Duvall, of Elisha," q.v.

DUVALL, Benjamin 3rd. Took the Oath of Allegiance before the Hon. Benjamin Hall in 1778 [Ref: O-274].
DUVALL, Charles (July 20, 1729 - 1814). Son of Benjamin and Sophia Duvall [Ref: ZC-173]. Took the Oath of Allegiance before the Hon. Thomas Williams in 1778 [Ref: O-302]. Charles married (1) Rebecca Beckett, and (2) Cassia Brashears by license dated Mar. 27, 1778 [Ref: X-906, ZB-69, ZE-61].
DUVALL, Charles. Ensign, Upper Battalion, Militia, Capt. Duvall's Company, June 27, 1781 [Ref: H-320].
DUVALL, Cornelius (Feb. 23, 1735, Maryland - c1810, Kentucky). Constable, Western Branch Hundred, 1778 [Ref: Z-30]. He married Keziah Duvall [Ref: X-906]. One Cornelius Duvall married Eleanor Ann Duvall by license dated Feb. 23, 1802 [Ref: ZB-69].
DUVALL, Daniel. Took the Oath of Allegiance (affirmed) before the Hon. James Beck in 1778 [Ref: O-252].
DUVALL, David (born Nov. 24, ----). Son of Joseph and Susannah Duvall, of Queen Anne's Parish [Ref: ZC-173]. Took the Oath of Allegiance before the Hon. James Beck in 1778 [Ref: O-255].
DUVALL, Edmund Bryce. See "Gabriel Duvall," q.v.
DUVALL, Eleanor Ann. See "Cornelius Duvall," q.v.
DUVALL, Elisha (Jan. 18, 1737 - 1786). Son of Samuel and Elizabeth Duvall [Ref: ZC-173]. Private, Select Militia, Upper Battalion, June 12, 1781 [Ref: S-6636 (Box 27, folder 82B)]. One Elisha Duvall married Rachell Belt by license dated June 17, 1785 [Ref: ZB-69]. The estate of one Elisha Duvall was probated on Aug. 27, 1786 [Ref: ZE-61]. See "Benjamin Duvall, of Elisha," q.v.
DUVALL, Elizabeth. See "John Duvall, Sr." and "Benjamin Duvall" and "Jacob Denune" and "Elisha Duvall" and "Jeremiah Duvall" and "Thomas Jones" and "Samuel Duvall," q.v.
DUVALL, Frederick Prussia Lewis (c1755-c1830). Son of Lewis Duvall (1721-c1789) and Alice Brown (1718-1811), Frederick married Mary Ann Hyatt in Baltimore County in 1799 and a daughter Nancy Duvall married John W. Lewis in 1830 [Ref: Ancestral chart of Muriel Elaine Lewis (of Tampa, Florida), in *Prince George's County Genealogical Society Bulletin*, Volume 25, No. 7 (Mar., 1994), pp. 135-137]. Took the Oath of Allegiance before the Hon. James Beck in 1778 [Ref: X-906, O-254, which latter source listed his name as "Fredrich P. L. Duvall"].
DUVALL, Gabriel (Dec. 6, 1752 - Mar. 6, 1844). Son of Benjamin Duvall and Susanna Tyler, he married (1) Mary Bryce, and (2) Jane Gibbon (1757-1834), and had a son Edmund Bryce Duvall (1790-1831, who changed the name spelling to "DuVal") and possibly a daughter Polly Duvall [Ref: U-290, U-291, Y-573, ZC-174, ZE-62]. He took the Oath of Allegiance before the Hon. David Craufurd in 1778 and rendered patriotic service relative to the hiring of carts and horses for the use of the military in 1777-1778 [Ref: O-272, C-454]. He held many public

offices, including: Convention Clerk, 1775-1776. Clerk of the Council of Safety, 1776. Clerk of the Lower House, 1777. Clerk for the Commission for the Sale of Confiscated British Property, 1781. Executive Council, 1782-1786. Member of the Lower House, 1787-1793. Prosecutor, Mayor's Court, Annapolis, 1781-1784. Recorder, Annapolis, 1788-1801. United States Congressman, 1794-1796. Judge of the General Court of Maryland, 1796. First Comptroller of the United States Treasury, 1802-1811. Associate Justice of the United States Supreme Court, 1811-1835 (resigned because of deafness). Staunch supporter of Thomas Jefferson [Ref: U-290, U-291]. Lived at "Marietta" on Bell Station Road near Route 450 and thought to be buried in the Duvall Family Cemetery on C. C. Beall's farm on Bell Station Road, but no tombstone has been found [Ref: Y-573, Y-611].

DUVALL, George. Private, 3rd Maryland Line, 1779, and discharged Jan. 12, 1780 [Ref: D-297].

DUVALL, Howard. Took the Oath of Allegiance before the Hon. Benjamin Hall in 1778 [Ref: O-274].

DUVALL, Isaac. Lieutenant, 3rd Maryland Line, 6th Company, under Capt. William Wilmot; commissioned Apr. 12, 1779 [Ref: D-296].

DUVALL, Jacob (1748/9 - died after 1806). Ensign, Militia, Capt. John Macgill's Company, Feb. 7, 1776. First Lieutenant, 25th Battalion, Capt. Marsh Duvall's Company, May 24, 1779 [Ref: M-72, A-139, E-414]. Took the Oath of Allegiance before the Hon. Benjamin Hall in 1778 [Ref: O-274]. Jacob Duvall married ---- Taylor [Ref: X-906].

DUVALL, Jacob, of John. Second Lieutenant, 25th Battalion, Capt. Marsh Duvall's Company, May 1, 1778 [Ref: M-72, E-62, N-34]. Took the Oath of Allegiance before the Hon. Thomas Williams in 1778 [Ref: O-302].

DUVALL, James. Took the Oath of Allegiance before the Hon. Benjamin Hall in 1778 [Ref: O-275].

DUVALL, Jeremiah (Aug. 24, 1741 - 1799). Son of Samuel and Elizabeth Duvall [Ref: ZC-174]. Took the Oath of Allegiance before the Hon. Osborn Sprigg [Ref: O-291]. The estate of one Jeremiah Duvall was probated on Jan. 19, 1799 [Ref: ZE-62].

DUVALL, Jeremiah (July 23, 1752 - Feb. 12, 1832, Pennsylvania). Took the Oath of Allegiance before the Hon. Thomas MacGill in 1778: O-306]. Jeremiah Duvall married Sarah Penn [Ref: X-906].

DUVALL, Jesse (Apr. 4, 1748 - Feb. 18, 1814). Took the Oath of Allegiance before the Hon. Benjamin Hall in 1778 [Ref: O-274]. On Mar. 23, 1782, the Council of Maryland ordered the Treasurer "to pay to Jesse Duvall the sum of seven pounds and ten shillings due him for the board of Benjamin Duvall, a draught from Prince George's County." [Ref: I-110]. Jesse Duvall married (1) unknown, and (2) Elizabeth Craycroft [Ref: X-906].

DUVALL, John. See "Marsh Mareen Duvall," q.v.

DUVALL, John Jr. (Feb. 22, 1745 - 1795). Son of John and Ann Duvall [Ref: ZC-174]. Took the Oath of Allegiance before the Hon. Benjamin Hall in 1778 [Ref: O-274, R-51, which latter source listed his name without the "Jr."]. Private, Select Militia, Upper Battalion, June 12, 1781 [Ref: S-6636 (Box 27, folder 82B)]. The estate of John Duvall, Jr. was probated on Sep. 13, 1795 [Ref: ZE-62].

DUVALL, John Sr. (Feb. 20, 1712/3 - 1791). Son of Mareen Jr. and Elizabeth Duvall [Ref: ZC-174]. Took the Oath of Allegiance before the Hon. Benjamin Hall in 1778 [Ref: O-274]. The estate of one John Duvall was probated on Mar. 10, 1791 [Ref: ZE-62].

DUVALL, Joseph (Jan. 16, 1733 -   ). Son of Mareen Jr. and Ruth Duvall [Ref: ZC-174]. Took the Oath of Allegiance before the Hon. Thomas Williams in 1778 [Ref: O-302]. Private, 2nd Maryland Line, from Feb. 4, 1777, until discharged on Feb. 4, 1780 [Ref: D-101]. See "James Mullikin" and "David Duvall," q.v.

DUVALL, Keziah. See "Cornelius Duvall," q.v.

DUVALL, Lewis (Dec. 3 or 21, 1721 - died after Aug. 6, 1789). Son of Mareen Duvall the Younger (died 1741) and Elizabeth Jacob (died 1752), Lewis married (1) Frances Hardesty, and (2) Alice Brown (1718-1811). A son "Frederick Prussia Lewis Duvall," q.v., married Mary Ann Hyatt, and a daughter Alice Duvall married Basil Burton (died 1823) [Ref: Ancestral Chart of Muriel Elaine Lewis (of Tampa, Florida), *Prince George's County Genealogical Society Bulletin* (Volume 25, No. 7, Mar., 1994, pp. 135-137), ZC-174]. Took the Oath of Allegiance before the Hon. David Craufurd in 1778 [Ref: O-272, R-47]. Source X-906 states that Lewis Duvall married Mrs. Alice Brown Hardesty.

DUVALL, Lewis (Oct. 18, 1745 - 1811). Probably the son of Mareen and Martha Duvall [Ref: ZC-174]. Took the Oath of Allegiance (affirmed) before the Hon. James Beck in 1778 [Ref: O-252, R-47]. Lewis Duvall married Ann Welch [Ref: X-906]. His estate was probated on Sep. 5, 1811 [Ref: ZE-62].

DUVALL, Mareen. Two men with this name took the Oath of Allegiance in 1778: one before the Hon. Benjamin Hall and another before the Hon. Osborn Sprigg [Ref: O-274, O-306]. One Mareen Duvall (1726-1807) lived his adult life in Montgomery County and married Mrs. Sarah Miles. In 1778 he took the Oath of Allegiance in that county and subsequently died there. "His headstone was moved to the exterior west wall of Holy Trinity Church at Collington." [Ref: Y-611, X-906]. Two men named Mareen Duvall left estates in Prince George's County: one was probated in 1783 and the other in 1789 [Ref: ZE-62]. See "Alexander Duvall" and "Benjamin Duvall" and "John Duvall" and "Joseph Duvall" and "Lewis Duvall," q.v.

DUVALL, Mareen Howard (Dec. 23, 1728 - c1809). Son of Mareen and Ruth Duvall. Constable in Horsepen Hundred in 1777 [Ref: Z-11]. Mareen Howard Duvall married Sarah Wheeler [Ref: X-906].

DUVALL, Marsh Mareen (Apr. 17, 1741 - c1803). Son of John and Ann Duvall [Ref: ZC-174]. Lieutenant, Militia, Capt. Joshua Selby's Company, 1776; served in Annapolis [Ref: M-208, B-403, which latter source mistakenly gave his name as "Marsh Wm. Duvall"]. Took the Oath of Allegiance before the Hon. Thomas Williams in 1778 [Ref: O-302]. Captain, 25th Battalion, Sep. 5, 1777 through at least May 1, 1778 [Ref: M-72, C-363, E-62, N-32]. Recruiting Officer, 1780 [Ref: F-57]. Appointed by the Council of Maryland to be the Tobacco Inspector at Queen Ann's Warehouse on Aug. 30, 1780 [Ref: F-271]. He married (1) Sarah Hall, and (2) Mrs. Susannah Ijams (Susanna Jeams) by license dated June 4, 1785 [Ref: X-906, ZB-70]. See "James Mullikin," q.v.

DUVALL, Martha. See "Lewis Duvall," q.v.

DUVALL, Nancy. See "Frederick Prussia Lewis Duvall," q.v.

DUVALL, Polly. See "Gabriel Duvall," q.v.

DUVALL, Rachel. See "John Lucas," q.v.

DUVALL, Richard. Private, 2nd Maryland Line, Capt. Alexander Truman's Company, 1782 [Ref: D-440].

DUVALL, Robert. Took the Oath of Allegiance before the Hon. Benjamin Hall in 1778 [Ref: O-274]. On July 2, 1781, the records of the Council of Maryland include the following letter from Robert Duvall of Prince George's County: "I am much obliged to his Excellency the Governor and Council, for their good opinion of my patriotism and zeal, in support of the Independence of America, and am sorry to inform you, that it is my being much indisposed that has prevented me from acting as a Recruiting Officer; having been under the Doctor's hands since the middle of May, but hope to be well shortly; therefore, if his Excellency the Governor and his Council have it in their power, and may think it expedient to invest me with full powers and authority, to raise a full company for three years or during the war, they may be sure of my exerting the earliest means to accomplish the matter, which I think I can do in a very little time." [Ref: H-333].

DUVALL, Ruth. See "Alexander Duvall" and "Joseph Duvall," q.v.

DUVALL, Samuel (July 2, 1740 - 1804). Son of Samuel and Elizabeth Duvall [Ref: ZC-175]. Private, 2nd Maryland Line, and discharged on Jan. 10, 1780 [Ref: D-101]. Private, Select Militia, Upper Battalion, June 12, 1781 [Ref: S-6636 (Box 27, folder 82B)]. One "Samuel Duvall from Prince George's County, draught to serve until the 10th of Dec. next, being deemed unfit for the service, is hereby discharged therefrom" by order of the Council of Maryland on Nov. 12, 1781 [Ref: G-666]. One Samuel Duvall married Mary Higgins [Ref: X-907]. See "Elisha Duvall," q.v.

DUVALL, Samuel. There were several men with this name in Queen Anne's Parish [Ref: ZC-174, ZC-175, ZE-63]. One took the Oath of Allegiance before the Hon. Thomas MacGill in 1778 [Ref: O-291].

DUVALL, Sarah. See "Benjamin Duvall" and Anthony Beck" and "James Beck," q.v.
DUVALL, Sophia. See "Charles Duvall" and "Benjamin Duvall," q.v.
DUVALL, Susannah. See "Benjamin Duvall" and "David Duvall" and "Gilbert Falconer," q.v.
DUVALL, Thomas (1739-1818). Took the Oath of Allegiance before the Hon. Benjamin Hall in 1778 [Ref: O-274, R-51]. The records of the Council of Maryland on June 22, 1778, state the following: "Thomas Duvall of Prince George's County a Draft from the Militia for nine Months agreeable to the late Act of Assembly, having procured Thomas Beall, son of Thomas, to enlist into the Service for nine months in his stead, he is therefore discharged." [Ref: E-145, E-146]. The estate of one Thomas Duvall was probated on Oct. 1, 1818 [Ref: ZE-63].
DUVALL Thomas Gabriel. At the County Court in August, 1778, he took the Oath of Allegiance at the same time he took the oath to become a practicing attorney at law in Prince George's County [Ref: Z-94].
DUVALL, William (1747-   ). Second Lieutenant, Maryland Line, Capt. John H. Lowe's Company, by July, 1776 [Ref: D-34, D-35]. Took the Oath of Allegiance before the Hon. Thomas Clagett in 1778 [Ref: O-264, R-74].
DYER, Amelia. See "Giles Green Dyer," q.v.
DYER, Ann. See "Francis Clements Dyer," q.v.
DYER, Edward (1730/40 - died before July 13, 1813). Took the Oath of Allegiance before the Hon. William Lyles, Jr. in 1778 [Ref: O-289]. Lieutenant, 2nd Maryland Line, Apr. 10, 1777. Captain and Brigade Quartermaster, Jan., 1779 [Ref: D-101]. Edward Dyer married Martha - --- [Ref: X-909]. See "Giles Green Dyer," q.v.
DYER, Eliza. See "Thomas Edelen Green," q.v.
DYER, Francis Clements (1746-1807). A son of Thomas Dyer and Henrietta Clements, he married Ann Clarkson and had these children: John Ethelred Dyer, Henry Edelen Dyer, William C. Dyer, James Corbin Dyer, Margaretta Dyer, Loretta Dyer, Sarah Ann Dyer, Maria Dyer, and Ann Eliza Dyer [Ref: ZA-308]. Served on a Grand Jury in 1777 [Ref: Z-29, which listed his name as "Francis Clermont Dyer"]. Took the Oath of Allegiance before the Hon. Thomas Clagett in 1778 [Ref: O-264]. "Francis Dyer" was an ensign in Capt. Thomas Dent's Company, 11th Battalion, May 1, 1778 [Ref: M-72, E-78]. "Francis Clements Dyer" was Deputy Sheriff of Prince George's County, 1786, and Justice of the Peace, 1805-1806 [Ref: ZA-308]. His estate was probated on Jan. 2, 1808 [Ref: ZE-64]. See "Giles Green Dyer," q.v.
DYER, George (1753, Maryland - died before Feb. 12, 1827, Virginia). "Lieutenant, a draft, June 15th, 1778" for continental service, Maryland Line [Ref: D-328]. Second Lieutenant, 11th Battalion, Capt. Richard Stonestreet's Company, May 1, 1778 through June, 1782 [Ref: M-72, N-32, E-62, L-19970 (Box 6, folder 21)]. Took the Oath of Allegiance

before the Hon. Thomas Clagett in 1778 [Ref: O-267]. He married Rachel Dalton [Ref: X-909]. One George Dyer married Sarah Clarkson by license dated May 27, 1784 [Ref: ZB-71].

DYER, Giles Green (Aug. 27, 1752 - 1819). A son of Thomas Dyer and Henrietta Clements, he married Susanna Smith and had these children: Thomas B. Dyer, Amelia (Dyer) Jameson, Mary (Dyer) Edelen, Lucy (Dyer) Boarman, Edward Dyer, Horatio Dyer, John R. Dyer, Francis C. Dyer, and Henrietta Dyer [Ref: X-909, ZA-307]. "Giles Green Dyer" took the Oath of Allegiance before the Hon. Thomas Clagett in 1778 [Ref: O-265]. "Giles Dyer" was a First Lieutenant, 11th Battalion, Capt. Richard Stonestreet's Company, May 1, 1778 to June, 1782 [Ref: M-72, E-62, N-32, L-19970 (Box 6, folder 21)]. The estate of "Giles G. Dyer" was probated on Oct. 13, 1829 [Ref: ZE-64].

DYER, Henrietta. See "Giles G. Dyer" and "John H. Beanes," q.v.

DYER, Henry (1750-   ). Private, Capt. Richard Stonestreet's Militia Company, 11th Battalion, June, 1782 [Ref: L-19970 (Box 6, folder 21), and R-79, which spelled his name "Dyar"]. See "Giles Green Dyer," q.v.

DYER, Henry Edelen. Took the Oath of Allegiance before the Hon. Thomas Clagett in 1778 [Ref: O-267]. See "Francis C. Dyer," q.v.

DYER, Horatio. See "Giles Green Dyer," q.v.

DYER, James. Private, 3rd Maryland Line, 1778 [Ref: D-103].

DYER, James Corbin. See "Francis Clements Dyer," q.v.

DYER, Jeremiah. Took the Oath of Allegiance before the Hon. Thomas Clagett in 1778 [Ref: O-268].

DYER, John. Ensign, 11th Battalion, Capt. Hezekiah Wheeler's Company, May 1, 1778. Second Lieutenant, May 24, 1779. Lieutenant, Select Militia, May 25, 1781 [Ref: M-72, N-32, E-62, E-414, G-445, and S-6636 (Box 31, folder 5), which latter source listed him as "Lt. John Dyar" on July 14, 1781]. Took the Oath of Allegiance before the Hon. Thomas Clagett in 1778 [Ref: O-265]. Lieutenant, 11th Militia Battalion, Capt. Hezekiah Wheeler's Company, April, 1781 [Ref: L-19970 (Box 6, folder 21), which spelled his name "Dyar"]. One John Dyer died before Apr. 13, 1791 [Ref: ZE-64].

DYER, John. Private, 3rd Maryland Line, Jan., 1777 to Nov., 1780, and private, 1st Maryland Line, 1781 [Ref: D-103, D-354].

DYER, John E. See "Francis Clements Dyer," q.v.

DYER, John R. See "Giles Green Dyer," q.v.

DYER, Loretta. See "Francis Clements Dyer," q.v.

DYER, Lucy. See "Giles Green Dyer," q.v.

DYER, Margaretta. See "Francis Clements Dyer," q.v.

DYER, Maria. See "Francis Clements Dyer," q.v.

DYER, Martha. See "Edward Dyer," q.v.

DYER, Mary. See "Middleton Belt" and "Giles Green Dyer" and "John Harris Gibbs," q.v.

DYER, Sarah Ann. See "Francis Clements Dyer," q.v.

103

DYER, Thomas (1744-   ). Second Lieutenant, 11th Battalion, Capt. Thomas Dent's Company, May 1, 1778 [Ref: M-72, E-62, N-32]. Took the Oath of Allegiance before the Hon. William Lyles, Jr. in 1778 [Ref: O-290, R-86, which spelled the name "Thomas Dyar"].

DYER, Thomas (c1734, Maryland - c1794, Virginia). He married Sarah Webster and rendered patriotic service by providing wheat for the military on Sep. 9, 1780 [Ref: Q-314, X-910].

DYER, Thomas. Sergeant, 2nd Maryland Line, May 1, 1778 to Jan., 1780 [Ref: D-101].

DYER, Thomas. See "Walter Dyer" and "Giles Green Dyer" and "Francis Clements Dyer," q.v.

DYER, Thomas, of Thomas. Took the Oath of Allegiance before the Hon. Thomas Clagett in 1778 [Ref: O-264].

DYER, Walter. Private, enrolled by Lt. John M. Burgess, Lower Battalion, on July 20, 1776, for continental service, Maryland Line [Ref: D-35]. Private, enrolled by Ensign Horatio Clagett on July 15, 1776, for continental service, Maryland Line [Ref: D-35, which spelled his name "Walter Dyar"]. Sergeant, 3rd Maryland Line, June 26, 1777; promoted to Lieutenant, Jan. 26, 1780 [Ref: D-103]. Lieutenant, Northern Detachment, 3rd Maryland Line, Capt. Horatio Clagett's Company, 1783 [Ref: D-501]. A son of Thomas Dyer and Henrietta Clements, Walter received payment for his services in the Revolutionary War from the Maryland Treasurer in December, 1816 [Ref: O-338, ZA-307, ZA-308].

DYER, William. Private, Capt. Hezekiah Wheeler's Company, 11th Militia Battalion, April, 1781 [Ref: L-19970 (Box 6, folder 21), which spelled the name "Dyar"]. See "Francis Clements Dyer," q.v.

DYSART, Patricia June. See "Azariah Gatton," q.v.

DYSON, Elizabeth. See "Azariah Gatton," q.v.

DYTCH (DYCHE), Mathias. Private, 3rd Maryland Line, 1781. Private, 2nd Maryland Line, Capt. Alexander Truman's Company, 1782-1783 [Ref: D-439, D-393, D-531].

DYTCH (DYCHE), Peter. Private, 4th Maryland Line, Rawlings' Regiment, July 27, 1776 - July, 1777 [Ref: D-105, D-302].

DYTCH (DYCHE, DYCH), William. Private, 3rd Maryland line, 1781. Artificer, 1782 [Ref: D-395, D-454].

EAGEN, Patrick. Private, 2nd Maryland Line, Capt. Alexander Truman's Company; prisoner of war, Sep. 8, 1781 [Ref: D-440].

EAGLIN, Jane. See "Joseph Clarkson," q.v.

EARLEY, Benjamin. "Benjamin Early" was a private in the 7th Maryland Line from June 6, 1778 to Mar. 16, 1779, when he was discharged [Ref: D-204]. "Benjamin Earley" married Jane Cooley by license dated Jan. 27, 1789 [Ref: ZB-72]. The estate of one Benjamin Earley was probated on May 14, 1807 [Ref: ZE-64].

EARLEY (EARLY), Martha. See "Francis Piles," q.v.

EARLEY, Samuel. Records of the Maryland Council on June 13, 1778 stated that "Samuel Earley who was taken up in Prince George's County as a Deserter from the Independent Company heretofore commanded by Major Allen Thomas Appearing on Examination of his Allegations and especially from the Information of Major Thomas to have been discharged from the Service soon after his Enlistment he is therefore discharged by this Board." [Ref: E-133]. This may be the "Samuel Earle" who was from Queen Anne's County [Ref: D-645].

EARLEY, William Jr. This name appeared twice on the same list and both took the Oath of Allegiance before the Hon. Fielder Bowie in 1778 [Ref: O-303, O-304, W-4648 (Box 4, folder 15)]. Perhaps one was William Earley, Sr., rather than both being William Earley, Jr. One William Earley died before Jan. 24, 1787 [Ref: ZE-65].

EASTON, Giles. Born in Prince George's County on Sep. 30, 1762, he lived in Montgomery County at the time of his enlistment in the Maryland Line. On Mar. 25, 1833 he applied for a pension (S10633) in Montgomery County and died there on Apr. 14, 1842 [Ref: P-1071].

EASTWOOD, Benjamin. Took the Oath of Allegiance before the Hon. Alexander Howard Magruder in 1778 [Ref: O-293].

EASTWOOD, John. Took the Oath of Allegiance before the Hon. Alexander Howard Magruder in 1778 [Ref: O-293]. Private, Capt. Benjamin Wailes' Militia Company, Lower Battalion; on duty guarding Magruder's Warehouse in the spring of 1782 [Ref: L-19970 (Box 6, folder 21)]. The estate of one John Eastwood was probated on Apr. 8, 1806 [Ref: ZE-65].

EDELEN, Barton. Private, Capt. Richard Stonestreet's Militia Company, 11th Battalion, June, 1782 [Ref: L-19970 (Box 6, folder 21)]. The estate of one Barton Edelen was probated on June 5, 1829 [Ref: ZE-65].

EDELEN, Barzeel. Third Sergeant, Capt. Richard Stonestreet's Militia Company, 11th Battalion, June, 1782 [Ref: L-19970 (Box 6, folder 21)].

EDELEN, Benedict. "Benedict Edelen" was a private in Capt. Richard Stonestreet's Militia Company, 11th Battalion, June, 1782 [Ref: L-19970 (Box 6, folder 21)]. "Bennedict Edelen" took the Oath of Allegiance before the Hon. Thomas Clagett in 1778 [Ref: O-265]. "Benedict Joseph Edelen" (c1754-1800) is listed in Reference X-926. The estate of one Benedict Edelen was probated by June 10, 1800 (date of account). [Ref: ZE-65].

EDELEN, Bennett. "Benet Edelen" was a private, Select Militia, Capt. Hezekiah Wheeler's Company, on July 14, 1781 [Ref: S-6636 (Box 31, folder 5)]. The estate of one "Bennett Edeline" was probated by Oct. 29, 1798 (date of inventory). [Ref: ZE-68].

EDELEN, Catherine. See "Christopher Edelen" and "Joseph Edelen, Jr.," q.v.

EDELEN, Christopher. Took the Oath of Allegiance before the Hon. William Lyles, Jr. in 1778 [Ref: O-289]. One Christopher Edelen was aged 53 and another was aged 20 in 1776 [Ref: R-79, R-87]. The estate of one "Christopher B. Edelen" was probated on Nov. 11, 1794 [Ref: ZE-65]. See "Richard Edelen," q.v.

EDELEN, Christopher, of John. Took the Oath of Allegiance before the Hon. Thomas Clagett in 1778 [Ref: O-267]. This might be the Christopher Edelen (1748, Maryland - died after 1810, Kentucky) who is listed in Reference X-926]. See "Christopher Edelen" above.

EDELEN, Clement. Private, 1st Maryland Line, 1776. Sergeant, when discharged on Dec. 27, 1779 [Ref: D-6, D-106]. He married Ann Simpson by license dated Nov. 6, 1780 [Ref: ZB-73].

EDELEN, Edward Jr. (1747-   ). Took the Oath of Allegiance before the Hon. Thomas Clagett in 1778 [Ref: O-265]. Rendered patriotic service by providing wheat for the military on May 9, 1783 [Ref: Q-598, R-5].

EDELEN, Elizabeth. See "Hezekiah Mudd" and "Dennis Osborn" and "Clement Wheeler," q.v.

EDELEN, George (1758-   ). Private, enrolled in the Flying Camp by Capt. Robert Bowie on July 27, 1776; nativity: Prince George's County; height 5' 7 1/2"; has own gun [Ref: D-36]. Paid for his services on Feb. 24, 1779 [Ref: E-308]. Fourth Sergeant, Capt. Richard Stonestreet's Militia Company, 11th Battalion, June, 1782 [Ref: L-19970 (Box 6, folder 21)]. One George Edelen married Rebecca Boarman by license dated Dec. 31, 1790 [Ref: ZB-73].

EDELEN, Henry. Took the Oath of Allegiance before the Hon. Thomas Clagett in 1778 [Ref: O-268]. Private, Maryland Line, by Feb. 24, 1779, when paid for his services "in cloathing." [Ref: E-308].

EDELEN, James Reed. Took the Oath of Allegiance before the Hon. Thomas Clagett in 1778 [Ref: O-267].

EDELEN, Jeremiah. Private, Select Militia, Capt. Hezekiah Wheeler's Company, July 14, 1781 [Ref: S-6636 (Box 31, folder 5)]. Private, Capt. Richard Stonestreet's Company, 11th Battalion, June, 1782 [Ref: L-19970 (Box 6, folder 21)]. One Jeremiah Edelen married Sally Jenkins by license dated Feb. 11, 1792 [Ref: ZB-73].

EDELEN, John. Private, 2nd Maryland Line, Capt. Patrick Sim's Company, 1776 [Ref: D-8]. Private, Select Militia, Capt. Hezekiah Wheeler's Company, July 14, 1781 [Ref: S-6636 (Box 31, folder 5)].

EDELEN, John Sr. "John Edelen" took the Oath of Allegiance before the Hon. William Lyles, Jr. in 1778 [Ref: O-289]. "John Edelen, Sr." was aged 62 in 1776 [Ref: R-41].

EDELEN, Joseph. Rendered patriotic service by providing wheat for the military on May 9, 1783 [Ref: Q-598].

EDELEN, Joseph Jr. (1757-1833). Took the Oath of Allegiance before the Hon. Thomas Clagett in 1778 [Ref: O-266]. Private in Capt. Hezekiah Wheeler's Company, 11th Militia Battalion, April, 1781 [Ref: L-19970 (Box 6, folder 21). Private, Select Militia, Capt. Hezekiah Wheeler's Company, July 14, 1781 [Ref: S-6636 (Box 31, folder 5)]. Some of the aforementioned sources did not include the "Jr." on his name]. One Joseph Edelen married Catherine Wathen by license dated Apr. 4, 1786, and a Joseph Edelen married Catherine Edelen by license dated Feb. 26, 1788 [Ref: ZB-73, X-926].

EDELEN, Joseph, of Christopher. Took the Oath of Allegiance before the Hon. Thomas Clagett in 1778 [Ref: O-267]. See "Joseph Edelen, Jr.," q.v.

EDELEN, Leonard (1754-   ). Private, enrolled in the Flying Camp by Capt. Robert Bowie on July 15, 1776; nativity: Prince George's County; height 5' 8"; has own gun [Ref: D-36]. Private, Capt. Hezekiah Wheeler's Company, 11th Militia Battalion, April, 1781 [Ref: L-19970 (Box 6, folder 21)]. Private, Select Militia, Capt. Hezekiah Wheeler's Company, July 14, 1781 [Ref: S-6636 (Box 31, folder 5)]. Took the Oath of Allegiance before the Hon. Thomas Clagett in 1778 [Ref: O-267].

EDELEN, Mary. See "Giles Green Dyer," q.v.

EDELEN, Mildred. See "Walter Boone," q.v.

EDELEN, Philip (1731-1789). Took the Oath of Allegiance before the Hon. William Lyles, Jr. in 1778 [Ref: O-289, R-74]. The estate of one Philip Edelen was probated on Feb. 11, 1789 [Ref: ZE-66].

EDELEN, Raphael C. See "John Goddard," q.v.

EDELEN, Rebecca. See "Bennett Gwynn," q.v.

EDELEN, Richard Jr. Took the Oath of Allegiance before the Hon. Thomas Clagett in 1778 [Ref: O-267].

EDELEN, Richard Sr. (Aug. 4, 1715 - died by Feb. 22, 1791). Took the Oath of Allegiance before the Hon. Thomas Clagett in 1778 [Ref: O-267, R-59]. A son of Christopher Edelen and Jane Jones, Richard married Sarah Stonestreet [Ref: X-926, ZC-20, ZE-67].

EDELEN, Richard Basil. Private, enrolled by Lt. John M. Burgess, Lower Battalion, on July 20, 1776, for continental service, Maryland Line [Ref: D-35]. Took the Oath of Allegiance before the Hon. Thomas Clagett in 1778 [Ref: O-268].

EDELEN, Samuel. Private, Select Militia, Capt. Hezekiah Wheeler's Company, July 14, 1781 [Ref: S-6636 (Box 31, folder 5)]. First Sergeant, Capt. Richard Stonestreet's Company, 11th Battalion, June, 1782 [Ref: L-19970 (Box 6, folder 21)]. One Samuel Edelen married Mary Smith by license dated Dec. 14, 1787 [Ref: ZB-74].

EDELEN, Sarah. See "Henry Rozer, Jr.," q.v.

EDELEN, Thomas Sr. (Nov. 12, 1720 -   ). Son of Thomas Edelen and Mary Blanford [Ref: ZC-20]. Took the Oath of Allegiance before the Hon. Thomas Clagett in 1778 [Ref: O-264, R-43].

EDELEN, William. Took the Oath of Allegiance before the Hon. William Lyles, Jr. in 1778 [Ref: O-290]. The estate of one William Edelen was probated on Apr. 12, 1791 [Ref: ZE-67].

EDGEWORTH, Philorlea. See "John Casey," q.v.

EDLSON, John. See "John Elson," q.v.

EDMONSTON, Brooke. See "Robert Orme," q.v.

EDMONSTON, Dorothy. See "Ninian Edmonston," q.v.
EDMONSTON, James (1745-1793). Took the Oath of Allegiance before the Hon. Christopher Lowndes in 1778 [Ref: O-284, R-55, which spelled the name "Edmonstone"]. Ensign, 25th Battalion, Capt. Richard Beall's Company, May 1, 1778 [Ref: N-34, M-73, E-62, which sources spelled the name both as "Edmonson" and "Edmonston"]. The estate of one James Edmonston was probated on Sep. 12, 1793 [Ref: ZE-68].
EDMONSTON, Mary. See "James Beall," q.v.
EDMONSTON, Ninian (1735 - Feb. 4, 1816). Took the Oath of Allegiance before the Hon. James Beck in 1778 [Ref: O-254, R-49]. Private (draft), continental service, 1780, Maryland Line [Ref: D-382, which spelled the name "Edmonson"]. Ninian Edmonston married Dorothy Brooke Edmonston [Ref: X-930, ZE-68].
EDMONSTON, Pamelia. See "Ignatius Brashears," q.v.
EDMONSTON, Priscilla. See "Robert Orme," q.v.
EDMONSTON, Rachel. See "Edward Beall," q.v.
EDWARDS, Peggy. See "Vachell Ijams," q.v.
ELDER, Ann. See "Henry Spalding" and "Bennett Gwynn," q.v.
ELLIOTT, John. Private, 2nd Maryland Line, Capt. Alexander Truman's Company, 1782 [Ref: D-440]. The estate of one John Elliott was probated on Apr. 12, 1794 [Ref: ZE-69].
ELLIOTT, Joseph. Private, 2nd Maryland Line, Capt. Alexander Truman's Company, 1782 [Ref: D-440].
ELLIOTT, Thomas. Private, Select Militia, Upper Battalion, June 12, 1781 [Ref: S-6636 (Box 27, folder 82B), which listed his name as "Ellet"].
ELLIS, Barnard. Private, 2nd Maryland Line, 1778 [Ref: D-106].
ELLIS, Benjamin. Private, enrolled by Ensign Alexander Truman on July 6, 1776, for continental service, Maryland Line [Ref: D-38].
ELLIS, Elijah. Private, Capt. Benjamin Wailes' Militia Company, Lower Battalion; on duty guarding Magruder's Warehouse in the spring of 1782 [Ref: L-19970 (Box 6, folder 21)]. An Elijah Ellis married Susanna Watson by license dated Dec. 27, 1779, an Elijah Ellis married Ann Cooksey by license dated July 9, 1802, and an Elijah Ellis married Martha Carrico by license dated July 27, 1809 [Ref: ZB-74, ZB-75].
ELLIS, John. Took the Oath of Allegiance before the Hon. Alexander Howard Magruder in 1778 [Ref: O-293]. Sergeant in Capt. Benjamin Wailes' Militia Company, Lower Battalion; on duty guarding Magruder's Warehouse in the spring of 1782 [Ref: L-19970 (Box 6, folder 21)].
ELLIS, Mary. See "Thomas Lewis," q.v.
ELLIS, Michael. Fifer, 2nd Maryland Line, Nov. 3, 1778 to at least Nov. 1, 1780 [Ref: D-106].
ELLIS, Robert. Private, 2nd Maryland Line, Mar. 4, 1777 through Apr. 14, 1779, when he reportedly "deserted" [Ref: D-106].
ELLISON, Thomas. Corporal, Northern Detachment, 3rd Maryland Line, Capt. Horatio Clagett's Company, 1783 [Ref: D-501].

ELMS, Polly. See "Samuel Luckett," q.v.
ELSBY, Sallie. See "Henry Boteler," q.v.
ELSON, Archibald (1740-1813). Took the Oath of Allegiance before the Hon. Richard Henderson in 1778 [Ref: O-278, R-50]. Archibald Elson married Hannah Roberts by license dated Feb. 24, 1782 [Ref: ZB-75]. His estate was probated on Apr. 15, 1813 [Ref: ZE-69].
ELSON, Joanna. See "John Elson," q.v.
ELSON, John. "John Elson" was a corporal in the 2nd Maryland Line, Capt. Patrick Sim's Company, 1776 [Ref: D-7]. "John Edlson" was a private, Capt. Hezekiah Wheeler's Company, 11th Militia Battalion, April, 1781 [Ref: L-19970 (Box 6, folder 21). One John Elson, son of John and Joanna, was born on Oct. 8, 1732 [Ref: ZC-175].
ELSON, Rachel. See "Zadock Moore," q.v.
ELSON, Sarah. See "John Baptist Kirby," q.v.
EMERSON, Elisha. See "James Emerson," q.v.
EMERSON, George. Private, Capt. Hezekiah Wheeler's Company, 11th Militia Battalion, April, 1781 [Ref: L-19970 (Box 6, folder 21)]. Took the Oath of Allegiance before the Hon. Osborn Sprigg in 1778 [Ref: O-307].
EMERSON, James (baptized Oct. 11, 1763, King George's Parish, Prince George's County, Maryland - died Oct. 28, 1836, Fayette County, Pennsylvania). Son of John and Penalopy Emerson [Ref: ZC-20]. Private, Capt. Hezekiah Wheeler's Company, 11th Militia Battalion, April, 1781 [Ref: L-19970 (Box 6, folder 21)]. Private, Select Militia, Capt. Hezekiah Wheeler's Company, July 14, 1781 [Ref: S-6636 (Box 31, folder 5)]. He applied for pension (R3339) in Fayette County, Pennsylvania, on Jan. 14, 1833, aged 71, a resident of Union Township, stating he was born in Prince George's County, Maryland, and served in the Maryland Line. He later moved to Berkeley County, Virginia near Martinsburg for 13 years and then moved to Fayette County around 1810. His widow (not named) died on July 18, 1838 and a son Elisha D. Emerson signed an affidavit on Sep. 7, 1852, in Fayette County, as one of the heirs of James Emerson [Ref: P-1114, which also spelled his name "Emberson"].
EMERSON, John (1706-   ). Took the Oath of Allegiance before the Hon. Thomas Clagett in 1778 [Ref: O-267, R-56]. See "James Emerson," q.v.
EMERSON, John. Private, Capt. Hezekiah Wheeler's Company, 11th Militia Battalion, April, 1781 [Ref: L-19970 (Box 6, folder 21)].
EMERSON, Penalopy. See "James Emerson," q.v.
EMERSON, Richard. Took the Oath of Allegiance before the Hon. William Lyles, Jr. in 1778 [Ref: O-289, which spelled the name "Emmerson"].
ENNIS, George. See "George Inness," q.v.
ESTEP, Benjamin Jr. "Benjamin Estep, Jr." was a private in Capt. Benjamin Wailes' Militia Company, Lower Battalion, and on duty guarding Magruder's Warehouse in the spring of 1782 [Ref: L-19970

(Box 6, folder 21)]. "Benjamin Estep" married Sarah Taylor by license dated Sep. 27, 1793 [Ref: ZB-75].

ESTEP, John. See "Benjamin Wailes," q.v.

ESTEP, Josiah. Private, Capt. Benjamin Wailes' Militia Company, Lower Battalion; on duty guarding Magruder's Warehouse in the spring of 1782 [Ref: L-19970 (Box 6, folder 21)].

EUBANKS, William. Took the Oath of Allegiance before the Hon. David Craufurd in 1778 [Ref: O-272].

EVANS, Edward. There were several men with this name who served in the Maryland Line [Ref: D-107, D-340, D-353, D-354, D-393, D-437]. The estate of one Edward Evans was probated on Aug. 23, 1792 in Prince George's County [Ref: ZE-69].

EVANS, Henry (1732-   ). Took the Oath of Allegiance before the Hon. Thomas Clagett in 1778 [Ref: O-264, R-17]. Second Lieutenant, Lower Battalion, Capt. Wheeler's Company, Sep. 1, 1777 [Ref: M-74, C-356, N-32].

EVANS, James. See "John Evans," q.v.

EVANS, Johannah. See "John Evans," q.v.

EVANS, John. Ensign, county militia, Capt. Michael Lowe's Company, Sep. 20, 1776 [Ref: B-287]. Took the Oath of Allegiance before the Hon. Osborn Sprigg in 1778 [Ref: O-308, R-40]. One John Evans (son of James and Johannah "Evens") was born on May 15, 1757 and another John Evans (son of Philip and Mary Evans) was born on Nov. 21, 1753 [Ref: ZC-20, ZD-113]. The estate of "John Evans (soldier)" was probated on Mar. 19, 1793, and the estate of another John Evans was probated on Sep. 15, 1817 [Ref: ZE-70]. Additional research will be necessary before drawing conclusions about which one rendered which patriotic service.

EVANS, Mary. See "William Hurley" and "John Evans," q.v.

EVANS, Philip. See "John Evans," q.v.

EVANS, Rebecca. See "Benjamin Bean," q.v.

EVANS, Ruth. See "Thomas Smith," q.v.

EVANS, Samuel. Private (draft), continental service, Maryland Line, 1781 [Ref: D-382].

EVANS, Sarah. See "John Hurley," q.v.

EVANS, Thomas. Private, 3rd Maryland Line, Capt. Horatio Clagett's Company, 1779 [Ref: D-295].

EVANS, Walter (1721-   ). Took the Oath of Allegiance before the Hon. Joshua Beall in 1778 [Ref: O-251, R-62].

EVANS, William. Private, 2nd Maryland Line, Capt. Patrick Sim's Company, 1776 [Ref: D-8].

EVERETT, Elisha. Private, 2nd Maryland Line, Capt. Patrick Sim's Company, 1776 [Ref: D-8, which spelled the name "Everit"]. Private, 1st Maryland Line, enlisted Mar. 12, 1778 and discharged on Apr. 18, 1779; "exchanged for Jefferson" *[sic]*. [Ref: D-106].

EVERETT, Joseph. Private, 2nd Maryland Line, enlisted May 28, 1778 and discharged on Dec. 18, 1778 [Ref: D-106, which spelled the name "Everitt"]. The estate of one Joseph Everett was probated on Sep. 8, 1815 [Ref: ZE-70].

EVERSFIELD, Charles (Apr. 15, 1750 - 1815). A physician and son of Rev. John Eversfield and Eleanor Clagett, Dr. Eversfield married Elizabeth Gantt by license dated Feb. 13, 1786, and their children were Elizabeth Eversfield, Eleanor Eversfield, and John Eversfield. Rndered civil service during the Revolutionary War [Ref: X-976, ZA-132, ZB-76, ZE-70].

EVERSFIELD, Deborah. See "Benjamin Berry," q.v.

EVERSFIELD, Eleanor. See "Elisha Berry" and "Charles Eversfield," q.v.

EVERSFIELD, Elizabeth. See "Charles Eversfield," q.v.

EVERSFIELD, John. See "Charles Eversfield," q.v.

EVERSFIELD, John Jr. Appointed by the Council of Maryland to be the Tobacco Inspector at Nottingham Warehouse on Sep. 23, 1780, and resigned by Oct. 7, 1780 [Ref: F-302, F-318]. Private, 2nd Guard, Capt. Henry Hill's Militia Company, Lower Battalion; on duty at Nottingham on the Patuxent, Apr. 12, 1781 [Ref: L-19970 (Box 6, folder 21), which listed his name without the "Jr."]. One John Eversfield married Barbara Brooke by license dated June 2, 1778, and a John Eversfield married Mary Ann Clagett by license dated Feb. 22, 1800 [Ref: ZB-76]. The estate of one John Eversfield (who appears to have been a Reverend) was probated on Mar. 3, 1781, and the estate of John Eversfield, Jr. was probated on Oct. 19, 1824 [Ref: ZE-70]. Additional research may be necessary before drawing conclusions. See "Fielder Bowie," q.v.

EVERSFIELD, Susannah. See "Allen Bowie, Sr.," q.v.

FAIRALL, Benjamin. See "John Igleheart," q.v.

FAIRBAIRN, William. Took the Oath of Allegiance before the Hon. Thomas Clagett in 1778 [Ref: O-268]. Private, 3rd Maryland Line, Capt. Horatio Clagett's Company, 1779; prisoner of war; exchanged by Aug. 1, 1781, at which time he was paid 5 pounds specie on his account, and was still in the service as of Dec. 14, 1781 when he was issued clothing [Ref: D-617, I-22, D-296, which latter source listed his name as "Wm. Fairburn"].

FAIRWEATHER, John. Private, Northern Detachment, 3rd Maryland Line, Capt. Horatio Clagett's Company, 1783 [Ref: D-502].

FAIVEL, Daniel. See "Daniel Farrell," q.v.

FAKES, John. Took the Oath of Allegiance before the Hon. William Berry in 1778 [Ref: O-258].

FALCONER, Alexander. See "Gilbert Falconer," q.v.

FALCONER, Gilbert (Jan. 15, 1722/3 -   ). Son of Alexander Falconer and Susanna Duvall [Ref: ZC-175]. Took the Oath of Allegiance before the Hon. Benjamin Hall in 1778 [Ref: O-274, which spelled his name "Falconar"]. In 1778, he rendered patriotic service by assisting the

Council of Maryland in delivering the pay of others who had been hired for their services [Ref: E-132].

FALCONER, Gilbert Jr. Took the Oath of Allegiance before the Hon. Thomas Williams in 1778 [Ref: O-302].

FALCONER, Susanna. See "Gilbert Falconer," q.v.

FALDO, Charles (1724-   ). Took the Oath of Allegiance before the Hon. Christopher Lowndes in 1778 [Ref: O-286, R-23].

FANE, Patrick. Private, 3rd Maryland Line, Capt. Horatio Clagett's Company, 1779 [Ref: D-295].

FARR, Nicholas. Took the Oath of Allegiance before the Hon. Fielder Bowie in 1778 [Ref: R-71, O-304, W-4648 (Box 4, folder 15)]. Private, Maryland Line, 1781 [Ref: D-408, D-509]. One Nicholas Farr married Tabitha White by license dated Feb. 13, 1805 [Ref: ZB-77]. One Nicholas Farr was aged 55 in the 1776 census [Ref: R-71]. The estate of one Nicholas Farr was probated on Oct. 13, 1841 [Ref: ZE-71]. Additional research may be necessary before drawing conclusions.

FARRELL, Cornelius. See "John Farrell," q.v.

FARRELL, Daniel. Took the Oath of Allegiance before the Hon. Osborn Sprigg in 1778 [Ref: O-307, which listed the name as "Faivel," but the original list (very light) at the Maryland State Archives (Box 4, folder 29) showed the name to be "Farrell"].

FARRELL, Ignatius (1740-   ). Private, 3rd Guard, Capt. Henry Hill's Militia Company, Lower Battalion; on duty at Nottingham on the Patuxent, Apr. 12, 1781 [Ref: L-19970, which spelled his name "Ignatious Fearil," and R-15, which spelled his name "Ignatius Farrell"].

FARRELL, John. "John Fearall" took the Oath of Allegiance before the Hon. Benjamin Hall in 1778 [Ref: O-274]. "John Farrell" applied for pension (R3450) in Huntington County, Pennsylvania, stating he served in the Maryland Line and married Lydia McGuire on Dec. 8, 1776. He died in November, 1809 in Shirley Township, Huntington County, and his widow died on Dec. 30, 1830 in Cambria County, Pennsylvania. Their surviving children in 1830 were Mary Donoughe, Thomas Farrell, Cornelius Farrell, and Ruth Weakland [Ref: P-1160]. One "John Farrall" married Susannah Wheeler by license dated Jan. 13, 1786 in Prince George's County [Ref: ZB-77]. The estate of "John Farrell" was probated on Feb. 13, 1782, and the estate of "John Fairall" was probated on July 21, 1812, both in Prince George's County [Ref: ZE-71]. Addititonal research may be necessary before drawing conclusions.

FARRELL, Thomas. See "John Farrell," q.v.

FARRIS, Henry. Took the Oath of Allegiance before the Hon. Benjamin Hall in 1778 [Ref: O-274].

FELTON, Thomas (1742, England -   ). Private, enlisted on June 4, 1781, for 3 years, continental service, Maryland Line; "Maryland, sent to Annapolis on furlough" on July 13, 1781 [Ref: D-382].

FENDALL, Elizabeth. See "Josias Beall," q.v.

FENDALL, Sarah. See "Thomas Contee" and "Benjamin Contee," q.v.
FENDER, Stephen. Took the Oath of Allegiance before the Hon. James Beck in 1778 [Ref: O-254].
FENLY, William (Oct. 24, 1761 - 1791). Son of Charles and Martha Fenley [Ref: ZC-22]. Private (draft), Middle Battalion, Militia, Aug., 1781. The estate of one William Fenly was probated on Nov. 15, 1791 [Ref: ZE-72]. See "Nicholas Waters," q.v.
FENNEL, John 1st. Corporal, Northern Detachment, 3rd Maryland Line, Capt. Horatio Clagett's Company, 1783 [Ref: D-501].
FERGUSON, James. Took the Oath of Allegiance before the Hon. Christopher Lowndes in 1778 [Ref: O-284, which spelled his name "James Furguson"]. One James Ferguson married Ruth Halsall by license dated Aug. 23, 1780 [Ref: ZB-78].
FERGUSON, James Jr. Private, Militia, 1776 [Ref: M-207, A-325, which spelled his name "James Furguson, Jr."].
FERGUSON, Jane. See "Elisha Berry," q.v.
FERGUSON, John (1725-   ). Took the Oath of Allegiance before the Hon. William Berry in 1778 [Ref: O-259, R-70].
FERGUSON, John. Private, Militia, 1776 [Ref: M-207, A-325, which spelled his name "Furguson"]. Private, 2nd Maryland Line, Apr. 1, 1779, and was taken prisoner on Aug. 16, 1780 (at the Battle of Camden). [Ref: D-109, which spelled his name "Jno. Fergusson"].
FERGUSON, Josias. Took the Oath of Allegiance before the Hon. William Lock Weems in 1778 [Ref: O-301, which spelled the name "Forgson"].
FERGUSSON, Ann S. See "Joseph Wilson," q.v.
FERGUSSON, Virlinda. See "Zephaniah Beall," q.v.
FERRALL, Ignatius. See "Ignatius Ferrall," q.v.
FERRELL, Elizabeth. See "John Cheney," q.v.
FIELD, Elisha. Private, 2nd Guard, Capt. Henry Hill's Militia Company, Lower Battalion; on duty at Nottingham on the Patuxent, Apr. 12, 1781 [Ref: L-19970 (Box 6, folder 21)]. The estate of "Elisha Fields" was probated on May 15, 1811 [Ref: ZE-72].
FIELDS, Margaret. See "Batson Naylor," q.v.
FINCH, Priscilla. See "Fielder Bowie" and "Allen Bowie," q.v.
FINCH, Thomas (1714-   ). Took the Oath of Allegiance before the Hon. William Berry in 1778 [Ref: O-258, R-52].
FINCH, William Jr. See "Fielder Bowie" and "Allen Bowie," q.v.
FINDLEY, Ann. See "Peter Boswell," q.v.
FINDLEY, Walter. The records of the Council of Maryland on Aug. 21, 1781, include a letter from Joshua Beall, County Lieutenant of Prince George's County, in which he stated "that Walter Findley was entered on board a vessel to go to sea, but as I had reasons of the same kind offered in classing the other battalions, which I was convinced was only to evade the draft, and as no vessel could at that time get out without the utmost risque from the enemy, I included him in the class" (for the

Middle Battalion of militia). A later entry in the same letter indicated that "I had Findley struck out of the Class and Jacob Vermillion put in." [Ref: H-433, H-434]. See "Matthew Clubb" and "Nicholas Waters," q.v.

FIRMAN, John. Took the Oath of Allegiance before the Hon. Osborn Sprigg in 1778 [Ref: O-308, W-4648 (Box 4, folder 29)].

FISHER, Abraham (1721-   ). Took the Oath of Allegiance before the Hon. Osborn Sprigg in 1778 [Ref: O-307, R-80].

FISHER, Eleanor. See "Edward Willett," q.v.

FISHER, John (1751-   ). Private, enrolled in the Flying Camp by Ensign William Shircliff on July 17, 1776; nativity: Germany; height 5' 6 1/2"; has own gun [Ref: D-36].

FISHER, Samuel. Private, Maryland Line, enlisted July 1, 1782 [Ref: D-426]. The estate of one Samuel Fisher was probated on Aug. 15, 1785 in Prince George's County [Ref: ZE-72].

FITZGERALD, John. Private, 4th Maryland Line, who had reportedly "deserted" on Oct. 26, 1780, but was paid for services rendered on Apr. 22, 1782 [Ref: I-144]. One John Fitzgerald married Jane Digges by license dated Jan. 2, 1779 [Ref: ZB-78].

FITZHUGH, William. Colonel who served on the Board of Patuxent Associator and signed a resolution at Nottingham on Apr. 21, 1781 relative to the defence of the rivers of Potomac and Patuxent and the completion of the fort at Drum Point [Ref: K-1814].

FITZSIMMONS, Thomas (1755-   ). Private, enrolled in the Flying Camp by Lieut. William D. Beall on Aug. 4, 1776; nativity: England; height: 5' 3 1/2"; black hair, brown complexion [Ref: D-37].

FLANAGAN, James. See "Smallwood Acton," q.v.

FLANAGIN, William. Private, 3rd Maryland Line, enlisted Apr. 9, 1777; served in Capt. Horatio Clagett's Company, December, 1779 [Ref: D-296].

FLINT, John. Private, 3rd Maryland Line, enlisted on Feb. 6, 1776 [Ref: D-10]. The estate of one John Flint was probated by Sep. 11, 1781 (date of inventory). [Ref: ZE-73].

FOARD, Charlotte. See "Butler Marlow," q.v.

FOARD, Mary. See "Benjamin Ward," q.v.

FOARD, William (1716-   ). Took the Oath of Allegiance before the Hon. Thomas Clagett in 1778 [Ref: O-265, R-42].

FOARD, William Jr. (1729-   ). Took the Oath of Allegiance before the Hon. Thomas Clagett in 1778 [Ref: O-267, R-19].

FOISTER, Basil. See "Basil Forster," q.v.

FOLLET, Benjamin. Drummer, 4th Maryland Line, enlisted Feb. 11, 1780, and died on June 17, 1781 [Ref: D-111, D-534, which spelled the name "Folliot"]. The estate of "Benjamin Follet (soldier)" was probated on July 24, 1793 in Prince George's County [Ref: ZE-73].

FOLLET, John. Private, German Regiment, 1779; 3rd Maryland Line, 1781; and 2nd Maryland Line, 1782 [Ref: D-208, D-395, D-447]. He may have served from Frederick rather than Prince George's County.

FOLLET, Joseph. Fifer, 4th Maryland Line, enlisted on Apr. 16, 1780, and died on July 25, 1782 [Ref: D-111, D-535, which spelled the name as "Folliot" and "Folliet"].

FORBIS, Sarah Moss. See "Alexander Truman," q.v.

FORBUS, John. Private, 3rd Maryland Line, Capt. Horatio Clagett's Company, 1779 [Ref: D-295].

FORCUM, Joseph. See "Azariah Gatton," q.v.

FORD, Archibald. Private, Maryland Line, by Feb. 24, 1779 when paid for his services "in cloathing." [Ref: E-308].

FORD, Eleanor. See "William Tong," q.v.

FORD, Notley. Private, enrolled by Lt. William Duvall, Lower Battalion, on July 18, 1776, for continental service, Maryland Line [Ref: D-35].

FORREST, Sarah. See "David Craufurd," q.v.

FORSTER (FOISTER), Basil. Took the Oath of Allegiance before the Hon. Benjamin Hall in 1778 [Ref: O-275, which spelled the name "Foister"].

FORSTER (FOISTER), Richard. "Richard Foister" took the Oath of Allegiance before the Hon. Thomas MacGill in 1778 [Ref: O-291]. "Richard Forster" married Priscilla Tyler by license dated Apr. 5, 1784 [Ref: ZB-78]. The estate of one Richard Forster was probated on Jan. 31, 1796 [Ref: ZE-74].

FOSSET, James. Took the Oath of Allegiance before the Hon. Benjamin Hall in 1778 [Ref: O-275].

FOWLER, Benjamin. Private in the county militia who participated in capturing an enemy boat and crew on Apr. 17, 1781 [Ref: M-209]. Private, Select Militia, Upper Battalion, June 12, 1781 [Ref: S-6636 (Box 27, folder 82B)].

FOWLER, Henry. Private, 1st Maryland Line, who was paid for his services "in cloathing" on Apr. 17, 1779 [Ref: E-351].

FOWLER, Isaac (1743-   ). Took the Oath of Allegiance before the Hon. William Berry in 1778 [Ref: O-258, R-46].

FOWLER, Jeremiah. In 1778 two men with this name took the Oath of Allegiance: one before the Hon. William Berry and one before the Hon. Benjamin Hall [Ref: O-258, O-274]. One Jeremiah Fowler, son of Thomas Fowler, was born on May 12, 1711 [Ref: ZC-176, R-46].

FOWLER, Jeremiah Jr. Took the Oath of Allegiance before the Hon. William Berry in 1778 [Ref: O-258].

FOWLER, Joseph. In 1778 two men with this name took the Oath of Allegiance: one (made his "X" mark) before the Hon. Truman Skinner and one signed before the Hon. William Berry [Ref: O-258, O-298].

FOWLER, Margaret. See "Philip Hopkins," q.v.

FOWLER, Richard. Took the Oath of Allegiance before the Hon. Christopher Lowndes in 1778 [Ref: O-284]. Richard Fowler married Ann Summers by license dated Jan. 16, 1779 [Ref: ZB-81].
FOWLER, Thomas (1746-   ). Took the Oath of Allegiance before the Hon. Benjamin Hall in 1778 [Ref: O-275, R-47]. See "Jeremiah Fowler," q.v.
FOWLER, Zadoc. Born in 1762 in Prince George's County, he moved to Frederick County in 1776 and allegedly enlisted in the Maryland Line. In 1834 he applied for a pension (R3714), but was rejected. [Ref: P-1248, and not listed in *Maryland Archives, Volume 18*].
FRAIL, John. Private, Capt. Alexander Truman's Company, stationed at Annapolis in 1781 and reported on "a list of men who have deserted since Mar. 1, 1781" [Ref: L-19970 (Box 7, folder 52)].
FRAIZER, Henry (1754-   ). Took the Oath of Allegiance before the Hon. Osborn Sprigg in 1778 [Ref: W-3538 (Box 4, folder 29), and O-306, which listed his name questionably as "Fraizer [Fraizen?]" and R-77, which spelled his name "Frazer"].
FRAIZER, John. Took the Oath of Allegiance before the Hon. Joshua Beall in 1778 [Ref: O-251]. See "John Fraser," q.v.
FRAIZER, Robert. Took the Oath of Allegiance before the Hon. Osborn Sprigg in 1778 [Ref: O-308, W-4648 (Box 4, folder 29)].
FRANCIS (FRANCES), Alexander. "Alexander Frances" was a private in the 3rd Maryland Line, Capt. Horatio Clagett's Company, December, 1779 [Ref: D-296]. "Alexander Francis" married Millicent Ann Loveless by license dated Dec. 22, 1783 [Ref: ZB-81].
FRANCIS (FRANCES), John (1719-   ). "John Frances" took the Oath of Allegiance before the Hon. Christopher Lowndes in 1778 [Ref: O-285, R-70]. One "John Francis" married Alice Crampkin [Cramphin?] by license dated Nov. 5, 1781 [Ref: ZB-81]. The estate of one "John Francis" was probated on Nov. 21, 1785 [Ref: ZE-75].
FRANKS, Henry (1751, Maryland - June 16, 1845, Ohio). Born at Piscataway in Prince George's County, Maryland, Henry Franks lived at Big Whitely near the Monogahela River about twenty miles from Besson Township, Pennsylvania at the time of his enlistment in the Pennsylvania Line. He married Margaret Van Buskirk and later lived in Hampshire and Ohio Counties, Virginia. He applied for a pension (S8522) in 1833 in Washington County, Ohio [Ref: P-1259]. It must also be noted that another Henry Franks was born on June 29, 1763 in Maryland, married Christina Mason, served as a private in the Pennsylvania Line, and died on May 5, 1836 in Ohio [Ref: X-1079].
FRASER, Alexander. Took the Oath of Allegiance (made his "X" mark) before the Hon. William Lock Weems in 1778 [Ref: O-301]. The estate of one "Alexander Frasier" was probated on May 24, 1796 [Ref: ZE-75].
FRASER, Anne. See "Allen Bowie, Sr.," q.v.
FRASER, George. Served on a Grand Jury in 1778 [Ref: Z-52].

FRASER, John. "John Fraser" took the Oath of Allegiance before the Hon. Thomas Clagett in 1778 [Ref: O-266]. "John T. Fraser" married Cassandra Evans by license dated Aug. 30, 1777 [Ref: ZB-82]. The estate of one "John Frazer" was probated on Dec. 18, 1820 [Ref: ZE-75]. See "John Frazier," q.v.
FRASER, William. Private (draft), continental service, Maryland Line, 1781 [Ref: D-382].
FRAZIER, Amelia. See "John Frazier," q.v.
FRAZIER, Daniel (1717-   ). Took the Oath of Allegiance before the Hon. Thomas Clagett in 1778 [Ref: O-266, R-76, which spelled his name "Fraser"].
FRAZIER, George Lanham. See "John Frazier," q.v.
FRAZIER, Hobart. Private, 2nd Maryland Line, from Feb. 1, 1778 until July 1, 1778, when he reportedly "deserted." [Ref: D-108].
FRAZIER, John. Took the Oath of Allegiance (made his "I" mark) before the Hon. Thomas Gantt, Jr. in 1778 [Ref: O-305, W-4648 (Box 4, folder 15)]. One John Frazier "went from Maryland to Newgate in Fairfax County, Virginia to enlist with Capt. John Jarrott for the Georgia Line." He married Mary Lanham on Oct. 24, 1789, in Prince George's County, Maryland and died testate on Jan. 12, 1820. Their children were John Lanham Frazier, Mary Frazier, Amelia Frazier, George Lanham Frazier, and William Frazier. His widow died July 23, 1838 and son John L. Frazier was her administrator in Prince George's County, Maryland [Ref: P-1262]. See "John Fraser," q.v.
FRAZIER, John Lanham. See "John Frazier," q.v.
FRAZIER, Lewin Jones. Took the Oath of Allegiance (made his "X" mark) before the Hon. Thomas Clagett in 1778 [Ref: O-268].
FRAZIER, Mary. See "John Frazier," q.v.
FRAZIER, William. Sergeant, Capt. Alexander H. Magruder's Militia Company, Lower Battalion; on duty guarding Magruder's Warehouse in the spring of 1782 [Ref: L-19970 (Box 6, folder 21)]. Took the Oath of Allegiance before the Hon. Thomas Gantt, Jr. in 1778 [Ref: O-305, W-4648 (Box 4, folder 15)]. See "John Frazier," q.v.
FREE, Catherine. See "Nicholas Free," q.v.
FREE, Elizabeth. See "Samuel Scott," q.v.
FREE, George. Private, Flying Camp, Upper District of Frederick County, July, 1776 [Ref: D-46]. The estate of one George Free was probated on Feb. 7, 1804 in Prince George's County [Ref: ZE-75, which also listed his name as "George A. Free"].
FREE, Nicholas (1735 - died before July 25, 1800). Took the Oath of Allegiance before the Hon. Christopher Lowndes in 1778 [Ref: O-283, R-70]. "Nicl. Fee" married Catherine Nigill on Feb. 2, 1790. He also served as a private in the 3rd Maryland Line in 1782 [Ref: D-451, D-508, X-1082, ZC-23].

FREELAND, Francis. "Francis Freland" took the Oath of Allegiance before the Hon. James Beck in 1778 [Ref: O-255]. The estate of one "Francis Freeland" was probated on Dec. 7, 1785 [Ref: ZE-75].
FREELAND, John. Served as a marine aboard a privateer, 1779-1781. Went to Kentucky c. 1817. [Ref: Pension Application R3773].
FREEMAN, Benjamin. Took the Oath of Allegiance before the Hon. Fielder Bowie in 1778 [Ref: O-303, W-4648 (Box 4, folder 15)].
FREEMAN, Lucy. See "William Manley," q.v.
FREEMAN, Mary. See "Richard Jones," q.v.
FREEMAN, Richard. See "Richard Jones," q.v.
FRENCH, Jeremiah. Private, 1st Maryland Line, 1780, and stationed at Camp James Island, South Carolina on Apr. 4, 1783 [Ref: D-355, D-442]. The estate of one Jeremiah French was probated on Apr. 26, 1794 in Prince George's County, Maryland [Ref: ZE-75].
FRY, Elizabeth. See "James Fry," q.v.
FRY, James (Oct. 20, 1746 - 1790). Son of Thomas and Elizabeth Fry [Ref: ZC-23]. Took the Oath of Allegiance before Hon. Fielder Bowie in 1778 [Ref: O-303, W-4648 (Box 4, folder 15)]. The estate of one James Fry was probated on Feb. 9, 1790 [Ref: ZE-76].
FRY, Joseph. See "Leonard Fry," q.v.
FRY, Leonard (c1750-   ). Took the Oath of Allegiance before Hon. Thomas Clagett in 1778 [Ref: R-75, O-266]. One Leonard Fry married Amey Day by license dated Dec. 8, 1803, in Prince George's County [Ref: ZB-83]. "Leonard Trueman Fry" was born on June 1, 1749, a son of Joseph and Elizabeth Fry, of King George's Parish, Prince George's County, Maryland [Ref: ZC-23]. It should be noted that there was a Leonard Fry (born circa 1750-1755) who married Catharine Schneck, served as a private in the Pennsylvania troops, and died in 1815 in Pennsylvania [Ref: X-1098].
FRY, Thomas. See "James Fry," q.v.
FULLER, Robert. Took the Oath of Allegiance before the Hon. Christopher Lowndes in 1778 [Ref: O-286].
FURNIVAL, Alexander. See "Zephaniah White," q.v.
FURROW, Samuel. Private, 2nd Maryland Line, Capt. Murdock's Company, Mar. 15, 1781 [Ref: D-366].
GAITHER, Basil. See "Azariah Gatton," q.v.
GAITHER, Benjamin. Took the Oath of Allegiance before the Hon. Benjamin Hall in 1778 [Ref: O-274]. The estate of one Benjamin Gaither was probated on Feb. 26, 1794 [Ref: ZE-76].
GAITHER, Ellen. See "Isaac Jones," q.v.
GAITHER, Lilah. See "Vachell Ijams," q.v.
GALE, Peter. Took the Oath of Allegiance before the Hon. Osborn Sprigg in 1778 [Ref: O-306].
GALER, Thomas (1739-1820). Took the Oath of Allegiance before the Hon. Christopher Lowndes in 1778 [Ref: O-286, R-49]. The estate of one

Thomas Galer was probated by Apr. 11, 1820 (date of account). [Ref: ZE-76].
GALLIHER, John. Private 6th Maryland Line, 1777-1780 [Ref: D-210].
GALWITH, Mary. See "Isaac Jenkins," q.v.
GALWITH, Rachel. See "Joseph Simpson, Jr.," q.v.
GALWORTH, John (1747-   ). Took the Oath of Allegiance before the Hon. Truman Skinner in 1778 [Ref: R-78, O-299, which latter source spelled his name "Galwith"]. One John Galwith served as a private in the Maryland Line from Anne Arundel County in 1776 [Ref: D-40].
GALWORTH, Peter. Private. 2nd Maryland Line, Capt. Patrick Sim's Company, 1776 [Ref: D-7].
GANTT, Ann (Anne). See "Thomas Gantt, Jr." and "Basil Waring, Jr." and "Basil Waring 3rd," q.v.
GANTT, Benjamin (1764-1808). Son of Thomas Gantt, Jr. and Susanna Mackall. Private, Capt. Alexander H. Magruder's Militia Company, Lower Battalion; on duty guarding Magruder's Warehouse in the spring of 1782. He subsequently moved to Georgia [Ref: U-343, U-344, L-19970 (Box 6, folder 21)].
GANTT, Benjamin. See "Benjamin Duvall" and "Samuel Scott," q.v.
GANTT, Betty. See "Thomas Gantt, Jr.," q.v.
GANTT, Charles. See "Thoma Gantt, Jr.," q.v.
GANTT, Daniel. See "Thomas Gantt, Jr.," q.v.
GANTT, Edward Jr. Took the Oath of Allegiance before the Hon. Thomas Williams in 1778 [Ref: O-302]. One Edward Gantt (son of Thomas Gantt, who died in 1765) was deceased by 1783 [Ref: U-341].
GANTT, Eleanor. See "Charles Eversfield" and "Leonard Townshend," q.v.
GANTT, Elizabeth. See "Thomas Gantt" and "Charles Eversfield," q.v.
GANTT, Erasmus. Son of Thomas Gantt (c1710-1785) and Eleanor Hillary. Born in Prince George's County (date unknown), moved to Washington County in 1794, and lived in Berkley County, Virginia in 1797. Served in the Lower House of the Maryland Legislature in 1784 and was a County Court Justice, 1787-1792 [Ref: U-340]. Took the Oath of Allegiance before the Hon. David Craufurd in 1778 [Ref: O-272]. On Aug. 12, 1781, he wrote to the Governor and requested an assignment to the cavalry. His letter is in the records of the Council of Maryland as follows: "In consequence of an Appointment from Your Excellency, to a Cornelcy *[sic]* in the Troop of Horse, which was directed for the Defence of Somerset & Worcester Counties, I was reduced to the Expenditure of a Considerable sum of money for Horses, and other necessary Equipments; trusting to your Excellency that in Case the plan of raising the Troops directed was not adopted I should meet your attention in some other appointment. The plan upon which the Regiment of Horse are to be raised by the State, renders a post in it far more reputable, than the Troop heretofore directed to be raised, therefore shall conceive myself honoured in your influence towards such an appointment." He

wrote a follow-up letter on Aug. 20, 1781, again offering his services as an officer in a Regiment of Horse and, as if to emphasize his zealousness, he stated "at present I am wholly unimployed." [Ref: H-413, Q-426].

GANTT, Fielder (c1730, Prince George's County - Nov. 12, 1807, Frederick County). Son of Thomas Gantt (died 1765) and Priscilla Brooke. Fielder was "of age" by 1753 and married Susanna ----. He spent his adult life in Frederick County, Maryland where he served in the Lower House, 1765-1766, 1779-1780, and was a County Court Justice, 1779-1785 [Ref: U-340, U-341, X-1121, which latter source misspelled his name as "Foelder Gantt"].

GANTT, George. Took the Oath of Allegiance which was recorded on a "return of Capt. Tapley of the brig *Royal*" and filed in court by the Hon. Thomas Gantt, Jr. in 1778 [Ref: O-305, W-4648 (Box 4, folder 15)]. He may be the George Gantt (son of Thomas) who died in 1779 [Ref: U-341]. He is also listed as being born circa 1715 and having died before June 15, 1779 [Ref: X-1121, ZE-77].

GANTT, George Jr. (c1760-c1805) Second Lieutenant, 11th Battalion, Capt. Alexander H. Magruder's Company, May 1, 1778 [Ref: M-77, E-62]. First Lieutenant, Lower Battalion, Capt. Alexander H. Magruder's Company, July 3, 1780 [Ref: M-77, F-210, N-33, which latter sources listed his name without the "Jr."]. Took the Oath of Allegiance before the Hon. Thomas Gantt, Jr. in 1778 [Ref: O-305, W-4648 (Box 4, folder 15)]. Lieutenant, Capt. Alexander H. Magruder's Militia Company, Lower Battalion; on duty guarding Magruder's Warehouse in the spring of 1782 [Ref: L-19970 (Box 6, folder 21)]. However, Reference X-1121 only lists his patriotic service and nothing about being a lieutenant. Additional research may be necessary before drawing conclusions.

GANTT, James (1754-   ). Took the Oath of Allegiance before the Hon. Thomas Clagett in 1778 [Ref: O-265, R-41].

GANTT, John. See "Thomas Gantt" and "Thomas Gantt, Jr.," q.v.

GANTT, Joseph. Private, Capt. Alexander H. Magruder's Militia Company, Lower Battalion; on duty guarding Magruder's Warehouse in the spring of 1782 [Ref: L-19970 (Box 6, folder 21)].

GANTT, Levi. Son of Thomas Gantt (c1710-1785) and Eleanor Hillary. Took the Oath of Allegiance before the Hon. Christopher Lowndes in 1778 [Ref: U-340, O-284, which spelled the name "Gant"]. Served on a Grand Jury in 1778 [Ref: Z-90]. The estate of one Levi Gantt was probated on Oct. 4, 1820 [Ref: ZE-77].

GANTT, Mary. See "Thomas Gantt, Jr.," q.v.

GANTT, Priscilla. See "Thomas Gantt" and "Jeremiah Belt," q.v.

GANTT, Rachel. See "Richard Brooke," q.v.

GANTT, Richard. See "Thomas Gantt, Jr.," q.v.

GANTT, Sarah. See "Osborn Sprigg," q.v.

GANTT, Susanna Mackall. See "Thomas Gantt, Jr.," q.v.

GANTT, Thomas. Private, Capt. Alexander H. Magruder's Militia Company, Lower Battalion; on duty guarding Magruder's Warehouse in the spring of 1782 [Ref: L-19970 (Box 6, folder 21)]. The estate of one Thomas Gantt was probated on May 3, 1808 and the estate of another Thomas Gantt was probated on July 17, 1820 [Ref: ZE-77]. Also see "Thomas Gantt, Jr.," q.v.

GANTT, Thomas (c1710-1785). Son of Thomas Gantt (died 1765) and Priscilla Brooke. He married (1) Rachel Smith and (2) Eleanor Hillary, and had these children: Thomas Gantt, Jr. (died 1808), Edward Gantt (c1741-1837, moved to Kentucky), John Gantt (moved to Berkley County, Virginia), Levi Gantt, Erasmus Gantt, Fielder Gantt, Rachel Brooke, Elizabeth Gantt, Priscilla Gantt, Ann Waring, and Sarah Sprigg [Ref: U-342]. Thomas served in the Maryland Legislature, Lower House, 1754-1758, was a Justice of the Court, 1738-1749, 1748-1751, and was a captain in the military by 1743. Took the Oath of Allegiance before the Hon. Thomas Gantt, Jr. in 1778 [Ref: U-342, O-305, X-1121, ZE-77, W-4648 (Box 4, folder 15)]. See "Osborn Sprigg," q.v., and the comment under "Thomas Gantt, Jr.," q.v.

GANTT, Thomas Jr. (1736-1808). Delegate to the Maryland Convention on July 26, 1775. House of Delegates, 1779. Justice of the County Court, 1777-1778. Administered the Oath of Allegiance in 1778 [Ref: A-3, C-273, U-70, U-80, O-305, Z-90, ZE-77, W-4648 (Box 4, folder 15)]. Justice of the Peace in 1779 [Ref: F-17]. First Lieutenant, 11th Battalion, Capt. Alexander Magruder's Company, May 24, 1779 [Ref: N-33, M-78, E-414, which misspelled his name "Thomas Gautt" and his captain's name as "Alexander H. McGuden"]. Served on the Board of Patuxent Associators and signed a resolution at Nottingham on Apr. 21, 1781 relative to the defence of the rivers of Potomac and Patuxent and the completion of the fort at Drum Point [Ref: K-1814, which spelled his name "Thomas Gant" without the "Jr."]. Thomas Gantt, 4th was an Ensign, 6th Maryland Line, commissioned Nov. 6, 1779 [Ref: F-10]. "Thomas Gantt, 4th, Jr. was born in Calvert County on Aug. 18, 1736 and died in Prince George's County on Dec. 12, 1800/7 *[sic]*. He married Susanna Mackall (1737-1777) and their son Charles Gantt (1771-1815) married Mary Parran." [Ref: SAR Application No. 137133 of George Blunt Breeden, of Baldwin, Maryland, approved on June 6, 1991]. He married second to Sarah Eleanor Potts in 1782. His children were Thomas Gantt (1760-1780), John Mackall Gantt, Benjamin Gantt (1764-1808, moved to Georgia), Richard Gantt (born 1767, moved to South Carolina), Daniel Gantt (born 1770, moved to Virginia), Charles Gantt (1773-1815), Thomas Gantt (born 1783), Betty Heighe Gantt (born 1756), Mary Newbern (born 1765), Ann Wood (born 1771), and Sarah Eleanor Beall (born 1787). [Ref: U-344, which source also pointed out identification problems with several men by the name of Thomas Gantt during the Revolutionary War. The will of Thomas Gantt was probated on May 30,

1808, in Prince George's County, so the date of death appears to be incorrect on the SAR application unless he died in December, 1807 and the will was not probated until May, 1808]. DAR papers only state that he died some time after 1800 [Ref: X-1121].

GANTT, Thomas 3rd (of Calvert County). Took the Oath of Allegiance which was recorded on a "return of Capt. Tapley of the brig *Royal*" and filed in court by the Hon. Thomas Gantt, Jr. in 1778 in Prince George's County [Ref: O-305 and W-4648 (Box 4, folder 15), both listing his name as "Thomas Gantt, ye 3d, of Calvert County"].

GANTT, Thomas 4th. See "Thomas Gantt, Jr.," q.v.

GARDNER, George Jr. Took the Oath of Allegiance before the Hon. David Craufurd in 1778 [Ref: O-272].

GARNER, John. Private, 1st Maryland Line, who was paid for his services "in cloathing" on Apr. 17, 1779 [Ref: E-351]. The estate of one John Garner was probated on Aug. 15, 1797 [Ref: ZE-77].

GARNER, Sarah. See "Thomas Delozier," q.v.

GARRETT, John. Private, 3rd Maryland Line, enlisted Feb. 28, 1777. Capt. Horatio Clagett's Company, December, 1779 [Ref: D-295].

GASSAWAY, Nicholas. Second Lieutenant, 3rd Maryland Line, Capt. Horatio Clagett's Company; commissioned Apr. 17, 1777, and still in the service (although sick and absent from muster) in December, 1779 [Ref: D-295]. His estate was probated on Apr. 9, 1793 [Ref: ZE-78]. See "Joseph Williams," q.v.

GATES, Eleanor. See "John Ryon," q.v.

GATES, James. Took the Oath of Allegiance in 1780 [Ref: J-111].

GATES, William. Private, 1st Maryland Line, enlisted June 4, 1778 and discharged Apr. 5, 1779 [Ref: D-112]. He was paid for his services "in cloathing" on Apr. 17, 1779 [Ref: E-351].

GATRILL, Delilah. See "Jeremiah Beall," q.v.

GATTON, Azariah (1750, Prince George's County, Maryland - 1807, Iredell County, North Carolina). A son of Thomas Gatton and Elizabeth ---- [Waters?], Azariah married Elizabeth Humphries on Feb. 2, 1769 and had these children: Nancy D. Gatton (born Nov., 1771 and married Isaac Ward), Angelenor Gatton (born Mar. 11, 1774 and married Basil Gaither), Sally Ann Gatton (born Mar. 5, 1776 and married James Ratledge), Benjamin Gatton (married Matilda Ratledge), James Gatton (never married), Elizabeth Gatton (married Joseph Forcum), Polly Gatton, Patsey Gatton, Lurary Gatton, Joseph H. Gatton (married Elizabeth Dyson and died in Wilson County, Tennessee in 1856), and Thomas Gatton. After the war Azariah went to North Carolina and patented land on Hunting Creek in 1786 in Rowan County [Ref: Information from Mrs. Patricia June Dysart, 7480 Neverland Lane, Redding, California 96002-4091, in 1996]. Azariah served on a Grand Jury in 1777 in Prince George's County [Ref: Z-29]. One "Azariah Gatton" was a private in the Maryland Line in 1781 [Ref: D-408]. An

"Azariah Gatting" married Mary Selby on June 23, 1794 in King George's Parish, Prince George's County. He was probably the son of James and Mary Gatton who was born in 1762 [Ref: ZC-24]. There is some uncertainty as to which Azariah served in the war. Additional research may be necessary before drawing conclusions.
GATTON, Benjamin. See "Azariah Gatton," q.v.
GATTON, Elizabeth. See "Azariah Gatton," q.v.
GATTON, James. See "Azariah Gatton," q.v.
GATTON, Joseph. See "Azariah Gatton," q.v.
GATTON, Lurary. See "Azariah Gatton," q.v.
GATTON, Mary. See "George Bean," q.v.
GATTON, Nancy. See "Azariah Gatton," q.v.
GATTON, Patsey. See "Azariah Gatton," q.v.
GATTON, Polly. See "Azariah Gatton," q.v.
GATTON, Sally. See "Azariah Gatton," q.v.
GATTON, Sylvester. Private, Northern Detachment, 3rd Maryland Line, Capt. Horatio Clagett's Company, 1783 [Ref: D-501].
GATTON, Thomas. See "Azariah Gatton" and George Bean," q.v.
GEARY, Samuel. Private (substitute), Maryland Line, discharged on Dec. 3, 1781 [Ref: I-10].
GENTLE, Mary. See "Thomas Gentle," q.v.
GENTLE, Stephen. See "Thomas Gentle," q.v.
GENTLE, Thomas. Took the Oath of Allegiance before the Hon. James Beck in 1778 [Ref: O-252]. One Thomas Gentle was aged 35 in the 1776 census of Prince George's County [Ref: R-28]. Another Thomas Gentle was born on Apr. 9, 1757, son of Stephen and Mary Gentle, of King George's Parish, Prince George's County [Ref: ZC-24].
GEORGE, William. Private, 6th Maryland Line; prisoner of war, exchanged by Aug. 20, 1781, at which time he was paid 5 pounds specie on his account. Private, 2nd Maryland Line, Capt. Alexander Truman's Company, 1782; died July 24, 1782 [Ref: D-439, D-617].
GERMAIN, John. First Corporal, 2nd Guard, Capt. Henry Hill's Militia Company, Lower Battalion; on duty at Nottingham on the Patuxent, Apr. 12, 1781 [Ref: L-19970 (Box 6, folder 21)].
GHISELIN, Margaret. See "Robert Bowie," q.v.
GIBBON, Jane. See "Gabriel Duvall," q.v.
GIBBONS, Daniel. Took the Oath of Allegiance in 1780 [Ref: J-111].
GIBBONS, John. Took the Oath of Allegiance before the Hon. Fielder Bowie in 1778 [Ref: O-304, W-4648 (Box 4, folder 15)]. The estate of one John Gibbons was probated in November, 1802 [Ref: ZE-79].
GIBBONS, Thomas. Took the Oath of Allegiance before the Hon. Osborn Sprigg in 1778 [Ref: O-308, W-4648 (Box 4, folder 29)]. The estate of one Thomas Gibbons was probated in April, 1789 [Ref: ZE-79].
GIBBONS, Walter. Private, Capt. Jesse Hellen's Militia Company, before May 23, 1782; guarded Magruder's Warehouse in the spring of 1782

[Ref: L-19970 (Box 6, folder 21)]. Took the Oath of Allegiance before the Hon. Fielder Bowie in 1778 [Ref: O-304. The original list at the Maryland State Archives (Box 4, folder 15) listed the name as "Gibbins"].

GIBBONS, William. Took the Oath of Allegiance before the Hon. Osborn Sprigg in 1778 [Ref: O-308, W-4648 (Box 4, folder 29)].

GIBBS, John Harris (June 20 or 22, 1753 -   ). Son of James and Ann Gibbs [Ref: ZC-24]. Took the Oath of Allegiance before the Hon. Thomas Clagett in 1778 [Ref: O-268]. Ensign, Lower Battalion, Capt. Richard Stonestreet's Company, June 12, 1781 [Ref: M-78, G-472, L-19970 (Box 6, folder 21)]. "John H. Gibbs" married Mary Henrietta Dyer by license dated July 20, 1778 [Ref: ZB-88].

GIBSON, Joseph. Private, 4th Maryland Line, Capt. Bowie's Company, from Apr. 1, 1777 until discharged Dec. 7, 1779 [Ref: D-115].

GILD, Whittington. Private, Northern Detachment, 3rd Maryland Line, Capt. Horatio Clagett's Company, 1783 [Ref: D-502].

GILL, James. Took the Oath of Allegiance before the Hon. George Lee in 1778 [Ref: O-279].

GILL, Moses (1757, Calvert County, Maryland - died after Nov. 3, 1832, Marion County, Missouri). Moses lived in Prince George's County when he enlisted in the Maryland Line (no date was given) and after 18 months moved with his father to Virginia and again enlisted in Fairfax County in the Virginia Line. After the war he lived in Virginia and then moved to Washington County, Ohio, Wood County, Virginia, and then to Marion County, Missouri, where he applied for a pension (S16823) on Nov. 3, 1832 [Ref: P-1351, but he is not listed in *Maryland Archives, Volume 18*]. Moses Gill also took the Oath of Allegiance before the Hon. George Lee in 1778 in Prince George's County [Ref: O-279].

GILL, Thomas. Took the Oath of Allegiance before the Hon. Thomas Clagett in 1778 [Ref: O-267]. Thomas Gill married Sarah Jones by license dated Aug. 30, 1777 [Ref: ZB-88].

GILPIN, Ann. See "Benjamin Gilpin," q.v.

GILPIN, Benjamin (1762, Fairfax County, Virginia - Apr. 20, 1840, Fayette County, Alabama). Born in late 1762 in Virginia, Benjamin was raised in Prince George's County, Maryland and enlisted in the Maryland Line in Montgomery County. After the war he moved to Rowan County, North Carolina where he lived for nearly 40 years and then moved to Putnam County, Georgia, where he lived until 1830. In Henry County, Alabama, he applied for a pension (S13155) on Mar. 21, 1837. He died on Apr. 24, 1840, and Richmond Gilpin was the administrator of his estate in Fayette County [Ref: P-1360]. Benjamin Gilpin, son of Edward and Ann Gilpin, was baptized in King George's Parish, Prince George's County, Maryland on May 6, 1764 [Ref: ZC-25].

GILPIN, Edward. Took the Oath of Allegiance before the Hon. Fielder Bowie in 1778 [Ref: O-304, W-4648 (Box 4, folder 15)]. See "Benjamin Gilpin," q.v.
GILPIN, Ignatious. Private, enrolled by Lt. William Duvall, Lower Battalion, on July 18, 1776, for continental service, Maryland Line [Ref: D-35].
GILPIN, Mary. See "Richard Walker," q.v.
GILPIN, Notley. Private, Select Militia, Capt. Hezekiah Wheeler's Company, July 14, 1781 [Ref: S-6636 (Box 31, folder 5)].
GILPIN, Richmond. See "Benjamin Gilpin," q.v.
GILPIN, William. Private, enrolled by Lt. William Duvall, Lower Battalion, on July 18, 1776, for continental service, Maryland Line [Ref: D-35]. Private, Select Militia, Capt. Hezekiah Wheeler's Company, July 14, 1781 [Ref: S-6636 (Box 31, folder 5)]. On Mar. 2, 1827, the Treasurer of the Western Shore of Maryland was directed to pay to William Gilpin, of Jefferson County, Virginia, during life, the half pay of a private for his services during the Revolutionary War [Ref: D-346].
GIM, Black Boy. Drummer, enrolled by Capt. Alexander H. Magruder, 11th Battalion, on July 14, 1776, for continental service, Maryland Line [Ref: D-38].
GLASGOW, William. Private, 3rd Maryland Line, enlisted May 16, 1778. Capt. Horatio Clagett's Company, December, 1779 [Ref: D-295].
GLOVER, Thomas. Took the Oath of Allegiance before the Hon. Osborn Sprigg in 1778 [Ref: O-306].
GLOYD, Joanna. See "John Ballard," q.v.
GODDARD, Barton. Private, 2nd Maryland Line, from May 30, 1778 until discharged on Apr. 3, 1779 [Ref: D-113, which spelled his name "Godthart"].
GODDARD, Benjamin. See "John Goddard," q.v.
GODDARD, Elinor. See "Patrick Beall," q.v.
GODDARD, John. Private, 3rd Maryland Line, 1780-1783 [Ref: D-115, D-430]. On Jan. 17, 1833, the Treasurer of the Western Shore was directed to pay to Raphael C. Edelen for the use of Benjamin Goddard, of Prince George's County, only child and representative of John Goddard, of said county, a revolutionary soldier who died Sep. 2, 1832, the amount of $16.89 due him at death, as a pensioner [Ref: O-346, O-347]. One John Goddard married Susannah Thorn by license dated Aug. 4, 1787, and a John Goddard married Elizabeth Knott by license dated July 15, 1795 [Ref: ZB-89].
GODFREY, Edmund. Private, 7th Maryland Line, 1776; discharged Jan. 5, 1777 [Ref: D-305].
GODFREY, William. Drummer, 7th Maryland Line, 1776; discharged Sep. 7, 1777 [Ref: D-305, D-211, which spelled his name "William Goodfrey"]. Took the Oath of Allegiance before the Hon. Thomas Williams in 1778 [Ref: O-302, which spelled the name "William Godphrey"].

GODMAN, ----. See "William Murdock Hall," q.v.
GOLD, Samuel (1750, Montgomery County, Maryland -   ). Private, enlisted Mar. 15, 1780, for 3 years or during war, in continental service, Maryland Line [Ref: D-333].
GOLD, William. Private, 2nd Maryland Line, Feb. 20, 1778 to at least Nov. 1, 1780 [Ref: D-113].
GORDON, Elizabeth (Eliza). See "James Truman," q.v.
GORDON, George. Took the Oath of Allegiance before the Hon. Christopher Lowndes in 1778 [Ref: O-288].
GORDON, John. Took the Oath of Allegiance before the Hon. James Beck in 1778 [Ref: O-252, which spelled the name "Gorden"]. Drummer, 3rd Maryland Line, by December, 1779 [Ref: D-296].
GORDON, Joseph. Private, Select Militia, Upper Battalion, June 12, 1781 [Ref: S-6636 (Box 27, folder 82B)]. Private, Militia, 1781; participated in capturing an enemy boat and crew on Apr. 17, 1781 [Ref: M-209].
GORDON, Josiah (1746-   ). Took the Oath of Allegiance before the Hon. William Berry in 1778 [Ref: O-259, R-32]. "Sergeant, a draft, June 15th, 1778" for continental service, Maryland Line [Ref: D-328, M-207, A-325].
GORDON, Mary. See "Tobias Belt" and "Sabrit Sollers," q.v.
GORDON, Mr. See "Christopher Beall," q.v.
GORDON, Thomas (1757-   ). Private, enrolled in the Flying Camp by Lieut. William D. Beall on Aug. 4, 1776; nativity: Scotland; height: 5' 2 1/2"; brown hair and brown complexion [Ref: D-37]. Another Thomas Gordon was aged 57 in 1776 [Ref: R-34]. One Thomas Gordon married Ann Hardy by license dated June 11, 1777 [Ref: ZB-90].
GORMAN, Abraham. See "Zekiel Meek," q.v.
GOVER, Frances. See "Robert Baden," q.v.
GRAHAM, John. Took the Oath of Allegiance before the Hon. David Craufurd in 1778 [Ref: O-272].
GRAHAM, Moses (1741-   ). Private, 2nd Maryland Line, Capt. Alexander Truman's Company, 1782 [Ref: D-440, R-61].
GRAHAME, Philip (1749, Maryland -   ). Private, enlisted May 28, 1781, for 3 years in continental service, Maryland Line; sent to Annapolis; on duty July 13, 1781 [Ref: D-381].
GRANT, John. Private, 2nd Maryland Line, Capt. Patrick Sim's Company, 1776 [Ref: D-8]. One John Grant married Ephana Claud by license dated Oct. 21, 1777 [Ref: ZB-90].
GRANT, Mary. See "John Riley," q.v.
GRAVES, John. Private, 2nd Guard, Capt. Henry Hill's Militia Company, Lower Battalion; on duty at Nottingham on the Patuxent, Apr. 12, 1781 [Ref: L-19970 (Box 6, folder 21)].
GRAVES, Lewis (1718-   ). Took the Oath of Allegiance before the Hon. William Lyles, Jr. in 1778 [Ref: O-290, R-56].
GRAY, Eleanor. See "William Kidwell," q.v.

GRAY, Jacob. Private, 2nd Maryland Line, from Mar. 4, 1777 to at least Nov. 1, 1780 [Ref: D-112].

GRAY, James. Private, 2nd Maryland Line, enlisted Dec. 24, 1776 [Ref: D-113]. One James Gray married Linny Osborn by license dated Feb. 7, 1785 [Ref: ZB-91].

GRAY, John. Corporal, Capt. Jesse Hellen's Militia Company; guarded Magruder's Warehouse in the spring of 1782 [Ref: L-19970 (Box 6, folder 21)].

GRAY, Joseph. Corporal, 2nd Maryland Line; reported dead on Feb. 28, 1778 [Ref: D-113].

GRAY, Rebecca. See "Thomas King," q.v.

GRAY, Thomas. Took the Oath of Allegiance before the Hon. Fielder Bowie in 1778 [Ref: O-304, W-4648 (Box 4, folder 15)].

GRAYER, Ananias. Private, Capt. Jesse Hellen's Militia Company, before May 23, 1782; guarded Magruder's Warehouse in the spring of 1782 [Ref: L-19970 (Box 6, folder 21)].

GRAYER, Benjamin. Took the Oath of Allegiance (made his "X" mark) before the Hon. Alexander Howard Magruder in 1778 [Ref: O-293]. Private, Capt. Benjamin Wailes' Militia Company, Lower Battalion; on duty guarding Magruder's Warehouse in the spring of 1782 [Ref: L-19970 (Box 6, folder 21)].

GREEN, Amos. Private, 2nd Maryland Line, Capt. Patrick Sim's Company, 1776 [Ref: D-7].

GREEN, Basil (1754-1782). Took the Oath of Allegiance before the Hon. Thomas Clagett in 1778 [Ref: O-265, R-42, which spelled the name "Bazell Green"]. Corporal, 11th Militia Battalion, Capt. Hezekiah Wheeler's Company, April, 1781 [Ref: L-19970 (Box 6, folder 21), which spelled the name "Basel Green"]. Basil Green married Sarah Ann Lanham by license dated Jan. 18, 1780 [Ref: ZB-91]. The estate of one Basil Green was probated by June 11, 1782 (date of inventory). [Ref: ZE-81].

GREEN, Edelen. Private, Capt. Hezekiah Wheeler's Company, 11th Militia Battalion, April, 1781 [Ref: L-19970 (Box 6, folder 21)].

GREEN, Elisha. Took the Oath of Allegiance before the Hon. Thomas MacGill in 1778 [Ref: O-291]. Elisha Green married Mary Clarke by license dated Mar. 1, 1783 [Ref: ZB-91]. The estate of one Elisha Green was probated on Apr. 26, 1790 [Ref: ZE-81].

GREEN, Jacob. Took the Oath of Allegiance before the Hon. James Beck in 1778 [Ref: O-253]. The estate of one Jacob Green was probated in 1802, another in 1809, and another in 1815 [Ref: ZE-81, ZE-82]. Additional research may be necessry before drawing conclusions as to which Jacob Green rendered patriotic service.

GREEN, James. See "Thomas Edelen Green," q.v.

GREEN, John. Private, 1st Maryland Line; paid for his services "in cloathing" on Apr. 17, 1779 [Ref: E-351]. This or another John Green was a private in the Maryland Line in 1781 [Ref: I-22].
GREEN, Mary Jane. See "Elijah Athey," q.v.
GREEN, Sarah. See "William Powell," q.v.
GREEN, Thomas Edelen (Mar. 9, 1745/46 -   ). Son of James Greene *[sic]* and Eliza Dyar [Ref: ZC-26]. Took the Oath of Allegiance before the Hon. Thomas Clagett in 1778 [Ref: O-266, R-87].
GREENFIELD, Dorothy. See "Benjamin Wailes," q.v.
GREENFIELD, Gabriel. Sergeant, Select Militia, Capt. Hezekiah Wheeler's Company, July 14, 1781 [Ref: S-6636 (Box 31, folder 5)]. Sergeant, Capt. Jesse Hellen's Militia Company; guarded Magruder's Warehouse in the spring of 1782 [Ref: L-19970 (Box 6, folder 21)]. The estate of "Gabriel P. T. Greenfield" was probated on June 27, 1815 [Ref: ZE-82].
GREENFIELD, Gerard Truman. Took the Oath of Allegiance which was recorded on a "return of Capt. Tapley of the brig *Royal*" and filed in court by the Hon. Thomas Gantt, Jr. in 1778 [Ref: O-305, W-4648 (Box 4, folder 15)]. The estate of "Gerrard T. Greenfield" was probated on Apr. 5, 1797 [Ref: ZE-82].
GREENFIELD, Thomas. See "Benjamin Wailes," q.v.
GREENFIELD, Thomas Smith. Took the Oath of Allegiance before the Hon. Thomas Gantt, Jr. in 1778 [Ref: O-305, W-4648 (Box 4, folder 15)]. His estate was probated on Sep. 10, 1806 [Ref: ZE-83].
GREENFIELD, Walter. Rendered patriotic service by providing wheat for the military on Aug. 9, 1780 [Ref: Q-308].
GREENFIELD, Walter Truman. Ensign, 11th Battalion, Capt. Jesse Hellen's Company, May 1, 1778 [Ref: M-80, E-78, N-32]. Took the Oath of Allegiance which was recorded on a "return of Capt. Tapley of the brig *Royal*" and filed in court by the Hon. Thomas Gantt, Jr. in 1778 [Ref: O-305, W-4648 (Box 4, folder 15)]. The estate of "Walter T. Greenfield" was probated in 1813 [Ref: ZE-83].
GREENFIELD, William. Rendered patriotic service by providing wheat for the military on Aug. 16, 1781 [Ref: Q-425].
GREENFIELD, William Truman. Took the Oath of Allegiance before the Hon. Thomas Gantt, Jr. in 1778 [Ref: O-305, W-4648 (Box 4, folder 15)]. Cadet, enrolled by Capt. Alexander H. Magruder, 11th Battalion, on July 18, 1776, for continental service, Maryland Line [Ref: D-38]. The estate of "William Trueman Greenfield" was probated on Sep. 3, 1794 [Ref: ZE-83].
GREENWELL, James (1722-   ). Took the Oath of Allegiance before the Hon. Christopher Lowndes in 1778 [Ref: O-283, R-49].
GREENWELL, Jesse. Private, 4th Maryland Line, who "died of his wounds in February, 1778." [Ref: D-115]. Just for the record it should be noted that there was also a Jesse Greenwell who married Luthy

Lowe by license dated Jan. 6, 1790, and a Jesse Greenwell who married
Ann Moore by license dated Jan. 21, 1795 [Ref: ZB-92].

GREENWOOD, James. Drummer, 2nd Maryland Line, Capt. Alexander
Truman's Company, 1782 [Ref: D-439].

GREER, Joseph. Private, 2nd Maryland Line, Capt. Murdock's Company,
Mar. 15, 1781 [Ref: D-366]. Private, 1st Maryland Line; wounded (lost
a leg) at the Siege of 96. His disability (invalid) pension commenced on
Nov. 15, 1783 and ended May 15, 1787 when he was reported dead [Ref:
D-634, D-635, K-1814]. The estate of Joseph Greer was probated on
Sep. 24, 1788 [Ref: ZE-83].

GREGORY, James. Private, 5th Maryland Line, "enlisted June 14, 1779
and joined Mar. 17, 1780." [Ref: D-210]. One James Gregory married
Ann Jones by license dated Dec. 13, 1792 [Ref: ZB-93].

GREGORY, John (1751, England -   ). Private (substitute), 1780,
continental service, Maryland Line [Ref: D-338].

GREGORY, Richard (1744-   ). Took the Oath of Allegiance before the
Hon. Thomas Clagett in 1778 [Ref: O-268, R-78].

GREGSBY, Wilkinson (1760, Maryland -   ). Private (substitute), 1780,
in continental service, Maryland Line [Ref: D-338, which spelled the
name "Wilkerson Greegsby"]. Private, 2nd Maryland Line, Capt.
Murdock's Company, Mar. 15, 1781 [Ref: D-366].

GRIEVES, Isaac. Private, 2nd Maryland Line, Capt. Alexander Truman's
Company, 1782 [Ref: D-440].

GRIFFIN, Darby. Private, 3rd Maryland Line, 1778 [Ref: D-279].

GRIFFIN, Michael. Private, Maryland Line; defective in June, 1780 [Ref:
D-415].

GRIFFIN, William. Private, Maryland Line, discharged on Dec. 3, 1781
[Ref: I-10].

GRIFFITH, Charles. Private, Northern Detachment, 3rd Maryland Line,
Capt. Horatio Clagett's Company, 1783; discharged Nov. 15, 1783 [Ref:
D-501].

GRIFFITH, Nancy. See "Burch Vermillion," q.v.

GRIMES, Catherine. See "Charles Grimes," q.v.

GRIMES, Charles (Aug. 31, 1757 -   ). Son of George and Catherine
Grimes [Ref: ZC-26]. Took the Oath of Allegiance before the Hon.
Fielder Bowie in 1778 [Ref: O-304, W-4648 (Box 4, folder 15)]. One
Charles Grimes married Ann Stone by license dated Feb. 17, 1787 [Ref:
ZB-94].

GRIMES, Charlotte. See "Thomas Taylor," q.v.

GRIMES, George (1726-   ). Took the Oath of Allegiance before the Hon.
Osborn Sprigg in 1778 [Ref: O-308, R-80, which latter source spelled his
name "Grymes"]. See "Charles Grimes," q.v.

GRIMES, John. Took the Oath of Allegiance before the Hon. Fielder
Bowie in 1778 [Ref: O-304, W-4648 (Box 4, folder 15)]. One John
Grimes married Martha Clements by license dated Jan. 11, 1785, and

a John Grimes married Sarah King by license dated Jan. 3, 1789 [Ref: ZB-94].
GRIMES, Mary. See "James Short" and "Thomas Taylor," q.v.
GRINDLE, William. Ensign, 11th Battalion, Capt. Benjamin Wailes' Company, May 24, 1779 [Ref: M-81, E-414, N-33].
GRINNARD, Paul. "Paul Grinnard" was a private, 2nd Maryland Line, Capt. Alexander Truman's Company, 1782 [Ref: D-440]. The estate of "Paul Grinard" was probated on May 14, 1794 [Ref: ZE-84].
GROVES, Samuel. Private, enrolled by Ensign Alexander Truman on July 3, 1776, for continental service, Maryland Line [Ref: D-38, which listed the name as "Samuel Grover"].
GROVES, Solomon. Served on a Grand Jury in 1778 [Ref: Z-90]. Took the Oath of Allegiance before the Hon. Benjamin Hall in 1778 [Ref: O-275, which listed the name as "Solomon Grove"].
GRUNDIE, William. Took the Oath of Allegiance before the Hon. Osborn Sprigg in 1778 [Ref: O-306].
GUDGEON, William. Corporal, Northern Detachment, 3rd Maryland Line, Capt. Horatio Clagett's Company, 1783 [Ref: D-501].
GUN, Henry. Private, 1st Guard, Capt. Henry Hill's Militia Company, Lower Battalion; on duty at Nottingham on the Patuxent, Apr. 12, 1781 [Ref: L-19970 (Box 6, folder 21)].
GUTTERIDGE, Diana. See "Thomas Bryan," q.v.
GUY, Mary. See "Thomas Webster," q.v.
GWYNN, Ann. See "Bennett Gwynn," q.v.
GWYNN, Bennett (1758-1826). Second Sergeant, 2nd Guard, Capt. Henry Hill's Militia Company, Lower Battalion, and on duty at Nottingham on the Patuxent, Apr. 12, 1781 [Ref: L-19970 (Box 6, folder 21), which spelled his name "Benit Gwynn"]. "Bennett Gwinn, son of Hooper Gwinn" was aged 19 by Nov., 1777 [Ref: Z-35]. He was married four times: (1) Mary Belt, and had a son Thomas Belt Gwynn; (2) Susanna Hilleary (by license dated Feb. 21, 1797) and had children John Hilleary Gwynn, Ann Gwynn, and William Henry Gwynn; (3) Rebecca Edelen (by license dated Aug. 29, 1807); and (4) Ann Teresa Elder, widow of Ignatius Boone (no date given). [Ref: ZA-344, ZA-345, ZB-95, ZE-84].
GWYNN, Benjamin. Took the Oath of Allegiance before the Hon. Osborn Sprigg in 1778 [Ref: O-306].
GWYNN, Hooper. See "Bennett Gwynn," q.v.
GWYNN, John. See "Bennett Gwynn" q.v.
GWYNN, Mary. See "Thomas Beall" and "Bennett Gwynn," q.v.
GWYNN, Rebecca. See "Bennett Gwynn," q.v.
GWYNN, Susanna. See "Henry Hilleary" and "Bennett Gwynn," q.v.
GWYNN, Thomas. Took the Oath of Allegiance before the Hon. Truman Skinner in 1778 [Ref: O-298]. See "Bennett Gwynn," q.v.
GWYNN, William. See "Bennett Gwynn," q.v.

HAGAN, Charles. Private (substitute), Maryland Line, discharged on Dec. 3, 1781 [Ref: I-10, which listed the name as "Hagin"].
HAGAN, James. Took the Oath of Allegiance (made his "X" mark) before the Hon. Truman Skinner in 1778 [Ref: O-299, which spelled the name "James Hagon"].
HAGAN, Raphael. Private, 1st Maryland Line, who was paid for his services "in cloathing" on Apr. 17, 1779 [Ref: E-351].
HAGAN, Sarah. See "Samuel T. Wilson," q.v.
HAGAN, Thomas. Took the Oath of Allegiance (made his "T" mark) before the Hon. Thomas Clagett in 1778 [Ref: O-266]. The estate of one Thomas Hagan was probated in 1815 [Ref: ZE-84].
HAGARTY, George. Private, 2nd Maryland Line, enlisted May 12, 1778; sergeant, Jan. 1, 1780 [Ref: D-119]. The estate of "George Hagarty (soldier)" was probated on Apr. 4, 1793 [Ref: ZE-84].
HAGARTY, Paul. Private, 2nd Maryland Line, Capt. Patrick Sim's Company, 1776. Private, 1st Maryland Line, enlisted Dec. 10, 1777 and discharged Dec. 27, 1777 [sic]. [Ref: D-8, D-117].
HALKERSTON, John. Second Lieutenant, 1st Independent Maryland Company, Jan. 2, 1776 [Ref: D-20]. This company apparently was composed of Charles and Calvert Countians. The estate of one John Halkerston (or Halkerstone) was probated in Prince George's County on Mar. 18, 1797 [Ref: ZE-84].
HALL, Amelia. See "John Read Magruder," q.v.
HALL, Ann. See "William Murdock Hall," q.v.
HALL, Anne. See "Basil Waring, Sr.," q.v.
HALL, Baruch. See "William Murdock Hall," q.v.
HALL, Benjamin. Major, Middle Battalion, Mar. 10, 1777 through Mar. 20, 1778 (refused another commission). [Ref: M-82, C-532, Q-152]. Justice who administered the Oath of Allegiance in 1778 [Ref: O-276]. He was paid by the Maryland Council "for the hire of his waggon and horses on account of the militia" on Jan. 5, 1778 [Ref: C-454]. See "John Hall," q.v.
HALL, Benjamin, of B. Took the Oath of Allegiance before the Hon. Thomas Boyd in 1778 [Ref: O-262]. This is probably Benjamin Hall, of Benjamin, who died before his father in 1780 [Ref: ZA-411].
HALL, Benjamin, of Francis (1719-1803). Eldest son of Francis Hall and Dorothy Lowe, he married Elinor Murdock in 1757 and had these children: William Murdock Hall (1759-c1792), Henry Lowe Hall (1761-1817), Anne (Hall) Clark, Eleanor (Hall) (Clarke) Magruder, and Catherine (Hall) Bowie [Ref: U-382, ZA-410]. Benjamin Hall was a Delegate to the first Maryland Convention, 1775-1776, Justice of the County Court, 1777-1779, and served in the House of Delegates in 1780 [Ref: A-3, U-70, U-73, U-82, C-273, and U-382, which latter source states that he was "probably born between 1730 and 1735." Yet, it also states he was a "Justice of Prince George's County in 1750-1751." This

year of birth is incorrect since he would have been commissioned a judge while still in his teens. Source ZA-410 states he was born in 1719, which should clarify the matter]. See "Addison Murdock" and "William Murdock Hall," q.v.

HALL, Clement 3rd. Took the Oath of Allegiance before the Hon. Joshua Beall in 1778 [Ref: O-251].

HALL, Eleanor. See "Francis Hall," q.v.

HALL, Elizabeth. See "William Murdock Hall," q.v.

HALL, Francis. Took the Oath of Allegiance before the Hon. Benjamin Hall in 1778 [Ref: O-276]. He was paid by the Maryland Council on Jan. 5, 1778 "for the hire of his cart and horses on account of the militia." [Ref: C-454]. There was a Francis Hall (c1696-1785) who had a son Francis Hall (1732-1798). [Ref: ZA-409, ZE-85]. Francis Hall, Jr. married Eleanor Hall by license dated June 25, 1791 [Ref: ZB-96]. Additional research may be necessary before drawing conclusions. See "Benjamin Hall, of Francis" and "Richard Bennett Hall," q.v.

HALL, Grafton. See "William Murdock Hall," q.v.

HALL, Henrietta. See "Henry Waring" and "John Waring," q.v.

HALL, Henry. See "Benjamin Hall, of Francis" and "John Hall," q.v.

HALL, Jacob. See "William Murdock Hall," q.v.

HALL, James. See "John Smith," q.v.

HALL, John. Took the Oath of Allegiance (made his "X" mark) before the Hon. Thomas Clagett in 1778 [Ref: O-269]. The "signer" was probably either John Hall (son of Henry and Martha Hall) who was born on Nov. 24, 1729, or John Hall (son of Benjamin and Sophia Hall) who was born on Nov. 30, 1732 [Ref: ZC-178].

HALL, John (1741-   ). Took the Oath of Allegiance before the Hon. Christopher Lowndes in 1778 [Ref: O-285, R-83].

HALL, John (Dec. 9, 1758, Anne Arundel County, Maryland - Feb. 8, 1835, Russell County, Kentucky). He lived in Prince George's County at the time of his enlistment and in 1779 moved to Caswell County, North Carolina and also enlisted there. He moved to Patrick County, Kentucky [sic] and then to Wayne County, Kentucky in 1800 and to Russell County in 1831. He applied for a pension (S1210) on Apr. 29, 1833, and died in 1835 [Ref: P-1481]. One John Hall was a private, 2nd Maryland Line, Capt. Alexander Truman's Company, 1782 [Ref: D-440].

HALL, Martha. See "Stephen West" and "William Murdock Hall" and "William Hall" and "John Hall," q.v.

HALL, Nathaniel (1728-1787). Took the Oath of Allegiance before the Hon. Osborn Sprigg in 1778 [Ref: O-306, R-36]. One Nathaniel Hall married Mary Hughes by license dated Dec. 23, 1777 [Ref: ZB-97]. The estate of one Nathaniel Hall was probated on Sep. 25, 1787 [Ref: ZE-86].

HALL, Philip (1735-   ). Took the Oath of Allegiance before the Hon. Osborn Sprigg in 1778 [Ref: O-306, R-53].

HALL, Regnal John Duckett. See "William Murdock Hall," q.v.
HALL, Richard Bennett. Captain, 25th Battalion, Militia, before June 18, 1776 and served through June 10, 1777 (resigned). [Ref: M-82, A-498, B-233]. Took the Oath of Allegiance before the Hon. Benjamin Hall in 1778 [Ref: O-276]. Richard Bennett Hall, son of Francis Hall, was born in 1760 and died in 1802. Although it may be possible, he certainly appears too young to be the captain in 1776 (only aged 16), but he may have been the signer in 1778 (aged 18). The estate of one Richard Bennett Hall was probated on Oct. 11, 1805, and the estate of another Richard Bennett Hall was probated on Jan. 15, 1827 [Ref: ZE-86]. Additional research will be necessary before drawing any conclusions. See Ref: ZA-413 and also "James Mullikin" and "John Rogers," q.v.
HALL, Richard Duckett. See "William Murdock Hall," q.v.
HALL, Sarah. See "Mareen Howard Duvall," q.v.
HALL, Sophia. See "John Hall," q.v.
HALL, Thomas. See "William Murdock Hall," q.v.
HALL, William (1715-1790). Took the Oath of Allegiance before the Hon. Richard Henderson in 1778 [Ref: O-277, R-46]. The estate of one William Hall was probated on Sep. 28, 1790 [Ref: ZE-86]. See "William Murdock Hall," q.v.
HALL, William, of Benjamin. Took the Oath of Allegiance before the Hon. Benjamin Hall in 1778 [Ref: O-274]. One William Hall married Martha Hall by license dated Jan. 13, 1779 [Ref: ZB-97]. The estate of one William Hall, of Benjamin, was probated on Jan. 4, 1792 [Ref: ZE-86].
HALL, William Murdock (Feb. 26, 1759 - Dec., 1791 or Jan., 1792). A son of Benjamin Hall (of Francis) and Elinor Murdock, he married Ann Duckett and had these children: Regnal John Duckett Hall, Grafton Hall, Benjamin Hall, Richard Duckett Hall, William Hall, Baruch Hall, Jacob Hall, Thomas Hall, Martha Hall, Ann Hall, Elizabeth (Hall) Howard, and ---- Godman (daughter who died before her father). [Ref: U-382, ZA-410, ZA-411]. William Murdock Hall took the Oath of Allegiance before the Hon. Benjamin Hall in 1778 [Ref: O-276]. The estate of one "William M. Hall" was probated on Dec. 15, 1800 [Ref: ZE-86].
HALLER, John Jr. Took the Oath of Allegiance before the Hon. Thomas Clagett in 1778 [Ref: O-265].
HALLEY, John. Private, Capt. Hezekiah Wheeler's Company, 11th Militia Battalion, April, 1781 [Ref: R-58, L-19970 (Box 6, folder 21)]. Private, Select Militia, Capt. Hezekiah Wheeler's Company, July 14, 1781 [Ref: S-6636 (Box 31, folder 5)]. There were two men named John Halley and both were aged 37 in 1776 [Ref: R-58, R-62]. The estate of one John Halley was probated in 1800 and the estate of another John Halley was probated in 1811 [Ref: ZE-86]. See "John Hawley," q.v. Additional research may be necessary before drawing conclusions.

HALLRIKALL, Balthezer. Took the Oath of Allegiance before the Hon. Christopher Lowndes in 1778 [Ref: O-282].
HALLRIKALL, Christian. Took the Oath of Allegiance before the Hon. Christopher Lowndes in 1778 [Ref: O-282].
HALLSALL, John. Took the Oath of Allegiance before the Hon. Christopher Lowndes in 1778 [Ref: O-286]. "John Halsal" married Lucy Downes by license dated Feb. 15, 1779 [Ref: ZB-98].
HALLSALL, John Jr. Took the Oath of Allegiance before the Hon. Christopher Lowndes in 1778 [Ref: O-286].
HALLSALL (HALSALL), Ruth. See "James Ferguson," q.v.
HALLSALL (HALSALL), Thomas. Took the Oath of Allegiance before the Hon. William Berry in 1778 [Ref: O-258].
HALLSALL (HALLSELL), Zachariah. Took the Oath of Allegiance before the Hon. Christopher Lowndes in 1778 [Ref: O-284].
HAMBLETON, Samuel. Private, enrolled by Capt. John H. Lowe on July 13, 1776, for continental service, Maryland Line [Ref: D-34].
HAMILTON, Andrew (Mar. 16, 1754 - Sep. 21, 1823). A son of Thomas and Ann Hamilton, he married Jane Burch (1752/3-1824) by license dated Apr. 17, 1783, and had a son Col. Samuel Hamilton (1783/4-1857). They are buried in the Hamilton Family Cemetery near Greenbelt, Maryland [Ref: Y-576, ZB-98, ZC-27, ZE-87]. Took the Oath of Allegiance before the Hon. James Beck in 1778 [Ref: O-255]. There was also an Andrew Hamilton who was aged 60 in 1776 [Ref: R-66], and an "Andrew Hamelton" who was the son of another Andrew Hamilton and was born on Mar. 7, 1763 [Ref: ZC-27]. See "Thomas Hamilton," q.v.
HAMILTON, Eliza. See "Alexius Sansbury," q.v.
HAMILTON, Francis. Took the Oath of Allegiance before the Hon. Truman Skinner in 1778 [Ref: O-299]. Constable, Mount Calvert Hundred, 1777 [Ref: Z-3]. Francis Hamilton married Susan Blanford by license dated Jan. 27, 1785 [Ref: ZB-98]. The estate of one Francis Hamilton was probated in 1819 [Ref: ZE-87].
HAMILTON, George. Took the Oath of Allegiance before the Hon. William Berry in 1778 [Ref: O-257].
HAMILTON, James. Took the Oath of Allegiance before the Hon. Truman Skinner in 1778 [Ref: O-299].
HAMILTON, Jane. See "Andrew Hamilton," q.v.
HAMILTON, John (1745-1779). Took the Oath of Allegiance before the Hon. Benjamin Hall in 1778 [Ref: O-275, R-32]. The estate of one John Hamilton was probated on Oct. 23, 1779 [Ref: ZE-87].
HAMILTON, Mary. See "Thomas Hamilton," q.v.
HAMILTON, Ruth. See "Roger Brook Beall," q.v.
HAMILTON, Samuel. See "Andrew Hamilton," q.v.
HAMILTON, Sarah. See "John Beck," q.v.
HAMILTON, Thomas (1714-1784). Took the Oath of Allegiance before the Hon. James Beck in 1778 [Ref: O-254, R-37]. His age in the 1776 census

was listed as 62, but if it is incorrect this may be the Thomas Hamilton who was born on May 21, 1710, son of Andrew Hamilton and his second wife Mary [Ref: ZC-27]. The estate of one Thomas Hamilton was probated in 1784 [Ref: ZE-87].

HAMILTON, Thomas. Physician who took the Oath of Allegiance before the Hon. Fielder Bowie in 1778 [Ref: O-303, W-4648 (Box 4, folder 15)]. One Thomas Hamilton married Ann Hodgkin by license dated Apr. 17, 1781 [Ref: ZB-98]. The estate of Dr. Thomas Hamilton was probated on Sep. 26, 1787 [Ref: ZE-87].

HAMILTON, William (1734-   ). Took the Oath of Allegiance before the Hon. William Berry in 1778 [Ref: O-259, R-66]. See "Alexander Beall, Jr." and "Osborn Sprigg," q.v.

HAMKINS, John. See "John Hawkins," q.v.

HAMMOND, Nancy. See "John Igleheart," q.v.

HAMMOND, Sarah. See "Thomas Hammond," q.v.

HAMMOND, Thomas (1762/1765-1832). Private, enlisted Apr. 28, 1781, aged 16, for 3 years in continental service; sent to Annapolis; on duty July 13, 1781 [Ref: D-381]. He applied for pension in Athens County, Ohio, on Nov. 10, 1819, aged 57, stating he enlisted in Prince George's County and later married Sarah Boyle on Jan. 28, 1793 in Montgomery County, Maryland. In 1828 they lived in Crawford County, Indiana and in 1831 they lived in Adams County, Illinois. His widow applied for pension (W4224) in Washington County, Ohio on Dec. 27, 1850, aged 76, stating Thomas had died in November, 1832. Sarah Hammond died on July 20, 1852, and although children were mentioned, none were actually named [Ref: P-1501].

HANCOCK, William (1701-   ). Took the Oath of Allegiance before the Hon. Benjamin Hall in 1778 [Ref: O-275, R-51].

HAND, William. Private, Maryland Line, enlisted Dec. 12, 1782 [Ref: D-429]. The estate of one William Hand was probated on May 5, 1794 [Ref: ZE-87].

HANNON, Henry. Private, enrolled by Ensign Horatio Clagett on July 15, 1776, for continental service, Maryland Line [Ref: D-35].

HANSON, Chloe. See "George Lee," q.v.

HANSON, Martha. See "Nathaniel Wilson," q.v.

HANSON, Samuel. Ensign, Middle Battalion, Capt. Clement Wheeler's Company, Nov. 13, 1779 [Ref: M-84, F-13]. One Samuel Hanson married Elizabeth Fendall Marshall by license dated July 29, 1788 and a Samuel Hanson married Sarah Beall by license dated June 9, 1795 [Ref: ZB-98].

HANSON, Thomas. Took the Oath of Allegiance before the Hon. George Lee in 1778 [Ref: O-279]. One "Thomas H. Hanson" married Rebecca Addison by license dated Mar. 21, 1778 [Ref: ZB-99]. The estate of Thomas H. Hanson was probated on Dec. 8, 1810 [Ref: ZE-88].

HARBIN, Abonijah. See "Edward Villars Harbin," q.v.

HARBIN, Allen Cort. See "Edward Villars Harbin," q.v.

HARBIN, Ann. See "Edward Villars Harbin," q.v.
HARBIN, Anthony. See "Edward Villars Harbin," q.v.
HARBIN, Edward. Private, Select Militia, Upper Battalion, June 12, 1781 [Ref: S-6636 (Box 27, folder 82B)].
HARBIN, Edward Villars. Took the Oath of Allegiance before the Hon. William Berry in 1778 [Ref: O-258, which spelled his name "Edward Villers Harben" and R-62, which spelled his name "Edward V. Herbin"]. Second Lieutenant, 25th Battalion, Capt. Josiah Shaw's Company, Sep. 5, 1777. First Lieutenant, Capt. John Weight's Company, May 1, 1778 [Ref: M-84, C-363, E-62, N-33, which sources spelled his name "Edward Vellis Harbin" and "Edward Villar Harbin" and "Edward Vallis Harbin"]. Edward Villars Harbin was born in 1731, son of William (1690-1733) and Mary Harbin, and married Lydia ----. The names of his children are mentioned in his will in North Carolina (date and county not stated) and they either went with him or followed him from Maryland to North Carolina: Reason or Rezin Harbin, Ann Harbin, and Edward Villars Harbin. A daughter Verlinda was born in Maryland on Sep. 23, 1763. The census of 1776 in Prince George's County listed five males between the ages of 4 and 21 and five females between the ages of 1 and 14 in his family. Verlinda Harbin married Allen Cort Harbin, and Reason or Rezin Harbin married Mary McNea [McNew] in 1778. Other sons of Edward Villars Harbin are believed to be James Harbin (who was in Indiana in 1850, born circa 1777 in Maryland), Adonijah Harbin (who was in Surry County, North Carolina in 1790), and Anthony Harbin. An inventory and account of sale of the property of Edward V. Harbin mentions Allen C. Harbin, Rezin Harbin, James Harbin, William Harbin, and Edward V. Harbin [Ref: Information compiled by Mrs. Blanche Taylor, 4519 Herder Street, Port Charlotte, Florida 33948, in 1990]. See "Joshua Harbin," q.v.
HARBIN, Elizabeth. See "Joshua Harbin," q.v.
HARBIN, James. See "Edward Villars Harbin," q.v.
HARBIN, John. See "Joshua Harbin," q.v.
HARBIN, Joshua. On Mar. 27, 1778, he was paid by the Council of Maryland for "the hire of his waggon for the Virginia Troops per certificate allowed by the Committee of Claims." The Council also paid "ten pounds and fifteen shillings for the use of Joshua Harbin per certificate allowed by the Auditor General" on June 10, 1778 [Ref: C-554, E-128]. This or perhaps another Joshua Harbin was born in Maryland (no date given), married Elizabeth ----, served as a private in the Maryland Line, rendered patriotic service, and died in Virginia some time before June 16, 1792 [Ref: X-1304]. He also might be the "Josh. Harbin" who enlisted in the Upper District of Frederick County (now Washington County) in July, 1776 [Ref: D-49]. There was a Joshua Harbin, son of William and Mary Harbin, who was born on Dec. 29, 1726 and married Elizabeth Ray on Mar. 1, 1753 [Ref: ZD-114, ZD-115, which

also spelled the name "Harvin"]. Joshua Harbin appears to have been a brother of "Edward Villars Harbin," q.v. If so, it appears that their brother John Harbin and family migrated to Camden, South Carolina where John died in 1797. Additional research may be necessary before drawing conclusions. See Henry C. Peden, Jr.'s *Marylanders to Carolina* (1994), pp. 74-75.

HARBIN, Mary. See "Joshua Harbin" and "Edward V. Harbin," q.v.

HARBIN, Rezin. Took the Oath of Allegiance before the Hon. Christopher Lowndes in 1778 [Ref: O-287]. Rezin Harbin married Mary MacNew by license dated Nov. 14, 1778 [Ref: ZB-99]. See "Edward Villars Harbin," q.v.

HARBIN, William. See "Joshua Harbin" and "Edward V. Harbin," q.v.

HARDACRE, William. Took the Oath of Allegiance before the Hon. Thomas Gantt, Jr. in 1778 [Ref: O-305, W-4648 (Box 4, folder 15)]. Private (drafted), continental service, Maryland Line, 1781 [Ref: D-382]. Private, Capt. Benjamin Wailes' Militia Company, Lower Battalion; on duty guarding Magruder's Warehouse in the spring of 1782 [Ref: L-19970 (Box 6, folder 21)].

HARDESTY, Alice. See "Lewis Duvall," q.v.

HARDESTY, Elizabeth. See "Robert Hardesty," q.v.

HARDESTY, Frances. See "Lewis Duvall," q.v.

HARDESTY, Robert (Oct. 28, 1727/30? - 1790). Took the Oath of Allegiance before the Hon. Benjamin Hall in 1778 [Ref: O-275]. The 1776 census of Prince George's County listed Robert Hardesty as being aged 49 [Ref: R-47]. Robert married Elizabeth ----, and his estate was probated on May 16, 1790 [Ref: X-1306, ZE-88].

HARDEY, Airy. See "Nathan Scarce," q.v.

HARDEY, Amey. See "George Hardey," q.v.

HARDEY, Ann. See "John Boone" and "Thomas Gordon," q.v.

HARDEY, Anthony (c1745 - 1819). Took the Oath of Allegiance before the Hon. Thomas Clagett in 1778 [Ref: O-268, R-83]. First Lieutenant, Militia, 1778 [Ref: N-36, which listed his name as "Anthr. Hardy"]. He married Lidde Lilly and rendered civil service [Ref: X-1308, which stated he died after 1788, but did not mention being a lieutenant]. The estate of one Anthony Hardey was probated on May 13, 1819 [Ref: ZE-88].

HARDEY, Baptist (July 16, 1753 -   ). Son of Ignatius and Rebecca Hardey [Ref: ZC-28, which spelled the name "Hardy"]. Took the Oath of Allegiance before the Hon. Osborn Sprigg in 1778 [Ref: O-307, R-64, which spelled his name "Babtist Hardey"]. Rendered patriotic service by providing wheat for the military on Sep. 4, 1780 [Ref: Q-314, which spelled the name "Hardy"]. "Baptist Hardey" married Ester Osborn by license dated Apr. 3, 1786 [Ref: ZB-99], but King George's Parish records indicate that "Baptist Hardy" married Ester Osborn on Feb. 19, 1786 [Ref: ZC-28].

HARDEY, Bennedict. Took the Oath of Allegiance before the Hon. Thomas Clagett in 1778 [Ref: O-264].

HARDEY, George (Sep. 6, 1760 - c1805). Son of John and Amey "Hardy" [Ref: ZD-114]. Took the Oath of Allegiance before the Hon. Osborn Sprigg in 1778 [Ref: R-63, O-300, O-308, which latter source listed his name as "George Harday"]. Private, 1st Maryland Line, enlisted on June 5, 1778, and discharged on Apr. 5, 1779 [Ref: D-118]. Private, 1st Maryland Line, who was paid for his services "in cloathing" on Apr. 17, 1779 [Ref: E-351]. George Hardey married Priscilla Jenkins by license dated July 13, 1786 [Ref: X-1309, ZB-99]. See "George Hardey, Sr.," q.v.

HARDEY, George Sr. Took the Oath of Allegiance before the Hon. Thomas Clagett in 1778 [Ref: O-264]. One George Hardey married Lucy Dent on Feb. 11, 1753, in King George's Parish, and had a son George Dent Hardey born Mar. 15, 1762 [Ref: ZC-27, ZC-28]. One "George Hardie" was born on Jan. 2, 1717, son of William, and one "George Hardie" was born on Mar. 7, 1723, son of George, of King George's Parish [Ref: ZC-28]. Additional research will be necessary before drawing conclusions. See "Thomas Hardey," q.v.

HARDEY, Henry Jr. Served on a Grand Jury in 1778 [Ref: Z-52]. The estate of "Henry Hardy" was probated in 1789 and the estate of "Henry Hardey" was probated in 1805 [Ref: ZE-88, ZE-89].

HARDEY, Ignatius (1737-   ). Took the Oath of Allegiance before the Hon. Osborn Sprigg in 1778 [Ref: R-81, O-307, which latter source spelled his name "Ignatious Hardey"]. See "Baptist Hardey" and "John Hardey, of Ignatius," q.v.

HARDEY, James (1752-1792). Private, enrolled in the Flying Camp by Lieut. Benjamin Brooks on July 17, 1776; nativity: Prince George's County; height 5' 10"; has own gun [Ref: D-36, which spelled the name "James Hardie"]. The estate of one James Hardey was probated on Aug. 20, 1792 [Ref: ZE-88].

HARDEY, John. See "George Hardey," q.v.

HARDEY, John Jr. Took the Oath of Allegiance before the Hon. David Craufurd in 1778 [Ref: O-270, which spelled his name "Hardy"].

HARDEY, John, of Ignatius (Apr. 28, 1759 -   ). Son of Ignatius and Rebecca Hardey [Ref: ZC-28]. Took the Oath of Allegiance before the Hon. Fielder Bowie in 1778 [Ref: O-304, W-4648 (Box 4, folder 15)].

HARDEY, Mary. See "Benjamin Ridgeway" and "Thomas Willcoxen," q.v.

HARDEY, Matilda. See "Henry Waring," q.v.

HARDEY, Rebecca. See "Baptist Hardey" and "John Hardey, of Ignatius" and John Darcey," q.v.

HARDEY, Thomas (Aug. 11, 1755 - 1781). Son of George Hardey and Lucy Dent [Ref: ZC-28]. "Thomas Dent Hardey" was a lieutenant in the 1st Maryland Line from July 19, 1777 to July 6, 1778, when he resigned [Ref: D-116]. "Thomas Hardy" married Margaret Wilcoxon by license dated Feb. 9, 1780 [Ref: ZB-100]. The estate of "Thomas Dent Hardey" was probated on Aug. 29, 1781 [Ref: ZE-88].

HARDEY, William. Took the Oath of Allegiance before the Hon. Benjamin Hall in 1778 [Ref: O-275, which spelled his name "Hardy"]. See "George Hardey," q.v.

HARDING, Edward (1723-). Took the Oath of Allegiance before the Hon. William Berry in 1778 [Ref: O-258, R-25, which spelled his name "Hardin" and gave his age as 53 in the 1776 census].

HARE, John. Private, Maryland Line, 1780, and died on May 27, 1781 [Ref: D-539]. The estate of "John Hare (soldier)" was probated on Mar. 7, 1793 [Ref: ZE-89].

HARE, Thomas. Private, 7th Maryland Line, enlisted Apr. 21, 1777 and discharged Apr. 27, 1780 [Ref: D-215]. Took the Oath of Allegiance before the Hon. Richard Henderson in 1778 [Ref: O-278]. The estate of "Thomas Hare (soldier)" was probated on Mar. 7, 1793 [Ref: ZE-89].

HARNESS, Daniel. Private, Northern Detachment, 3rd Maryland Line, Capt. Horatio Clagett's Company, 1783 [Ref: D-501].

HARPER, Sarah. See "Richard Brooke," q.v.

HARRINGTON, Levin. Private, 1st Maryland Line, who was paid for his services "in cloathing" on Apr. 15, 1779 [Ref: E-347]. Private, Northern Detachment, 3rd Maryland Line, Capt. Horatio Clagett's Company, 1783 [Ref: D-501].

HARRINGTON, Richard. Private, 1st Maryland Line, who was paid for his services "in cloathing" on Apr. 15, 1779 [Ref: E-347]. Private, Northern Detachment, 3rd Maryland Line, Capt. Horatio Clagett's Company, 1783 [Ref: D-502].

HARRIS, Ann. See "Lewin Jones," q.v.

HARRIS, Basil (Mar. 27, 1763 - 1800). Son of James and Eady Harris [Ref: ZC-29]. Private, Capt. Hezekiah Wheeler's Company, 11th Militia Battalion, April, 1781 [Ref: L-19970 (Box 6, folder 21), which spelled his name "Basel"]. Private, Select Militia, Capt. Hezekiah Wheeler's Company, July 14, 1781 [Ref: S-6636 (Box 31, folder 5)]. The estate of one Basil Harris was probated on Sep. 9, 1800. "Mrs. Edy Harriss" died in 1799 [Ref: ZE-89].

HARRIS, Eady. See "Basil Harris," q.v.

HARRIS, George. Took the Oath of Allegiance before the Hon. Fielder Bowie in 1778 [Ref: O-303, which spelled his name "Harriss"].

HARRIS, James. Private, Capt. Hezekiah Wheeler's Company, 11th Militia Battalion, April, 1781 [Ref: L-19970 (Box 6, folder 21)]. Took the Oath of Allegiance before the Hon. Fielder Bowie in 1778 [Ref: O-304, W-4648 (Box 4, folder 15)]. See "Basil Harris," q.v.

HARRIS, John Jr. (1726-1805). Took the Oath of Allegiance before the Hon. Thomas Clagett in 1778 [Ref: O-265, R-16]. There was also a "John Harris" who was aged 95 in 1776 [Ref: R-53]. The estate of one John Harris was probated on Mar. 12, 1805 [Ref: ZE-89].

139

HARRIS, Josias (1756-). Corporal, 3rd Maryland Line, in Capt. Horatio Clagett's Company, 1779; enlisted May 26, 1778, for 3 years [Ref: D-295]. Sergeant, Select Militia, Capt. Hezekiah Wheeler's Company, July 14, 1781 [Ref: R-43, S-6636 (Box 31, folder 5)].

HARRIS, Richard. Private, enlisted Jan. 7, 1780, for 3 years or during war, in continental service, Maryland Line [Ref: D-333].

HARRIS, Thomas. Private, Northern Detachment, 3rd Maryland Line, Capt. Horatio Clagett's Company, 1783 [Ref: D-501].

HARRIS, William (1746-). Took the Oath of Allegiance before the Hon. William Lyles, Jr. in 1778 [Ref: O-290, R-42].

HARRIS, William (1755-). Private, enrolled in the Flying Camp by Lieut. William D. Beall on July 22, 1776; nativity: England; height: 5' 7"; black hair, fair complexion [Ref: D-37]. He was involved in recruiting at Bladensburg on Feb. 22, 1780 [Ref: D-332, which spelled his name "Harriss"].

HARRIS, William. Private, enlisted Jan. 27, 1780, for 3 years or during war, in continental service, Maryland Line [Ref: D-333].

HARRIS, William 1st. Private, 2nd Maryland Line, Capt. Alexander Truman's Company, 1782 [Ref: D-439].

HARRISON, Elisha. Took the Oath of Allegiance before the Hon. David Craufurd in 1778 [Ref: O-271]. Surgeon's Mate, 4th Maryland Line, Oct. 15, 1781 [Ref: D-481]. One Elisha Harrison married Sarah Beall by license dated Mar. 25, 1796 [Ref: ZB-101].

HARRISON, Elizabeth. See "Ignatius Brashears," q.v.

HARRISON, Jane Contee. See "William Murdock," q.v.

HARRISON, John. Took the Oath of Allegiance before the Hon. Fielder Bowie in 1778 [Ref: O-303, W-4648 (Box 4, folder 15)]. Justice of the Peace in 1779 [Ref: F-17]. Served on the Board of Patuxent Associators and signed a resolution at Nottingham on Apr. 21, 1781 relative to the defence of the rivers of Potomac and Patuxent and the completion of the fort at Drum Point [Ref: K-1814].

HARRISON, Joseph. Took the Oath of Allegiance before the Hon. David Craufurd in 1778 [Ref: O-272].

HARRISON, Mr. ----. On Feb. 16, 1778, the Maryland Council ordered "that the Commissary of Provisions deliver to Mr. Harrison of Prince George's County 15 bushels of salt for the Continental Army." [Ref: C-501].

HARRISON, Thomas. Private, 2nd Maryland Line, enlisted on Mar. 2, 1776, and discharged (sick in Maryland) on Nov. 1, 1780 [Ref: D-119]. One Thomas Harrison married Mary Stamp by license dated May 30, 1783 [Ref: ZB-102].

HARRISON, Walter H. Took the Oath of Allegiance before the Hon. James Mullikin in 1778 [Ref: O-296].

HARRISON, William (1737, Maryland -   ). Private, enlisted May 30, 1781, for 3 years in continental service, Maryland Line; sent to Annapolis; on duty July 13, 1781 [Ref: D-382].
HARVEY, Alexander. Took the Oath of Allegiance (made his "X" mark) before the Hon. James Mullikin in 1778 [Ref: O-296]. Alexander Harvey married Rebecca McCauley by license dated July 19, 1777 [Ref: ZB-102].
HARVEY, Barbara. See "John Harvey," q.v.
HARVEY, Elinor. See "Henry Harvey," q.v.
HARVEY, Elizabeth. See "George Walls," q.v.
HARVEY, Henry (Oct. 1, 1755 - 1813). Son of Thomas and Elinor Harvey [Ref: ZC-29, which spelled the name "Harvy"]. Took the Oath of Allegiance before the Hon. Osborn Sprigg in 1778 [Ref: O-306, R-15]. Henry Harvey married Sarah Ann McDaniel by license dated Apr. 20, 1791 [Ref: X-1340, ZB-102, ZE-90].
HARVEY, James. Two men with this name (both born in 1746) took the Oath of Allegiance in 1778: one before the Hon. Fielder Bowie and one before the Hon, Osborn Sprigg [Ref: O-304, O-306, R-14, R-15]. One James Harvey was constable in Mount Calvert Hundred in 1778 [Ref: Z-57]. One James Harvey married Ann Selby by license dated Mar. 25, 1796 [Ref: ZB-102]. The estate of one James Harvey was probated by Aug. 14, 1787 (date of inventory) and the estate of another James Harvey was probated on Dec. 13, 1814 [Ref: ZE-90].
HARVEY, John (1752 - died after 1801). Private, Capt. Alexander H. Magruder's Militia Company, Lower Battalion; on duty guarding Magruder's Warehouse in the spring of 1782 [Ref: L-19970 (Box 6, folder 21), R-30]. Private, Select Militia, Capt. Hezekiah Wheeler's Company, July 14, 1781 [Ref: S-6636 (Box 31, folder 5)]. He married Barbara ---- [Ref: X-1340].
HARVEY, Lenny. See "Thomas Burch," q.v.
HARVEY, Newman. Took the Oath of Allegiance before the Hon. Osborn Sprigg in 1778 [Ref: O-308, W-4648 (Box 4, folder 29)]. The estate of Newman Harvey was probated on Feb. 20, 1809 [Ref: ZE-90].
HARVEY, Thomas (1721-   ). Took the Oath of Allegiance before the Hon. Fielder Bowie in 1778 [Ref: O-304, R-15]. See "Henry Harvey," q.v.
HARVEY, William Groom. Took the Oath of Allegiance before the Hon. Fielder Bowie in 1778 [Ref: O-303, W-4648 (Box 4, folder 15)]. Served on a Grand Jury in 1777 [Ref: Z-23]. The estate of "William G. Harvey" was probated on Oct. 13, 1801 [Ref: ZE-90].
HARVIN, Clement. Took the Oath of Allegiance before the Hon. Osborn Sprigg in 1778 [Ref: O-306].
HARWOOD, Benjamin. Second Lieutenant, 25th Battalion, Capt. Hezekiah Magruder's Company, May 1, 1778. Captain, Upper Battalion, June 24, 1780 through June 27, 1781 (resigned). [Ref: M-85, E-62, F-203, H-320, N-34]. Took the Oath of Allegiance before the Hon. Thomas

Williams in 1778 [Ref: O-302]. The estate of one Benjamin Harwood was probated in 1812 [Ref: ZE-90].
HARWOOD, Eleanor. See "John Smith Brookes," q.v.
HARWOOD, Sarah. See "Thomas Harwood," q.v.
HARWOOD, Thomas (Dec. 8, 1726 - May 15, 1791). Son of Thomas and Sarah Harwood [Ref: ZC-179]. Captain in the Horse Troops by Sep. 1, 1781 [Ref: M-85, G-596, H-407]. Thomas Harwood served on the Board of Patuxent Associators and signed a resolution at Nottingham on Apr. 21, 1781, relative to the defence of the rivers of Potomac and Patuxent and the completion of the fort at Drum Point [Ref: K-1814]. He married Rachel Sprigg [Ref: X-1342].
HARWOOD, Thomas Jr. (c1757-   ). "Thomas Harwood, Jr." was also referred to as "Thomas Harwood III" and he was probably born in Prince George's County. He lived alternately in Prince George's and Calvert Counties and his patriotic service was principally in Calvert County [Ref: U-421, U-422]. One Thomas Harwood married Ann Whyte by license dated Oct. 29, 1778, in Prince George's County [Ref: ZB-103].
HASE, William. Took the Oath of Allegiance before the Hon. Fielder Bowie in 1778 [Ref: O-304, which mistakenly listed the name as "---Hale;" yet, the original list at the Maryland State Archives (Box 4, folder 15) clearly shows the name as "William Hase"].
HASWELL, William (1730-   ). Took the Oath of Allegiance before the Hon. William Lyles, Jr. in 1778 [Ref: O-290, R-74, which spelled his name "William Hazwell"].
HATFIELD, Francis (1724-1785). Took the Oath of Allegiance before the Hon. Christopher Lowndes in 1778 [Ref: O-285, R-19]. The estate of Francis Hatfield was probated in May, 1785 [Ref: ZE-91].
HATTON, Basil (Aug. 8, 1760 - 1840). Private, enrolled by Lt. William Duvall, Lower Battalion, on July 18, 1776, for the continental service, Maryland Line [Ref: D-35, which spelled the name "Bassil Hatten"]. He was pensioned in Prince George's County and paid in the District of Columbia in 1831 [Ref: T-50]. He also applied for a pension (S8665) on Apr. 4, 1833 and stated that he was born on Aug. 8, 1760 in Prince George's County and lived there at the time of enlistment. He stated he also enlisted in Fairfax County, Virginia and served in the 3rd Georgia Regiment [Ref: P-1564]. The estate of one Basil Hatton was probated on Aug. 19, 1840 in Prince George's County [Ref: ZE-91].
HATTON, George. Took the Oath of Allegiance before the Hon. Thomas Clagett in 1778 [Ref: O-267]. The estate of one George Hatton was probated on Apr. 10, 1804 [Ref: ZE-91].
HATTON, Henry (Feb. 6, 1755 - 1824). Son of Joseph and Mary Hatton [Ref: ZC-30]. Took the Oath of Allegiance before the Hon. Thomas Clagett in 1778 [Ref: O-267]. The estate of one Henry Hatton was probated on Nov. 15, 1824 [Ref: ZE-91].

HATTON, John. Private, 4th Maryland Line, Oct. 26, 1779; reportedly "deserted" in July, 1780 [Ref: D-124].

HATTON, Joseph (June 3, 1721 - 1792). Took the Oath of Allegiance before the Hon. William Lyles, Jr. in 1778 [Ref: O-289, R-85]. He married Mary ---- [Ref: X-1354]. The estate of Joseph Hatton, Sr. was probated on Aug. 15, 1792 [Ref: ZE-91]. See "Henry Hatton" and "Josias or Josiah Hatton" and "Nathaniel Hatton," q.v.

HATTON, Joseph Jr. Took the Oath of Allegiance before the Hon. Thomas Clagett in 1778 [Ref: O-267]. "Joseph Hatton" married Martha Jones by license dated Oct. 4, 1777 [Ref: ZB-103]. The estate of one Joseph Hatton was probated in 1811 [Ref: ZE-91].

HATTON, Josias or Josiah (July 1, 1757 - Oct. 16, 1798). Son of Joseph and Mary Hatton [Ref: ZC-30, which spelled his name "Josiah Hatton"]. Private, enlisted Jan. 30, 1776, in the Third Company of Regular Maryland Troops under Capt. Barton Lucas [Ref: D-10, which spelled his name "Josiah Hatton"]. "Josias Hatton" is buried in the Hatton Family Cemetery on Route 223 near Piscataway, Maryland [Ref: Y-614]. The estate of "Josias Hatton" was probated on Jan. 9, 1799, and the inventory of the estate of "Josiah Hatton" was filed on Feb. 13, 1799 [Ref: ZE-91].

HATTON, Lucy. See "Nathaniel Hatton," q.v.

HATTON, Mary. See "Joseph Hatton" and "Henry Hatton" and "Josias or Josiah Hatton," q.v.

HATTON, Nathaniel (Mar. 3, 1723 - 1794). Son of Joseph and Lucy Hatton [Ref: ZC-30]. Took the Oath of Allegiance before the Hon. Thomas Clagett in 1778 [Ref: O-267, R-87, which latter source stated he was aged 55 in 1776]. The estate of one Nathaniel Hatton was probated on Nov. 19, 1794 [Ref: ZE-91].

HAVENER (HAVANOR), Dominick (1730-   ). "Dominic Havanor" took the Oath of Allegiance before the Hon. Thomas Clagett in 1778 [Ref: O-268, R-81, which latter source spelled his name "Dominicar Haviner"]. "Dominick Havener" married Eleanor Upton by license dated Jan. 31, 1789 [Ref: ZB-104].

HAWKINS, George Fraser (1741-1785). Son of John Hawkins, Jr. and Susannah Fraser. He married Susannah Trueman Somerville by 1769 and had these children: John Trueman Hawkins, George Fraser Hawkins, Peggy (Hawkins) Hawkins, and Susannah Greenfield Hawkins [Ref: U-423]. County Court Justice, 1769-1773. Took the Oath of Allegiance before the Hon. William Lyles, Jr. in 1778. Served in the House of Delegates, 1781-1783. County Coroner, 1785 [Ref: O-290, R-75, U-86, U-87, U-423, I-163, which also spelled his name "George Frazier Hawkins"]. The estate of "George F. Hawkins" was probated on Sep. 13, 1785 [Ref: ZE-92].

HAWKINS, Henry. Ensign, 3rd Maryland Line, Northern Detachment, Capt. Horatio Clagett's Company, 1783 [Ref: D-501]. One Henry

Hawkins married Jennett Swann by license dated Dec. 26, 1790 [Ref: ZB-104].
HAWKINS, James (1735-   ). Took the Oath of Allegiance before the Hon. Thomas Clagett in 1778 [Ref: O-266, R-86]. First Lieutenant, 11th Battalion, Capt. Hezekiah Wheeler's Company, May 1, 1778 [Ref: M-86, E-78, N-32].
HAWKINS, John. Cornet, Horse Troops, by Sep. 1, 1781 [Ref: M-83, G-596, which mistakenly listed his name as "John Hamkins," and H-407, which listed his name as "John Hawkins, Esq."].
HAWKINS, John T. See "George Fraser Hawkins," q.v.
HAWKINS, Peggy H. See "George Fraser Hawkins," q.v.
HAWKINS, Sarah. See "William Beanes," q.v.
HAWKINS, Susan Anne. See "John Fraser Bowie," q.v.
HAWKINS, Susannah G. See "George Fraser Hawkins," q.v.
HAWKINS, Thomas. Private, Capt. Alexander Truman's Company, who was stationed at Annapolis in 1781 and was reported on "a list of men who have deserted since Mar. 1, 1781." [Ref: L-19970 (Box 7, folder 52)]. The estate of one Thomas Hawkins was probated in 1822 in Prince George's County [Ref: ZE-92].
HAWLEY, Absalom. Took the Oath of Allegiance before the Hon. Christopher Lowndes in 1778 [Ref: O-288].
HAWLEY, John. Took the Oath of Allegiance before the Hon. Christopher Lowndes in 1778 [Ref: O-288].
HAWLEY, William. Took the Oath of Allegiance before the Hon. Christopher Lowndes in 1778 [Ref: O-288].
HAYE, Cephas. See "Cephas Hoye," q.v.
HAYE, Dorsett. See "Dorsett Hoye," q.v.
HAYE, Sabrit. See "Sabrit Hoye," q.v.
HAYE, Thomas. See "Thomas Hoye," q.v.
HAYES, John Hawkins (Feb. 13, 1759 - Sep. 29, 1838). Took the Oath of Allegiance before the Hon. Thomas Clagett in 1778 in Prince George's County [Ref: O-268, which spelled his name "John Hawkins Hayse"]. He applied for a pension in St. Mary's County on Aug. 14, 1832, stating he was born there on Feb. 13, 1759 and lived in Prince George's County at the time of his enlistment in the Maryland Line. After the war he lived for two or three years in Virginia and then returned to St. Mary's County. In 1853 his widow Teresa Hayes applied for a pension (W2544), stating John had died on Sep. 29, 1838. She also received his bounty land (warrant no. 2433-160-55) in 1855 [Ref: P-1580].
HAYES, Thomas. "Thomas Hays" took the Oath of Allegiance before the Hon. William Berry in 1778 [Ref: O-259]. "Thomas Hayes" married Rebecca Padgett by license dated Sep. 9, 1784 [Ref: ZB-105]. The estate of one "Thomas Hays" was probated in 1814 [Ref: ZE-93].
HAYES, Teresa. See "John Hawkins Hayes," q.v.

HAYES, William. "William Hays" took the Oath of Allegiance before the Hon. David Craufurd in 1778 [Ref: O-272]. "William Hayes" married Rachel Alexander by license dated Sep. 5, 1795 [Ref: ZB-106].

HAYS, Eleanor. See "John Kidwell," q.v.

HAYLEY, Caleb. Private, Militia, Capt. Joshua Robert Selby's Company, 1776. On Sep. 10, 1776, he petitioned the Council of Safety, stating while in Annapolis he fell at night when he went with others to relieve the guards, has been sick seven weeks since then and desires payment for his time. His injury has left him "entirely incapable of labouring and as he has no other method of getting a livelihood he is now reduced to a most deplorable condition." Statement was endorsed by his commander who stated "Caleb Haley was under duty out of the 25th Battalion of Amaricka [America] when he received his hurt and moreover I think he is deserving of some assistance." [Ref: M-208, B-402, B-403].

HEAD, John. He applied for a pension (S39680) in Prince George's County, Maryland, on May 30, 1818, aged about 60, stating he had enlisted at Annapolis, Maryland. In 1820 he lived at New Hampton in Hunterdon County, New Jersey, and stated he was aged 65 and had a wife with him (no name was given). By 1825 he was in Northampton County, Pennsylvania, and was still there in 1828 [Ref: P-1585].

HEARN, Nancy. See "Jeremiah Igleheart," q.v.

HEARON, John. Took the Oath of Allegiance before the Hon. Christopher Lowndes in 1778 [Ref: O-285].

HEITMAN, Francis B. See "Alexander Truman," q.v.

HELLEN, Jesse. Captain, Militia, 11th Battalion, May 1, 1778 [Ref: M-86, E-62]. Guarded Magruder's Warehouse in the spring of 1782, by order of Major John H. Beane [Ref: L-19970 (Box 6, folder 21), and N-32, which spelled the name "Hillen"]. Took the Oath of Allegiance before the Hon. Alexander Howard Magruder in 1778 [Ref: O-293, which spelled the name "Hellin"]. Served on a Grand Jury in 1778 [Ref: Z-52]. The estate of "Jessie Hellen" was probated on June 18, 1818 [Ref: ZE-93].

HELLEN, William (c1750-1780). He rendered patriotic service and married Dorcas Johnson [Ref: X-1386].

HENDERSON, Ariana. See "Patrick Sim" and "Richard Henderson," q.v.

HENDERSON, Janet. See "Richard Henderson," q.v.

HENDERSON, Richard (Feb. 5, 1736, Scotland - July, 1802). Third son of Rev. Richard Henderson (Minister of the Parish of Blantyre in the Shire of Lanerk in Scotland) and Janet Cleland, he married Sarah Brice in King George's Parish, Prince George's County, on Nov. 19, 1761 [Ref: ZC-31, Z-1392]. Their children were: Richard Henderson (born Nov. 1, 1762), Sarah Henderson (born May 15, 1764), Janet Henderson (born Sep. 2, 1765), and Ariana Henderson (born Dec. 20, 1766). Richard Henderson was Commanding Officer of the Bladensburgh Company in August, 1775 [Ref: M-86, A-49]. Court Justice, 1777-1778, who

administered the Oath of Allegiance in 1778 [Ref: C-273, Z-90, O-278, R-22]. Justice of the Peace in 1779 [Ref: F-17].
HENDERSON, Sarah. See "Richard Henderson," q.v.
HENNESS, Margaret. See "William Mockbee, Jr.," q.v.
HENNIS, Rebecca. See "John Wightt," q.v.
HENRY, Mary. See "William Lowe," q.v.
HENRY, Sarah. See "Elias Lowe," q.v.
HENRY, Thomas Sr. Took the Oath of Allegiance before the Hon. William Berry in 1778 [Ref: O-258]. One "Thomas Henry" was aged 73 and another "Thomas Henry" was aged 23 in 1776 [Ref: R-72].
HEPBURN, Samuel. First Lieutenant, Middle Battalion, Capt. John Brooks Company, May 1, 1778. Captain, June 24, 1780 [Ref: M-87, E-56, E-63, F-203, N-35]. Rendered patriotic service by providing wheat for the military on Sep. 2, 1780 [Ref: Q-314]. Took the Oath of Allegiance before the Hon. David Craufurd in 1778 [Ref: O-271]. Justice of the Peace in 1779 [Ref: F-17]. The estate of Samuel Hepburn was probated on Mar. 14, 1807 [Ref: ZE-94].
HERRINDON, Elizabeth. See "Vachell Ijams," q.v.
HEWIT, Susan. See "Benjamin Burch," q.v.
HEWIT, William. See "Benjamin Burch," q.v.
HEWITT, James. Took the Oath of Allegiance before the Hon. Christopher Lowndes in 1778 [Ref: O-283]. Private, 2nd Maryland Line, Capt. Murdock's Company, Mar. 15, 1781 [Ref: D-366].
HEWITT, Thomas. Matross in Capt. Marbury's Company of Artillery, 1777 [Ref: D-575]. Bombardier in the Frederick German Artillery, 1782 [Ref: D-581]. The estate of one Thomas Hewitt was probated in Prince George's County in 1797 [Ref: ZE-94].
HEYDER, William. Private, 2nd Maryland Line, Capt. Patrick Sim's Company, 1776 [Ref: D-8].
HICKEY, Charles (1737, Ireland -   ). Private, enlisted Feb. 23, 1781, for 3 years in the continental service, Maryland Line; "Pennsylvania, sent to Annapolis" *[sic]* and on duty July 13, 1781 [Ref: D-381, which spelled his name "Charles Hickie"]. Private, 2nd Maryland Line, 1782 [Ref: D-446].
HICKEY, Francis. Took the Oath of Allegiance before the Hon. Fielder Bowie in 1778 [Ref: O-304, W-4648 (Box 4, folder 15)]. Private, 1st Maryland Line, enlisted May 2, 1778 and discharged Feb. 14, 1779 [Ref: D-118]. On Feb. 24, 1779 he was paid for his services "in cloathing." [Ref: E-308].
HICKEY, Leonard. Private, enrolled by Ensign Alexander Truman on July 7, 1776, for continental service, Maryland Line [Ref: D-38]. See "Thomas Mayhew," q.v.
HICKEY, Thomas. Private, 4th Maryland Line, enlisted Apr. 26, 1778; corporal, Apr. 1, 1779; and reportedly "deserted" on Jan. 2, 1780 [Ref: D-123].

HICKEY, William. Private, 6th Maryland Line, enlisted Dec. 5, 1776, and reportedly "deserted" on Apr. 13, 1777 [Ref: D-282].

HICKINGS, John. Private, Northern Detachment, 3rd Maryland Line, Capt. Horatio Clagett's Company, 1783 [Ref: D-502].

HICKSON, John (1765, Maryland -). Private, enlisted June 5, 1781, for 3 years in continental service, Maryland Line; sent to Annapolis; on furlough July 13, 1781 [Ref: D-382].

HIDE, Benjamin. Private, Capt. Alexander H. Magruder's Militia Company, Lower Battalion; on duty guarding Magruder's Warehouse in the spring of 1782 [Ref: L-19970 (Box 6, folder 21)].

HIDE, George. Private, Capt. Alexander H. Magruder's Militia Company, Lower Battalion; on duty guarding Magruder's Warehouse in the spring of 1782 [Ref: L-19970 (Box 6, folder 21)].

HIGDON, Benjamin (1724-1795). Took the Oath of Allegiance (made his "BH" mark) before the Hon. Thomas Clagett in 1778 [Ref: O-265, R-53]. The estate of one Benjamin Higdon was probated on Feb. 3, 1795 [Ref: ZE-95].

HIGDON, Thomas. Private, 3rd Maryland Line, Capt. Horatio Clagett's Company, 1779 [Ref: D-295].

HIGDON, Truman. Took the Oath of Allegiance before the Hon. Fielder Bowie in 1778 [Ref: O-304, W-4648 (Box 4, folder 15)].

HIGDON, William. Private, 1st Maryland Line, who was paid for his services "in cloathing" on Apr. 17, 1779 [Ref: E-351].

HIGGINS, Eleanor. See "Samuel Higgins" and "Benjamin Duvall," q.v.

HIGGINS, Mary. See "Samuel Duvall," q.v.

HIGGINS, Richard. Took the Oath of Allegiance before the Hon. Thomas Williams in 1778 [Ref: O-302].

HIGGINS, Samuel. Took the Oath of Allegiance before the Hon. James Mullikin in 1778 [Ref: O-296]. He might be the Samuel Higgins who was born in England circa 1752 and died in Maryland in 1785. If so, his wife was Eleanor ----, and he served as a private in the Maryland troops [Ref: X-1417]. The estate of one Samuel Higgins was probated on May 7, 1785 [Ref: ZE-95].

HIGGINS, William (1747-1795). Took the Oath of Allegiance before the Hon. James Beck in 1778 [Ref: R-48, O-255, which spelled his name "Higins"]. The estate of one William Higgins was probated on Feb. 2, 1795 [Ref: ZE-95].

HILL, ----. See "Nicholas Brooke," q.v.

HILL, Abner. Private, 2nd Maryland Line, May 20, 1778; reported to have "died at Fishkill" in 1778 [Ref: D-119].

HILL, Anne T. See "Henry Hill, Jr.," q.v.

HILL, Clement (Jan. 4, 1707 - Feb. 12, 1782). Took the Oath of Allegiance before the Hon. David Craufurd in 1778 [Ref: O-272]. Clement Hill, Sr. married Mary Digges (1715-1756) and had one son, "Clement Hill, Jr.," q.v. [Ref: X-1421, ZA-433].

HILL, Clement Jr. (Nov. 6, 1743 - Feb. 6, 1807). Took the Oath of Allegiance before the Hon. David Craufurd in 1778 [Ref: O-272]. Second Lieutenant, Middle Battalion, Capt. William Berry's Company, May 1, 1778 [Ref: M-87, E-63, N-35, which also referred to him as "Clement Hill 3rd"]. Clement Hill, Jr., only son of Clement Hill, married Eleanor Brent in 1774 [Ref: ZA-433, X-1421, which latter source listed her name as "Eleanor Brant"].

HILL, Clement B. See "Henry Hill, Jr.," q.v.

HILL, Edward. Private, 2nd Maryland Line, May 29, 1778; reported dead on Dec. 2, 1778 [Ref: D-119].

HILL, Henrietta Margaret. See "Benjamin Ogle," q.v.

HILL, Henry. Took the Oath of Allegiance before the Hon. Truman Skinner in 1778 [Ref: O-298]. The estate of one Henry Hill was probated on Apr. 26, 1796 [Ref: ZE-95].

HILL, Henry Jr. (c1750 - Apr. 27, 1822). Lieutenant who served on a General Courts-Martial for the trial of Capt. Richard Bennett Hall, Lieut. Jeremiah Ryley, Lieut. Jonathan Wright, and Lieut. James Mullikin on July 25, 1776, at Upper Marlboro [Ref: A-553, which listed his name without the "Jr."]. Second Lieutenant, Lower Battalion, Capt. Thomas Dent's Company, Aug. 1, 1777. Captain, 11th Battalion, May 1, 1778. Captain, 1st Guard, Lower Battalion; on duty at Nottingham on the Patuxent, Apr. 12, 1781 [Ref: M-87, E-78, C-356, N-32, L-19970 (Box 6, folder 21), X-1422]. Took the Oath of Allegiance before the Hon. Truman Skinner in 1778 [Ref: O-297]. Henry Hill married "Hetta" Brooke [Esther Maxwell Brooke] by license dated Apr. 23, 1781 and died on Apr. 27, 1822 [Ref: ZB-108, ZA-450, which states he died in 1832, but *Index to Probate Records of Prince George's County, 1696-1900* lists an account for Henry Hill in November, 1822]. Hester Hill applied for a pension (W14907) on Oct. 17, 1838 in Washington, DC, aged 78, a resident of Prince George's County, Maryland. She died on Aug. 15, 1842, leaving the following children: Anne T. Hill, Joseph Benedict Hill, Clement B. Hill, and Henrietta J. Kennedy [Ref: P-1634, ZA-450].

HILL, Henry 3rd. Private, 1st Guard, Capt. Henry Hill's Militia Company, Lower Battalion; on duty at Nottingham on the Patuxent, Apr. 12, 1781 [Ref: L-19970, which spelled his name "Henry Hill Thd"]. Private, Select Militia, Capt. Hezekiah Wheeler's Company, July 14, 1781 [Ref: S-6636 (Box 31, folder 5), which listed him as "Henry Hill Junr."].

HILL, Hester. See "Henry Hill, Jr.," q.v.

HILL, James. Private, 2nd Maryland Line, 1778-1780 [Ref: D-119]. The estate of "James Hill (soldier)" was probated on July 24, 1793 [Ref: ZE-95].

HILL, Job. Took the Oath of Allegiance which was recorded on a "return of Capt. Tapley of the brig *Royal*" and filed in court by the Hon. Thomas Gantt, Jr. in 1778 [Ref: O-305, W-4648 (Box 4, folder 15)].

HILL, John, of James. Took the Oath of Allegiance before the Hon. James Beck in 1778 [Ref: O-256]. One "John Hill" was aged 58 in 1776 [Ref: R-28]. The estate of one John Hill was probated on Aug. 23, 1800 [Ref: ZE-95].
HILL, Joseph. Took the Oath of Allegiance (made his "X" mark) before the Hon. Thomas Clagett in 1778 [Ref: O-266].
HILL, Joseph Benedict. See "Henry Hill, Jr.," q.v.
HILL, Philip. Lieutenant, 1st Maryland Line, 1780, and Lieutenant, 3rd Maryland Line, 1781 [Ref: D-356, D-363]. The estate of one Philip Hill was probated on Apr. 14, 1801 [Ref: ZE-96].
HILL, Richard. Private, 2nd Maryland Line; discharged Jan. 10, 1780 [Ref: D-119]. Private, Select Militia, Upper Battalion, June 12, 1781 [Ref: S-6636 (Box 27, folder 82B)]. Private, Militia, 1781; participated in capturing an enemy boat and crew on Apr. 17, 1781 [Ref: M-208].
HILL, Richard. Second Lieutenant, Middle Battalion, Capt. Zachariah Berry's Company, June 24, 1780 [Ref: M-87, F-203]. Took the Oath of Allegiance before the Hon. Christopher Lowndes in 1778 [Ref: O-287].
HILL, Thomas. Took the Oath of Allegiance (made a mark that looked like a "3" that was almost closed at the bottom) before the Hon. Thomas Clagett in 1778 [Ref: O-268].
HILLAND, Mark. Private, 4th Maryland Line, Capt. Bowie's Company; reportedly "deserted" on Apr. 1, 1778 [Ref: D-123].
HILLEARY (HILLARY), Ashburn or Ausburn (Apr. 11, 1759, Prince George's County, Maryland - Feb. 6, 1847, Fayette County, Pennsylvania). He applied for a pension in 1832 in Fayette County, Pennsylvania, stating he was born in Prince George's County and had served in Frederick County under his brother Capt. Edward Hillary *[sic]* in the Maryland Line. He married Eleanore King on May 1, 1802 and at the age of 25 they moved to Fayette County, Pennsylvania and settled in Springhill Township. No children were mentioned. On Apr. 12, 1852, aged 80, "Eleanore Hillary" applied for a widow's pension (W8219) in Fayette County, Pennsylvania [Ref: P-1641].
HILLEARY, Ann. See "Henry Hilleary" and Samuel Wheeler," q.v.
HILLEARY, Cassandra. See "Henry Hilleary, Sr.," q.v.
HILLEARY, Dennis. See "Henry Hilleary, Sr.," q.v.
HILLEARY, Edward. See "Ashburn Hilleary," q.v.
HILLEARY, Eleanor. See "Erasmus Gantt" and "Thomas Gantt" and "Levi Gantt" and "Ashburn Hilleary" and "Henry Hilleary," q.v.
HILLEARY, Elizabeth. See "James Waring," q.v.
HILLEARY, George. See "Henry Hilleary, Sr.," q.v.
HILLEARY, Henry Jr. Private, Militia; participated in capturing an enemy boat and crew on Apr. 17, 1781 [Ref: M-208]. Private, Select Militia, Upper Battalion, June 12, 1781 [Ref: S-6636 (Box 27, folder 82B), which spelled his name "Henry Hillery Junr."].

HILLEARY, Henry Sr. (Feb. 15, 1726/7 - 1783). Youngest son of Thomas and Eleanor Hilleary, Jr., he married Cassandra Magruder in 1751 and had these children: Walter Hilleary, John Hilleary, Nathan Hilleary, Dennis Hilleary and George Hilleary (twins), Sarah (Hilleary) Wheeler, Susanna (Hilleary) Gwynn and Eleanor (Hilleary) Woodward (twins), Cassandra (Hilleary) Beall, Henry Hilleary, Rebecca (Hilleary) Belt, Ann (Hilleary) Wheeler, and Elizabeth (Hilleary) Waring [Ref: X-1427, ZA-460, ZA-461, ZC-179]. Henry took the Oath of Allegiance before the Hon. Thomas Williams in 1778 [Ref: O-302]. He was commissioned a first lieutenant in the Maryland Line on Apr. 21, 1779 [Ref: E-55, ZA-461].

HILLEARY, John (1741 - Dec. 27, 1782). Took the Oath of Allegiance before the Hon. Osborn Sprigg in 1778 [Ref: O-306]. Private, 2nd Maryland Line, Capt. Alexander Truman's Company, 1782 [Ref: D-440, which spelled his name "Hillary"]. John Hilleary married Mary ---- [Ref: X-1427]. See "Henry Hilleary, Sr.," q.v.

HILLEARY, Mary. See "John Hilleary," q.v.
HILLEARY, Nathan. See "Henry Hilleary, Sr.," q.v.
HILLEARY, Rebecca. See "Henry Hilleary, Sr.," q.v.
HILLEARY, Rignal (c1750 - Aug. 11, 1783). Ensign, Maryland Line; prisoner of war until exchanged Oct. 25, 1780. Lieutenant, 3rd Maryland Line, 1782 [Ref: X-1427, D-450, D-616, which latter source listed his name as "Reg. Hillery"]. Rignal died in service and his widow (no name was given) received a pension equal to his half pay according to an "official letter" (paper torn with the signature missing) dated June 25, 1790, at Annapolis [Ref: D-628, which listed his name as "Rignal Hillary"]. "Affidavit of Joseph Cross, of Prince George's County, Maryland, dated June 14, 1830, stated that Rignal Hillery died in 1783 at Annapolis on his way home after the Army of the South was destroyed. Elizabeth Magruder, a daughter, signed power of attorney to Rignal Magruder in Washington, DC, but there was no date on the document and her place of residence was not shown." [Ref: P-1641]. The estate of Rignal Hilleary was probated in 1786 [Ref: ZE-96].

HILLEARY, Sarah. See "Henry Hilleary, Sr.," q.v.
HILLEARY, Susanna. See "Bennett Gwynn," q.v.
HILLEARY, Tilghman. Took the Oath of Allegiance before the Hon. Thomas Williams in 1778 [Ref: O-302]. "Tilghman Hilliary" married Ann Wheeler by license dated Jan. 9, 1782 [Ref: ZB-110]. The estate of one Tilghman Hilleary was probated in 1835 [Ref: ZE-97].

HILLEARY, Walter (1752-1821/3). Eldest son of Henry Hilleary and Cassandra Magruder, he married Elizabeth Magruder before July 23, 1794 [Ref: ZA-416]. Took the Oath of Allegiance before the Hon. Thomas Williams in 1778 [Ref: O-302]. Walter and wife Elizabeth (1752-1820) are buried in the Hilleary Cemetery at 3800 Lottsford Road near the Catholic Rest Home [Ref: Y-578, Y-612, which states he died in

1821, while Reference ZA-461 states he died in 1824]. The estate of Walter Hilleary was probated on Dec. 16, 1823 [Ref: ZE-97].
HILLEARY, William. Took the Oath of Allegiance before the Hon. David Craufurd in 1778 [Ref: O-272].
HILLEN, Jesse. See "Jesse Hellen," q.v.
HILTON, Andrew. See "Truman Hilton," q.v.
HILTON, James. See "Truman Hilton," q.v.
HILTON, Judith. See "Truman Hilton," q.v.
HILTON, Moneky. See "Truman Hilton," q.v.
HILTON, Samuel. Private, Smallwood's Regiment, Maryland Line, 1777, and died on Jan. 10, 1778 [Ref: D-121]. The estate of Samuel Hilton was probated by Dec. 5, 1778 (date of inventory). [Ref: ZE-97].
HILTON, Truman. "Truman Hilton" was a private in the 1st Maryland Line, enlisted Mar. 6, 1776 [Ref: D-7]. One "Trueman Hilton" was baptized on Feb. 4, 1753, son of Andrew and Judith Hilton, and another "Trueman Hilton" was born on Mar. 7, 1758, son of James and Moneky [Monica] Hilton [Ref: ZC-31].
HINDS, James. Private, enrolled by Lt. John M. Burgess, Lower Battalion, on July 20, 1776, for continental service, Maryland Line [Ref: D-35].
HINES, Elizabeth. See "John Peirce," q.v.
HINES, Samuel. See "Basil Wright," q.v.
HINNESS, George. See "George Inness," q.v.
HINNESS, John. Private, 2nd Maryland Line, from July 28, 1777 until Aug. 16, 1780, when he was taken prisoner (at the Battle of Camden). [Ref: D-126]. "John Hinness" took the Oath of Allegiance before the Hon. Osborn Sprigg in 1778 [Ref: O-308, which listed the name with uncertainty as "Hinness [Henness, Inness?]," but the original list at the Maryland State Archives (Box 4, folder 29), listed the name as "Hinness"].
HINSON, Christopher. Corporal, Northern Detachment, 3rd Maryland Line, Capt. Horatio Clagett's Company, 1783 [Ref: D-501].
HINTER, Joseph. Took the Oath of Allegiance before the Hon. Thomas Williams in 1778 [Ref: O-302].
HINTHS, Edward. Private, 2nd Maryland Line, Capt. Murdock's Company, Mar. 15, 1781 [Ref: D-366].
HINTON, Charles. Took the Oath of Allegiance (made his "X" mark) before the Hon. James Beck in 1778 [Ref: O-253].
HINTON, John (Nov. 27, 1730 - 1787). Took the Oath of Allegiance (made his "I" mark with an equidistant horizontal line through the middle) before the Hon. James Beck in 1778 [Ref: O-253, ZC-180]. The estate of one John Hinton was probated on Mar. 31, 1787 [Ref: ZE-97].
HINTON, John Jr. Took the Oath of Allegiance before the Hon. James Beck in 1778 [Ref: O-254]. There was one John Hinton who served in

Capt. Richard Smith's Company, Flying Camp (now Montgomery County) in October, 1776 [Ref: D-648].
HINTON, Mary. See "John Spires," q.v.
HINTON, Rachel. See "James Ball," q.v.
HINTON, Sarah. See "John Taylor," q.v.
HINTON, Thomas (1730-   ). Took the Oath of Allegiance before the Hon. Benjamin Hall in 1778 [Ref: O-275, R-37].
HITCH, Christopher (c1736 - died before July 22, 1805, Virginia). Took the Oath of Allegiance before the Hon. David Craufurd in 1778 [Ref: O-270]. He married "Susannah/Rebecca" *[sic]*. [Ref: X-1436].
HOBBS, Austin. Took the Oath of Allegiance before the Hon. David Craufurd in 1778 [Ref: O-272].
HOBBS, John (c1760, Maryland - 1808, New York). Took the Oath of Allegiance before the Hon. Osborn Sprigg in 1778 [Ref: O-306]. He married Charlotte ---- [Ref: X-1442].
HOBKIRK, William. Private, Capt. Alexander H. Magruder's Militia Company, Lower Battalion; on duty guarding Magruder's Warehouse in the spring of 1782 [Ref: L-19970 (Box 6, folder 21)]. Took the Oath of Allegiance before the Hon. James Beck in 1778 [Ref: O-253].
HODGE, James. See "James Hodges, Jr.," q.v.
HODGE, Lucy. See "Dennis Osborn," q.v.
HODGE, Nathan. Took the Oath of Allegiance before the Hon. Thomas Williams in 1778 [Ref: O-302]. The estate of one Nathan Hodge was probated in 1785 [Ref: ZE-97].
HODGES, Charity. See "Charles Ramsey Hodges," q.v.
HODGES, Charles Ramsey (Feb. 18, 1704 - 1794). Son of Thomas and Charity Hodges [Ref: ZC-180]. Took the Oath of Allegiance before the Hon. James Mullikin in 1778 [Ref: O-295]. The estate of one "Charles R. Hodges" was probated in 1794 [Ref: ZE-97].
HODGES, James Jr. "James Hodges, Jr." took the Oath of Allegiance before the Hon. David Craufurd in 1778 [Ref: O-271]. "James Hodge" married Martha Brashears by license dated Jan. 22, 1790 [Ref: ZB-110]. The estate of one "James Hodges" was probated in 1803 [Ref: ZE-97].
HODGES, Jemima. See "Thomas Ramsey Hodges," q.v.
HODGES, John Ramsey. Took the Oath of Allegiance before the Hon. Benjamin Hall in 1778 [Ref: O-276]. The estate of one "John Hodges" was probated by Feb. 10, 1809 [Ref: ZE-98].
HODGES, Joseph Ramsey. Took the Oath of Allegiance before the Hon. James Mullikin in 1778 [Ref: O-296]. The estate of one "Joseph R. Hodges" was probated on Jan. 28, 1809 [Ref: ZE-98].
HODGES, Nathan. See "Nathan Hodge," q.v.
HODGES, Sarah. See "Thomas Belt," q.v.
HODGES, Thomas. See "Charles Ramsey Hodges," q.v.
HODGES, Thomas Ramsey (1737-1807). Took the Oath of Allegiance before the Hon. David Craufurd in 1778 [Ref: O-270]. He married

Jemima ---- [Ref: X-1447]. "Thomas Ramsey Hodges" married Deborah Berry by license dated Dec. 30, 1797. "Thomas Ramsey Hodges, Jr." married Sarah Magruder Clagett by license dated Mar. 14, 1805 [Ref: ZB-111]. The estate of one "Thomas R. Hodges" was probated on Feb. 6, 1807, and the estate of another "Thomas R. Hodges" was probated on Mar. 20, 1821 [Ref: ZE-98].

HODGKIN, Ann. See "Thomas Hamilton," q.v.

HODGKIN, George. Took the Oath of Allegiance before the Hon. George Lee in 1778 [Ref: O-279, which spelled the name "Hodgkins"].

HODGKIN, John Allen. Took the Oath of Allegiance before the Hon. George Lee in 1778 [Ref: O-279, which spelled the name "Hodgkins"]. The estate of "John A. Hodgkin" was probated on Oct. 28, 1785 [Ref: ZE-98, which also listed the name as "John Allen Hodgkins" in 1789].

HODGKIN, Ralph. Took the Oath of Allegiance before the Hon. George Lee in 1778 [Ref: O-279, which spelled the name "Hodgkins"].

HODGKIN, Theodore. Private, 2nd Guard, Capt. Henry Hill's Militia Company, Lower Battalion; on duty at Nottingham on the Patuxent, Apr. 12, 1781 [Ref: L-19970 (Box 6, folder 21), which spelled the name "Hogkins"]. Theodore Hodgkin married Mary J. Curcaurd by license dated Apr. 9, 1787 [Ref: ZB-111].

HODGKIN, Thomas. Took the Oath of Allegiance before the Hon. Fielder Bowie in 1778 [Ref: O-304, which had spelled the name "Hodgken," but the original list at the Maryland State Archives (Box 4, folder 15) shows the name as "Hodgkin"].

HODGKIN, Thomas, of Philip. Took the Oath of Allegiance before the Hon. Fielder Bowie in 1778 [Ref: O-304 (which spelled the name "Hodgken"), but the original list at the Maryland State Archives (Box 4, folder 15) shows the name as "Thomas Hodgkin, of Philip"].

HOGAN, Edmond. Took the Oath of Allegiance before the Hon. Christopher Lowndes in 1778 [Ref: O-285].

HOGGIN, John (1756-   ). Private, enrolled by Capt. John H. Lowe on July 13, 1776, for continental service, Maryland Line [Ref: R-10, D-35, which spelled the name "Hoggins"].

HOGGIN, Peter (1726-   ). Took the Oath of Allegiance before the Hon. Thomas Clagett in 1778 [Ref: O-266, R-10].

HOLLAND, Jacob. Private, 2nd Maryland Line, Capt. Patrick Sim's Company, 1776 [Ref: D-8]. There was also a Jacob Holland who was born in 1763 in Maryland, married Sarah Miller, served as a private in the South Carolina troops, and died in Alabama in 1852 [Ref: X-1459]. See Revolutionary War pension S10866 [Ref: P-1679]. Additional research may be necessry before drawing conclusions.

HOLLAND, John. Took the Oath of Allegiance before the Hon. David Craufurd in 1778 [Ref: O-272].

HOLLAND, William. Private, Northern Detachment, 3rd Maryland Line, Capt. Horatio Clagett's Company, 1783 [Ref: D-502]. There were three men named William Holland who served in Maryland: one was born in 1763 and died in 1839 in Tennessee, another was born circa 1760-1762 and died in 1838 in Maryland, and another was born in 1757 and died in 1822 in South Carolina [Ref: X-1459]. Additional research may be necessary before drawing conclusions.

HOLLEY, Benjamin. See "Francis Holley," q.v.

HOLLEY, Francis (c1755, Maryland - May 7, 1807, Alabama). Private, Maryland Line. Martha Holley Thompson applied for pension (R10549) in Morgan County, Alabama on Dec. 15, 1842, aged 78, stating she married first to Francis Holley on Feb. 2, 1780 on the Noley Chuckey River in North Carolina. He served in the Maryland Line initially, moved to North Carolina and then to Georgia where he enlisted again. Francis died on May 7, 1807, leaving these children: Rebeckah Holley (born May 20, 1781), Mary Holley (born May 8, 1783), James Holley (born June 24, 1785), Shirell Holley (born Nov. 4, 1787), John Holley (born Feb. 8, 1790), Benjamin Holley (born Feb. 27, 1792), Patsy Holley (born Mar. 8, 1794), and Sarah Holley (born Aug. 13, 1796). Martha married second to "Electious Thompson," q.v., who was aged 78 on Jan. 7, 1826 and died on Dec. 30, 1840. Shirell Holley, son of Francis, filed an affidavit in 1842 in Alabama [Ref: P-1681]. Another source states that Francis Holley married Martha Sherrell, served as a soldier and spy in North Carolina, and died July 5, 1807 [Ref: X-1460].

HOLLEY, James. See "Francis Holley," q.v.

HOLLEY, John. See "Francis Holley," q.v.

HOLLEY, Martha. See "Electious Thompson" and "Francis Holley," q.v.

HOLLEY, Mary. See "Thomas Long" and Francis Holley," q.v.

HOLLEY, Patsy. See "Francis Holley," q.v.

HOLLEY, Rebeckah. See "Francis Holley," q.v.

HOLLEY, Sarah. See "Francis Holley," q.v.

HOLLEY, Shirell. See "Francis Holley," q.v.

HOLLEY, Thomas. Private, Select Militia, Upper Battalion, June 12, 1781 [Ref: S-6636 (Box 27, folder 82B)]. Private, Militia, 1781; participated in capturing an enemy boat and crew on Apr. 17, 1781 [Ref: M-208, which spelled the name "Thomas Holly"].

HOLLYDAY, Ann. See "Walter Brooke Cox," q.v.

HOLLYDAY, Clement. First Lieutenant and Paymaster, 5th Maryland Line, from Dec. 10, 1776 to Feb. 25, 1779 (when he resigned). He appears to have been from the Upper District of Frederick County [Ref: D-48, D-49, D-212]. One Clement Hollyday married Hedwick Priggs by license dated Dec. 18, 1784, in Prince George's County [Ref: ZB-112]. The estate of one Clement Hollyday was probated in November, 1825, in Prince George's County [Ref: ZE-99].

HOLLYDAY, John. Private, 2nd Maryland Line, Capt. Alexander Truman's Company, 1782 [Ref: D-440, which spelled the name "Holliday"].

HOLLYDAY, Leonard. Physician who served on the Board of Patuxent Associators and signed a resolution at Nottingham on Apr. 21, 1781 relative to the defence of the rivers of Potomac and Patuxent and the completion of the fort at Drum Point [Ref: K-1814]. Took the Oath of Allegiance before the Hon. Fielder Bowie in 1778 [Ref: O-303, W-4648 (Box 4, folder 15)]. The estate of one Leonatd Hollyday was probated on Dec. 3, 1793 [Ref: ZE-99].

HOLLYDAY, Leonard Jr. Took the Oath of Allegiance before the Hon. Fielder Bowie in 1778 [Ref: O-303, W-4648 (Box 4, folder 15)]. Served on the Board of Patuxent Associators and signed a resolution at Nottingham on Apr. 21, 1781 relative to the defence of the rivers of Potomac and Patuxent and the completion of the fort at Drum Point [Ref: K-1814].

HOLMES (HOMS), Henry. Private, 3rd Maryland Line, enlisted Mar. 7, 1778. Private, Capt. Horatio Clagett's Company, December, 1779 [Ref: D-296].

HOLMES, Ruth (Lewis). See "James Lucas," q.v.

HOLMES, William. First Lieutenant, 25th Battalion, Capt. Josiah Shaw's Company, Sep. 5, 1777 through Dec. 17, 1777, or Jan. 13, 1778, when he resigned [Ref: M-88, B-337, C-363].

HOLWECK, Helen Summers. See "John Wheat," q.v.

HOOFMAN, John. Private, 9th Company of Light Infantry, enlisted Jan. 26, 1776 [Ref: D-19]. He married Mary Scott by license dated Apr. 24, 1781 [Ref: ZB-112].

HOOK, Mary. See "Stephen Riley," q.v.

HOOKER, Priscilla. See "George Cole," q.v.

HOOKER, Robert. Private, 2nd Guard, Capt. Henry Hill's Militia Company, Lower Battalion; on duty at Nottingham on the Patuxent, Apr. 12, 1781 [Ref: L-19970 (Box 6, folder 21)].

HOOPER, John. Took the Oath of Allegiance before the Hon. Fielder Bowie in 1778 [Ref: O-304, W-4648 (Box 4, folder 15)]. One John Hooper married Elizabeth Dove by license dated June 6, 1778, a John Hooper married Mary Ann Dove by license dated Feb. 20, 1784, and a John Hooper married Elizabeth Brown by license dated July 7, 1788 [Ref: ZB-112].

HOOPER, Jonah. Private, 2nd Guard, Capt. Henry Hill's Militia Company, Lower Battalion; on duty at Nottingham on the Patuxent, Apr. 12, 1781 [Ref: L-19970 (Box 6, folder 21)].

HOOPER, Jonas. Took the Oath of Allegiance before the Hon. Fielder Bowie in 1778 [Ref: O-303, which mistakenly listed the name "Jonas Hooker;" yet, the original list at the Maryland State Archives (Box 4, folder 15) clearly shows the name as "Jonas Hooper"].

HOOPER, Thomas. Private, Capt. Alexander H. Magruder's Militia Company, Lower Battalion; on duty guarding Magruder's Warehouse in the spring of 1782 [Ref: L-19970 (Box 6, folder 21)]. One Thomas

155

Hooper married Elizabeth Bedder [Beddo] by license dated Aug. 18, 1784 [Ref: ZB-112].

HOPE, Ralph. Private, 4th Maryland Line, 1782-1783 [Ref: D-458, D-486]. The estate of one Ralph Hope was probated on Apr. 12, 1794 [Ref: ZE-100].

HOPKINS, Ann. See "Richard Tarman, Jr.," q.v.

HOPKINS, Francis. Private, 3rd Maryland Line, Capt. Horatio Clagett's Company, 1779 [Ref: D-295]. One Francis Hopkins married Mary Sansbury by license dated Jan. 29, 1786 [Ref: ZB-112].

HOPKINS, Philip. Took the Oath of Allegiance (made his mark that looked like a "P" laying on it side) before the Hon. Truman Skinner in 1778 [Ref: O-298]. One Philip Hopkins married Margaret Fowler by license dated June 6, 1794, a Philip Hopkins married Susanna Ryon by license dated Aug. 22, 1798, and a Philip Hopkins married Rebecca Weeden by license dated Nov. 3, 1807 [Ref: ZB-112, ZB-113].

HOPKINS, Richard. Took the Oath of Allegiance before the Hon. Osborn Sprigg in 1778 [Ref: O-308, W-4648 (Box 4, folder 29)].

HOPPER, Joseph. Private, enrolled by Lt. William Duvall, Lower Battalion, on July 18, 1776, for continental service, Maryland Line [Ref: D-35, which listed his name as "Joseph Hoppes"].

HOPPER, Robert. Took the Oath of Allegiance before the Hon. James Beck in 1778 [Ref: O-255].

HORNER, John. Took the Oath of Allegiance before the Hon. Christopher Lowndes in 1778 [Ref: O-286].

HORSEY, Elizabeth. See "Thomas Sim Lee," q.v.

HORSON, Thomas. Fifer, 2nd Maryland Line, Capt. Patrick Sim's Company, 1776 [Ref: D-7].

HOSKINS, John. Private, Smallwood's Regiment, Maryland Line, enlisted Apr. 25, 1778, and reported missing on Aug. 16, 1780 (at the Battle of Camden). [Ref: D-121]. The estate of one "John Allen Hoskins" was probated on Oct. 10, 1790 [Ref: ZE-100].

HOSKINS, Randall. Private, 1st Maryland Line, who was paid for his services "in cloathing" on Apr. 17, 1779 [Ref: E-351].

HOSKINS, Zepha. Private, Smallwood's Regiment, Maryland Line, enlisted May 30, 1778 and discharged Apr. 14, 1779 [Ref: D-121].

HOSKINSON, George. Took the Oath of Allegiance before the Hon. Richard Henderson in 1778 [Ref: O-277]. "George Hoskins" was aged 43 in 1776 [Ref: R-50].

HOSPER, Thomas. Took the Oath of Allegiance before the Hon. Osborn Sprigg in 1778 [Ref: O-306].

HOWARD, Elizabeth. See "Alexander Howard Magruder" and "Fielder Bowie" and "William Murdock Hall," q.v.

HOWARD, Ignatious. Private, enrolled by Lt. William Duvall, Lower Battalion, on July 18, 1776, for continental service, Maryland Line [Ref: D-35].

HOWARD, Joseph. Private, 1st Maryland Line, 1777-1780 [Ref: D-116]. The estate of "Joseph Howard (soldier)" was probated on Apr. 17, 1793 [Ref: ZE-100].
HOWARD, William Stevens. See "Alexander Howard Magruder," q.v.
HOWE, David (c1763-   ). Private, Maryland Line, enlisted in April, 1779, for 3 years, Capt. Nathaniel Magrudy's [Magruder's] Company, and was present at Yorktown when Cornwallis surrendered in 1781. He reenlisted in the 4th Maryland Regiment on Feb. 23, 1782, for 3 years, served under Capt. David Luckett, marched to Pittsburgh, Pennsylvania, and was discharged there in 1785 *[sic]*. Applied for and received pension S7041 on Mar. 1, 1834, aged 70, at Deer Township, Allegheny County, Pennsylvania. His service was verified by fellow soldiers John Clevidence and John Bell who were also in Allegheny County, Pennsylvania in 1834 [Ref: D-417, V-1947 (Volume 35, No. 2, p. 63)]. See "John Cleverdence," q.v.
HOWE, Walter. Private, 1st Maryland Line, enlisted Feb. 18, 1777 and discharged Jan. 11, 1780 [Ref: ZE-116]. The estate of one Walter Howe was probated on Mar. 31, 1794 [Ref: ZE-100].
HOWELL, John. Took the Oath of Allegiance before the Hon. Osborn Sprigg in 1778 [Ref: O-306].
HOWELL, Mary. See "Alexander Truman," q.v.
HOWERTON, Sarah. See "John Owens," q.v.
HOWN, Henry. Took the Oath of Allegiance before the Hon. Fielder Bowie in 1778 [Ref: O-304, W-4648 (Box 4, folder 15)].
HOWN, Henry Jr. Took the Oath of Allegiance which was recorded on a "return of Capt. Tapley of the brig *Royal*" and filed in court by the Hon. Thomas Gantt, Jr. in 1778 [Ref: O-305, W-4648 (Box 4, folder 15)].
HOXTON, Julia. See "Theodore Middleton," q.v.
HOXTON, Walter. Took the Oath of Allegiance before the Hon. Alexander Howard Magruder in 1778 [Ref: O-293]. The estate of Walter Hoxton was probated on May 28, 1788 [Ref: ZE-101].
HOXTON, Walter Hyde. Took the Oath of Allegiance before the Hon. Alexander Howard Magruder in 1778 [Ref: O-293]. Sergeant in Capt. Benjamin Wailes' Militia Company, Lower Battalion; on duty guarding Magruder's Warehouse in the spring of 1782 [Ref: L-19970 (Box 6, folder 21)]. The estate of Walter H. Hoxton was probated by Apr. 12, 1785 (date of inventory). [Ref: ZE-101].
HOYE, Cephas. Private, 7th Maryland Line, enlisted Jan. 24, 1776 and "on attachment duty at the magazine." He enlisted again in the 1st Maryland Line on Dec. 10, 1776, but "never joined." [Ref: D-16, D-117]. Took the Oath of Allegiance before the Hon. Fielder Bowie in 1778 [Ref: O-303, which mistakenly listed his name as "Haye;" the original list at the Maryland State Archives (Box 4, folder 15) shows the name as "Hoye"]. First Sergeant, 2nd Guard, Capt. Henry Hill's Militia Company, Lower Battalion; on duty at Nottingham on the Patuxent, Apr. 12, 1781

[Ref: L-19970 (Box 6, folder 21), which spelled the name "Sephris Hoy"]. One "Cephas Hoye" married Sarah Collings by license dated Dec. 27, 1784, and one "Cephus Hoye" married Elizabeth Ryon by license dated Sep. 9, 1786 [Ref: ZB-114]. The estate of Cephas Hoye was probated on May 3, 1791 [Ref: ZE-101, which source also listed him as "Cephlias Hoye"].

HOYE, Dorsett. Took the Oath of Allegiance before the Hon. Fielder Bowie in 1778 [Ref: O-304, which mistakenly listed his name as "Dorsett Haye;" yet, the original list at the Maryland State Archives (Box 4, folder 15) shows the name as "Hoye"]. The estate of Dorsett Hoye was probated on Feb. 3, 1795 [Ref: ZE-101].

HOYE, Sabrit. Took the Oath of Allegiance before the Hon. Fielder Bowie in 1778 [Ref: O-303, which mistakenly spelled his name "Haye." The original list at the Maryland State Archives (Box 4, folder 15) shows the name as "Hoye"].

HOYE, Thomas (1760-1807). Ensign, Militia, Mar. 16, 1776 [Ref: M-86, which misspelled his name "Hoge," and Ref: A-246 and A-253, which misspelled his name "Haye"]. Second Lieutenant, 11th Battalion, Capt. Robert Bowie's Company, May 1, 1778 [Ref: M-88, E-62, which misspelled his name "Hoge"]. Second Lieutenant, 11th Battalion, Capt. John Beanes' Company, May 24, 1779 [Ref: N-33, M-90, E-414, which spelled his name "Hoye"]. Served under Capt. William Beatty at Camden, South Carolina, in April, 1781 [Ref: Q-386, which spelled his name "Hoy"]. Took the Oath of Allegiance before the Hon. Fielder Bowie in 1778 [Ref: O-303, which mistakenly spelled his name "Haye. The original list at the Maryland State Archives (Box 4, folder 15) shows the name as "Hoye"]. Constable, Mattapony Hundred, 1778 [Ref: Z-30]. Thomas Hoye married Agnes Scott by license dated Apr. 22, 1786 [Ref: ZB-114, X-1513]. The estate of Thomas Hoye was probated on Apr. 28, 1807 [Ref: ZE-101].

HUGAR, William (1743-   ). Took the Oath of Allegiance before the Hon. Truman Skinner in 1778 [Ref: R-39, O-299, which latter source spelled the name "William Huger"]. Private, 2nd Guard, Capt. Henry Hill's Militia Company, Lower Battalion; on duty at Nottingham on the Patuxent, Apr. 12, 1781 [Ref: L-19970 (Box 6, folder 21)].

HUGGINS, Samuel. Private, 6th Maryland Line; sick in the Brick House Hospital at Reading, Pennsylvania, Nov. 17, 1777 [Ref: D-618]. The estate of one Samuel Huggins was probated by Apr. 17, 1790 (date of account) in Prince George's County [Ref: ZE-101].

HUGHES, Benjamin. See "Ignatius Brashears," q.v.

HUGHES, John. Private, enlisted 1780 [Mar. 15?] for the duration of the war, in continental service, Maryland Line [Ref: D-333]. The estate of one John Hughes was probated by May 15, 1809 (date of account). [Ref: ZE-101].

HUGHES, Joseph (1726-). Took the Oath of Allegiance before the Hon. William Berry in 1778 [Ref: O-258, R-46].
HUGHES, Mary. See "Nathaniel Hall," q.v.
HUGHES, Samuel. Private, 3rd Maryland Line, Capt. Horatio Clagett's Company, 1779 [Ref: D-295].
HUGHES, Theophilus. Private, Militia, 1776 [Ref: M-207, A-325].
HULL, Casimir. Private, German Regiment, Maryland Line, 1778, and discharged on July 26, 1779 [Ref: D-217].
HULL, John. Private, 5th Maryland Line, enlisted May 12, 1778; fifer, Apr. 1, 1779; drummer, 1780-1783 [Ref: D-213, D-538].
HULL, Nathaniel. Private, 4th Maryland Line, 1777-1780; discharged Jan. 15, 1781 [Ref: D-124, D-538]. The estate of "Nathaniel Hull (soldier)" was probated on July 24, 1793 [Ref: ZE-102].
HULL, William. Private, 4th Maryland Line, 1778 [Ref: D-123].
HUMBERSTONE, Richard. Took the Oath of Allegiance before the Hon. David Craufurd in 1778 [Ref: O-271]. The estate of one Richard Humberstone was probated in July, 1793 [Ref: ZE-102].
HUMPHREY (HUMFREY), Henry (Feb. 7, 1747 -). Son of Henry and Sarah Humfrey [Ref: ZC-32]. Took the Oath of Allegiance before the Hon. Thomas Clagett in 1778 [Ref: O-265, which spelled his name "Humfrey," and R-77, which spelled his name "Humphry"]. See "John Humphrey" and "Thomas Humphrey," q.v.
HUMPHREY (HUMFREY), John (Jan. 23, 1757 -). Son of Henry and Sarah Humfrey [Ref: ZC-32]. "John Humfrey" took the Oath of Allegiance before the Hon. Thomas Clagett in 1778 [Ref: O-265].
HUMPHREY, Sarah (Sallie). See "John Humphrey" and "Henry Humphrey" and "John Ranter" and "Thomas Humphrey" and "John Igleheart," q.v.
HUMPHREY (HUMFREY), Thomas (Feb. 22, 1759 -). Son of Henry and Sarah Humfrey [Ref: ZC-32, which listed his name as "Thomas Talbot Humfrey"]. "Thomas Humfrey" took the Oath of Allegiance before the Hon. Thomas Clagett in 1778 [Ref: O-265]. "Thomas Humphrys" was a private in the 7th Maryland Line from July 20, 1778 to Feb. 22, 1779, when he was discharged [Ref: D-217]. "Thomas Humphries" married Margaret Burch by license dated Nov. 22, 1781 [Ref: ZB-114].
HUMPHREY, Winnifred. See "John Igleheart," q.v.
HUNGERFORD, Elizabeth. See "Philip Jenkins," q.v.
HUNT, James (1735-). Took the Oath of Allegiance before the Hon. Christopher Lowndes in 1778 [Ref: O-283, R-18]. Private, Maryland Line, by Feb. 24, 1779, when paid for his services "in cloathing." [Ref: E-308]. Private, Northern Detachment, 3rd Maryland Line, Capt. Horatio Clagett's Company, 1783 [Ref: D-501]. One James Hunt married Unie Loveless by license dated Jan. 12, 1793 [Ref: ZB-114].

HUNTER, George. Private, Capt. Alexander Truman's Company, 1781; stationed at Annapolis and reported on "a list of men who have deserted since Mar. 1, 1781." [Ref: L-19970 (Box 7, folder 52)].
HUNTER, Richard. Took the Oath of Allegiance (made his mark that looked like a large "+" sign) before the Hon. Thomas Boyd in 1778 [Ref: O-261]. One Richard Hunter married Rachel Whiten by license dated Jan. 19, 1782 [Ref: ZB-115].
HURDLE, Leonard. Took the Oath of Allegiance before the Hon. Christopher Lowndes in 1778 [Ref: O-285].
HURDLE, Robert. Took the Oath of Allegiance before the Hon. William Berry in 1778 [Ref: O-259].
HURLEY, Caleb. Constable in Hynson Hundred in 1778 [Ref: Z-30].
HURLEY, Daniel. Private, Maryland Line, enlisted Oct. 14, 1781 [Ref: D-424]. One Daniel Hurley, son of William and Rachel, was born Aug. 15, 1760. Another Daniel Hurley, son of Thomas and Jane, was born June 9, 1762 [Ref: ZC-32]. One Daniel Hurley married Amelia Bayne by license dated Dec. 21, 1784 [Ref: ZB-115]. Another Daniel Hurley married Mary Jones on Sep. 10, 1797, in King George's Parish. One Daniel Hurley died Apr. 25, 1793 [Ref: ZC-32, ZE-102]. Additional research may be necessary before drawing conclusions.
HURLEY, Isaiah. Private, Militia, 1776 [Ref: M-207, A-325].
HURLEY, Jane. See "Daniel Hurley," q.v.
HURLEY, John (1751, Ireland - died before 1815, Maryland). Private, enrolled in the Flying Camp by Lieut. William D. Beall on July 19, 1776; nativity: Ireland; height: 5' 6"; well made with dark hair, fair complexion [Ref: D-37]. One John Hurley married Amelia Lewis [Ref: X-1550], and a John Hurley married Sarah Evans by license dated Dec. 19, 1787 [Ref: ZB-115].
HURLEY, Rachel. See "Daniel Hurley," q.v.
HURLEY, Salem (1756 - died after 1832). Took the Oath of Allegiance before the Hon. Osborn Sprigg in 1778 [Ref: O-300 and O-308, which listed the name as "Sabn. Hurley," but the original list at the Maryland State Archives (Box 4, folder 29) shows the name to be either "Sabm." or "Salm." Since "Salem Hurley" lived in the area and also served in the Revolutionary War, this appears to be him]. "Salem Hurly" applied for a pension (S10893) in Washington, DC on Dec. 4, 1832, and stated he served in the Maryland Line and in the naval service. He was born in Prince George's County and lived there until July, 1832, when he moved to Washington, DC [Ref: P-1783]. Salem Hurley married Amma *[sic]* Summers by license dated Dec. 8, 1784 [Ref: ZB-115].
HURLEY, Thomas. See "Daniel Hurley," q.v.
HURLEY, William (1750-1799). Private, 7th Maryland Line, 1780 [Ref: D-217]. One William Hurley married Mary Evans by license dated Aug. 12, 1778, a William Hurley married Rebecca Soper by license dated Dec. 21, 1790, and a William Hurley married Sarah Soper by license dated Aug.

12, 1795 [Ref: ZB-116, X-1150]. The estate of one William Hurley was probated on Sep. 10, 1799 [Ref: ZE-102]. William Hurley took the Oath of Allegiance before the Hon. Osborn Sprigg in 1778 [Ref: O-306, R-85]. One William Hurley was aged 37 in the 1776 census [Ref: R-85]. Additional research may be necessary before drawing conclusions. See "Daniel Hurley," q.v.

HUTCHINSON, Elizabeth. See "Thomas Conner," q.v.

HUTCHINSON, Samuel. Private (draft), continental service, 1781, Maryland Line [Ref: D-382]. Samuel Hutchinson married Ann Brown by license dated June 3, 1786 [Ref: ZB-116].

HUTCHINSON, William (1721-   ). Took the Oath of Allegiance before the Hon. Osborn Sprigg in 1778 [Ref: O-308, W-4648 (Box 4, folder 29)].

HUTCHINSON, William (1751-1831). Private, enrolled in the Flying Camp by Lieut. Benjamin Brooks on July 17, 1776; nativity: Prince George's County; height 5' 6"; has own gun [Ref: D-36, which spelled his name "Hutcheson"]. Took the Oath of Allegiance before the Hon. David Craufurd in 1778 [Ref: O-270, R-38, which sources spelled his name "Hutchison"]. Constable, Upper Marlborough Hundred, 1778 [Ref: Z-30, which spelled his name "Hutchinson"]. Private, Northern Detachment, 3rd Maryland Line, Capt. Horatio Clagett's Company, 1783 [Ref: D-501]. William Hutchinson married Christian Willett by license dated Apr. 18, 1780 [Ref: ZB-116] The estate of one William Hutchinson was probated on Nov. 8, 1839 [Ref: ZE-103, which also spelled the name "Hutcheson"].

HYATT, Charles. See "William Hyatt, Sr.," q.v.

HYATT, Christopher (1751-1808). Took the Oath of Allegiance before the Hon. Benjamin Hall in 1778 [Ref: O-275, R-47, which spelled his name "Hyat"]. He married (1) Lucy Beckett Peach by license dated Sep. 10, 1777, and (2) Sarah Clarke by license dated Sep. 3, 1793 [Ref: ZB-116, X-1557]. The estate of one Christopher Hyatt was probated on Aug. 11, 1808 [Ref: ZE-103].

HYATT, Mary. See "Frederick Prussia Lewis Duvall" and "Lewis Duvall," q.v.

HYATT, Sarah. See "William Hyatt, Sr.," q.v.

HYATT, William Jr. (1748-   ). Took the Oath of Allegiance before the Hon. Benjamin Hall in 1778 [Ref: O-275, R-48, which spelled his name "Hyat"].

HYATT, William Sr. (Feb. 18, 1717 - 1794). Son of Charles and Sarah Hyatt, of Queen Anne's Parish [Ref: ZC-180]. Took the Oath of Allegiance before the Hon. Benjamin Hall in 1778 [Ref: O-275, R-47, which latter source spelled his name "Hyat" and gave his age in 1776 as 57]. "William Hyatt" married Elizabeth Walker [Ref: X-1557, which stated he died before Nov. 9, 1794]. The estate of one William Hyatt was probated on Nov. 7, 1794 [Ref: ZE-103].

HYDE, Priscilla. See "Thomas Lawson," q.v.

HYMAS, Barbara. See "Lewin Jones," q.v.

IGLEHART, Dennis. See "John and William Igleheart," q.v.
IGLEHART, Elizabeth. See "Jeremiah and "John Igleheart," q.v.
IGLEHART, Jacob. See "John Igleheart," q.v.
IGLEHART, James. See "Jeremiah and "John Igleheart," q.v.
IGLEHART, Jemima. See "John Igleheart," q.v.
IGLEHART, Jesse. See "Jeremiah Igleheart," q.v.
IGLEHART, John. See "Jeremiah and "John Igleheart," q.v.
IGLEHART, Levi. See "John Igleheart," q.v.
IGLEHART, Martha. See "John Igleheart," q.v.
IGLEHART, Mary. See "Jeremiah Igleheart," q.v.
IGLEHART, Nathan. See "William Igleheart," q.v.
IGLEHART, Rezin. See "Jeremiah and William Igleheart," q.v.
IGLEHART, Richard. See "John Igleheart," q.v.
IGLEHART, Susanna. See "Jeremiah and William Igleheart," q.v.
IGLEHEART, Cornelius. See "Jacob and "Jeremiah Igleheart," q.v.
IGLEHEART, Jacob. Son of Jacob Igleheart and Jane Perry. Took the Oath of Allegiance before the Hon. Benjamin Hall in 1778 [Ref: O-275]. Jacob Igleheart married Mary ---, but they had no children. His estate was probated on Jan. 30, 1799 [Ref: ZE-103, which spelled the name "Ingleheart"]. In the final account in 1804 his surviving siblings were listed as his heirs, viz., John Igleheart, Ann Cross, Sarah James, James Igleheart, and Mary Cross. It also mentioned his two deceased brothers Jeremiah Igleheart and William Igleheart (who had a son Cornelius Igleheart). [Ref: Unpublished manuscript entitled "Iglehart-Igleheart" compiled by Mrs. Robert Emory Costen, 13 Rosemar Drive, Ellicott City, Maryland 21043, a copy of which is in the Maryland Historical Society Library].
IGLEHEART, James. See "Jacob Igleheart," q.v.
IGLEHEART, Jeremiah (c1750-c1802). Son of Jacob Igleheart and Jane Perry. Took the Oath of Allegiance before the Hon. Christopher Lowndes in 1778 [Ref: O-288]. He married Mary ---- [Ref: X-1561], and had these children: Elizabeth Iglehart (born Apr. 18, 1775 and married Christopher Sipe), James Iglehart (married Ann Burton), Jesse Iglehart (born Feb. 18, 1781 and married Sarah Burton), John Iglehart (born 1784 and married Harriet Beall), Susanna Iglehart (born 1786 and married William Burton), Cornelius Iglehart (married Nancy Hearn), Rezin Iglehart (married Hester Watkins), and Mary Iglehart (baptized Apr. 23, 1792). [Ref: Prince George's County Guardian Accounts, 1802-1805, folio 49, and an unpublished manuscript by Mrs. Robert Emory Costen]. See "Jacob Igleheart," q.v.
IGLEHEART, John (1745-1810). Son of Jacob Igleheart and Jane Perry. Took the Oath of Allegiance before the Hon. Thomas Williams in 1778 [Ref: O-302, which spelled his name "Iglehart"]. He married Mary Denune [Ref: X-1561]. The estate of one "John W. Igleheart" was probated in 1811 [Ref: ZE-103]. The children of John Igleheart (or

Iglehart) were: Martha Iglehart (born Aug. 28, 1765 and married Benjamin Fairall), James Iglehart (born July 21, 1767 and married Sallie Humphrey), John Iglehart (born June 23, 1770 and married Rachel Nichols), Richard Iglehart (born Sep. 11, 1772 and married Nancy Hammond), Jacob Iglehart (born Mar. 30, 1774 and married (1) Ann Beall and (2) Esther Soper), Jemima Iglehart (born Mar. 31, 1776 and married William Boyd), William Iglehart (born Oct. 13, 1778 and married Ann Smith), Elizabeth Iglehart (born circa 1782 and married Abraham Boyd), Levi Iglehart (born Oct. 13, 1786 and married Eleanor Taylor), and Dennis Iglehart (born in 1793 and married Winnifred Humphrey). Most of these families moved to Ohio County, Kentucky. See "Jacob Igleheart," q.v.

IGLEHEART, Mary. See "Jeremiah and John Igleheart," q.v.

IGLEHEART, Susannah. See "Jacob Wheeler," q.v.

IGLEHEART, William (1754-1786). Son of Jacob Igleheart and Jane Perry, he married Susanna Soper on Mar. 17, 1781. Their children were Nathan Iglehart, Rezin Iglehart, and Dennis Iglehart. Susanna Iglehart, widow of William Iglehart, married Jacob Wheeler on June 2, 1787. "William Idlehart" took the Oath of Allegiance before the Hon. James Beck in 1778 [Ref: O-255]. See additional information and sources under "Jacob Igleheart," q.v.

IJAMS, Burgess. See "Vachell Ijams," q.v.

IJAMS, John. Private, 1st Maryland Line, 1779-1780 [Ref: D-126, which questioned the name as being Iiams or Irons]. The estate of one John Ijams was probated on Februry 6, 1789 [Ref: ZE-103]. See "Vachell Ijams," q.v.

IJAMS, Joseph. See "Vachell Ijams," q.v.

IJAMS, Martha. See "Vachell Ijams," q.v.

IJAMS, Margaret. See "Thomas Woodard," q.v.

IJAMS, Susannah. See "Marsh Mareen Duvall," q.v.

IJAMS, Vachell (Jan., 1759/60, Maryland - Feb. 20, 1833, Alabama). His pension record (S32337) stated that he lived with his father (not named) in Anne Arundel County at the time of enlistment in the Maryland Line. He later moved to Prince George's County, Maryland with his father and enlisted there. He then moved to Rowan County, North Carolina and also enlisted there. In 1823 he moved to Lauderdale County, Alabama, filed for a pension on Aug. 2, 1832, and died on Feb. 20, 1833. He had married Martha ---- in 1791 in North Carolina and she died in 1838. Their surviving children were William Ijams, Joseph Ijams, Pearson Ijams, Peggy Edwards, Ann Ijams, and Elizabeth Herrindon. Also mentioned: son-in-law David C. McClamaugh, but his wife was not named; John D. Ijams, son of Joseph Ijams; and Burgess Ijams, relationship not stated [Ref: P-1796]. Vachell Ijams married (1) Lilah Gaiter [Gaither], and (2) Martha Cunningham [Ref: X-1561]. His name is spelled "Vachel Jeems" on the pension rolls [Ref: Thomas M. Owen's

163

Revolutionary Soldiers in Alabama (1975 edition; originally published in 1911), page 62].

IJAMS, William. See "Vachell Ijams," q.v.

INNESS, George. "George Inness was a substitute to serve for three years, June 15th, 1778" in the continental service, Maryland Line [Ref: D-328]. "George Ennis" had enlisted as a substitute for "Robert Orme," q.v. [Ref: E-150].

INNESS, John. See "John Hinness," q.v.

IRVINGTON, Jeremiah (1741 - Dec. 1, 1827). Private, 1st Maryland Line, Feb. 28, 1777; discharged Feb. 20, 1780 [Ref: D-146]. Applied for a pension (S34936) in Prince George's County on Apr. 12, 1821, "aged 70 or thereabouts." with a wife (not named) aged 60 [Ref: P-1807]. Pension commenced on Sep. 7, 1818 [Ref: T-39, which listed his name as "Jeremiah Ivington, alias Nivington, alias Nithington"]. The estate of "Jeremiah Irvington" was probated in Prince George's County on July 5, 1828 [Ref: ZE-104].

ISAAC, Jemima (Gemima). See "Mordecai Isaac," q.v.

ISAAC, Richard (Jan. 21, 1720/1 - 1792). Son of Richard and Sarah Isaac, of Queen Anne's Parish [Ref: ZC-181]. Took the Oath of Allegiance before the Hon. James Beck in 1778 [Ref: O-255, R-21]. "Richard Isaacs" married Sarah Jacobs [Ref: X-1570]. The estate of "Richard Isaac" was probated on June 25, 1792 [Ref: ZE-104].

ISAAC, Sarah. See "John Ray" and "Richard Isaac," q.v.

IVORY, Charles. Private, Maryland Line, 1778 [Ref: D-318]. The estate of one Charles Ivory was probated in 1785 [Ref: ZE-104].

JACKSON, Alexander (1722-1803). Took the Oath of Allegiance before the Hon. Christopher Lowndes in 1778 [Ref: O-285, R-73]. He married Deborah Mauduitt [Manduitt?]. [Ref: X-1574]. The estate of Alexander Jackson was probated on Oct. 21, 1803 [Ref: ZE-104].

JACKSON, James (1760, Maryland -   ). Private, enlisted May 28, 1781, for 3 years in continental service, Maryland Line; sent to Annapolis; on duty July 13, 1781 [Ref: D-381].

JACKSON, Jasper. Private, Select Militia, Upper Battalion, June 12, 1781 [Ref: S-6636 (Box 27, folder 82B)]. The estate of "Jasper M. Jackson" was probated on June 17, 1812 [Ref: ZE-105].

JACKSON, John. There were several men with the name who served in the Maryland Line [Ref: D-10, D-65, D-125, D-128, D-219, D-220]. The estate of one "John Jackson (soldier)" was probated on Apr. 4, 1793, in Prince George's County [Ref: ZE-105].

JACKSON, Mary. See "Thomas Cramphin," q.v.

JACKSON, Nehemiah. Took the Oath of Allegiance before the Hon. Fielder Bowie in 1778 [Ref: O-304, which questions the last name. The original list at the Maryland State Archives (Box 4, folder 15) is unclear; the name could be "Jackson" or perhaps "Tasker"].

JACKSON, Peter. Private, Northern Detachment, 3rd Maryland Line, Capt. Horatio Clagett's Company, 1783 [Ref: D-502].

JACKSON, William (1750-1829). Took the Oath of Allegiance before the Hon. Christopher Lowndes in 1778 [Ref: O-286, R-74]. Ensign, Militia, 1778 [Ref: N-34]. Second Lieutenant, Upper Battalion, Capt. Selby's Company, June 27, 1781 [Ref: H-320]. The estate of one William Jackson was probated on June 9, 1829 [Ref: ZE-105].

JACKSON, William. Took the Oath of Allegiance before the Hon. Osborn Sprigg in 1778 [Ref: O-307, which spelled the name "Jacson"]. The estate of one "William John Jackson" was probated on Jan. 4, 1796 [Ref: ZE-105].

JACOB, Benjamin. Took the Oath of Allegiance before the Hon. Benjamin Hall in 1778 [Ref: O-274]. There were apparently three men with this name who resided in Queen Anne's Parish: one was born in 1710, one was born in 1724, and one married Elenor Odell in 1771 [Ref: ZC-181]. Additional research may be necessary before drawing conclusions.

JACOB, Charles. Took the Oath of Allegiance before the Hon. David Craufurd in 1778 [Ref: O-271].

JACOB, Elizabeth. See "Lewis Duvall," q.v.

JACOB, Gemima. See "Mordecai Jacob," q.v.

JACOB, George. On Feb. 2, 1780, the Council of Maryland ordered "that the Collector of the tax for Prince George's County pay to Lieut. George Jacob of the 6th Regiment two thousand dollars to be expended in the recruiting service and accounted for." [Ref: F-75]. The estate of one George Jacob was probated on Mar. 29, 1785 [Ref: ZE-105].

JACOB, Isaac. Took the Oath of Allegiance before the Hon. Benjamin Hall in 1778 [Ref: O-274]. The estate of one Isaac Jacob was probated on Mar. 29, 1785 [Ref: ZE-105].

JACOB, Jemima. See "Mordecai Jacob," q.v.

JACOB, Jesse. Sergeant, 6th Maryland Line; prisoner of war who was exchanged by Sep. 3, 1781, at which time he was paid five pounds specie on his account. Sergeant, 2nd Maryland Line, Capt. Alexander Truman's Company, 1782 [Ref: D-439, D-616, which listed his name as "Jacobs"].

JACOB, Joel. Took the Oath of Allegiance before the Hon. Benjamin Hall in 1778 [Ref: O-276].

JACOB, Mordecai (Sep. 9, 1748 -   ). Son of Mordicai Jacob (died in 1771) and Gemima [Jemima] Isaac, of Queen Anne's Parish [Ref: ZC-181, ZE-105]. Took the Oath of Allegiance before the Hon. Thomas Williams in 1778 [Ref: O-302]. Ensign, 25th Battalion, Capt. Marsh Duvall's Company, May 24, 1779 [Ref: M-91, E-414, N-34, which also spelled his name "Jacobs"].

JACOB, Zachariah. Took the Oath of Allegiance (made his "X" mark) before the Hon. Thomas Boyd in 1778 [Ref: O-261]. Private, 3rd Maryland Line, enlisted on May 13, 1778 and served to at least Nov. 1, 1780 [Ref: D-127].

165

JACOBS, Ruth. See "John Mills," q.v.
JACOBS, Sarah. See "Richard Isaac," q.v.
JAMES, John (1738-   ). Took the Oath of Allegiance before the Hon. George Lee in 1778 [Ref: O-279, R-76].
JAMES, John (1751-   ). Private, enrolled in the Flying Camp by Lieut. Benjamin Brooks on July 25, 1776; nativity: Prince George's County; height 5' 4" [Ref: D-36].
JAMES, Philip. Private, Militia, 1776 [Ref: M-207, A-325]. Took the Oath of Allegiance before the Hon. Christopher Lowndes in 1778 [Ref: O-288].
JAMES, Sarah. See "Jacob Igleheart," q.v.
JAMESON, Amelia. See "Giles Green Dyer," q.v.
JAMISON, Ann E. See "Rinaldo Johnson," q.v.
JAMISON, Richard (1731-   ). Took the Oath of Allegiance before the Hon. William Berry in 1778 [Ref: O-259, R-25, which spelled his name "Richard Jameston"].
JARBOE, James. Private, enrolled by Lt. John M. Burgess, Lower Battalion, on July 20, 1776, for continental service, Maryland Line [Ref: D-35]. One "James Jarboe" was aged 40 and a "James Jarbo" was aged 45 in 1776. Both were residents of Prince George's County [Ref: R-75].
JARMAIN, Ann. See "George Lanham," q.v.
JARROTT, John. See "John Frazier," q.v.
JEAMS, Susanna. See "Marsh Mareen Duvall," q.v.
JEANS, Edward (1711-   ). Took the Oath of Allegiance before the Hon. Christopher Lowndes in 1778 [Ref: O-285, R-27].
JEANS, Joseph. Took the Oath of Allegiance before the Hon. Christopher Lowndes in 1778 [Ref: O-287]. Private, Col. Rawlings' Regiment, Maryland Line, 1777, and Sergeant from Oct. 1, 1779, to at least July, 1781 [Ref: D-128, D-350, D-351].
JEEMS, Vachel. See "Vachell Ijams," q.v.
JEFFERSON, Luke (1732-   ). Took the Oath of Allegiance before the Hon. George Lee in 1778 [Ref: O-279, R-66].
JEFFRIES, Alexander. "Alexander Jeffreys" took the Oath of Allegiance before the Hon. David Craufurd in 1778 [Ref: O-272]. The estate of "Alexander Jeffries" was probated on July 27, 1807 [Ref: ZE-106].
JEFFRIES, David. Private, 4th Maryland Line, 1778 [Ref: D-128].
JEFFRIES, John. Took the Oath of Allegiance before the Hon. Osborn Sprigg in 1778 [Ref: O-308, which spelled the name "Jeffrais," but the original list (very light) at the Maryland State Archives (Box 4, folder 29) shows the name to be more like "Jeffries"].
JEFFRIES, William. Private, 5th Maryland Line; sick in the Court House Hospital in Reading, Pennsylvania, on Nov. 17, 1777 [Ref: D-619]. The estate of one "William Jeffreys" was probated in 1807 in Prince George's County, Maryland [Ref: ZE-105].

JENKERSON, Edward (1736-   ). Private, enrolled in the Flying Camp by Lieut. William D. Beall on July 19, 1776; nativity: England; height: 5' 11"; red hair, brown complexion [Ref: D-37].

JENKINS, Bartholomew. Took the Oath of Allegiance before the Hon. William Berry in 1778 [Ref: O-259, which spelled the name "Bartholomew Jinkins"].

JENKINS, Edward. Took the Oath of Allegiance before the Hon. Thomas Clagett in 1778 [Ref: O-267]. The estate of one Edward Jenkins was probated on May 30, 1797 [Ref: ZE-106].

JENKINS, Enoch (1731-1789). Took the Oath of Allegiance before the Hon. Christopher Lowndes in 1778 [Ref: O-283, R-24]. The estate of Enoch Jenkins was probated on Jan. 4, 1790 [Ref: ZE-106].

JENKINS, Francis Jr. (1747-1790?). Took the Oath of Allegiance before the Hon. Thomas Clagett in 1778 [Ref: O-265]. "Francis Jenkins, Sr." was aged 57 in 1776 [Ref: R-21, R-38]. One Francis Jenkins married Martha Day by license dated Oct. 28, 1780 [Ref: ZB-120]. The estate of one Francis Jenkins was probated on Mar. 1, 1785, and the estate of another Francis Jenkins was probated on Mar. 23, 1790 [Ref: ZE-106].

JENKINS, George. Private, enrolled by Lt. William Duvall, Lower Battalion, on July 18, 1776, for continental service, Maryland Line [Ref: D-35, which spelled his name "George Jinkens"].

JENKINS, Isaac. Private, 1st Maryland Line, enlisted May 5, 1779 and reported missing Aug. 16,1 780 (at the Battle of Camden). He may have been the Isaac Jenkins who enlisted [or reenlisted] on Sep. 12, 1782 [Ref: D-126, D-423]. One Isaac Jenkins married Mary Galwith by license dated June 5, 1787 [Ref: ZB-120].

JENKINS, John (1723-1789). Took the Oath of Allegiance before the Hon. Christopher Lowndes in 1778 [Ref: O-283, R-32]. The estate of one John Jenkins was probated on Dec. 8, 1789 [Ref: ZE-106].

JENKINS, Joseph (May 22, 1755 -   ). Son of John and Frances Jenkins [Ref: ZC-34]. Took the Oath of Allegiance before the Hon. Thomas Williams in 1778 [Ref: O-302]. The records of the Maryland Council on Mar. 27, 1778, contains the following: "It appears that Joseph Jenkins, son of John Jenkins, of Prince George's County, was born in this State, that he was long since duly enrolled in Capt. Andrew Beall's Company of Militia, and on the 28th day of Feb. last took the Oath of Fidelity and Support to this State agreeable to the Laws thereof, and from any thing that appears he hath been always a Resident and Subject to the State and the said Joseph Jenkins complaining to this Board that he hath been drafted in Virginia for a Soldier as an Inhabitant and Subject thereof and threatened to be taken from his Home as such, on no other ground than his having travelled into the Back Parts of Virginia with an Intention of Purchasing a piece of Land for his father which he did not accomplish. This Board desirous of Affording to the Subjects of this State the Protection due to them do Order that the said Joseph Jenkins be not taken as a Soldier under the said Draft or treated with any Violence but that if any Officer claims him as a Soldier in Consequence of the said Draft that the Evidence if any of his being Subject thereto be laid before the Government and Council that the same may be considered and Justice done therein the said Joseph Jenkins giving Security before some Justice of the Peace for Prince George's County in one hundred and fifty pounds for his Appearance before this Board on due Notice given to him for that Purpose or left in writing at his fathers Dwelling House." [Ref: C-554, C-555]. One Joseph Jenkins married Margery Wilson by license dated June 25, 1780 [Ref: ZB-120].

JENKINS, Philip (c1755, Maryland - died after 1822, Tennessee). Private, 2nd Maryland Line, Capt. Patrick Sim's Company, 1776 [Ref: D-8]. He married Elizabeth Hungerford [Ref: X-1591].

JENKINS, Priscilla. See "George Hardey," q.v.

JENKINS, Richard (1741-   ). Took the Oath of Allegiance before the Hon. Thomas Clagett in 1778 [Ref: O-267, R-41].

JENKINS, Sally. See "Jeremiah Edelen," q.v.

JENKINS, Thomas. Private, enrolled by Capt. John H. Lowe on July 13, 1776, for continental service, Maryland Line [Ref: D-35]. Private, 1st Maryland Line, who was paid for his services "in cloathing" on Apr. 17, 1779 [Ref: E-351]. Private, Select Militia, Capt. Hezekiah Wheeler's Company, July 14, 1781 [Ref: S-6636 (Box 31, folder 5)]. One Thomas Jenkins married Mildred Atcherson by license dated Nov. 10, 1787 [Ref: ZB-120]. The estate of one Thomas Jenkins was probated in 1843 [Ref: ZE-107].

JENKINS, William. Took the Oath of Allegiance (made his "X" mark) before the Hon. Thomas Clagett in 1778 [Ref: O-269].

JENKINS, William (1743-1803?). Private, Capt. Richard Stonestreet's Militia Company, 11th Battalion, June, 1782 [Ref: L-19970 (Box 6, folder 21)]. Took the Oath of Allegiance before the Hon. Osborn Sprigg in 1778 [Ref: O-307, R-38]. One William Jenkins married Dorcas Masters by license dated Dec. 31, 1778 [Ref: ZB-121]. The estate of one William Jenkins was probated in 1791, another William Jenkins in 1803, and one William Jenkins Sr. in 1821 [Ref: ZE-107]. Additional research may be necessary before drawing conclusions.

JENKINS, Zachariah (1726-1792). Took the Oath of Allegiance before the Hon. Christopher Lowndes in 1778 [Ref: O-285, R-43]. The estate of Zachariah Jenkins was provated on Nov. 6, 1792 [Ref: ZE-107].

JENKINS, Zadock (1742-1811). Took the Oath of Allegiance before the Hon. Osborn Sprigg in 1778 [Ref: O-307, R-80]. One Zadock Jenkins married Ann Summers by license dated Jan. 12, 1798 [Ref: ZB-121]. The estate of one Zadock Jenkins was probated on Jan. 3, 1812 [Ref: ZE-107, which also misspelled the name as "Zadvik"].

JENNINGS, Charles. "A draft, June 15th, 1778" for continental service, Maryland Line [Ref: D-328, which spelled his name "Charles Jenings"].

Took the Oath of Allegiance before the Hon. William Berry in 1778 [Ref: O-259, which spelled his name "Charles Ginings"]. The records of the Council of Maryland on June 22, 1778, state that Charles Jennings was "a Draft from Prince George's County who had gone home again. We have sent Mr. Gordon after him and request that you [the County Lieutenant] give him any necessary assistance." [Ref: E-146].

JENNINGS, Richard. Private, Northern Detachment, 3rd Maryland Line, Capt. Horatio Clagett's Company, 1783 [Ref: D-501].

JERAC, Jacob. See "Jacob Jover (Jerac?)," q.v.

JERAC, John. See "John Jover (Jerac?)," q.v.

JETT, Mary B. See "Alexander Truman," q.v.

JEWELL, David. See "Jonathan Jewell," q.v.

JEWELL, Elizabeth. See "Jonathan Jewell," q.v.

JEWELL, Jonathan (1762-1847). Born in Prince George's County, a son of David Jewell, Jonathan moved with his family to Loudoun County, Virginia in 1776 (following his father's death). He served in the Revolutionary War and was present at the siege and surrender of Yorktown, but having lost his papers, his pension application was rejected. In 1790 he took up a land grant on the Barren River in Barren County, Kentucky. His wife's name was recorded as Elizabeth in 1819, but his will in 1847 named Nancy as his wife [Ref: *Traces* (Quarterly Publication of the South Central Kentucky Historical and Genealogical Society), Volume 16, No. 3 (1988), p. 84]. Elizabeth Jewell, with the consent of her father Jonathan, married Franklin Settle in Barren County, Kentucky on Oct. 28, 1818. One Jonathan Jewell married Ann Colman [Coleman] on Feb. 15, 1831 [Ref: *Marriage Records of Barren County, Kentucky, 1799-1849*, by Martha Powell Reneau (1984), pp. 143, 233].

JOHNS, Aquilla. Naval Lieutenant aboard the ship *Defence* in 1777 [Ref: D-657]. The estate of one Aquilla Johns was probated in 1820 in Prince George's County [Ref: ZE-107]. See "Hannibal Lusk," q.v.

JOHNS, William. Took the Oath of Allegiance before the Hon. Fielder Bowie in 1778 [Ref: O-304, W-4648 (Box 4, folder 15)].

JOHNSON, Alexis. See "Thomas Johnson," q.v.

JOHNSON, Benjamin. Private, enrolled by Lt. William Duvall, Lower Battalion, on July 18, 1776, for continental service, Maryland Line [Ref: D-35, which spelled his name "Benjamin Jonson"]. Took the Oath of Allegiance before the Hon. William Lyles, Jr. in 1778 [Ref: O-290]. Private, 3rd Maryland Line, Capt. Horatio Clagett's Company, 1779 [Ref: D-295]. One Benjamin Johnson married Anne Sansbury by license dated Feb. 11, 1792 [Ref: ZB-121].

JOHNSON, Dorcas. See "William Hellen," q.v.

JOHNSON, Elizabeth. See "Thomas Johnson" and "Valentine Lynn," q.v.

JOHNSON, George. Private, 6th Maryland Line, enlisted May 10, 1778 and reported missing on Aug. 16, 1780 (at the Battle of Camden). [Ref:

D-219]. The estate of "George Johnson (soldier)" was probated on Mar. 21, 1793, in Prince George's County [Ref: ZE-107].

JOHNSON, James. Private, enrolled by Ensign Horatio Clagett on July 15, 1776, for continental service, Maryland Line [Ref: D-35]. One James Johnson married Catherine West by license dated Dec. 5, 1782 [Ref: ZB-122]. The estate of one James Johnson was probated on June 24, 1790 [Ref: ZE-107].

JOHNSON, John. There were several men with this name who served in the Maryland Line [Ref: D-14, D-126, D-128, D-218, D-219, D-310]. The estate of one "John Johnson (soldier)" was probated on Mar. 21, 1793, and perhaps another estate of "John Johnson (soldier)" was probated on Aug. 5, 1793, in Prince George's County [Ref: ZE-108]. Additional research may be necessary before drawing conclusions.

JOHNSON, Magruder. Served on a Grand Jury in 1778 [Ref: Z-52].

JOHNSON, Margery. See "Thomas Johnson," q.v.

JOHNSON, Richard. Private, 2nd Maryland Line, Capt. Patrick Sim's Company, 1776 [Ref: D-8].

JOHNSON, Rinaldo (c1755-1811). Son of Thomas Johnson (of Baltimore County) and Ann Riston (who moved to Prince George's County circa 1755), he married (1) Rebecca Trueman by license dated Feb. 4, 1779 (died in 1781), and (2) Ann Eilbeck Mason, and had these children by his second wife: Thomas Rinaldo Johnson, Ann Eilbeck Jamison, and Sarah Williams. Rinaldo served in these capacities: Clerk of the Committee of Observation in 1775. Clerk pro tem of the Committee of Correspondence in 1776. House of Delegates, 1781-1782. County Justice, 1782-1800. Associate Justice, 1804-1805. Orphans Court Justice, 1782-1794 [Ref: U-86, U-493, U-494, ZB-122]. The estate of Rinaldo Johnson was probated on Feb. 25, 1812 [Ref: ZE-108].

JOHNSON, Sarah. See "Benjamin Brookes," q.v.

JOHNSON, Thomas (1741-1796?). Private, enrolled in the Flying Camp by Lieut. Benjamin Brooks on Aug. 8, 1776; nativity: England; height 5' 10"; has own gun [Ref: D-36]. One Thomas Johnson or Johnston was a soldier in the Maryland Line. His widow Margery applied for pension (W13555) on Oct. 31, 1837, aged 93, in Washington, DC, stating she and Thomas were married in Prince George's County opposite Alexandria before the Revolution and he enlisted at Bladensburg where he then lived. On Dec. 6, 1837 John and Nancy Perkins, of Washington, DC, made affidavit that Thomas and Margery Johnston had several children and that they knew two sons and two daughters but all were deceased in 1837 except one son Alexis Johnston. Alexis made affidavit in 1837 that he was aged 52 and that he had a sister Elizabeth who was aged at least 14 years older than he was and she died about 1840 *[sic]*, aged 64 [Ref: P-1858]. There was also a Thomas Johnson, aged 30, in Prince George's County in 1776 [Ref: R-85]. The estate of one Thomas Johnson was probated on Jan. 25, 1796 and another estate of a Thomas Johnson was probated on Oct. 1, 1801 [Ref: ZE-108]. Additional research may be necessary before drawing conclusions. See "Rinaldo Johnson," q.v.

JOHNSON, T. Jr. See "Hannibal Lusk," q.v.

JOHNSON, William. There were several men with this name who served in the Maryland Line [Ref: D-16, D-32, D-125, D-126, D-220, D-322, D-341]. The estate of "William Johnson (soldier)" was probated on Aug. 5, 1793, in Prince George's County [Ref: ZE-108].

JOHNSTON, Alexis. See "Thomas Johnson," q.v.

JOHNSTON, Elizabeth. See "Thomas Johnson," q.v.

JONES, Alexander (1744-   ). Private in the Virginia Line who pensioned in Prince George's County, Maryland in 1818 [Ref: T-39].

JONES, Amos. See "Richard Jones," q.v.

JONES, Amy. See "Josiah or Josias Jones," q.v.

JONES, Ann. See "Thomas Jones" and "Richard Jones" and "James Gregory" and "Elisha Loveless," q.v.

JONES, Benjamin. There were several men with this name who served in the Maryland Line [Ref: D-218, D-219]. One Benjamin Jones married Ruth Young by license dated Oct. 11, 1786 in Prince George's County [Ref: ZB-123]. Additional research may be necessary before drawing conclusions about his military service.

JONES, Charles (1751-1801). Took the Oath of Allegiance before the Hon. Thomas Clagett in 1778 [Ref: O-267, R-42]. The estate of one Charles Jones was probated on Nov. 30, 1801 [Ref: ZE-108]. See "John Jones," q.v.

JONES, Daniel (1752-   ). Private, Maryland Militia, who pensioned in Prince George's County and was paid in the District of Columbia in 1831 [Ref: T-50]. One Daniel Jones married Susanna Bradley by license dated Nov. 16, 1778 in Prince George's County [Ref: ZB-123].

JONES, David (1755-1814). Private, Maryland Line. Born in Prince George's County and lived there at time of his enlistment in the Revolutionary War. He applied for a pension (S8769) on July 20, 1832, aged 67 [Ref: P-1869]. Private, Capt. Benjamin Wailes' Militia Company, Lower Battalion; on duty guarding Magruder's Warehouse in the spring of 1782 [Ref: L-19970 (Box 6, folder 21)]. The estate of one David Jones was probated on June 25, 1814 [Ref: ZE-108].

JONES, Edward. Private, 2nd Maryland Line, Capt. Patrick Sim's Company, 1776 [Ref: D-9]. The estate of one Edward Jones was probated on Mar. 31, 1777 [Ref: ZE-108].

JONES, Edward, of John (Mar. 19, 1746/7 -   ). Son of John and Sarah Jones [Ref: ZD-116]. Took the Oath of Allegiance before the Hon. Thomas Clagett in 1778 [Ref: O-268].

JONES, Edward and Eliz. See "William Jones," q.v.

JONES, Elizabeth. See "Richard Jones" and "Thomas Jones" and "Mareen Carrick" and "John Jones" and "Samuel Jones" and "Richard Lyles," q.v.

171

JONES, Evan. The records of the Council of Maryland on June 12, 1778, indicate that Evan Jones was paid by the State Treasurer the money "due him and his company whilst in service per the payroll examined and passed by the A. G. [Auditor General]." [Ref: E-132]. See "John Jones," q.v.
JONES, Frances. See "Thomas Jones," q.v.
JONES, Francis (1725-   ). Took the Oath of Allegiance before the Hon. George Lee in 1778 [Ref: O-279, R-84].
JONES, Frederick. See "Thomas Jones," q.v.
JONES, Garrettson. See "Thomas Jones," q.v.
JONES, George. There were several men with this name who served in the Maryland Line [Ref: D-458, D-488, D-542]. One George Jones married Ann Roberts by license dated Janury 4, 1785, a George Jones married Elizabeth Sinclair by license dated Aug. 25, 1787, and a George Jones married Elizabeth Wilson by license dated Jan. 29, 1788, in Prince George's County [Ref: ZB-124]. Additional research may be necessary before drawing conclusions.
JONES, Henry (1737-1778). Took the Oath of Allegiance before the Hon. George Lee in 1778 [Ref: O-279, R-69]. The estate of one Henry Jones was probated by Ann Jones on Mar. 25, 1778 (date of inventory) and a final administrative account was filed by Ann Beam on Apr. 24, 1786 [Ref: ZE-109].
JONES, Henry Culver. See "Richard Jones," q.v.
JONES, Isaac (Feb. 7, 1756, Maryland - Jan. 14, 1801). Private (draft) in the continental service, 1781, Maryland Line [Ref: D-382]. Isaac Jones married Ellen Gaither [Ref: X-1621].
JONES, James. Private, 3rd Maryland Line, Capt. Horatio Clagett's Company, 1779 [Ref: D-295]. Private (substitute), continental service, 1781 [Ref: D-382]. One James Jones married Rosanah Smith by license dated Mar. 19, 1785 [Ref: ZB-124].
JONES, Jane. See "Richard Edelen," q.v.
JONES, John (1754, England -   ). Private, enlisted May 21, 1781, for 3 years in continental service; sent to Annapolis; on duty July 13, 1781 [Ref: D-381]. Took the Oath of Allegiance before the Hon. Christopher Lowndes in 1778 [Ref: O-285].
JONES, John (1731-   ). Took the Oath of Allegiance (made his "I" mark) before the Hon. Thomas Clagett in 1778 [Ref: O-266, R-77].
JONES, John (Oct. 7, 1760 -   ). Son of Evan Jones [Ref: ZD-116]. Private, 2nd Maryland Line, Capt. Murdock's Company, Mar. 15, 1781 [Ref: D-366].
JONES, John. See "Basil Wright" and "Edward Jones," q.v.
JONES, John Courts (Sep. 11, 1754 -   ). Son of Charles and Elizabeth Jones, of Prince George's Parish [Ref: ZD-116]. He was a second lieutenant in the Upper District of Frederick County (now Washington

County) in July, 1776 [Ref: D-48. Also see *Maryland Archives, Volume 18* for more details about his military service].

JONES, Joseph (1731-1818). Ensign, 25th Militia Battalion, Jan. 3, 1776. Captain, Upper Battalion, May 24, 1779 through June 24, 1780 (succeeded). [Ref: R-50, M-93, E-414, F-203, N-32, D-360]. The estate of one "Joseph Jones, Sr." was probated on Jan. 18, 1819 [Ref: ZE-109].

JONES, Josiah or Josias (1754-1820). "Josiah Jones" took the Oath of Allegiance before the Hon. Christopher Lowndes in 1778 [Ref: O-283, R-51]. One "Josias Jones" married Amy Jones by license dated Mar. 23, 1785 [Ref: Zb-124]. The estate of one "Josiah Jones" was probated on Aug. 8, 1820 [Ref: ZE-109].

JONES, Lewin (Sep. 24, 1746 - 1815, Fairfax County, Virginia). Son of William and Mary Jones [Ref: ZC-36]. He married Ann Harris (1757-1842), daughter of Benjamin Harris (died 1793) and wife Sarah Ann (died 1811), on Jan. 28, 1779, in Prince George's County, and a son Lewin Jones (1781-1833) married Jane Wigginton (1791-1880). [Ref: Ancestral Chart of Barbara (Perine) Hymas (of Sterling, Virginia), *Prince George's County Genealogical Society Bulletin*, Volume 25, No. 3 (Nov., 1993, pp. 64-65), ZC-36]. Private, Capt. Hezekiah Wheeler's Company, 11th Militia Battalion, April, 1781 [Ref: L-19970 (Box 6, folder 21)]. Took the Oath of Allegiance before the Hon. Thomas Clagett in 1778 [Ref: O-267].

JONES, Lewis. The estate of "Lewis Jones (soldier)" was probated in Prince George's County on Sep. 5, 1792 [Ref: ZE-109]. One Lewis Jones was a private, 2nd Maryland Line, enlisted on July 6, 1779 and discharged on Feb. 23, 1779 *[sic]*, and another Lewis Jones was a private, 3rd Maryland Line, enlisted on Feb. 21, 1777 and discharged on Feb. 21, 1780 ("time expired"). [Ref: D-126, D-127]. See "Thomas Jones," q.v.

JONES, Martha. See "Elias Lazenby" and "Joseph Hatton," q.v.

JONES, Mary. See "Richard Jones" and "Thomas Lyles" and "Daniel Hurley" and "Notley Jones" and "Lewin Jones" and "William Patterson," q.v.

JONES, Nancy. See "Basil Wright," q.v.

JONES, Notley. Took the Oath of Allegiance before the Hon. Christopher Lowndes in 1778 [Ref: O-284]. One Notley Jones was aged 51 and another was aged 27 in 1776 [Ref: R-25, R-77]. Notley Jones, son of William and Mary, was born Sep. 6, 1746 [Ref: ZC-36].

JONES, Philip (1744-   ). Matross in the Virginia Line who was pensioned in Prince George's County, Maryland in 1820, aged 76 [Ref: T-39].

JONES, Philip (1758-1827?). "Philip Jones, pension nos. S36029 and S34941, Continental and Maryland Line, applied June 19, 1820 in Washington, DC, aged 62; however, on Apr. 4, 1820, he was of Prince George's County, Maryland." [Ref: P-1879]. One Philip Jones took the

Oath of Allegiance (made his "P" mark) before the Hon. Thomas Clagett in 1778 [Ref: O-267]. There was also a "Philip Lewin Jones" who was aged 27 in 1776 [Ref: R-42]. The estate of one Philip Jones was probated on Mar. 7, 1827 [Ref: ZE-109]. Additional research may be necessry before drawing conclusions.

JONES, Penelopy. See "Thomas Jones," q.v.
JONES, Philip. See "Thomas Jones," q.v.
JONES, Phillemon. See "Thomas Jones," q.v.
JONES, Ralph. Took the Oath of Allegiance before the Hon. Christopher Lowndes in 1778 [Ref: O-286].
JONES, Rebecca. See "John Taylor," q.v.
JONES, Richard (Feb. 2, 1757, England - Apr. 18, 1821, Ontario County, New York). Private, enlisted on May 9, 1781, for 3 years in the Maryland Line, continental service, and sent to Annapolis; on duty July 13, 1781. Private, Capt. Alexander H. Magruder's Militia Company, Lower Battalion; on duty guarding Magruder's Warehouse in the spring of 1782 [Ref: D-381, L-19970 (Box 6, folder 21)]. Richard married Susannah Culver (Oct. 21, 1756 - June 11, 1851) in February, 1778, in Montgomery County, Maryland. They lived in Prince George's County at the time of his service, later lived near Colesville in Montgomery County, and in 1805 they moved to Hopewell in Ontario County, New York. Their children were: Mary Jones (born Feb. 12, 1779), Elizabeth Jones (born Oct. 30, 1784 and died Apr. 2, 1789), Henry Culver Jones (born July 28, 1788), Ann Jones (born Aug. 8, 1791), Amos Jones (born May 19, 1793), Thomas Culver Jones (born Apr. 15, 1795). Susannah Jones received pension W20190 and died in 1851, leaving these children: Henry C. Jones (aged 65, of Erie County, New York); Ann Shelell [Shekell?], aged 62; Amos Jones, aged 60; and, Thomas C. Jones, aged 58 (the last three lived in Ontario County, New York). Also mentioned were Richard Freeman (born Oct. 1, 1801) and Mary Freeman (born Aug. 28, 1807), but no relationship was stated [Ref: P-1879]. See "Thomas Jones," q.v.
JONES, Richard (1736-   ). Private, enrolled by Ensign Alexander Truman on July 7, 1776, for continental service, Maryland Line [Ref: D-38, R-67]. See "Samuel Jones," q.v.
JONES, Roger. Private, Capt. Benjamin Wailes' Militia Company, Lower Battalion; on duty guarding Magruder's Warehouse in the spring of 1782 [Ref: L-19970 (Box 6, folder 21)].
JONES, Samuel (Mar. 29, 1728 - 1803 or 1806?). Son of Richard and Elizabeth Jones [Ref: ZC-182]. Took the Oath of Allegiance before the Hon. Richard Henderson in 1778 [Ref: O-277, R-46]. The estate of one Samuel Jones was probated on Feb. 15, 1803, and the estate of another Samuel Jones was probated on Nov. 6, 1806 [Ref: ZE-110].
JONES, Sarah. See "Charles Boteler, Jr." and "Edward Jones" and "Thomas Gill," q.v.

JONES, Silvester (1741-   ). Took the Oath of Allegiance before the Hon. Osborn Sprigg in 1778 [Ref: O-306, R-65].

JONES, Susannah. See "Richard Jones" and "Thomas Conner," q.v.

JONES, Thomas (May 16, 1732 -   ). Son of Richard and Rachel Jones of Queen Anne's Parish [Ref: ZC-182]. Took the Oath of Allegiance (affirmed) before the Hon. Benjamin Hall in 1778 [Ref: O-275].

JONES, Thomas (Jan. 23, 1757 - died after 1833). Thomas Jones, aged 78 in 1833, applied for pension (R20304) in Prince George's County, stating he lived in Charles County at the time of his enlistment in the Maryland Line. His application was rejected [Ref: P-1883]. One Thomas Jones, son of Philip and Penelopy, was born Jan. 23, 1757, in Prince George's County [Ref: ZC-36].

JONES, Thomas (Oct. 23, 1743 - Jan. 1, 1813). Son of William and Mary Jones [Ref: ZC-36]. Private, Maryland Line. He lived in Prince George's County at time of enlistment, married Elizabeth Duvall on Feb. 1, 1777 at Bladensburg, and had these children: Lewis Jones (born Nov. 10, 1777), Thomas Jones (born Apr. 28, 1780), Frances Jones (born Oct. 29, 1782), Garrettson and Ann Jones (twins born Mar. 14, 1786), Frederick Jones (born Oct. 24, 1788), Phillemon Jones (born Jan. 21, 1779), and Richard Jones (born July 15, 1800). Elizabeth Jones applied for pension (W9487) in Baltimore, Maryland on Oct. 17, 1840, aged 85, at which time all of her children were married and she had 47 grandchildren [Ref: R-9, Z-1627, P-1882, which latter source mistakenly listed her name as "Dinall" instead of "Duvall"]. The estate of Thomas Jones was probated on Mar. 13, 1813 [Ref: ZE-110].

JONES, Thomas Culver. See "Richard Jones," q.v.

JONES, William (Apr. 17, 1716 - 1789). Son of Edward and "Eliz(?)" Jones [Ref: ZC-37]. Took the Oath of Allegiance (made a horizontal "I" mark with an equidistant vertical line through the middle) before the Hon. Thomas Clagett in 1778 [Ref: O-268, R-42]. The estate of one William Jones was probated on Jan. 20, 1790 in Prince George's County [Ref: ZE-110]. See "Lewin Jones" and "Notley Jones," q.v.

JONES, William (1764, Maryland - died after 1820, Virginia). Private (substitute), 1780, continental service, and private in the 2nd Maryland Line, Capt. William Murdock's Company, Mar. 15, 1781 [Ref: D-338, D-366]. On Feb. 12, 1820, the Treasurer of the Western Shore was directed to pay to William Jones, formerly of Prince George's County, Maryland, now residing in the State of Virginia, quarterly, for life, half pay of a private, for his services during the war [Ref: O-361]. One William Jones married Darkey Mockbee by license dated June 25, 1791, and a William Jones married Sabret King by license dated Feb. 11, 1793 [Ref: ZB-125].

JONES, Zachariah. Two men by this name took the Oath of Allegiance in 1778: one before the Hon. Christopher Lowndes and one before the Hon. David Craufurd [Ref: O-271, O-288].

JOURDAN, Anne. See "Basil Beall," q.v.
JOURDAN, Elise. See "Moses Orme" and "Robert Orme," q.v.
JOVER (JERAC?), Jacob. Took the Oath of Allegiance before the Hon. Christopher Lowndes in 1778 [Ref: O-284].
JOVER (JERAC?), John. Took the Oath of Allegiance before the Hon. Christopher Lowndes in 1778 [Ref: O-285].
KAINE, Edward (1756, England -   ). Private, enrolled in the Flying Camp by Lieut. William D. Beall on July 16, 1776; nativity: England; height: 5' 5"; brown hair, fair complexion [Ref: D-37]. See "Edward Cain," q.v.
KANE, Mary. See "Smallwood Acton," q.v.
KEADLE, Elizabeth. See "William Keadle" and "John Moore," q.v.
KEADLE, James Gibson. Took the Oath of Allegiance before the Hon. David Craufurd in 1778 [Ref: O-272].
KEADLE, Thomas. Private (substitute), continental service, 1781 [Ref: D-382]. Thomas Keadle married Mary Perry by license dated June 15, 1784 [Ref: ZB-126].
KEADLE, William (c1750 - died after Mar. 11, 1794). Took the Oath of Allegiance before the Hon. David Craufurd in 1778 [Ref: O-271]. Constable in Charlotte Hundred in 1778 [Ref: Z-30]. He married Elizabeth ---- [Ref: X-1639].
KEARNES, Thomas. Private, 2nd Maryland Line, Capt. Alexander Truman's Company, 1782; "not heard of since Mar. muster, then waiter to General Gates." [Ref: D-440].
KEETCH, George. Took the Oath of Allegiance (made his "X" mark) before the Hon. Thomas Clagett in 1778 [Ref: O-267]. A "George Keath" was aged 51 in 1776 in Prince George's County [Ref: R-78].
KEITCH, John (1737-1783?). Private, Maryland Line, enlisted June 5, 1781, for 3 years in continental service; sent to Annapolis; was on furlough on July 13, 1781 [Ref: D-382, D-396, D-453]. The estate of one "John Keech" was probated by July 16, 1783 (date of inventory). [Ref: ZE-110].
KEITH, Duncan. Corporal, 3rd Maryland Line, in Capt. Horatio Clagett's Company, July 1, 1779 [Ref: D-130, D-295].
KEITH, Elizabeth. See "John Contee," q.v.
KEITH, James. "James Keth" took the Oath of Allegiance before the Hon. Osborn Sprigg in 1778 [Ref: O-307]. The estate of one "James Keith" was probated on June 19, 1790 [Ref: ZE-110].
KELLEE, Joseph (1760, Maryland -   ). Private (recruit), 1780, in continental service, Maryland Line [Ref: D-338].
KELLY, James (1753, Maryland -   ). Private, enlisted on May 29, 1781, for 3 years in continental service, Maryland Line; sent to Annapolis; reportedly "deserted" before July 13, 1781 [Ref: D-382].
KELOUGH, Mary. See "John Boswell," q.v.

KELSON, George. Private, 2nd Maryland Line, Capt. Alexander Truman's Company, 1782 [Ref: D-440]. Received bounty land warrant 11427-100-1 in February, 1790; "no pension papers." [Ref: P-1917].
KENNEDY, Henrietta. See "Henry Hill, Jr.," q.v.
KENNEDY, Monica. See "Samuel Luckett," q.v.
KENT, Alice Lee. See "Benjamin Contee," q.v.
KERRICK, Benjamin H. (c1765-c1838). Fifer, 2nd Maryland Line, Capt. Alexander Truman's Company, 1782 [Ref: D-439]. He received bounty land warrant #11429-100-25 in September, 1789, and also applied for and received a pension (S46386) on Nov. 4, 1828, in Spencer County, Kentucky. He also served in the 6th Maryland Line [Ref: P-1932, X-498, and Anderson C. Quisenberry's *Revolutionary Soldiers in Kentucky* (1896), p. 158].
KERRICK, Joseph. Private, 2nd Maryland Line, Capt. Alexander Truman's Company, 1782; died Dec. 27, 1782 [Ref: D-439].
KETCHLY, David. Took the Oath of Allegiance before the Hon. James Beck in 1778 [Ref: O-255].
KEY, Theophilus. Private, Capt. Benjamin Wailes' Militia Company, Lower Battalion; on duty guarding Magruder's Warehouse in the spring of 1782 [Ref: L-19970 (Box 6, folder 21)].
KIDWELL, Alexander. Took the Oath of Allegiance before the Hon. David Craufurd in 1778 [Ref: O-271].
KIDWELL, Benjamin (May 25, 1754, Wales - Feb. 10, 1810). Private, 3rd Maryland Line, enlisted May 26, 1778; Capt. Horatio Claggett's Company, December, 1779; furloughed Jan. 4, 1780. Benjamin Kidwell married Elizabeth Mudd, probably in Prince George's County [Ref: D-130, D-296, and a query in the *Maryland Genealogical Society Bulletin*, Volume 33, No. 4 (Fall, 1992), page 828, submitted by Dr. Richard D. Mudd, 1001 Hoyt Avenue, Saginaw, Michigan 48607]. Source X-1673 states Benjamin died on Dec. 10, 1810, not Feb. 10, 1810. The estate of another Benjamin Kidwell was probated on July 30, 1792 [Ref: ZE-111]. Additional research may be necessary before drawing conclusions.
KIDWELL, Elijah. Private, enrolled by Ensign Horatio Clagett on July 15, 1776, for continental service, Maryland Line [Ref: D-35].
KIDWELL, Hezekiah (c1760, Maryland - c1810/18, Kentucky). Private, Capt. Jesse Hellen's Militia Company, before May 23, 1782; guarded Magruder's Warehouse in the spring of 1782 [Ref: L-19970 (Box 6, folder 21)]. Took the Oath of Allegiance before the Hon. Osborn Sprigg in 1778 [Ref: O-308, which spelled his name "Cidwell"]. Hezekiah Kidwell married Susannah ---- [Ref: X-1673].
KIDWELL, James. Private, enrolled by Lt. William Duvall, Lower Battalion, on July 18, 1776, for continental service, Maryland Line [Ref: D-35]. One James Kidwell married Mary Mudd by license dated Dec. 18, 1790 [Ref: ZB-128].

KIDWELL, John. Private, Capt. Jesse Hellen's Militia Company, by May 23, 1782; guarded Magruder's Warehouse in the spring of 1782 [Ref: L-19970 (Box 6, folder 21)]. One John Kidwell married Mary Lawson by license dated Feb. 22, 1784, and a John Kidwell married Eleanor Hays by license dated Jan. 5, 1785 [Ref: ZB-128].

KIDWELL, Marshall. Private, Capt. Jesse Hellen's Militia Company, before May 23, 1782; guarded Magruder's Warehouse in the spring of 1782 [Ref: L-19970 (Box 6, folder 21)].

KIDWELL, Richard. Private, Capt. Jesse Hellen's Militia Company, before May 23, 1782; guarded Magruder's Warehouse in the spring of 1782 [Ref: L-19970 (Box 6, folder 21)].

KIDWELL, Susannah. See "Hezekiah Kidwell," q.v.

KIDWELL, William. Private, Capt. Jesse Hellen's Militia Company, by May 23, 1782; guarded Magruder's Warehouse in the spring of 1782 [Ref: L-19970 (Box 6, folder 21)]. One William Kidwell married Eleanor Gray by license dated Jan. 4, 1783 [Ref: ZB-128].

KILLEGAN, James. Private, 2nd Maryland Line, enlisted May 9, 1779 and served until June, 1782 [Ref: D-129, D-461]. The estate of one James Killegan was probated on May 17, 1794 [Ref: ZE-111].

KING, Ann. See "Zadock Moore," q.v.

KING, Benjamin. Took the Oath of Allegiance before the Hon. Osborn Sprigg in 1778 [Ref: O-300].

KING, Cassandra. See "Zadock Riston," q.v.

KING, Dradin. See "James King," q.v.

KING, Eleanor. See "John King" and "Ashburn Hilleary," q.v.

KING, Franncis. See "Thomas King," q.v.

KING, Henry. Private, 1st Guard, Capt. Henry Hill's Militia Company, Lower Battalion; on duty at Nottingham on the Patuxent, Apr. 12, 1781 [Ref: L-19970 (Box 6, folder 21)]. Took the Oath of Allegiance before the Hon. Osborn Sprigg in 1778 [Ref: O-308, W-4648 (Box 4, folder 29)]. The estate of one Henry King was probated by May 7, 1787 (date of Inventory). [Ref: ZE-112].

KING, James. Private, Capt. Hezekiah Wheeler's Company, 11th Militia Battalion, April, 1781 [Ref: L-19970 (Box 6, folder 21)]. Private, Select Militia, Capt. Hezekiah Wheeler's Company, July 14, 1781 [Ref: S-6636 (Box 31, folder 5)]. Took the Oath of Allegiance before the Hon. Osborn Sprigg in 1778 [Ref: O-307]. "James King, taylor" was aged 28 in 1776 [Ref: R-56]. The estate of one James King was probated on Jan. 31, 1828 [Ref: ZE-112].

KING, John (1702-1789). Took the Oath of Allegiance before the Hon. Osborn Sprigg in 1778 [Ref: O-308, R-82]. The estate of one John King was probated on Jan. 12, 1790 [Ref: ZE-112].

KING, John (1738-1816). Took the Oath of Allegiance before the Hon. Alexander Howard Magruder in 1778 [Ref: O-293, R-78]. He married

Eleanor ---- [Ref: X-1685]. The estate of "John King, Sr." was probated on Jan. 31, 1816 [Ref: ZE-112].
KING, John (1751 - 1821 or 1831?). Private (draft), continental service, 1780 [Ref: D-382, R-87]. One John King married Susanna Leach by license dated Nov. 25, 1777, and a John King married Keziah Upton by license dated June 6, 1779 [Ref: ZB-129]. The estate of one John King was probated on Jan. 16, 1821, and the estate of another John King was probated on Apr. 4, 1831 [Ref: ZE-112]. Additional research may be necessary before drawing conclusions.
KING, Leonard. Private, Capt. Alexander H. Magruder's Militia Company, Lower Battalion; on duty guarding Magruder's Warehouse in the spring of 1782 [Ref: L-19970 (Box 6, folder 21)]. Leonard King married Susanna Watson by license dated Nov. 15, 1780 [Ref: ZB-129].
KING, Margaret. See "Thomas King," q.v.
KING, Philip. Private, 2nd Maryland Line, Capt. Patrick Sim's Company, 1776 [Ref: D-8].
KING, Richard (1691 - after 1778). Took the Oath of Allegiance before the Hon. Osborn Sprigg in 1778 [Ref: O-307, R-48].
KING, Ruth. See "Thomas Simpson," q.v.
KING, Sabret. See "William Jones," q.v.
KING, Sarah. See "John Grimes," q.v.
KING, Susanna. See "John Biggs," q.v.
KING, Thomas. There were several men with this name: (1) Took the Oath of Allegiance before the Hon. Christopher Lowndes in 1778 [Ref: O-285]. (2) Took the Oath of Allegiance (made his "+" mark) before the Hon. Truman Skinner in 1778 [Ref: O-297]. (3) Took the Oath of Allegiance before the Hon. Benjamin Hall in 1778 [Ref: O-276]. One Thomas King was a private (draft) in the Maryland Line, continental service, in 1780 [Ref: D-382]. One Thomas King married Mary Mitchell by license dated Oct. 16, 1787, and a Thomas M. King married Rebecca Gray by license dated Jan. 18, 1790 [Ref: ZB-130]. Also, Thomas King, son of Francis and Margaret King, of Queen Anne's Parish, was born on Nov. 5, 1720 [Ref: ZC-182]. Additional research may be necessary before drawing conclusions.
KING, William. Second Lieutenant, Militia, Capt. Michael Lowe's Company, Sep. 20, 1776. Quartermaster, Horse Troops, June 9, 1781 [Ref: M-95, B-287, G-467]. Took the Oath of Allegiance before the Hon. Truman Skinner in 1778 [Ref: O-298].
KING, William. Took the Oath of Allegiance (made his "X" mark) before the Hon. Thomas Clagett in 1778 [Ref: O-267].
KIRBY (KERBY), Francis (1758 - Oct. 14, 1831). "Richard Kerby" was a patriot who was paid for manufacturing salt on Sep. 2, 1782. He is buried in the St. John's Churchyard at Broad Creek, Prince George's County [Ref: Y-613]. "Francis Kirby" married Elizabeth Collard by license dated Jan. 11, 1783 [Ref: ZB-130].

KIRBY (KERBY), John Baptist (1750 - Apr. 1, 1828). "John Baptist Kerby" was a private, 6th Company of Maryland Troops, Feb. 24, 1776 [Ref: D-15]. "John Baptist Cirby" took the Oath of Allegiance before the Hon. William Berry in 1778 [Ref: O-259]. He is buried in the St. John's Churchyard at Broad Creek, Prince George's County [Ref: U-614, ZE-111]. "John Baptist Kirby" married Sarah Elson by license dated Sep. 23, 1779 [Ref: ZB-130].

KIRBY, Richard. Served on a Grand Jury in 1778 [Ref: Z-52, Z-90]. One Richard Kirby married Susanna Talburt by license dated Sep. 9, 1783 [Ref: ZB-130]. The estate of one Richard Kirby was probated on Oct. 22, 1785 and the estate of another Richard Kirby was probated on July 20, 1797 [Ref: ZE-112]. See "Richard Carbury (Carby)," q.v.

KIRK, James. Private, Northern Detachment, 3rd Maryland Line, Capt. Horatio Clagett's Company, 1783 [Ref: D-502]. The estate of one James Kirk was probated on May 17, 1793 [Ref: ZE-112].

KNIGHT, Eleasa. See "George Knight," q.v.

KNIGHT, George. Took the Oath of Allegiance before the Hon. Christopher Lowndes in 1778 [Ref: O-288]. Private, 2nd Maryland Line, 1778; discharged on Oct. 1, 1780 [Ref: D-129]. In 1778 Eleasa Knight petitioned the Prince George's County Court and was allowed ten pounds current money because her husband [not named] "has gone to camp and left her without subsistence." [Ref: Z-97].

KNIGHTON, John. Private (draught), Major Higgins' Battalion, Capt. Mullikin's Company, continental service, 1781 [Ref: D-399].

KNIGHTON, Keizer (1743-   ). Took the Oath of Allegiance (made his "X" mark) before the Hon. Thomas Clagett in 1778 [Ref: O-269, R-76, which spelled the name "Nighton"].

KNIGHTON, William. Private, Col. Grayson's Regiment, Capt. Grant's Company, continental service, 1780-1781 [Ref: D-602].

KNOTT, Elizabeth. See "John Goddard," q.v.

LACKLIN, Leonard. Private, enrolled by Capt. John H. Lowe on July 13, 1776, for continental service, Maryland Line [Ref: D-34, which spelled the name "Lenard Lacklin"].

LAMAR, Priscilla. See "James Drane, Jr.," q.v.

LAMAR, Richard. Took the Oath of Allegiance before the Hon. Benjamin Hall in 1778 [Ref: O-276]. One Richard Lamar married Ann Drane by license dated Nov. 9, 1790 [Ref: ZB-131]. The estate of one Richard Lamar was probated on May 15, 1807, and the estate of another Richard Lamar was probated on Feb. 13, 1821 [Ref: ZE-113].

LAMAR, William (1755 - Jan. 8, 1838). Rendered patriotic service by providing supplies to Capt. Robert Bowie on Aug. 10, 1781, in Prince George's County [Ref: Q-422]. Private in 1776, Ensign in 1777, Lieutenant in 1777, Quartermaster in 1778, and Captain by 1782. This might be the William Lamar who applied for and received pension S46388 in Allegheny County in 1828 (and bounty land in 1800). If so, he married Margaret Worthington and served in the 1st and 7th Maryland Lines [Ref: Q-599, P-1997, X-1729, D-50, D-224]. There was also a William Lamar who married Sarah Peirce by license dated Mar. 29, 1804 [Ref: ZB-131].

LAMAR, William Bishop (Aug. 3, 1745, Maryland - Aug. 29, 1812, Tennessee). Took the Oath of Allegiance before the Hon. James Mullikin in 1778 [Ref: O-295]. William Bishop Lamar married Elizabeth Smith [Ref: X-1729].

LANE, John. Took the Oath of Allegiance before the Hon. Fielder Bowie in 1778 [Ref: O-304, W-4648 (Box 4, folder 15)]. John Lane married Margaret Burnes by license dated Feb. 21, 1781 [Ref: ZB-132].

LANE, Thomas. Private, enrolled by Capt. Alexander H. Magruder, 11th Battalion, on Aug. 19, 1776, for continental service, Maryland Line [Ref: D-38].

LANGLEY, John Francis. Took the Oath of Allegiance (made his "X" mark) before the Hon. Thomas Clagett in 1778 [Ref: O-266].

LANGLEY, Joseph. Took the Oath of Allegiance before the Hon. Thomas Clagett in 1778 [Ref: O-268].

LANGLEY, Joseph Acseveris(?). Took the Oath of Allegiance (made his "X" mark) before the Hon. Thomas Clagett in 1778 [Ref: O-268].

LANHAM, Aaron. Rendered patriotic service by providing wheat for the military on Sep. 2, 1780 [Ref: Q-314].

LANHAM, Ann Roby. See "Henry Barnes," q.v.

LANHAM, Archibald (1751-   ). Took the Oath of Allegiance before the Hon. William Berry in 1778 [Ref: O-258, R-49].

LANHAM, Catherine. See "William Lanham," q.v.

LANHAM, Charity. See "Solomon Lanham," q.v.

LANHAM, Darby. Private, 2nd Maryland Line, Capt. Alexander Truman's Company, 1782 [Ref: D-439, which spelled his name "Leneham"].

LANHAM, Edward (Feb. 28, 1732 -   ). Son of Edward Lanham [Ref: ZC-39]. Took the Oath of Allegiance before the Hon. Thomas Clagett in 1778 [Ref: O-266]. Private, Select Militia, Capt. Hezekiah Wheeler's Company, July 14, 1781 [Ref: S-6636 (Box 31, folder 5)]. See "Josias Lanham" and "Notley Lanham" and "Richard Lanham," q.v.

LANHAM, Edward (1750-1791). Captain, Militia, Middle Battalion, May 24, 1779 [Ref: M-96, E-414, R-75]. Edward Lanham married Susannah Page [Ref: X-1742]. The estate of Edward Lanham was probated on Apr. 7, 1791 [Ref: ZE-114].

LANHAM, Eleanor. See "Henry Lanham," q.v.

LANHAM, Eli. Private, enrolled by Capt. John H. Lowe on July 13, 1776, for continental service, Maryland Line [Ref: D-35]. Took the Oath of Allegiance (made his "X" mark) before the Hon. Thomas Clagett in 1778 [Ref: O-268, which spelled his name "Elie Lanham"].

LANHAM, Elias (1751-   ). Took the Oath of Allegiance (made his "X" mark) before the Hon. Thomas Clagett in 1778 [Ref: O-268, R-7].

Private, enrolled by Capt. John H. Lowe on July 13, 1776, for continental service, Maryland Line [Ref: D-35].

LANHAM, Elisha (June 23, 1725 -   ). Son of John Lanham and Mary Dickinson [Ref: ZC-39]. Took the Oath of Allegiance before the Hon. Thomas Clagett in 1778 [Ref: O-266, R-10]. Served on a Grand Jury in 1777 [Ref: Z-29].

LANHAM, Elizabeth. See "John D. Lanham" and "Henry Lanham," q.v.

LANHAM, George (c1760 - 1792?). Took the Oath of Allegiance (made his "X" mark) before the Hon. Thomas Clagett in 1778 [Ref: O-266]. George Lanham married Ann Jarmain by license dated Feb. 23, 1781 [Ref: X-1742, ZB-132]. The estate of one George Lanham was probated by Apr. 7, 1792 (date of account). [Ref: ZE-114].

LANHAM, Henry (May 28, 1761 - Nov. 20, 1849). Son of Shadrick and Sarah Lanham [Ref: ZC-39]. Private, 2nd Maryland Line, Capt. Patrick Sim's Company, 1776 [Ref: D-8]. One Henry Lanham married Eleanor (Millia) ----. [Ref: X-1742]. There was also a Henry Dickerson Lanham, son of Jessey and Elizabeth Lanham, of Prince George's Parish, who was born on July 25, 1760 [Ref: ZD-116]. The estate of one Henry Lanham was probated in 1778 [Ref: ZE-114]. Additional research may be necessary before drawing conclusions.

LANHAM, Hezekiah. Private, Capt. Hezekiah Wheeler's Company, 11th Militia Battalion, April, 1781 [Ref: L-19970 (Box 6, folder 21)]. Took the Oath of Allegiance before the Hon. William Lyles, Jr. in 1778 [Ref: O-290].

LANHAM, Hilliary. "Hillary Lanham" was a private in the Maryland Line, enlisted Sep. 13, 1781 [Ref: D-424]. "Hilliary Lanham" married Elizabeth Upton by license dated Apr. 5, 1783 [Ref: ZB-132].

LANHAM, Jeremiah. Took the Oath of Allegiance before the Hon. Christopher Lowndes in 1778 [Ref: O-285].

LANHAM, Jessey. See "Henry Lanham," q.v.

LANHAM, John. Private, 1st Maryland Line, Dec. 10, 1776 until discharged on Dec. 27, 1779 [Ref: D-131]. See "Elisha Lanham" and "William Lanham," q.v.

LANHAM, John Downs (Aug. 13, 1758 -   ). A son of Josias and Elizabeth Lanham, he married Susannah Allen on Feb. 27, 1791 [Ref: ZC-39]. Private, 2nd Maryland Line, Capt. Patrick Sim's Company, 1776 [Ref: D-8, which listed him as "John D. Lanham"].

LANHAM, Josias (Sep. 2, 1728 -   ). Son of Edward Lanham [Ref: ZC-40]. Took the Oath of Allegiance before the Hon. Thomas Clagett in 1778 [Ref: O-265, R-57]. See "John Downs Lanham" and "Solomon Lanham," q.v.

LANHAM, Kinsey. Corporal, 4th Maryland Line, 1782 [Ref: D-458].

LANHAM, Leah. See "Stephen Lanham," q.v.

LANHAM, Mary. See "John Frazier" and "Solomon Lanham," q.v.

LANHAM, Moses. Took the Oath of Allegiance before the Hon. Christopher Lowndes in 1778 [Ref: O-286].

LANHAM, Nathan (1724-   ). Took the Oath of Allegiance before the Hon. Christopher Lowndes in 1778 [Ref: O-286, R-25].

LANHAM, Notley (Oct. 11, 1724 - 1783?). Son of Edward Lanham [Ref: ZC-40, which spelled his name "Nottley Lanham"]. Took the Oath of Allegiance before the Hon. Christopher Lowndes in 1778 [Ref: O-284]. The estate of one "Nolley Lanham" was probated by Feb. 21, 1783 (date of inventory). [Ref: ZE-114].

LANHAM, Richard (July 16, 1737 - 1819?). Son of Edward and "Susane(?)" *[sic]* Lanham [Ref: ZC-40]. Private, 1st Maryland Line, from June 5, 1778 until discharged Apr. 5, 1779 [Ref: D-132]. Private, 1st Maryland Line, who was paid for his services "in cloathing" on Apr. 17, 1779 [Ref: E-351]. The estate of one Richard Lanham was probated on Aug. 23, 1819 [Ref: ZE-114].

LANHAM, Robert. Private, Select Militia, Upper Battalion, June 12, 1781 [Ref: S-6636 (Box 27, folder 82B)]. Private, Militia, 1781; participated in capturing an enemy boat and crew on Apr. 17, 1781 [Ref: M-209].

LANHAM, Samuel (1746-   ). Took the Oath of Allegiance before the Hon. Joshua Beall in 1778 [Ref: O-251, R-71]. Constable in Oxon Hundred, 1777-1778 [Ref: Z-3, Z-30].

LANHAM, Sarah. See "Shadrick Lanham" and "Henry Lanham" and "Basil Green" and "Stephen Lanham," q.v.

LANHAM, Shadrick (1729, Maryland - died after 1814, Indiana). Took the Oath of Allegiance before the Hon. William Berry in 1778 [Ref: O-259, R-27]. Shadrick Lanham married Sarah ---- [Ref: X-1743]. See "Henry Lanham," q.v.

LANHAM, Solomon (1755-   ). Took the Oath of Allegiance before the Hon. Thomas Clagett in 1778 [Ref: O-267]. This name is listed twice in the census of 1776, both men aged 21 [Ref: R-7, R-75]. One Solomon Lanham married Charity Lanham by license dated Jan. 14, 1778 [Ref: ZB-133]. One Solomon Lanham, son of Josias and Mary Lanham, was born Jan. 2, 1753 or 1754 (recorded twice in King George's Parish, but with a different year). [Ref: ZC-40].

LANHAM, Stephen Sr. (May 28, 1726 - died after Sep. 9, 1806). Son of Thomas and Sarah Lanham, he rendered patriotic service and married (1) Leah ----, and (2) Susannah ---- [Ref: X-1743, ZC-40]. See "Thomas Lanham," q.v.

LANHAM, Susannah. See "Stephen Lanham" and "Richard Lanham," q.v.

LANHAM, Thomas (1757 - died after Mar. 25, 1840, Madison County, Kentucky). Private, Maryland Line. He applied for and received a pension (S30534) in Madison County, Kentucky on June 8, 1836, stating that he was born in Prince George's County and lived there with his parents (not named) at the time of his enlistment. After the war he moved near Wheeling, Virginia, and then moved to Kentucky. His brother Stephen Lanham also made affidavit in Kentucky in 1836 and stated that he (Stephen) was born in Prince George's County in 1760 [Ref: P-2012]. Thomas Lanham married Patience Sappington [Ref: X-1743]. See "Stephen Lanham," q.v.

LANHAM, William (c1750 - 1821/1826?). Took the Oath of Allegiance before the Hon. Christopher Lowndes in 1778 [Ref: O-286, R-70]. William Lanham, son of John and Catherine Lanham, was baptized on Feb. 4, 1753, in King George's Parish [Ref: ZC-40]. The estate of one William Lanham was probated on Jan. 22, 1821 and the estate of this or perhaps another William Lanham was probated on Oct. 16, 1826 [Ref: ZE-115].

LANN, Thomas (1760-   ). Private, enrolled in the Flying Camp by Capt. Robert Bowie on July 4, 1776; nativity: Maryland; height: 5' 4" [Ref: D-37].

LANSDALE, ----. See "Thomas Boyd," q.v.

LANSDALE, Charles (1742-c1795/1800). Took the Oath of Allegiance before the Hon. Thomas Clagett in 1778 [Ref: R-12, O-266, which latter source listed his name as "Landsdale"]. He also delivered money by order of the Maryland Council to the Purchaser of Provisions for Prince George's County in April, 1778 [Ref: E-56]. He married Catherine Wheeler [Ref: X-1744].

LANSDALE, Cornelia. See "Thomas Lancaster Lansdale," q.v.

LANSDALE, Eliza. See "Thomas Lancaster Lansdale," q.v.

LANSDALE, Isaac. Took the Oath of Allegiance before the Hon. Thomas Boyd in 1778 [Ref: O-262]. See "Thomas Lancaster Lansdale," q.v.

LANSDALE, John. Took the Oath of Allegiance before the Hon. James Mullikin in 1778 [Ref: O-296]. Second Lieutenant, Upper Battalion, Militia, Capt. Tyler's Company, June 27, 1781 [Ref: H-320, which spelled his name "Lansdell"].

LANSDALE, John Jr. Took the Oath of Allegiance before the Hon. James Mullikin in 1778 [Ref: O-295]. Constable, Patuxent Hundred, 1777 [Ref: Z-3].

LANSDALE, Margaret. See "Thomas Lancaster Lansdale," q.v.

LANSDALE, Martha. See "Thomas Lancaster Lansdale," q.v.

LANSDALE, Philip. See "Thomas Lancaster Lansdale," q.v.

LANSDALE, Richard (1723-1781). Took the Oath of Allegiance before the Hon. James Beck in 1778 [Ref: O-255, R-47]. The estate of one Richard Lansdale was probated on Mar. 12, 1781 [Ref: ZE-115].

LANSDALE, Thomas Lancaster (Nov. 10, 1748 - Jan. 17, 1803). A son of Isaac Lansdale (and grandson of Isaac Lansdale, the immigrant), Thomas married Cornelia Van Horn on Feb. 12, 1782 and had these children living in 1827: William M. Lansdale (born Dec. 1, 1782, married Eliza C. Moylan on Mar. 10, 1807, and lived in Harford County in 1827); Cornelia Lansdale (born May 7, 1784, married Philip I. Thomas on Nov. 8, 1804, and lived in Anne Arundel County in 1827); Violetta Lansdale (born

Feb. 2, 1787, married Samuel Sprigg [no date], and lived in Prince George's County in 1827); Eliza Lansdale (born May 8, 1789, married ---- Cox, and lived in New York City in 1827); Philip Lansdale (born Aug. 8, 1791 and lived in Anne Arundel County in 1827). Thomas Lansdale died in Prince George's County on Jan. 17, 1803, and Cornelia Lansdale applied for and received pension W13604 on Aug. 24, 1838, in Washington, DC. Also, Dr. John M. Thomas (grandson) lived in Washington, DC in 1838 [Ref: P-2013]. First Lieutenant of a Baltimore Company in the Flying Camp, July to December 1776; taken prisoner at Fort Washington. Captain, 4th Maryland Regiment, Dec. 10, 1776. Major, 3rd Maryland Regiment, May 22, 1779. Served to Nov. 15, 1783. "Died Jan. 19, 1805. Buried in the Lansdale Cemetery, Route 197, near Belair, Prince George's County. Tombstone now missing." Cornelia V. Lansdale died at her birthplace at Lothian in Anne Arundel County [Ref: Y-582, Y-612]. Source X-1744 lists a Thomas Lancaster Lansdale (1727-1785) who married Martha ---- and was also a major during the war. Source ZC-182 lists a Thomas Lancaster Lansdale, son of Isaac and Margaret Lansdale, of Queen Anne's Parish, who was born Nov. 5, 1727. See Henry C. Peden, Jr.'s *Revolutionary Patriots of Baltimore Town and Baltimore County, 1775-1783*, pp. 154-155. The estate of Thomas Lansdale was probated on Jan. 27, 1803 in Prine George's County [Ref: ZE-115, which also referred to him as "Major Thomas Lansdale"]. Additional research may be necessary before drawing conclusions.

LANSDALE, Violetta. See "Thomas Lancaster Lansdale," q.v.

LANSDALE, William. Took the Oath of Allegiance before the Hon. James Beck in 1778 [Ref: O-253]. See "Thomas Lansdale," q.v.

LARKIN, Elias. Took the Oath of Allegiance before the Hon. Fielder Bowie in 1778 [Ref: O-304, W-4648 (Box 4, folder 15)].

LASHLY, Mary. See "John Wood," q.v.

LAURIE, Gaven. Took the Oath of Allegiance before the Hon. William Berry in 1778 [Ref: O-258].

LAW, Patrick. Private, Militia, 1776 [Ref: M-207, A-325].

LAWS, George. Private, 2nd Maryland Line, enlisted June 2, 1778, and in service to at least Nov. 1, 1780 [Ref: D-133].

LAWS, William. Private, 2nd Maryland Line, enlisted May 18, 1777 and served to at least Jan. 1, 1781 [Ref: D-133, D-357]. One William Laws married Martha Walker by license dated May 26, 1784 [Ref: ZB-134].

LAWSON, ----. See "John Hawkins Lowe," q.v.

LAWSON, Elizabeth. See "George Lee," q.v.

LAWSON, John. Took the Oath of Allegiance (made his "X" mark) which was recorded on a "return of Capt. Tapley of the brig *Royal*" and filed in court by the Hon. Thomas Gantt, Jr. in 1778 [Ref: O-305, W-4648 (Box 4, folder 15)].

LAWSON, Mary. See "John Kidwell," q.v.

LAWSON, Thomas. Took the Oath of Allegiance (made his "T" mark) before the Hon. Thomas Gantt, Jr. in 1778 [Ref: O-305, W-4648 (Box 4, folder 15)].

LAWSON, Thomas Jr. "Thomas Lawson, Jr." was a private, Capt. Jesse Hellen's Militia Company, before May 23, 1782; guarded Magruder's Warehouse in the spring of 1782 [Ref: L-19970 (Box 6, folder 21)]. Took the Oath of Allegiance before the Hon. Truman Skinner in 1778 [Ref: O-297]. "Thomas Lawson" married Priscilla Hyde by license dated Feb. 26, 1791 [Ref: ZB-134].

LAWSON, William. Took the Oath of Allegiance before the Hon, Osborn Sprigg in 1778 [Ref: O-306, and the original list (very light) at the Maryland State Archives (Box 4, folder 29), which actually listed the name as either "Losson" or "Lasson"]. William Lawson married Eleanor Simpson by license dated Nov. 16, 1778 [Ref: ZB-134].

LAY, John. Private, enrolled by Ensign Horatio Clagett on July 15, 1776, for continental service, Maryland Line [Ref: D-35].

LAZENBY, Elias (Mar. 18, 1752, Maryland - died before Jan. 7, 1820, Georgia). Ensign, 25th Battalion, Capt. Thomas Richardson's Company, Apr. 10, 1776 [Ref: M-96, A-320, which spelled his name "Lazinbey"]. Second Lieutenant, June 9, 1777 [Ref: M-98, which mistakenly listed his name as "Logenby"]. He married Martha Jones and later lived and served in Montgomery County [Ref: X-1758, Also see Henry C. Peden, Jr.'s *Revolutionary Patriots of Montgomery County, 1775-1783*, page 195].

LEACH, Susannah. See "John King," q.v.

LEACH, Thomas. See "John Spires," q.v.

LEASURE, Nancy. See "Nathan Scarce," q.v.

LEASURE, Robert. See "Nathan Scarce," q.v.

LEE, Archibald. See "Thomas Sim Lee," q.v.

LEE, Elizabeth. See "Thomas Sim Lee," q.v.

LEE, George (1736, Prince George's County - 1807, Charles County). Son of Philip Lee and Elizabeth Lawson. He married Chloe Hanson by 1760 and had "at least daughters, born in 1764 and 1766" [Ref: U-525]. Delegate to the Maryland Convention on July 26, 1775 [Ref: A-3, U-70]. Commissioned a Second Major, 25th Battalion, Jan. 13, 1776, but returned the commission to Col. Joshua Beall on Jan. 30, 1776, stating "I was nominated by the officers of the companies of which the lower battalion is composed as a field officer of that battalion and as the gentleman thought me unworthy of a commission there, I beg leave to return the one they sent me. I never aspired after a commission anywhere, but as the gentlemen officers aforesaid thought proper to mention me in their return, I should have done all in my power to render them satisfaction had I been appointed. I hope my refusal to act under this commission may not be construed into any disrespect shown to you and those under your command as I can assure you nothing of the sort is intended." [Ref: M-97, A-126]. Justice of the County Court, 1777 [Ref: C-273]. Justice who administered the Oath of Allegiance in 1778 [Ref: O-279, R-43]. Surveyor General of the Western Shore, 1768-1771. Justice, Charles County, 1764-1766, 1769-1770. Sheriff, Charles County, 1771-1774. Justice, Prince George's County, 1779-1780. Justice, Charles County, 1784-1795 [Ref: U-525, U-526]. The estate of one George Lee was probated in Prince George's County on Sep. 30, 1807 [Ref: ZE-116].

LEE, Henry. Took the Oath of Allegiance (made his "H" mark) before the Hon. Alexander Howard Magruder in 1778 [Ref: O-293]. One Henry Lee married Elizabeth Cave by license dated Dec. 15, 1781 [Ref: ZB-134].

LEE, Ignatius. See "Thomas Sim Lee," q.v.

LEE, Mary Digges. She was the wife of Gov. Thomas Sim Lee "who by his patriotic zeal was able to send supplies and recruits to the Continental Army" and she [Mary] "inspired the women of Maryland to send extra supplies." [Ref: Y-613]. See "Thomas Sim Lee," q.v.

LEE, Philip. See "George Lee," q.v.

LEE, Robert. Private, Capt. Benjamin Wailes' Militia Company, Lower Battalion; on duty guarding Magruder's Warehouse in the spring of 1782 [Ref: L-19970 (Box 6, folder 21)].

LEE, Sarah Russell. See "Benjamin Contee," q.v.

LEE, Thomas Sim (Oct. 29, 1745, Upper Marlboro, Prince George's County at his father's home or at "Blenheim" in Charles County on his grandfather's estate - died on Oct. 9, 1819, at "Needwood," Frederick County). A son of Col. Thomas Lee and Christian Sim, he married Mary Digges in 1771 and had these children: Ignatius Digges Lee (died 1789), Archibald Lee (1778-1781), Archibald Lee (1781-1839), Thomas Lee (of Anne Arundel County), William Lee (of Cecil County), John Lee (1788-1871), Mary Christian Ringgold (moved to Louisiana), and Elizabeth Digges Horsey (moved to Delaware). [Ref: U-529]. Thomas held many public offices, including the following: Delegate to the Maryland Convention, 1775-1776. Clerk of the County Court, 1766-1776. Lower House of the Legislature, 1787-1788. State Senator, 1791-1796. Executive Council, 1777-1779. Governor of Maryland, 1779-1782, 1792-1794 (elected in 1798 but declined to accept). [Ref: A-7, U-70, U-74, U-530]. Also, on Mar. 16, 1777, "The Council proceeded to the choice of a member in the room of Charles Carroll, Sr., Esq., who resigned and the Hon. Thomas Sim Lee, Esq., was elected, who appearing was qualified by taking the Oaths, and subscribing to the Declaration directed by the Form of Government, and taking the Oath prescribed by the General Assembly" [Ref: C-189]. His military service: First Major, 11th Battalion, Jan. 13, 1776. Colonel, Lower Battalion, Feb. 4, 1777 to Mar. 26, 1777 (resignation accepted by the Council). [Ref: M-97, C-113, C-189, Y-613, X-1773, which latter two sources state that he died on Nov. 9, 1819,

187

while Source U-530 states that he died on Oct. 9, 1819. Source ZA-524 states he died Oct. 19, 1819].

LEE, William. See "Thomas Sim Lee," q.v.

LEECH, Benjamin. Corporal, Capt. Alexander H. Magruder's Militia Company, Lower Battalion; on duty guarding Magruder's Warehouse in the spring of 1782 [Ref: L-19970 (Box 6, folder 21)]. There was also a Benjamin Leech who was a sergeant at this same time.

LEECH, Benjamin. Sergeant, Capt. Alexander H. Magruder's Militia Company, Lower Battalion; on duty guarding Magruder's Warehouse in the spring of 1782 [Ref: L-19970 (Box 6, folder 21)]. This name appeared twice on the same muster roll; one Benjamin Leech was a corporal and another Benjamin Leech was a sergeant.

LEECH, Charles. Private, enrolled by Capt. Alexander H. Magruder, 11th Battalion, on July 23, 1776, for continental service, Maryland Line [Ref: D-38].

LEECH, Jeremiah. "Jeremiah Leech" was a private in Capt. Alexander H. Magruder's Militia Company, Lower Battalion; on duty guarding Magruder's Warehouse in the spring of 1782 [Ref: L-19970 (Box 6, folder 21)]. "Jeremiah Leitch" was a private (substitute) in the continental service, 1781, Maryland Continental Line [Ref: D-382].

LEEKE, Frank. Took the Oath of Allegiance before the Hon. David Craufurd in 1778 [Ref: O-271]. Served on the Board of Patuxent Associators and signed a resolution at Nottingham on Apr. 21, 1781 relative to the defence of the rivers of Potomac and Patuxent and the completion of the fort at Drum Point [Ref: K-1814, which spelled his name "Franke Leeke"]. Judge of the Orphans Court in 1779; referred to as "Esq." in 1780 [Ref: F-17, F-103]. The estate of Frank Leeke was probated on May 22, 1790 [Ref: ZE-117, which also referred to him as "Francis Leeke" in a 1791 account].

LEEKE, Henry. "Henry Leeke" was a private in the 1st Maryland Line, 1776; sergeant, Apr. 17, 1777; and discharged on Dec. 10, 1779 [Ref: D-131]. "Henry Leek" was a corporal in Capt. Patrick Sim's Company, 2nd Maryland Line, on Jan. 29, 1776 [Ref: D-7].

LEITCH, Margaret. See "William Sydebotham," q.v.

LETCHWORTH, Joseph. Took the Oath of Allegiance before the Hon. Alexander Howard Magruder in 1778 [Ref: O-293]. One Joseph Letchworth was a sergeant in the 6th Maryland Line who enlisted on June 21, 1777, and reportedly died on Apr. 3, 1778 [Ref: D-284].

LETCHWORTH, Levin. Corporal in Capt. Benjamin Wailes' Militia Company, Lower Battalion; on duty guarding Magruder's Warehouse in the spring of 1782 [Ref: L-19970 (Box 6, folder 21)].

LETTMAN, John (1749-   ). Private (draft), continental service, 1781 [Ref: D-382]. Discharged from the Maryland Line in 1781 [Ref: D-409, R-52].

LETTMAN, William. Private, 2nd Maryland Line, 1778, and reported to have been "killed at Eutaw." [Ref: D-133].
LEVI, Alexander. Private, 4th Maryland Line, enlisted on Apr. 22, 1778; stationed at Camp James Island, South Carolina on Apr. 4, 1783 [Ref: D-135, D-355]. The estate of one Alexander Levi was probated on May 17, 1794 in Prince George's County [Ref: ZE-117].
LEWIS, Amelia. See "John Hurley," q.v.
LEWIS, Benjamin. Drummer, 2nd Maryland Line, Capt. Patrick Sim's Company, 1776 [Ref: D-7].
LEWIS, George. Took the Oath of Allegiance before the Hon. George Lee in 1778 [Ref: O-279].
LEWIS, John W. See "Frederick Prussia Lewis Duvall," q.v.
LEWIS, Muriel. See "Lewis Duvall" and "Frederick Prussia Lewis Duvall," q.v.
LEWIS, Ruth Holmes. See "James Lucas," q.v.
LEWIS, Thomas (1742, Maryland - c1814, North Carolina). Took the Oath of Allegiance before the Hon. Osborn Sprigg in 1778 [Ref: O-308, R-78]. He married Mary Ellis [Ref: X-1796]. It should be noted that the estate of one Thomas Lewis was probated in Prince George's County, Maryland on Oct. 17, 1820 [Ref: ZE-118].
LILLY, Lidde. See "Anthony Hardey," q.v.
LILLY, William. See "William Tilley," q.v.
LINCOLN, John. Private, 2nd Maryland Line, Capt. Alexander Truman's Company, 1782; waiter to Capt. Smith [Ref: D-440]. Took the Oath of Allegiance before the Hon. Osborn Sprigg in 1778 [Ref: O-307, which questionably listed it as "Lintern, Lintem, Linkem[?]," but the original list at the Maryland State Archives (Box 4, folder 29) looks like "Lincum" or possibly "Linken"].
LINDSAY (LINDSEY), John (Mar. 15, 1758 -   ). Son of Samuel and Sarah Lindsey [Ref: ZC-41]. Private, 2nd Maryland Line, Capt. Patrick Sim's Company, 1776 [Ref: D-7].
LINDSEY, Samuel (1728-   ). Took the Oath of Allegiance before the Hon. William Lyles, Jr. in 1778 [Ref: O-290, R-74]. See "John Lindsay," q.v.
LINDSEY, Sarah. See "John Lindsay," q.v.
LINTON, Isaac. Took the Oath of Allegiance before the Hon. David Craufurd in 1778 [Ref: O-272].
LISBY, Samuel. Took the Oath of Allegiance before the Hon. Osborn Sprigg in 1778 [Ref: O-307].
LITTLEFORD, Mary. See "Thomas Walker, Jr.," q.v.
LITTLEMORE, Richard. Took the Oath of Allegiance before the Hon. Thomas Clagett in 1778 [Ref: O-267].
LITTLETON, Jane. See "Francis Bird," q.v.
LIVINGSTON, Anna. See "George Digges," q.v.
LLOYD, Elizabeth. See "Thomas Lloyd," q.v.

LLOYD, Hannah. See "Thomas Lloyd," q.v.
LLOYD, Mary. See "Thomas Lloyd," q.v.
LLOYD, Thomas (c1755, Lancaster, Pennsylvania - Jan. 19, 1827, Philadelphia). Private, 4th Maryland Line. Born in Lancaster, Pennsylvania, he lived in Upper Marlborough, Maryland at the time of his enlistment in the Maryland Line and married Mary Carson on Oct. 2, 1780, in Lancaster, Pennsylvania. He died Jan. 19, 1827 at Philadelphia and his widow applied for pension (W4672) on Feb. 10, 1846, in Delaware County, Pennsylvania. She died there on Oct. 10, 1849, leaving children Elizabeth Lloyd, Mary Lloyd, Hannah B. Lloyd, and Jane A. Rudolph [Ref: P-2099, D-135].
LOCKER, Elizabeth. See "James Locker" and "Philip Locker," q.v.
LOCKER, James (Mar. 11, 1755 -   ). Son of Philip and Elizabeth Locker [Ref: ZC-42]. Private, enrolled by Capt. John H. Lowe on July 13, 1776, for continental service, Maryland Line [Ref: D-35, R-11].
LOCKER, Jesse. Private, Northern Detachment, 3rd Maryland Line, Capt. Horatio Clagett's Company, 1781-1783 [Ref: D-397, D-501].
LOCKER, Philip (June 29, 1753-   ). Son of Philip and Elizabeth Locker [Ref: ZC-43]. Private, Maryland Line, enrolled by Capt. John H. Lowe on July 13, 1776, for continental service, Maryland Line. Discharged on Dec. 3, 1781 [Ref: D-34, I-10, R-11]. See "James Locker," q.v.
LODDENBURGHE, Valentine. "Valentine Lottenburg" took the Oath of Allegiance before the Hon. Benjamin Hall in 1778 [Ref: O-274]. The estate of "Valentine Loddenburgh" was probated on Feb. 9, 1782 [Ref: ZE-118].
LOGAN, Margaret. See "Christopher Beall," q.v.
LOMAX, John. Private, Select Militia, Capt. Hezekiah Wheeler's Company, July 14, 1781 [Ref: S-6636 (Box 31, folder 5)].
LOMAX, Stephen. Private, Capt. Hezekiah Wheeler's Company, 11th Militia Battalion, April, 1781 [Ref: L-19970 (Box 6, folder 21)].
LOMAX, Theophilus. Private, 5th Maryland Line, enlisted Mar. 31, 1777; sergeant, 1780-1783 [Ref: D-223, D-545]. The estate of one Theophilus Lomax was probated on Apr. 14, 1794 [Ref: ZE-119].
LONG, Catharine. See "Charles Beaven," q.v.
LONG, Joseph. Private, 2nd Maryland Line, Capt. Alexander Truman's Company, 1782 [Ref: D-440].
LONG, Thomas. Private, Capt. Hezekiah Wheeler's Company, 11th Militia Battalion, April, 1781 [Ref: L-19970 (Box 6, folder 21)]. Took the Oath of Allegiance before the Hon. Fielder Bowie in 1778 [Ref: O-304, W-4648 (Box 4, folder 15)]. One Thomas Long married Mary Holley in King George's Parish on July 30, 1791, and a Thomas Long died on Sep. 1, 1795 [Ref: ZC-43, ZE-119].
LONG, William. Private, enrolled by Lt. John M. Burgess, Lower Battalion, on July 20, 1776, for continental service, Maryland Line [Ref:

D-35]. One William Long married Rebecca Pickrell by license dated Feb. 11, 1781 [Ref: ZB-137].

LONGLY, Edward (1732-   ). Private, enrolled by Lt. John M. Burgess, Lower Battalion, on July 20, 1776, for continental service, Maryland Line [Ref: D-35, R-42].

LOSSON, William. See "William Lawson," q.v.

LOTTENBURG, Valentine. See "Valentine Loddenburgh," q.v.

LOVE, David. Sergeant, Northern Detachment, 3rd Maryland Line, Capt. Horatio Clagett's Company, 1783 [Ref: D-501].

LOVE, John. There were several men with this name who served in the Maryland Line [Ref: D-57, D-133, D-224, D-299, D-349, D-354]. The estate of "John Love (soldier)" was probated on Jan. 2, 1793 in Prince George's County [Ref: ZE-119].

LOVEJOY, John (Jan., 1740 - Apr. 20, 1808). Private in Capt. Jesse Hellen's Militia Company, and guarded Magruder's Warehouse in the spring of 1782 [Ref: L-19970 (Box 6, folder 21), which spelled his name "Lovjoy"]. He took the Oath of Allegiance before the Hon. Fielder Bowie in 1778 [Ref: O-304, W-4648 (Box 4, folder 15)]. He married Mrs. Rebecca (Naylor) Ransom [Ref: X-1845, which source stated he rendered patriotic service, but it did not cite his service as a private in the militia]. The estate of John Lovejoy was probated by July 12, 1808 [Ref: ZE-119].

LOVELESS, Elisha. Private, 1st Maryland Line. Muster rolls of the Maryland Troops state he enlisted on May 22, 1778 and was reported dead on Jan. 16, 1779 [Ref: D-132]. However, he was paid for his services on Feb. 24, 1779 [Ref: E-308]. "Elisha Lovelace" married Anne Jones on Jan. 8, 1789 (license dated Jan. 6, 1789) in Prince George's County [Ref: ZB-137, ZC-43]. It should be noted that "William Lovless" and "Elias Lovless" served in the Maryland Line in 1778 and were from Charles County [Ref: D-331].

LOVELESS, Millicent. See "Alexander Francis," q.v.

LOVELESS, Unie. See "James Hunt," q.v.

LOVELESS, William. Private, 2nd Guard, Capt. Henry Hill's Militia Company, Lower Battalion; on duty at Nottingham on the Patuxent, Apr. 12, 1781 [Ref: L-19970 (Box 6, folder 21), which spelled his name "Lovelis"]. See "Elisha Loveless," q.v.

LOWE, Alla. See "John Tolson Lowe," q.v.

LOWE, Ann. See "Dennis Lowe" and "Basil Lowe," q.v.

LOWE, Bartley. See "John Tolson Lowe," q.v.

LOWE, Basil (Mar. 21, 1758, Maryland - Sep. 22, 1846, Edgefield, South Carolina). Son of Henry and Ann Lowe [Ref: ZC-44]. Corporal, Maryland Line, enlisted in 1782, served in the First Partizan Legion commanded by Brigadier General Armand, Marquis de la Rouerie, and was discharged Nov. 15, 1783 [Ref: D-594]. Basil applied for pension on June 4, 1818, in Edgefield, South Carolina, stating he lived in Prince George's

County with his father (not named) during the Revolutionary War and married Trecy Wood about 3 years after the war. Around 1798 or 1799 they moved with his father's family to South Carolina. In 1821 Basil was aged 62 and had 6 children (no names were given) who were all married and lived away from home. His widow Trecy (Teresa) Lowe applied for pension (W9136) in Edgefield District, South Carolina, on Oct. 11, 1847, aged 79, stating Basil had died Sep. 22, 1846. In 1849 she lived with a daughter Mrs. Elizabeth McBride at Aiken, Barnwell District, South Carolina. Soldier's brother Dennis Lowe made affidavit in 1839 that he had lived in Prince George's County, Maryland and enlisted with Basil [Ref: P-2131, which also listed his name as "Bazel Low"]. Took the Oath of Allegiance before the Hon. George Lee in 1778 [Ref: O-279]. Basil Lowe married Tracey [Teresa] Wood by license dated Aug. 15, 1785 [Ref: X-1849, ZB-138]. See "John Tolson Lowe," q.v.

LOWE, Dennis (1764/66, Maryland - died after 1820, South Carolina or Georgia). Private, Maryland Line, enlisted in 1782 and served in the First Partizan Legion commanded by Brig. General Armand, Marquis de la Rouerie, and was discharged Nov. 15, 1783 [Ref: D-594]. He applied for pension (S38917) in Edgefield District, South Carolina, on Oct. 4, 1820, aged about 56, stating that he enlisted in Prince George's County, Maryland and was a son of Henry Lowe. In 1820 Dennis mentioned 5 children (no names were given) and stated only one was under age, but all 5 lived in Georgia [Ref: P-2131, P-2132, which also listed his name as "Dennis Low"]. Dennis Low, son of Henry Jr. and Ann Low (Lowe), was baptized in King George's Parish on Aug. 24, 1766 [Ref: ZC-44]. See "John Tolson Lowe" and "Basil Lowe," q.v.

LOWE, Dorothy. See "Benjamin Hall, of Francis," q.v.

LOWE, Elias. Took the Oath of Allegiance before the Hon. Joshua Beall in 1778 [Ref: O-251]. Elias Lowe married Sarah Henry by license dated Aug. 9, 1785 [Ref: ZB-138].

LOWE, Elizabeth and Ellen. See "John Tolson Lowe," q.v.

LOWE, Fanny and Fernando. See "John Tolson Lowe," q.v.

LOWE, Henry. Took the Oath of Allegiance before the Hon. Osborn Sprigg in 1778 [Ref: O-307]. "Henry Lowe" was aged 43 and "Harry Lowe" was aged 27 in 1776 [Ref: R-84]. One "Henry Low" married Peggy Low on Apr. 8, 1792, in King George's Parish [Ref: ZC-44]. See "John Tolson Lowe" and "Dennis Lowe" and "Basil Lowe," q.v.

LOWE, Hezekiah. See "John Tolson Lowe," q.v.

LOWE, J. Westly. See "John Tolson Lowe," q.v.

LOWE, James. Private, enrolled by Capt. John H. Lowe on July 13, 1776, for continental service, Maryland Line [Ref: D-35]. Took the Oath of Allegiance before the Hon. Thomas Clagett in 1778 [Ref: O-268].

LOWE, John. There were several men with this name: (1) One took the Oath of Allegiance before the Hon. George Lee in 1778 [Ref: O-279]. (2) One was appointed by the Council of Maryland to be the Tobacco

Inspector at Broad Creek Warehouse on Aug. 30, 1780 [Ref: F-271]. (3) One was a private in the Northern Detachment, 3rd Maryland Line, Capt. Horatio Clagett's Company, 1783 [Ref: D-501]. (4) "John Lowe (Patuxent)" took the Oath of Allegiance before the Hon. William Berry in 1778 [Ref: O-259]. One John Lowe was aged 60 and another was aged 52 in 1776 [Ref: R-66, R-74]. One John Lowe, son of John, was baptized on Apr. 6, 1752, in King George's Parish [Ref: ZC-44]. Additional research may be necessary before drawing conclusions. See "John Lowe, Jr." and "John Hawkins Lowe" and "John Tolson Lowe," q.v.

LOWE, John Jr. Served on a Grand Jury in 1778 [Ref: Z-52, Z-90].

LOWE, John Hawkins (1732, Maryland - 1820, Pennsylvania). Captain in the Maryland Line, 1776. Major in the Militia, 1778. Lieutenant Colonel, Nov. 15, 1779 [Ref: D-34, N-32, N-35]. Took the Oath of Allegiance before the Hon. George Lee in 1778 [Ref: O-279]. John Hawkins Lowe married ---- Lawson [Ref: X-1850]. There was also a John H. Lowe who married Barbara Magruder on Jan. 3, 1788 (by license dated Jan. 2, 1788) in Prince George's County and died before Dec. 5, 1788 [Ref: ZB-138, ZC-44, ZE-120]. Additional research may be necessary before drawing conclusions.

LOWE, John Tolson (Sep. 30, 1754, Maryland - Dec. 20, 1824, Florida). Son of Henry Jr. and Ann Lowe [Ref: ZC-44]. Sergeant, 1778; ensign, 1780, 2nd Maryland Line; lieutenant, 1781, 1st Maryland Line; retired Jan. 1, 1783 [Ref: D-132, which listed his name as "J. Tolson Lowe," and D-358 and D-478, which listed his name as "John T. Lowe," and D-476, which mistakenly listed his name as "John F. Lowe"]. He lived with his father Henry at the time of enlistment in Prince George's County and married Susannah Riddle (born June 7, 1768) on July 11, 1784. Some time thereafter they moved to South Carolina (about 15 miles from Edgefield) and in 1804 they moved to Florida. Susannah Lowe applied for and received pension W24575 on Sep. 5, 1854 while living with a son-in-law Judge William M. Reed in Hamilton County, Florida and stated her husband had died Dec. 20, 1824 in Nassau County, Florida, opposite the village of St. Mary's in Camden County, South Carolina. She stated that her husband had built mills on Bells River some 4 miles from St. Mary's, Georgia, and his heirs (not named) received 16,000 acres of land from the United States which was confirmed at Washington, DC in 1839. They had 16 children with the oldest being born on Apr. 1, 1785 and the youngest being born on Jan. 8, 1808 in Florida (no names were given). In 1846 their children living were: J. Wesly (or Westly) Lowe, of Columbia County, Rebecca Reed, Eliza Smith, and Ellen Miller (all living in Florida); Bartley or Bartly M. Lowe (former President of the Branch State Bank in Huntsville, Alabama and in 1846 lived in New Orleans, Louisiana). The other children mentioned were Hezekiah Lowe, Fernando Lowe, Thomas Lowe, Alla Lowe, and Fanny Lowe; also an Abraham B. Smith, of Hamilton County, Florida (no relationship was stated). Susannah further stated that John Lowe's brothers Basil Lowe and Dennis Lowe also served in the Revolutionary War. His brother Basil, sisters Elizabeth and Ellen, and uncle John Lowe were present at their wedding in 1784. Philip (or Philamon) E. Lowe lived at Wellburn in Suwanee County, Florida, and was an heir in 1877 [Ref: X-1850, P-2132, which latter source also listed his name as "John Tolason Lowe"]. "John Lowe" married Susannah Riddle by license dated July 10, 1784, in Prince George's County [Ref: ZB-138].

LOWE, Luthy. See "Jesse Greenwell," q.v.

LOWE, Mary. See "Thomas Brown," q.v.

LOWE, Michael (1741 - died after 1818). Captain, Militia, 1776 [Ref: B-287]. Served on a General Courts-Martial for the trial of Capt. Richard Bennett Hall, Lieut. Jeremiah Ryley, Lieut. Jonathan Wright, and Lieut. James Mullikin, at Upper Marlboro on July 25, 1776 [Ref: A-553, R-17]. He married Anne Magruder [Ref: X-1850].

LOWE, Nathan. Private, enrolled by Lt. John M. Burgess, Lower Battalion, on July 20, 1776, for continental service, Maryland Line [Ref: D-35]. Took the Oath of Allegiance before the Hon. Osborn Sprigg in 1778 [Ref: O-306]. The estate of one Nathan Lowe was probated on Mar. 31, 1784 [Ref: ZE-120].

LOWE, Nehemiah (1756 - before 1851). Private, Maryland Line. He applied for pension (R6489) on Nov. 20, 1844 in Montgomery County, Maryland, stating he lived in Prince George's County and enlisted there in the Revolutionary War. On Apr. 15, 1851, aged 81, his widow applied for a pension, stating she was born in Prince George's County, maiden name Amelia MacBee, and married on Nov. 22, 1791. Nehemiah's date of death was not stated. His application for pension was rejected [Ref: P-2132, and he is not listed in *Maryland Archives, Volume 18*].

LOWE, Nicholas (1748-   ). Private (draft), continental service, Maryland Line, 1780 [Ref: D-382, R-83, which latter source spelled his name "Nickolas"].

LOWE, Peggy. See "Henry Lowe," q.v.

LOWE, Philip (or Philamon). See "John Tolson Lowe," q.v.

LOWE, Richard (1746-   ). Private, 2nd Maryland Line, Capt. Patrick Sim's Company, 1776 [Ref: D-8]. Took the Oath of Allegiance before the Hon. William Berry in 1778 [Ref: O-259, R-83].

LOWE, Samuel. See "Zephaniah Lowe," q.v.

LOWE, Sephina (Sophana). See "Zephaniah Lowe," q.v.

LOWE, Susannah. See "William Digges" and "John Tolson Lowe," q.v.

LOWE, Thomas. See "John Tolson Lowe," q.v.

LOWE, Tracey (Teresa). See "Basil Lowe," q.v.

LOWE, William (1721-   ). Took the Oath of Allegiance before the Hon. Joshua Beall in 1778 [Ref: O-251, R-20].

LOWE, William. Private, 7th Maryland Line, from Feb. 17, 1777 to Mar., 1778 [Ref: D-224]. One William Lowe married Mary Henry by license dated Apr. 19, 1783 [Ref: ZB-139].

LOWE, Zadock. Took the Oath of Allegiance before the Hon. Joshua Beall in 1778 [Ref: O-251].

LOWE, Zephaniah (Mar. 12, 1754 - 1793). Son of Samuel (died 1782) and Sephina [Sophana] Lowe (died 1781). [Ref: ZC-44, ZE-120]. Took the Oath of Allegiance before the Hon. Osborn Sprigg in 1778 [Ref: O-307]. Constable in Western Branch Hundred, 1777 [Ref: Z-3]. The estate of Zephaniah Lowe was probated on Sep. 2, 1793 [Ref: ZE-120].

LOWNDES, Christopher (baptized June 19, 1713, England - Jan. 8, 1785, Maryland). County Court Justice, 1753-1785. Administered the Oath of Allegiance in 1778 [Ref: C-273, O-281, R-18, Z-90], and authenticated enlistment certificates in 1780 [Ref: D-332]. Also furnished cordage for ships during the war. Lived at "Bostwick" in Bladensburg (3900 block of 48th Street) and is buried in Addison Chapel Churchyard, Addison Road and 62nd Place, at Seat Pleasant [Ref: Y-612, C-298]. He married Elizabeth Tasker [Ref: X-1852].

LOWNDES, Rebecca. See "Benjamin Stoddert," q.v.

LUCAS, Adam (1743-   ). Took the Oath of Allegiance (made his "X" mark) before the Hon. Thomas Clagett in 1778 [Ref: R-40, O-263, which latter source spelled the name "Adam Lewcas"]. Private, Capt. Richard Stonestreet's Militia Company, 11th Battalion, June, 1782 [Ref: L-19970 (Box 6, folder 21)].

LUCAS, Ann. See "Barton Lucas," q.v.

LUCAS, Barton (Jan. 29, 1729/30 - 1785). Son of Thomas and Ann Lucas [Ref: ZD-117]. Colonel, Upper Battalion, Militia, 1778-1780 [Ref: N-33, D-333]. The estate of Barton Lucas was probated on May 16, 1785 [Ref: ZE-121].

LUCAS, Basil (Aug. 20, 1757, Maryland - July 6, 1841, Virginia). Sergeant, 2nd Maryland Line, 1778, and discharged Jan. 10, 1780 [Ref: D-133]. He applied for and received pension S18097 on May 11, 1833, in Berkeley County, Virginia, stating that his name was on the pension roll of Maryland in 1831. He married Elizabeth ---- on Feb. 26, 1786 (no children were named). [Ref: P-2136, X-1853, which latter source mistakenly stated he was born in Virginia].

LUCAS, Dorothy. See "John Lucas," q.v.

LUCAS, Elizabeth. See "Basil Lucas," q.v.

LUCAS, James (1760, Maryland - 1820, Virginia). Took the Oath of Allegiance before the Hon. Benjamin Hall in 1778 [Ref: O-275]. Sergeant by Dec. 25, 1779, and even though he had reportedly "deserted," he was actually discharged on Jan. 10, 1780 [Ref: D-133]. He married Mrs. Ruth Holmes (Lewis) [sic]. [Ref: X-1854].

LUCAS, John (June 26, 1750 - Sep. 22, 1823). Sergeant, 2nd Maryland Line, 1778-1780 [Ref: D-133]. He married (1) Mary Simmons by license dated Dec. 14, 1780, and (2) Mrs. Rachel (Belt) Marriott [Ref: ZB-139, X-1854, which latter source referred to him as "John Lucas 2nd"]. He applied for a pension (S34967) in Anne Arundel County on June 30, 1818, and died on Sep. 22, 1823, leaving a widow Rachel who was still living in 1838. Osbourne Lucas made an inquiry in 1838 and stated John and Rachel were married in Prince George's County (no date given). In 1859 Mr. M. Bannon, a Baltimore attorney, made inquiry in behalf of a Dorothy Lucas, but no relationship was stated. The widow never applied for a pension [Ref: P-2137, X-1854].

LUCAS, John (1756 - Feb. 5, 1826). Private, 2nd Maryland Line, enlisted on May 15, 1778 and served to at least Nov. 1, 1780 [Ref: D-133]. He applied for pension (S36052) in Washington, DC on Mar. 30, 1818, aged 62, stating he enlisted at Bladensburg. In 1820 he had a wife aged 60 and a daughter aged 13 (no names were given). [Ref: P-2137]. Private, Select Militia, Upper Battalion, June 12, 1781 [Ref: S-6636 (Box 27, folder 82B)]. He might be the John Lucas who married Rachel Duvall by license dated Sep. 12, 1787 [Ref: ZB-139]. There was a John Lucas who was born in Maryland on Sep. 7, 1760, was a private in Pennsylvania, and died in Ohio on June 15, 1836 [Ref: X-1854]. There were several men with this name in Maryland who served in the Revolutionary War [Ref: P-2137]. Additional research may be necessary before drawing conclusions.

LUCAS, Lindoras. Took the Oath of Allegiance before the Hon. Benjamin Hall in 1778 [Ref: O-274].

LUCAS, Morris William. Took the Oath of Allegiance before the Hon. Christopher Lowndes in 1778 [Ref: O-288].

LUCAS, Osbourne. See "John Lucas," q.v.

LUCAS, Rachel. See "John Lucas," q.v.

LUCAS, Samuel. Took the Oath of Allegiance before the Hon. Thomas Williams in 1778 [Ref: O-302, which spelled the name "Lucass"].

LUCAS, Thomas. Two men with this name took the Oath of Allegiance in 1778: one before the Hon. Osborn Sprigg [Ref: O-307, which had listed the name as "Lucas [Lewis?]," but the original list (very light and faded) at the Maryland State Archives (Box 4, folder 29), shows the name more likely to be "Lucas"]; and another Thomas Lucas took the oath before the Hon. Thomas Williams [Ref: O-302, which spelled the name "Lucass"]. One Thomas Lucas (1732 - Jan. 11, 1819, Maryland) is cited in Source X-1854 (wife's name not known). The estate of one Thomas Lucas was probated in Prince George's County on Oct. 2, 1784 [Ref: ZE-121]. Additional research may be necessary before drawing conclusions. See "Barton Lucas," q.v.

LUCKETT, Ann (Anna). See "Samuel Luckett," q.v.

LUCKETT, David (c1750 - Oct. 7, 1799). Ensign, 1st Maryland Line, by 1780. Lieutenant, 1781, 4th Maryland Line, through 1783. [Ref: D-132, D-365, D-521]. On May 7, 1824, his heirs received bounty land warrant

#1086-200, stating he died "many years prior." His wife was Susannah -----, and their surviving children in 1824 were Will G. Luckett, Luther Luckett, David L. Luckett, Juliet Simpson, and Catharine Simpson. "all of Kentucky." [Ref: P-2139, X-1856]. See "John Cleverdence" and "David Howe" and "Samuel Luckett," q.v.

LUCKETT, Elizabeth. See "Samuel Luckett," q.v.

LUCKETT, Frances. See "Samuel Luckett," q.v.

LUCKETT, John. See "Samuel Luckett," q.v.

LUCKETT, Luther. See "David Luckett," q.v.

LUCKETT, Nancy. See "Samuel Luckett," q.v.

LUCKETT, Samuel (June 12, 1756, Maryland - Aug. 22, 1828, Barren County, Kentucky). Private, Jan. 24, 1776, and sergeant, 1st Maryland Line, from Dec. 10, 1776 to Dec. 27, 1779, when discharged [Ref: D-6, D-132]. He applied for pension (S36051) in Barren County, Kentucky on May 12, 1818, and in 1820 had a wife Elizabeth (born May 9, 1769) and referred to these children: Samuel Luckett (born Mar. 2, 1801), John Luckett (born May 19, 1803), David Luckett (born Sep. 26, 1805), Nancy Luckett (born Jan. 13, 1808, married Lodaway Creek on Jan. 26, 1828), and Anna Luckett (born June 17, 1811). In 1818 a William Luckett made affidavit in Barren County (no relationship was stated but this was Samuel's son). [Ref: P-2139, and *Marriage Records of Barren County, Kentucky, 1799-1849*, by Martha Powell Reneau (1984), p. 55]. The will of Samuel Luckett was written on Apr. 17, 1828 and probated in October, 1828, in Barren County, naming his wife Elizabeth and children Ann Ware Luckett, David Luckett, William Luckett, Frances H. Luckett, Samuel Luckett, Susanna Parnell, Polly Elms, John L. Luckett, and Nancy Creek [Ref: *Kentucky Court and Other Records*, by Mrs. William Breckenridge Ardery (1926), page 14]. Source X-1856 states that Samuel Luckett married (1) Monica Kennedy and (2) Elizabeth Cox, and that he was a lieutenant in the Maryland Line. However, *Maryland Archives, Volume 18* indicates that he was discharged as a sergeant in 1779 [Ref: D-132]. Additional research may be necessary before drawing conclusions.

LUCKETT, Susannah. See "David Luckett," q.v.

LUCKETT, Thomas H. Captain, Maryland Line, 1780-1783 [Ref: D-521]. In April, 1816, bounty land warrant #653-400-10 was issued to Thomas H. Luckett and other heirs "of the deceased soldier of the Maryland Line" (not named) in Washington, DC [Ref: P-2139]. Source X-1856 lists two men by the name of "Thomas Hussey Luckett" with different dates and different wives, although both men served in Maryland and died in Virginia. One married Elizabeth Noland, served as a captain the Maryland Line and died in Virginia in December, 1786. The other was born circa 1733, married Eleanor Douglas, rendered patriotic service in Maryland and died in Virginia before Jan. 27, 1800.

LUCKETT, Will G. See "David Luckett," q.v.

LUCKETT, William. See "Samuel Luckett," q.v.
LUSBY, Samuel. Bombardier, Frederick German Artillery, 1782 [Ref: D-581]. The estate of one Samuel Lusby was probated on Apr. 4, 1809 in Prince George's County [Ref: ZE-121].
LUSK, Hannibal (Captain). On Jan. 26, 1781, the records of the Council of Maryland include the parole of Capt. Lusk, as follows: "I do hereby acknowledge myself to be a prisoner of war on my parole to His Excellency of Maryland, and that I am hereby engaged until I shall be exchanged or otherwise released therefrom to remain at Bladensburgh in Prince George's and I shall not in the mean time do or cause any thing to be done prejudicial to the success of the Armies or Navies of the United States of America or either of them or have intercourse or hold correspondence with their or either of their enemies and that upon a summons from His Excellency the Governor of Maryland or other person having authority thereto, that I will surrender myself to him or them at such time and place as shall hereafter be required. Witness my hand this 26th day of Jan., 1781, Hannl. Lusk; witness: T. Johnson, Jr." On Jan. 27, 1781, the Council replied: "Permission is hereby given to the within named Captain Lusk to go into New York to solicit his exchange for Aquila Johns, late Commander of the *Buckskin Merchantman*, now prisoner of war on parole to Commodore Gayton; in case the exchange should not be effected, the said Captain to return when required. He is also permitted to take with him William Willson, a lad of about twelve years of age, on his procuring a citizen of this State to be exchanged for said Willson." [Ref: H-40, H-41].
LYLES, Archibald. See "Richard Lyles," q.v.
LYLES, Henry. Guide for the militia in 1781, and participated in capturing an enemy boat and crew on Apr. 17, 1781 [Ref: M-208].
LYLES, James (1763, Maryland -   ). Private, enlisted in May, 1781, for duration of the war, in continental service, Maryland Line; sent to Annapolis; on duty July 13, 1781 [Ref: D-381].
LYLES, Mary. See "Thomas Lyles" and "Joseph Coomes," q.v.
LYLES, Richard (Sep. 29, 1757, Maryland - died before 1853, Kentucky). Second Lieutenant in the 25th Militia Battalion, Capt. Joseph Jones' Company, May 24, 1779, and First Lieutenant, Upper Battalion, Capt. Benjamin Harwood's Company, June 24, 1780 [Ref: M-99, E-414, F-203, N-34]. Took the Oath of Allegiance before the Hon. Thomas Williams in 1778 [Ref: O-302]. He applied for pension (R6543) on Oct. 14, 1835, in Logan County, Kentucky, stating he was born in Prince George's County, Maryland and lived there at the time of his enlistment. On Apr. 26, 1853, Archibald M. Lyles, of McCracken County, Kentucky, signed a power of attorney as the only heir of Richard Lyles, but did not state the relationship [Ref: P-2149]. He married (1) Harriet Magruder by license dated Jan. 11, 1786, and (2) Elizabeth Jones [Ref: ZB-140, X-1863, which latter source stated that he served as a surgeon's mate].

LYLES, Thomas (Sep. 29, 1754, Maryland - Feb. 4, 1840, Tennessee). Ensign, Militia, 1778. Second Lieutenant, 1779. First Lieutenant, Upper Battalion, Capt. Tyler's Company, June 27, 1781 [Ref: N-34, H-320]. Took the Oath of Allegiance before the Hon. Benjamin Hall in 1778 [Ref: O-276]. He applied for pension (R6544) on Sep. 9, 1834, in Jefferson County, Tennessee, stating he was born in Prince George's County, Maryland and lived there at the time of his enlistment. After the war he moved to Jefferson County, Tennessee. On Nov. 2, 1853, Zachariah A. Lyles signed a power of attorney as an heir of Thomas Lyles, but he did not state their relationship [Ref: P-2149]. Thomas married (1) Eleanor Duckett by license dated Apr. 10, 1779, (2) Mary Jones by license dated Oct. 23, 1790, and (3) Mary ---- [Ref: X-1864, ZB-140].

LYLES, William Jr. (1750 - Dec. 27, 1815). Second Major, Lower Battalion, Feb. 4, 1777. Major, Upper Battalion, Sep. 1, 1777. Lieutenant Colonel, Lower Battalion, Oct. 7, 1780 [Ref: M-99, N-32, C-113, C-356, F-318, which latter source listed his name without the "Jr."]. County Court Justice, 1777 [Ref: C-273]. He administered the Oath of Allegiance in 1778 [Ref: O-290]. "On Nov. 19, 1779, he was licensed to purchase provisions for the Continental Army in Prince George's County and to superintend the Post at Piscataway Creek to cure said provisions." [Ref: F-20]. Lieutenant Colonel, 11th Battalion, April, 1781, "in command when the British were up the Potomack River." Lieutenant Colonel, Lower Battalion, 1781 [Ref: L-19970 (Box 6, folder 21), which listed his name without the "Jr."]. On Apr. 12, 1781, at his estate near the mouth of the Piscataway River, the enemy landed about 100 men from their ships in the Potomac River and burned all his buildings. He is buried in St. John's Churchyard at Broad Creek [Ref: Y-614]. Source X-1864 lists a William Lyles born in 1750 who rendered civil service and married (1) Unknown, and (2) Sarah Magruder, but it did not state that he was a lieutenant colonel in the militia. The estate of one William Lyles was probated on Jan. 31, 1816 [Ref: ZE-122]. Additional research may be necessary before drawing conclusions.

LYLES, Zachariah. Private, 2nd Maryland Line, from June 11, 1779 to at least Nov. 1, 1780 [Ref: D-133]. See "Thomas Lyles," q.v.

LYNCH (LINCH), Amelia. See "Thomas Simpson," q.v.

LYNCH, John Smith. Private, Capt. Benjamin Wailes' Militia Company, Lower Battalion, and on duty guarding Magruder's Warehouse in the spring of 1782 [Ref: L-19970 (Box 6, folder 21)].

LYNCH, Smith. Private, Capt. Alexander H. Magruder's Militia Company, Lower Battalion, and on duty guarding Magruder's Warehouse in the spring of 1782 [Ref: L-19970 (Box 6, folder 21)].

LYNN, Jane. See "Richard Brooke," q.v.

LYNN, Valentine. Private, 9th Company of Light Infantry, enlisted Jan. 22, 1776 [Ref: D-19]. "Valen Linn" was a private in the 1st Maryland

Line, enlisted on Dec. 10, 1776, promoted to corporal on Apr. 12, 1777, discharged on Oct. 11, 1777, rejoined in July, 1778, reduced to a private on Sep. 15, 1778, and was discharged on Dec. 27, 1779 [Ref: D-131]. "Valentine Lynn" married Elizabeth Johnson by license dated Sep. 21, 1795 [Ref: ZB-140].

LYNN, William. Private, 9th Company of Light Infantry, enlisted Jan. 22, 1776 [Ref: D-19].

LYON, Isaac. Private, 3rd Maryland Line, Capt. Horatio Clagett's Company, 1779 [Ref: D-295].

LYON, Hugh. Clerk for the Committee of Observation in 1776 [Ref: R-89]. Deputy Clerk of the Prince George's County Court in 1778 [Ref: Z-95]. The estate of Hugh Lyon was probated on Nov. 28, 1786 [Ref: ZE-122].

MACBEE, Amelia. See "Nehemiah Lowe," q.v.

MACCASTLE, Mary. See "James Short," q.v.

MACDANIEL, John. Private, enrolled by Lt. William Duvall, Lower Battalion, on July 18, 1776, for continental service, Maryland Line [Ref: D-35].

MACDONALD, Alex. See "Edward Burch," q.v.

MACGILL, Elizabeth. See "Elijah Rawlings," q.v.

MACGILL, John. See "John McGill," q.v.

MACGILL, Thomas. See "Thomas McGill," q.v.

MACKALL, Susanna. See "Thomas Gantt, Jr.," q.v.

MACKINTOSH, John (1726-). Took the Oath of Allegiance before the Hon. Christopher Lowndes in 1778 [Ref: O-286, R-52, which spelled the name "Mackentoush"].

MADAN, William. Private, Northern Detachment, 3rd Maryland Line, Capt. Horatio Clagett's Company, 1783 [Ref: D-501].

MADDOCKE, James (1734 - after 1798). Took the Oath of Allegiance before the Hon. Osborn Sprigg in 1778 [Ref: O-306, X-1875].

MADDOX, Nathan (c1760, Maryland - died before Nov. 12, 1829, Ohio). Private in Capt. Benjamin Wailes' Militia Company, Lower Battalion; on duty guarding Magruder's Warehouse in the spring of 1782 [Ref: L-19970 (Box 6, folder 21)]. Nathan Maddox married Michel [sic] Robey [Ref: X-1875].

MAGILL, Thomas. See "Thomas McGill," q.v.

MAGRUDER, Alexander (1716 - Nov. 10, 1779). Took the Oath of Allegiance before the Hon. Alexander Howard Magruder in 1778 [Ref: O-293]. He married Elizabeth Howard and one of their children was "Alexander Howard Magruder," q.v. [Ref: X-1877, ZE-123].

MAGRUDER, Alexander Howard (Sep. 15, 1745 - Aug. 17, 1782). Son of Alexander Magruder (1716-1779) and Elizabeth Howard (1721-1803, daughter of William Stevens Howard and Sarah Briscoe Truman). He probably married Jane Truman and had children Alexander Magruder, Henry Magruder, and Anne or Nancy Magruder (who married Capt.

Thomas Marshall Dent). [Ref: Henry C. Peden, Jr.'s *Truman and Related Families of Early Maryland* (1987), p. 28, and DAR National No. 554450]. Alexander H. Magruder held several positions during the Revolutionary War era: Justice of the County Court, 1770-1782. Served on the Committee of Observation, 1775-1776 [Ref: C-273, U-567, U-568, Z-90]. Captain, 6th Maryland Line, 1776 [Ref: D-34, D-38]. Captain, 11th Battalion, Militia, May 1, 1778, through 1782 [Ref: M-100, E-62, N-33, L-19970 (Box 6, folder 21)]. Administered the Oath of Allegiance in 1778 [Ref: O-292]. He served on the Board of Patuxent Associators and signed a resolution at Nottingham on Apr. 21, 1781 relative to the defence of the rivers of Potomac and Patuxent and the completion of the fort at Drum Point [Ref: K-1814, U-568]. Judge of the Orphans Court in 1779. Served in the House of Delegates, 1780-1781 [Ref: F-17, U-84]. Justice of the Peace in 1781 [Ref: Q-463]. See "John Clagett," q.v.

MAGRUDER, Allitha. See "Walter Drane," q.v.

MAGRUDER, Anne. See "John Contee" and "Dennis Magruder" and "Alexander Truman" and "Alexander Howard Magruder" and "James Truman" and "Thomas Truman" and "Michael Lowe," q.v.

MAGRUDER, Barbara. See "John Hawkins Lowe," q.v.

MAGRUDER, Cassandra. See "Henry Hilleary, Sr." and "Walter Hilleary," q.v.

MAGRUDER, Dennis (July 1, 1758/9 - May 21, 1836). Took the Oath of Allegiance before the Hon. Osborn Sprigg in 1778 [Ref: O-307, R-8]. First Lieutenant, Middle Battalion, Capt. John Casey's Company, May 1, 1778 [Ref: M-100, E-63, N-36]. He married Anne Contee in 1779 [Ref: U-231, X-1877, ZE-123].

MAGRUDER, Edward (1748-1784). Took the Oath of Allegiance before the Hon. Thomas Clagett in 1778 [Ref: O-264, R-83]. He was also involved in recruiting in 1780 [Ref: G-63]. The estate of Edward Magruder was probated by Sep. 28, 1784 (date of inventory). [Ref: ZE-123]. See "Thomas Walls," q.v.

MAGRUDER, Eleanor (Clarke). Her first husband was Dr. David Clarke and her second husband was ---- Magruder. See "Benjamin Hall, of Francis" and "John Magruder Burgess," q.v.

MAGRUDER, Elizabeth. See "Rignal Hilleary" and "Osborn Williams" and "Richard Alexander Contee" and "Walter Hilleary" and "James Somervell" and "Nathaniel Magruder" and "Samuel Magruder," q.v.

MAGRUDER, Enoch. Sergeant, Rawlings' Regiment, Maryland Line, 1779 [Ref: D-145]. Enoch Magruder married Elizabeth Sprigg by license dated Feb. 27, 1780 [Ref: ZB-142, which also listed the year as 1781]. The estate of one Enoch Magruder was probated on Nov. 1, 1786, and the estate of another Enoch Magruder was probated on Apr. 11, 1829 [Ref: ZE-124]. See "Thomas Duckett," q.v.

MAGRUDER, George Fraser (Mar., 1733/4 - c1799). Took the Oath of Allegiance before the Hon. Thomas Williams in 1778 [Ref: O-302].

Rendered patriotic service by providing wheat for the military on Sep. 2, 1780 [Ref: Q-314, which spelled the name "George Frazer Magruder"]. He married Eleanor Bowie [Ref: X-1877]. The estate of one "George Magruder" was probated on Feb. 12, 1800 in Prince George's County [Ref: ZE-124]. It must be noted that George Fraser Magruder was mistakenly listed as a patriot in Henry C. Peden, Jr.'s *Revolutionary Patriots of Montgomery County, 1775-1783*, but he was apparently a patriot in Prince George's County.

MAGRUDER, Harriet. See "Richard Lyles," q.v.

MAGRUDER, Haswell (1736-1811). Constable in New Scotland Hundred, 1777-1778 [Ref: Z-3, Z-30]. He married (1) Charity Beall, and (2) Ann Allen by license dated Apr. 18, 1802 [Ref: X-1877, ZB-142]. The estate of one Haswell Magruder was probated on May 11, 1811 [Ref: ZE-124, which also spelled his name "Hoswell"].

MAGRUDER, Henderson. Captain, 25th Battalion, Jan. 3, 1776 to May 24, 1778 or 1779 (resigned). [Ref: M-100, E-62, E-414, N-34]. Took the Oath of Allegiance before the Hon. James Mullikin in 1778 [Ref: O-295]. The estate of one Henderson Magruder was probated on Apr. 7, 1829 [Ref: ZE-124]. See "Jeremiah Magruder," q.v.

MAGRUDER, Henry. Captain who served on a General Courts-Martial for the trial of Capt. Richard Bennett Hall, Lieut. Jeremiah Ryley, Lieut. Jonathan Wright, and Lieut. James Mullikin on Aug. 23, 1776, at Upper Marlboro [Ref: B-233, M-100]. See "Alexander Howard Magruder," q.v.

MAGRUDER, Hezekiah. Took the Oath of Allegiance before the Hon. Alexander Howard Magruder in 1778 [Ref: O-293]. There was also a Hezekiah Magruder who took the Oath of Allegiance in Montgomery County in 1778, served there as a first lieutenant in the militia, and died some time before Nov. 4, 1806 [Ref: X-1877].

MAGRUDER, James. Took the Oath of Allegiance before the Hon. David Craufurd in 1778 [Ref: O-271]. There was also a James Magruder who took the Oath of Allegiance in Montgomery County in 1778 [Ref: X-1877]. See "Jeremiah Magruder" and "John Read Magruder," q.v.

MAGRUDER, Jeremiah (1731-1798). Son of James Magruder and Barbara Combs, he married Mary Tyler and had these children: Henderson Magruder, Elizabeth Williams, and Christiana Worthington. He was a corporal in the Foot Militia, 1749. County Court Justice, 1773-1778. Committee of Observation, 1775-1776. House of Delegates, 1777-1783 [Ref: C-273, U-76, U-78, U-80, U-82, U-87, U-568, ZE-124].

MAGRUDER, John Read (June 17, 1736 - Sep. 24, 1811). Son of James Magruder and Barbara Contee, he married Barbara Contee and their daughter Jane Contee married William Beanes Marbury, son of "Luke Marbury," q.v. [Ref: U-568, U-573, X-1877]. He served on the Board of Patuxent Associators and signed a resolution at Nottingham on Apr. 21, 1781 relative to the defence of the rivers of Potomac and Patuxent and the completion of the fort at Drum Point [Ref: K-1814]. Clerk of Prince

George's County Court in 1778 [Ref: Z-55]. The estate of "John Read Magruder" was probated on Nov. 23, 1811 [Ref: ZE-125]. "John Read Magruder, Jr." married Amelia Hall by license dated Sep. 13, 1794 [Ref: ZB-142].

MAGRUDER, Margaret. See "Nathaniel Magruder," q.v.

MAGRUDER, Mary. See "Thomas Duckett Boyd" and "John Contee" and "Thomas Clagett" and "Thomas Duckett," q.v.

MAGRUDER, Nathaniel (c1730-1785). He was one of four men elected by the Convention of Maryland on July 3, 1776, to be Judges of the Election in Prince George's County for representatives to the new convention for the express purpose of forming a new government. Nathaniel is buried in the Magruder-McGregor Family Cemetery at "Dunblane" on Westphalia Road near Forestville [Ref: Y-585, Y-613]. Nathaniel rendered patriotic service by providing wheat for the military on Aug. 8, 1780 [Ref: Q-307]. He married Margaret Magruder [Ref: X-1877]. "Nathaniel Magrudy" was a captain in the Maryland Line in 1779-1780. There was also a Nathaniel Magruder, son of Ninian and Elizabeth Magruder, of Queen Anne's Parish, who was born Nov. 30, 1721 [Ref: ZC-184]. See "David Howe," q.v.

MAGRUDER, Nathaniel. Private, Capt. Alexander H. Magruder's Militia Company, Lower Battalion; on duty guarding Magruder's Warehouse in the spring of 1782 [Ref: L-19970 (Box 6, folder 21)].

MAGRUDER, Nathaniel Beall. Ensign, State Infantry, Col. Rawlings' Regiment, 1779-1780 [Ref: M-100, F-83, F-149]. It is not clear whether he was from Prince George's County or Montgomery County. Additional research may be necessary before drawing conclusions.

MAGRUDER, Ninian. See "Nathaniel Magruder" and "Samuel Magruder," q.v.

MAGRUDER, Robert (Oct. 11, 1711 -   ). Son of Samuel and Elinor Magruder [Ref: ZC-184]. Took the Oath of Allegiance before the Hon. Osborn Sprigg in 1778 [Ref: O-307].

MAGRUDER, Samuel (Feb. 24, 1708 - 1782/1790?). Son of Ninian and Elizabeth Magruder [Ref: ZC-184]. Took the Oath of Allegiance before the Hon. Osborn Sprigg in 1778 [Ref: O-307]. The estate of one "Samuel H. Magruder" was probated by Dec. 10, 1782 (date of inventory) and the estate of a "Samuel Magruder" was probated on Nov. 2, 1790 [Ref: ZE-125]. See "Robert Magruder," q.v.

MAGRUDER, Sarah. See "Thomas Clagett" and "William Lyles" and "John Osborn," q.v.

MAGRUDER, Susannah. See "William Waters," q.v.

MAGRUDER, Thomas (1738-1809). Took the Oath of Allegiance before the Hon. David Craufurd in 1778 [Ref: O-272, R-82]. The estate of one Thomas Magruder was probated on May 17, 1809 [Ref: ZE-126].

MAGRUDER, Zadock (1729-1811). Born in Prince George's County, he served as a colonel of troops in both Frederick and Montgomery

203

Counties. See Source U-571 for details about his service, plus Henry C. Peden, Jr.'s *Revolutionary Patriots of Montgomery County*. Also see Source ZA-543 for his ancestry and family information].

MAHON, Francis. Took the Oath of Allegiance before the Hon. Thomas Williams in 1778 [Ref: O-302].

MAHONEY, Clement. Private, 2nd Maryland Line, Jan. 22, 1778; in hospital when his time expired; joined muster in April, 1778, and was discharged on Jan. 10, 1780 (and again on Apr. 1, 1780?). [Ref: D-138].

MAHONEY, Edward (1743-1818?). Private, 6th Maryland Line, Mar. 8, 1777, and discharged on Mar. 8, 1780 [Ref: D-230]. His pension commenced on Apr. 9, 1818 [Ref: T-39]. One Edward Mahoney married Alis Taylor by license dated Dec. 18, 1786 [Ref: ZB-143]. The estate of one "Edward Mahorney" was probated on Nov. 5, 1818 [Ref: ZE-126].

MAHONY, John. Took the Oath of Allegiance before the Hon. Truman Skinner in 1778 [Ref: O-297]. John Mahony married Elizabeth Moore by license dated May 14, 1785 [Ref: ZB-143].

MALONE, James. Took the Oath of Allegiance before the Hon. Christopher Lowndes in 1778 [Ref: O-285].

MALOY, Roger. Private, 2nd Maryland Line, Capt. Murdock's Company, Mar. 15, 1781 [Ref: D-366].

MANDWELL, Philip. Private, 3rd Maryland Line, Capt. Horatio Clagett's Company, December, 1779, and reportedly "deserted" on Jan. 3, 1780 [Ref: D-296].

MANDITT (MAUDITT, MANDUITT), Deborah. See "Alexander Jackson" and "Leonard M. Deakins," q.v.

MANGUN, James (c1760-1820). Took the Oath of Allegiance before the Hon. Truman Skinner in 1778 [Ref: O-298]. He married Sarah ---- [Ref: X-1884]. The estate of James Mangun was probated on Oct. 13, 1820 [Ref: ZE-126, which also spelled the name "Mangunn"].

MANGUN, John Smith. "John Smith Mangun" took the Oath of Allegiance (made his "X" mark) before the Hon. Truman Skinner in 1778 [Ref: O-297]. "John Mangun" married Elizabeth Piles by license dated Aug. 4, 1785 [Ref: ZB-144]. The estate of "John Mangunn" was probated on Nov. 12, 1831 [Ref: ZE-126].

MANGUN, Sarah. See "James Mangun," q.v.

MANLEY, Jonathan. Private, Militia, 1776 [Ref: M-207, A-325].

MANLEY, Jonathan Jr. Took the Oath of Allegiance before the Hon. William Berry in 1778 [Ref: O-259].

MANLEY, William (Nov. 24, 1761, Maryland - 1824, Georgia). Private, 2nd Maryland Line, Capt. William Murdock's Company, Mar. 15, 1781 [Ref: D-366, which spelled his name "Manly"]. He married Lucy Freeman [Ref: X-1885]. There was also a William Manley who married Sarah Brown on Jan. 8, 1789 (by license dated Jan. 7, 1789) in King George's Parish [Ref: ZB-144, ZC-46].

MANNING, John (1736-1809). Took the Oath of Allegiance before the Hon. William Lyles, Jr. in 1778 [Ref: O-290, R-40]. The estate of one John Manning was probated on Feb. 3, 1809 [Ref: ZE-126].
MANSFIELD, Henry. Private, 2nd Maryland Line, Capt. Murdock's Company, Mar. 15, 1781 [Ref: D-366].
MANTLE (MAUNTLE), George. Private, 2nd Maryland Line, Capt. Alexander Truman's Company, 1780-1782 [Ref: D-439, D-354].
MANTLE, John (1756-1792). Private, enrolled in the Flying Camp by Lieut. William D. Beall on July 20, 1776; nativity: England; height: 5' 6"; brown hair, fair complexion, very well made [Ref: D-37]. Private, enlisted Jan. 31, 1780, for 3 years or during war, in continental service, Maryland Line [Ref: D-333]. He was probably the "Serjeant Mantle" who was involved in recruiting at Bladensburg on Feb. 22, 1780 [Ref: D-332]. 2nd Maryland Line, Capt. Alexander Truman's Company, 1782 [Ref: D-439]. The estate of one John Mantle was probated on Sep. 22, 1792 [Ref: ZE-126].
MARBURY, Caroline. See "Luke Marbury," q.v.
MARBURY, Elizabeth. See "Ignatius Wheeler" and "Luke Marbury," q.v.
MARBURY, Henrietta. See "Luke Marbury," q.v.
MARBURY, Luke (1745-1809). Only child of Luke Marbury and Elizabeth Beanes, he married his first cousin Elizabeth Beanes, daughter of William Beanes, in 1770, and had these children: William Beanes Marbury, Elizabeth (Marbury) Sothoron, Henrietta Beanes (Marbury) Clagett, and Caroline (Marbury) Marshall [Ref: U-573, ZA-551, ZE-127]. Luke Marbury was very active during the Revolutionary era: Delegate to the Maryland Convention, 1775-1776 [Ref: U-70, U-74]. Committee of Observation, 1775. Captain, Militia, Mar. 15, 1776. Lieutenant Colonel, Lower Battalion, Feb. 4, 1777. County Lieutenant, July 1, 1777. Colonel, Sep. 1, 1777, and was taken prisoner at the Battle of Germantown on Oct. 4, 1777; exchanged Mar. 26, 1781 [Ref: R-42, M-100, C-113, C-304, C-356, C-429, U-573, D-616, which latter source misspelled his name as "Luke Mabury"]. Served on a General Courts-Martial for the trial of Capt. Richard Bennett Hall, Lieut. Jeremiah Ryley, Lieut. Jonathan Wright, and Lieut. James Mullikin on July 25, 1776, at Upper Marlboro [Ref: A-553]. Justice of the County Court, 1777 [Ref: C-273]. Colonel, Lower Battalion, Militia, 1778 [Ref: N-32]. He is probably buried in the family cemetery at the rear of his home "Wyoming" at the corner of Thrift and Tippett Roads, but no tombstone has been found [Ref: Y-586, Y-613].
MARBURY, William. Captain of an artillery company, 1777-1778 [Ref: D-575]. The estate of one William Marbury was probated in Prince George's County in 1823 [Ref: ZE-127]. See "Luke Marbury," q.v.
MARLOW, Ann M. See "Josias Fendall Beall," q.v.
MARLOW, Butler (1754 - after 1820). Private (substitute), 2nd Maryland Line, continental service, 1780-1781; discharged on Dec. 3, 1781 [Ref: D-

140, D-382, D-410, I-10]. He applied for pension (S34974) in Prince George's County on Sep. 6, 1820, aged 66, with a wife aged 54 and four daughters aged 16, 14, 12, and 10 years (no names were given). [Ref: P-2191, which listed his name as "Butler or Butler Dunning Marlow"]. "Buttler Marlow" married Charlotte Foard by license dated Dec. 21, 1782, and "Butler D. Marlowe" married Elizabeth Webster by license dated Aug. 30, 1796 [Ref: ZB-145]. It should be noted that Source X-869 mistakenly indexed his name as "Butler Marlow Downing."

MARLOW, John. Private, enrolled by Lt. John M. Burgess, Lower Battalion, on July 20, 1776, for continental service, Maryland Line [Ref: D-35, which spelled his name "Marlowe"]. See "Middleton Marlow" and "Thomas Dorset Marlow" and "William Marlow," q.v.

MARLOW, John. Private, enrolled by Ensign Horatio Clagett on July 15, 1776, for continental service, Maryland Line [Ref: D-35].

MARLOW, John Jr. (June 3, 1757 -   ). Son of John and Lidea or Elenor Marlow [Ref: ZC-46]. Took the Oath of Allegiance before the Hon. Thomas Clagett in 1778 [Ref: O-268]. One "John Marlow" was aged 52 in 1776 [Ref: R-44]. One John Marlow married Elizabeth Baden by license dated Oct. 29, 1791 [Ref: ZB-145].

MARLOW, John H. Took the Oath of Allegiance before the Hon. George Lee in 1778 [Ref: O-279].

MARLOW, Lidea. See "John Marlow" and "Middleton Marlow" and "Thomas Dorset Marlow" and "William Marlow," q.v.

MARLOW, Middleton (Sep. 21, 1746 -   ). Son of John and Lidea or Elenor Marlow [Ref: ZC-46]. Private, 2nd Maryland Line, Capt. Patrick Sim's Company, 1776 [Ref: D-8, D-136].

MARLOW, Randolph. Private, enrolled by Capt. Alexander H. Magruder, 11th Battalion, on July 10, 1776, continental service, Maryland Line [Ref: D-38].

MARLOW, Richard. See "William Marlow," q.v.

MARLOW, Samuel. Private, 2nd Maryland Line, 1778; discharged on Sep. 29, 1779 [Ref: D-139]. The estate of one "Samuel H. Marlow" was probated on Feb. 24, 1800, and the estate of a "Samuel Marlowe" was probated in 1818 [Ref: ZE-127, ZE-128].

MARLOW, Thomas Dorset (June 24, 1755 - 1790). Son of John and Lidea or Elenor Marlow [Ref: ZC-46]. Private, enrolled by Capt. John H. Lowe on July 13, 1776, for continental service, Maryland Line [Ref: D-34]. Took the Oath of Allegiance before the Hon. George Lee in 1778 [Ref: O-279]. "Thomas D. Marlow" married Margaret Clagett by license dated Mar. 10, 1787 [Ref: ZB-145]. The estate of "Thomas Dorsett Marlow" was probated on Apr. 9, 1790 [Ref: ZE-127, D-128, which also listed his name as "Darsett Marlow"].

MARLOW, William (1765-1816?). Private, enlisted May 25, 1781, for the duration of the war, in continental service; sent to Annapolis and on duty July 13, 1781 [Ref: D-381]. This or perhaps another William

Marlow was a private, 4th Maryland Regiment, having enlisted in 1782 for 3 years, and sworn in Feb. 25, 1782 [Ref: D-417]. Sergeant, Northern Detachment, 3rd Maryland Line, Capt. Horatio Clagett's Company, 1783 [Ref: D-501]. One William Marlow took the Oath of Allegiance before the Hon. George Lee in 1778 [Ref: O-279]. One William Marlow married Mary Willett by license dated Dec. 29, 1786 [Ref: ZB-145]. "William Berrey Marlow," son of Richard and Lidea Marlow, was baptized on Apr. 5, 1767 and married Delilah Strong on Feb. 13, 1796 in King George's Parish. Another William Marlow, son of John and Lidea Marlow, was born on May 15, 1759 [Ref: ZC-46]. The estate of one "William Marlowe" was probated on Apr. 9, 1816 [Ref: ZE-128]. Additional research may be necessary before drawing conclusions.

MARR, Charles (1750-   ). Took the Oath of Allegiance before the Hon. Christopher Lowndes in 1778 [Ref: O-284, R-58].

MARRIOTT, Rachel (Belt). See "John Lucas," q.v.

MARSHALL, Benjamin. Took the Oath of Allegiance before the Hon. Christopher Lowndes in 1778 [Ref: O-285]. One Benjamin Marshall married Sarah Upton by license dated Jan. 17, 1778 [Ref: ZB-145].

MARSHALL, Benjamin (1755, Prince George's County, Maryland - Mar. 29, 1834, Hardy County, Virginia). He applied for pension in Hardy County, Virginia on Mar. 11, 1834, stating he was born in Prince George's County, Maryland in 1755, married Elizabeth ---- about 1775 in Montgomery County, Maryland, and lived in Hampshire County (the part that became Hardy County), Virginia at the time of his enlistment in the Virginia Line. His widow applied for a pension (W4279) on Aug. 29, 1838, aged 78, in Hardy County, stating that Benjamin died on Mar. 29, 1834. She died on Oct. 10, 1845, leaving these children: Hanson or Henson Marshall, Mary Tucker, Samuel Marshall (aged 43 in 1840), Elizabeth Marshall, and Emily Marshall; also a son Thomas Marshall died before his mother [Ref: P-2196].

MARSHALL, Caroline. See "Luke Marbury," q.v.

MARSHALL, Elizabeth. See "Benjamin Marshall" and Samuel Hanson," q.v.

MARSHALL, Emily. See "Benjamin Marshall," q.v.

MARSHALL, Hanson. See "Benjamin Marshall," q.v.

MARSHALL, Mary. See "Richard Clagett," q.v.

MARSHALL, Richard. Took the Oath of Allegiance before the Hon. William Berry in 1778 [Ref: O-257]. The estate of one Richard Marshall was probated on Oct. 27, 1812 [Ref: ZE-128].

MARSHALL, Samuel. See "Benjamin Marshall," q.v.

MARSHALL, Thomas. Took the Oath of Allegiance before the Hon. William Berry in 1778 [Ref: O-257]. See "Benjamin Marshall," q.v.

MARSON, John. Took the Oath of Allegiance before the Hon. James Beck in 1778 [Ref: O-254].

MARTHIS, William. Private, Militia, 1776 [Ref: M-207, A-325].

MARTIN, Ann. See "Adam Wykall," q.v.
MARTIN, Anna Statia. See "Alexis Boone," q.v.
MARTIN, Henry. Took the Oath of Allegiance before the Hon. Fielder Bowie in 1778 [Ref: O-304, W-4648 (Box 4, folder 15)].
MARTIN, Jacob. Took the Oath of Allegiance before the Hon. Osborn Sprigg in 1778 [Ref: O-308, which spelled it "Jacob Marton"].
MARTIN, Ignatius. Private, 1st Maryland Line, enlisted Mar. 18, 1777, and reportedly died on Aug. 27, 1777 [Ref: D-137]. The estate of "Ignatius Martin (soldier)" was probated on Aug. 1, 1792 in Prince George's County [Ref: ZE-128].
MARTIN, John (1733-   ). Took the Oath of Allegiance before the Hon. Osborn Sprigg in 1778 [Ref: O-308, R-69].
MARTIN, John Elias. Took the Oath of Allegiance before the Hon. Christopher Lowndes in 1778 [Ref: O-282]. The estate of John Elias Martin was probated on Sep. 27, 1782 [Ref: ZE-128].
MARTIN, John Jr. Private, enlisted Feb. 12, 1780, for 3 years or during war, in continental service, Maryland Line [Ref: D-333].
MARTIN, Leonard. Private, 1st Maryland Line, enlisted June 1, 1778 and discharged Feb. 14, 1779. On Feb. 24, 1779 he was paid for his services [Ref: D-138, E-308].
MARTIN, Michael. Private, 3rd Maryland Line, 1779 [Ref: D-297].
MARTIN, Pleasant. See "Smallwood Acton," q.v.
MARTIN, Sarah Ann. See "John Connolly," q.v.
MARTIN, Smith. Private in Capt. Hezekiah Wheeler's Company, 11th Militia Battalion, April, 1781 [Ref: L-19970 (Box 6, folder 21)]. Private, Select Militia, Capt. Hezekiah Wheeler's Company, July 14, 1781 [Ref: S-6636 (Box 31, folder 5)].
MARTIN, Thomas (1736-   ). Took the Oath of Allegiance (made his "X" mark) before the Hon. Thomas Clagett in 1778 [Ref: O-268, R-3].
MARTIN, William. Private, 4th Maryland Line, enlisted May 22, 1776 [Ref: D-11]. The estate of "William Martin (soldier)" was probated on Jan. 2, 1793 in Prince George's County [Ref: ZE-129].
MASON, Ann. See "Rinaldo Johnson," q.v.
MASON, Christina. See "Henry Franks," q.v.
MASON, Elizabeth. See "Richard Smith," q.v.
MASTERS, Dorcas. See "William Jenkins," q.v.
MASTERS, John. Private, enrolled by Capt. John H. Lowe on July 13, 1776, for continental service, Maryland Line [Ref: D-35]. John Masters married Prescella Bayne by license dated June 3, 1778 [Ref: ZB-146].
MATTHEWS, John. Took the Oath of Allegiance before the Hon. David Craufurd in 1778 [Ref: O-272].
MATTHEWS, William. Private, Militia, 1776 [Ref: M-207, A-325, which spelled the name "William Mathews"]. Took the Oath of Allegiance before the Hon. Thomas Williams in 1778 [Ref: O-302].

MATTINGLEY, Clement (1748-   ). Took the Oath of Allegiance before the Hon. Fielder Bowie in 1778 [Ref: R-79, O-304, W-4648 (Box 4, folder 15)].

MATTINGLEY, Joseph. Private, 1st Maryland Line, enlisted Dec. 10, 1776, promoted to sergeant on May 24, 1777, and discharged on Dec. 27, 1779 [Ref: D-136]. "Joseph Mattinly" married Margaret Scott by license dated Jan. 24, 1785 [Ref: ZB-147].

MATTINGLEY, Philip. Private, 2nd Maryland Line, from May 31, 1778 until discharged on Apr. 3, 1779 [Ref: D-139].

MATTINGLEY, Thomas. Private, 2nd Maryland Line, from May 31, 1778 until discharged on Apr. 3, 1779 [Ref: D-139].

MAUDUITT (MANDITT, MANDUITT) Deborah. See "Alexander Jackson" and "Leonard M. Deakins," q.v.

MAULDEN, Willimina M. See "John Baden," q.v.

MAXWELL, James. Corporal, 2nd Maryland Line, Capt. Alexander Truman's Company, 1782 [Ref: D-439].

MAY, Hannah. Rendered patriotic service (not specified) for which the Council of Maryland directed the Western Shore Treasurer on Nov. 12, 1781, "to pay her one pound of the bills emitted under the Act for the emission of bills of credit, etc. and of the money appropriated for the present campaign due her per account passed by the Deputy Auditor." [Ref: G-666]. On Apr. 26, 1782 she received the sum of one pound, two shillings and five pence from the State Treasurer for services rendered [Ref: I-148].

MAY, Joseph. Private in the Maryland Line by Feb. 24, 1779, when he was paid for his services "in cloathing." [Ref: E-308].

MAY, Richard. Private, 1st Maryland Line, who was paid for his services "in cloathing" on Apr. 17, 1779 [Ref: E-351].

MAYCH, Ann. See "Elisha Riston," q.b.

MAYHEW, Bazil. Private, Capt. Jesse Hellen's Militia Company, before May 23, 1782; guarded Magruder's Warehouse in the spring of 1782 [Ref: L-19970 (Box 6, folder 21)].

MAYHEW, Bryan, or Brian (Oct. 10, 1756, Maryland - July 4, 1833, Kentucky). "Bryan Mayhew" was a private who was enrolled by Capt. Alexander Howard Magruder, 11th Battalion, on Aug. 5, 1776, for continental service in the Maryland Line [Ref: D-38]. "Brian Mayhew" married (1) Ann Conley, and (2) Ann Dophey [Ref: X-1931].

MAYHEW, Charity. See "William Mayhew," q.v.

MAYHEW, Henry (Mar. 6, 1760 -   ). Son of William and Sarah Ann Mayhew [Ref: ZC-48]. Private, Capt. Benjamin Wailes' Militia Company, Lower Battalion; on duty guarding Magruder's Warehouse in the spring of 1782 [Ref: L-19970 (Box 6, folder 21)].

MAYHEW, James (1724-   ). Took the Oath of Allegiance before the Hon. William Berry in 1778 [Ref: O-259, R-65]. Source X-1931 also lists a James Mayhew who was born in Maryland in 1735, rendered patriotic service, and died in Virginia before Feb. 4, 1794. One James Mayhew married Mary Ryon by license dated May 14, 1788 [Ref: ZB-147].

MAYHEW, John (1726-   ). Took the Oath of Allegiance before the Hon. William Berry in 1778 [Ref: O-259, R-63, which spelled his name "John Mahew"]. "Johne Mayhew" married Massy Soper by license dated Dec. 9, 1795 [Ref: ZB-147]. See "Jonathan Mayhew," q.v.

MAYHEW, John Jr. Private, Militia, 1776 [Ref: M-207, A-325].

MAYHEW, Jonathan (c1756 - died after 1820). Private, 1st Maryland Line, 1776-1779; reenlisted, 3rd Maryland Line, Jan. 9, 1779, and served to 1781. Applied for a pension (S36054) in Washington County, Maryland on Apr. 9, 1818, aged about 62, stating he lived in Prince George's County at the time of his enlistment. In 1820 he had a wife aged 59 (not named) and a daughter Sara Matilda Mayhew, aged 16. On July 3, 1820, he moved to Washington, DC [Ref: P-2235, which listed his name as "Jonathan Mayhugh," D-142 and D-296, which listed his name as "Jona. Mahugh," and E-351, which listed his name as "Jonathan Mahew"]. Source X-1931 states John Mayhew (Feb. 13, 1758, Maryland - 1838, North Carolina) married Elizabeth Self, was a private in Virginia, and received a pension. It appears that Jonathan and John were the same person since Jonathan was the only Maryland pensioner by that name [Ref: P-2235]. "John Mayhew, Jr." is yet another possibility. Additional research may be necessary before drawing conclusions.

MAYHEW, Mary. See "William Cage," q.v.

MAYHEW, Sarah. See "Jonathan Mayhew" and" Henry Mayhew," q.v.

MAYHEW, Thomas. Private, 1st Maryland Line, enlisted on Dec. 10, 1776 and "exchanged for L. Hickey" [Ref: D-137]. Private, 3rd Maryland Line, from July 20, 1778 to Jan. 23, 1779, when he was discharged [Ref: D-142],

MAYHEW (MAHEW), Verlinda. See "Wilson Cage," q.v.

MAYHEW, William (1733-1794). Took the Oath of Allegiance (made his "W" mark) before the Hon. Alexander Howard Magruder in 1778 [Ref: O-293, R-61, which latter source spelled his name "Mahew"]. Private, enrolled by Capt. Alexander H. Magruder, 11th Battalion, on Aug. 1, 1776, for continental service, Maryland Line [Ref: D-38]. The estate of one William Mayhew was probated on June 20, 1794 in Prince George's County [Ref: ZE-129]. There was also a William Mayhew who rendered patriotic service in Maryland, married Charity ----, and died after 1800 in South Carolina [Ref: X-1931]. Additional research may be necessary before drawing conclusions. See "Henry Mayhew," q.v.

MAYNARD, Samuel. Captain who served on the Board of the Patuxent Associators and signed a resolution at Nottingham on Apr. 21, 1781 relative to the defence of the rivers of Potomac and Patuxent and the completion of the fort at Drum Point [Ref: K-1814].

McATEE, John. Sergeant, 11th Militia Battalion, Capt. Hezekiah Wheeler's Company, April, 1781 [Ref: L-19970 (Box 6, folder 21)]. Took

the Oath of Allegiance before the Hon. William Lyles, Jr. in 1778 [Ref: O-289]. The estate of one John McAtee was probated on Dec. 17, 1794 [Ref: ZE-130].
McATEE, Joseph. Private, Maryland Line, by Aug. 25, 1780, at which time the State Treasurer paid "Joseph McKettee, a recruit from Prince George's County" over eleven hundred pounds to be delivered to Joshua Beall, County Lieutenant [Ref: F-264].
McAWAY, Charles. Private, 4th Maryland Line, from Aug. 18, 1777 to at least Nov. 1, 1780 [Ref: D-143].
McBRIDE, Elizabeth. See "Basil Lowe," q.v.
McCABE, James. Private, Maryland Line, recruited by the Lieutenant of Frederick County on Apr. 9, 1778 [Ref: D-315]. The estate of one James McCabe was probated in Prince George's County on Aug. 28, 1800 [Ref: ZE-130].
McCANN, John. Private, 3rd Maryland Line, Capt. Horatio Clagett's Company, 1779 [Ref: D-295].
McCANN, Michael. Private, 2nd Maryland Line, Capt. Alexander Truman's Company, 1782 [Ref: D-439].
McCARTY, Timothy. Took the Oath of Allegiance (made his "X" mark) before the Hon. James Mullikin in 1778 [Ref: O-296].
McCAULEY, Rebecca. See "Alexander Harvey," q.v.
McCLAIN, John. Private, Northern Detachment, 3rd Maryland Line, Capt. Horatio Clagett's Company, 1783 [Ref: D-501].
McCLAMAUGH, David C. See "Vachell Ijams," q.v.
McCOLLEY, George Sr. Took the Oath of Allegiance before the Hon. James Beck in 1778 [Ref: O-254, which spelled it "Macolley"].
McCOLLEY, Zachariah. Took the Oath of Allegiance before the Hon. Thomas Williams in 1778 [Ref: O-302, which spelled it "McColly"].
McCOY, James. See "James McKay," q.v.
McCOY, John. Took the Oath of Allegiance before the Hon. David Craufurd in 1778 [Ref: O-271]. The estate of one John McCoy was probated on Dec. 3, 1793 [Ref: ZE-130].
McDANIEL, John (1737-   ). Constable in King George Hundred, 1777 [Ref: Z-3]. Took the Oath of Allegiance before the Hon. Thomas Clagett in 1778 [Ref: O-265, R-85]. Private in Capt. Hezekiah Wheeler's Company, 11th Militia Battalion, April, 1781 [Ref: L-19970 (Box 6, folder 21)].
McDANIEL, Sarah Ann. See "Henry Harvey," q.v.
McDANIEL, Walter (1747, Anne Arundel County, Maryland - after 1833, Brown County, Ohio). Applied for pension (R6683) in Brown County, Ohio on Apr. 30, 1833, stating he was born in 1747 in Anne Arundel County, Maryland and lived in Prince George's County at the time of his enlistment in the Maryland Line. After the war he moved to Virginia and then to Ohio; no family information given in his pension application (which was rejected). [Ref: P-2264; not listed in *Maryland Archives*,

Volume 18]. Source X-1957 mistakenly stated he was born in Massachusetts (typographical error) and died after Mar. 4, 1847, which meant he was over 100 years old. Also stated he was a private, minuteman (militiamen), and pensioner, so his rejected application must have been subsequently accepted. Additional research may be necessary before drawing conclusions.

McDANIEL, Walter (1755-   ). Took the Oath of Allegiance before the Hon. Thomas Clagett in 1778 [Ref: O-267, R-85]. If the age is incorrect, this could be the Walter McDaniel (born 1747) above.

McDONALD, Allen. Private, 6th Maryland Line, enlisted Apr. 28, 1778 and served to Apr., 1779 [Ref: D-230]. The estate of one Allen McDonald was probated on Sep. 24, 1807 [Ref: ZE-130].

McDONALD, Dunkin. See "John McDonald," q.v.

McDONALD, Elinor. See "John McDonald," q.v.

McDONALD, James. Took the Oath of Allegiance (made his "X" mark) before the Hon. Thomas Boyd in 1778 [Ref: O-262].

McDONALD, John (Oct. 19, 1750 -   ). Son of Dunkin and Elinor McDonald [Ref: ZC-49]. Took the Oath of Allegiance before the Hon. Fielder Bowie in 1778 [Ref: O-304, W-4648 (Box 4, folder 15)].

McDONNALD, John (1743-   ). Private, enrolled in the Flying Camp by Lieut. William D. Beall on Aug. 18, 1776; nativity: England; height: 5' 6"; brown hair, brown complexion [Ref: D-37].

McDONNALD, John (1746-   ). Private, enrolled in the Flying Camp by Lieut. William D. Beall on July 30, 1776; nativity: Maryland; height: 5' 8"; brown hair, brown complexion [Ref: D-37].

McDOWELL, Catherine. See "Levin Claridge," q.v.

McDOWELL, John (1725-   ). Took the Oath of Allegiance before the Hon. Truman Skinner in 1778 [Ref: R-44, O-297, which spelled the name "John McDowall"].

McDOWELL, Lucinda. See "Ignatius Brashears," q.v.

McELDERRY, Mary. See "Thomas Clagett" and "Jacob Duckett," q.v.

McFERRAN, John C. See "Alexander Truman," q.v.

McFERRAN, Margaret. See "Alexander Truman," q.v.

McGILL, John. Captain, 25th Battalion, 1776 [Ref: B-14, M-102, which latter source spelled his name "MacGill"]. Second Major, Upper Battalion, in July, 1776 [Ref: B-16]. "John MacGill" took the Oath of Allegiance before the Hon. Thomas Williams in 1778 [Ref: O-302].

McGILL, John. "John MacGill" was a private in the militia in Capt. Joshua Selby's Company, 1776, and served in Annapolis [Ref: M-208, B-403]. He participated in capturing an enemy boat and crew on Apr. 17, 1781 [Ref: M-209, which spelled his name "Magill"].

McGILL, John Jr. Private, Select Militia, Upper Battalion, June 12, 1781 [Ref: S-6636 (Box 27, folder 82B), which spelled his name "MacGill"].

McGILL, Thomas (1746-1787?). "Thomas MacGill" was a member of the Committee of Safety on Aug. 3, 1775 [Ref: A-49]. "Thomas Magill" was a County Court Justice in 1777 [Ref: C-273], and administered the Oath of Allegiance in 1778 [Ref: O-291]. "Thomas Magill" took the Oath of Allegiance before the Hon. Christopher Lowndes in 1778 [Ref: O-284]. "Thomas McGill" was aged 30 in 1776 [Ref: R-72]. The estate of one "Thomas McGill" was probated by Apr. 4, 1787 (date of inventory). [Ref: ZE-131].

McGINNIS, Andrew (1759, Ireland -   ). Private (substitute), 1780, in continental service, Maryland Line [Ref: D-338].

McGLOCKLAIN, Mark. Private, 3rd Maryland Line, Capt. Horatio Clagett's Company, December, 1779 [Ref: D-296].

McGREGOR, Alexander. Private, Northern Detachment, 3rd Maryland Line, Capt. Horatio Clagett's Company, 1783 [Ref: D-502].

McGUIRE, Lydia. See "John Fearall," q.v.

McHANDY, Thomas. Private, 2nd Maryland Line, Capt. Alexander Truman's Company, 1782, and reportedly died on Aug. 28, 1782 [Ref: D-439]. The estate of one Thomas McHandy was probated on May 17, 1793 [Ref: ZE-131].

McKAY, James (1752/4, Prince George's County, Maryland - Aug. 2, 1833, Clermont County, Ohio). He applied for a pension (S16199) in Clermont County, Ohio on Aug. 6, 1832, aged 80, stating that he was born in Prince George's County and lived in Frederick County at the time of his enlistment in the Maryland Line [Ref: P-2285]. Source X-1970 states he was born in 1754 and married (1) Margaret Denhem Burke and (2) Elizabeth Brown. Although "James McKay" is not listed in Henry C. Peden, Jr.'s *Revolutionary Patriots of Frederick County, 1775-1783*, "James McCoy" and "William McKay" are both listed in Capt. Meroney's Company of the Flying Camp in 1776. Additional research may be necessary before drawing conclusions.

McKAY, William. See "James McKay," q.v.

McKENSEY, James. Took the Oath of Allegiance before the Hon. Osborn Sprigg in 1778 [Ref: O-307].

McKETTEE, Joseph. See "Joseph McAtee," q.v.

McKINSEE, Benjamin. Took the Oath of Allegiance before the Hon. Fielder Bowie in 1778 [Ref: O-303, which questioned the name as "Mc--- ?;" yet, the original list at the Maryland State Archives (Box 4, folder 15) shows the name rather clearly as "McKinsee"].

McKNESS, Samuel. Took the Oath of Allegiance before the Hon. George Lee in 1778 [Ref: O-279].

McKNIGHT, John. Private, 4th Maryland Line, enlisted Feb. 23, 1779 [Ref: D-145]. The estate of "John McKnight (soldier)" was probated on July 24, 1793 [Ref: ZE-131].

McLANE, John (1712-   ). Took the Oath of Allegiance before the Hon. Christopher Lowndes in 1778 [Ref: R-59, O-287, which latter source spelled his name "MacClain"].

McLANE, John (1745-   ). Private, enrolled in the Flying Camp by Lieut. William D. Beall on July 17, 1776; nativity: Prince George's County; height: 5' 8" [Ref: D-37, which spelled his name "MacClane"]. See "John McClain," q.v.

McLAUGHLIN, John. Corporal, 4th Maryland Line, enlisted May 3, 1776 [Ref: D-11, which spelled his name "McGlaughlin"]. This or another John McLaughlin was a private in the 7th Maryland Line, 1777-1780 [Ref: D-233]. Took the Oath of Allegiance before the Hon. James Beck in 1778 [Ref: O-253]. The estate of one "John McLackland" was probated on Feb. 10, 1790, and the estate of "John McLaughlin (soldier)" was probated on July 24, 1793 [Ref: ZE-131]. Additional research may be necessary before drawing conclusions.

McLAUGHLIN, Peter. Took the Oath of Allegiance before the Hon. James Mullikin in 1778 [Ref: O-295].

McLAUGHLIN, William. Private, 2nd Maryland Line, from Sep. 1, 1777 to at least Nov. 1, 1780 [Ref: D-138].

McLURK, Daniel. Took the Oath of Allegiance before the Hon. Osborn Sprigg in 1778 [Ref: O-307].

McMANIS, Barney. Private, 7th Maryland Line, enlisted Dec. 25, 1776, and died on Aug. 18, 1780 (after the Battle of Camden). [Ref: D-233, D-305, which also spelled his name "McMannis"]. The estate of "Barny McManus (soldier)" was probated on Feb. 20, 1792 in Prince George's County [Ref: ZE-131].

McMANIS, Henry. Private, 6th Maryland Line, 1778 [Ref: D-228].

McMANIS, Thomas. Private, 7th Maryland Line, enlisted June 4, 1777 and discharged May 12, 1780 [Ref: D-231].

McNEW, Basil (1748-1817). Took the Oath of Allegiance before the Hon. Christopher Lowndes in 1778 [Ref: O-288, R-46, which listed his name as "Bazell Macnew"]. The estate of "Basil McNew" was probated on Apr. 9, 1817 [Ref: ZE-132].

McNEW (MacNEW), Mary. See "Rezin Harbin," q.v.

McNEW, Moses. Private, 2nd Maryland Line, Capt. Patrick Sim's Company, 1776 [Ref: D-8]. The estate of "Moses McNew (soldier)" was probated on July 18, 1792 [Ref: ZE-132].

McPHERSON, William (1765, Maryland -   ). Private, enlisted May 23, 1781, for 3 years in continental service, Maryland Line; sent to Annapolis; on duty July 13, 1781 [Ref: D-381].

McSWAIN, Samuel. Private, enrolled by Capt. John H. Lowe on July 13, 1776, for continental service, Maryland Line [Ref: D-34].

MEARS, William. Took the Oath of Allegiance before the Hon. Thomas Williams in 1778 [Ref: O-302].

MEDLEY, John Baptist. Took the Oath of Allegiance before the Hon. Benjamin Hall in 1778 [Ref: O-276, which spelled his name "John Baptis Medley"].

MEEK, Zekiel. On Apr. 27, 1782, the Western Shore Treasurer was ordered "to pay to Abraham Gorman 53 pounds and 14 shillings to be delivered over to Zekiel Meek as ordered by the Council of Maryland under the Act for the Emission of Bills of Credit." [Ref: I-149].

MEEKS, Thomas (1756, Maryland - Sep. 14, 1838, Indiana). Sergeant, 6th Maryland Line, July 21, 1777 until Apr. 7, 1780, when discharged [Ref: D-228]. Private, Capt. Richard Stonestreet's Militia Company, 11th Battalion, June, 1782 [Ref: L-19970 (Box 6, folder 21), which spelled the name "Thomas Meaks"]. "Thomas Meek" married Martha Davis [Ref: X-1996]. It should be noted that there were several men with the name of Meek or Meeks in Maryland during the Revolutionary War, but they were primarily from Kent County and Anne Arundel County. Additional research may be necessary before drawing conclusions.

MEFFORD, Jacob (Oct., 1764, Maryland - Dec. 14, 1844, Kentucky). Private, Northern Detachment, 3rd Maryland Line, Capt. Horatio Clagett's Company, 1783 [Ref: D-502, which spelled the name "Mifford"]. He married Eleanor ---- [Ref: X-1997]. It appears that Jacob was of French descent and had enlisted in Frederick County, Maryland. It must be noted that he was inadvertently omitted from Henry C. Peden's *Revolutionary Patriots of Frederick County, 1775-1783*. For more information consult Source P-2321.

MELVIN, Peter. Private, 2nd Maryland Line, enlisted Feb. 4, 1777. Private, 1st Maryland Line, 1780-1783 [Ref: D-139, D-357, D-495]. The estate of one Peter Melvin was probated on Feb. 21, 1785 [Ref: ZE-132].

MERRY, John (1758, Maryland -   ). Private, enlisted on May 28, 1781, for 3 years in continental service, Maryland Line; sent to Annapolis; on duty July 13, 1781 [Ref: D-382].

MICHELL, John. Took the Oath of Allegiance before the Hon. Fielder Bowie in 1778 [Ref: O-304. The original list at the Maryland State Archives also spelled his name "Michell" but there is a line drawn across the name as if one were crossing a "T" which is not there, i.e., spelling the name as "John Mitchell" rather than "Michell"].

MIDDLETON, Smith (1720-1794). Took the Oath of Allegiance before the Hon. George Lee in 1778 [Ref: O-279, R-75]. The estate of Smith Middleton was probated on Apr. 8, 1794 [Ref: ZE-13].

MIDDLETON, Theodore (Mar. 3, 1758, Charles County, Maryland - Jan. 28, 1844, Prince George's County, Maryland). Second Lieutenant, Middle Battalion, Capt. Samuel H. Beans' Company, May 1, 1778. Captain of Infantry "for the defense of the Chesapeake Bay" on Apr. 27, 1781 [Ref: M-103, M-104, E-63, G-418, N-36]. He applied for and received a pension (S11075) on Feb. 20, 1833, in Prince George's County, Maryland, and was paid in the District of Columbia. Theodore Middleton married Julia Hoxton and a son, W. H. Middleton, was mentioned in 1855 [Ref: T-50, P-2344, X-2019].

MIDDLETON, W. H. See "Theodore Middleton," q.v.

MIER, Elizabeth. See "Joseph Waters," q.v.
MILBURN, Nicholas (1750-1830). Private, 2nd Maryland Line, Capt. Alexander Truman's Company, 1782, and was promoted to corporal on Apr. 1, 1782 [Ref: D-440]. He married Jane ---- [Ref: X-2020].
MILES, Frederick. Private, 9th Company of Infantry, enlisted on Jan. 22, 1776 [Ref: D-19]. Private, 2nd Maryland Line, enlisted Apr. 25, 1778; corporal, Jan. 10, 1780; and discharged May 1, 1781 [Ref: D-140]. Took the Oath of Allegiance before the Hon. Thomas Williams in 1778 [Ref: O-302]. One Frederick Miles married Elizabeth White by license dated Dec. 31, 1781, and Frederick Miles married Ruth Brashears by license dated Feb. 11, 1784 [Ref: ZB-150]. There may have been two men with this name. Additional research may be necessary before drawing conclusions.
MILES, Henry. There were two men with this name who enlisted in the Maryland Line from Charles County in July, 1776 [Ref: D-32]. One Henry Miles married Henrietta Blanford by license dated June 9, 1783, in Prince George's County [Ref: ZB-150]. Additional research may be necessary before drawing conclusions.
MILES, James. Private, enrolled by Lt. William Duvall, Lower Battalion, on July 18, 1776, for continental service, Maryland Line [Ref: D-35].
MILES, Jesse (July 1, 1763, Prince George's County, Maryland - Apr. 11, 1838, Bullitt County, Kentucky). He moved to Berkley County, Virginia with his father Richard and was drafted into the militia in 1781 (also served as a substitute for his father). He moved to Nelson County, Kentucky in 1793 and then to Bullitt County, where he received pension S1235 in 1833 [Ref: P-2346].
MILES, John. Took the Oath of Allegiance before the Hon. Truman Skinner in 1778 [Ref: O-298], and rendered patriotic service by providing wheat for the military on Apr. 17, 1783 [Ref: Q-425]. One John Miles was born in Maryland circa 1758, rendered patriotic service, married Peggy ----, and died in Georgia on Sep. 22, 1825 [Ref: X-2021]. There was also a John Miles who married Jane Pearce by license dated Nov. 30, 1780, and a John Miles who married Rebecca Pearce by license dated Jan. 21, 1783 [Ref: ZB-150].
MILES, Mary. See "Francis Mitchell," q.v.
MILES, Morris. Took the Oath of Allegiance before the Hon. Thomas Williams in 1778 [Ref: O-302]. The estate of Morris Miles was probated on Aug. 6, 1788 [Ref: ZE-132].
MILES, Nathan. Took the Oath of Allegiance before the Hon. Thomas Williams in 1778 [Ref: O-302].
MILES, Nicholas (1741-   ). Ensign, 11th Battalion, Capt. Henry Hill's Company, May 1, 1778. Second Lieutenant, May 24, 1779 [Ref: M-104, E-62, E-414, N-32]. Took the Oath of Allegiance before the Hon. Thomas Clagett in 1778 [Ref: O-264, R-87].
MILES, Peggy. See "John Miles," q.v.

MILES, Richard. See "Jesse Miles," q.v.
MILES, Sarah. See "Mareen Duvall," q.v.
MILES, Shadrick. Took the Oath of Allegiance before the Hon. Osborn Sprigg in 1778 [Ref: O-306].
MILLAR, Andrew (1751-   ). Private, enrolled in the Flying Camp by Lieut. Benjamin Brooks on July 17, 1776; nativity: Prince George's County; height 5' 11"; has own gun [Ref: D-36].
MILLARD, William. Took the Oath of Allegiance before the Hon. James Mullikin in 1778 [Ref: O-296]. William Millard married Elizabeth Webb by license dated June 22, 1780 [Ref: ZB-151]. The estate of one William Millard was probated on June 20, 1797 [Ref: ZE-133].
MILLEMON, George. See "Stephen Riley," q.v.
MILLER, Andrew. Took the Oath of Allegiance before the Hon. David Craufurd in 1778 [Ref: O-272]. See "Andrew Millar," q.v.
MILLER, Ellen. See "John Tolson Lowe," q.v.
MILLER, Jacob. Private, enrolled by Lt. John M. Burgess, Lower Battalion, on July 20, 1776, for continental service, Maryland Line [Ref: D-35].
MILLER, Jacob. Private, enrolled by Ensign Horatio Clagett on July 15, 1776, for continental service, Maryland Line [Ref: D-35].
MILLER, John. Private, enrolled by Lt. John M. Burgess, Lower Battalion, on July 20, 1776, for continental service, Maryland Line [Ref: D-35]. Took the Oath of Allegiance before the Hon. William Berry in 1778 [Ref: O-258].
MILLER, John. Private, enrolled by Ensign Alexander Truman on July 5, 1776, for continental service, Maryland Line [Ref: D-38]. Private, 4th Maryland Line, enlisted Feb. 12, 1778 [Ref: D-144].
MILLER, Philip. Ensign, 7th Maryland Line, 1777 [Ref: D-233]. The estate of one Philip Miller was probated by Mar. 23, 1785 (date of inventory) in Prince George's County [Ref: ZE-133].
MILLER, Sarah. See "Jacob Holland," q.v.
MILLS, John. Private, 2nd Maryland Line, Capt. Patrick Sim's Company, 1776 [Ref: D-8]. Took the Oath of Allegiance (made his mark that looked like a backwards "N") before the Hon. Thomas Boyd in 1778 [Ref: O-261]. "John Mills married Ruth Jacobs on Jan. 3, 1778 and John Mills married Elizabeth Waters on Jan. 18, 1782. Walter Mills, born 1783, married in Rowan County, North Carolina and died after 1860 in Casey County, Kentucky." [Ref: Query from Elizabeth Wahle, 720 El Verano Drive, Walnut Creek, California 94598 in *Prince George's County Genealogical Society Bulletin*, Volume 25, No. 8 (Apr., 1994), p. 150]. John Mills married Elizabeth Waters by license dated Jan. 18, 1782 [Ref: ZB-151].
MILLS, Walter. See "John Mills," q.v.
MILLS, William. Took the Oath of Allegiance before the Hon. Benjamin Hall in 1778 [Ref: O-274].

MILLS, Zachariah (1760-1824). Took the Oath of Allegiance (made his mark that looked like a backwards "C") before the Hon. James Beck in 1778 [Ref: O-253]. One Zachariah Mills applied for a pension (S35000) in Prince George's County on Sep. 21, 1818, aged 58, stating he had enlisted in Queen Anne's County and served in the Maryland Line. In 1821 he lived in Anne Arundel County with a wife aged 44 and two small children (names not given). [Ref: P-2370]. One Zachariah Mills married Elizabeth Waters by license dated Dec. 21, 1787 [Ref: ZB-151]. The estate of one "Zacharich Mills" was probated on Mar. 8, 1824 in Prince George's County [Ref: ZE-133].

MINNING, John. Private, 3rd Maryland Line, Capt. Horatio Clagett's Company, 1779; reported "deserted" on Dec. 1, 1779 [Ref: D-296].

MINNISS, John. Took the Oath of Allegiance before the Hon. Osborn Sprigg in 1778 [Ref: O-307, which questioned whether his name was "Hinness?"]. There was, in fact, a "John Minniss" who was aged 36 in the census of 1776 of Prince George's County [Ref: R-82].

MITCHELL, Amelia. See "Benjamin Ray," q.v.

MITCHELL, Ann. See "James Beall," q.v.

MITCHELL, Benjamin. Took the Oath of Allegiance before the Hon. David Craufurd in 1778 [Ref: O-271].

MITCHELL, Benjamin Notly. Took the Oath of Allegiance (made his "N" mark) before the Hon. Thomas Clagett in 1778 [Ref: O-264].

MITCHELL, Charles (1758-   ). Private, enrolled in the Flying Camp by Lieut. Benjamin Brooks on July 6, 1776, aged 18; nativity: Maryland; height 5' 5"; brown hair, fair skin; has own gun [Ref: D-36]. Took the Oath of Allegiance before the Hon. Thomas Williams in 1778 [Ref: O-302, which listed the name as "Charles Mitchel"]. One Charles Mitchell applied for a pension (S47519) in the District of Columbia on June 2, 1818, aged 62, and a resident of Maryland, stating he had enlisted in Prince George's County and served in the Maryland Line [Ref: P-2377].

MITCHELL, David (Feb. 9, 1752 -   ). Son of John and Elizabeth Mitchell [Ref: ZC-184]. Took the Oath of Allegiance before the Hon. James Beck in 1778 [Ref: O-255, which spelled the name "Mitchel"].

MITCHELL, Edward (1754-1815). Private, enrolled in the Flying Camp by Lieut. Benjamin Brooks on July 20, 1776; nativity: Prince George's County; height 5' 6"; has own gun [Ref: D-36]. The estate of one Edward Mitchell was probated on July 4, 1815 [Ref: ZE-133].

MITCHELL, Elizabeth. See "David Mitchell," q.v.

MITCHELL, Francis. Private, 1st Maryland Line, enlisted Dec. 10, 1776 and discharged Dec. 27, 1776 [Ref: D-136]. Francis Mitchell married Mary Miles by license dated Apr. 26, 1786 [Ref: ZB-152].

MITCHELL, James. Private, 2nd Maryland Line, Capt. Patrick Sim's Company, 1776 [Ref: D-7].

MITCHELL, John. Took the Oath of Allegiance before the Hon. Thomas Williams in 1778 [Ref: O-302]. Private (draft), continental service,

Maryland Line, 1781 [Ref: D-382]. One John Mitchell married Drury Sweney by license dated May 10, 1788, and a John Mitchell married Rebeccah Clubb by license dated Jan. 29, 1791 [Ref: ZB-152]. See "John Michell" and "David Mitchell," q.v.

MITCHELL, John Jr. Took the Oath of Allegiance before the Hon. James Beck in 1778 [Ref: O-255, which listed the name as "John Mitchel, Junr."]. See "John Mitchell," q.v.

MITCHELL, John Sr. Took the Oath of Allegiance before the Hon. James Beck in 1778 [Ref: O-256, which listed the name as "John Mitchel, Senr."].

MITCHELL, Joseph Jr. Took the Oath of Allegiance before the Hon. Thomas Clagett in 1778 [Ref: O-265].

MITCHELL, Joseph Sr. (1724-1790). Took the Oath of Allegiance (made his "I" mark with an equidistant horizontal line through the middle) before the Hon. Thomas Clagett in 1778 [Ref: O-267, R-38]. The estate of one Joseph Mitchell was probated on Apr. 13, 1790 [Ref: ZE-134].

MITCHELL, Mary. See "Thomas King," q.v.

MITCHELL, Mordecai Miles. Took the Oath of Allegiance before the Hon. David Craufurd in 1778 [Ref: O-272]. He married Sarah Wilson by license dated Nov. 26, 1779 [Ref: ZB-152].

MITCHELL, Nathan (1756-). Private, enrolled in the Flying Camp by Lieut. Benjamin Brooks on July 17, 1776; nativity: Prince George's County; height 6'; has own gun [Ref: D-36].

MITCHELL, Priscilla. See "Thomas Upton," q.v.

MITCHELL, Richard. Two men with this name took the Oath of Allegiance in 1778: one before the Hon. Truman Skinner and one before the Hon. Osborn Sprigg [Ref: O-298, O-306].

MITCHELL, Sarah. See "Francis Mudd" and "Thomas Stallions," q.v.

MITCHELL, Theodore. Took the Oath of Allegiance before the Hon. Thomas Williams in 1778 [Ref: O-302, which spelled the name "Mitchel"]. He married Mary Wells by license dated Nov. 27, 1777 [Ref: ZB-153].

MITCHELL, Thomas. Private, enrolled by Lt. John M. Burgess, Lower Battalion, on July 20, 1776, for continental service, Maryland Line [Ref: D-35]. Took the Oath of Allegiance before the Hon. Osborn Sprigg in 1778 [Ref: O-307]. One Thomas Mitchell married Eleanor Edelen by license dated Nov. 9, 1778, and a Thomas Mitchell married Eleanor Mockbee by license dated Dec. 22, 1783 [Ref: ZB-153]. The estate of one Thomas Mitchell was probated on Aug. 14, 1827 [Ref: ZE-134].

MITCHELL, Thomas L. (1754 - Sep. 1, 1829). Took the Oath of Allegiance in 1778. He is buried in Addison Chapel Churchyard, Addison Road and 62nd Place, at Seat Pleasant [Ref: Y-612]. One "Thomas Lee Mitchell" married Elizabeth Wilson by license dated Oct. 2, 1802 [Ref: ZB-153]. The estate of "Thomas L. Mitchell" was probated on Feb. 16, 1830 [Ref: ZE-134].

MITCHELL, William. Took the Oath of Allegiance before the Hon. David Craufurd in 1778 [Ref: O-272]. One William Mitchell married Mary White by license dated Dec. 10, 1792 [Ref: ZB-153].
MOBERLY, Leven. Private, Capt. Jesse Hellen's Militia Company, before May 23, 1782, and guarded Magruder's Warehouse in the spring of 1782 [Ref: L-19970 (Box 6, folder 21)].
MOBERLY, Thomas. Private (draft), continental service, Maryland Line, 1780 [Ref: D-382, which spelled his name "Mobberly"]. Private, Capt. Jesse Hellen's Militia Company, before May 23, 1782; guarded Magruder's Warehouse in the spring of 1782 [Ref: L-19970 (Box 6, folder 21), which spelled his name "Moberley"].
MOCKBEE (MACBEE), Amelia. See "Nehemiah Lowe," q.v.
MOCKBEE, Alexander. See "Zadock Mockbee," q.v.
MOCKBEE, Ann. See "Basil Mockbee" and "Zadock Mockbee," q.v.
MOCKBEE, Basil. Took the Oath of Allegiance before the Hon. Osborn Sprigg in 1778 [Ref: O-307, which listed the name "Barie Mockbee," but the original list (very light) at the Maryland State Archives (Box 4, folder 29) looks more like "Basil" rather than "Barie"]. "Basil Mockbee" married Ann Mockbee by license dated Nov. 5, 1779 [Ref: ZB-153].
MOCKBEE, Brock. Took the Oath of Allegiance before the Hon. Osborn Sprigg in 1778 [Ref: O-307, which listed the name as "Booth." The original list at the Maryland State Archives (Box 4, folder 29) is very light, so it might actually be "Brock" instead of "Booth"]. The estate of one Brock Mockbee was probated on May 4, 1790 in Prince George's County [Ref: ZE-134]. See "William Mockbee," q.v.
MOCKBEE, Charles. Private, Select Militia, Upper Battalion, June 12, 1781 [Ref: S-6636 (Box 27, folder 82B)].
MOCKBEE, Darkey. See "William Jones," q.v.
MOCKBEE, Ed. See "William Nicholls Mockbee," q.v.
MOCKBEE, Eleanor. See "Thomas Mitchell," q.v.
MOCKBEE, Elizabeth. See "William Mockbee," q.v.
MOCKBEE, James. Private, Militia, 1776 [Ref: M-207, A-325, which spelled the name "Mockbe"]. Took the Oath of Allegiance before the Hon. David Craufurd in 1778 [Ref: O-272].
MOCKBEE, John. Took the Oath of Allegiance before the Hon. David Craufurd in 1778 [Ref: O-272]. John Mockbee married Margaret Robinson by license dated Aug. 20, 1777 [Ref: ZB-153].
MOCKBEE, Joseph. Private (draft), continental service, Maryland Line, 1781 [Ref: D-382]. Took the Oath of Allegiance before the Hon. William Berry in 1778 [Ref: O-259, which spelled the name "Mackbee"]. The estate of one Joseph Mockbee was probated on Dec. 8, 1795 [Ref: ZE-134].
MOCKBEE, Mary. See "Zadock Mockbee," q.v.
MOCKBEE, Philip. See "Zadock Mockbee," q.v.
MOCKBEE, Rachel. See "John Ridgeway," q.v.

MOCKBEE, Sarah. See "William Nicholls Mockbee," q.v.
MOCKBEE, Thomas. See "Zadock Mockbee," q.v.
MOCKBEE, Walter. See "Zadock Mockbee," q.v.
MOCKBEE, William. "William Mocbee" took the Oath of Allegiance before the Hon. Osborn Sprigg in 1778 [Ref: O-306]. "William Mockbee" was a private, 2nd Maryland Line, 1778-1780 [Ref: D-139]. One "William Mockbee" married Ann Clarke by license dated Feb. 29, 1780, and "William Mockbee, Jr." married Margaret Henness by license dated Dec. 24, 1780 [Ref: ZB-153]. William Mockbee, son of Brock and Elizabeth Mockbee, of Queen Anne's Parish, was born on Apr. 22, 1730 [Ref: ZC-185]. See "Zadock Mockbee," q.v.
MOCKBEE, William Nicholls (Sep. 16, 1759 -   ). Son of Ed *[sic]* and Sarah Mockbee, of Prince George's Parish [Ref: ZD-118]. Took the Oath of Allegiance before the Hon. Osborn Sprigg in 1778 [Ref: O-307, which listed his name as "William N. Mockbee"].
MOCKBEE, Zadock. Took the Oath of Allegiance before the Hon. Osborn Sprigg in 1778 [Ref: O-306, which listed his name as "Macbee," and W-4648 (Box 4, folder 29), which listed it as "Mocbee"]. "Zadoc Mockebie" married Ann ---- and had these children listed in the King George's Parish register: Alexander Mockbee (born Mar. 23, 1778), William Mockbee (born Apr. 29, 1780), Mary Mockbee (born Feb., 18 178?), Philip Soper Mockbee (born Aug. 31, 178?), Thomas M. Mockbee (born May 2, 178?), Walter Evans Mockbee (born Aug. 13, 1789), and Ann Mockbee (born June 21, 1792). [Ref: ZC-50].
MOLTON, William. Second Lieutenant, Lower Battalion, Capt. Jesse Hellen's Company, Sep. 1, 1777 [Ref: M-105, C-356].
MOODIE, Henry Hume. Took the Oath of Allegiance before the Hon. David Craufurd in 1778 [Ref: O-272].
MOODIE, William. Took the Oath of Allegiance before the Hon. Osborn Sprigg in 1778 [Ref: O-306].
MOONE, John Smith. Took the Oath of Allegiance (made his "I" mark with an equidistant horizontal line through the middle) before the Hon. Thomas Clagett in 1778 [Ref: O-268].
MOONEY, Patrick. One Patrick Mooney was a private, 6th Maryland Line, enlisted on Apr. 3, 1777 and was reported missing on Aug. 16, 1780 (at the Battle of Camden). [Ref: D-230]. Another Patrick Mooney was a private, 7th Maryland Line, enlisted Aug. 15, 1777 and reportedly "deserted" on July 8, 1780 [Ref: D-232]. The estate of one "Patrick Mooney (soldier)" was probated on Mar. 7, 1793 in Prince George's County [Ref: ZE-134].
MOORE, Alexander C. (1754 - after 1832). Private, Maryland Line. He applied for pension (S11091) on Sep. 10, 1832, in Washington, DC, stating he was born in Prince George's County and lived near Upper Marlborough at the time of his enlistment. He moved to what is now Washington, DC after the war [Ref: P-2397].

221

MOORE, Ann. See "Jesse Greenwell," q.v.
MOORE, Benjamin (1712-1784). Took the Oath of Allegiance before the Hon. Osborn Sprigg in 1778 [Ref: O-307, R-82]. The estate of one Benjamin Moore was probated on June 8, 1784 [Ref: ZE-134].
MOORE, Elijah. Two men with this name took the Oath of Allegiance in 1778: one before the Hon. Fielder Bowie and another (made his "X" mark) before the Hon. Thomas Clagett [Ref: O-266, O-304, W-4648 (Box 4, folder 15)].
MOORE, Elizabeth. See "John Mahony," q.v.
MOORE, George Jr. Took the Oath of Allegiance before the Hon. William Berry in 1778 [Ref: O-258]. Ensign, Upper Battalion, Militia, Capt. Sheckell's Company, June 27, 1781 [Ref: H-320].
MOORE, George Sr. Took the Oath of Allegiance before the Hon. William Berry in 1778 [Ref: O-258]. He rendered patriotic service by providing wheat for the military on Sep. 2, 1780 [Ref: Q-314]. The estate of one George Moore was probated on Mar. 29, 1783 [Ref: ZE-134].
MOORE, James (1736-1784). Took the Oath of Allegiance before the Hon. Osborn Sprigg in 1778 [Ref: R-82, O-307, which latter source listed his name as "James Moore, Sr."]. Served on a Grand Jury in 1777 [Ref: Z-29]. The estate of "James Moore, Sr." was probated on Sep. 28, 1784 [Ref: ZE-135].
MOORE, James. "James More" was apparently recruited for military service by Aug. 28, 1780 when the County Lieutenant reported to the Council of Maryland that he (More) "is supposed to have stole a horse & gone off. I imployed a man to go after him and furnished him with money in case he could here of him, but as we could then get no intelligence of him, or which way he had gone, I thought it would be spending the publick money to very little purpose. I have since heard he has been seen on his way to Carolina." [Ref: G-63].
MOORE, James, of Benjamin. Took the Oath of Allegiance before the Hon. Osborn Sprigg in 1778 [Ref: O-307]. The estate of James Moore, of Benjamin, was probated on May 23, 1794 [Ref: ZE-135].
MOORE, Jeremiah (1749-1793). Private, Militia, 1776 [Ref: M-207, A-325]. Took the Oath of Allegiance before the Hon. William Berry in 1778 [Ref: O-258, R-26]. The estate of Jeremiah Moore was probated on Dec. 3, 1793 [Ref: ZE-135].
MOORE, John (1760, England - 1793, Maryland). Private, 7th Maryland Line, "served seven years." Buried in Trinity Episcopal Churchyard at Upper Marlboro [Ref: Y-613]. Private (substitute), 1780, in continental service, Maryland Line [Ref: D-338]. Private, 2nd Maryland Line, Capt. William Murdock's Company, Mar. 15, 1781 [Ref: D-366]. He married Elizabeth Cadle [Ref: X-2064]. Also see the following entries about three men by the name of John Moore.
MOORE, John. Three men with this name took the Oath of Allegiance in 1778: one before the Hon. James Beck [Ref: O-254], one before the

Hon. Osborn Sprigg [Ref: O-306], and another before the Hon. Fielder Bowie [Ref: O-304, W-4648 (Box 4, folder 15)]. One John Moore married Elizabeth Keadle by license dated Mar. 3, 1783 [Ref: ZB-154]. See "John Moore (1760-1793)," q.v.

MOORE, John 5th. Private, Northern Detachment, 3rd Maryland Line, Capt. Horatio Clagett's Company, 1783 [Ref: D-502].

MOORE, Joseph. Took the Oath of Allegiance before the Hon. Osborn Sprigg in 1778 [Ref: O-307].

MOORE, Sarah. See "James Thompson," q.v.

MOORE, Thomas (1745-   ). Took the Oath of Allegiance before the Hon. Thomas Clagett in 1778 [Ref: O-268, R-86]. Private, Capt. Hezekiah Wheeler's Company, 11th Militia Battalion, April, 1781 [Ref: L-19970 (Box 6, folder 21)].

MOORE, William. Second Lieutenant, 25th Battalion, May 1, 1778, Capt. Joseph Carlton's Company. First Lieutenant, May 24, 1779, Capt. Josiah Shaw's Company. Captain, Upper Battalion, June 24, 1780 to June 27, 1781, by which time he had moved from the county [Ref: M-105, C-78, C-414, G-492, H-320, N-33]. Took the Oath of Allegiance before the Hon. William Berry in 1778 [Ref: O-258].

MOORE, Zachariah (1762, Maryland - Aug. 28, 1837, Missouri). Private, Militia; participated in capturing an enemy boat and crew on Apr. 17, 1781. Private, Select Militia, Upper Battalion, June 12, 1781 [Ref: M-208, S-6636 (Box 27, folder 82B)]. Private in the Maryland Line, 1782. Sergeant, 1783; discharged Sep. 7, 1783 [Ref: D-509, D-549]. On Mar. 3, 1802, Campbell County, Kentucky, he signed a power of attorney and it was stated he was formerly of Prince George's County, Maryland where he had enlisted in the war. He applied for a pension (S18987) in St. Clair County, Missouri on Sep. 20, 1828 [Ref: P-2410]. Zachariah Moore married Elsie Bourne [Ref: X-2069].

MOORE, Zadock. Took the Oath of Allegiance before the Hon. Osborn Sprigg in 1778 [Ref: O-307]. One Zadock Moore married Ann King by license dated Mar. 6, 1779, a Zadock Moore married Mary Soper by license dated June 6, 1779, and a Zadock Moore married Rachel Elson by license dated Nov. 22, 1782 [Ref: ZB-155]. The estate of one Zadock Moore was probated by Mar. 26, 1790 (date of account). [Ref: ZE-135]. Additional research may be necessary before drawing conclusions.

MORAN, Benjamin. Private, 2nd Maryland Line, Capt. Alexander Truman's Company; died on Feb. 2, 1782 [Ref: D-440, which spelled the name "Mooren"]. The estate of "Benjamin Moran (soldier)" was probated on Apr. 17, 1793 [Ref: ZE-135].

MORAN, William. Private, Maryland Line; defective on Mar. 6, 1781 [Ref: D-414]. Source X-2070 lists two William Moran's who served as privates in the Maryland Line: one William Moran (1748-1824) died in Virginia and the other William Moran (c1724-1797) died in North Carolina.

MORELICK, Moses. See "John Dove," q.v.

MORGAN, John Hunt. See "Alexander Truman," q.v.
MORGAN, Marmaduke. Took the Oath of Allegiance before the Hon. Osborn Sprigg in 1778 [Ref: O-308, which spelled it "Morgin"].
MORRIS, Barton (1756-   ). Private, 2nd Guard, Capt. Henry Hill's Militia Company, Lower Battalion; on duty at Nottingham on the Patuxent, Apr. 12, 1781 [Ref: R-78, L-19970 (Box 6, folder 21), which latter source spelled his name "Bartain Morris"].
MORRIS, John. Sergeant, 3rd Maryland Line, Capt. Horatio Clagett's Company, 1779 [Ref: D-295, which spelled his name "Jno. Morriss"].
MORRIS, Martha Dent. See "John Simpson," q.v.
MORRIS, Samuel. Private, enrolled by Lt. William Duvall, Lower Battalion, on July 18, 1776, for continental service, Maryland Line [Ref: D-35].
MORRISON, John. Fifer, 1st Maryland Line, enlisted Apr. 9, 1778 [Ref: D-138]. The estate of one John Morrison was probated on Apr. 10, 1794 [Ref: ZE-136].
MORSELL, Kidd (1754 - Jan. 9, 1815). Took the Oath of Allegiance in Harford County in 1778. He is buried "in the back yard next door to Johnnie Smith's in Beltsville [Prince George's County, Maryland] but gravestone could no longer be found in 1982." [Ref: Y-589, and *Revolutionary Patriots of Harford County, Maryland, 1775-1783*, by Henry C. Peden, Jr. (1985), page 164]. One Kidd Morsell married Margaret Buchan by license dated Mar. 29, 1803, in Prince George's County [Ref: ZB-156]. The estate of one Kidd Morsell was probated on Feb. 7, 1815 in Prince George's County [Ref: ZE-136].
MORSON, William. Took the Oath of Allegiance before the Hon. David Craufurd in 1778 [Ref: O-270].
MORTON, Richard. Took the Oath of Allegiance before the Hon. Osborn Sprigg in 1778 [Ref: O-306].
MORTON, Samuel. Took the Oath of Allegiance before the Hon. Alexander Howard Magruder in 1778 [Ref: O-293].
MORTON, Thomas. Took the Oath of Allegiance before the Hon. Alexander Howard Magruder in 1778 [Ref: O-293]. The estate of one Thomas Morton was probated on June 22, 1782 [Ref: ZE-136].
MORTON, William. Second Lieutenant, Militia, 1777 [Ref: N-32]. Rendered patriotic service by providing wheat for the military on Aug. 16, 1781 [Ref: Q-425]. Took the Oath of Allegiance before the Hon. Truman Skinner in 1778 [Ref: O-297]. The estate of one William Morton was probated on May 20, 1815 [Ref: ZE-136].
MOYLAN, Eliza C. See "Thomas Lansdale," q.v.
MUDD, Ann. See "John Williams," q.v.
MUDD, Bennett (or Benedict?). "Bent. Mudd" was a private, 1st Maryland Line, enlisted on Feb. 9, 1779; sergeant, July 1, 1780 [Ref: D-138]. "Bennett Mudd" was paid for his services "in cloathing" on Apr. 17, 1779

[Ref: E-351]. The estate of one "Benedict Mudd" was probated in 1822 [Ref: ZE-136].
MUDD, Elizabeth. See "Benjamin Kidwell," q.v.
MUDD, Francis (1746-1779). Took the Oath of Allegiance before the Hon. Truman Skinner in 1778 [Ref: O-298, R-75]. He married Sarah Mitchell [Ref: X-2101]. The estate of Francis Mudd was probated by July 3, 1779 (date of inventory and account). [Ref: ZE-136].
MUDD, Henry Lowe. Private, 2nd Guard, Capt. Henry Hill's Militia Company, Lower Battalion; on duty at Nottingham on the Patuxent, Apr. 12, 1781 [Ref: L-19970 (Box 6, folder 21), which listed his name as "H. L. Mudd"]. Took the Oath of Allegiance before the Hon. Truman Skinner in 1778 [Ref: O-298].
MUDD, Hezekiah. Took the Oath of Allegiance before the Hon. Osborn Sprigg in 1778 [Ref: O-307]. Private, 2nd Guard, Capt. Henry Hill's Militia Company, Lower Battalion; on duty at Nottingham on the Patuxent, Apr. 12, 1781 [Ref: L-19970 (Box 6, folder 21)]. He was paid for his services in August, 1781 [Ref: G-569]. Hezekiah Mudd married Elizabeth Edelen by license dated May 12, 1779 [Ref: ZB-156].
MUDD, Jeremiah. Private, Maryland Line, 1781 [Ref: I-22].
MUDD, Mary. See "James Kidwell," q.v.
MUDD, Melinda. See "William Shircliff," q.v.
MUDD, Richard D. See "Benjamin Kidwell," q.v.
MUDD, Thomas (1740-1814). Took the Oath of Allegiance before the Hon. Thomas Clagett in 1778 [Ref: O-264, R-41]. Private, 1st Guard, Capt. Henry Hill's Militia Company, Lower Battalion; on duty at Nottingham on the Patuxent, Apr. 12, 1781 [Ref: L-19970 (Box 6, folder 21)]. The estate of one Thomas Mudd was probated on June 29, 1814 [Ref: ZE-136].
MUDD, William (1757-   ). Private, enrolled in the Flying Camp by Capt. Robert Bowie on Aug. 3, 1776; nativity: Prince George's County; height 5' 4"; has own gun [Ref: D-36, which spelled the name "Mud"].
MULLAN, Edward. Private, enrolled by Capt. Alexander H. Magruder, 11th Battalion, on July 4, 1776, for continental service, Maryland Line [Ref: D-38].
MULLIKIN, Archibald (Dec., 1753 -   ). Son of Lewis and Mary Mulliken, of Prince George's Parish in Prince George's County [Ref: ZD-118]. "Archibald Mullihan" was a private in the Upper District of Frederick County in July, 1776 [Ref: D-50].
MULLIKIN, James. Justice of the County Court, 1777-1778 [Ref: Z-90, C-273]. Captain, Militia, 25th Battalion, to at least May 1, 1778 [Ref: M-106, N-34, E-62, which latter source spelled his name "James Mullican"]. One Lieutenant James Mullikin, of Capt. Boyd's Company, was tried (with other officers) at a General Courts-Martial on July 25 and Aug. 23, 1776. Apparently, Capt. Richard B. Hall claimed Lieut. Mullikin was creating divisions in the company and struck and abused one of the

privates. The outcome of the courts-martial, however, was not stated. See "John Rogers," q.v. [Ref: A-498, A-553, B-233]. Also, James Mullikin was a Justice who administered the Oath of Allegiance in 1778 [Ref: O-294]. The records of the Council of Maryland on Apr. 1, 1779, stated the following: "After three Days spent in examining Witnesses on both Sides on a Memorial presented to the Governor and Council by James Draine, Marsh Marine Duvall, Benjamin Belt, Joseph Duvall, and James Draine Junr. against James Mullikin, praying that he might be removed from the Magistracy of Prince George's County, It was recommended by his Excellency and the Council to the Parties, to make up and settle all Differences subsisting between them and in the future to live in Peace. Whereupon the Memorialists agree to withdraw their Memorial and We the Subscribers agree that all Differences and Disputes which have heretofore subsisted between Us be buried in Oblivion and that we will not revive the same and that this shall be published in the News Paper." [Ref: E-335].

MULLIKIN, Jane. See "Basil Waring 3rd," q.v.

MULLIKIN, John. Took the Oath of Allegiance before the Hon. Christopher Lowndes in 1778 [Ref: O-283]. "John Mullican" was aged 70 and "John Mullican, Jr." was aged 40 in 1776 [Ref: R-33]. There was also a John Mullikin, son of Lewis and Mary Mullikin, who was born on Jan. 23, 1752, in Prince George's Parish [Ref: ZD-118]. Additional research may be necessary before drawing conclusions.

MULLIKIN, Lewis (Mar. 6, 1757 -   ). Son of Lewis and Mary Mullikin, of Prince George's Parish in Prince George's County [Ref: ZD-118]. "Lewis Mullican" was a private in the Upper District of Frederick County in July, 1776 [Ref: D-44]. See "Archibald Mullikin" and "John Mullikin," q.v.

MULLIKIN, Mary. See "William Bowie" and "Archibald Mullikin" and "Allen Bowie, Sr." and "Lewis Mullikin" and "John Mullikin," q.v.

MULLIKIN, Samuel (1749-   ). Took the Oath of Allegiance before the Hon. Fielder Bowie in 1778 [Ref: O-304, W-4648 (Box 4, folder 15), and R-77, which listed his name as "Mullican"].

MULLIKIN, Thomas (1738-   ). "Thomas Mullikin" took the Oath of Allegiance before the Hon. Christopher Lowndes in 1778 [Ref: O-283]. "Thomas Mullican" was aged 38 in 1776 [Ref: R-33].

MULLIKIN, William (1734-1789). Took the Oath of Allegiance before the Hon. William Berry in 1778 [Ref: O-258, R-51, which spelled his name "Mullican"]. The estate of one William Mullikin was probated on Oct. 5, 1789 [Ref: ZE-137].

MULLIKIN, William Jr. Took the Oath of Allegiance before the Hon. Christopher Lowndes in 1778 [Ref: O-283]. Private, Militia, 1776 [Ref: M-207, A-325]. One "William Mulliken" married Ann Barrett by license dated Mar. 25, 1780 [Ref: ZB-157]. The estate of one William Mullikin was probated on Oct. 7, 1823 [Ref: ZE-137].

MULLOWNEY, Darby. Private, enrolled by Capt. John H. Lowe on July 13, 1776, for continental service, Maryland Line [Ref: D-35].

MULLOY, Roger (1758, England -   ). Private (substitute), 1780, continental service, Maryland Line [Ref: D-338].

MUNDLEY, John. Took the Oath of Allegiance before the Hon. Osborn Sprigg in 1778 [Ref: O-307].

MURDOCK, Addison (July 31, 1731 - 1793). A son of William Murdock and Ann Addison (first wife), of Queen Anne's Parish, Addison never married. He was the brother-in-law of "Benjamin Hall, of Francis," q.v., and attended the Maryland Convention in 1774, served on the Committee of Correspondence in 1774-1775, and served on the Committee of Observation in 1775. He was commissioned First Major, 25th Battalion, on Jan. 13, 1776, but in a letter to the Council dated Jan. 23, 1776, he stated, "I have been honored by the convention with the enclosed commission which I now return to you, with a prayer to be excused from accepting it. The precarious and declining state of my health renders me incapable of executing the office, either with benefit to my country, or reputation to myself, and therefore, I think it my duty to refuse it." [Ref: M-106, A-109, ZA-563, ZC-186, ZE-138]. Addison took the Oath of Allegiance before the Hon. Benjamin Hall in 1778 [Ref: O-276].

MURDOCK, Elinor. See "Benjamin Hall, of Francis," q.v.

MURDOCK, John (May 16, 1733 - died by Aug. 3, 1791). A son of William Murdock and Ann Addison (first wife), of Queen Anne's Parish, Col. John Murdock married Ann Belt in 1751 and inherited his father's lands in Frederick County. His obituary in the *Maryland Gazette* on Aug. 3, 1791 stated "He was descended from an ancient family in this state, appointed to the most honorable position previous to the Revolution and was a patriot, statesman, and soldier." [Ref: ZA-563, ZA-567, ZC-186]. He was the father of "William Murdock," q.v.

MURDOCK, William. Lieutenant, 2nd Maryland Line, Apr. 1, 1780. Captain, Maryland State Regiment, Mar. 15, 1781 [Ref: D-366, D-379, which spelled his name both "William Murdoch and Murdock"]. Jane Contee (Harrison) (Murdock) Clagett, widow of both William Murdoch (or Murdock) and Zadock Clagett, applied for a pension in Washington, DC on Nov. 29, 1837, aged 71. She stated that her maiden name was Jane Contee Harrison and she married William Murdoch (or Murdock) on May 27, 1783 in Frederick County. He died in February, 1792 and she married secondly to Zadock Clagett who died in June, 1796 [Ref: P-2456, although Source ZA-567 indicates he died by Feb. 22, 1791, and was a captain and member of the Society of the Cincinnati].

MURDOCK, William. See "Addison Murdock" and "John Murdock," q.v.

MURPHY, John. Took the Oath of Allegiance before the Hon. Benjamin Hall in 1778 [Ref: O-275].

MURRAY, John. There were several men with this name who served in the Maryland Line [Ref: D-58, D-142, D-144, D-231, D-426, D-451]. The estate of one John Murray was probated in Prince George's County in 1804 [Ref: ZE-138].
MURRAY, Margaret. See "John Sutherland," q.v.
NAGLE, Jacob. See "Richard Nagle," q.v.
NAGLE, John. See "Richard Nagle," q.v.
NAGLE, Richard (c1747, Ireland - Feb. 22, 1837, Pennsylvania). Private, Maryland Line. Pension file of John Farrell or Fearall (R3450) includes a statement by John and Jacob Nagle, of Cambria County, Pennsylvania, that their father Richard served with John Farrell (who died in 1809 in Huntington County, Pennsylvania) in the Maryland Line [Ref: P-1160]. It appears that Richard Nagle enlisted in Frederick County [Ref: P-2468, X-2120].
NAILOR, Joshua. See "Joshua Naylor," q.v.
NALLY, Aaron. Took the Oath of Allegiance before the Hon. Christopher Lowndes in 1778 [Ref: O-287].
NAYDIN, Hester. See "Thomas Naydin," q.v.
NAYDIN, Thomas (1737-   ). Took the Oath of Allegiance before the Hon. Thomas Clagett in 1778 [Ref: O-266, R-9, which spelled his name "Thomas Neydin"]. On May 8, 1782, the records of the Council of Maryland contain this entry: "Permission is hereby granted to Thomas Naydin of Prince George's County in the State of Maryland to apply for His Excellency General Washington or the Commanding Officers at the out Posts of the American Army, for License to go into New York City for the purpose of obtaining a Passage from thence to Great Britain and to take with him his wife Hester Naydin and daughter [not named] about seven years of age." [Ref: I-159].
NAYLOR, Adelphia. See "Joshua Naylor," q.v.
NAYLOR, Ann. See "Joshua Naylor" and "Samuel Perrie Wailes" and "Walter Watson," q.v.
NAYLOR, Batson (May, 1759, Maryland - Nov. 7, 1830, North Carolina). Son of Batson Naylor (died 1769) and Margaret Fields. Private, 2nd Guard, Capt. Henry Hill's Militia Company, Lower Battalion; on duty at Nottingham on the Patuxent, Apr. 12, 1781 [Ref: L-19970 (Box 6, folder 21)]. Took the Oath of Allegiance before the Hon. Fielder Bowie in 1778 [Ref: O-304, W-4648 (Box 4, folder 15)]. Batson Naylor married Mrs. Eleanor Smith Austin (widow) by license dated Nov. 6, 1778 [Ref: X-2124, but it cited only his patriotic service and not his military service; ZB-159, which misspelled his name as "Batson"; and information from Joseph Y. Rowe, 69 Mattingly Avenue, Indian Head, Maryland 20640, in 1989]. See "Benjamin Naylor," q.v.
NAYLOR, Benjamin G. Private, Capt. Benjamin Wailes' Militia Company, Lower Battalion; on duty guarding Magruder's Warehouse in the spring of 1782 [Ref: L-19970 (Box 6, folder 21)]. Benjamin Naylor, son of

Batson Naylor and Margaret Fields, and brother of "Batson Naylor," q.v., was born Sep. 25, 1760 in Maryland, married Deborah Selby, and died in Kentucky on Mar. 26, 1839 [Ref: X-2124, and information from Joseph Y. Rowe, of Indian Head, Maryland, 1989]. See "Joshua Naylor" and "Samuel P. Wailes," q.v.

NAYLOR, George. Private, enrolled by Ensign Alexander Truman on July 4, 1776, for continental service, Maryland Line [Ref: D-38]. Took the Oath of Allegiance before the Hon. Truman Skinner in 1778 [Ref: O-298]. First Lieutenant, Militia, 1778 [Ref: N-32, which spelled the name "Nailor"]. It must be cautioned that there were several men named George Naylor, so this information could apply to any of them. One George Naylor married Eleanor Berry by license dated June 2, 1785, and a George Naylor married Elizabeth Adams by license dated Jan. 23, 1802 [Ref: ZB-159]. The estate of one George Naylor was probated in 1788 and the estate of one George Naylor was probated in 1809 [Ref: ZE-138]. Additional research may be necessary before drawing conclusions. See "Joshua Naylor," q.v., and the other George Naylors that follow herein.

NAYLOR, George Jr. Took the Oath of Allegiance before the Hon. Fielder Bowie in 1778 [Ref: O-303, W-4648 (Box 4, folder 15)]. "George Nailor, Junr." was a Recruiting Officer in 1780 [Ref: F-57]. Source X-2124 lists two George Naylor's who died in Kentucky. See comment under "George Naylor," q.v.

NAYLOR, George, of Batson. Took the Oath of Allegiance before the Hon. Fielder Bowie in 1778 [Ref: O-304, W-4648 (Box 4, folder 15)]. Private, Capt. Benjamin Wailes' Militia Company, Lower Battalion; on duty guarding Magruder's Warehouse in the spring of 1782 [Ref: L-19970 (Box 6, folder 21)]. See "George Naylor," q.v.

NAYLOR, George, of James. Took the Oath of Allegiance before the Hon. Alexander Howard Magruder in 1778 [Ref: O-293].

NAYLOR, George, of Swanky. Private, Capt. Benjamin Wailes' Militia Company, Lower Battalion; on duty guarding Magruder's Warehouse in the spring of 1782 [Ref: L-19970 (Box 6, folder 21)].

NAYLOR, Isaac. "Isaac Naylor" was a private, Capt. Benjamin Wailes' Militia Company, Lower Battalion, and on duty guarding Magruder's Warehouse in the spring of 1782 [Ref: L-19970 (Box 6, folder 21)]. "Isaac Nailor" was a private in Rawlings' Regiment, Maryland Line, from 1777 until discharged on Aug. 9, 1779 [Ref: D-148]. See "Nicholas Naylor," q.v.

NAYLOR, James. See "Joshua Naylor," q.v.

NAYLOR, Jemimah. See "Joshua Naylor," q.v.

NAYLOR, John Lawson. First Lieutenant, 11th Battalion, Capt. Henry Hill's Company, May 1, 1778 [Ref: M-106, E-62, which listed his name as "John Nailer"]. First Lieutenant, 3rd Guard, Capt. Henry Hill's Militia Company, Lower Battalion; on duty at Nottingham on the Patuxent, Apr. 12, 1781 [Ref: L-19970 (Box 6, folder 21)]. Took the Oath of

Allegiance before the Hon. Fielder Bowie in 1778 [Ref: O-303, W-4648 (Box 4, folder 15)].

NAYLOR, Joshua (1751 or 1756 - June 24, 1835, Montgomery County, North Carolina). Private, 1st Maryland Line, 1775-1776; corporal, 4th Maryland Line, Aug. 1, 1777; discharged on May 20, 1780, in Prince George's County, Maryland. He married Mourning Stoggins on June 11, 1782 in Montgomery County, North Carolina. The names and ages of their children who were living in 1822 were: Wade Hampton Naylor, aged 15; Nancy Naylor, aged 12 or 13; Jemimah Naylor, aged 11; Joshua Naylor, aged 9; and, George Naylor, aged 5. "Joshua Nailor" applied for a pension (S41914) on July 4, 1820, aged 64, and received it on Feb. 1, 1822. He died on June 24, 1835 and was buried in Lane's Chapel in Montgomery County, North Carolina. His widow made an affidavit in Stanly County, North Carolina on Jan. 7, 1861, aged 96, stating Joshua was born in 1751, died in 1835, and was married in 1782. They had seven children: George Naylor, Wade Hampton Naylor, Joshua Naylor, Jemima Naylor, and Adelphia Naylor (but the other two children were not mentioned by name). [Ref: P-2468, X-2124, D-147, D-16, and the *DAR Magazine* (1929), Vol. 63, No. 2, p. 103)].

NAYLOR, Joshua (1745-1816). Took the Oath of Allegiance before the Hon. Osborn Sprigg in 1778. Joshua married Susanna ---- and their five children were James Naylor (born Oct. 9, 1774 and married Priscilla Wilson), Joshua Naylor, Benjamin Naylor, Ann Naylor, and Susanna Naylor [Ref: X-2124, O-308, which spelled his name "Nailor," and *Maryland State Society DAR Directory of Members and Ancestors, 1892-1965*, p. 540 (1966)]. There was also a Joshua Naylor who married Martha Nutwell by license dated Jan. 17, 1780, and a Joshua Naylor who married Martha Baden by license dated Dec. 2, 1799 [Ref: ZB-159, ZE-138].

NAYLOR, Mary S. See "Nicholas Naylor," q.v.

NAYLOR, Mourning. See "Joshua Naylor," q.v.

NAYLOR, Nancy. See "Walter Watson" and "Joshua Naylor," q.v.

NAYLOR, Nicholas. Private, 9th Company of Light Infantry, enlisted Jan. 22, 1776. Corporal, Sergeant, and Quartermaster Sergeant, 1st Maryland Line, from Dec. 10, 1776 to at least Nov., 1780 [Ref: D-19, D-146]. Nicholas Naylor married Mary Selby by license dated Feb. 15, 1783 [Ref: ZB-160]. "Nicholas Naler *[sic]* was listed on tax records of Fayette County, Kentucky on July 2, 1789. An Adair County Circuit Court record states that in a deposition taken in Fayette County on Mar. 22, 1806, Isaac Naylor, aged 56 on Nov. 13, 1805, speaks of his brother Nicholas Naylor. In 1806-1807 Nicholas sold his land in Adair County and moved to Barren County where he appeared in the 1810 census." [Ref: Information from Mrs. Mary S. Naylor, 68870 Thomas Street, White Pigeon, Michigan 49099, in 1987. Also see Henry C. Peden, Jr.'s *Marylanders to Kentucky, 1775-1825*, page 108].

NAYLOR, Samuel. Took the Oath of Allegiance before the Hon. David Craufurd in 1778 [Ref: O-272, which spelled the name "Nayler"].
NAYLOR, Susanna. See "Joshua Naylor," q.v.
NAYLOR, Wade H. See "Joshua Naylor," q.v.
NEAGLE, James. Private, 2nd Maryland Line, Capt. Alexander Truman's Company, 1782; on report as "not heard of since Mar. muster, then sick in Virginia." [Ref: D-440].
NEAGLE, Morris. Private, 4th Maryland Line, 1778; taken prisoner on Aug. 16, 1780 (at the Battle of Camden) and "continued to the end of the war." [Ref: D-147, D-286]. The estate of Morris Neagle was probated on May 17, 1794 [Ref: ZE-139].
NEAL, Joseph. Sergeant, Northern Detachment, 3rd Maryland Line, Capt. Horatio Clagett's Company, 1783; reduced to a private on Nov. 15, 1783 [Ref: D-501].
NEAL, Thomas. Took the Oath of Allegiance before the Hon. Christopher Lowndes in 1778 [Ref: O-288]. Thomas Neal married Elizabeth Whitemore by license dated Aug. 7, 1779 [Ref: ZB-160].
NEALE, Eleanor. See "Henry Rozer," q.v.
NEGRO Absolom. Private (draft), continental service, 1781, Maryland Line [Ref: D-382].
NEGRO Jim. See "Gim, Black Boy," q.v.
NELSON, Mary Brook. See "Joseph Sim," q.v.
NELSON, Robert. Private, 2nd Maryland Line, Capt. Patrick Sim's Company, 1776 [Ref: D-8].
NEIL, Doras. Took the Oath of Allegiance before the Hon. George Lee in 1778 [Ref: O-279].
NEVITT, Charles. "Charles Nevet" took the Oath of Allegiance before the Hon. Thomas Clagett in 1778 [Ref: O-266]. "Charles Nevitt" married Levinah Bowling by license dated Jan. 18, 1780 [Ref: ZB-160].
NEVITT, John Jr. (1747-   ). "John Nevet, Jr." took the Oath of Allegiance before the Hon. Thomas Clagett in 1778 [Ref: O-265, R-12]. "John Nevitt" was a private in Capt. John Sprigg Belt's Company, Maryland Line, 1780-1781 [Ref: D-353].
NEVITT, John Sr. (1723-1803?). "John Nevet, Sr." took the Oath of Allegiance (made his "X" mark) before the Hon. Thomas Clagett in 1778 [Ref: O-264, R-13]. The estate of one "John Nevitt" was probated on Apr. 28, 1803 [Ref: ZE-139].
NEVILL, John Jr. Sergeant, 11th Militia Battalion, Capt. Hezekiah Wheeler's Company, April, 1781 [Ref: L-19970 (Box 6, folder 21)].
NEWBERN, Mary. See "Thomas Gantt, Jr.," q.v.
NEWELL, James. Private, Northern Detachment, 3rd Maryland Line, Capt. Horatio Clagett's Company, 1783 [Ref: D-501].
NEWHOUSE, John. Took the Oath of Allegiance (made his mark that looked like backwards "N") which was recorded on a "return of Capt.

Tapley of the brig *Royal*" and filed in court by the Hon. Thomas Gantt, Jr. in 1778 [Ref: O-305, W-4648 (Box 4, folder 15)].

NEWMAN, Butler. Took the Oath of Allegiance before the Hon. Osborn Sprigg in 1778 [Ref: O-307]. Butler Newman married Verlinder ---- [Stonestreet?] and had these children listed in the King George's Parish register: George Newman (born Oct. 23, 1760), Butler Stonestreet Newman (born Mar. 29, 1763), Mary Elenor Newman (born May 19, 1765), Elizabeth Newman (baptized Nov. 29, 1767), and Jane Newman (born Apr. 28, 1773). [Ref: ZC-52]. The estate of Butler Newman was probated by Aug. 4, 1781 (date of inventory) by Verlinda Newman [Ref: ZE-139].

NEWMAN, Elizabeth. See "Butler Newman," q.v.

NEWMAN, George. Private, enrolled by Ensign Horatio Clagett on July 15, 1776, for continental service, Maryland Line [Ref: D-35]. See "Butler Newman," q.v.

NEWMAN, Jane. See "Butler Newman," q.v.

NEWMAN, Mary Elenor. See "Butler Newman," q.v.

NEWMAN, Verlinder. See "Butler Newman," q.v.

NEWTON, Ann. See "Nathaniel Newton," q.v.

NEWTON, Basil. Private, Northern Detachment, 3rd Maryland Line, Capt. Horatio Clagett's Company, 1783 [Ref: D-501]. Although Capt. Horatio Clagett was from Prince George's County it appears that Basil Newton was from Calvert County. See information in Henry C. Peden, Jr.'s *Revolutionary Patriots of Calvert and St. Mary's Counties, Maryland, 1775-1783*, page 202.

NEWTON, John (1754 - June, 1824). Private, Maryland Line; pension commenced in Prince George's County on Apr. 9, 1818 [Ref: T-39, D-40, D-369, D-392, D-453, D-507]. John Newton married Eleanor Callahan by license dated May 27, 1781 [Ref: ZB-161].

NEWTON, Joseph. See "Nathaniel Newton," q.v.

NEWTON, Nathaniel (Aug. 1, 1736 - 1809). Son of Joseph and Ann Newton [Ref: ZC-52]. Took the Oath of Allegiance before the Hon. Thomas Clagett in 1778 [Ref: O-268, R-86]. The estate of one Nathaniel Newton was probated on Feb. 14, 1809 [Ref: ZE-139].

NEWTON, Thomas. Private, 4th Maryland Line, 1778; reported to have "deserted" on May 3, 1780 [Ref: D-147].

NEWTON, William. Private, 2nd Maryland Line, from Dec. 10, 1776 to at least Nov. 1, 1780 [Ref: D-146].

NICHOLAS, Elizabeth. See "Thomas Darnall, Sr.," q.v.

NICHOLS, Edward. Took the Oath of Allegiance before the Hon. David Craufurd in 1778 [Ref: O-271, which spelled the name "Nicols"].

NICHOLS, Ann. See "John Nichols" and "Thomas Nichols, Jr." and "William Nichols," q.v.

NICHOLS, Cassandra. See "William Nichols," q.v.

NICHOLS, Henry (1725-   ). Took the Oath of Allegiance (made his "N" mark) before the Hon. Thomas Clagett in 1778 [Ref: R-75, O-267, which spelled the name "Henry Nicholls"].
NICHOLS, John (Jan. 21, 1720 -   ). Son of Thomas and Ann "Nicholls" of Prince George's Parish [Ref: ZD-118]. Took the Oath of Allegiance (made his "X" mark) before the Hon. James Mullikin in 1778 [Ref: O-295].
NICHOLS, Philip. Took the Oath of Allegiance before the Hon. Benjamin Hall in 1778 [Ref: O-275]. The estate of one Philip Nicholl (Nicholls) was probated on Aug. 3, 1807 [Ref: ZE-139].
NICHOLS, Rachel. See "John Igleheart," q.v.
NICHOLS, Richard. Took the Oath of Allegiance before the Hon. Benjamin Hall in 1778 [Ref: O-274].
NICHOLS, Samuel. Took the Oath of Allegiance before the Hon. Thomas MacGill in 1778 [Ref: O-291]. The estate of one Samuel Nicholls was probated by May 4, 1778 (date of account). [Ref: ZE-139].
NICHOLS, Simon. See "Thomas Nichols," q.v.
NICHOLS, Staly. Took the Oath of Allegiance before the Hon. David Craufurd in 1778 [Ref: O-272, which spelled the name "Nicols"]. The estate of "Staley Nicholls" was probated on Apr. 20, 1798 [Ref: ZE-140].
NICHOLS, Thomas (Sep. 22, 1758 -   ). Son of Simon and Ann "Nicholls" of Prince George's Parish [Ref: ZD-118]. Rendered patriotic service (unspecified) and was paid ten pounds, fifteen shillings by the Council of Maryland "for his use" on June 10, 1778 [Ref: E-128]. See "John Nichols" and "William Nichols," q.v.
NICHOLS, Thomas Jr. (Nov. 12, 1724 -   ). Son of Thomas and Ann "Nicholls" of Prince George's Parish [Ref: ZD-118]. Rendered patriotic service (unspecified) and was paid ten pounds, fifteen shillings by the Council of Maryland "for his use" on June 10, 1778 [Ref: E-128].
NICHOLS, William (Jan. 17, 1727 - 1792?). Son of Thomas and Ann "Nicholls" of Prince George's Parish [Ref: ZD-188]. Took the Oath of Allegiance before the Hon. David Craufurd in 1778 [Ref: O-271, which spelled the name "Nicols"]. The estate of one "William Nicholls" was probated on Mar. 31, 1792 [Ref: ZE-140]. See "William Nichols, Jr.," q.v.
NICHOLS, William (Sep. 18, 1759 -   ). Son of Thomas and Cassandra "Nicholls" of Prince George's Parish [Ref: ZD-118]. Ensign, Middle Battalion, Capt. Humphrey Belt's Company, May 1, 1778. First Lieutenant, May 24, 1779, Capt. Joseph Clagett's Company [Ref: M-107, E-63, E-414, N-35, which spelled the name "Nicholls"]. Took the Oath of Allegiance before the Hon. James Mullikin in 1778 [Ref: O-295]. See "William Nichols, Jr.," q.v.
NICHOLS, William Jr. Took the Oath of Allegiance before the Hon. Thomas Boyd in 1778 [Ref: O-262]. Constable, Patuxent Hundred, 1778 [Ref: Z-30, which spelled his name "Nicholls"]. Additional research may

be necessary before drawing conclusions regarding the patriotic services of the three aforementioned William Nichols.
NICHOLS, William, of Clark. Took the Oath of Allegiance before the Hon. Thomas MacGill in 1778 [Ref: O-291].
NICHOLSON, Anthony. Private, 4th Maryland Line, enlisted Feb. 10, 1778, and reported dead in February, 1779 [Ref: D-147].
NICHOLSON, George. Private, 4th Maryland Line, enlisted Mar. 7, 1778, and reported dead on Sep. 16, 1779 [Ref: D-147].
NICHOLSON, Henry. Private, 2nd Maryland Line, Apr. 4, 1778; corporal, Jan. 10, 1780; served to at least Nov. 1, 1780 [Ref: D-146, which spelled his name "Henry Nickleson"].
NICHOLSON, John. There were several men with this name who served in the Maryland Line [Ref: D-23, D-234, D-269, D-272, D-353, D-393, D-422]. The estate of one John Nicholson was probated on July 26, 1793 in Prince George's County [Ref: ZE-140].
NICHOLSON, Nicholas (1736-   ). Private, 1st Maryland Line, enlisted Dec. 10, 1776 and discharged on Dec. 27, 1779. Reenlisted Apr. 15, 1780; sergeant by Nov., 1780. Sergeant, 3rd Maryland Line, 1781-1782 [Ref: D-146, D-395, D-452]. Took the Oath of Allegiance before the Hon. Truman Skinner in 1778 [Ref: O-299, R-83, which latter source spelled his name "Nickleson].
NICHOLSON, Stephen. Private, 2nd Maryland Line, 1778; corporal, Feb. 1, 1779; sergeant, Jan. 10, 1780; taken prisoner on Aug. 16, 1780 (at the Battle of Camden). [Ref: D-146, which spelled his name "Nickleson"].
NIGILL, Catherine. See "Nicholas Free," q.v.
NITHINGTON, Jeremiah. See "Jeremiah Irvington," q.v.
NOBLE, Mary. See "John Baynes," q.v.
NOLAND, Elizabeth. See "Thomas H. Luckett," q.v.
NORMAN, Joseph. Took the Oath of Allegiance before the Hon. William Lyles, Jr. in 1778 [Ref: O-290].
NORTHEY, Ann. See "William Slye," q.v.
NORTHEY, Mary. See "Clement Ryon," q.v.
NORTHEY, Nathaniel. Private, 1st Guard, Capt. Henry Hill's Militia Company, Lower Battalion; on duty at Nottingham on the Patuxent, Apr. 12, 1781 [Ref: L-19970 (Box 6, folder 21)]. Took the Oath of Allegiance (made his "N" mark) before the Hon. Truman Skinner in 1778 [Ref: O-299, which listed it as "Nathan Nothey"].
NORTON, George. Private, 2nd Maryland Line, Mar. 1, 1777 until discharged on Mar. 8, 1780 [Ref: D-146].
NORTON, Lawrence. Private, 4th Maryland Line, Apr. 21, 1778, and reportedly "deserted" in July, 1780 [Ref: D-147].
NORTON, Robert (1747-   ). Took the Oath of Allegiance before the Hon. George Lee in 1778 [Ref: O-279, R-68].
NORTON, Sarah. See "Butler E. Stonestreet," q.v.

NORTON, William Sr. (1716 - died after Feb. 21, 1778). Took the Oath of Allegiance before the Hon. Thomas Clagett in 1778 [Ref: O-266, R-77]. His second wife was Elinor Stonestreet [Ref: X-2164].
NOTHEY, Nathan. See "Nathaniel Northey," q.v.
NOWELL, James. Private, 2nd Maryland Line, Capt. Alexander Truman's Company, 1782; waiter to Major Hardman [Ref: D-440]. The estate of one James Nowell was probated on May 18, 1810 [Ref: ZE-140].
NOWLAN, Patrick. Private, 2nd Maryland Line, Capt. Patrick Sim's Company, 1776 [Ref: D-8].
NUTHALL, Mary. See "Richard Duckett" and "Baruch Duckett," q.v.
NUTWELL, Catherine. See "Thomas Watson," q.v.
NUTWELL, Martha. See "Joshua Naylor," q.v.
OAKLEY, John. Took the Oath of Allegiance before the Hon. Thomas Williams in 1778 [Ref: O-302]. Brigade Major in the militia who participated in capturing an enemy boat and crew on Apr. 17, 1781 [Ref: M-108, M-208, H-193]. Select Militia, Upper Battalion, June 12, 1781 [Ref: S-6636 (Box 27, folder 82B), which listed his name as "John Oakely"]. County Surveyor, Jan. 7, 1783 [Ref: I-339].
OARD, Peter. Private, enrolled by Ensign Horatio Clagett on July 15, 1776, for continental service, Maryland Line [Ref: D-35].
ODELL, Elenor. See "Benjamin Jacob," q.v.
ODELL, Mary (Polly). See "Thomas Duckett," q.v.
ODEN, Benjamin. Private, Select Militia, Upper Battalion, June 12, 1781 [Ref: S-6636 (Box 27, folder 82B)]. Participated earlier in capturing an enemy boat and crew on Apr. 17, 1781 [Ref: M-208]. Benjamin Oden married Rachel Sophia West (daughter of Stephen West) by license dated Jan. 25, 1791 [Ref: U-879, ZB-162]. The estate of one Benjamin Oden was probated in 1836 [Ref: ZE-141].
ODEN, Elizabeth. See "Edward Lloyd Wailes," q.v.
ODEN, Martha. See "Osburn Brashears," q.v.
ODEN, Meshac. See "Edward Lloyd Wailes," q.v.
ODEN, Rachel. See "Stephen West," q.v.
ODEN, Sarah. See "Edward Lloyd Wailes," q.v.
ODLE, Rigdon. Private (substitute), Maryland Line, discharged on Dec. 3, 1781 [Ref: I-10, D-411].
OFFUTT, Jane. See "Basil Waring 3rd," q.v.
OFFUTT, Sarah. See "David Craufurd," q.v.
OGDEN, Andrew. Private, enrolled by Lt. John M. Burgess, Lower Battalion, on July 20, 1776, for continental service, Maryland Line [Ref: D-35].
OGDEN, John. Took the Oath of Allegiance before the Hon. Truman Skinner in 1778 [Ref: O-299]. Second Sergeant, 1st Guard, Capt. Henry Hill's Militia Company, Lower Battalion, and was on duty at Nottingham on the Patuxent on Apr. 12, 1781 [Ref: L-19970 (Box 6, folder 21),

which spelled his name "Ogdon"]. Private, Maryland Line, discharged on Dec. 3, 1781 [Ref: I-10].

OGDEN, Robert (1750-). Took the Oath of Allegiance before the Hon. Truman Skinner in 1778 [Ref: O-299, R-38]. "Robert Ogdon" married Ann Wynn by license dated Oct. 17, 1778 [Ref: ZB-162].

OGLE, Benjamin (Jan. 27, 1749 - July 6, 1809). Took the Oath of Allegiance before the Hon. Benjamin Hall in 1778 [Ref: O-274]. He rendered patriotic service on Dec. 24, 1781, when the Council of Maryland ordered the Western Shore Treasurer to pay to Benjamin Ogle, Esq., 1600 pounds of money "appropriated for the present campaign," said money to be delivered to the Commissary of Prince George's County [Ref: I-32]. Lived at his country estate "Belair" in Bowie, Maryland, and is probably buried there, but no tombstone has been found. He was a Third Lieutenant in Capt. Samuel Harvey Howard's Independent Company of Militia in the City of Annapolis, and subsequently the Governor of Maryland, 1798-1801 [Ref: Y-612]. Source X-2179 states he was born on Feb. 7, 1749, died on July 7, 1809, and his second wife was Henrietta Margaret Hill.

OHLER, Elizabeth. See "Benjamin Biggs," q.v.

OLBEE, John. See "John Albee," q.v.

OLDER, George (1752-). Private, enrolled in the Flying Camp by Capt. Robert Bowie on July 21, 1776; nativity: Maryland; height: 5' 10" [Ref: D-37].

OLIVE, James (1758-). Private, enrolled in the Flying Camp by Lieut. William D. Beall on Aug. 9, 1776; nativity: England; height: 5' 7"; brown hair, fair complexion [Ref: D-37].

OLIVER, Cornelius. Private, Capt. Alexander H. Magruder's Militia Company, Lower Battalion; on duty guarding Magruder's Warehouse in the spring of 1782 [Ref: L-19970 (Box 6, folder 21)]. Cornelius Oliver married Elizabeth Wells by license dated Jan. 9, 1784 [Ref: ZB-163].

OLIVER, Hezekiah. Took the Oath of Allegiance (made his "H" mark) before the Hon. Alexander Howard Magruder in 1778 [Ref: O-293].

OLIVER, Martha. See "Samuel Wells," q.v.

O'NEAL, Nathaniel. Took the Oath of Allegiance before the Hon. Truman Skinner in 1778 [Ref: O-299]. "Nathaniel O'Neall" married Ann Taylor by license dated June 5, 1789 [Ref: ZB-163].

O'NEIL, Elizabeth. See "Basil Waring, Sr.," q.v.

O'NEIL, William. Took the Oath of Allegiance before the Hon. George Lee in 1778 [Ref: O-279]. The estate of one "William O'Neale" was probated in 1815 [Ref: ZE-141].

ONION, Henry. Private, Select Militia, 1781; participated in capturing an enemy boat and crew on Apr. 17, 1781 [Ref: M-209, which spelled the name "Henry Onions"]. Private, Select Militia, Upper Battalion, June 12, 1781 [Ref: S-6636 (Box 27, folder 82B)]. Took the Oath of Allegiance before the Hon. Osborn Sprigg in 1778 [Ref: O-306].

ONIONS, John. Private, 1st Maryland Line, 1780-1781 [Ref: D-354].
ORDE, William. Private, enrolled by Lt. John M. Burgess, Lower Battalion, on July 20, 1776, for continental service, Maryland Line [Ref: D-35].
ORDE, Peter. See "Peter Oard," q.v.
ORFORD, Jane. See "Basil Waring, Jr.," q.v.
ORME, Ann. See "Robert Orme" and "Nathan Orme" and "Samuel Willett," q.v.
ORME, Archibald. See "Robert Orme," q.v.
ORME, Deborah. See "Robert Orme," q.v.
ORME, Dorothy. See "Robert Orme," q.v.
ORME, Eli. See "Robert Orme," q.v.
ORME, Elizabeth. See "Robert Orme," q.v.
ORME, Hezekiah. Took the Oath of Allegiance before the Hon. Fielder Bowie in 1778 [Ref: O-304, W-4648 (Box 4, folder 15)]. The estate of Hezekiah Orme was probated on Apr. 13, 1791 [Ref: ZE-142].
ORME, John. Two men with this name took the Oath of Allegiance in 1778: one before the Hon. James Beck and another before the Hon. Fielder Bowie [Ref: O-252, O-304, W-4648 (Box 4, folder 15)].
ORME, James. See "Robert Orme," q.v.
ORME, Joseph. Private, 2nd Maryland Line, 1778 [Ref: D-148].
ORME, Mary. See "Ignatius Brashears," q.v.
ORME, Moses. Ensign, 11th Battalion, May 1, 1778, Capt. John Perry's Company. First Lieutenant, May 24, 1779, Capt. Benjamin Wailes' Company [Ref: M-108, E-62, E-414, N-33]. He rendered patriotic service by providing wheat for the military on Aug. 9, 1780 [Ref: Q-308]. See "Moses Orme, Jr.," q.v.
ORME, Moses Jr. (c1730-c1782). Took the Oath of Allegiance before the Hon. Alexander Howard Magruder in 1778 [Ref: O-293]. One Moses Orme was a private in the 2nd Maryland Line in 1778; discharged on Jan. 10, 1780 [Ref: D-148, which listed his name without the "Jr."]. Source X-2188 states Moses married (1) Verlinda Taylor and (2) Priscilla Taylor, rendered patriotic service, and died before Feb. 12, 1782; however, it does not mention military service. Perhaps the soldier was Moses' son Moses who was born in 1755. For additional information on this family see Elise Greenup Jourdan's *Early Families of Southern Maryland, Volume I*, page 144. It should be noted that there was also a Moses Orme who married Elizabeth Brashears by license dated Feb. 27, 1795 [Ref: ZB-163]. Additional research may be necessary before drawing conclusions.
ORME, Nathan. Private in the militia, Lower District of Frederick County, July, 1776 [Ref: D-42]. The estate of one Nathan Orme was probated in Prince George's County by Dec. 21, 1778 (date of account) by Ann H. Orme [Ref: ZE-142]. See "Robert Orme," q.v.

ORME, Richard. Took the Oath of Allegiance before the Hon. Fielder Bowie in 1778 [Ref: O-303, W-4648 (Box 4, folder 15)].
ORME, Robert (Aug. 12, 1744 - Sep. 13, 1820). Took the Oath of Allegiance before the Hon. James Beck in 1778 [Ref: O-256, R-49]. Records of the Council of Maryland on June 22, 1778, state that Robert Orme was "a Draft from Prince George's County who had gone home again. We have sent Mr. Gordon after him and request you [County Lieutenant] give him any necessary assistance." [Ref: E-146]. After procuring George Ennis to serve as his substitute, Robert Orme was discharged from the service on June 25, 1778 [Ref: E-150, X-2188, which latter source does not mention his military service]. Robert Orme married Priscilla Edmonston (1739-1813) on Feb. 4, 1769, and their children were: Deborah Orme (born Nov. 4, 1769 and married Brooke Edmonston); James Orme (born Nov. 24, 1770); Dorothy Orme (born Sep. 21, 1772); Robert Orme (born June 21, 1774); Nathan Orme (born Mar. 5, 1776); Ann Henrietta Orme (born Jan. 10, 1778 and married Basil Belt); Eli Orme (born Jan. 10, 1779); Elizabeth Orme (born Nov. 6, 1781); and, Archibald Edmonston Orme (born July 25, 1783). [Ref: Elise Greenup Jourdan's *Early Families of Southern Maryland, Volume I*, page 149]. The estate of Robert Orme was probated on Oct. 22, 1820 [Ref: ZE-142].
ORME, Ruth. See "Leonard M. Deakins," q.v.
ORME, Sabinah. See "John Smith Selby," q.v.
ORME, Samuel. "Samuel Orme" took the Oath of Allegiance before the Hon. Alexander Howard Magruder in 1778 [Ref: O-293]. "Samuel Oram" was a drummer in the 4th Maryland Line in 1778-1780 [Ref: D-149].
ORME, Samuel Taylor (1750-1817). Sergeant in Capt. Benjamin Wailes' Militia Company, Lower Battalion, and on duty guarding Magruder's Warehouse in the spring of 1782 [Ref: L-19970 (Box 6, folder 21)]. He married Martha Ransom [Ref: X-2188].
ORME, Thomas. Took the Oath of Allegiance (made his "T" mark that looked like an upside down "L") before the Hon. Truman Skinner in 1778 [Ref: O-299, which spelled his name "Thomas Orm"].
ORME, William. Corporal, 2nd Maryland Line, 1778; discharged on Jan. 10, 1780 [Ref: D-148, which spelled the name "Orm"]. Private, Capt. Jesse Hellen's Militia Company, before May 23, 1782; guarded Magruder's Warehouse in the spring of 1782 [Ref: L-19970 (Box 6, folder 21)]. Took the Oath of Allegiance before the Hon. Fielder Bowie in 1778 [Ref: O-304, W-4648 (Box 4, folder 15)]. The estate of one William Orme was probated on Jan. 15, 1817 [Ref: ZE-142].
ORMOND, William. Private, 2nd Maryland Line. His name appeared on a list of applicants for invalid pensions returned by Maryland to the House of Representatives on May 22, 1794. He served in the 2nd Maryland Regiment and was wounded at the Battle of Monmouth in

June, 1778. He lived in Prince George's County in 1794 and 1795 [Ref: P-2545].

OSBORN, Dennis. Took the Oath of Allegiance before the Hon. Osborn Sprigg in 1778 [Ref: O-306]. One Dennis Osborn married Lucy Hodge by license dated Dec. 16, 1784, and Dennis Osborn married Elizabeth Edelen by license dated Sep. 9, 1801 [Ref: ZB-163]. The estate of one "Dennis Osbourn" was probated on Mar. 18, 1817 [Ref: ZE-142].

OSBORN, Francis. Private, 2nd Maryland Line, Capt. Patrick Sim's Company, 1776 [Ref: D-8]. Took the Oath of Allegiance before the Hon. Osborn Sprigg in 1778 [Ref: O-306]. Francis Osborn married Charity Pope by license dated July 19, 1778 [Ref: ZB-164].

OSBORN, John. Took the Oath of Allegiance before the Hon. Osborn Sprigg in 1778 [Ref: O-306]. One John Osborn married Sarah Magruder by license dated Jan. 12, 1788 [Ref: ZB-164]. The estate of one "John Osborn" was probated in 1790 and the estate of one "John Osbourn" was probated in 1824 [Ref: ZE-142, ZE-143].

OSBORN, Linny. See "James Gray," q.v.

OUCHTERLONEY (OUCHTERLONG), Agnes. See "Samuel Collard," q.v.

OWEN, Benjamin Jr. Took the Oath of Allegiance before the Hon. James Beck in 1778 [Ref: O-252, which spelled the name "Owens"].

OWEN, Benjamin Sr. (1716-1794). Took the Oath of Allegiance before the Hon. James Beck in 1778 [Ref: O-252, R-48]. The estate of one "Benjamin Owens" was probated in 1794 [Ref: ZE-143].

OWEN, Elizabeth. See "Zachariah Berry," q.v.

OWEN, Thomas M. See "Vachell Ijams," q.v.

OWEN, Zachariah. Took the Oath of Allegiance before the Hon. James Beck in 1778 [Ref: O-255]. Constable in Upper Marlborough Hundred and Charlotte Hundred in 1778 [Ref: Z-3]. He may be the Zachariah Owen (or Owens) who was born circa 1757 in Maryland and died in Kentucky in 1822; name of wife not known [Ref: X-2203].

OWENS, John. Private, 3rd Maryland Line, enlisted Mar. 11, 1778 [Ref: D-148]. One John Owens married Sarah Howerton by license dated Mar. 8, 1780 [Ref: ZB-165].

OWENS, Joseph. Private, 1st Maryland Line, enlisted June 5, 1778 and discharged in February, 1779 [Ref: D-148, which spelled the name "Owings"]. One Joseph Owens married Jane Waters by license dated Feb. 19, 1787 [Ref: ZB-165]. The estate of one Joseph Owens was probated on Oct. 17, 1811 [Ref: ZE-143].

OWENS, Paris. Private, Northern Detachment, 3rd Maryland Line, Capt. Horatio Clagett's Company, 1783 [Ref: D-502]. "Parris Owens" enlisted on Sep. 7, 1782, and "Paris Owens" enlisted on Sep. 14, 1782 [Ref: D-425, D-429]. Additional research may be necessary before drawing conclusions as to whether or not there were one or two men named Paris Owens.

239

OWENS, Stephen. Private, 2nd Maryland Line, Capt. Alexander Truman's Company, 1782; waiter to Lieutenant Lynn [Ref: D-440].

OWENS, William. Took the Oath of Allegiance before the Hon. David Craufurd in 1778 [Ref: O-271].

PADDY, John. Private, Capt. Benjamin Wailes' Militia Company, Lower Battalion; on duty guarding Magruder's Warehouse in the spring of 1782 [Ref: L-19970 (Box 6, folder 21)].

PADGETT, Hezekiah. Took the Oath of Allegiance before the Hon. Truman Skinner in 1778 [Ref: O-299]. The estate of one Hezekiah Padgett was probated on Nov. 25, 1794 [Ref: ZE-143].

PADGETT, Rebecca. See "Thomas Hayes," q.v.

PAGE, Anthony (1744-1800). Took the Oath of Allegiance before the Hon. James Beck in 1778 [Ref: O-254, R-30]. The estate of one Anthony Page was probated on Apr. 7, 1800 [Ref: ZE-144].

PAGE, Daniel. Took the Oath of Allegiance before the Hon. Osborn Sprigg in 1778 [Ref: O-306]. Daniel Page married Leonora Piles by license dated Nov. 16, 1777 [Ref: ZB-166]. The estate of one Daniel Page was probated on Apr. 9, 1793 [Ref: ZE-144].

PAGE, Susannah. See "Edward Lanham," q.v.

PAGGATT, Benjamin. Private, enrolled on July 18, 1776, by Capt. Alexander H. Magruder, 11th Battalion, for continental service, Maryland Line [Ref: D-38].

PALLOZZI, Julia. See "Ignatius Brashears," q.v.

PALMER, Jacob. Private, Rawlings' Regiment, Maryland Line, enlisted May 5, 1779, and "died in November 1780 per certificate of Adamson Tannaker." [Ref: D-154]. The estate of "Jacob Palmer (soldier)" was probated on July 24, 1793 [Ref: ZE-144].

PARKER, Ann. See "Richard Clagett," q.v.

PARKER, Elizabeth. See "Leonard Townshend," q.v.

PARKER, John (1728-1793?). Took the Oath of Allegiance before the Hon. Christopher Lowndes in 1778 [Ref: O-287, R-25]. The estate of one John Parker was probated on Dec. 3, 1793 [Ref: ZE-144].

PARKER, John Jr. (1753-   ). Took the Oath of Allegiance before the Hon. Christopher Lowndes in 1778 [Ref: O-284, R-24]. One John Parker served as a private in the 2nd Maryland Line from Apr. 18, 1778 until Apr., 1780, when he was transferred to the Invalids Corps [Ref: D-151].

PARKER, Mary. See "Peter B. Cage," q.v.

PARKINS, Thomas. See "Thomas Perkins," q.v.

PARKINS, William. See "William Perkins," q.v.

PARNELL, Susanna. See "Samuel Luckett," q.v.

PARRAN, Mary. See "Thomas Gantt, Jr.," q.v.

PARRIOTT, Dennis. See "Christopher Parrott," q.v.

PARRIOTT, Isabella. See "Christopher Parrott," q.v.

PARRIOTT, John. See "Christopher Parrott," q.v.

PARRIOTT, Joseph. See "Christopher Parrott," q.v.

PARROTT, Christopher (Mar. 25, 1755, Prince George's County, Maryland - Oct. 1, 1820, Hampshire County, Virginia). Sergeant, 2nd Maryland Line, 1777, who was discharged Jan. 10, 1780, but reenlisted to take up deserters until Aug., 1780. Christopher Parriott (or Parrott) married Martha Clarke, daughter of Abraham Clarke, on Jan. 21, 1781 (license dated Jan. 20, 1781), at Marlboro in Prince George's County. "Christopher Parrott" died in Hampshire County, Virginia in 1820 and his widow Martha Parrott (who received pension W18713) died in Marshall County, Virginia on Dec. 19, 1839. Their surviving children in 1850 were John Parriott, Ann Davis (widow), Amelia Turner (widow), Joseph S. Parriott (aged 50), and Dennis M. Parriott (aged 52). Also mentioned was a granddaughter Isabella T. Parriott [Ref: P-2605, D-150, X-2237, V-1944 (Vol. 32, No. 4, p. 102), ZB-167].

PARROTT, Martha. See "Christopher Parrott," q.v.

PARROTT, Samuel. Took the Oath of Allegiance before the Hon. David Craufurd in 1778 [Ref: O-271, which spelled the name "Parret"].

PARSLOW, John. Took the Oath of Allegiance before the Hon. James Beck in 1778 [Ref: O-253]. The estate of one "John Parslows" was probated on Sep. 2, 1794 [Ref: ZE-145].

PATTERSON, Elizabeth. See "Alexander Duvall," q.v.

PATTERSON, Thomas. The records of the Council of Maryland on June 22, 1778, state that Thomas Patterson from Prince George's County was retained (among others from other counties) and "send on board the Galleys." [Ref: E-144].

PATTERSON, William. There were several men named William Patterson who served in the Maryland Line [Ref: D-153, D-465, D-500, D-551]. One William Patterson married Mary Jones by license dated Nov. 23, 1779, in Prince George's County [Ref: ZB-167]. Additional research may be necessary before drawing conclusions.

PEACH, Joseph. See "Richard Peach" and "William Peach," q.v.

PEACH, Lucy. See "Christopher Hyatt," q.v.

PEACH, Mary. See "Richard Peach" and "William Peach," q.v.

PEACH, Richard (Dec. 25, 1738 - 1820?). Son of Joseph and Mary Peach [Ref: ZC-187]. Took the Oath of Allegiance before the Hon. Benjamin Hall in 1778 [Ref: O-275]. The estate of one Richard Peach was probated in May 9, 1820 [Ref: ZE-145].

PEACH, William (Aug. 25, 173? - 1795). Son of Joseph and Mary Peach [Ref: ZC-187]. Took the Oath of Allegiance before the Hon. James Beck in 1778 [Ref: O-256]. One William Peach served in the 4th Maryland Line as a sergeant on Aug. 2, 1777, reduced to private on Oct. 31, 1779, and reportedly "deserted" on Apr. 22, 1780; however, upon showing just cause, he was discharged [Ref: D-153]. The estate of one William Peach was probated on Feb. 28, 1795 and the estate of one William Peach, Jr. was probated on Mar. 12, 1795 [Ref: ZE-145].

PEACOCK, John. Took the Oath of Allegiance before the Hon. William Berry in 1778 [Ref: O-259].
PEACOCK, William. Took the Oath of Allegiance (made his "X" mark) before the Hon. Thomas Clagett in 1778 [Ref: O-265]. One William Peacock married Penelope Holly by license dated June 28, 1792 [Ref: ZB-167].
PEARCE, Elizabeth. See "Joseph Ambler," q.v.
PEARCE, James. See "James Peirce, Jr.," q.v.
PEARCE, Jane. See "Allen Brightwell" and "John Miles," q.v.
PEARCE, John. Private, 1st Maryland Line, 1777-1780; discharged on Sep. 7, 1780 [Ref: D-149]. The estate of one John Pearce was probated on July 26, 1793 [Ref: ZE-145].
PEARCE, Mary. See "Richard Brightwell," q.v.
PEARCE, Rebecca. See "John Miles," q.v.
PEARCE, Shadrick. See "Shadrick Scarce," q.v.
PEARCE, William. Private, 3rd Maryland Line, enlisted Jan. 29, 1776 [Ref: D-1]. The estate of one William Pearce was probated by Aug. 7, 1784 (date of inventory). [Ref: ZE-145].
PEARRE, James (1727-1796). Took the Oath of Allegiance before the Hon. Christopher Lowndes in 1778 [Ref: O-283]. "He married Mercy (Masse?, Marcia?) ----. In 1762 his father deeded his 100 acres in Frederick (now Montgomery) County; he sold it in 1771. Inherited part of the Prince George's County land but sold it late in 1785. In 1785-6 moved to Georgia, where he died, leaving a will." [Ref: "The Early Pearres of Maryland," by Nancy Pearre Lesure, *Maryland Genealogical Society Bulletin*, Vol. 34, No. 1 (1993), page 97].
PEARRE, John (1746-   ). Took the Oath of Allegiance before the Hon. Christopher Lowndes in 1778 [Ref: O-282, R-74, which spelled the name "John Pear"]. He may be the John Pearre who was a brother of the above James Pearre (1727-1796). He also sold his inherited land in Prince George's County later in 1785 and moved to Georgia. However, he was born circa 1735, not 1746]. See "John Perry," q.v.
PEARY, Howard. Took the Oath of Allegiance before the Hon. Osborn Sprigg in 1778 [Ref: O-306].
PEARY, Samuel. Took the Oath of Allegiance before the Hon. Osborn Sprigg in 1778 [Ref: O-306].
PEARY, Thomas. Took the Oath of Allegiance before the Hon. Osborn Sprigg in 1778 [Ref: O-307].
PEDEN, Elmore. See "Alexander Truman," q.v.
PEDEN, Henry C. Jr. See "Alexander Truman" and "Basil Newton" and "Aaron Spaulding" and "Kidd Morsell" and "Thomas L. Lansdale" and "Elias Lazenby" and "George Fraser Magruder" and "Zadock Magruder" and "James McKay" and "Jacob Mefford" and "John Sprigg Belt" and "Nicholas Naylor," q.v.
PEDEN, William Henry. See "Alexander Truman," q.v.

PEIRCE, Elizabeth. See "Thomas Cave, Jr.," q.v.
PEIRCE, George. Took the Oath of Allegiance before the Hon. William Berry in 1778 [Ref: O-258, which spelled the name "Peerce"].
PEIRCE, Henry Culver. Took the Oath of Allegiance before the Hon. Christopher Lowndes in 1778 [Ref: O-284].
PEIRCE, James Jr. Private, Select Militia, Upper Battalion, June 12, 1781 [Ref: S-6636 (Box 27, folder 82B), which spelled his name "James Pearce, Jr."].
PEIRCE, John Jr. "John Peirce, Jr." was a private in Capt. Benjamin Wailes' Militia Company, Lower Battalion; on duty guarding Magruder's Warehouse in the spring of 1782 [Ref: L-19970 (Box 6, folder 21)]. "John Peirce" married Elizabeth Hines by license dated Feb. 3, 1786 [Ref: ZB-168].
PEIRCE, Sarah. See "William Lamar," q.v.
PEIRCE, Thomas (1726-1785?). Took the Oath of Allegiance before the Hon. William Berry in 1778 [Ref: O-258, R-61, which spelled the name "Pearce" and "Peerce"]. Private, Capt. Benjamin Wailes' Militia Company, Lower Battalion; on duty guarding Magruder's Warehouse in the spring of 1782 [Ref: L-19970 (Box 6, folder 21)]. "Thomas Pearce" married Elizabeth Ambler by license dated Jan. 21, 1783 [Ref: ZB-168]. The estate of one "Thomas Pearce" was probated on June 6, 1785 [Ref: ZE-146].
PEIRCE, William. "William Peerce" took the Oath of Allegiance before the Hon. William Berry in 1778 [Ref: O-258]. "William Pearce was a constable in Rock Creek Hundred in 1777 [Ref: Z-3].
PENN, Jacob. Private, 2nd Maryland Line, Capt. Patrick Sim's Company, 1776 [Ref: D-8].
PENN, Sarah. See "Jeremiah Duvall," q.v.
PENNIFIELD, Thomas. Private who served from Montgomery County and married Easther Beanes by license dated July 20, 1790, in Prince George's County [Ref: ZB-168, D-342].
PENNOCK, John Private, 3rd Maryland Line, enlisted Jan. 9, 1779; Capt. Horatio Clagett's Company, December, 1779 [Ref: E-351, D-295, which latter source listed the name as "Jona. Pemnick"].
PENNY, James. Private, enrolled by Capt. John H. Lowe on July 13, 1776, for continental service, Maryland Line [Ref: D-35].
PENNY, John. Private, 2nd Maryland Line, 1780 [Ref: D-151, which spelled his name "John Penney"].
PERKINS, John. See "Thomas Johnson," q.v.
PERKINS, Nancy. See "Thomas Johnson," q.v.
PERKINS, Thomas (1756-   ). Private, 2nd Maryland Line, Capt. Patrick Sim's Company, 1776 [Ref: D-8]. Took the Oath of Allegiance before the Hon. Osborn Sprigg in 1778 [Ref: O-306, R-82, which latter source listed the name as "Parkins"].

PERKINS, William. Took the Oath of Allegiance before the Hon. James Beck in 1778 [Ref: O-254, which listed the name as "Parkins"].
PERRIE, John. See "John Perry," q.v.
PERRIE, Simon. See "Simon Perry," q.v.
PERRY, Charles. See "Ignatius Perry," q.v.
PERRY, Easter. See "Benjamin Warman," q.v.
PERRY, Edward (June 19, 1751 -   ). Son of Edward and Elizabeth Perry [Ref: ZC-188]. Took the Oath of Allegiance before the Hon. David Craufurd in 1778 [Ref: O-270]. Edward Perry married Susanna Clarke by license dated July 12, 1777 [Ref: ZB-169].
PERRY, Elizabeth. See "Edward Perry," q.v.
PERRY, Ignatius (Dec. 25, 1740 -   ). "Ignatious Perrey" was the son of Charles and Rachel "Perrey" of Prince George's Parish [Ref: ZD-119]. "Ignatius Perry" took the Oath of Allegiance before the Hon. James Mullikin in 1778 [Ref: O-295].
PERRY, James. Private, 2nd Maryland Line, Capt. Patrick Sim's Company, 1776 [Ref: D-8]. One James Perry, son of John and Priscilla Perry, was born on June 10, 1747 [Ref: ZC-188].
PERRY, James Jr. Private, Militia; participated in capturing an enemy boat and crew on Apr. 17, 1781 [Ref: M-208].
PERRY, Jane. See "Jacob Igleheart," q.v.
PERRY, John (Sep. 19, 1737 -   ). Son of John and Priscilla Perry [Ref: ZC-188]. Captain, Militia, 11th Battalion, May 1, 1778 to May 24, 1779 (succeeded). [Ref: M-110, M-111, E-62, E-414, R-72, N-33]. "John Perrie" took the Oath of Allegiance before the Hon. Alexander Howard Magruder in 1778 [Ref: O-293]. On May 6, 1783, the Council of Maryland granted "permission to John Perrie of Prince George's County to go into New York." [Ref: I-47]. See "John Pearre" and "James Perry" and "Robert Perry" and "Zadock Perry," q.v.
PERRY, Joseph. Took the Oath of Allegiance before the Hon. Thomas Williams in 1778 [Ref: O-302]. He rendered patriotic service by providing wheat for the military on Aug. 16, 1781 [Ref: Q-425].
PERRY, Priscilla. See "James Perry" and "John Perry" and "Clement Beall" and "Robert Perry" and "Zadock Perry," q.v.
PERRY, Rachel. See "Ignatius Perry," q.v.
PERRY, Robert (May 29, 1742 -   ). Son of John and Priscilla Perry [Ref: ZC-188]. Took the Oath of Allegiance before the Hon. William Lock Weems in 1778 [Ref: O-301].
PERRY, Samuel. Took the Oath of Allegiance before the Hon. Thomas Williams in 1778 [Ref: O-302].
PERRY, Simon. Private, 1st Maryland Line, enlisted May 12, 1778 and in service in 1781 [Ref: I-22, D-330, D-150, which latter source spelled the name "Perrie"].
PERRY, William. Took the Oath of Allegiance before the Hon. Benjamin Hall in 1778 [Ref: O-276].

PERRY, Zadock (Nov. 10, 1750 -   ). Son of John and Priscilla Perry [Ref: ZC-188]. Took the Oath of Allegiance before the Hon. David Craufurd in 1778 [Ref: O-272].
PETER, Jonathan H. Took the Oath of Allegiance before the Hon. Fielder Bowie in 1778 [Ref: O-304, but the original list at the Maryland State Archives (Box 4, folder 15) shows the name may actually be "Jonathan H. Peters"].
PETERS, Elizabeth. See "Uriah Vermillion," q.v.
PHEALEAN, Peter (1750-   ). Private, enrolled in the Flying Camp by Lieut. William D. Beall on July 19, 1776; nativity: England; height: 5' 8"; black hair, fair complexion [Ref: D-37].
PHELPS, Robert (1731-   ). Took the Oath of Allegiance before the Hon. Osborn Sprigg in 1778 [Ref: R-88, O-307, which latter source spelled his name "Robert Felphs"].
PHILLIPS, Bedder or Beddoe (1740-   ). Took the Oath of Allegiance before the Hon. Osborn Sprigg in 1778 [Ref: R-67, which listed his name as "Obeddo Philips," but Source O-308 and the original list at the Maryland State Archives (Box 4, folder 29) shows the name to be "Bedder Phillips"]. The King George Parish register lists "Bedder Phillips husband of Verlinder...." *[sic]* which is then followed by two children, John Dawson Phillips, son of Bedder and Verlinder (born Sep. 30, 1756), and Vialinder Phillops, daughter of Lurana and Bedder Phillops (baptized Nov. 6, 1768) [Ref: ZC-55].
PHILLIPS, George. Private, 7th Maryland Line, enlisted Mar. 18, 1777 [Ref: D-239]. The estate of "George Phillips (soldier)" was probated in July 24, 1793 [Ref: ZE-147].
PHILLIPS, James (1754-   ). Private, enrolled in the Flying Camp by Lieut. William D. Beall on July 22, 1776; nativity: England; height: 5' 6"; black hair, yellow complexion [Ref: D-37].
PHILLOPS, John. See "Bedder Phillips," q.v.
PHILLOPS, Lurana. See "Bedder Phillips," q.v.
PHILLOPS, Verlinder. See "Bedder Phillips," q.v.
PHOEBE, Mary Ann. See "James Webster," q.v.
PICKENS, Elizabeth. See "George Upton," q.v.
PICKRELL, Rebecca. See "William Long," q.v.
PICKRELL, Richard. Private, enrolled by Capt. John H. Lowe on July 13, 1776, for continental service, Maryland Line [Ref: D-35].
PILES, Ann. See "Samuel Townshend," q.v.
PILES, Elizabeth. See "John Smith Mangun" and "James Drane" and "William Wall" and "Edward Sprigg," q.v.
PILES, Francis. Took the Oath of Allegiance before the Hon. Fielder Bowie in 1778 [Ref: O-303, W-4648 (Box 4, folder 15)]. One Francis Piles married Martha Early by license dated Apr. 6, 1795 [Ref: ZB-170]. The estate of one Francis Piles was probated on Apr. 7, 1819 [Ref: ZE-148].

245

PILES, Henry. Took the Oath of Allegiance before the Hon. Christopher Lowndes in 1778 [Ref: O-288]. Henry Piles married Elizabeth Wallingford by license dated Aug. 6, 1779 [Ref: ZB-171].
PILES, Leonora. See "Daniel Page," q.v.
PINDELL, Elizabeth. See "Thomas Pindell," q.v.
PINDELL, Jane. See "Thomas Pindell," q.v.
PINDELL, Philip (1758-   ). Private, enrolled in the Flying Camp by Capt. Robert Bowie on Aug. 1, 1776; nativity: Maryland; height: 5' 9"; has own gun [Ref: D-37]. "Philip Pindall" married Priscilla Pratt by license dated Nov. 1, 1796 [Ref: ZB-171]. See "Thomas Pindell," q.v.
PINDELL, Thomas. Took the Oath of Allegiance before the Hon. Thomas Boyd in 1778 [Ref: O-262]. There were two men with this name in Queen Anne's Parish: one was born on Mar. 15, 1723/4 (son of Philip and Elizabeth Pindell) and one was born on Sep. 28, 1728 (son of Thomas and Jane Pindell). [Ref: ZC-188]. The estate of one "Thomas Pindle" was probated on Oct. 12, 1779 [Ref: ZE-149, which source also spelled the name "Pindell" and "Pindall"]. Additional research may be necessary before drawing conclusions.
PINGSTON, Thomas (1749, England -   ). Private (substitute), 1780, in continental service, Maryland Line [Ref: D-338]. Private, 2nd Maryland Line, Capt. Murdock's Company, Mar. 15, 1781 [Ref: D-366].
PLUMMER, Ebenezer. Took the Oath of Allegiance (made his mark that resembled an elongated "C" with a horizontal line through it, or a large curved "E" with a tail on it) before the Hon. Thomas Boyd in 1778 [Ref: O-261]. The estate of one "Abiezer Plummer" was probated on Oct. 8, 1778 [Ref: ZE-149].
PLUMMER, John. Took the Oath of Allegiance before the Hon. Thomas Boyd in 1778 [Ref: O-261]. John Plummer married Ann Digges by license dated Nov. 28, 1780 [Ref: ZB-172]. The estate of one John Plummer was probated on July 10, 1813 [Ref: ZE-149].
PLUMMER, Joseph. Took the Oath of Allegiance before the Hon. Thomas Boyd in 1778 [Ref: O-261]. The estate of one Joseph Plummer was probated on Apr. 18, 1789 [Ref: ZE-149].
PLUMMER, Thomas. Took the Oath of Allegiance before the Hon. James Mullikin in 1778 [Ref: O-295].
PONSONBY, Richard. Took the Oath of Allegiance before the Hon. Christopher Lowndes in 1778 [Ref: O-282].
POOL, James. Private, Northern Detachment, 3rd Maryland Line, Capt. Horatio Clagett's Company, 1783 [Ref: D-502].
POPE, Amelia. See "Joseph Pope," q.v.
POPE, Charity. See "Francis Osborn," q.v.
POPE, Joseph (1725-1798). "Joseph Pope" took the Oath of Allegiance before the Hon. Christopher Lowndes in 1778 [Ref: O-287, R-65]. "Joseph Pope, Jr." married Amelia Pope by license dated Dec. 11, 1787

[Ref: ZB-172]. The estate of one Joseph Pope was probated on June 6, 1798 [Ref: ZE-149].

POPE, Joshua. Private, Select Militia, Upper Battalion, June 12, 1781 [Ref: S-6636 (Box 27, folder 82B)]. The estate of one Joshua Pope was probated on Aug. 10, 1809 [Ref: ZE-150].

POPE, Nathaniel (1736-1813). Took the Oath of Allegiance before the Hon. Christopher Lowndes in 1778 [Ref: O-287, R-65]. The estate of one Nathaniel Pope was probated on Dec. 3, 1813 [Ref: ZE-150].

POPE, William. On Dec. 3, 1780 the County Lieutenant reported to the Council of Maryland that "I should be glad to know if one William Pope does not stand as a deserter on the Maryland Rolls. I have understood he went off in that carriter [sic], and is now returned." [Ref: G-198].

POPHAM, Samuel. Private, 4th Maryland Line, 1777. Matross in the artillery, 1777-1778 [Ref: D-153, D-577]. Samuel Popham married Delia Crutchly by license dated Dec. 25, 1783 [Ref: ZB-172].

POTTENGER, Elizabeth. See "Allen Bowie, Jr.," q.v.

POTTENGER, Robert. Took the Oath of Allegiance before the Hon. James Mullikin in 1778 [Ref: O-296]. One Robert Pottenger married Mary Buchanan by license dated Feb. 15, 1785 [Ref: ZB-172]. The estate of Dr. Robert Pottenger was probated on Mar. 16, 1801 [Ref: ZE-150, which also spelled the name "Pottinger"].

POTTENGER, Susannah. See "Richard Simmons," q.v.

POTTER, William. Private, Capt. Alexander Truman's Company, stationed at Annapolis in 1781 and reported on "a list of men who have deserted since Mar. 1, 1781." [Ref: L-19970 (Box 7, folder 52)]. One William Powell married Sarah Green by license dated Mar. 17, 1785 [Ref: ZB-173].

POTTS, Sarah. See "Thomas Gantt, Jr.," q.v.

POWELL, Joseph. Took the Oath of Allegiance before the Hon. James Beck in 1778 [Ref: O-253].

POWELL, William. Private, Northern Detachment, 3rd Maryland Line, Capt. Horatio Clagett's Company, 1783 [Ref: D-501].

POWER, Walter. Private, enrolled by Lt. William Duvall, Lower Battalion, on July 18, 1776, for continental service, Maryland Line [Ref: D-35].

PRATHER, Benjamin. Took the Oath of Allegiance before the Hon. Christopher Lowndes in 1778 [Ref: O-286]. Benjamin Prather married Rachel Walker by license dated Jan. 15, 1782 [Ref: ZB-173].

PRATHER, Elizabeth. See "James Prather" and "Jeremiah Prather," q.v.

PRATHER, James (Jan. 27, 1735 - 1791). Son of Thomas and Elizabeth Prather [Ref: ZC-189]. Took the Oath of Allegiance before the Hon. William Berry in 1778 [Ref: O-258]. The census enumerator in 1776 reported that "James Prather refused to give in a list of his family." [Ref: R-89]. The estate of one James Prather was probated om July 22, 1791 [Ref: ZE-150].

PRATHER, Jeremiah (July 7, 173? -   ). Son of Jonathan Smith Prather and wife Elizabeth [Ref: ZC-189]. Took the Oath of Allegiance before the Hon. Thomas Boyd in 1778 [Ref: O-262].
PRATHER, Jonathan Smith. See "Jeremiah Prather," q.v.
PRATHER, Nathan (1742-1813). Took the Oath of Allegiance before the Hon. James Beck in 1778 [Ref: O-254, R-45]. Served on a Grand Jury in 1778 [Ref: Z-90]. The estate of one Nathan Prather was probated on Mar. 5, 1813 [Ref: ZE-151].
PRATHER, Thomas. See "James Prather," q.v.
PRATHER, Zachariah. Private, 2nd Maryland Line, enlisted May 1, 1778, and promoted to sergeant on Jan. 10, 1780 [Ref: D-151]. Zachariah Prather married Rosamond Callahane by license dated Mar. 2, 1778 [Ref: ZB-173].
PRATHER, Zephaniah (1741-1807). Took the Oath of Allegiance before the Hon. William Berry in 1778 [Ref: O-258, R-48]. The estate of one Zephaniah Prather was probated on Sep. 1, 1807, and was administered by a Zephaniah Prather [Ref: ZE-151].
PRATT, Eleanor. See "Cephas Sheckell," q.v.
PRATT, Priscilla. See "Philip Pindell," q.v.
PRESTON, Stephen. Private, 3rd Maryland Line, Capt. Horatio Clagett's Company, December, 1779 [Ref: D-296, which spelled the name "Priston"].
PRICE, Benedict. See "Benoni Price," q.v.
PRICE, Benoni (1726-1783). Took the Oath of Allegiance before the Hon. Christopher Lowndes in 1778 [Ref: O-282, which misspelled his name as "Benomi Price," and R-30, which spelled his name "Benoney Price"]. Benoni Price married Mary ---- [Beall?] by 1754 and these children are listed in the King George's Parish register: Ignatius Price (born Sep. 15, 1754), Reason Price (baptized in 1761), Loyd Beall Price (baptized Oct. 23, 1763), Fredrick Price (baptized Aug. 18, 1765), and Benedict Beall Price (baptized May 10, 1767). [Ref: ZC-57]. The estate of "Benoni Price" was probated on Aug. 28, 1783 [Ref: ZE-151, which also spelled his name "Benone"].
PRICE, Fredrick. See "Benoni Price," q.v.
PRICE, Ignatius (Sep. 15, 1754-   ). Son of Benoni and Mary Price [Ref: ZC-57]. Took the Oath of Allegiance before the Hon. James Beck in 1778 [Ref: R-30, O-254]. See "Benoni Price," q.v.
PRICE, Loyd. See "Benoni Price," q.v.
PRICE, Mary. See "Benoni Price," q.v.
PRICE, Reason. See "Benoni Price," q.v.
PRICE, Richard. Private, 3rd Maryland Line, 1781 [Ref: D-396]. One Richard Price married Rachel Willett by license dated Dec. 17, 1782 [Ref: ZB-173].
PRICE, Stephen. Sergeant, 2nd Maryland Line, Capt. Alexander Truman's Company, 1782 [Ref: D-439].

PRIDIX, John. Private, Capt. Alexander Truman's Company, stationed at Annapolis in 1781 and reported on "a list of men who have deserted since Mar. 1, 1781" [Ref: L-19970 (Box 7, folder 52)].
PRIESTLEY, Thomas. Took the Oath of Allegiance before the Hon. Osborn Sprigg in 1778 [Ref: O-306].
PRIGGS, Hedwick. See "Clement Hollyday," q.v.
PRIGGS, John. Quartermaster in the 11th Battalion, Jan. 13, 1776 [Ref: M-113, which listed his name as "John F. A. Priggs"]. "John Priggs" served on the Board of Patuxent Associators who signed a resolution at Nottingham on Apr. 21, 1781 relative to the defence of the rivers of Potomac and Patuxent and the completion of the fort at Drum Point [Ref: K-1814]. "Fredrick Augustus Priggs, son of John Fred. Augustus Priggs," was born on Oct. 27, 1749 and was baptized on Mar. 10, 1749/50 in Prince George's Parish [Ref: ZD-120]. The estate of "John F. A. Priggs" was probated on June 14, 1796 [Ref: ZE-152].
PROCTER, Elanor. See "Osburn Brashears," q.v.
PROCTOR, Charles. Private, 1st Maryland Line, enlisted on May 29, 1778, and reportedly died on Nov. 3, 1778 [Ref: ZE-150]. The estate of a Charles Proctor was probated in Prince George's County on Sep. 10, 1818 [Ref: ZE-152].
PUMPHRY, Ann. See "John Brashears," q.v.
PURCE, Mary. See "Richard Brightwell," q.v.
PURDY, Edward. Private, enlisted Feb. 19, 1780, for 3 years or during war, in continental service, Maryland Line [Ref: D-333]. Defective from the Maryland Line on Mar. 1, 1781 [Ref: D-414].
PURDY, Henry (1746-   ). Private, Militia, 1776 [Ref: M-207, A-325, R-73, which latter source spelled his name "Purdie"].
PURDY, Henry (Apr. 23, 1762 -   ). Son of Henry and Sarah Purdy [Ref: ZC-57]. Private, enlisted Feb. 19, 1780, for 3 years or during war, in continental service, Maryland Line [Ref: D-333]. Private, 2nd Maryland Line, Capt. Alexander Truman's Company, 1782 [Ref: D-439]. See "John Purdy, of Henry," q.v.
PURDY, John. Private, 2nd Maryland Line, Capt. Alexander Truman's Company, 1782 [Ref: D-439]. There was also a Sgt. John Purdy who reportedly "deserted" from the 2nd Maryland Line on Mar. 4, 1778 [Ref: D-151].
PURDY, John, of Henry. Private, enlisted Feb. 12, 1780, for 3 years or during war, in continental service, Maryland Line [Ref: D-333]. This might be "John Hosey Purdey" who was a son of Henry and Sarah Purdy. However, he was born on May 19, 1764, and would have been almost 16 years old at time of enlistment [Ref: ZC-57].
PURDY, Sarah. See "Henry Purdy" and "John Purdy, of Henry," q.v.
QUEEN, James. Took the Oath of Allegiance before the Hon. Christopher Lowndes in 1778 [Ref: O-284].

QUEEN, John. Corporal, 2nd Maryland Line, 1778; sergeant, July 1, 1779; in service to at least Nov., 1780 [Ref: D-116, D-154, which source spelled his name both as "Gwinn" and "Queen."]

QUEEN, Joseph. Ensign, 25th Battalion, May 1, 1778, Capt. John Weight's Company. Ensign, Select Militia, Upper Battalion, June 12, 1781, Capt. Osburn Williams' Company [Ref: M-113, N-33, E-62, G-475, G-488, S-6636 (Box 27, folder 82B)]. Participated in capturing an enemy boat and crew on Apr. 17, 1781 [Ref: M-208, which listed his name only as "J. Queen"]. Took the Oath of Allegiance before the Hon. Christopher Lowndes in 1778 [Ref: O-284]. The estate of one Joseph Queen was probated on Feb. 5, 1802 [Ref: ZE-152]. See "Edmond Turner," q.v.

QUEEN, Marshall. Took the Oath of Allegiance before the Hon. Christopher Lowndes in 1778 [Ref: O-283].

QUEEN, Richard (1725-1794). Took the Oath of Allegiance before the Hon. Christopher Lowndes in 1778 [Ref: O-282, R-60, X-2390, which latter source stated wife's name was unknown]. The estate of one Richard Queen was probated on Oct. 7, 1794 [Ref: ZE-152].

QUEEN, Walter (1755-   ). Took the Oath of Allegiance before the Hon. William Berry in 1778 [Ref: O-258, R-60]. Constable, Rock Creek Hundred, 1778 [Ref: Z-30]. Served on a Grand Jury in 1777 [Ref: Z-29].

QUERNEY, Lawrence. Private, 2nd Maryland Line, Capt. Patrick Sim's Company, 1776 [Ref: D-7].

QUISENBERRY, Anderson C. See "Benjamin H. Kerrick," q.v.

RANKEN, George. Took the Oath of Allegiance before the Hon. David Craufurd in 1778 [Ref: O-271].

RANKIN, Robert. Took the Oath of Allegiance (made his "R" mark) before the Hon. Thomas Clagett in 1778 [Ref: O-265].

RANKINS, Daniel. Private, 2nd Maryland Line, Capt. Patrick Sim's Company, 1776 [Ref: D-8]. Private, Select Militia, Capt. Hezekiah Wheeler's Company, July 14, 1781 [Ref: S-6636 (Box 31, folder 5)]. This might be the Daniel Rankin who was born in Maryland in 1752 and died in Ohio on Apr. 30, 1833; if so, his wife was Eleanor Tongue [Ref: X-2404].

RANSOM, Martha. See "Samuel Taylor Orme," q.v.

RANSOM, Rebecca Naylor. See "John Lovejoy," q.v.

RANTER, James. Private, 2nd Guard, Capt. Henry Hill's Militia Company, Lower Battalion; on duty at Nottingham on the Patuxent, Apr. 12, 1781 [Ref: L-19970 (Box 6, folder 21)].

RANTER, John. Private (draft), continental service, 1781 [Ref: D-382]. Private, 2nd Guard, Capt. Henry Hill's Militia Company, Lower Battalion; on duty at Nottingham on the Patuxent, Apr. 12, 1781 [Ref: L-19970 (Box 6, folder 21)]. Served on a Grand Jury in 1777 [Ref: Z-23]. John Ranter (also listed as John Ranten) married Sarah Ann Humphrey by license dated Dec. 9, 1778 [Ref: ZB-176]. Took the Oath of Allegiance before the Hon. Truman Skinner in 1778 [Ref: O-299].

RATLEDGE, James. See "Azariah Gatton," q.v.
RATLEDGE, Matilda. See "Azariah Gatton," q.v.
RAWLINGS, Aaron (June 28, 1738 - July 4, 1798). Private, Northern Detachment, 3rd Maryland Line, Capt. Horatio Clagett's Company, 1783 [Ref: D-501]. He married Mary Somers [Ref: X-2409].
RAWLINGS, Benjamin. Private, enrolled by Capt. Alexander H. Magruder, 11th Battalion, on July 25, 1776, for continental service, Maryland Line [Ref: D-38].
RAWLINGS, Elijah. Private, enrolled by Ensign Alexander Truman on July 4, 1776, for continental service, Maryland Line [Ref: D-38]. Elijah Rawlings married Elizabeth MacGill by license dated Aug. 6, 1778 [Ref: ZB-176].
RAWLINGS, Elizabeth. See "Richard Alexander Contee" and "John Smith," q.v.
RAWLINGS, Gassaway. See "Richard Alexander Contee," q.v.
RAWLINGS, James. Took the Oath of Allegiance before the Hon. James Beck in 1778 [Ref: O-255].
RAWLINGS, John. Private, enrolled by Capt. Alexander H. Magruder, 11th Battalion, on Aug. 1, 1776, for continental service, Maryland Line [Ref: D-38]. "Jona. Rawlings" was a private in the 2nd Maryland Line who was taken prisoner on Aug. 16, 1780 (at the Battle of Camden). [Ref: D-156].
RAWLINGS, Nevitt. Private, enrolled by Ensign Alexander Truman on July 4, 1776, for continental service, Maryland Line [Ref: D-38].
RAWLINGS, Susannah. See "Thomas Duckett," q.v.
RAWLINGS, Thomas. Private, Capt. Benjamin Wailes' Militia Company, Lower Battalion; on duty guarding Magruder's Warehouse in the spring of 1782 [Ref: L-19970 (Box 6, folder 21)].
RAWLINGS, William. Private, Capt. Alexander H. Magruder's Militia Company, Lower Battalion; on duty guarding Magruder's Warehouse in the spring of 1782 [Ref: L-19970 (Box 6, folder 21)]. Took the Oath of Allegiance in 1780 [Ref: J-118].
RAY, Ann. See "John Ray," q.v.
RAY, Basil (1754-   ). Private, enrolled in the Flying Camp by Capt. Robert Bowie in July, 1776; nativity: Maryland; height: 5' 8"; has own gun [Ref: D-37]. Basil Ray married Rebecca Wall by license dated Jan. 19, 1782 [Ref: ZB-177].
RAY, Benjamin (Nov. 7, 1739 - 1785?). Son of John and Sarah Ray [Ref: ZD-120]. Took the Oath of Allegiance (made his "B" mark) before the Hon. James Mullikin in 1778 [Ref: O-296]. The estate of one Benjamin Ray was probated by Oct. 1, 1785 (date of inventory). [Ref: ZE-153].
RAY, Benjamin Jr. "Benjamin Ray, Jr." took the Oath of Allegiance before the Hon. James Beck in 1778 [Ref: O-253]. "Benjamin Ray" was a private in the Maryland Line in 1781 [Ref: D-411]. "Benjamin Ray" married Amelia Mitchell by license dated Dec. 25, 1782 [Ref: ZB-177].

RAY, David. Private, 4th Maryland Line, 1777-1780 [Ref: D-158].
RAY, Elizabeth. See "John Ray," q.v.
RAY, James. Private in county militia, 1776 [Ref: M-207, A-325]. Private, 2nd Maryland Line, enlisted Mar. 4, 1777 [Ref: D-156].
RAY, Jesse. Matross, Capt. William Marbury's Artillery, 1777, and Bombardier, Frederick German Artillery, 1782-1783 [Ref: D-575, D-582]. Jesse Ray married Mary Wall by license dated Jan. 24, 1782 [Ref: ZB-177].
RAY, John Sr. (Aug. 10, 1707 - 1779). Son of William Jr. and Elizabeth Ray [Ref: ZC-190]. Took the Oath of Allegiance before the Hon. Richard Henderson in 1778 [Ref: O-278, R-23]. He married Sarah Wilson [Ref: X-2411]. However, there was also a John Ray who married Sarah Isaac by license dated Mar. 24, 1787. He may have been the John Ray born on Aug. 6, 173?, son of William and Ann Ray [Ref: ZB-177, ZC-190]. There was also another John Ray, son of John and Sarah Ray, who was born on June 24, 1732 [Ref: ZD-120]. The estate of one "John Ray" was probated on Apr. 19, 1779 and the estate of one "John Rae" was probated on Feb. 17, 1801 [Ref: ZE-153, Z-154]. Additional research may be necessary before drawing conclusions as to which ones rendered patriotic service. See "Benjamin Ray" and "John Ray" and "Josias Ray" and "William Ray," q.v.
RAY, Josias (Jan. 4, 1757, Maryland - died before Jan. 23, 1815, Washington, DC). Son of John and Sarah Ray [Ref: ZD-120]. Private, Militia, 1776 [Ref: M-207, A-325]. Took the Oath of Allegiance before the Hon. William Berry in 1778 [Ref: O-258]. Josias Ray married Sarah - --- [Ref: X-2412].
RAY, Phillip. Took the Oath of Allegiance before the Hon. Osborn Sprigg in 1778 [Ref: O-307, which listed the name as "Phillip Ray [Kay?]," but the original list (very light) at the Maryland State Archives (Box 4, folder 29) shows the name to be "Phillip Ray"].
RAY, Samuel (May 5, 1753 -   ). Son of John and Sarah Ray [Ref: ZD-120]. Private, 3rd Maryland Line, 1776 [Ref: D-10, D-155].
RAY, Sarah. See "Josias Ray" and "Benjamin Ray" and "John Ray" and "Samuel Ray" and "William Ray," q.v.
RAY, Thomas (1745-   ). Took the Oath of Allegiance before the Hon. William Berry in 1778 [Ref: O-259, R-64].
RAY, William (Sep. 19, 1741 -   ). Son of John and Sarah Ray [Ref: ZD-120]. Took the Oath of Allegiance before the Hon. Truman Skinner in 1778 [Ref: O-298]. Served on a Grand Jury in 1777 and 1778 [Ref: Z-29, Z-90]. See "John Ray," q.v.
READ, William M. Private, Capt. Benjamin Wailes' Militia Company, Lower Battalion; on duty guarding Magruder's Warehouse in the spring of 1782 [Ref: L-19970 (Box 6, folder 21)].
READER, John. Sergeant, 2nd Maryland Line, Capt. Murdock's Company, Mar. 15, 1781 [Ref: D-366].

REDMAN, Alice. Rendered patriotic service (not specified) and was paid one pound, two shillings and five pence by the State Treasurer on Apr. 26, 1782 [Ref: I-148].
REDMAN, Chloe. See "John Redman, Jr.," q.v.
REDMAN, John (1716-   ). Took the Oath of Allegiance before the Hon. William Lyles, Jr. in 1778 [Ref: O-289, R-53].
REDMAN, John Jr. (1746, Maryland - 1816, Ohio). Soldier in the Maryland troops. He married Chloe ---- [Ref: X-2419]. John Redman was a matross in Major Brown's Artillery in 1782, and served with Thomas Redman (who was probably his brother). [Ref: D-584, R-85].
REDMAN, Thomas. Matross, Major Brown's Artillery, 1782. He served with John Redman (who was probably his brother). [Ref: D-583].
REED, Rebecca. See "John Tolson Lowe," q.v.
REED, William. See "William M. Read" and "John T. Lowe," q.v.
REESE, Levy. Private, 2nd Maryland Line, Capt. Murdock's Company, Mar. 15, 1781 [Ref: D-366].
RENEAU, Martha. See "Jonathan Jewell" and "Samuel Luckett," q.v.
REVELL, Randall. Sergeant, 2nd Maryland Line, 1777; discharged June 10, 1780 [Ref: D-156].
REVELLE, Charles. Drummer, 2nd Maryland Line, Capt. Murdock's Company, Mar. 15, 1781 [Ref: D-366].
REYNOLDS, Margaret. See "Alexander Truman," q.v.
REYNOLDS, William. See "Alexander Truman," q.v.
RHODES, Mildred. See "Benjamin Burch," q.v.
RHODES, William. See "Benjamin Burch," q.v.
RICHARDS, George. Took the Oath of Allegiance (made his mark that resembled a large "+" sign) before the Hon. Thomas Boyd in 1778 [Ref: O-262].
RICHARDS, Martha. See "Jonathan Sasser," q.v.
RICHARDSON, Elisha. Private, 1st Maryland Line, enlisted Apr. 23, 1777 and discharged Dec. 27, 1779 [Ref: D-155]. The estate of Elisha Richardson was probated on Jan. 12, 1811 [Ref: ZE-155].
RICHARDSON, Thomas (1743-1820). Justice of the County Court, 1777 [Ref: C-273]. Took the Oath of Allegiance before the Hon. James Beck in 1778 [Ref: O-256, R-47]. Captain, Militia, 25th Battalion, Mar. 18, 1776 to 1779 (when he resigned). [Ref: M-115, A-260, E-78, N-34]. Captain who served on a General Courts-Martial for the trial of Capt. Richard Bennett Hall, Lieut. Jeremiah Ryley, Lieut. Jonathan Wright, and Lieut. James Mullikin on Aug. 23, 1776, at Upper Marlboro [Ref: B-233]. He also rendered patriotic service by providing wheat for the military on Aug. 7, 1780 [Ref: Q-307]. The estate of one Thomas Richardson was probated on Jan. 11, 1820 [Ref: ZE-155].
RICHMOND, Christopher. Clerk, Smallwood's Regiment, stationed at the headquarters in Annapolis in 1776 [Ref: D-5]. Paymaster, 1st Maryland Line, Jan. 1, 1777; Lieutenant, May 27, 1778; and Captain, Oct., 1781

[Ref: D-155]. The estate of one Christopher Richmond was probated in Prince George's County on Apr. 28, 1796 [Ref: ZE-155].
RIDDELL, James. Took the Oath of Allegiance before the Hon. Richard Henderson in 1778 [Ref: O-278].
RIDDLE, Elizabeth. See "Jacob Riddle," q.v.
RIDDLE, Jacob. Took the Oath of Allegiance before the Hon. James Beck in 1778 [Ref: O-255]. Jacob Riddle married Sarah ---- by 1764 and had two children listed in the King George's Parish register: Jacob Riddle (born May 26, 1764 and baptized Aug. 5, 1764) and Elizabeth Lunn Riddle (baptized May 31, 1767). [Ref: ZC-58].
RIDDLE, Sarah. See "Jacob Riddle," q.v.
RIDDLE, Susannah. See "John Tolson Lowe," q.v.
RIDDLE, Virlinda. See "Samuel Tyler," q.v.
RIDER, Adam. Private, 2nd Maryland Line, Capt. Alexander Truman's Company, 1782 [Ref: D-439].
RIDER, James. Private, 2nd Maryland Line, from May 15, 1778 until discharged on Dec. 24, 1778 [Ref: D-156].
RIDGELY, Ann. See "Thomas Snowden," q.v.
RIDGELY, Basil. Private, 2nd Maryland Line, Capt. Patrick Sim's Company, 1776 [Ref: D-8].
RIDGELY, Richard. In the County Court in August, 1778, he took the Oath of Allegiance at the same time he took the oath to become a practicing attorney at law in Prince George's County [Ref: Z-90].
RIDGEWAY, Benjamin. Took the Oath of Allegiance before the Hon. Osborn Sprigg in 1778 [Ref: O-307]. "Benjamin Ridgway" married Mary Hardey by license dated Dec. 14, 1779 [Ref: ZB-181].
RIDGEWAY, Elizabeth. See "Jonathan Ridgeway," q.v.
RIDGEWAY, John. Second Lieutenant, Militia, June 9, 1777, Capt. Hezekiah Magruder's Company [Ref: M-116]. Took the Oath of Allegiance before the Hon. Benjamin Hall in 1778 [Ref: O-276]. "John Ridgeway" married Rachel Mockbee by license dated Dec. 2, 1778 [Ref: ZB-180]. See "Jonathan Ridgeway," q.v.
RIDGEWAY, Jonathan (1717-1807). Son of John and Elizabeth Ridgeway [Ref: ZC-58, ZC-191]. Took the Oath of Allegiance before the Hon. Fielder Bowie in 1778 [Ref: O-304, R-77, which latter source states he was aged 57 in 1776]. The estate of one "Jonathan Ridgway" was probated on Oct. 16, 1807 [Ref: ZE-156].
RIDGEWAY, Mary. See "Basil Wheat," q.v.
RIGHT, Bazzell. See "Basil Wright," q.v.
RILEY, Christian Berket (1736-   ). Took the Oath of Allegiance before the Hon. Christopher Lowndes in 1778 [Ref: O-283, R-70, which latter source listed his name as "Christian B. Reyly"].
RILEY, James. Private, 3rd Maryland Line, enlisted on Nov. 17, 1778. Private, Capt. Horatio Clagett's Company, in December, 1779 [Ref: D-

296]. "James Ryley" took the Oath of Allegiance before the Hon. Christopher Lowndes in 1778 [Ref: O-287].

RILEY, Jeremiah (1730-   ). Took the Oath of Allegiance before the Hon. Joshua Beall in 1778 [Ref: O-251, R-62, which spelled his name "Jeremiah Reyley"]. "Jeremiah Ryley" was a lieutenant, 25th Battalion, Capt. Boyd's Company, May 23, 1776 until July 7, 1776 (courts-martial). [Ref: M-116, A-440, A-553, B-233]. See "John Rogers," q.v.

RILEY, John. Private, 6th Maryland Regiment, enlisted Aug. 26, 1781, for 3 years, and was sworn in Aug. 26, 1781 [Ref: D-417]. One John Riley married Mary Grant by license dated Dec. 10, 1788, and a John Riley married Willicy Clarke by license dated Aug. 2, 1790 [Ref: ZB-181].

RILEY, Johnson Michael. Took the Oath of Allegiance before the Hon. David Craufurd in 1778 [Ref: O-271, which spelled his name "Rieley"]. Served on a Grand Jury in 1778 [Ref: Z-90].

RILEY, Margaret. See "Tobias Talbott," q.v.

RILEY, Mary. See "Stephen Riley," q.v.

RILEY, Michael. Served on a Grand Jury in 1778 [Ref: Z-52].

RILEY, Stephen (Mar. 6, 1759, Lower Marlborough, Calvert County, Maryland - Mar. 2, 1840, Baltimore, Maryland). He applied for a pension in May 25, 1833 in Baltimore, stating that he was born in Calvert County, lived at Bladensburg at the time of enlistment, and after the war lived in Baltimore. He married Mary Hook on Jan. 2, 1783 in Baltimore and died there in 1840. His widow applied for pension (W9255) on Oct. 20, 1843, aged 80, and a George Millemon made affidavit in Baltimore in 1843, aged 73, but no relationship was given [Ref: P-2892].

RISDEN, John. Took the Oath of Allegiance before the Hon. William Berry in 1778 [Ref: O-259].

RISDEN, Zaddock. See "Zadock Riston," q.v.

RISDON, Zedekiah. Private, Maryland Line, 1781 [Ref: I-22].

RISTON, Ann. See "Rinaldo Johnson," q.v.

RISTON, Benjamin. See "Zadock Riston," q.v.

RISTON, Elisha. Took the Oath of Allegiance before the Hon. Osborn Sprigg in 1778 [Ref: O-307]. Elisha Riston married Ann Maych [sic] by license dated Feb. 6, 1790 [Ref: ZB-181].

RISTON, Zadock (1756-c1839). Took the Oath of Allegiance before the Hon. Osborn Sprigg in 1778 [Ref: O-307]. Private (substitute), Maryland Line, continental service, 1781 [Ref: D-382]. "Zedock Reston" was discharged from the Maryland Line in 1781 [Ref: D-411]. He was paid 15 pound and 5 shillings by the State Treasurer on Apr. 27, 1782 [Ref: I-149]. "Zadock Riston or Rister" applied for pension (S35348) in Prince George's County on Apr. 18, 1818, aged 62. In 1820 he stated he had with him three grandchildren whose father had went away, and also a daughter lived with him (no names were given). On Mar. 23, 1827 he moved to Washington, DC where relatives lived [Ref: P-2897]. On Feb.

24, 1830, the Western Shore Treasurer was directed to pay "Zaddock Risden, alias Riston," who was a soldier of the Revolutionary War, of Prince George's County, during life, quarterly, half pay of a private, for his services during that war. On Mar. 26, 1839, the Treasurer was directed to pay to Benjamin Riston and Cassandra Ann King, or order, only children of Zadock Riston, late of Prince George's County, deceased, a pensioner, the balance of pension due him from the State of Maryland at the time of his death, and which he was entitled to under a resolution of the General Assembly [Ref: O-385, O-386]. Zadock Riston married Elizabeth Bartly by license dated Jan. 7, 1786 [Ref: ZB-181].

RITCHIE, James. Took the Oath of Allegiance before the Hon. David Craufurd in 1778 [Ref: O-271].

RITCHIE, John. Private, 5th Maryland Line, enlisted Dec. 5, 1776; still in service in January, 1780 [Ref: D-240]. The estate of one John Ritchie was probated in January, 1832 [Ref: ZE-156].

ROBERTS, Ann. See "George Jones," q.v.

ROBERTS, Evan. Took the Oath of Allegiance before the Hon. Fielder Bowie in 1778 [Ref: O-303, W-4648 (Box 4, folder 15)].

ROBERTS, Hannah. See "Archibald Elson," q.v.

ROBERTS, Horatio. Private, 7th Maryland Line, enlisted Feb. 2, 1780, and was reported missing on Aug. 16, 1780 (at the Battle of Camden). [Ref: D-243]. The estate of one Horatio Roberts was probated on May 26, 1794 [Ref: ZE-156].

ROBERTS, Howard. Took the Oath of Allegiance before the Hon. Osborn Sprigg in 1778 [Ref: O-307].

ROBERTS, John. Took the Oath of Allegiance before the Hon. Osborn Sprigg in 1778 [Ref: O-308, W-4648 (Box 4, folder 29)]. The estate of one John Roberts was probated on Apr. 10, 1787 [Ref: ZE-156].

ROBERTS, Sarah. See "Samuel Busey," q.v.

ROBERTS, Thomas. Took the Oath of Allegiance before the Hon. Thomas MacGill in 1778 [Ref: O-291].

ROBERTS, William (1753-   ). Private, enrolled in the Flying Camp by Lieut. Benjamin Brooks on Aug. 20, 1776; nativity: England; height 5' 6" [Ref: D-36].

ROBERTSON, Charles. Private, Maryland Line, discharged on Dec. 3, 1781. Issued clothing on Dec. 14, 1781 [Ref: I-10, I-22].

ROBERTSON, John. Took the Oath of Allegiance before the Hon. William Berry in 1778 [Ref: O-258]. Private, 3rd Maryland Line, Capt. Horatio Clagett's Company, 1779 [Ref: D-295].

ROBEY, Absalom. Took the Oath of Allegiance before the Hon. Christopher Lowndes in 1778 [Ref: O-287].

ROBEY, Acton. Private, 1st Maryland Line, who was paid for his services "in cloathing" on Apr. 17, 1779 [Ref: E-351].

ROBEY, Elizabeth. See "Thomas Darnall, Jr.," q.v.

ROBEY, John (1714-   ). Took the Oath of Allegiance before the Hon. Christopher Lowndes in 1778 [Ref: O-287, R-60].

ROBEY, John. Private, 1st Maryland Line, on May 13, 1778, and taken prisoner in January, 1780, reenlisted [sic] and was discharged on Jan. 9, 1782 [Ref: D-155, D-392]. In December, 1815, the Treasurer of the Western Shore was directed to pay John Roby, during life, half pay of a private, for the services rendered his country during the Revolutionary War [Ref: O-386].

ROBEY, Joseph. Private, 1st Maryland Line, June 14, 1779; fifer, Oct. 1, 1779; died Sep. 25, 1780 [Ref: D-155].

ROBEY, Leonard. Took the Oath of Allegiance before the Hon. Christopher Lowndes in 1778 [Ref: O-287].

ROBEY, Mary. See "John Boswell," q.v.

ROBEY, Michel. See "Nathan Maddox," q.v.

ROBEY, Mildred. See "Zachariah Burch," q.v.

ROBEY, Rachel. See "Roby Tucker," q.v.

ROBEY, Thomas (1759-   ). Private, enrolled in the Flying Camp by Capt. Robert Bowie on Aug. 3, 1776; nativity: Prince George's County; height 5' 5 1/2" [Ref: D-36].

ROBINSON, Benjamin. Took the Oath of Allegiance before the Hon. William Lyles, Jr. in 1778 [Ref: O-289]. The estate of Benjamin Robinson was probated on Feb. 21, 1810 [Ref: ZE-157].

ROBINSON, James. Took the Oath of Allegiance before the Hon. Osborn Sprigg in 1778 [Ref: R-83, O-306, which latter source spelled his name "James Robison"].

ROBINSON, John. Two men with the name took the Oath of Allegiance in 1778: one before the Hon. Thomas Clagett and another before the Hon. James Beck [Ref: O-254, O-265]. One John Robinson was aged 30 in the 1776 census of Prince George's County [Ref: R-25].

ROBINSON, John Crown. Took the Oath of Allegiance before the Hon. James Mullikin in 1778 [Ref: O-295].

ROBINSON, Jonathan. Private, 2nd Maryland Line, Capt. Patrick Sim's Company, 1776 [Ref: D-7].

ROBINSON, Margaret. See "John Mockbee," q.v.

ROBINSON, Milley. See "Thomas Wise," q.v.

ROBINSON, Robert (1745, Maryland -   ). Private, enlisted May 19, 1781, for 3 years in continental service, Maryland Line; sent to Annapolis; on duty July 13, 1781 [Ref: D-381].

ROBINSON, Sarah. See "Charles Boteler, Jr.," q.v.

ROBISON, James. Took the Oath of Allegiance before the Hon. Osborn Sprigg in 1778 [Ref: O-307].

ROBISON, Benjamin. Took the Oath of Allegiance before the Hon. Osborn Sprigg in 1778 [Ref: O-308, W-4648 (Box 4, folder 29)].

ROBISON, Stephen. Took the Oath of Allegiance before the Hon. Osborn Sprigg in 1778 [Ref: O-306, which spelled it "Robeson"].

RODERY, John. Private, 2nd Maryland Line, Capt. Patrick Sim's Company, 1776 [Ref: D-8].
ROGERS, Byrd. See "Alexander Truman," q.v.
ROGERS, Charles. See "Alexander Truman," q.v.
ROGERS, Daniel. See "John Rogers," q.v.
ROGERS, Henry. See "Alexander Truman," q.v.
ROGERS, Janie. See "Alexander Truman," q.v.
ROGERS, John (1723 - Sep. 23, 1789). Probably the son of Capt. William Rogers (1699-1749), John married Margaret Lee Clark and had these children: William Rogers, Thomas Rogers, Daniel Rogers, John Rogers, Lucy Rogers, and Margaret Rogers Chandler. He served as a Delegate to the Maryland Convention, 1774-1776 [Ref: A-7, U-70, U-72, U-703]. As Second Major, 11th Battalion (commissioned Jan. 13, 1776), he served as President on a General Courts-Martial for the trial of Capt. Richard Bennett Hall, Lieut. Jeremiah Ryley, Lieut. Jonathan Wright, and Lieut. James Mullikin on July 25, 1776, at Upper Marlboro [Ref: A-553, M-117]. He also served on the Committee of Correspondence in 1774, Committee of Observation in 1775, and member of the Executive Council in 1777. He was appointed Judge, Court of Admiralty, 1776, but declined, and was Chancellor of Maryland between 1778 and 1789 [Ref: U-703]. A memorial marker was presented by the Prince George's County American Revolution Bicentennial Commission in 1977 and located beside the walkway in front of the Prince George's County Administration Building in Upper Marlboro, Maryland. It noted that "John Rogers was one of only three Maryland delegates to the Continental Congress who voted on July 2, 1776 to declare America's independence and on July 4, 1776 to approve the Declaration of Independence. On July 4, 1776 the Maryland Convention in Annapolis elected Charles Carroll of Carrollton to replace Rogers, who was ill. Because the Declaration was not signed by anyone until Aug. 2, 1776, it is Carroll's name and not that of John Rogers which appears on this most revered American document. John Rogers is the only delegate to the Continental Congress who voted for the Declaration of Independence but was denied the privilege of signing it." [Ref: Y-617]. John Rogers, attorney of Prince George's County, died in Annapolis and was "much lamented" in the *Maryland Gazette* on Sep. 29, 1789 and Oct. 1, 1789 [Ref: ZA-157].
ROGERS, Lucy. See "John Rogers," q.v.
ROGERS, Margaret. See "John Rogers," q.v.
ROGERS, Mary. See "Alexander Truman," q.v.
ROGERS, Peter. See "Alexander Truman," q.v.
ROGERS, Philip. See "Alexander Truman," q.v.
ROGERS, Sarah. See "Alexander Truman," q.v.
ROGERS, Thomas. See "John Rogers," q.v.
ROGERS, William. See "Alexander Truman" and "John Rogers," q.v.

ROLAND, George. Took the Oath of Allegiance before the Hon. Osborn Sprigg in 1778 [Ref: O-306]. The estate of "George Rowling, Sr." was probated on Nov. 9, 1782, and inventories and accounts in 1783 spelled his name "Roland" and "Rowland." [Ref: ZE-158].
ROLANDS, Gorder [Gordon?]. Took the Oath of Allegiance before the Hon. Christopher Lowndes in 1778 [Ref: O-288].
ROPER, Ann. See "Ishom Coleman," q.v.
ROSE, Susan. See "William Rose," q.v.
ROSE, Thomas. Took the Oath of Allegiance before the Hon. Thomas Boyd in 1778 [Ref: O-262]. One Thomas Rose married Mary Smith by license dated Oct. 22, 1777 [Ref: ZB-183]. See "William Rose," q.v.
ROSE, William. Sergeant, 2nd Maryland Line, Capt. Alexander Truman's Company, 1782 [Ref: D-439]. There was also a William Rose who was Sergeant Major in the 1st Maryland Line by July, 1781, but it appears that he may have been from Charles County [Ref: H-354]. One William Rose was born on Dec. 23, 1724, son of Thomas and Susan Rose, of Queen Anne's Parish in Prince George's County [Ref: ZC-191].
ROSS, Joseph. Lieutenant, Select Militia, Capt. Osborn Williams' Company, June 25, 1781 [Ref: M-117, G-488].
ROSS, William (1740-1828?). Took the Oath of Allegiance before the Hon. William Berry in 1778 [Ref: O-259, R-34]. The estate of one William Ross was probated on May 12, 1828 [Ref: ZE-158].
ROUGHTON, Job. Took the Oath of Allegiance which was recorded on a "return of Capt. Tapley of the brig *Royal*" and filed in court by the Hon. Thomas Gantt, Jr. in 1778 [Ref: O-305, W-4648 (Box 4, folder 15)].
ROWAN, William. Took the Oath of Allegiance before the Hon. David Craufurd in 1778 [Ref: O-272].
ROWE, Joseph Y. See "Batson Naylor" and "Benjamin Naylor," q.v.
ROWLAND, Elizabeth. See "Jacob Rowland," q.v.
ROWLAND, Jacob (c1726, Pennsylvania - died after Jan. 17, 1792, Maryland). Private, 2nd Maryland Line, Capt. Alexander Truman's Company, 1782 [Ref: D-440]. He married Elizabeth --- [Ref: X-2527].
ROWLAND, William. Private, 4th Maryland Line, from Apr. 23, 1777 until discharged on Mar. 1, 1780 [Ref: D-158].
ROZER, Edward. See "Henry Rozer," q.v.
ROZER, Eleanor. See "Henry Rozer," q.v.
ROZER, Francis Hall. See "Henry Rozer, Jr.," q.v.
ROZER, Henry (1725-1802). Son of Notley Rozer who died in 1727. Henry took the Oath of Allegiance before the Hon. George Lee in 1778 [Ref: O-279, R-85], and was a Justice of the Peace in 1779 [Ref: F-17, which spelled his name "Rozier"]. He married Eleanor Neale (first wife; name of second wife was not given) and had sons Notley Rozer, Henry Rozer, Edward Rozer, and Thomas Whetenhall Rozer [Ref: ZA-572]. See "Henry Rozer, Jr.," q.v.

ROZER, Henry Jr. (c1755-1802?). A son of Henry Rozer and Eleanor Neale, he took the Oath of Allegiance before the Hon. George Lee in 1778 [Ref: O-279]. Second Lieutenant, Militia, 1778; resigned by 1779 [Ref: N-36, which spelled his name "Henry Rozier"]. Second Lieutenant, Middle Battalion, May 1, 1778, Capt. John Casey's Company [Ref: M-117, E-63]. "Henry Rozer, of Notley Hall, son of Henry" died testate in 1802, but no wife was mentioned, only a daughter Maria Rozer, wife of Francis Hall Rozer (who was the son of Francis Hall and assumed the Rozer name upon his marriage, and who had several children) and also a son Thomas Whetenhall Rozer (son of Henry Rozer). There was a Henry Rozer, Jr. who married Sarah Edelen by license dated Sep. 13, 1779 [Ref: ZA-573, ZB-184]. Therefore, it should be noted that some information about Henry Rozer, Jr. may be confused with Henry Rozer (son of Notley Rozer) and Henry Rozer, of Notley Hall (son of Henry Rozer).

ROZER, Maria. See "Henry Rozer, Jr.," q.v.

ROZER, Notley. See Henry Rozer" and "Henry Rozer, Jr.," q.v.

ROZER, Thomas. See "Henry Rozer," q.v.

RUDOLPH, Jane. See "Thomas Lloyd," q.v.

RUE, William. Private, Northern Detachment, 3rd Maryland Line, Capt. Horatio Clagett's Company, 1783 [Ref: D-501].

RUMBALD, John (1762, Maryland -   ). Private (substitute), 1780, continental service, Maryland Line [Ref: D-338].

RUMWILL, John. Private, 2nd Maryland Line, Capt. Murdock's Company, Mar. 15, 1781 [Ref: D-366].

RUSSELL, Abraham. Private, enrolled by Capt. John H. Lowe on July 13, 1776, for continental service, Maryland Line [Ref: D-35]. Took the Oath of Allegiance before the Hon. Benjamin Hall in 1778 [Ref: O-276].

RUSSELL, Ann. See "William Russell" and "Sabrit Sollers," q.v.

RUSSELL, Benjamin. Took the Oath of Allegiance (made his "X" mark) before the Hon. William Lock Weems in 1778 [Ref: O-301].

RUSSELL, James. Private, 3rd Maryland Line, 1781 [Ref: D-392]. The estate of one James Russell was probated in 1801 [Ref: ZE-159].

RUSSELL, John. Private, 2nd Maryland Line, Capt. Patrick Sim's Company, 1776 [Ref: D-8]. Took the Oath of Allegiance (made his "I" mark with an equidistant horizontal line through the middle) before the Hon. William Lock Weems in 1778 [Ref: O-301]. The estate of one John Russell was probated in 1806 [Ref: ZE-159].

RUSSELL, Philip. Took the Oath of Allegiance (made his mark that resembled a "T") before the Hon. William Lock Weems in 1778 [Ref: O-301]. The estate of one Philip Russell was probated in 1779 [Ref: ZE-159]. There was also a Philip Russell who married Elizabeth Dove by license dated Feb. 17, 1781 [Ref: ZB-184].

RUSSELL, William. Took the Oath of Allegiance (made his mark in the form of a backwards "R") before the Hon. William Lock Weems in 1778

[Ref: O-301]. William Russell was born before 1725 and married Ann ---- [Ref: X-2542].

RUTTER, Jonathan. Took the Oath of Allegiance (made his "X" mark) which was recorded on a "return of Capt. Tapley of the brig *Royal*" and filed in court by the Hon. Thomas Gantt, Jr. in 1778 [Ref: O-305, W-4648 (Box 4, folder 15)].

RYAN, George (1761, England -   ). Private (substitute), 1780, continental service, Maryland Line [Ref: D-338]. See "George Ryon," q.v.

RYLEY, Christian. See "Christian Berket Riley," q.v.

RYLEY, Jeremiah. See "Jeremiah Riley," q.v.

RYLEY, John. See "John Riley," q.v.

RYON, Clement. "Clement Ryon" took the Oath of Allegiance before the Hon. Osborn Sprigg in 1778 [Ref: O-306]. "Clement Ryan" married Mary Northy by license dated Feb. 1, 1779 [Ref: ZB-184].

RYON, Darby. Took the Oath of Allegiance before the Hon. Fielder Bowie in 1778 [Ref: W-4648 (Box 4, folder 15), and O-303, which latter source spelled the name "Darby Ryan"]. "Darby Ryon" married Ann Addison Sim by license dated Dec. 31, 1779 [Ref: U-737, ZB-184]. See "Joseph Sim," q.v.

RYON, Elisha. Took the Oath of Allegiance before the Hon. Osborn Sprigg in 1778 [Ref: O-300]. Elisha Ryon married Sarah Sansbury by license dated Feb. 16, 1779 [Ref: ZB-185].

RYON, Elizabeth. See "Cephas Hoye," q.v.

RYON, George. Private, 2nd Maryland Line, Capt. Murdock's Company, Mar. 15, 1781 [Ref: D-366]. See "George Ryan," q.v.

RYON, James. Took the Oath of Allegiance before the Hon. Benjamin Hall in 1778 [Ref: O-276, which spelled his name "Ryan"]. The estate of one James Ryon was probated in 1781 [Ref: ZE-159].

RYON, James Brown. Took the Oath of Allegiance before the Hon. Osborn Sprigg in 1778 [Ref: O-307].

RYON, John. Private, Capt. Hezekiah Wheeler's Company, 11th Militia Battalion, 1781 [Ref: L-19970 (Box 6, folder 21)]. Took the Oath of Allegiance before the Hon. Osborn Sprigg in 1778 [Ref: O-307]. One John Ryon married Eleanor Gates by license dated Mar. 7, 1786 [Ref: ZB-185].

RYON, John. Took the Oath of Allegiance (made a horizontal "I" mark with an equidistant vertical line through the middle) before the Hon. Thomas Clagett in 1778 [Ref: O-267]. The estate of one John Ryon was probated in 1781 [Ref: ZE-159].

RYON, John, of Joseph. Private (draft), continental service, 1781 [Ref: D-382].

RYON, John, of Nathaniel. Took the Oath of Allegiance before the Hon. Fielder Bowie in 1778 [Ref: O-304, which listed his name as "John Ryon," but the original list at the Maryland State Archives (Box 4, folder 15) listed the name as "John Ryon, of Natl."].

RYON, John, of Sol. Private, 2nd Guard, Capt. Henry Hill's Militia Company, Lower Battalion; on duty at Nottingham on the Patuxent, Apr. 12, 1781 [Ref: L-19970 (Box 6, folder 21)].

RYON, John, of William. Private, 2nd Guard, Capt. Henry Hill's Militia Company, Lower Battalion; on duty at Nottingham on the Patuxent, Apr. 12, 1781 [Ref: L-19970 (Box 6, folder 21)].

RYON, Joseph. Private, 2nd Guard, Capt. Henry Hill's Militia Company, Lower Battalion; on duty at Nottingham on the Patuxent, Apr. 12, 1781 [Ref: L-19970 (Box 6, folder 21)].

RYON, Mary. See "James Mayhew," q.v.

RYON, Nathaniel. Took the Oath of Allegiance before the Hon. Fielder Bowie in 1778 [Ref: W-4648 (Box 4, folder 15) and O-303, which latter source spelled the name "Ryan"]. The estate of one Nathaniel Ryon was probated in 1791 [Ref: ZE-159].

RYON, Philip. Private, Capt. Richard Stonestreet's Militia Company, 11th Battalion, June, 1782 [Ref: L-19970 (Box 6, folder 21)]. Took the Oath of Allegiance before the Hon. Osborn Sprigg in 1778 [Ref: O-300]. Philip Ryon married Joanna Alder by license dated Mar. 23, 1778 [Ref: ZB-185].

RYON, Sarah. See "Charles Walker," q.v.

RYON, Susannah. See "Philip Hopkins," q.v.

RYON, Thomas. Took the Oath of Allegiance before the Hon. David Craufurd in 1778 [Ref: O-272].

SABOLLE, Joseph. Private, enlisted Feb. 19, 1780, for 3 years or during war, in continental service, Maryland Line [Ref: D-333].

SADLER, James. Took the Oath of Allegiance before the Hon. Fielder Bowie in 1778 [Ref: O-303, W-4648 (Box 4, folder 15)].

SADLER, Rebecca. See "Abraham Turner," q.v.

SADLER, Thomas. Private (draft), Maryland Line, continental service, 1780. Discharged on Dec. 3, 1781 [Ref: I-10, D-382].

SADLER, William. Took the Oath of Allegiance before the Hon. Fielder Bowie in 1778 [Ref: O-304, W-4648 (Box 4, folder 15)].

SAMPSON, Jacob. Took the Oath of Allegiance before the Hon. James Beck in 1778 [Ref: O-255].

SANDERS, Bennett. Private, 1st Maryland Line, who was paid for his services "in cloathing" on Apr. 17, 1779 [Ref: E-351].

SANDERS, Elizabeth. See "Richard Alexander Contee," q.v.

SANDERS, Harriet. See "Edward Lloyd Wailes," q.v.

SANDERS, John. Took the Oath of Allegiance before the Hon. Osborn Sprigg in 1778 [Ref: O-307]. Drummer and Fifer, 3rd Maryland Line, Capt. Horatio Clagett's Company, 1779 [Ref: D-295].

SANSBURY, Alexius. Second Corporal, 1st Guard, Capt. Henry Hill's Militia Company, Lower Battalion; on duty at Nottingham on the Patuxent, Apr. 12, 1781 [Ref: L-19970, which spelled his name "Sandsbuary"]. "Alexius Sansbury" married Eliza Hamilton by license

dated Feb. 16, 1789 [Ref: ZB-186]. The estate of "Alexius Sansbury" was probated on May 26, 1818 [Ref: ZE-160].
SANSBURY, Anne. See "Benjamin Johnson," q.v.
SANSBURY, Benjamin. Private, Select Militia, Upper Battalion, June 12, 1781 [Ref: S-6636 (Box 27, folder 82B)]. Private, Militia, 1781; participated in capturing an enemy boat and crew on Apr. 17, 1781 [Ref: M-208].
SANSBURY, Eleanor. See "Thomas Sansbury" and "Ignatius Boone," q.v.
SANSBURY, Francis. Took the Oath of Allegiance before the Hon. Osborn Sprigg in 1778 [Ref: O-307, which spelled the name "Sandsburry"].
SANSBURY, Isaac (1732-   ). Took the Oath of Allegiance before the Hon. Christopher Lowndes in 1778 [Ref: R-34, O-282, which spelled the name "Isaac Sansberrie"]. Second Lieutenant, 25th Battalion, May 1, 1778, Capt. Richard Beall's Company [Ref: M-118, E-62, N-34, which latter source spelled the name "Sansberry"]. Served on a Grand Jury in 1778 [Ref: Z-52].
SANSBURY, John. Private, Select Militia, Upper Battalion, June 12, 1781 [Ref: S-6636 (Box 27, folder 82B)]. Private, Militia, 1781; participated in capturing an enemy boat and crew on Apr. 17, 1781 [Ref: M-209].
SANSBURY, Mary. See "Francis Hopkins," q.v.
SANSBURY, Richard. Private, 4th Maryland Line, 1777; discharged on Dec. 14, 1779 [Ref: D-165]. Took the Oath of Allegiance before the Hon. Fielder Bowie in 1778 [Ref: O-304, and the original list at the Maryland State Archives (Box 4, folder 15), which spelled his name "Richard Sandsbury"].
SANSBURY, Sarah. See "Thomas Blacklock" and "Elisha Ryon," q.v.
SANSBURY, Thomas (c1740-1781). Took the Oath of Allegiance before the Hon. Osborn Sprigg in 1778 [Ref: O-307, which spelled his name "Sandsburry"]. Private, Militia, and participated in capturing an enemy boat and crew on Apr. 17, 1781 [Ref: M-208]. Private, Select Militia, Upper Battalion, June 12, 1781 [Ref: S-6636 (Box 27, folder 82B)]. Took the Oath of Allegiance before the Hon. Truman Skinner in 1778 [Ref: O-298]. Served on a Grand Jury in 1778 [Ref: Z-90]. He married Eleanor ---- [Ref: X-2564]. The estate of Thomas Samsbury was probated on Mar. 15, 1781 [Ref: ZE-160].
SANSBURY, William (1736-1824?). Took the Oath of Allegiance before the Hon. Christopher Lowndes in 1778 [Ref: O-285, R-49, which spelled the name "Sansberry"]. The estate of "William Sansberry" was probated on Apr. 6, 1824 [Ref: ZE-160].
SAPP, Robert. Private, 2nd Maryland Line, Capt. Patrick Sim's Company, 1776 [Ref: D-9].
SASSELL, ----. See "Anthony Thomas," q.v.
SASSER (SASSCER), Amy. See "Charles Beaven," q.v.
SASSER, Elizabeth. See "Jonathan Sasser," q.v.

SASSER, Jonathan. Took the Oath of Allegiance before the Hon. Fielder Bowie in 1778 [Ref: O-304, which mistakenly listed the name as "Jonathan Soper." The original list at the Maryland State Archives (Box 4, folder 215) shows the name as "Jonathan Sasser"]. "Jonathan Throne Sasser" *[sic]* married (1) Elizabeth Sasser by license dated Sep. 29, 1783, and (2) Martha Richards by license dated Jan. 16, 1797, and died circa 1841 [Ref: X-2568, ZB-187]. The estate of one "Jonathan Thorne Sasscer" *[sic]* was probated on Feb. 13, 1815 [Ref: ZE-160]. Additional research may be necessary before drawing conclusions.

SASSER, Robert. Private, Capt. Alexander H. Magruder's Militia Company, Lower Battalion; on duty guarding Magruder's Warehouse in the spring of 1782 [Ref: L-19970 (Box 6, folder 21)].

SASSER (SASSCER), Sarah. See "Charles Beaven," q.v.

SASSER, Thomas William. Private, enrolled by Capt. Alexander H. Magruder, 11th Battalion, on July 3, 1776, for continental service, Maryland Line [Ref: D-38].

SASSER, William. Private, enrolled by Capt. Alexander H. Magruder, 11th Battalion, on July 18, 1776, for continental service, Maryland Line [Ref: D-38]. "William Sasser, Sr." took the Oath of Allegiance before the Hon. Truman Skinner in 1778 [Ref: O-297, which spelled the name "William Sasscer, Sr."]. The estate of one "William Sasscer" was probated on Sep. 19, 1796 [Ref: ZE-161].

SASSER, William Jr. Took the Oath of Allegiance (made his "X" mark) before the Hon. Truman Skinner in 1778 [Ref: O-299, which spelled the name "William Sasscer, Jr."]. The estate of one "William Sasscer" was probated on May 7, 1821 [Ref: ZE-161].

SATTERFIELD, William. Private, 7th Maryland Line, enlisted June 7, 1777; corporal, Dec. 25, 1777; sergeant, Mar. 1, 1780; and was reported missing on Aug. 16, 1780 (at the Battle of Camden). [Ref: D-248]. The estate of "William Sattersfield" was probated on Mar. 10, 1794, in Prince George's County [Ref: ZE-161].

SAUNDERS, Elizabeth. See "Edward Boteler," q.v.

SCARCE, Nathan (1741-1804). Took the Oath of Allegiance before the Hon. Fielder Bowie in 1778 [Ref: R-81, O-304, which questionably listed the name only as "Nathan ----" because the ink is smeared on the original list at the Maryland State Archives (Box 4, folder 15); nonetheless, the name appears to be "Nathan Scarce"]. Nathan Scarce married Susannah Casteel (1763-1804) and a son Rezin Scarce (c1788-1832) married Airy Hardey (c1785-1854) and lived in Luzerne County, Pennsylvania, and Steuben County, New York, and Fairfax County, Virginia [Ref: Ancestral chart of Robert Donald and Nancy Elizabeth (Frinks) Leasure, of Abington, Virginia, in the *Prince George's County Genealogical Society Bulletin*, Volume 25, No. 6 (Feb., 1994), pp. 110-111]. The estate of Nathan Scarce was probated on Dec. 5, 1804 [Ref: ZE-161]. It should be noted that Sources ZB-190 and ZE-163 have mistakenly indexed some names as "Searce" when they should have been indexed as "Scarce."

SCARCE, Rebecca. See "John Summers," q.v.
SCARCE, Rezin. See "Nathan Scarce," q.v.
SCARCE, Sarah. See "Nathan Summers," q.v.
SCARCE, Shadrick. Took the Oath of Allegiance before the Hon. Osborn Sprigg in 1778 [Ref: O-308, which questionably listed the name as "Pearse [?], [Searce?]," but in the original list (very light) at the Maryland State Archives (Box 4, folder 29) the name appears to look more like "Scarce"].
SCHNECK, Catharine. See "Leonard Fry," q.v.
SCISSELL, ----. See "Anthony Thomas," q.v.
SCOFIELD, William. Private, 7th Maryland Line, enlisted on June 28, 1777, and reportedly "deserted" on June 30, 1777 [Ref: D-249]. The estate of one "William Scholfield" was probated on Nov. 24, 1783 [Ref: ZE-161, which also spelled the name "Schoolfield"].
SCOTT, Agnes. See "Thomas Hoye," q.v.
SCOTT, Ann. See "Bazil Wilson," q.v.
SCOTT, Elizabeth. See "Samuel Scott," q.v.
SCOTT, Henry. Private in the militia in 1776 [Ref: M-207, A-325]. One Henry Scott was aged 49 in 1776 [Ref: R-71]. The estate of one Henry Scott was probated on May 20, 1777 [Ref: ZE-162].
SCOTT, James. There were several men with this name who served in the Maryland Line [Ref: D-31, D-246, D-249, D-343, D-396, D-422]. The estate of one James Scott was probated on Apr. 10, 1794 in Prince George's County [Ref: ZE-162]
SCOTT, Margaret. See "Joseph Mattingley," q.v.
SCOTT, Richard. Private, 1st Guard, Capt. Henry Hill's Militia Company, Lower Battalion; on duty at Nottingham on the Patuxent, Apr. 12, 1781 [Ref: L-19970 (Box 6, folder 21)].
SCOTT, Richard Keen. Constable in Grubb Hundred, 1777 [Ref: Z-3]. The estate of "Richard K. Scott" was probated on Feb. 19, 1788 [Ref: ZE-162].
SCOTT, Samuel (1745-   ). Private, 2nd Maryland Line, Mar. 15, 1781. Private, Northern Detachment, 3rd Maryland Line, Capt. Horatio Clagett's Company, 1783; discharged on June 20, 1783 [Ref: D-366, D-502, D-555]. His pension commenced on May 27, 1818 [Ref: T-39]. On Feb. 21, 1834, the Treasurer of the Western Shore was directed to pay to Benjamin L. Gantt for the use of Mrs. Elizabeth Scott, widow of the late Samuel Scott, of Prince George's County, a revolutionary soldier, the amount of $14.44 due him at death as a pensioner. On Mar. 4, 1834, the Treasurer was directed to pay to Mrs. Elizabeth Scott, widow of Samuel Scott, during life, quarterly, half pay of a private, for the services of her husband during the Revolutionary War. On Jan. 19, 1848, the State Treasurer was directed to pay to order of William Scott,

one of the legal representatives of Elizabeth Scott, late of Prince George's County, deceased, the balance of pension money due at her death [Ref: O-389]. One Samuel Scott married Ann Dickson Wilson by license dated Nov. 19, 1784, and a Samuel Scott married Elizabeth Free by license dated Apr. 19, 1796 [Ref: ZB-189].

SCOTT, Thomas. Private, 3rd Maryland Line, enlisted Jan. 20, 1776 [Ref: D-9]. The estate of one Thomas Scott was probated on May 1, 1794 in Prince George's County [Ref: ZE-162].

SCOTT, William. See "Samuel Scott," q.v.

SEABURN, Zachariah. Took the Oath of Allegiance before the Hon. Benjamin Hall in 1778 [Ref: O-275].

SEARCY, Milley. See "John Connolly," q.v.

SEEGO (SEEGS?), Thomas. The estate of one "Thomas Seegs (soldier)" was probated in Prince George's County on Apr. 13, 1793 [Ref: ZE-163]. "Thomas Seego" was a private, 4th Maryland Line, enlisted on July 22, 1782 [Ref: D-467]. "Thomas Scego" was still in service in 1783 [Ref: D-503, D-567, which also spelled his name "Sergo"].

SELBY, Agnes. See "Nathan Selby," q.v.

SELBY, Ann. See "Thomas Dorsett" and "James Harvey," q.v.

SELBY, Elizabeth. See "William Wilson Selby," q.v.

SELBY, James Wilson (1747, Maryland - died after 1809, Kentucky). "James Wilson Selby" took the Oath of Allegiance before the Hon. Christopher Lowndes in 1778 [Ref: O-288]. "James Selbey" was aged 29 in 1776 [Ref: R-46]. He married Ruth ---- [Ref: X-2609].

SELBY, John. Constable in Mount Calvert Hundred, 1778 [Ref: Z-30].

SELBY, John Smith. Sergeant, 7th Maryland Line, enlisted on Mar. 9, 1776 [Ref: D-15]. He married Sabinah Orme by license dated Apr. 14, 1780 [Ref: ZB-191]. The estate of John Smith Selby was probated by May 3, 1785 (date of inventory). [Ref: ZE-163].

SELBY, Joseph. Captain who served on a General Courts-Martial for the trial of Capt. Richard Bennett Hall, Lieut. Jeremiah Ryley, Lieut. Jonathan Wright, and Lieut. James Mullikin on Aug. 23, 1776, at Upper Marlboro [Ref: B-233]. Took the Oath of Allegiance before the Hon. Fielder Bowie in 1778 [Ref: O-304, W-4648 (Box 4, folder 15)]. The estate of one Joseph Selby was probated on June 1, 1786 [Ref: ZE-163].

SELBY, Joshua Wilson (1741-1816). "Joshua Wilson Selby" took the Oath of Allegiance before the Hon. Christopher Lowndes in 1778 [Ref: O-283]. "Joshua Selby" was aged 35 in 1776 [Ref: R-47]. The estate of "Joshua Wilson Selby" was probated on Feb. 20, 1816 [Ref: ZE-163].

SELBY, Josiah. Ensign, Upper Battalion, Militia, Capt. Selby's Company, June 27, 1781 [Ref: H-320].

SELBY, Josiah Wilson. Captain, 25th Battalion, July 20, 1776 to at least May 1, 1778 [Ref: M-119, B-84, E-62, N-34]. Took the Oath of Allegiance before the Hon. William Berry in 1778 [Ref: O-258].

SELBY, Lingan Wilson. Took the Oath of Allegiance before the Hon. William Berry in 1778 [Ref: O-258]. "Lingan Selbey" was aged 23 in 1776 [Ref: R-46].
SELBY, Mary. See "Nicholas Naylor" and "Azariah Gatton," q.v.
SELBY, Nathan (1735, Maryland - died after 1810, Virginia). Took the Oath of Allegiance before the Hon. William Berry in 1778 [Ref: O-258, R-46, which spelled his name "Selbey"]. Nathan Selby married Agnes ---- [Ref: X-2609].
SELBY, Richard. Rendered patriotic service by providing wheat for the military on Aug. 9, 1780 [Ref: Q-308].
SELBY, Ruth. See "James Wilson Selby," q.v.
SELBY, William Magruder (1709-1783). Took the Oath of Allegiance before the Hon. William Berry in 1778 [Ref: O-258, R-48, which listed the name as "William M. Selbey"]. "William Magruder Selby" married Martha Wilson [Ref: X-2609]. The estate of "William M. Selby" was probated on Jan. 21, 1783 [Ref: ZE-164].
SELBY, William Wilson (1729-1800). First Lieutenant, Militia, 25th Battalion, May 1, 1778, Capt. Josiah Selby's Company [Ref: M-119, E-62, N-34]. Constable, Eastern Branch Hundred, 1777 [Ref: Z-3]. Took the Oath of Allegiance before the Hon. Christopher Lowndes in 1778 [Ref: O-288]. "William W. Selbey" was aged 47 in 1776 [Ref: R-46]. He married Elizabeth ---- [Ref: X-2609]. The estate of William Wilson Selby was probated on June 25, 1800 [Ref: ZE-164].
SELF, Elizabeth. See "Jonathan Mayhew," q.v.
SELMAN, John. Private, Maryland Line, discharged on Dec. 3, 1781 [Ref: I-10].
SERGANT, Benjamin. Took the Oath of Allegiance before the Hon. Osborn Sprigg in 1778 [Ref: O-306].
SETTLE, Franklin. See "Jonathan Jewell," q.v.
SEWELL, James. Private, 2nd Maryland Line, Capt. Alexander Truman's Company, 1782 [Ref: D-440].
SHACKELFORD, Sarah Ann. See "Edward Lloyd Wailes," q.v.
SHANKS, Thomas (1747-   ). Took the Oath of Allegiance before the Hon. Christopher Lowndes in 1778 [Ref: O-287, R-72].
SHARPLESS, Robert. Corporal, 2nd Maryland Line, Capt. Alexander Truman's Company, 1782; prisoner of war, wounded, and exchanged by Apr. 15, 1782, at which time he was "paid 5 pounds specie on his account." [Ref: D-439, D-617].
SHAW, Angus. Took the Oath of Allegiance before the Hon. Christopher Lowndes in 1778 [Ref: O-287].
SHAW, Basil (1756 or 1758, Maryland - after July 29, 1834, Haywood County, North Carolina). Took the Oath of Allegiance before the Hon. Christopher Lowndes in 1778 [Ref: O-285, R-48, which spelled his name "Bazell Shaw"]. The records of the Council of Maryland on Aug. 21, 1781, include a letter from the County Lieutenant in which he stated

that "I this day had the petition of Basil Shaw put into my hands, he was drafted against another marryed man who had a wife and children and has been out in the service of his country and is a very industrious man. Shaw, from the best information I could get, is a very idle, lasey fellow, who is rather a burden than help to his family, for which reason I chose him to go into service. I shall inquire farther into the matter from some persons whose names are to his petition." [Ref: H-435]. He applied for a pension, but was rejected (R9436) on Apr. 2, 1834, in Haywood County, North Carolina. He stated he enlisted in the Maryland Line in Prince George's County, Maryland, but it could not be verified. He later moved to Pittsylvania County, Virginia and 13 years later moved to Newberry District, South Carolina for another 13 years. He then moved to Rutherford County, North Carolina for 26 years and to Haywood County, North Carolina in February, 1831. He was aged 86 on July 29, 1834 [Ref: P-3086, and should not be confused with Basil Shaw, of Montgomery County, Maryland who served in the Maryland Line and moved to Nashville, Tennessee. He applied for and received a pension (S16526) in Hall County, Georgia in 1833, aged 72].

SHAW, Charles (1739-   ). Took the Oath of Allegiance before the Hon. Christopher Lowndes in 1778 [Ref: O-285, R-51]. Private (draft), continental service, Maryland Line, 1781 [Ref: D-382].

SHAW, Elizabeth. See "Joseph Shaw," q.v.

SHAW, John. There were several men with this name who served in the Maryland Line [Ref: D-6, D-70, D-160, D-248, D-661]. One John Shaw was born on Sep. 17, 1755, son of John and Sarah Shaw, of King George's Parish in Prince George's County [Ref: ZC-61]. Additional research may be necessary before drawing conclusions. See "Joseph Shaw," q.v.

SHAW, Joseph (May 28, 1737 - 1785). Son of John and Elizabeth Shaw [Ref: ZC-62]. Took the Oath of Allegiance (made his "X" mark) before the Hon. Thomas Clagett in 1778 [Ref: O-265, R-41]. The estate of one Joseph Shaw was probated on Aug. 21, 1785 [Ref: ZE-164].

SHAW, Josiah (1745-   ). Captain, 25th Battalion, Sep. 5, 1777 to June 24, 1780 [Ref: M-120, C-363, C-414, F-203, R-36].

SHAW, Josias. First Lieutenant, Aug. 23, 1776, Capt. Beall's Company, and First Lieutenant, 25th Battalion, May 1, 1778, Capt. Joseph Carlton's Company. Captain, May 24, 1779 [Ref: M-120, B-232, C-78, N-32, N-33].

SHAW, Josias. Private, Militia, 1776 [Ref: M-207, A-325]. Took the Oath of Allegiance before the Hon. Thomas Williams in 1778 [Ref: O-302].

SHAW, Sarah. See "John Shaw," q.v.

SHAW, William. Private, Select Militia, Upper Battalion, June 12, 1781 [Ref: S-6636 (Box 27, folder 82B)]. Private, Militia, 1781; participated in capturing an enemy boat and crew on Apr. 17, 1781 [Ref: M-208].

SHEAN, Patrick. Private, 4th Maryland Line, enlisted Dec. 1, 1776; corporal, Sep. 1, 1779; reported missing on Aug. 16, 1780 (at the Battle of Camden). [Ref: D-165].
SHEAN, Timothy. Private, 4th Maryland Line, enlisted Dec. 7, 1776, and reported missing on Aug. 16, 1780 (at the Battle of Camden). [Ref: D-165, D-415]. The estate of one Timothy Shean was probated on Mar. 10, 1794 [Ref: ZE-165].
SHECKELL (SHEKELL, SHELELL?), Ann. See "Richard Jones," q.v.
SHECKELL, Cephas. "Cephas Sheckell" took the Oath of Allegiance before the Hon. Benjamin Hall in 1778 [Ref: O-276]. "Cephas Shekells" married Eleanor Pratt by license dated Sep. 14, 1780, and a "Cephas Shekells" married Eleanor Boyd by license dated Sep. 27, 1796 [Ref: ZB-192].
SHECKELL, Ezekial. Took the Oath of Allegiance before the Hon. Richard Henderson in 1778 [Ref: O-278].
SHECKELL, Richard. Took the Oath of Allegiance before the Hon. Benjamin Hall in 1778 [Ref: O-276].
SHECKELL, Samuel (1750-   ). Second Lieutenant, Upper Battalion, June 24, 1780, Capt. William Moore's Company. Captain, July 2, 1781 [Ref: M-120, G-492, F-203, which latter source spelled his name "Samuel Sheckles," and R-21 spelled his name "Samuel Shackells"]. Took the Oath of Allegiance before the Hon. Christopher Lowndes in 1778 [Ref: O-283, which spelled his name "Samuel Shekill"]. He was appointed by the Council of Maryland to be one of the two Tobacco Inspectors at Bladensburg Warehouse on Aug. 30, 1780 [Ref: F-271, which spelled his name "Saml. Shekells"]. Captain, Upper Battalion, June 27, 1781 [Ref: H-320].
SHEE, Murphy. Private, Maryland Line, 1782; confined by Capt. Alexander Truman at Bacon's Bridge, South Carolina, on Apr. 19, 1782, and charged with plundering [Ref: D-417].
SHELELL (SHEKELL?), Ann. See "Richard Jones," q.v.
SHELL (STULL?), Richard. Private, 3rd Maryland Line, Capt. Horatio Clagett's Company, December, 1779 [Ref: D-296].
SHELTON, Thomas. Took the Oath of Allegiance before the Hon. James Beck in 1778 [Ref: O-254].
SHEPPARD, Valinda. See "Rezin Beall," q.v.
SHERIDAN, Thomas. Private, 2nd Maryland Line, Capt. Alexander Truman's Company, 1782 [Ref: D-439].
SHERIFF, John (1736-   ). Took the Oath of Allegiance before the Hon. Benjamin Hall in 1778 [Ref: O-274, R-54, which spelled the name "John Sherife"].
SHERIFF, Samuel. Took the Oath of Allegiance before the Hon. Thomas MacGill in 1778 [Ref: O-291].
SHERRELL, Martha. See "Francis Holley," q.v.

SHERWOOD, John. Private, enrolled by Capt. John H. Lowe on July 13, 1776, for continental service, Maryland Line [Ref: D-35, D-67].
SHERWOOD, Susanna. See "John Callihorn," q.v.
SHIRCLIFF (SHERKLIFF), Dorothy. See "Joseph Coomes," q.v.
SHIRCLIFF, William. Private in Capt. Hezekiah Wheeler's Company, 11th Militia Battalion, April, 1781 [Ref: L-19970 (Box 6, folder 21), which spelled his name "William Shercliff"]. Ensign, Select Militia, Capt. Hezekiah Wheeler's Company, by June 8, 1781 [Ref: M-121, G-466, S-6636 (Box 31, folder 5)].
SHIRCLIFF, William (c1750 - Jan. 13, 1808). Ensign, Maryland Line, Capt. Robert Bowie's Company, in place of Colmore Beans by convention appointment on July 6, 1776 [Ref: D-34]. "William Shercliff" was a first lieutenant in the 4th Maryland Line from Dec. 10, 1776, until he resigned in February, 1778 [Ref: D-166]. "William Shircliff" married Melinda Mudd [Ref: X-2653].
SHIRTLEY, Joseph. Private, 3rd Maryland Line, under Col. Thomas Williams. His widow (no name given) reported he had been killed at the Battle of Germantown on Oct. 4, 1777. Her disability payment began June 6, 1778 and was stopped Aug. 14, 1781, but no reason was given in this record [Ref: D-634, D-635, K-1814].
SHITES, James. Took the Oath of Allegiance (made his mark that looked like the letters "uep" or "ues" connected together) before the Hon. William Lock Weems in 1778 [Ref: O-301].
SHORT, George. Took the Oath of Allegiance before the Hon. Christopher Lowndes in 1778 [Ref: O-285].
SHORT, Isaac (1740-   ). Took the Oath of Allegiance before the Hon. Christopher Lowndes in 1778 [Ref: O-285, R-49].
SHORT, James. Private, 7th Maryland Line, enlisted June 30, 1778 for 9 months and reportedly "deserted" in January, 1780 [Ref: D-249, D-309]. One James Short married Mary Grimes by license dated Feb. 9, 1779, and a James Short married Mary Maccastle by license dated Dec. 12, 1791 [Ref: ZB-193]. The estate of one James Short was probated on Mar. 28, 1808 [Ref: ZE-165].
SHREEVES, Mary. See "Humphrey Beckett," q.v.
SHUGAR, William. "William Shugar" was a private, enrolled by Lt. William Duvall, Lower Battalion, on July 18, 1776, for continental service, Maryland Line [Ref: D-35]. "William Sugars" was a private in the 3rd Maryland Line, enlisted on Apr. 25, 1778 [Ref: D-165].
SHUGART, Peter. Corporal, 2nd Maryland Line, Capt. Alexander Truman's Company, 1782; "deserted" on July 2, 1782 [Ref: D-439].
SILK, Samuel. Took the Oath of Allegiance (made his "X" mark) before the Hon. Truman Skinner in 1778 [Ref: O-297]. Private, 3rd Maryland Line, 1781-1782 [Ref: D-394, D-454]. Samuel Silk married Elizabeth Collings by license dated July 26, 1779 [Ref: ZB-194].
SIM, Anthony. See "Joseph Sim," q.v.

SIM, Joseph (c1725 - Nov. 27, 1793). Son of Dr. Patrick Sim and Mary Brooke. He married (1) Catherine Murdock by 1754, and (2) Lettice Wardrop Thomson, who was twice a widow (died in 1776). His children were Patrick Sim, William Sim, Joseph Sim, Anthony Sim, Thomas Sim, Ann Addison Ryon, and Mary Brooke Nelson [Ref: U-737]. Served as Clerk of the Prince George's County Court, 1749-1767. Justice, Provincial Court, 1773. Member of Lower House, 1771, 1773-1776. Committee of Observation, 1775. State Senate, 1776-1781. Colonel, militia, May 5, 1774, and Colonel, 11th Battalion, from Jan. 13, 1776 until Sep. 23, 1776 (resigned). Contributed money and tobacco to support the Revolutionary Army in 1780 [Ref: M-121, B-296, D-38, A-13, U-70, U-72, U-80, U-82, U-84, U-736, U-737]. "Col. Joseph Sim and his son Col. Patrick Sim are probably buried at "Sim's Delight" now called "Bellefields" on Duley Station Road." [Ref: Y-614]. Source X-2667 only lists the first wife.

SIM, Patrick. Captain, 2nd Maryland Line, on Jan. 20, 1776 [Ref: D-7, which listed his name as "Patk. Sims"]. Colonel, Middle Battalion, Mar. 10, 1778 to 1779 [Ref: M-121, C-532, N-35, which spelled his name "Simm"]. Took the Oath of Allegiance before the Hon. David Craufurd in 1778 [Ref: O-271]. His pension commenced on Apr. 9, 1818 and he died on Jan. 7, 1819 [Ref: T-39, which spelled his name "Sims"]. One Patrick Sim married Mary Carroll by license dated July 11, 1777, and a Patrick Sim married Arianna Henderson by license dated Aug. 28, 1787 [Ref: ZB-194]. The estate of "Col. Patrick Sim" was probated on Jan. 18, 1819 [Ref: ZE-166]. See "Joseph Sim," q.v.

SIM, Thomas. See "Joseph Sim," q.v.

SIM, William. See "Joseph Sim," q.v.

SIMMONS, Isaac. Took the Oath of Allegiance before the Hon. James Mullikin in 1778 [Ref: O-296]. Constable in Collington Hundred, 1778 [Ref: Z-30]. Isaac Simmons married Susanna Simmons by license dated Nov. 19, 1777 [Ref: ZB-194].

SIMMONS, Jacob. Took the Oath of Allegiance before the Hon. James Mullikin in 1778 [Ref: O-296]. Jacob Simmons married Eleanor Cross by license dated Apr. 19, 1780 [Ref: ZB-194].

SIMMONS, Jesse. Took the Oath of Allegiance before the Hon. James Mullikin in 1778 [Ref: O-296].

SIMMONS, Jonathan (Aug. 9, 1735 -   ). Son of Jonathan Simmons and Elizabeth Swearingen, of Queen Anne's Parish [Ref: ZC-192]. Took the Oath of Allegiance before the Hon. Thomas Williams in 1778 [Ref: O-302, and R-29, which latter source states he was aged 31 in the 1776 census of Prince George's County. Therefore, either the enumerator made an error or there were two Jonathan Simmons]. Additional research may be necessary before drawing conclusions. See "Richard Simmons," q.v.

SIMMONS, Mary. See "John Lucas," q.v.

SIMMONS, Richard. Two men by this name took the Oath of Allegiance in 1778: one before the Hon. Thomas Williams and another before the Hon. James Beck [Ref: O-254, O-302]. One Richard Simmons (c1720 - Apr. 2, 1782) married (1) Susannah Pottenger, and (2) Mary Willett by license dated Mar. 7, 1779 [Ref: X-2671, ZB-194]. The estate of one Richard Simmons was probated on Apr. 1, 1784 and was administered by Jonathan Simmons [Ref: ZE-166].

SIMMONS, Robert. There were two men with this name who took the Oath of Allegiance in 1778: one before the Hon. Fielder Bowie and another before the Hon. Thomas Williams [Ref: O-302, O-304, W-4648 (Box 4, folder 15)]. "Robert Simmonds" was a private, 3rd Guard, Capt. Henry Hill's Militia Company, Lower Battalion; on duty at Nottingham on the Patuxent, Apr. 12, 1781 [Ref: L-19970 (Box 6, folder 21)]. One "Robert Simmons" married Catherine Baldwin by license dated May 9, 1781 [Ref: ZB-194].

SIMMONS, Samuel (c1742-1781). Took the Oath of Allegiance before the Hon. James Mullikin in 1778 [Ref: O-296]. He married Verlinda Willett [Ref: X-2671]. The estate of Samuel Simmons was probated on May 21, 1781 by Verlinda Simmons [Ref: ZE-166].

SIMMONS, Susanna. See "Isaac Simmons," q.v.

SIMMONS, Van (1752-   ). Took the Oath of Allegiance before the Hon. Christopher Lowndes in 1778 [Ref: O-283, R-49].

SIMMS, Edward (1738-   ). Took the Oath of Allegiance before the Hon. Thomas Clagett in 1778 [Ref: O-268, R-12].

SIMMS, Ignatius. Private, Capt. Richard Stonestreet's Militia Company, 11th Battalion, June, 1782 [Ref: L-19970 (Box 6, folder 21), which spelled his name "Sims"].

SIMMS, Marmaduke. Took the Oath of Allegiance (made his "M" mark) before the Hon. Thomas Clagett in 1778 [Ref: O-266].

SIMPKINS, Thomas. Private, 2nd Maryland Line, Capt. Patrick Sim's Company, 1776 [Ref: D-8].

SIMPSON, Ann. See "Clement Edelen," q.v.

SIMPSON, Catharine. See "David Luckett," q.v.

SIMPSON, Eleanor. See "William Lawson," q.v.

SIMPSON, Gilbert (1730-1787). Took the Oath of Allegiance before the Hon. Fielder Bowie in 1778 [Ref: R-88, O-304, W-4648 (Box 4, folder 15)]. The estate of one Gilbert Simpson was probated on Sep. 25, 1787 by Joseph Simpson [Ref: ZE-166].

SIMPSON, Greenbury (1749-   ). Private, enrolled in the Flying Camp by Capt. Robert Bowie on July 16, 1776; nativity: Prince George's County; height 6' 1/4"; has own gun [Ref: D-36].

SIMPSON, John (1725-   ). First Lieutenant, 11th Battalion, Sep. 1, 1777 to at least May 1, 1778, Capt. Thomas Dent's Company [Ref: M-121, C-356, E-78, N-32, R-87].

SIMPSON, John (1742-   ). Private, Select Militia, Capt. Hezekiah Wheeler's Company, July 14, 1781 [Ref: S-6636 (Box 31, folder 5), T-17, R-81]. One John Simpson married Rebecca Whiting by license dated Sep. 9, 1784, and a John Simpson married Mary Dent Morris (by license dated Apr. 10, 1788) on Apr. 22, 1788 [Ref: ZB-195, ZC-62].
SIMPSON, John, of Green. Took the Oath of Allegiance before the Hon. Thomas Clagett in 1778 [Ref: O-264].
SIMPSON, Joseph Jr. "Joseph Simpson, Jr." took the Oath of Allegiance (made his "X" mark) before the Hon. Thomas Clagett in 1778 [Ref: O-266]. "Joseph Simpson" married Rachel Galwith by license dated Jan. 31, 1788 [Ref: ZB-195]. See "Gilbert Simpson," q.v.
SIMPSON, Juliet. See "David Luckett," q.v.
SIMPSON, Thomas. Private, Capt. Richard Stonestreet's Militia Company, 11th Battalion, June, 1782 [Ref: L-19970 (Box 6, folder 21)]. Sergeant, Select Militia, Capt. Hezekiah Wheeler's Company, July 14, 1781 [Ref: S-6636 (Box 31, folder 5)]. Took the Oath of Allegiance before the Hon. Thomas Clagett in 1778 [Ref: O-267]. One Thomas Simpson married Ruth King (by license dated Apr. 7, 1787) on Apr. 10, 1787, and a Thomas Simpson married Amelia Linch by license dated Sep. 17, 1787 [Ref: ZB-195, ZC-63]. One Thomas Simpson was born on Oct. 5, 1763 and was baptized on Nov. 13, 1763 (parents not named in register). [Ref: ZC-63]. The estate of one Thomas Simpson was probated on Sep. 10, 1821 [Ref: ZE-167].
SINCLAIR, Andrew. Private, 4th Maryland Line, 1777; discharged on June 14, 1778 [Ref: D-166, which spelled the name "Sinklair"].
SINCLAIR, Elizabeth. See "Nathaniel Sinclair" and "George Jones" and "William Sinclair," q.v.
SINCLAIR, Mordecai. Took the Oath of Allegiance before the Hon. Osborn Sprigg in 1778 [Ref: O-300]. The estate of one "Mordicai Sinclair" was probated on Feb. 2, 1791 [Ref: ZE-167].
SINCLAIR, Nathaniel (Jan. 31, 1707 -   ). Son of William and ELizabeth Sinkler *[sic]* and twin of "William Sinclair," q.v. [Ref: ZC-192]. Took the Oath of Allegiance before the Hon. Fielder Bowie in 1778 [Ref: O-304, W-4648 (Box 4, folder 15)].
SINCLAIR, William (Jan. 31, 1707 -   ). Son of William and Elizabeth Sinkler *[sic]* and twin of "Nathaniel Sinclair," q.v. [Ref: ZC-192]. Took the Oath of Allegiance before the Hon. Osborn Sprigg in 1778 [Ref: O-308, which spelled the name "Sinclear"].
SIPE, Christopher. See "Jeremiah Igleheart," q.v.
SISCILL, Phillip (1736-c1803). Took the Oath of Allegiance before the Hon. William Berry in 1778 [Ref: O-259, R-35, which spelled his name "Philip Cissell"]. He married Elizabeth Thomas [Ref: X-521]. "Philip Cissil" was a militia private in 1776 [Ref: M-207, A-325].
SISSELL, Ann. See "Ninian Beall," q.v.

SISSILL, Joshua (c1733, Maryland - died by Apr. 19, 1814, Ohio). Private, enrolled by Capt. John H. Lowe on July 13, 1776, in the Maryland Line [Ref: D-35]. He married Mary ---- [Ref: X-521].
SISTER Charles (Elizabeth Anne). See "Henry Waring," q.v.
SISTER Mary Samuel (Josephine Jane). See "Henry Waring," q.v.
SKINNER, Priscilla. See "Truman Skinner," q.v.
SKINNER, Thomas. Captain who served on a General Courts-Martial for the trial of Capt. Richard Bennett Hall, Lieut. Jeremiah Ryley, Lieut. Jonathan Wright, and Lieut. James Mullikin on Aug. 23, 1776, at Upper Marlboro [Ref: B-233]. The estate of one Thomas Skinner was probated on Apr. 28, 1835 [Ref: ZE-167].
SKINNER, Truman (Apr. 13, 1737 - Oct. 6, 1780). Captain who served on a General Courts-Martial for the trial of Capt. Richard Bennett Hall, Lieut. Jeremiah Ryley, Lieut. Jonathan Wright, and Lieut. James Mullikin on July 25, 1776, at Upper Marlboro [Ref: A-553]. Court Justice, 1777-1778 [Ref: C-273, Z-90]. Administered the Oath of Allegiance in 1778 [Ref: O-299]. Stored arms and ammunition at his home in July, 1780 [Ref: G-4, which listed him as "Col. Trueman Skinner"]. First Major, Lower Battalion, Feb. 4, 1777. Lieutenant Colonel, 11th Battalion, from Sep. 1, 1777 to about Oct. 6, 1780, when he was reported deceased by the County Lieutenant [Ref: M-121, N-32, E-414, C-113, C-356, E-62, F-318, G-135]. Truman Skinner married Priscilla Skinner [Ref: X-2683]. His estate was probated on June 12, 1781 [Ref: ZE-167].
SKIPPER, John. Private, 1st Maryland Line, enlisted Dec. 10, 1776 and died in August, 1777 [Ref: D-160, which spelled the name "Skepper"].
SKIPPER, William. Private, 2nd Maryland Line, Capt. Patrick Sim's Company, 1776 [Ref: D-8]. Private, 1st Maryland line, enlisted Feb. 22, 1777, and reportedly "deserted" [Ref: D-160].
SLATER, Jonathan. Justice of the County Court, 1777 [Ref: C-273].
SLATER, Sarah Contee. See "Thomas Contee," q.v.
SLYE, William. Private, 7th Maryland Line, enlisted Apr. 30, 1778; corporal, July, 1780; missing on Aug. 16, 1780 (at the Battle of Camden); discharged on Apr. 30, 1781 [Ref: D-249]. William Slye married Ann Northey by license dated June 19, 1783 [Ref: ZB-196].
SMALLWOOD, Ann. See "Elijah Coe" and "John Wynn" and "William Wynn," q.v.
SMALLWOOD, Bayne (baptized Mar. 1, 1752, Maryland - died after 1820, Virginia). Son of Thomas and Mary Smallwood [Ref: ZC-63]. Private, enrolled by Lt. William Duvall, Lower Battalion, on July 18, 1776, for continental service, Maryland Line [Ref: D-31, D-35]. He married (1) Mary Wynn, and (2) Marsilva Coe by license dated Dec. 19, 1780 [Ref: X-2694, ZB-196].
SMALLWOOD, Hester. See "Henry Acton," q.v.

SMALLWOOD, John (Jan. 2, 1763 - 1812/1824?). Son of Eliga [sic] and Sarah Smallwood [Ref: ZC-63]. Private, 1st Maryland Line, 1780. Private, 3rd Maryland Line, 1781 [Ref: D-358, D-396]. One John Smallwood married Cloe Wilson (by license dated Dec. 15, 1787) on Dec. 16, 1787 [Ref: ZC-63, ZB-196, which latter source listed her name as "Clour Wilson"]. The estate of one John Smallwood was probated on June 4, 1812, and the estate of a John Smallwood was probated on Feb. 3, 1824 [Ref: ZE-168].

SMALLWOOD, Ledstone. Private, enrolled by Ensign Horatio Clagett on July 15, 1776, for continental service, Maryland Line [Ref: D-35].

SMALLWOOD, Mary. See "Bayne Smallwood," q.v.

SMALLWOOD, Mildred. See "William Smallwood Wynn," q.v.

SMALLWOOD, Milicent. See "William Wynn," q.v.

SMALLWOOD, Rebecca. See "Hezekiah Wynn," q.v.

SMALLWOOD, Sarah. See "John Smallwood," q.v.

SMALLWOOD, Thomas. See "Bayne Smallwood," q.v.

SMALLWOOD, Walter Bean (1763, Maryland -   ). Private, enlisted June 5, 1781, for 3 years, continental service, Maryland Line; sent to Annapolis; on furlough, July 13, 1781 [Ref: D-382]. Private, 2nd Maryland Line, Capt. Alexander Truman's Company, 1782 [Ref: D-440].

SMITH, Abraham B. See "John Tolson Lowe," q.v.

SMITH, Ann. See "Anthony Drane" and "John Smith" and "Joseph Sparrow" and "John Igleheart," q.v.

SMITH, Anthony (1728-1791). Took the Oath of Allegiance before the Hon. James Beck in 1778 [Ref: O-253, R-50]. The estate of one Anthony Smith was probated on May 18, 1791 [Ref: ZE-168].

SMITH, Charles. Ensign, Select Militia, Capt. Hezekiah Wheeler's Company, from May 25, 1781 until June 8, 1781, when he resigned [Ref: M-122, G-445].

SMITH, Edward B. Private, enrolled by Lt. William Duvall, Lower Battalion, on July 18, 1776, for continental service, Maryland Line [Ref: D-35].

SMITH, Eleanor. See "Joshua Beall," q.v.

SMITH, Eliza. See "John Tolson Lowe," q.v.

SMITH, Elizabeth. See "John Smith" and "Richard Smith" and "William Bowie" and "William Lamar" and "Thomas Swain," q.v.

SMITH, Grissel. See "John Smith" and "Samuel Smith," q.v.

SMITH, Henrietta. See "David Young," q.v.

SMITH, Henry (Feb. 26, 1759, Prince George's County, Maryland -died after July 1, 1834, Shelby County, Kentucky). He applied for a pension (S31374) on July 1, 1834 in Shelby County, Kentucky, stating he was born in Prince George's County, Maryland and lived in Frederick County at the time of his enlistment in the Maryland Line. In 1800 he moved to Jefferson County, Virginia and in 1808 he moved to Shelby County, Kentucky [Ref: P-3188].

SMITH, Henry (Feb. 4, 1757 -   ). Son of James and Mary Smith [Ref: ZC-64]. Took the Oath of Allegiance before the Hon. Christopher Lowndes in 1778 [Ref: O-285].
SMITH, Isaac. Took the Oath of Allegiance (made his "I" mark) which was recorded on a "return of Capt. Tapley of the brig *Royal*" and filed in court by the Hon. Thomas Gantt, Jr. in 1778 [Ref: O-305, W-4648 (Box 4, folder 15)]. Private, Capt. Alexander H. Magruder's Militia Company, Lower Battalion; on duty guarding Magruder's Warehouse in the spring of 1782 [Ref: L-19970 (Box 6, folder 21)]. Served on a Grand Jury in 1778 [Ref: Z-90]. The estate of one Isaac Smith was probated on June 3, 1823 [Ref: ZE-168].
SMITH, James (Sep. 5, 1759 -   ). Son of James and Mary Smith [Ref: ZC-64]. Private (draft), continental service, 1781, Maryland Line [Ref: D-382]. See "Henry Smith," q.v.
SMITH, James. Took the Oath of Allegiance before the Hon. Osborn Sprigg in 1778 [Ref: O-306, R-6]. One James Smith was aged 44 in 1776 and another James Smith was aged 52 in 1776 [Ref: R-6, R-44].
SMITH, James Haddock (1733-1806). Took the Oath of Allegiance before the Hon. David Craufurd in 1778 [Ref: O-271]. James Haddock Smith married Ann Burgess [Ref: X-2700]. The estate of "James H. Smith" was probated on Nov. 4, 1806 [Ref: ZE-168].
SMITH, John. There were several men with this name: (1) Private, Capt. Hezekiah Wheeler's Company, 11th Militia Battalion, April, 1781 [Ref: L-19970 (Box 6, folder 21)]. (2) Private, Capt. Jesse Hellen's Militia Company, before May 23, 1782; guarded Magruder's Warehouse in the spring of 1782 [Ref: L-19970 (Box 6, folder 21)]. (3) Took the Oath of Allegiance before the Hon. Osborn Sprigg in 1778 [Ref: O-308, W-4648 (Box 4, folder 29)]. (4) Took the Oath of Allegiance before the Hon. Christopher Lowndes in 1778 [Ref: O-285]. (5) Took the Oath of Allegiance before the Hon. James Beck in 1778 [Ref: O-256]. One John Smith was aged 53 in 1776 [Ref: R-83]. One John Smith married Elizabeth Rawlings by license dated Aug. 20, 1777 [Ref: ZB-198]. One John Smith, son of Samuel and Grissel Smith, of King George's Parish, was born on Dec. 15, 1735 [Ref: ZC-64]. One John Smith, son of William and Elizabeth Smith, of Queen Anne's Parish, was born on June 3, 1732 [Ref: ZC-192]. One John Smith, son of Nicholas Smith, was born on Jan. 8, 1723, in Prince George's Parish [Ref: ZD-121]. More men named John Smith are profiled below. Additional research will be necessary before drawing conclusions about patriotic service.
SMITH, John (1758, Prince George's County, Maryland - died after 1832, Iredell County, North Carolina). He applied for a pension (R9768) on Nov. 20, 1832 in Iredell County, North Carolina, but it was rejected. His application stated he lived in Maryland at the time of his enlistment into the Maryland Line and Maryland Sea Service, and in 1792 he moved to North Carolina [Ref: P-3199].

SMITH, John (July 17, 1760, Prince George's County, Maryland - died prior to Jan. 2, 1840, Harrison County, Virginia). Applied for a pension (S6117) on Aug. 25, 1832 in Harrison County, Virginia, stating he was born in Maryland and at the age of 5 he moved with his father (no name given) to Frederick County where he lived at the time of his enlistment in the Maryland Line. There he married and lived for 2 years after the war and then moved to Washington County, Maryland for 2 more years, to Allegheny County, Maryland for 11 years, and then to Harrison County, Virginia [Ref: P-3198].

SMITH, John (baptized on Aug. 18, 1765 - died between 1828 and 1842). Son of John and Ann Smith [Ref: ZC-64]. Private, enlisted June 18, 1781, for 3 years in continental service, Maryland Line; on duty July 13, 1781 [Ref: D-382]. On Feb. 24, 1823, the Treasurer of the Western Shore was directed to pay to John Smith, of Prince George's County, half pay of a corporal, during life, for his services during the Revolutionary War in the 3rd Maryland Line [Ref: D-394, T-54]. Applied for pension (S46521) on Oct. 10, 1828, in Prince George's County, a resident of Piscataway. His date of death was not given, but it stated he had lived in Prince George's County for 50 years. The last pension payment was made on Sep. 4, 1842 to James P. Hall, attorney [Ref: P-3198, T-54].

SMITH, Joseph. There were several men with this name who served in the Maryland Line [Ref: D-50, D-66, D-159, D-160, D-165, D-265, D-270, D-317, D-330, D-517, D-600, D-617, D-660]. The estate of one "Joseph Smith (soldier)" was probated on Apr. 13, 1793 in Prince George's County [Ref: ZE-169].

SMITH, Joseph. Took the Oath of Allegiance before the Hon. David Craufurd in 1778 [Ref: O-270]. Served on a Grand Jury, 1777-1778 [Ref: Z-23, Z-90]. The estate of one Joseph Smith was probated on Aug. 12, 1801 by Walter Smith [Ref: ZE-169].

SMITH, Lawrence. Took the Oath of Allegiance before the Hon. Benjamin Hall in 1778 [Ref: O-275].

SMITH, Lewis. Private, Capt. Hezekiah Wheeler's Company, 11th Militia Battalion, April, 1781 [Ref: L-19970 (Box 6, folder 21)].

SMITH, Lucy. See "Richard Brooke," q.v.

SMITH, Margaret Hamilton. See "Richard Waters," q.v.

SMITH, Mary. See "Alexis Boone" and "Samuel Edelen" and "Thomas Rose" and "Henry Smith" and "James Smith," q.v.

SMITH, Matthew. Private, Maryland Line, by Feb. 24, 1779 when paid for his services "in cloathing." [Ref: E-308].

SMITH, Michael. Private, Capt. Alexander Truman's Company, who was stationed at Annapolis in 1781 and reported on a list of men who "deserted" since Mar. 1, 1781 [Ref: L-19970 (Box 7, folder 52)].

SMITH, Nacey. See "Luke Adams," q.v.

SMITH, Nicholas. See "John Smith," q.v.

SMITH, Patrick. Colonel who served on the Board of the Patuxent Associators and signed a resolution at Nottingham on Apr. 21, 1781 relative to the defence of the rivers of Potomac and Patuxent and the completion of the fort at Drum Point [Ref: K-1814].
SMITH, Rachel. See "Thomas Gantt," q.v.
SMITH, Rebecca. See "Richard Smith" and "Dennis Coghlan," q.v.
SMITH, Reubin. Private, 4th Maryland Line, enlisted Oct. 24, 1779. Private, 1st Maryland Line, 1781-1783 [Ref: D-167, D-358]. The estate of Reubin Smith was probated on May 1, 1794 [Ref: ZE-170].
SMITH, Richard (July 15, 1728 - 1794). Son of William Smith and Elizabeth Mason [Ref: ZC-192]. Took the Oath of Allegiance before the Hon. Thomas Boyd in 1778 [Ref: O-262, which listed his name as "Ri Smith"]. In the Smith Family Cemetery located on Poplar Ridge Farm on Queen Anne Road (near Defense Highway about 2 miles from Queen Anne Bridge over the Patuxent River) are buried Dr. Richard Smith and Rebecca Smith (1726 - Sep. 9, 1815). [Ref: Y-595]. The estate of "Dr. Richard Smith" was probated on July 12, 1794 [Ref: ZE-170]. See "Joseph Williams" and "Richard Williams," q.v.
SMITH, Rosanah. See "James Jones," q.v.
SMITH, Samuel. There were several men with this name who served in the Maryland Line [Ref: D-164, D-164, D-314, D-315, D-392]. One Samuel Smith, son of Samuel and Grissel, was born on Apr. 8, 1755 in Prince George's County [Ref: ZC-64]. Additional research may be necessary before drawing conclusions. See "John Smith," q.v.
SMITH, Sarah. See "James Wear," q.v.
SMITH, Susanna. See "Giles G. Smith" and "Charles Smith," q.v.
SMITH, Thomas. Sergeant, Capt. Alexander H. Magruder's Militia Company, Lower Battalion; on duty guarding Magruder's Warehouse in the spring of 1782 [Ref: L-19970 (Box 6, folder 21)]. Took the Oath of Allegiance before the Hon. Thomas Gantt, Jr. in 1778 [Ref: O-305, W-4648 (Box 4, folder 15)]. One Thomas Smith married Ruth Evans by license dated Aug. 18, 1777 [Ref: ZB-199]. The estate of one Thomas Smith was probated on Dec. 1, 1789, and another was probated on June 5, 1815 [Ref: ZE-170].
SMITH, Thomas. Took the Oath of Allegiance before the Hon. Benjamin Hall in 1778 [Ref: O-275]. Private, 2nd Maryland Line, Capt. Murdock's Company, Mar. 15, 1781 [Ref: D-366]. Private, 2nd Maryland Line, Capt. Alexander Truman's Company, 1782, and waiter to Major Hardman [Ref: D-440, which listed him as "Thomas Smith 1st"]. The estate of one Thomas Smith was probated on Dec. 1, 1789, and another was probated on June 5, 1815 [Ref: ZE-170].
SMITH, Ursula. See "John White," q.v.
SMITH, Walter. See "Joseph Smith," q.v.
SMITH, William. Took the Oath of Allegiance before the Hon. David Craufurd in 1778 [Ref: O-271]. The estate of one William Smith was

probated on Mar. 10, 1794, and another was probated on June 1, 1812 [Ref: ZE-170]. See "John Smith" and Richard Smith," q.v.

SNOWDEN, Deborah. See "Richard Brooke," q.v.

SNOWDEN, Margaret. See "John Contee," q.v.

SNOWDEN, Ned. Private (draught), Maryland Line, who was discharged on Dec. 3, 1781. He was paid eight pounds, eleven shillings and eight pence on May 13, 1782 [Ref: I-10, I-164, D-412].

SNOWDEN, Thomas (1731-1803). Second Major, 25th Battalion, Mar. 18, 1776, and First Major, Upper Battalion, July 9, 1776. He served as the President on a General Courts-Martial for the trial of Capt. Richard Bennett Hall, Lieut. Jeremiah Ryley, Lieut. Jonathan Wright, and Lieut. James Mullikin on Aug. 23, 1776, at Upper Marlboro [Ref: A-260, B-16, B-233, M-123]. He married Ann Ridgely, an heiress, and upon their marriage their estate became known as "Montpelier." It was here that George Washington stopped on his way to the Constitutional Convention in 1787 [Ref: Y-596, Y-611, Y-616, citing a bronze plaque placed by The Army-Navy Chapter, DAR, at the grave of Thomas Snowden in the Birmingham Manor Cemetery located across the Patuxent River in Anne Arundel County on the edge of Fort Meade. Also see Thomas' obituary in the *Maryland Gazette* on Oct. 29, 1803, Annapolis, Maryland]. A son, Richard Snowden, is buried in the Snowden Family Cemetery-Oaklands located on Contee Road in Laurel, Maryland [Ref: Y-597, X-2735]. The estate of "Thomas Snowden (Major)" was probated on Nov. 22, 1803 [Ref: ZE-171].

SOLLERS, John. Private, enrolled by Capt. Alexander H. Magruder, 11th Battalion, on July 4, 1776, for continental service, Maryland Line [Ref: D-38].

SOLLERS, Sabrit. "Sabrit Sollers" took the Oath of Allegiance before the Hon. Fielder Bowie in 1778 [Ref: O-304, W-4648 (Box 4, folder 15)]. One "Sabrett Sollars" married Ann Russell by license dated Mar. 3, 1786, and a "Sabret Sollars" married Mary Gordon by license dated May 10, 1787 [Ref: ZB-200].

SOMERS, Mary. See "Aaron Rawlings," q.v.

SOMERVELL, James (Apr. 19, 1758 - May 4, 1815). Captain, 6th Maryland Line. In November, 1785, the Maryland General Assembly granted half pay of a captain to "James Somerville for disability acquired in the service, late a captain in the Maryland Line in the Continental Army." On Mar. 12, 1828, the Treasurer of the Western Shore was directed to pay to James Somervell, of Prince George's County, son and one of the heirs of Captain James Somervell, an officer of the Maryland Line during the Revolution, such sum as may appear to be due to him on the pension list of Maryland at the time of his decease [Ref: O-395, T-17]. "James Somervell" married Anne Truman (Trueman). [Ref: X-2739]. "James Somerville" married Elizabeth Hawkins Magruder by license dated Nov. 7, 1792, in Prince George's County, and was active

in Calvert County during the war [Ref: ZB-200, D-33, D-34]. One James Somerville was a lieutenant in the 6th Maryland Line on Feb. 20, 1777, promoted to captain on June 1, 1779, and was wounded at the Battle of Camden on Aug. 16, 1780 [Ref: D-246]. The estate of James Somervell was probated on Nov. 17, 1815 in Prince George's County [Ref: ZE-171].
SOMERVILLE, Susannah. See "George Fraser Hawkins," q.v.
SOMMERS, John Dent. See "John Summers," q.v.
SOMMERS, John Smith. See "John Summers," q.v.
SOPER, Abraham. Took the Oath of Allegiance before the Hon. Osborn Sprigg in 1778 [Ref: O-306, which spelled the name "Soaper"].
SOPER, Alexander. Served on a Grand Jury in 1777 [Ref: Z-29]. The estate of one Alexander Soper was probated on Oct. 28, 1806 [Ref: ZE-171]. See "Leonard Soper," q.v.
SOPER, Charles. Took the Oath of Allegiance before the Hon. Thomas Williams in 1778 [Ref: O-302]. One Charles Soper married Mary ---- and had a son Joseph Belt Soper baptized in 1767 [Ref: ZC-65].
SOPER, Esther. See "John Igleheart," q.v.
SOPER, John (1724-1801). Took the Oath of Allegiance before the Hon. Osborn Sprigg in 1778 [Ref: R-64, O-306, which spelled the name "Soaper"]. The estate of John Soper was probated on June 26, 1801 [Ref: ZE-171]. See "Leonard Soper" and "Nathan Soper," q.v.
SOPER, Joseph. See "Charles Soper," q.v.
SOPER, Leonard (1742-1809). Took the Oath of Allegiance before the Hon. Osborn Sprigg in 1778 [Ref: R-82, O-306, which spelled the name "Soaper"]. One Leonard Soper married Elizabeth ---- and had these children listed in King George's Parish register: Mary Soper (baptized Apr. 19, 1767), Alexander Soper (born Mar. 7, 1772), John Soper (born Sep. 2, 1773), and Leven Soper (born Feb. 4, 1787) *[sic]*. [Ref: ZC-65]. The estate of Leonard Soper was probated on Sep. 6, 1809 [Ref: ZE-172].
SOPER, Leen. See "Leonard Soper," q.v.
SOPER, Martha. See "Nathan Soper," q.v.
SOPER, Mary. See "Zadock Moore" and "Leonard Soper," q.v.
SOPER, Massy. See "John Mayhew," q.v.
SOPER, Nathan. Took the Oath of Allegiance before the Hon. James Mullikin in 1778 [Ref: O-296]. Nathan Soper married Ann Darcey by license dated Nov. 21, 1791 [Ref: ZB-201]. The church record states her name was Ann Dersey [Dorsey?] and they were married on Nov. 26, 1791. Nathan Soper, son of John and Martha Soper, was baptized on Apr. 11, 1762, in King George's Parish [Ref: ZC-65]. The estate of one Nathan Soper was probated in 1824 [Ref: ZE-172].
SOPER, Rebecca. See "William Soper," q.v.
SOPER, Sarah. See "William Soper," q.v.
SOPER, Susannah. See "Thomas Darnall, Sr.," q.v.

SOPER, Thomas. Took the Oath of Allegiance before the Hon. William Berry in 1778 [Ref: O-259].
SOTHORON, Elizabeth. See "Luke Marbury," q.v.
SOTHORON, Harriet. See "William Clagett," q.v.
SOUTHER, Christopher. Took the Oath of Allegiance before the Hon. Benjamin Hall in 1778 [Ref: O-274]. The estate of one Christopher Souther was probated on Mar. 22, 1781 [Ref: ZE-172].
SOUTHER, Valentine. Musician, 2nd Maryland Line, who enlisted in June, 1780 and reportedly "deserted" on Aug. 14, 1780 [Ref: D-161].
SOUTHER, William. Private (draft), Maryland Line, discharged on Jan. 3, 1782 [Ref: D-412, I-37].
SOUTHWELL, Lana. See "William Stewart," q.v.
SPALDING, Aaron. Private, 2nd Maryland Line, Jan. 1, 1777. Sergeant by May, 1780 [Ref: D-161]. In December, 1815, the Treasurer of the Western Shore was directed to pay to Aaron Spalding, during life, half pay of a sergeant [Ref: O-395]. It appears there were two men named Aaron Spalding who served in the revolution. See Henry C. Peden, Jr.'s *Revolutionary Patriots of Calvert and St. Mary's Counties, Maryland, 1775-1783*, p. 249.
SPALDING, Henry (1749 - after 1811). Private, 2nd Maryland Line, Jan. 10, 1777 until discharged on Jan. 10, 1780 [Ref: D-162]. In November, 1811, the Treasurer of the Western Shore was directed "to pay to Henry Spalding, late a private in the Revolutionary War, the half pay of a private, as a provision to him in his indigent situation and advanced life." [Ref: O-395]. There was also a Henry Spalding who served on a Grand Jury in 1778 [Ref: Z-52], and took the Oath of Allegiance before the Hon. Thomas Clagett in 1778 [Ref: O-267, R-87]. Source X-2746 lists a Henry Spalding (1747-1816) who married Ann Elder and was a private in the Maryland Line. Additional research may be necessary before drawing conclusions.
SPALDING, James. Took the Oath of Allegiance before the Hon. Thomas Clagett in 1778 [Ref: O-267]. The estate of one James Spalding was probated on Sep. 6, 1800 [Ref: ZE-172].
SPALDING, John (1752-1820). Took the Oath of Allegiance before the Hon. Thomas Clagett in 1778 [Ref: O-265, R-87]. Corporal, Select Militia, Capt. Hezekiah Wheeler's Company, July 14, 1781 [Ref: S-6636 (Box 31, folder 5)]. The estate of one John Spalding was probated om Nov. 13, 1820 [Ref: ZE-172].
SPALDING, William. Private, Select Militia, Capt. Hezekiah Wheeler's Company, July 14, 1781 [Ref: S-6636 (Box 31, folder 5)]. Took the Oath of Allegiance before the Hon. Thomas Clagett in 1778 [Ref: O-267]. Another William Spalding was a private in the 1st Maryland Line and was reported dead Nov. 26, 1778 [Ref: D-161]. The estate of one William Spalding was probated on July 30, 1792 [Ref: ZE-172].

SPARROW, Joseph (1733-   ). Took the Oath of Allegiance before the Hon. Christopher Lowndes in 1778 [Ref: O-286, R-59]. One Joseph Sparrows married Ann Smith by license dated Dec. 9, 1778 [Ref: ZB-202].
SPARROW, Solomon (Oct. 5, 1746 - died before Feb. 27, 1818). Took the Oath of Allegiance before the Hon. Thomas Boyd in 1778 [Ref: O-262, X-2750]. The estate of Solomon Sparrow was probated on June 8, 1820 [Ref: ZE-172, which source misspelled the name as "Sparron").
SPARROW, Thomas. Took the Oath of Allegiance before the Hon. William Lock Weems in 1778 [Ref: O-301].
SPEAK, Nathan. Private, 2nd Maryland Line, Capt. Alexander Truman's Company, 1782; "died Oct. 6, 1782, furlough Nov. 2, 1780" [Ref: D-440].
SPEAKS, Ally and Casey. See "Hezekiah Speaks," q.v.
SPEAKS, Eleanor and Elizabeth. See "Hezekiah Speaks," q.v.
SPEAKS, Hezekiah (1757, Prince George's County, Maryland - Jan. 1, 1837, Bourbon County, Kentucky). He applied for a pension on Sep. 17, 1832, aged 75, in Bourbon County, Kentucky, stating that he was born in Prince George's County, Maryland and lived in Montgomery County at the time of his enlistment in the Maryland Line. He died in 1837 and his widow Eleanor (daughter of Edward Tucker, of Montgomery County, Maryland) applied for pension (W8748) on Dec. 30, 1842, aged 80, in Bourbon County, stating they married near Georgetown, Maryland "about the first of the year" in 1783. Their children in 1842 were John Speaks (aged 59, if alive), Elizabeth ---- (aged 56), William Speaks (aged 54, if alive), Sarah ---- (aged 51), Eleanor ---- (aged 49), Nancy ---- (aged 47), Mary ---- (aged 45, if alive), Casey ---- (aged 42, if alive), and Ally Ashford (aged 40, wife of Michael Ashford). Also mentioned was a John Tucker (in 1832), but no relationship was stated [Ref: P-3261, X-2750].
SPEAKS, John. See "Hezekiah Speaks," q.v.
SPEAKS, Mary. See "Hezekiah Speaks," q.v.
SPEAKS, Nancy. See "Hezekiah Speaks," q.v.
SPEAKS, Sarah. See "Hezekiah Speaks," q.v.
SPEAKS, William. See "Hezekiah Speaks," q.v.
SPEARS, Thomas. Took the Oath of Allegiance before the Hon. Fielder Bowie in 1778 [Ref: O-304, which questionably listed the name as "Thos. S----." The original list at the Maryland State Archives (Box 4, folder 15) is unclear in the ending so the name could be "Thomas Spears" or perhaps even "Thomas Speans"].
SPENCER, John (1740, Scotland -   ). Private (substitute), 1780, continental service, Maryland Line [Ref: D-338].
SPINK, Ann. See "Edward Burch," q.v.
SPIRES, John (1761, Maryland - Dec. 27, 1821, Indiana County, Pennsylvania). Private (substitute), Maryland Line, continental service, 1781 [Ref: D-382]. He applied for pension in Indiana County, Pennsylvania on Apr. 17, 1818, aged 57, stating that he served in the

Maryland Line and married Mary Hinton on Aug. 24, 1784 near Bladensburg, Maryland. They lived in Prince George's County until 1794 when they moved to Indiana County, Pennsylvania. In 1820 his wife Mary was aged 56 and the children living at home were Mary Spires (aged 16) and Hinton Spires (aged 12), plus a granddaughter Nancy Stone (aged 3). John's widow applied for pension (W3731) on Apr. 25, 1849, aged 83, stating John died on Dec. 27, 1821 and their children were all born before Jan. 1, 1794: Susan or Susanna Spires (born about 1786), Richard Spires (born about 1787 or 1788), Joseph Spires, John or Jonathan Spires, and Lawson Spires (all but Lawson were listed again in 1850). Thomas Leach, aged 64, born in and a resident of Prince George's County in 1850, stated his mother (not named) was a sister of Mary Hinton who married soldier John Spires. Also, in 1850, a Francis Anderson stated he was born near Bladensburg in 1786 and a John Anderson stated he was born about 7 miles from Bladensburg on Apr. 5, 1782 (although no relationships were stated they were probably sons-in-law of John Spires the soldier). [Ref: P-3274].

SPIRES, Jonathan. See "John Spires," q.v.
SPIRES, Joseph. See "John Spires," q.v.
SPIRES, Lawson. See "John Spires," q.v.
SPIRES, Mary. See "John Spires," q.v.
SPIRES, Richard. See "John Spires," q.v.
SPIRES, Susan. See "John Spires," q.v.
SPRIGG, Edward (c1721-1790). Son of Thomas Sprigg and Margery Wight. Served on the Committee of Observation in 1774 and the Committee of Correspondence in 1775. Commissioner of the Tax in 1778, 1779, 1781, 1782 and 1783. Judge of the Court of Appeals for Tax Assessments, 1778. Took the Oath of Allegiance before the Hon. David Craufurd in 1778 [Ref: O-271, U-761]. Rendered patriotic service (not specified) and the Council of Maryland ordered the State Treasurer on Apr. 24, 1782 to pay him 171 pounds and 10 pence "agreeable to the Act to adjust the Debts due from this State." [Ref: I-146]. It must be noted that there was also an Edward Sprigg, son of Edward Sprigg and Elizabeth Pile, who was born on June 12, 1723 in Queen Anne's Parish. He died prior to Oct. 10, 1784 (date account filed). [Ref: ZE-173, which also listed an estate probated for another Edward Sprigg on Apr. 10, 1790]. Therefore, it is possible that the Edward Sprigg born in 1723 may have rendered the unspecified patriotic service and was paid in 1782 as mentioned above, or perhaps not. Additional research will be necessary before drawing conclusions.
SPRIGG, Elizabeth. See "Enoch Magruder" and "Thomas Watkins," q.v.
SPRIGG, John (Nov. 26, 1716 - 1787?). Son of Thomas Jr. and Margery Sprigg [Ref: ZC-192]. Took the Oath of Allegiance before the Hon. Osborn Sprigg in 1778 [Ref: O-306]. The estate of one John Sprigg was

probated on Sep. 20, 1787 [Ref: ZE-173, which also listed another estate probated for a John Sprigg in 1799].

SPRIGG, John Clark. He was paid by order of the Council of Safety for services rendered "for collecting the number of souls in part of Prince George's County" [enumerating inhabitants] on Sep. 6, 1776 [Ref: B-259]. Second Lieutenant, Middle Battalion, May 1, 1778, Capt. John Brooks' Company. First Lieutenant, June 24, 1780, Capt. Samuel Hepburn's Company [Ref: M-124, E-63, F-203, N-35, which latter sources spelled his name "John Clarke Sprigg"]. Took the Oath of Allegiance before the Hon. Osborn Sprigg in 1778 [Ref: O-307]. The estate of John Clark Sprigg was probated on Mar. 24, 1781 [Ref: U-154, ZE-173]. See "William S. Bowie," q.v.

SPRIGG, Margaret. See "Robert Bowie" and "Walter Bowie," q.v.

SPRGG, Margery. See "John Sprigg," q.v.

SPRIGG, Osborn (c1741-1815). Son of Osborn Sprigg and Rachel Belt. He married (1) Martha Craufurd (widow of both William Hamilton and Charles Clark, and daughter of David Craufurd), and (2) in 1779, Sarah Gantt (daughter of Thomas Gantt) by license dated Apr. 3, 1779 [Ref: U-764, ZA-595, ZB-203]. Osborn Sprigg served in these capacities: Delegate to Maryland Convention, 1774-1776. House of Delegates, 1777. Justice of the County Court, 1777 [Ref: C-273, A-3, U-70, U-74, U-765]. Administered the Oath of Allegiance in 1778 [Ref: O-308, W-4648 (Box 4, folder 29)]. Justice of the Peace in 1779 [Ref: F-17]. Constitution Ratification Convention, 1788. Commissioner of the Tax, appointed 1792, 1798 [Ref: U-765]. The estate of Osborn Sprigg was probated on May 11, 1815 [Ref: ZE-173, which also spelled his name "Osborne" and "Osbourn"].

SPRIGG, Philip. First Lieutenant, Militia, 1779 [Ref: N-35]. Took the Oath of Allegiance before the Hon. Osborn Sprigg in 1778 [Ref: O-306].

SPRIGG, Rachel. See "Thomas Harwood," q.v.

SPRIGG, Samuel. See "Thomas Lansdale," q.v.

SPRIGG, Sarah. See "Thomas Gantt," q.v.

SPRIGG, Thomas. See "Edward Sprigg" and "John Sprigg," q.v.

SPRIGG, Violetta. See "Thomas Lansdale," q.v.

ST. CLARE, Robert (1723-   ). Took the Oath of Allegiance before the Hon. George Lee in 1778 [Ref: O-279, R-67, which latter source spelled his name "Robert St. Clair"].

STACKHOUSE, John. Private, 6th Maryland Line, enlisted Apr. 2, 1780. Private, 2nd Maryland Line, Capt. Alexander Truman's Company, 1782; discharged Apr. 2, 1783 [Ref: D-248, D-440].

STALLIONS (STALLINGS), Samuel. Private, 1st Guard, Capt. Henry Hill's Militia Company, Lower Battalion; on duty at Nottingham on the Patuxent, Apr. 12, 1781 [Ref: L-19970 (Box 6, folder 21)]. Took the Oath of Allegiance (made his "X" mark) before the Hon. Truman Skinner in 1778 [Ref: O-299, which spelled the name "Stallings"].

STALLIONS (STALLINGS), Thomas. Took the Oath of Allegiance before the Hon. Fielder Bowie in 1778 [Ref: O-304, W-4648 (Box 4, folder 15)]. "Thomas Stallings" was a private in the 2nd Maryland Line until discharged on Jan. 15, 1778 [Ref: D-164]. "Thomas Stallings, Jr." married Sarah Mitchell by license dated Nov. 25, 1791 [Ref: ZB-203]. The estate of "Thomas Stallings, Jr." was probated on Dec. 14, 1803 and the estate of "Thomas Stallings" was probated on Oct. 14, 1806 [Ref: ZE-174].
STALLIONS (STALLINGS), Thomas Harvey. Private, 1st Guard, Capt. Henry Hill's Militia Company, Lower Battalion; on duty at Nottingham on the Patuxent, Apr. 12, 1781 [Ref: L-19970 (Box 6, folder 21)]. Took the Oath of Allegiance before the Hon. Osborn Sprigg in 1778 [Ref: O-306, which spelled the name "Thomas H. Stallion"]. The estate of "Thomas Harvey Stallings" was probated on May 19, 1818 [Ref: ZE-174].
STAMP, John. Private, Capt. Alexander H. Magruder's Militia Company, Lower Battalion; on duty guarding Magruder's Warehouse in the spring of 1782 [Ref: L-19970 (Box 6, folder 21)]. The estate of John Stamp was probated on July 22, 1801 [Ref: ZE-174].
STAMP, Mary. See "Thomas Harrison," q.v.
STANDAGE, Elizabeth. See "Zadock Talbott," q.v.
STANDAGE, Hezekiah. Took the Oath of Allegiance before the Hon. Osborn Sprigg in 1778 [Ref: O-307, which listed the name as "Hezk. Standage [Handage?]," but the original list at the Maryland State Archives (Box 4, folder 29) shows the name to be "Standage"].
STANDAGE, Margaret. See "Henry Talbott," q.v.
STANDAGE, Thomas (1713-   ). Took the Oath of Allegiance before the Hon. Fielder Bowie in 1778 [Ref: R-68, O-304, W-4648 (Box 4, folder 15)].
STANDLEY, Michael. Private, Maryland Line, Jan. 1, 1782 [Ref: D-465, D-414, which latter source indicated that Michael Standley was a resident of Frederick County when he reportedly "defected" from the Maryland Line in June, 1780; yet, he was in service in 1782]. The estate of one "Michael Stanly" was probated on Apr. 26, 1794, in Prince George's County [Ref: ZE-174].
STANDLEY, Roger. Private, 2nd Maryland Line, May 20, 1778, and reported dead on Oct. 10, 1778 [Ref: D-163].
STEEL, Alexander (1763, Maryland -   ). Private, enlisted May 26, 1781, for 3 years in continental service, Maryland Line; sent to Annapolis; on duty July 13, 1781 [Ref: D-381]. Private, 2nd Guard, Capt. Henry Hill's Militia Company, Lower Battalion; on duty at Nottingham on the Patuxent, Apr. 12, 1781 [Ref: L-19970 (Box 6, folder 21)].
STEPHENS, Edward. Private, enrolled by Capt. Alexander H. Magruder, 11th Battalion, on July 18, 1776, for continental service in the Maryland Line [Ref: D-38].

STEPHENS, George (1745, England -   ). Private (substitute), 1780, in continental service, Maryland Line [Ref: D-338, which spelled his name "Stephins"]. Took the Oath of Allegiance before the Hon. James Beck in 1778 [Ref: O-253]. See "George Stevens," q.v.

STEPHENS, Hugh. Private, enrolled by Capt. Alexander H. Magruder, 11th Battalion, on July 15, 1776, for continental service, Maryland Line [Ref: D-38].

STEPHENS, James. Private, Maryland Line, enlisted Oct. 8, 1782 [Ref: D-427]. The estate of one James Stephens was probated on June 18, 1810, in Prince George's County [Ref: ZE-175].

STEPHENS, Rebecca. See "Thomas Stevens," q.v.

STEPHENS, Thomas. See "Thomas Stevens," q.v.

STEPHENS, William Jr. (1750-   ). "William Stephens, Jr." took the Oath of Allegiance before the Hon. Thomas Clagett in 1778 [Ref: R-85, O-265]. "William Stephens" married Ann Taylor by license dated Dec. 31, 1785 [Ref: ZB-204]. "William Stevens" married Rebecca Tilley by license dated Jan. 15, 1785 [Ref: ZB-204].

STEPHENS, William Sr. (1714-   ). Took the Oath of Allegiance before the Hon. Thomas Clagett in 1778 [Ref: O-269, R-53]. See "Thomas Stevens," q.v.

STEVENS, George. Private, 2nd Maryland Line, Capt. Murdock's Company, Mar. 15, 1781 [Ref: D-366].

STEVENS, Henry. Took the Oath of Allegiance in 1780 [Ref: J-120].

STEVENS, Thomas. "Thomas Stevens" was a constable in King George Hundred in 1778 [Ref: Z-30]. "Thomas Stephens," son of William and Rebecca Stephens, was born on Aug. 1, 1745 [Ref: ZC-66].

STEVENS, William. See "William Stephens, Jr.," q.v.

STEVENSON, Alexander. Drummer, 2nd Maryland Line, Capt. Alexander Truman's Company, 1782 [Ref: D-439].

STEWARD, James 1st. Private, 2nd Maryland Line, Capt. Alexander Truman's Company, 1782; died Dec. 1, 1782 [Ref: D-439].

STEWARD, Joseph. Private, 2nd Maryland Line, Capt. Patrick Sim's Company, 1776 [Ref: D-8].

STEWARD, Stephen. In November, 1776, he offered his services to the Council of Safety in a letter from Prince George's County to the Maryland Council in which he stated, in part, "I intend to set off to Baltimore by water to look after the rigen, cables, iron hoops and boats for the provence vessels I understand the Defense, Prise, Ship, Captain Walker has some small guns and cohornes. If you have no particular use for them, and will give me an order for them I can fit out these two schooners with guns. If you want me to do anything for you at Baltimore plese to request me and I will comply with your orders." He also mentioned his clerk, Mr. Wasteney [Ref: B-440]. The records of the Maryland Council on May 20, 1778, state the following: "Joseph Winterson was brought before this Board as a Deserter and no Evidence being produced of his being enlisted and a letter from Stephen Steward inducing a Belief that he did not enlist it is ordered that he be permitted to go at large on his own business." [Ref: E-97]. He apparently was owner of a galley that had been appropriated for the defence of the bay in 1781 [Ref: G-617].

STEWART, Charles. "Charles Stewart" took the Oath of Allegiance (made his "CS" mark) before the Hon. Truman Skinner in 1778 [Ref: O-298]. "Charles Steuart" married Elizabeth Calvert by license dated June 14, 1780 [Ref: ZB-204].

STEWART, James. Took the Oath of Allegiance (made his "|" mark) before the Hon. Truman Skinner in 1778 [Ref: O-299].

STEWART, William. "William Stewart" was a private, Capt. Alexander H. Magruder's Militia Company, Lower Battalion; on duty guarding Magruder's Warehouse in the spring of 1782 [Ref: L-19970 (Box 6, folder 21)]. "William Steuart" married Lana Southwell by license dated Feb. 21, 1778 [Ref: ZB-204].

STODDERT, Ann. See "William Truman Stoddert," q.v.

STODDERT, Benjamin C. (1751 - Dec. 18, 1813). Major in the Pennsylvania Line [Source X-2819 states Maryland Line] who was wounded at the Battle of Brandywine. He served as Secretary of the Board of War of Continental Congress in 1779-1781, and the first Secretary of the Navy, 1798-1801. Benjamin lived at "Bostwick" in Bladensburg and at "Beall's Pleasure" as well as his home in George Town. He is buried in Addison Chapel Churchyard at Seat Pleasant [Ref: Y-612, X-2819]. "Benjamin C. Stoddart" married Rebecca Lowndes by license dated June 7, 1781 [Ref: ZB-205]. The estate of "Benjamin Stoddert" was probated on Dec. 25, 1813 [Ref: ZE-175].

STODDERT, John. See "William Truman Stoddert," q.v.

STODDERT, Johanna. See "William Truman Stoddert," q.v.

STODDERT, Susanna. See "William Truman Stoddert," q.v.

STODDERT, Thomas. See "William Truman Stoddert," q.v.

STODDERT, William Truman (Mar. 15, 1736/7 -   ). Son of John and Marianne Stoddert [Ref: ZC-66]. Lieutenant, 4th Maryland Line, commissioned May 21, 1779 and still in service in January, 1781 [Ref: D-364, D-380]. William married Elizabeth ---- and had these children listed in King George's Parish register: Susanna Truman Stoddert (born Dec. 4, 1759), Thomas James John Stoddert (born Feb. 19, 1763), and Johanna Truman Stoddert (born Aug. 30, 1756). [Ref: ZC-66].

STOGGINS, Mourning. See "Joshua Naylor," q.v.

STONE, Ann. See "Charles Grimes," q.v.

STONE, David. Took the Oath of Allegiance before the Hon. William Berry in 1778 [Ref: O-259]. Served on a Grand Jury in 1777 [Ref: Z-23].

STONE, Joseph (1739-   ). Took the Oath of Allegiance before the Hon. Osborn Sprigg in 1778 [Ref: O-306, R-78].

STONE, Leonoa. See "Nathaniel Talbott," q.v.

STONE, Mary. See "Edward Taylor," q.v.
STONE, Nancy. See "John Spires," q.v.
STONE, Nicholas. Took the Oath of Allegiance before the Hon. Osborn Sprigg in 1778 [Ref: O-307, which mistakenly listed the name as "Victr. Stone," but the original list (very light) at the Maryland State Archives (Box 4, folder 29) listed the name "Nichs. Stone"].
STONE, Rachel. See "Walter Watson," q.v.
STONE, Richard (1714-   ). Took the Oath of Allegiance before the Hon. William Berry in 1778 [Ref: O-259, R-70].
STONESTREET, Butler. See "Butler Edelen Stonestreet" and "Henry Stonestreet" and "Richard Stonestreet," q.v.
STONESTREET, Butler Edelen (Feb. 3, 1756, Maryland - June 7, 1826, Kentucky). Son of Butler and ---- Stonestreet [Ref: ZC-67]. Private who was enrolled by Ensign Horatio Clagett on July 15, 1776, for continental service, Maryland Line [Ref: D-35, X-2828, which latter source states he was born on June 7, 1755]. "Buttler E. Stonestreet" married Sarah Norton by license dated Jan. 6, 1778 [Ref: ZB-206].
STONESTREET, Edward (baptized Jan. 14, 1753 -   ). Son of Edward and Elinor Stonestreet [Ref: ZC-67]. Took the Oath of Allegiance before the Hon. Christopher Lowndes in 1778 [Ref: O-287]. Edward Stonestreet married Margery Weight by license dated May 10, 1780 [Ref: ZB-206].
STONESTREET, Elinor. See "Edward Stonestreet" and "William Norton, Sr.," q.v.
STONESTREET, Henry (Sep. 11, 1752 -   ). Son of Butler and ---- Stonestreet [Ref: ZC-67]. Took the Oath of Allegiance before the Hon. Thomas Clagett in 1778 [Ref: O-265, R-85]. Adjutant, 1782 [Ref: Q-514].
STONESTREET, John (1751-   ). Took the Oath of Allegiance before the Hon. Thomas Clagett in 1778 [Ref: O-265, R-76]. Ensign, 11th Battalion, May 1, 1778, Capt. Richard Stonestreet's Company [Ref: M-126, E-62, N-32].
STONESTREET, Joseph (1740-   ). Took the Oath of Allegiance before the Hon. William Lyles, Jr. in 1778 [Ref: O-290, R-75].
STONESTREET, Richard (May 26, 1754 - 1815). Son of Butler and ---- Stonestreet [Ref: ZC-67]. Second Lieutenant, Lower Battalion, Sep. 1, 1777, Capt. Samuel Baynes' Company. Captain, May 1, 1778 [Ref: M-126, C-356, E-62]. Captain, 11th Militia Battalion, 1782 [Ref: L-19970 (Box 6, folder 21), N-32]. Took the Oath of Allegiance before the Hon. George Lee in 1778 [Ref: O-279, R-57]. Recruiting Officer, 1780 [Ref: F-57]. The estate of Richard Stonestreet was probated on Apr. 28, 1815 [Ref: ZE-175].
STONESTREET, Sarah. See "Richard Edelen, Sr.," q.v.
STONESTREET, William. Private, 6th Maryland Line, enlisted Apr. 1, 1778 [Ref: D-247]. Private, 2nd Maryland Line, Capt. Alexander Truman's Company, 1782 [Ref: D-440].

STOOPS, Andrew. Private, 7th Maryland Line, enlisted May 29, 1777 [Ref: ZE-248]. The estate of Andrew Stoops was probated on July 27, 1793, in Prince George's County [Ref: ZE-176].

STRONG, Delilah. See "William Marlow," q.v.

STUART, John (1751-1810?). Took the Oath of Allegiance before the Hon. Christopher Lowndes in 1778 [Ref: O-286, R-71]. The estate of a "Dr. John Stuart" was probated in July, 1810 [Ref: ZE-176].

STULL, Richard. See "Richard Shell (Stull?)," q.v.

SUFFOLK, Richard. Private, 3rd Maryland Line, Capt. Horatio Clagett's Company, 1779 [Ref: D-295].

SUIT, Edward (Aug. 15, 1760 -   ). Son of Nathaniel Suit and Mary Burch [Ref: ZC-67]. Private, 2nd Maryland Line, July 8, 1779; corporal, Feb. 1, 1780; in service to at least Nov., 1780 [Ref: D-163, which spelled the name "Suite"].

SUIT, Jesse Burch (Sep. 27, 1753 -   ). Son of Nathaniel Suit and Mary Burch [Ref: ZC-67]. Private, 2nd Maryland Line, enlisted Jan. 20, 1777, promoted to sergeant in June, 1780, reduced to private on Oct. 7, 1779, and again promoted to sergeant in the 3rd Maryland Line, 1st Company, by Aug. 28, 1781 [Ref: D-161, D-392, which source also spelled his name "Sute" and "Suite"].

SUIT, Nathaniel (Mar. 10, 1756 - 1817). Son of Nathaniel Suit and Mary Burch [Ref: ZC-67]. Private, Militia, 1776 [Ref: M-207, A-325]. The estate of Nathaniel Suit was probated on Dec. 10, 1817 [Ref: ZE-176]. See "Jesse Burch Suit" and "Edward Suit," q.v.

SULLIVAN, Solomon. Private, Northern Detachment, 3rd Maryland Line, Capt. Horatio Clagett's Company, 1783 [Ref: D-501].

SULLIVAN, Thomas. Took the Oath of Allegiance before the Hon. Fielder Bowie in 1778 [Ref: O-304, W-4648 (Box 4, folder 15)]. One Thomas Sullivan was a private in the 3rd Maryland Line on June 18, 1779, and reportedly "deserted" on Feb. 2, 1780 [Ref: D-165].

SUMMERS, Amma. See "Salem Hurley," q.v.

SUMMERS, Ann. See "John Summers" and "Richard Fowler" and "Zadock Jenkins," q.v.

SUMMERS, John. Took the Oath of Allegiance before the Hon. Osborn Sprigg in 1778 [Ref: O-306]. One John Summers was born circa 1720 and died circa 1787. He married Mary ---- [Ref: X-2854]. There were also several men with this name who served in the Maryland Line [Ref: D-246, D-266, D-347, D-357, D-445, D-484]. "John Dent Sommers" was born on July 13, 1754, son of Thomas and Rachel Sommers. "John Smith Sommers" was born on Oct. 2, 1748, son of James and Mary Sommers [Ref: ZC-64]. "John Smith Summers" was born on Oct. 2, 1748, son of John [sic] and Mary Summers [Ref: ZC-67]. "John Summers" married Rebecca Scarce on Feb. 27, 1792, King George's Parish [Ref: ZC-67]. "Jonathan Summers" married Ann ---- by 1783 [Ref: ZC-67]. The estate of one "John Summers" was probated on Nov. 13, 1786, and another on

Jan. 10, 1787 [Ref: ZE-176, ZE-177]. Additional research may be necessary before drawing conclusions. See "John Wheat," q.v.

SUMMERS, Josiah. Took the Oath of Allegiance before the Hon. Osborn Sprigg in 1778 [Ref: O-307].

SUMMERS, Mary. See "John Summers" and "Nathan Summers" and "John Wheat," q.v.

SUMMERS, Nathan (c1740-1784/1790?). Took the Oath of Allegiance before the Hon. Osborn Sprigg in 1778 [Ref: O-307]. One "Nathan Summers" married Mary ---- [Ref: X-2855, which stated he died by 1790]. The estate of "Nathaniel Summers" was probated on Mar. 31, 1784, and another was probated on Apr. 13, 1790. An account on the estate of "Nathan Summers" was filed by "Nathan Summers" on June 28, 1791 [Ref: ZE-177]. One "Nathaniel Summers" married Sarah Scarce by license dated Jan. 2, 1793 [Ref: ZB-207]. Additional research may be necessary before drawing conclusions.

SUMMERS, Rachel. See "John Summers," q.v.

SUMMERS, Thomas. Private, 2nd Maryland Line, 1777, and discharged on Jan. 10, 1780 [Ref: D-162].

SUTHERLAND, John (1747/8, Scotland - Jan. 2, 1842, Washington County, Pennsylvania). He applied for a pension (S6173) on Jan. 29, 1834, aged 86, at Cross Creek Township in Washington County, Pennsylvania, stating he was born in Scotland and came to America in 1773. He settled in Prince George's County and lived there at the time of his enlistment in the Maryland Line. In 1783 he moved to North Strabane Township in Washington County [Ref: P-3392]. He married Susannah ---- [Ref: X-2858]. There was also a John Sutherland who married Margaret Murray by license dated Nov. 30, 1780, in Prince George's County [Ref: ZB-208].

SWAIN, John. First Corporal, 1st Guard, Capt. Henry Hill's Militia Company, Lower Battalion; on duty at Nottingham on the Patuxent, Apr. 12, 1781 [Ref: L-19970 (Box 6, folder 21)]. One John Swain was a private in the 3rd Maryland Line on Sep. 8, 1777. He reportedly "deserted one muster," but then rejoined in February, 1778 [Ref: D-164].

SWAIN, Joshua. Took the Oath of Allegiance (made his mark that resembled a large "+" sign) before the Hon. James Beck in 1778 [Ref: O-253].

SWAIN, Thomas. Private (draft), continental service, Maryland Line, 1781 [Ref: D-382]. Private, 1st Guard, Capt. Henry Hill's Militia Company, Lower Battalion; on duty at Nottingham on the Patuxent, Apr. 12, 1781 [Ref: L-19970 (Box 6, folder 21)]. Rendered patriotic service by providing wheat for the military on May 9, 1783 [Ref: Q-598]. Thomas Swain married Elizabeth Smith by license dated Feb. 17, 1779 [Ref: ZB-208]. The estate of one "Thomas Swaine" was probated on Aug. 18, 1787 [Ref: ZE-177].

SWAIN, Willby. Took the Oath of Allegiance before the Hon. James Beck in 1778 [Ref: O-256].
SWALES (SWAILS), John (1742 - Oct. 30, 1788). "John Swales" was a private in the Northern Detachment, 3rd Maryland Line, Capt. Horatio Clagett's Company, in 1783 [Ref: D-501]. "John Swails" married Eleanor ---- [Ref: X-2860].
SWANN, Edward. Took the Oath of Allegiance before the Hon. Thomas Gantt, Jr. in 1778 [Ref: O-305, W-4648 (Box 4, folder 15)]. The estate of one Edward Swann was probated on May 10, 1803 [Ref: ZE-178].
SWANN, James. Sergeant, Militia, Capt. Jesse Hellen's Company; guarded Magruder's Warehouse in the spring of 1782 [Ref: L-19970 (Box 6, folder 21)]. Took the Oath of Allegiance before the Hon. Thomas Gantt, Jr. in 1778 [Ref: O-305, W-4648 (Box 4, folder 15)]. The estate of one James Swann was probated on Feb. 14, 1805 [Ref: ZE-178].
SWANN, Jennett. See "Henry Hawkins," q.v.
SWANN, John T. Private, Capt. Alexander H. Magruder's Militia Company, Lower Battalion; on duty guarding Magruder's Warehouse in the spring of 1782 [Ref: L-19970 (Box 6, folder 21)]. The estate of a "John Swann" was probated on Feb. 14, 1786 [Ref: ZE-178].
SWANN, Leonard. Took the Oath of Allegiance before the Hon. William Lyles, Jr. in 1778 [Ref: O-290, which spelled the name "Swan"]. Private, 3rd Maryland Line, enlisted May 3, 1778; Capt. Horatio Clagett's Company, December, 1779 [Ref: D-296].
SWANN, Samuel. Took the Oath of Allegiance before the Hon. Fielder Bowie in 1778 [Ref: O-304, W-4648 (Box 4, folder 15)].
SWEARINGEN, Ann. See "Elisha Williams," q.v.
SWEARINGEN, Elizabeth. See "Jonathan Simmons," q.v.
SWEENEY, Notley. Private (draught), Lt. Clemons' Company, Major Higgins' Battalion, continental service, 1781 [Ref: D-399]. The estate of one Notley Sweeney was probated in 1852 [Ref: ZE-178].
SWEENEY, Zachariah. "Zachariah Sweany" took the Oath of Allegiance before the Hon. David Craufurd in 1778 [Ref: O-270]. The estate of "Zachariah Sweeney" was probated on July 10, 1826 [Ref: ZE-178].
SWENEY, Drury. See "John Mitchell," q.v.
SYDEBOTHAM, William (1738-1792?). Took the Oath of Allegiance before the Hon. Christopher Lowndes in 1778 [Ref: R-71, O-286, which latter source spelled the name "Sudebotham"]. One William Sydebotham married Margaret Leitch by license dated Sep. 23, 1778 [Ref: ZB-210]. The estate of one "William Sydebothan" [sic] was probated on June 19, 1792, and an inventory on the estate of "William Sydebotham" was filed on Dec. 15, 1807 [Ref: ZE-178].
SYMMER, Alexander. Took the Oath of Allegiance before the Hon. David Craufurd in 1778 [Ref: O-271].
TALBOTT, Benjamin. Private, enrolled by Capt. John H. Lowe on July 13, 1776, for continental service, Maryland Line [Ref: D-35]. Took the

Oath of Allegiance before the Hon. Osborn Sprigg in 1778 [Ref: O-308, which listed the name as "Talburt"]. See "Charles Talbott," q.v.

TALBOTT, Charles (Feb. 15, 1761 - Feb. 15, 1844, Montgomery County, Maryland). Son of Paul and Martha Talbut [sic], of King George's Parish, Prince George's County [Ref: ZC-69]. He applied for pension (S11519) on June 30, 1843, aged 84, in Washington, DC "as he lived near the Montgomery County and Washington, DC line." He stated he lived in Prince George's County at the time of his enlistment in the Maryland troops and after the war he moved to Frederick County and later moved to Montgomery County. Paul Talbott made an affidavit in 1845 in Washington, DC, that he was the eldest son of Charles Talbott who had died in 1844 leaving these children: Paul Talbott and Benjamin Talbott (both of Montgomery County, Maryland) and Charles Talbott, Jr. (of the State of New York). [Ref: P-3415].

TALBOTT, Coxon. Private, 2nd Maryland Line, Capt. Patrick Sim's Company, 1776. Private, 1st Maryland Line, enlisted Dec. 10, 1776, and reportedly died on May 23, 1777 [Ref: D-7, D-168].

TALBOTT, Elinor. See "Notley Talbott," q.v.

TALBOTT, Henry (1751, Prince George's County - died after 1832, Washington, DC). "Henry Talbott, or Talburt" applied for a pension (S11511) on Dec. 31, 1832, in Washington, DC, stating he lived in Prince George's County at the time of his enlistment in the Maryland Line. In 1830 he moved to Washington, DC [Ref: P-3415]. "Henry Talburt" took the Oath of Allegiance in 1780 [Ref: J-121]. One "Henry Talburt" married Margaret Standage by license dated Sep. 26, 1780 [Ref: ZB-211].

TALBOTT, John (1725-   ). Served on a grand Jury in 1778 [Ref: Z-90, R-80, which latter source spelled his name "Talbot"]. One "John Talbot" married Ann Davis by license dated Oct. 1, 1777 [Ref: ZB-211].

TALBOTT, John, of Paul. Took the Oath of Allegiance before the Hon. Thomas Clagett in 1778 [Ref: O-267].

TALBOTT, Margaret. See "Osborne Talbott," q.v.

TALBOTT, Martha. See "Charles Talbott," q.v.

TALBOTT, Nathaniel (1720-   ). Took the Oath of Allegiance before the Hon. Fielder Bowie in 1778 [Ref: R-77, which spelled the name as "Talbot," and O-304, which spelled the name "Talbert;" yet, the original list at the Maryland State Archives (Box 4, folder 15) shows the name as "Talburt"]. One "Nathan Talburt" married Leonoa [sic] Stone by license dated Apr. 19, 1783 [Ref: ZB-211]. The estate of "Nathaniel Talbert" was probated in 1822 [Ref: ZE-179].

TALBOTT, Notley (Sep. 13, 1757 -   ). Son of Thomas and Elinor Talbott, of King George's Parish in Prince George's County [Ref: ZC-69]. "Notley Talbot (Talbort)" served as a private in the Upper District of Frederick County in July, 1776 [Ref: ZC-49].

TALBOTT, Osborne (Mar. 3, 1755 -   ). Son of Thomas and Margaret Talbott [Ref: ZC-69]. Private, enrolled by Capt. John H. Lowe on July 13, 1776, for continental service, Maryland Line [Ref: D-35, which listed the name as "Osburn Talburt"].

TALBOTT, Paul. Took the Oath of Allegiance before the Hon. Osborn Sprigg in 1778 [Ref: O-307, which spelled the name "Tolbert"]. The estate of a "Paul Talburt" was probated on Feb. 19, 1778, and the estate of a "Paul Talbert" was probated on Dec. 4, 1832 [Ref: ZE-179]. See "Charles Talbott," q.v.

TALBOTT, Sarah. See "William Talbott," q.v.

TALBOTT, Thomas. Took the Oath of Allegiance in 1780 [Ref: J-121, which spelled the name "Talburt"]. See "Notley Talbott" and "Osborne Talbott," q.v.

TALBOTT, Tobias (1747-   ). "Tobias Talbott" took the Oath of Allegiance in 1780 [Ref: J-121, R-68, which latter source spelled the name "Tobias Talbot"]. One "Tobias Talbert" married Margaret Riley by license dated Aug. 9, 1800 [Ref: ZB-210].

TALBOTT, William. Private, 4th Maryland Line, 1777, and died on Aug. 2, 1778 [Ref: ZE-290]. The estate of one "William Talburt" was probated by Feb. 23, 1782 (date of inventory filed by Sarah Talburt). [Ref: ZE-179],

TALBOTT, Zadock. "Zadock Talburt" took the Oath of Allegiance in 1780 [Ref: J-121]. "Zadock Talbert" married Elizabeth Standage by license dated Dec. 30, 1778 [Ref: ZB-210]. "Mrs. Zadoc Tolburt funeral July 24, 1796" *[sic]*, King George's Parish [Ref: ZC-71].

TALBURT, Susannah. See "Thomas Burch" and "Richard Kirby," q.v.

TANNAKER, Adamson. See "Jacob Palmer," q.v.

TANNER, Ignatius Nevett. Took the Oath of Allegiance before the Hon. Fielder Bowie in 1778 [Ref: O-304, W-4648 (Box 4, folder 15), which listed the name as "Tannar"].

TANNER, James. See "Basil Wright," q.v.

TANNER, Nancy. See "Basil Wright," q.v.

TANNICLIFF, William. "William Teanneclift" was a private enrolled by Ensign Alexander Truman on July 8, 1776, for continental service, Maryland Line [Ref: D-38]. The estate of one "William Tannicliff" was probated on Nov. 3, 1781 [Ref: ZE-179].

TANNIHILL, James (1705-1780). Took the Oath of Allegiance before the Hon. William Berry in 1778 [Ref: O-259, R-66, which spelled the name "Tawnihill"]. The estate of "James Tannehill, Sr." was probated on Dec. 12, 1780 by William Tannihill [Ref: ZE-179, which also spelled the name "Tannahill"].

TANNIHILL, James. Private (draft), continental service, 1781 [Ref: D-382]. Took the Oath of Allegiance before the Hon. Christopher Lowndes in 1778 [Ref: O-286, which spelled the name "Tannehill"].

TANNIHILL, William. See "James Tannihill,"q.v.

TANNIHILL, Zachariah. Sergeant, 3rd Maryland Line, enlisted Jan. 29, 1776 [Ref: D-9, which spelled the name "Zacha. Tannahill"].
TAPLEY, Captain. Commander of the brig *Royal* who administered the Oath of Allegiance to his crew in 1778 and his return was filed in court by the Hon. Thomas Gantt, Jr. in 1778 [Ref: O-305, W-4648 (Box 4, folder 15)].
TARMAN, Henrietta. See "William Taylor," q.v.
TARMAN, Henry. Private, 3rd Maryland Line, 1778-1779 [Ref: D-170].
TARMAN, Richard Jr. Private, Maryland Line, 1781 [Ref: D-412]. One Richard Tarman married Ann Hopkins by license dated May 30, 1795, and one Richard Tarman married Margaret Brant by license dated Feb. 12, 1795 [Ref: ZB-211].
TARMAN, Richard Sr. Private, Maryland Line, 1781 [Ref: D-412].
TARMAN, Susannah. See "John Albee," q.v.
TASCO, Richard. Private, 3rd Maryland Line, Capt. Horatio Clagett's Company, 1779-1781 [Ref: D-295, D-354].
TASKER, Elizabeth. See "Christopher Lowndes," q.v.
TASKER, Nehemiah. See "Nehemiah Jackson," q.v.
TATE, James. Private, Militia; participated in capturing an enemy boat and crew on Apr. 17, 1781 [Ref: M-209]. Private, Select Militia, Upper Battalion, June 12, 1781 [Ref: S-6636 (Box 27, folder 82B)]. Took the Oath of Allegiance before the Hon. James Beck in 1778 [Ref: O-253, which spelled the name "James Taitt"].
TAYLOR, ----. See "Jacob Duvall," q.v.
TAYLOR, Alis. See "Edward Mahoney," q.v.
TAYLOR, Ann. See "Nathaniel O'Neal" and "William Stephens," q.v.
TAYLOR, Benjamin. Sergeant, 11th Militia Battalion, Capt. Hezekiah Wheeler's Company. Apr., 1781 [Ref: L-19970 (Box 6, folder 21)]. Took the Oath of Allegiance before the Hon. William Lyles, Jr. in 1778 [Ref: O-290]. The estate of one Benjamin Taylor was probated on Mar. 12, 1805 [Ref: ZE-180].
TAYLOR, Edward. Private, 2nd Maryland Line, 1778 [Ref: D-189]. One Edward Taylor married Mary Stone by license dated Jan. 13, 1784 [Ref: ZB-212].
TAYLOR, Eleanor. See "Benjamin Boyd," q.v.
TAYLOR, Elizabeth. See "John Igleheart," q.v.
TAYLOR, George. Private, 2nd Maryland Line, Capt. Alexander Truman's Company, 1782 [Ref: D-440].
TAYLOR, Griffith. Private, 3rd Maryland Line, enlisted Apr. 20, 1778 and served to at least Nov. 1, 1780 [Ref: D-170].
TAYLOR, John. Private, enrolled by Lt. John M. Burgess, Lower Battalion, on July 20, 1776, for continental service, Maryland Line [Ref: D-35]. Took the Oath of Allegiance before the Hon. Osborn Sprigg in 1778 [Ref: O-306]. One John Taylor married Rebecca Jones by license dated Aug. 23, 1780, a John Taylor married Sarah Hinton by license

dated Feb. 6, 1784, and a John Taylor married Mary Crook by license dated Feb. 16, 1798 [Ref: ZB-212]. The estate of one John Taylor was probated on July 9, 1795 [Ref: ZE-180]. Additional research may be necessary before drawing conclusions.

TAYLOR, Mary Ann. See "Thomas Brown," q.v.

TAYLOR, Priscilla. See "Moses Orme, Jr.," q.v.

TAYLOR, Richard. Private, 2nd Guard, Capt. Henry Hill's Militia Company, Lower Battalion; on duty at Nottingham on the Patuxent, Apr. 12, 1781 [Ref: L-19970 (Box 6, folder 21)]. Took the Oath of Allegiance before the Hon. Truman Skinner in 1778 [Ref: O-299]. This or perhaps another Richard Taylor was a private in the Maryland Line (substitute) who was discharged on Dec. 3, 1781 [Ref: I-10]. Also, one "Richard Taylor, a substitute from Prince George's County, was paid fourteen pounds, eighteen shillings, and four pence of the bills emitted under the Act for the emission of Bills of Credit" on Feb. 22, 1782 [Ref: I-83].

TAYLOR, Robert 2nd. Sergeant, 2nd Maryland Line, Capt. Alexander Truman's Company, 1782 [Ref: D-439].

TAYLOR, Sarah. See "Thomas Brown" and "Benjamin Estep," q.v.

TAYLOR, Snowden. Private, 3rd Maryland Line, 1777, and discharged Dec. 6, 1779 [Ref: D-169].

TAYLOR, Thomas. There were several men with this name who served in the Maryland Line. One Thomas Taylor was a private, 2nd Maryland Line, 1778, and another Thomas Taylor was a private, 3rd Maryland Line, 1777-1780 [Ref: D-169, D-170, D-412]. One Thomas Taylor married Mary Grimes by license dated Dec. 21, 1785, and a Thomas Taylor married Charlotte Grimes by license dated May 22, 1804, in Prince George's County [Ref: ZB-213]. The estate of one Thomas Taylor was probated on Oct. 15, 1830 [Ref: ZE-180]. Additional research may be necessary before drawing conclusions.

TAYLOR, Verlinda. See "Moses Orme, Jr.," q.v.

TAYLOR, William. Private, 1st Guard, Capt. Henry Hill's Militia Company, Lower Battalion; on duty at Nottingham on the Patuxent, Apr. 12, 1781 [Ref: L-19970 (Box 6, folder 21)]. Took the Oath of Allegiance before the Hon. Truman Skinner in 1778 [Ref: O-298]. Served on a Grand Jury in 1777 [Ref: Z-23]. One William Taylor married Henrietta Tarman by license dated Jan. 9, 1794 [Ref: ZB-213]. The estate of one William Taylor was probated on Mar. 7, 1810 [Ref: ZE-180].

TAYMAN, Benjamin. Private, 6th Maryland Line, enlisted on July 1, 1778, and was reported as "dead or deserted" (no date was given). [Ref: D-252, which listed the name "Benja. Taymon"]. The estate of "Benjamin Tayman" was probated on Jan. 13, 1796 [Ref: ZE-180].

TENANT, James. Private (substitute), Maryland Line, discharged on Dec. 3, 1781 [Ref: D-412, I-10].

TENANT, Thomas. Took the Oath of Allegiance before the Hon. William Berry in 1778 [Ref: O-258].
TENNALLY (TENLEY), Charles. Took the Oath of Allegiance before the Hon. Thomas Clagett in 1778 [Ref: O-265].
TENNALLY, John (1749-   ). Took the Oath of Allegiance before the Hon. Thomas Clagett in 1778 [Ref: O-266, R-13]. Ensign, Middle Battalion, May 1, 1778, Capt. Michael Lowe's Company. Second Lieutenant, May 24, 1779 [Ref: R-13, M-129, E-63, which latter source spelled the name "Tinnerly" and E-414, which mistakenly listed the captain's name as "Michael Lower" and Ref: N-36, which mistakenly spelled the name "Timerly"].
TENNALLY, Josias. Took the Oath of Allegiance before the Hon. Thomas Clagett in 1778 [Ref: O-264].
TENNALLY, William (1747-   ). Took the Oath of Allegiance (made his "X" mark) before the Hon. Thomas Clagett in 1778 [Ref: O-266].
THOMAS, Alexander. Took the Oath of Allegiance (made his "A" mark) before the Hon. Thomas Gantt, Jr. in 1778 [Ref: O-305, W-4648 (Box 4, folder 15)].
THOMAS, Anthony. Private, Flying Camp, 1776, from Frederick County [Ref: D-46]. One Anthony Thomas married ---- Sassell [Scissell?] by license dated Jan. 30, 1782, in Prince George's County [Ref: ZB-214].
THOMAS Caleb. Private (draft), Maryland Line, 1781, from Charles County [Ref: D-376]. One Caleb Thomas married Mary Cave by license dated Dec. 29, 1784, in Prince George's County [Ref: ZB-214].
THOMAS, Cornelia. See "Thomas Lansdale," q.v.
THOMAS, Elizabeth. See "William Tong" and "John Thomas" and "Philip Siscill" and "Nathan Walker," q.v.
THOMAS, Henry. See "John Thomas," q.v.
THOMAS, John. Corporal, 2nd Maryland Line, Capt. Alexander Truman's Company, 1782 [Ref: D-439, which listed him as "John Thomas 1st"]. One John Thomas, son of William and Elizabeth, was born on June 7, 1736, and another John Thomas, son of Henry and Lucey, was born on July 17, 1762 [Ref: ZC-70]. See "Thomas Lansdale," q.v.
THOMAS, Lucey. See "John Thomas," q.v.
THOMAS, Philip. See "Thomas Lansdale," q.v.
THOMAS, Thomas. Took the Oath of Allegiance before the Hon. Christopher Lowndes in 1778 [Ref: O-288]. Private, 3rd Maryland Line, 1778-1780 [Ref: D-170, D-171].
THOMAS, William. See "John Thomas," q.v.
THOMPSON, Charles. Private, 1st Maryland Line, who was paid for his services "in cloathing" on Apr. 17, 1779 [Ref: E-351]. Private, Select Militia, Capt. Hezekiah Wheeler's Company, July 14, 1781 [Ref: S-6636 (Box 31, folder 5)].
THOMPSON, Clark. Private, Capt. Richard Stonestreet's Militia Company, 11th Battalion, 1782 [Ref: L-19970 (Box 6, folder 21)].

THOMPSON, Electious (1755, Prince George's County, Maryland - Dec. 30, 1840, Morgan County, Alabama). "Electious Thompson" applied for pension (S32017) on Aug. 27, 1832, in Morgan County, Alabama, stating he was born in Prince George's County, Maryland and lived in St. Mary's County at the time of his enlistment in the Maryland Line. After the war he moved to Loudoun County, Virginia, then to North Carolina, then to Floyd County, Kentucky, and finally to Alabama. His widow Martha made affidavit on Mar. 26, 1841 that Electious had died on Dec. 30, 1840. She had also applied for pension as the former widow of Francis Holley (R10549) who served in the North Carolina Line [Ref: P-3473]. "Elexis Thompson" took the Oath of Allegiance before the Hon. Christopher Lowndes in 1778 [Ref: O-288]. "Electius Thompson" married (1) Mary Elizabeth Alexander by license dated Aug. 14, 1780, in Prince George's County, and (2) Martha (Sherrell) Holly [Ref: X-2922, ZB-216].

THOMPSON, Francis. Private, 2nd Maryland Line, Capt. Patrick Sim's Company, 1776 [Ref: D-8].

THOMPSON, James. There were several men with this name who served in the Maryland Line, 1777-1780 [Ref: D-6, D-50, D-168, D-412]. One "James Fraser Thompson" married Sarah Moore by license dated June 5, 1778, in Prince George's County [Ref: ZB-216]. Additional research may be necessary before drawing conclusions.

THOMPSON, John. There were several men with this name in the 1776 census of Prince George's County: "John Thompson" was aged 60, "John Thompson, Sr." was aged 67, and "John Thompson, Jr." was aged 40 [Ref: R-34, R-45, R-78]. One "John Thomson" took the Oath of Allegiance before the Hon. Osborn Sprigg in 1778 [Ref: O-306]. One "John Thompson" took the Oath of Allegiance before the Hon. Christopher Lowndes in 1778 [Ref: O-285]. John Thompson, son of William and Mary, was born on Sep. 3, 1753 [Ref: ZC-70]. Additional research will be necessary before drawing conclusions.

THOMPSON, Martha. See "Francis Holley" and "Electious Thompson," q.v.

THOMPSON, Mary. See "John Thompson," q.v.

THOMPSON, Richard. Private, Capt. Richard Stonestreet's Militia Company, 11th Battalion, June, 1782 [Ref: L-19970 (Box 6, folder 21)]. One Richard Thompson married Rachel Burgess by license dated Oct. 20, 1779 [Ref: ZB-217].

THOMPSON, Samuel. Private, Capt. Richard Stonestreet's Militia Company, 11th Battalion, June, 1782 [Ref: L-19970 (Box 6, folder 21)]. One Samuel Thompson married Ann Walker by license dated Feb. 10, 1790 [Ref: ZB-217].

THOMPSON, William. Took the Oath of Allegiance before the Hon. Truman Skinner in 1778 [Ref: O-297]. Private, 1st Guard, Capt. Henry Hill's Company, Lower Battalion, Militia, 1781; on duty at Nottingham

297

on the Patuxent, Apr. 12, 1781 [Ref: L-19970, which spelled his name "Tomson"]. See "John Thompson," q.v.
THOMPSON, William (1738-   ). Took the Oath of Allegiance before the Hon. Osborn Sprigg in 1778 [Ref: O-306, R-78].
THOMSON, Lettice. See "Joseph Sim," q.v.
THORN, Benjamin (1733-   ). Took the Oath of Allegiance (made his "X" mark) before the Hon. Thomas Clagett in 1778 [Ref: O-267, R-76].
THORN, Cassandra. See "Thomas Thorn," q.v.
THORN, Eleanor. See "Thomas Thorn," q.v.
THORN, Ephraim (1733-1779). Took the Oath of Allegiance before the Hon. Christopher Lowndes in 1778 [Ref: O-284, R-24]. The estate of Ephraim Thorn was probated on Oct. 25, 1779 [Ref: ZE-182].
THORN, Henry. Took the Oath of Allegiance before the Hon. Christopher Lowndes in 1778 [Ref: O-284]. One Henry Thorn married Elizabeth Wilson by license dated May 29, 1779 [Ref: ZB-217]. The estate of one Henry Thorn was probated on June 25, 1788 [Ref: ZE-182]. See "Zachariah Thorn," q.v.
THORN, Hezekiah. See "Thomas Thorn," q.v.
THORN, James. Took the Oath of Allegiance before the Hon. Thomas Clagett in 1778 [Ref: O-268]. The estate of one James Thorn was probated on Mar. 1, 1781 (date of inventory) by Susanna Thorn [Ref: ZE-182]. See "Thomas Thorn," q.v.
THORN, Joshua. See "Thomas Thorn," q.v.
THORN, Martha. See "Zachariah Thorn," q.v.
THORN, Mary. See "Henry Thorn," q.v.
THORN, Rachel. See "Thomas Thorn," q.v.
THORN, Susanna. See "James Thorn" and "Thomas Thorn" and "John Goddard," q.v.
THORN, Thomas (circa 1730 - died after Sep. 14, 1788). A son of James Thorn (died 1781) and Susanna Thorn (died 1788), Thomas married first to Rachel ---- and had two children, Hezekiah Thorn (born July 3, 1763) and Thomas Thorn (born Feb. 3, 1766). He married second to Cassandra ---- and had these children recorded in the King George's Parish register: Joshua Thorn (born Dec. 9, 1771), Rachel Thorn (born Apr. 10, 1773), William Thorn (born Oct. 20, 1774), and Eleanor Thorn (born Jan. 20, 1776) [Ref: ZC-70, ZC-71, X-2930, ZE-182]. Took the Oath of Allegiance before the Hon. Joshua Beall in 1778 [Ref: O-251, R-20].
THORN, Walter. See "Zachariah Thorn," q.v.
THORN, William. See "Thomas Thorn," q.v.
THORN, Zachariah. Took the Oath of Allegiance (made his "X" mark) before the Hon. Thomas Clagett in 1778 [Ref: O-267]. Zachariah Thorn married Martha ---- by 1768 and had these children listed in the King George's Parish register: Henry Burch Thorn (baptized on Apr. 3, 1768), Walter Thorn (born Aug. 14, 1773), and Zachariah Thorn (born Dec. 25, 1775). [Ref: ZC-71].

THOROUGHGOOD, John. Private, 2nd Maryland Line, 1778; corporal, July 1, 1778; discharged and reenlisted as a sergeant on Jan. 1, 1780 [Ref: D-169]. Reported "defective" in June, 1780, but he was present at the muster on Nov. 1, 1780 [Ref: D-415, D-169].
THRALLS (THRALL), Richard (Apr. 23, 1753, Maryland - July 26, 1835, Virginia). "Richard Thrall" took the Oath of Allegiance before the Hon. Christopher Lowndes in 1778 [Ref: O-285]. The Census of 1776 in Prince George's County noted that "Richard Thrawls refused to give in a list of his family." [Ref: R-89]. He may have lived in Hancock, Maryland at the time of his enlistment and applied for a pension (S6240) on Apr. 23, 1833, in Monongalia County, Virginia, stating he served in the Virginia Line. Richard Thralls married Lucy Mulliken (by license dated Dec. 31, 1787) on Jan. 3, 1788, in King George's Parish, Prince George's County, Maryland [Ref: X-2933, P-3489, P-3490, ZB-217, ZC-71].
TILLEY, Charles. Took the Oath of Allegiance before the Hon. Christopher Lowndes in 1778 [Ref: O-286]. The estate of one Charles Tilley was probated on Sep. 10, 1804 [Ref: ZE-182].
TILLEY, John. Private in the militia in 1776 [Ref: M-207, A-325]. Took the Oath of Allegiance before the Hon. Christopher Lowndes in 1778 [Ref: O-287, which spelled the name "Tilly"]. Constable in Bladensburg Hundred, 1778 [Ref: Z-30]. The estate of one John Tilley was probated on Feb. 2, 1807 [Ref: ZE-182].
TILLEY, Rebecca. See "William Stevens," q.v.
TILLEY, Robert. First Lieutenant, Upper Battalion, Militia, Capt. Sheckell's Company, June 27, 1781 [Ref: H-320]. The estate of one Robert Tilley was probated on Apr. 8, 1794 [Ref: ZE-183].
TILLEY, Thomas Jr. (1751-   ). Private in the militia in 1776 [Ref: M-208, A-325]. Took the Oath of Allegiance before the Hon. Christopher Lowndes in 1778 [Ref: R-74, O-284, which source listed the name as "Thomas Tilly, Jr."]. There was also a "Thomas Tilley" who was aged 48 in 1776 [Ref: R-72]. The estate of one Thomas Tilley was probated on Oct. 4, 1791 [Ref: ZE-183].
TILLEY, William. Private, 4th Maryland Line, Apr. 12, 1778 until Jan. 10, 1780, when he reportedly "deserted" [Ref: D-110, D-135, which source seems to have misspelled his name as "William Filley" on one occasion and "William Lilly" on another].
TILLEY, Zachariah. Took the Oath of Allegiance before the Hon. Christopher Lowndes in 1778 [Ref: O-288]. Private (draft), in continental service, 1781; discharged from the Maryland Line on Dec. 11, 1781 [Ref: D-382, D-412, I-18]. The estate of one Zachariah Tilley was probated on July 15, 1815 [Ref: ZE-183].
TILLS, Samuel (1726-   ). Took the Oath of Allegiance (made his "X" mark) before the Hon. Thomas Clagett in 1778 [Ref: O-269, R-53].

TIPPITTS, Peter. Private, 3rd Maryland Line, Capt. Horatio Clagett's Company, December, 1779 [Ref: D-296].
TODD, Charles. Took the Oath of Allegiance before the Hon. David Craufurd in 1778 [Ref: O-272].
TOMLIN, Hugh. Private, 2nd Maryland Line, Capt. Patrick Sim's Company, 1776 [Ref: D-7, D-168].
TOMPKINS, Jane. See "Joseph Digges," q.v.
TONG, Benjamin. See "William Tong," q.v.
TONG, Elizabeth. See "William Tong," q.v.
TONG, Hiram. See "William Tong," q.v.
TONG, Theodore. See "William Tong," q.v.
TONG, William (Aug. 9, 1756, Prince George's County, Maryland - Feb. 8, 1848, Mount Vernon, Illinois). He applied for pension on Nov. 23, 1833 in Madison County, Missouri, stating he was born in Prince George's County, Maryland and lived there at the time of his enlistment in the Maryland Line. In 1791 he moved to Washington County, Maryland, in 1807 he moved to Ohio County, Kentucky, and in 1819 he moved to Madison County, Missouri. He married Elizabeth Thomas in Washington County, Maryland (marriage bond issued May 18, 1795) and in 1835 he stated he had 22 children and numerous grandchildren and great-grandchildren (no names were given). His widow applied for pension (W1333) on Dec. 4, 1848, aged 73, in Madison County, Missouri, stating that William died on Feb. 8, 1848 in Mount Vernon, Illinois, and they had raised 13 children (no names were given). In 1848 Theodore F. Tong and Mrs. Ann Cooper, of Madison County, Missouri, stated they were children of William Tong by his first wife (no name was given). In 1840 Benjamin O. Tong, of Washington, DC was mentioned, and in 1853 Hiram N. Tong, of Madison County, Missouri, but no relationships were stated. Elizabeth Tong also applied for and received bounty land warrant #26479-160-55 in 1855 [Ref: P-3516]. William Tong took the Oath of Allegiance before the Hon. Thomas Clagett in 1778 [Ref: O-267]. Source X-2955 states William Tong was born on Aug. 8, 1756, and married (1) Eleanor Ford, and (2) Elizabeth Thomas.
TONGUE, Eleanor. See "Daniel Rankins," q.v.
TONGUE, Mary. See "Milburn Coe," q.v.
TOWNLEY, Henry. Private, 3rd Maryland Line, enlisted June 4, 1778, reported missing on Aug. 16, 1780 (at the Battle of Camden) but subsequently rejoined the regiment [Ref: D-170].
TOWNSHEND, Daniel. See "Samuel Townshend, Jr.," q.v.
TOWNSEND, Mary. See "Benjamin Burch," q.v.
TOWNSHEND, Leonard (c1760 - Oct. 8, 1816). Took the Oath of Allegiance before the Hon. Osborn Sprigg in 1778 [Ref: O-306]. He married (1) Eleanor Young, (2) Elizabeth Parker, and (3) Eleanor Gantt [Ref: X-2964, which source mistakenly indicates he took the Oath in

Massachusetts (typographical error), but it was Maryland]. See "Samuel Townshend," q.v.

TOWNSHEND, Samuel (Nov. 4, 1714 - 1804). Took the Oath of Allegiance before the Hon. Truman Skinner in 1778 [Ref: O-297, R-39]. He and wife Ann Piles (1729-1801), and also their son William Townshend (1768-1849), are buried in the Townshend Family Cemetery "located off Route 5 near T. B." [Ref: Y-600, X-2965, which latter source spelled her name "Pyles"]. The estate of Samuel Townshend was probated on Oct. 11, 1804 and was administered by Leonard Townshend in 1805 [Ref: ZE-184]. See "Samuel Townshend, Jr.," q.v.

TOWNSHEND, Samuel Jr. Took the Oath of Allegiance before the Hon. David Craufurd in 1778 [Ref: O-272, which spelled the name "Samuel Townsend, Jr."]. Private, 2nd Guard, Capt. Henry Hill's Militia Company, Lower Battalion; on duty at Nottingham on the Patuxent, Apr. 12, 1781 [Ref: L-19970 (Box 6, folder 21), which listed the name without the "Jr."]. The estate of Samuel Townshend, Jr. was probated by Nov. 23, 1805 by Daniel Townshend, and the estate of Samuel Townshend was administered by Daniel Townshend (et al) in 1808 [Ref: ZE-183, ZE-184]. *Ed. Note:* Unless Samuel and Samuel Jr. died around the same time, there may be a discrepancy here. Additional research may be necessary before drawing conclusions.

TOWNSHEND, Sarah. See "Samuel Bonifant," q.v.

TOWNSHEND, William. See "Samuel Townshend," q.v.

TRACY, Elizabeth. See "John Conner," q.v.

TRACY, William. Private, 6th Maryland Line, enlisted Feb. 26, 1778, and discharged May 13, 1778 [Ref: D-291]. One William Tracy married Mary Scissell by license dated Sep. 18, 1777 [Ref: ZB-220].

TRAMMEL, Dennis (1763, Maryland -   ). Private (substitute), 1780, in continental service, Maryland Line [Ref: D-338, which spelled the name "Dinnis Tramel"]. Private, 3rd Maryland Line, 1782 [Ref: D-450].

TRICE, Mary. See "Alexander Truman," q.v.

TROWELL, William. Took the Oath of Allegiance before the Hon. Thomas Williams in 1778 [Ref: O-302].

TRUMAN, Alexander (c1750, Maryland - 1792, Ohio). Son of Henry Truman and Ann Magruder, of Prince George's County, and grandson of Thomas Truman and Sarah Briscoe. Alexander was an Ensign, 6th Maryland Line, Capt. Alexander H. Magruder's Company, in June, 1776, and Captain, 2nd Maryland Line, from Dec. 10, 1776 to Jan. 1, 1783, when he retired [Ref: D-439, D-479, N-32, D-34, D-38, which spelled his name "Alex. Trueman"]. He married Margaret Reynolds, daughter of William Reynolds (owner of Reynolds Tavern in Annapolis; died testate in 1777) and Mary Howell (second wife of William Reynolds) in Anne Arundel County by license dated May 29, 1781. Their children were Alexander Magruder Truman (who lived in Lafayette County, Missouri in 1836), Thomas Truman, and Mary Ann Truman. Margaret Truman, wife of Alexander, died in 1786. Alexander rejoined the United States Army in June, 1790, and was wounded in a battle with the Indians in November, 1791, in Ohio. He was promoted to major and while on a peace mission back to the Miami Valley of Ohio he was shot and killed by Indians in April, 1792 (about 5 miles west of the present town of Sidney). Guardianships were appointed for his three orphaned children in Maryland and they eventually migrated westward. Mary Ann Truman (1785-1822) and her brothers moved to Kentucky circa 1800 and settled on land granted to them by the Federal government (bounty land warrant #2156-300) due to their father's service. Mary Ann Truman met and married Byrd (or Bird) Rogers, Jr. (1770-1835), a son of Byrd Rogers and Mary Trice, of Virginia, who were in Fayette County, Kentucky in 1800. Byrd Rogers, Sr. died there in February, 1801. Byrd Rogers, Jr. and wife Mary Ann moved to Barren County. They are buried near the main highway intersection at Griderville. Their children were: William Byrd Rogers (1804-1884, who married Nancy Elizabeth Bagby, 1806-1889); Peter Rogers (who died in Charleston, Illinois); Philip Rogers; Mary B. Rogers (who married Dr. Jett and died in 1875); John Rogers; Margaret Rogers (who married John Calvin McFerran); and, Henry M. Rogers. Charles Bagby Rogers (1840-1919) was a son of William Byrd Rogers and a great-grandson of Major Alexander Truman. He was a Confederate soldier under Gen. John Hunt Morgan in the Civil War (War Between the States, 1861-1865) and married Sarah Moss Forbis (1843-1921) in 1863. Their daughter Janie Terry Rogers (1867-1960) married Elmore "Mote" Peden (1865-1941) in 1887 and their son William Henry Peden (1891-1944) married Pearl Eugenia Crenshaw (1892-1976) in 1913. They lived in and around Glasgow, Barren County, Kentucky. Captain (later Major) Alexander Truman was an Original Member of the Society of the Cincinnati in 1783, and that membership has been held since 1986 by his 5th great-grandson Henry Clint Peden, Jr. (born 1946, Baltimore City), now of Bel Air, Harford County, Maryland [Ref: P-3544; *The Draper Manuscripts, Frontier War Papers* (Section 5U, page 105 and more); *Marylanders to Kentucky*, by Henry C. Peden, Jr. (1991), pp. 147-148; *Genealogy of the Pedens of Kentucky, 1756-1986*, by Henry C. Peden, Jr. (1986); *Truman and Related Families of Early Maryland*, by Henry C. Peden, Jr. (1987); *DAR Genealogical Records Committee Report, 1955-1956*, pp. 54-55, at the DAR Library, Washington, DC; *Harry Wright Newman Collection* at the Charles County Community College, Learning Resources Center, LaPlata, Maryland; and, *Historical Register of Officers of the Continental Army, 1775-1783*, by Francis B. Heitman (1914), p. 549, citing *The American State Papers, Indian Affairs*, Vol. I, p. 243]. See "Henry Truman, Jr." and "Edward Truman," q.v.

TRUMAN, Ann. See "James Truman" and "James Somervell," q.v.

TRUMAN, Edward. Took the Oath of Allegiance before the Hon. William Berry in 1778 [Ref: O-259]. He was a son of Henry Truman and a brother of "Alexander Truman," q.v. Edward was born circa 1753 and had a son Edward Truman, Jr. [Ref: Henry C. Peden, Jr.'s *Truman and Related Families of Early Maryland* (1987), p. 34].

TRUMAN, Henry. Took the Oath of Allegiance before the Hon. Alexander Howard Magruder in 1778 [Ref: O-293, which spelled the name "Trueman"]. See "Alexander Truman" and "James Truman" and "Thomas Truman" and "Henry Truman, Jr." and "Edward Truman," q.v.

TRUMAN, Henry Jr. Private, Lower Battalion, Capt. Benjamin Wailes Militia Company; on guard at Magruder's Warehouse on June 8, 1782 [Ref: L-19970 (Box 6, folder 21)]. Son of Henry Truman and brother of "Alexander Truman" and "James Truman," q.v. One Henry Truman married Ann Beavin by license dated Apr. 3, 1790 [Ref: ZB-220].

TRUMAN, James (1742, Prince George's County - Dec. 22, 1789, Charles County, Maryland). A son of Henry Truman and Ann Magruder, he married Elizabeth Gordon (or Eliza Gorden), and daughter Anne Magruder Truman married George Dent. Took the Oath of Allegiance before the Hon. Alexander Howard Magruder in 1778 [Ref: Henry C. Peden, Jr.'s *Truman and Related Families in Early Maryland* (1987), page 25; and O-293, which source spelled the name "Trueman"].

TRUMAN, Jane. See "Alexander Howard Magruder," q.v.

TRUMAN, Margaret. See "Alexander Truman," q.v.

TRUMAN, Mary. See "Alexander Truman," q.v.

TRUMAN, Sarah. See "Alexander Howard Magruder," q.v.

TRUMAN, Thomas (c1744-1777). Son of Henry Truman and Ann Magruder. Captain who served on a General Courts-Martial for the trial of Capt. Richard Bennett Hall, Lieut. Jeremiah Ryley, Lieut. Jonathan Wright, and Lieut. James Mullikin on July 25, 1776, at Upper Marlboro [Ref: A-553]. Justice of the County Court, 1766-1777 [Ref: Dielman-Hayward Files at the Maryland Historical Society, and C-273, which spelled his name "Trueman"]. The estate of "Thomas Truman" was probated on Oct. 21, 1777 [Ref: ZE-184, which also spelled the name "Trueman"]. See *Truman and Related Families of Early Maryland*, by Henry C. Peden, Jr. (1987).

TRUSTY, John. Private, 3rd Maryland Line, 1777-1780 [Ref: D-171]. The estate of one John Trusty was probated on July 24, 1793, in Prince George's County [Ref: ZE-185].

TRUNCHELL, William. Took the Oath of Allegiance before the Hon. Christopher Lowndes in 1778 [Ref: O-285].

TUCKER, Benjamin (1745-   ). Took the Oath of Allegiance before the Hon. Christopher Lowndes in 1778 [Ref: O-284, R-60]. One Benjamin Tucker married Ann Wornald by license dated Feb. 11, 1778, in Prince George's County [Ref: ZB-220]. There was also a Benjamin Tucker who served as a private in the militia of the Lower District of Frederick County (now Montgomery County) in July, 1776 [Ref: D-42].

TUCKER, Edward. See "Hezekiah Speaks," q.v.

TUCKER, Eleanor. See "Hezekiah Speaks," q.v.

TUCKER, Henry. Private, Maryland Line, enlisted Aug. 17, 1781 [Ref: D-404]. The estate of one Henry Tucker was probated on Jan. 24, 1793, in Prince George's County [Ref: ZE-185].

TUCKER, Hester. See "Roby Tucker," q.v.

TUCKER, John. Private, 2nd Guard, in Capt. Henry Hill's Militia Company, Lower Battalion; on duty at Nottingham on the Patuxent, Apr. 12, 1781 [Ref: L-19970 (Box 6, folder 21)]. See "Hezekiah Speaks," q.v.

TUCKER, John. Private, 3rd Guard, Capt. Henry Hill's Militia Company, Lower Battalion; on duty at Nottingham on the Patuxent, Apr. 12, 1781 [Ref: L-19970 (Box 6, folder 21)]. See "Hezekiah Speaks," q.v.

TUCKER, Mary. See "Benjamin Marshall," q.v.

TUCKER, Roby (1753, Maryland - died after Nov. 14, 1837, North Carolina). Took the Oath of Allegiance before the Hon. Christopher Lowndes in 1778 [Ref: O-287, R-59, which spelled his name "Robey Tucker"]. He married (1) Hester ----, and (2) Rachel Robey [Ref: X-2986].

TUCKER, Thomas. Took the Oath of Allegiance before the Hon. Osborn Sprigg in 1778 [Ref: O-308, R-27]. One Thomas Tucker was aged 41 in 1776 and another was aged 64 in 1776 [Ref: R-27, R-30].

TUELL, Henry. Private, Militia, 1776 [Ref: M-208, A-325]. Took the Oath of Allegiance before the Hon. James Beck in 1778 [Ref: O-252].

TUELL, Rachel. See "William Tuell, Jr.," q.v.

TUELL, William (1714-   ). Took the Oath of Allegiance before the Hon. Christopher Lowndes in 1778 [Ref: O-286, R-62].

TUELL, William Jr. (1738 - Oct. 4, 1777). Private, enrolled by Lt. John M. Burgess, Lower Battalion, on July 20, 1776, for the continental service, Maryland Line [Ref: D-35]. His widow (no name was given) reported he was a private in the 3rd Maryland Line when killed at the Battle of Germantown on Oct. 4, 1777 while serving under Capt. Horatio Clagett. She received a disability payment until July 31, 1784, but the reason for stopping it was not stated [Ref: D-634, D-635, K-1814, which listed his name as "Wm. Tuel"]. "William Tuell, Jr." was aged 38 in the 1776 census of Prince George's County, and his wife was named Rachel [Ref: R-68].

TURNBULL, John (1747-   ). Took the Oath of Allegiance before the Hon. Christopher Lowndes in 1778 [Ref: O-282, R-73]. Quartermaster, Upper Battalion, Apr. 8, 1781 [Ref: M-208, M-131, H-172].

TURNER, Abraham. "Abram Turner" was a private in the 2nd Maryland Line from May 24, 1778 until reported dead on Sep. 30, 1778 [Ref: D-

169, D-320]. There was an "Abraham Turner" who married Rebecca Sadler by license dated Nov. 27, 1781 [Ref: ZB-221].

TURNER, Amelia. See "Christopher Parrott," q.v.

TURNER, Ann. See "William Webster, Jr.," q.v.

TURNER, Benjamin (1729-   ). Took the Oath of Allegiance before the Hon. Osborn Sprigg in 1778 [Ref: O-307, R-42].

TURNER, Edmond (1714-1788). Took the Oath of Allegiance before the Hon. Christopher Lowndes in 1778 [Ref: O-284, R-24]. The estate of one Edmond Turner was probated on Oct. 9, 1788 and administered by Joseph Queen in 1788, 1790 and 1801 [Ref: ZE-185].

TURNER, Edward. See "John Turner," q.v.

TURNER, Elisha (1750-   ). Took the Oath of Allegiance before the Hon. Truman Skinner in 1778 [Ref: O-299, R-39]. Private, 2nd Guard, Capt. Henry Hill's Militia Company, Lower Battalion; on duty at Nottingham on the Patuxent, Apr. 12, 1781 [Ref: L-19970 (Box 6, folder 21)].

TURNER, Elizabeth. See "John Turner," q.v.

TURNER, Jeremiah. Took the Oath of Allegiance before the Hon. James Beck in 1778 [Ref: O-256]. On Aug. 20, 1781, a petition to the Governor about Jeremiah Turner is included in the records of the Council of Maryland, as follows: "Humbly sheweth -- As a Draughted Man Your Petitioner begs leave to Represent to your Excellency his Situation and Circumstances, now at present depending (to wit) he being a Married Man and having the care and Management for three Orphans, who are Minors, whose Concern is Pritty considerable, and should he be forced from them and his family they must unavoidably suffer greatly beyond Comprehention, as there is near Twenty slaves under his direction, the Crop and Stock must Principly be lost in his Absence, therefore he begs your Excellency will favourably hear his and the familys Grievance, & redress them for which favour he will forever be in Duty Bound to Pray &c. We whose Names are hereunto subscribed do recommend to your Honours the above Petitioner case to bear a Preportion to the Representation above -- and clear from any Dissemulation or Disaffection to our Cause, and that his an industrious Diligent Honest Man." Signed by Thomas Beall, Thomas G. Watkins, Archibald Elson, and Resin Beall. [Ref: H-431, H-432, Q-418].

TURNER, Jesse. Private, Capt. Alexander H. Magruder's Militia Company, Lower Battalion; on duty guarding Magruder's Warehouse in the spring of 1782 [Ref: L-19970 (Box 6, folder 21)]. Private, Select Militia, Capt. Hezekiah Wheeler's Company, July 14, 1781 [Ref: S-6636 (Box 31, folder 5)]. Took the Oath of Allegiance before the Hon. Fielder Bowie in 1778 [Ref: O-304, W-4648 (Box 4, folder 15)].

TURNER, John. Two men with this name took the Oath of Allegiance before the Hon. James Beck in 1778 [Ref: O-255, O-256]. One John Turner was aged 38 in 1776 [Ref: R-47]. There were also two John Turners in Queen Anne's Parish, one of whom was deceased by 1777 (account filed). One John Turner was born on Mar. 29, 1715 (son of Edward and Susanna Turner) and the other was born on Mar. 3, 1720/1 (son of John Jr. and Elizabeth Turner). [Ref: ZC-194]. Additional research may be necessary before drawing conclusions.

TURNER, Jonathan (1740-   ). Took the Oath of Allegiance before the Hon. Thomas Clagett in 1778 [Ref: O-266, R-57].

TURNER, Josiah. Took the Oath of Allegiance before the Hon. James Beck in 1778 [Ref: O-256].

TURNER, Philip. Ensign, Upper Battalion, June 24, 1780, Capt. James Mullikin's Militia Company [Ref: M-131, F-203]. Took the Oath of Allegiance before the Hon. James Mullikin in 1778 [Ref: O-296]. Served on a Grand Jury in 1778 [Ref: Z-90]. One Philip Turner married Rachel Williams by license dated Sep. 14, 1787 [Ref: ZB-221]. The estate of one Philip Turner was probated on May 21, 1796 [Ref: ZE-185]. See "Thomas Williams," q.v.

TURNER, Rachel. See "Philip Turner" and "Thomas Williams," q.v.

TURNER, Richard. Private, 3rd Maryland Line, enlisted on Apr. 28, 1777; corporal, Mar. 16, 1778; sergeant, Aug. 29, 1778; and was taken prisoner on Aug. 16, 1780 (at the Battle of Camden). [Ref: D-170]. The estate of one Richard Turner was probated on Mar. 10, 1794, in Prince George's County [Ref: ZE-186].

TURNER, Susanna. See "John Turner," q.v.

TURNER, William (1749-   ). Took the Oath of Allegiance before the Hon. Thomas Clagett in 1778 [Ref: O-265, R-41]. Private, Militia; participated in capturing an enemy boat and crew on Apr. 17, 1781 [Ref: M-209]. Private, Select Militia, Upper Battalion, June 12, 1781 [Ref: S-6636 (Box 27, folder 82B)]. Private (draft), Maryland Line, continental service, 1781 [Ref: D-382]. One William Turner married Dorcas Batt by license dated Feb. 21, 1784 [Ref: ZB-222].

TURTIN (TURTON), John (1745-   ). Private, 2nd Guard, Capt. Henry Hill's Militia Company, Lower Battalion; on duty at Nottingham on the Patuxent, Apr. 12, 1781 [Ref: L-19970, R-6].

TYLER, Edward (Mar. 2, 175? - 1825). Son of Robert and Mary Tyler [Ref: ZC-194]. Private, 2nd Maryland Line, enlisted on Jan. 10, 1778; corporal, May 15, 1778; and discharged on Jan. 10, 1780 [Ref: D-169, which spelled his name "Tiler"]. The estate of one Edward Tyler was probated on Aug. 25, 1825 [Ref: ZE-186].

TYLER, Eleanor. See "Robert Tyler," q.v.

TYLER, Elizabeth. See "Humphrey Belt," q.v.

TYLER, Henrietta. See "Robert Tyler," q.v.

TYLER, John (Aug. 19, 1759 -   ). Son of Robert and Mary Tyler [Ref: ZC-194]. Took the Oath of Allegiance before the Hon. Thomas Williams in 1778 [Ref: O-302].

TYLER, John, of Samuel. Private, Select Militia, Upper Battalion, June 12, 1781 [Ref: S-6636 (Box 27, folder 82B)].

TYLER, Mary. See "John Tyler" and "Edward Tyler" and "Thomas Tyler" and "William Tyler," q.v.

TYLER, Millicent. See "Colmore Beanes" and Robert Tyler," q.v.

TYLER, Priscilla. See "Richard Forster," q.v.

TYLER, Richard. Private (substitute), continental service, 1781, Maryland Line [Ref: D-382].

TYLER, Robert (Nov. 5, 1727 - died "on or about" Dec. 14, 1777). A son of Robert Tyler (1704-1741) and Mary Wade, Robert married Eleanor Bradley in 1759 and had two children, Robert Bradley Tyler and Millicent Beanes [Ref: U-846]. Served as a Delegate to the Maryland Convention, 1774-1776, Committee of Correspondence, 1774, and Committee of Observation, 1775. He was a Lieutenant Colonel, 25th Battalion, on Jan. 13, 1776, and Colonel, Upper Battalion, from July 9, 1776 to at least Sep. 11, 1777 [Ref: A-3, U-70, U-72, M-131, C-369, U-846, ZE-187]. Source X-3003 stated that Robert's second wife was Henrietta ----, but this source may have him confused with "Robert Bradley Tyler," q.v., whose wife was Henrietta Beanes unless, of course, it is a different Henrietta. Additional research may be necessary before drawing conclusions.

TYLER, Robert Sr. Took the Oath of Allegiance before the Hon. James Beck in 1778 [Ref: O-255]. See "John Tyler" and "Edward Tyler" and "Thomas Tyler" and "William Tyler," q.v. q.v.

TYLER, Robert Bradley (July 1, 1759 - 1793). Son of Robert Tyler, Jr. and Elinor Bradley, he married (1) Henrietta Beanes by license dated Dec. 1, 1779, and (2) Dryden Gorden Belt by license dated Mar. 17, 1783 [Ref: U-846, ZB-222, ZC-195]. Served as a Captain, Upper Battalion, June 27, 1781 [Ref: M-131, O-401, H-320, D-412]. Took the Oath of Allegiance before the Hon. James Mullikin in 1778 [Ref: O-296]. Source X-3003 states he was a private, but "Robert B. Tyler" was commissioned a captain by the Council of Maryland in 1781 [Ref: G-492]. The estate of Robert Bradley Tyler was probated on Feb. 23, 1793 [Ref: ZE-187].

TYLER, Samuel (Jan. 22, 1737 - Oct. 1, 1805). "Samuel Tyler, Esquire, aged 68, of Prince George's County, 'A Revolutionary Patriot,' appointed Register of Wills for Prince George's County by Act of Legislature, in 1777, died on Oct. 1, 1805 [Ref: D-634, D-635, V-1937 (Volume 25, No. 2, p. 58, citing a newspaper article dated Oct. 11, 1805)]. Samuel Tyler married Susanna Duvall on Feb. 21, 1762 [Ref: ZC-195]. Another Samuel Tyler married Virlinda Riddle by license dated Jan. 19, 1782, and a Samuel Tyler married Susanna Waters by license dated Dec. 25, 1783, in Prince George's County [Ref: ZB-222]. The estate of Samuel Tyler was probated on Oct. 29, 1805 [Ref: ZE-187].

TYLER, Susanna. See "Gabriel Duvall" and "Samuel D. Beck," q.v.

307

TYLER, Thomas (Oct. 3, 1749 -   ). Son of Robert and Mary Tyler [Ref: ZC-195]. Took the Oath of Allegiance before the Hon. James Beck in 1778 [Ref: O-255].
TYLER, William (Aug. 20, 1733 -   ). Son of Robert Jr. and Mary Tyler [Ref: ZC-195]. Took the Oath of Allegiance before the Hon. Thomas Williams in 1778 [Ref: O-302].
TYNDOLL, Samuel. Took the Oath of Allegiance before the Hon. Fielder Bowie in 1778 [Ref: W-4648 (Box 4, folder 15); however, this name was inadvertently omitted from the list in Ref: O-304].
UNDERWOOD, William. Private, Capt. Hezekiah Wheeler's Company, 11th Militia Battalion, April, 1781 [Ref: L-19970 (Box 6, folder 21)]. The estate of William Underwood was probated on Aug. 30, 1788 [Ref: ZE-187].
UNFUG, Irene Beall. See "Zachariah Berry," q.v.
UPTON, Eleanor. See "Dominick Havener," q.v.
UPTON, Elizabeth. See "Hilliary Lanham," q.v.
UPTON, George. Took the Oath of Allegiance before the Hon. Osborn Sprigg in 1778 [Ref: O-300]. One George Upton married Elizabeth Pickens by license dated Jan. 6, 1778 [Ref: ZB-223].
UPTON, Keziah. See "John King," q.v.
UPTON, Sarah. See "Francis Wheat" and "Benjamin Marshall," q.v.
UPTON, Thomas (1754-1807). Took the Oath of Allegiance before the Hon. Osborn Sprigg in 1778 [Ref: O-300, R-64]. One Thomas Upton married Priscilla Mitchell by license dated Feb. 19, 1798 [Ref: ZB-223]. The estate of one Thomas Upton was probated on Dec. 31, 1807 [Ref: ZE-187].
URQUEHART, William. Took the Oath of Allegiance before the Hon. David Craufurd in 1778 [Ref: O-271]. The estate of one "William Urquhart" was probated on Nov. 15, 1778 [Ref: ZE-187, which source also listed the name as "Urguhart" and "Urquart"].
URQUHART, Andrew. Private, 3rd Maryland Line, 1777 [Ref: D-172].
USHER, William. On Aug. 19, 1780, the Council of Maryland determined that "William Usher, of Prince George's County, has been adjudged altogether unfit for military service and [is] therefore returned.... and ought not be admitted to the credit of the county." [Ref: F-258]. The County Lieutenant responded on Aug. 28, 1780, stating "William Ussher was a substitute I passed. I thought him rather old, but finding from the information of those who knew him that he had always been a healthy hearty man, I lookt on him as a man that might be usefull in the Army." [Ref: G-63].
UTCHERSON, Edward. Private, Capt. Richard Stonestreet's Militia Company, 11th Battalion, June, 1782 [Ref: L-19970 (Box 6, folder 21)]. See "Edward Atcheson," q.v.

UTCHERSON, James. Private, Capt. Richard Stonestreet's Militia Company, 11th Battalion, June, 1782 [Ref: L-19970 (Box 6, folder 21)]. See "James Atcheson," q.v.
VAN BUSKIRK, Margaret. See "Henry Franks," q.v.
VAN HORN, Cornelia. See "Thomas Lancaster Lansdale," q.v.
VANE, John. Private, Northern Detachment, 3rd Maryland Line, Capt. Horatio Clagett's Company, 1783 [Ref: D-501].
VAUGHAN, Susanna. See "Zadock Brashears," q.v.
VEACH (VEITCH), John (June 21, 1732 - Sep. 11, 1784). Private, 2nd Maryland Line, Capt. Patrick Sim's Company, 1776 [Ref: D-8]. Took the Oath of Allegiance before the Hon. Christopher Lowndes in 1778 [Ref: O-283]. John Veach married Mary Conn [Ref: X-3048]. His estate was probated on Feb. 14, 1785, in Prince George's County [Ref: ZE-188]. Also see Laurence R. Guthrie's *We Veitches, Veatches, Veaches, Veeches* (Redmond, Oregon: 1974).
VERMILLION, Ann. See "Burch Vermillion," q.v.
VERMILLION, Benjamin. Private, 2nd Maryland Line, Capt. Patrick Sim's Company, 1776 [Ref: D-8]. One Benjamin Vermillion married Priscilla Farr by license dated Jan. 8, 1787 [Ref: ZB-224].
VERMILLION, Burch. Took the Oath of Allegiance before the Hon. Thomas Clagett in 1778 [Ref: O-267]. Source X-3050 lists Francis Burch Vermillion (c1758, Maryland - c1842, Missouri) who rendered patriotic service in Maryland. If this is the same person, he was married to (1) Ann Wood, (2) Ann Williams, and (3) Nancy Griffith. "Robert Virmilion" was born on Mar. 26, 1785, son of Burch and Ann, of King George's Parish in Prince George's County, Maryland [Ref: ZC-74].
VERMILLION, Edward (Howard?). Took the Oath of Allegiance before the Hon. Osborn Sprigg in 1778 [Ref: O-306, which listed the name as "Howard" but the original list (very light) at the Maryland State Archives (Box 4, folder 29) looked like the name might be "Edward" rather than "Howard"]. Neither one left an estate in Prince George's County. Additional research will be necessary before drawing any conclusions.
VERMILLION, Elizabeth. See "Robert Vermillion," q.v.
VERMILLION, Francis. See "Burch Vermillion," q.v.
VERMILLION, Howard. See "Edward Vermillion," q.v.
VERMILLION, Jacob. Private (drafted), Upper Battalion, Militia, Aug. 21, 1781 [Ref: H-434]. See "Walter Findley," q.v.
VERMILLION, Penelope. See "Francis Burch," q.v.
VERMILLION, Robert (1725-1779). Took the Oath of Allegiance before the Hon. William Lyles, Jr. in 1778 [Ref: O-290, R-58, which spelled the name "Vermilion"]. Robert Vermillion married Elizabeth ---- and had a son Robert born on Jan. 26, 1755 [Ref: ZC-74]. The estate of one Robert Vermillion was probated on June 19, 1779 [Ref: ZE-188]. See "Burch Vermillion," q.v.

309

VERMILLION, Samuel (Apr. 6, 1755, Maryland - Feb. 8, 1837, North Carolina). Private, 1st Maryland Line, Dec. 10, 1776 until Mar. 12, 1777, when he reportedly "deserted, joined," but he was still on the rolls in 1782 [Ref: X-3050, D-7, D-463, D-172, which latter source mistakenly listed him as "Saul Vermillion"].
VERMILLION, Sarah. See "Stephen Whitmore," q.v.
VERMILLION, Uriah (Oct. 4, 1761, Maryland - Oct. 31, 1844, Ohio). Private, Capt. Hezekiah Wheeler's Company, 11th Militia Battalion, April, 1781 [Ref: L-19970 (Box 6, folder 21)]. Uriah married (1) Susannah Barker and (2) Mrs. Elizabeth Shumate Peters [Ref: X-3050].
VERMILLION, William. Private (drafted), Middle Battalion, Militia, Aug. 21, 1781 [Ref: H-434].
VINCENT, Elizabeth. See "Humphrey Belt," q.v.
VINCENT (VINSON), John. Private, enrolled by Ensign Horatio Clagett on July 15, 1776, for continental service, Maryland Line [Ref: D-35]. The estate of "John Vincent" was probated on Mar. 14, 1793, in Prince George's County [Ref: ZE-188].
WADE, Charity. See "Zachariah Wade," q.v.
WADE, George (May 22, 1744 -   ). Son of Zachariah and Mary Wade [Ref: ZC-74]. Took the Oath of Allegiance before the Hon. William Lyles, Jr. in 1778 [Ref: O-289, R-14]. Private, enrolled by Capt. John H. Lowe on July 13, 1776, for continental service, Maryland Line; served in Rawlings' Regiment, 1779 [Ref: D-35, D-180].
WADE, Henry. Private, enrolled by Capt. John H. Lowe on July 13, 1776, for continental service, Maryland Line [Ref: D-35].
WADE, James. Private, 3rd Maryland Line, enlisted on June 2, 1777 and reported missing on Aug. 16, 1780 (at the Battle of Camden). [Ref: D-176]. The estate of one James Wade was probated on Mar. 22, 1794, in Prince George's County [Ref: ZE-188].
WADE, Lancelot (Nov. 11, 1757 -   ). Son of Zachariah and Mary Wade, he married Patty Fenly on Aug. 13, 1786 in King George's Parish [Ref: ZC-74]. "Lanct. Wade" was a private, 1st Maryland Line, enlisted June 4, 1778, and discharged Apr. 5, 1779 [Ref: D-173].
WADE, Mary. See "Robert Tyler," q.v.
WADE, Richard. Private, 3rd Maryland Line, enlisted Feb. 5, 1776 [Ref: D-10]. The estate of one Richard Wade was probated in 1785 [Ref: ZE-189]. Another Richard Wade died in King George's Parish in Prince George's County on Jan. 3, 1798 [Ref: ZC-74].
WADE, Robert (1736-1782?). Took the Oath of Allegiance before the Hon. William Lyles, Jr. in 1778 [Ref: O-289, R-53]. Captain who served on a General Courts-Martial for the trial of Capt. Richard Bennett Hall, Lieut. Jeremiah Ryley, Lieut. Jonathan Wright, and Lieut. James Mullikin on July 25, 1776, at Upper Marlboro [Ref: A-553, M-132, which latter source did not list his first name, but indicated there was a Captain Wade in Prince George's County prior to July 8, 1776]. The

estate of "Robert Wade, Sr." was probated on Jan. 26, 1782, in Prince George's County [Ref: ZE-189].

WADE, Robert Jr. (1726-1793?). Took the Oath of Allegiance before the Hon. Thomas Clagett in 1778 [Ref: O-267, R-84]. The estate of one Robert Wade was probated on Mar. 5, 1793 [Ref: ZE-189].

WADE, Zachariah (1720-   ). Took the Oath of Allegiance before the Hon. William Lyles, Jr. in 1778 [Ref: O-289, R-14]. Zachariah Wade married Nancy Noble on Nov. 3, 17-- [1743?] and had these children listed in the King George's Parish register: George Wade (born May 22, 1744), Zachariah Meeks Wade (born Apr. 4, 1748), Charity Wade (born July 11, 1753), and Lancelot Wade (born Nov. 11, 1757). [Ref: ZC-74].

WADE, Zachariah Meeks (Apr. 4, 1748 -   ). Son of Zachariah and Mary Wade [Ref: ZC-74, which listed his name as "Zacha. Meeks Wade"]. Private, enrolled by Ensign Horatio Clagett on July 15, 1776, for continental service, Maryland Line [Ref: D-35, which listed his name as "Zacharias Meek Wade"]. Took the Oath of Allegiance before the Hon. Thomas Clagett in 1778 [Ref: O-268].

WAHLE, Elizabeth. See "John Mills," q.v.

WAILES, Ann Perrie. See "Benjamin Wailes" and "Samuel Wailes" and "Levin Covington Wailes," q.v.

WAILES, Benjamin. A son of Levin Wailes and Ann Perrie, Benjamin married Susannah ---- [Bussey?] and had the following children: Ann Perrie Wailes (married Thomas Clark), Levin Covington Wailes, John Wailes, Rebecca Wailes (married George Burroughs), George Wailes (married Dorothy Greenfield), Catherine Wailes (married John Estep), Hezekiah Bussey Wailes, and Sarah Ann Wailes (married Thomas Greenfield). [Ref: "The Wailes Family of Early Maryland and Some of Their Relatives on the Eastern and Western Shores," by Ernest C. Allnutt, Jr., Lt. Col. AUS, Ret., *Maryland Genealogical Society Bulletin*, Volume 36, No. 2 (Spring, 1995), pp. 145-196, which contains much more documented information on the Wailes family]. Benjamin served as a Second Lieutenant, Lower Battalion, on Sep. 1, 1777, Capt. William Wilkinson's Company; First Lieutenant, 11th Battalion, May 1, 1778, Capt. John Perry's Company; and Captain, May 24, 1779 [Ref: X-3073, M-132, C-356, E-62, E-414, N-33, which spelled his name "Wales"]. Took the Oath of Allegiance before the Hon. Alexander Howard Magruder in 1778 [Ref: O-293]. He was also appointed by the Council of Maryland to be the Tobacco Inspector at Magruder's Warehouse on Aug. 30, 1780 [Ref: F-271, which spelled his name "Wales"]. The estate of Benjamin Wailes was probated on June 25, 1789 [Ref: ZE-189]. See "Edward Lloyd Wailes" and "Samuel Perrie Wailes" and "Levin Covington Wailes," q.v.

WAILES, Catherine. See "Benjamin Wailes," q.v.

WAILES, Edward Lloyd (Sep. 25, 1758, Prince George's County, Maryland - Jan. 27, 1809, Oglethorpe County, Georgia). A son of Benjamin Wailes and Sarah Howard, he married Sarah Biggs Oden by license dated Mar. 22, 1780, in Prince George's County. Sarah was born in November, 1763 (daughter of Meshac and Elizabeth Oden) and she married Edward Wailes on Mar. 28, 1780. Their children were: Elizabeth Howard Wailes (born Mar. 21, 1781), Sarah Biggs Wailes (born Aug. 28, 1783 and died Dec. 22, 1783), Sarah Ann Wailes (born Mar. 20, 1785), and Harriet Wailes (born June 13, 1787). Edward's widow Sarah received pension W4375 for his service in the Maryland Line and died on June 16, 1840 in Madison County, Georgia, leaving children Harriet Sanders (aged 57, of Madison County) and Sarah Ann Shackelford (aged 49, of Jackson County, Georgia). They both made affidavits in 1845 that their father Edward Lloyd Wailes had lived in Prince George's County, Maryland during the Revolutionary War and also lived there for several years thereafter. In 1796 he moved to Columbia County, Georgia, and in 1797 he moved to Elbert County, the part which later became Madison County. While on a visit to Oglethorpe County, Georgia, he died on Jan. 27, 1809 [Ref: P-3634, ZB-225]. Edward Lloyd Wailes was a Second Lieutenant, 11th Battalion, Capt. Benjamin Wailes' Company, May 24, 1779, and Quartermaster in 1782. After the Revolution he was again on active duty as Adjutant of Prince George's County militia in the Whiskey Rebellion of 1794 in Bedford County, Pennsylvania. He was also Sheriff of the county from 1789 to 1792 [Ref: X-3073, M-132, E-414, N-33, Q-518, L-19970 (Box 6, folder 21), and "The Wailes Family of Early Maryland and Some of Their Relatives on the Eastern and Western Shores," by Ernest C. Allnutt, Jr., Lt. Col. AUS, Ret., *Maryland Genealogical Society Bulletin*, Volume 36, No. 2 (Spring, 1995), pp. 145-196, which contains well documented information on the Wailes family].

WAILES, Elizabeth. See "Edward Lloyd Wailes," q.v.
WAILES, George. Took the Oath of Allegiance (made his "X" mark) before the Hon. Alexander Howard Magruder in 1778 [Ref: O-293]. See "Benjamin Wailes," q.v.
WAILES, Harriet. See "Edward Lloyd Wailes," q.v.
WAILES, Hezekiah. See "Benjamin Wailes" and Samuel Perrie Wailes," q.v.
WAILES, John. See "Benjamin Wailes" and "Samuel Perrie Wailes," q.v.
WAILES, John Perrie. See "Levin Covington Wailes," q.v.
WAILES, Leonard. See "Samuel Perrie Wailes," q.v.
WAILES, Levin Covington. A son of "Capt. Benjamin Wailes," q.v., he married his second cousin Sarah Perrie by license dated Dec. 17, 1789, and had a son John Perrie Wailes and a daughter Anne Perrie Wailes. Levin was a private in the Lower Battalion, Capt. Benjamin Wailes' Company (commanded by his father) and was on active duty May 27, 1782, defending Magruder's Warehouse. "He was too young to sign the Oath of Fidelity and Support in 1778." [Ref: L-19970 (Box 6, folder 21); "The Wailes Family of Early Maryland and Some of Their Relatives on

the Eastern and Western Shore," by Ernest C. Allnutt, Jr., Lt. Col. AUS, Ret., *Maryland Genealogical Society Bulletin*, Volume 36, No. 2 (Spring, 1995), pp. 145-196, which contains well documented information on the Wailes family]. See "Samuel Perrie Wailes" and "Benjamin Wailes," q.v.

WAILES, Rebecca. See "Benjamin Wailes," q.v.

WAILES, Samuel Perrie (c1746-1807). A son of Levin Wailes and Anne Perrie, he married Ann Naylor by license dated Feb. 8, 1783, and had these children: Ann Perrie Wailes (married her cousin Benjamin Naylor and moved to Indiana); Benjamin Wailes (married Sophia Wilson and served in the War of 1812); Samuel Perrie Wailes (married Mary Susanna Wilson, widow, and died in Iowa); Levin Covington Wailes (unmarried; served in the War of 1812); John Perrie Wailes (married Sophia Elizabeth Wilson; died in Kansas); Hezekiah Wailes (unmarried; died in Iowa); and, Leonard Covington (served in War of 1812, married Elizabeth Dougherty and died in Iowa). [Ref: ZB-225, and "The Wailes family of Early Maryland and Some of Their Relatives on the Eastern and Western Shores," by Ernest C. Allnutt, Jr., Lt. Col. AUS, Ret., *Maryland Genealogical Society Bulletin*, Volume 36, No. 2 (Spring, 1995), pp. 145-196, which contains more documented information on the Wailes family]. Samuel Wailes took the Oath of Allegiance before the Hon. Alexander Howard Magruder in 1778 [Ref: O-293]. Served as an Ensign in the militia, Lower Battalion, on Mar. 7, 1780, Capt. Benjamin Wailes' Company, and was on duty guarding Magruder's Warehouse in the spring of 1782 [Ref: M-132, F-210, L-19970 (Box 6, folder 21)]. Also, Source X-3074 states Samuel Perrie Wailes was born circa 1762, married Ann Naylor, served as an ensign in the Revolutionary War, and died some time before Aug. 17, 1810 in Maryland. Actually, he was born circa 1746 and his estate was probated on May 28, 1807. An inventory dated Aug. 18, 1807 listed his name as "Samuel P. Wailes" and the administratrix was Ann Wailes [Ref: ZE-189].

WAILES, Sarah. See "Edward L. Wailes" and "Benjamin Wailes," q.v.

WALKER, Ann. See "Samuel Thompson," q.v.

WALKER, Catharine. See "Richard Walker" and "John Walker," q.v.

WALKER, Charles (baptized May 10, 1752 - died 1794). Son of Isaac and Elizabeth Walker [Ref: ZC-75]. Took the Oath of Allegiance before the Hon. David Craufurd in 1778 [Ref: O-272, R-38]. Source X-3075 stated that Charles Walker was a private in the Maryland Line, married Mrs. Sarah Wilson Ryon, and died after 1790. Actually, he enlisted in the 7th Maryland Line in 1778 and was discharged on Mar. 1, 1779. His estate was probated on June 27, 1794 by Sarah Walker [Ref: D-258, ZE-189].

WALKER, Edward. One Edward Walker was a private, 7th Maryland Line, 1776, one Edward Walker was a private, 2nd Maryland Line, 1777, and another Edward Walker was a private, 6th Maryland Line, 1778-1780 [Ref: D-174, D-256]. Perhaps one of them was "Edward Lanham

Walker" who was born in 1760, son of John and Rachel Walker, of King George Parish in Prince George's County [Ref: ZC-75].

WALKER, Elizabeth. See "William Hyatt" and "Charles Walker," q.v.

WALKER, Francis. See "John Walker," q.v.

WALKER, Isaac (1721-1807). Ensign, 25th Battalion, Sep. 5, 1777, Capt. Josiah Shaw's Company. Second Lieutenant, May 1, 1778, Capt. Thomas Richardson's Company. First Lieutenant, May 24, 1779, Capt. Richard Beall's Company [Ref: M-132, C-363, E-62, E-414, N-34]. Took the Oath of Allegiance before the Hon. Benjamin Hall in 1778 [Ref: O-275, R-54]. His son, Nathan Walker, was a private. They are buried in the Walker Cemetery on the south corner of the Capital Beltway and Kenilworth Avenue [Ref: Y-603, Y-611]. See "Charles Walker," q.v.

WALKER, Isaac. The records of the Council of Maryland on Aug. 21, 1781, include a letter from the County Lieutenant regarding draft problems in the Upper Battalion. He had to draw the class twice and "the lot fell on Isaac Walker, a young single man, rather than on Thomas Williams, a married man." Later, Isaac Walker objected to going into service as he was not drafted the first time and he challenged the legality of the second draft [Ref: H-434]. One Isaac Walker married Eleanor Bradford by license dated July 27, 1790 [Ref: ZB-225]. The estate of one Isaac Walker was probated in 1797, another in 1807, and perhaps another in 1810 [Ref: ZE-189]. Additional research may be necessary before drawing conclusions. See "Charles Walker" and "Thomas Devin Williams," q.v.

WALKER, Isaac Jr. Constable in the Eastern Branch Hundred in 1778 [Ref: Z-30]. See "Isaac Walker," q.v.

WALKER, Isaac, of Joseph. Took the Oath of Allegiance before the Hon. James Beck in 1778 [Ref: O-256]. See "Isaac Walker," q.v.

WALKER, John (Oct. 17, 1758 - 1790?). Son of Francis and Catherine Walker [Ref: ZC-75]. Private, 2nd Maryland Line, Capt. Patrick Sim's Company, 1776. Sergeant, Capt. Murdock's Company, Mar. 15, 1781 [Ref: D-8, D-366]. The estate of one John Walker was probated on Mar. 22, 1794 [Ref: ZE-190]. See "Edward Walker," q.v.

WALKER, Joseph (1722-1783?). Took the Oath of Allegiance before the Hon. James Beck in 1778 [Ref: O-256, R-52, which listed his name as "Joseph Walker, Sr."]. Appointed by the Council of Maryland to be the Auctioner for Prince George's County on Mar. 2, 1781 [Ref: G-334]. He served on the Board of Patuxent Associators and signed a resolution at Nottingham on Apr. 21, 1781 relative to the defence of the rivers of Potomac and Patuxent and the completion of the fort at Drum Point [Ref: K-1814]. The estate of one Joseph Walker was probated by Dec. 12, 1783 (date of inventory) and another was probated on Nov. 1, 1792 [Ref: ZE-190]. Additional research may be necessary before drawing conclusions.

WALKER, Joseph Jr. Took the Oath of Allegiance before the Hon. David Craufurd in 1778 [Ref: O-271]. The estate of one Joseph Walker was probated on Nov. 29, 1803 [Ref: ZE-190]. See "Joseph Walker," q.v.

WALKER, Martha. See "David Craufurd" and "William Laws," q.v.

WALKER, Nathan (1756 - Dec. 28, 1842). Son of Isaac Walker. Private, Upper Battalion, Capt. Thomas Beall's Company, 1778-1779. Buried in the Walker Cemetery [Ref: Y-603, Y-611]. He married (1) Nancy Baggerly, and (2) Elizabeth Thomas [Ref: X-3079]. The estate of Nathan Walker was probated on Feb. 4, 1843 [Ref: ZE-190]. See "Isaac Walker," q.v.

WALKER, Rachel. See "Richard Walker" and "Edward Walker" and "Benjamin Prather," q.v.

WALKER, Rebekah. See "James Beck," q.v.

WALKER, Richard. Ensign, 25th Battalion, May 24, 1779, Capt. Thomas Beall's Company [Ref: M-132, E-414]. Took the Oath of Allegiance before the Hon. James Beck in 1778 [Ref: O-256]. One Richard Walker married Mary Gilpin by license dated Aug. 23, 1778, and another Richard Walker married Catharine Walker by license dated Dec. 24, 1796 [Ref: ZB-226]. The estate of one Richard Walker was probated on Nov. 11, 1807 by Rachel Walker [Ref: ZE-190]. Additional research may be necessary before drawing conclusions.

WALKER, Thomas Jr. Took the Oath of Allegiance (made his "X" mark) before the Hon. Thomas Clagett in 1778 [Ref: O-266]. One Thomas Walker married Mary Littleford by license dated Dec. 24, 1780 [Ref: ZB-226].

WALKER, William (1752-   ). Private (draft), continental service, Maryland Line, 1780 [Ref: D-382, R-78].

WALL, John. Private, 2nd Maryland Line, Capt. Anderson's Company, sick with "fever inflam." in hospital at New Windsor on Dec. 7, 1778 [Ref: D-620]. The estate of one John Wall was probated on Oct. 12, 1813, in Prince George's County [Ref: ZE-190].

WALL, Mary. See "Jesse Ray," q.v.

WALL, Rebecca. See "Basil Ray," q.v.

WALL, Robert Sr. Took the Oath of Allegiance (made his "X" mark) before the Hon. Truman Skinner in 1778 [Ref: O-299]. The estate of one Robert Wall was probated on Apr. 25, 1780 [Ref: ZE-190]. See "Robert Waugh," q.v.

WALL, William. Private, 3rd Guard, Capt. Henry Hill's Militia Company, Lower Battalion; on duty at Nottingham on the Patuxent, Apr. 12, 1781 [Ref: L-19970 (Box 6, folder 21)]. One William Wall married Elizabeth Piles by license dated Jan. 9, 1786 [Ref: ZB-227]. The estate of one William Wall was probated on February 17, 1815 [Ref: ZE-191].

WALLACE, Eleanor L. See "Thomas Clagett," q.v.

WALLACE, Michael. First Surgeon's Mate (and Surgeon), 1st Maryland Line, from Jan. 3, 1776 to some time in 1777 when he resigned due to

315

illness [Ref: D-5, D-173]. One Michael Wallace married Eleanor Contee by license dated Aug. 18, 1780 [Ref: ZB-227].
WALLACE, Richard (1740-   ). Took the Oath of Allegiance before the Hon. Christopher Lowndes in 1778 [Ref: O-286, R-71, which spelled the name "Richard Walace"].
WALLACE, Susanna and Thomas. See "Thomas Walliss," q.v.
WALLINGFORD, Elizabeth. See "Henry Piles," q.v.
WALLINGFORD, George. "George Wallingford" took the Oath of Allegiance before the Hon. Osborn Sprigg in 1778 [Ref: O-307]. "George Warringford" was aged 23 in 1776 [Ref: R-65].
WALLINGFORD, James. Private, 4th Maryland Line, from Jan. 6, 1777 until discharged on Jan. 6, 1780 [Ref: D-178, which listed his name as "Jas. Wallingsford"].
WALLISS, Thomas (baptized June 2, 1751 -   ). Son of Thomas and Susanna Walliss [Ref: ZC-75]. Private, 2nd Maryland Line, 1778 [Ref: D-175, which spelled the name "Wallis"].
WALLS, Andrew. Took the Oath of Allegiance before the Hon. Christopher Lowndes in 1778 [Ref: O-283].
WALLS, Benjamin. See "George Walls," q.v.
WALLS, George (Feb. 14, 1752 - May 11, 1831). He lived in Charles County, Maryland at the time of his enlistment in the Maryland Line, but also served as a private, 2nd Guard, in Capt. Henry Hill's Company, Lower Battalion, Prince George's County Militia, on duty at Nottingham on the Patuxent, Apr. 12, 1781. George married Martha Naylor (born Feb. 14, 1762) in Prince George's County on Mar. 28, 1784, and they had these children, according to her pension application (W8972) on June 21, 1845: Margaret Baden Walls (born Jan. 30, 1787 and married Josiah Wilson on Jan. 30, 1817); Jane N. Walls (born May 23, 1791); William Batson Walls (born July 3, 1793 and died Jan. 29, 1823); George Naylor Walls (born Aug. 22, 1796, married Sarah Club on Jan. 20, 1824, and lived in Prince George's County in 1845); Naylor Davis Walls (born Nov. 12, 1798 and died testate on Jan. 15, 1835); Benjamin Baden Walls (born July 6, 1801, married Elizabeth Harvey on July 30, 1835, had a daughter Martha Ann Rebecca Walls born on June 10, 1836, and he died testate on Sep. 16, 1836); Elizabeth Ann Walls (born Nov. 11, 1803); and, Martha Ann Walls (born Mar. 18, 1807). Also mentioned was Elizabeth Baden (born in September, 1764 and died Sep. 25, 1835), wife of John Baden, but the relationship to George Walls was not stated [Ref: P-3660, L-19970 (Box 6, folder 21)]. The estate of George Walls was probated on June 12, 1831 [Ref: ZE-191].
WALLS, Margaret. See "George Walls," q.v.
WALLS, Martha. See "George Walls," q.v.
WALLS, Naylor. See "George Walls," q.v.
WALLS, Thomas (1745, Maryland -   ). Took the Oath of Allegiance before the Hon. Truman Skinner in 1778 [Ref: O-297, which spelled the

name "Wall"]. Private (substitute), in continental service, Maryland Line, 1780 [Ref: D-338]. On Aug. 19, 1780, the Council of Maryland determined that "Thomas Wall, of Prince George's County, has been adjudged altogether unfit for military service and [is] therefore returned... and ought not be admitted to the credit of the county." [Ref: F-258]. The County Lieutenant then responded on Aug. 28, 1780, stating "Thomas Walls I understood by some persons since I sent him off, that Edward Magruder the head of the class who procured him, gave him 400 pounds more than they had agreed for, to conceal his sore leg from Colonel Addison the field officer who passed him. This has occasioned a dispute with many of the class about paying for him, and as there has been but a small part of the money paid I shall endeavour to prevent any farther payments." [Ref: G-63].

WALLS, William. See "George Walls," q.v.

WALSH, Thomas. Private, 2nd Maryland Line, Capt. Patrick Sim's Company, 1776 [Ref: D-8].

WALTZ, Michael. Private, 2nd Maryland Line, Capt. Patrick Sim's Company, 1776 [Ref: D-8].

WARD, Andrew. Took the Oath of Allegiance before the Hon. Truman Skinner in 1778 [Ref: O-298].

WARD, Benjamin. Private, 3rd Maryland Line, 1781 [Ref: D-395]. One Benjamin Ward married Mary Foard by license dated July 17, 1784 [Ref: ZB-228].

WARD, Innocent. See "John Ward," q.v.

WARD, John. There were several men with this name who served in the Maryland Line [Ref: D-6, D-51, D-412, D-423, D-486, D-660]. One John Ward was baptized in King George's Parish on Aug. 18, 1751, son of John and Innocent Ward, and another Jonathan Ward was born there on May 23, 1751, son of John Ward [Ref: ZC-76]. Additional research may be necessary before drawing conclusions.

WARD, Jonathan. See "John Ward," q.v.

WARD, Thomas. Private, 1st Maryland Line, enlisted May 20, 1778 and discharged on Feb. 14, 1779 [Ref: D-173]. On Feb. 24, 1779 he was paid for his services "in cloathing" [Ref: E-308].

WARE, Hugh. Private, Northern Detachment, 3rd Maryland Line, Capt. Horatio Clagett's Company, 1782-1783 [Ref: D-466, D-502, D-561]. The estate of Hugh Ware was probated on Mar. 14, 1793 [Ref: ZE-191].

WARFIELD, Elizabeth. See "Joseph Wells," q.v.

WARFIELD, John Jr. Took the Oath of Allegiance before the Hon. Fielder Bowie in 1778 [Ref: O-303, W-4648 (Box 4, folder 15)]. One John Warfield married Ann Carrick by license dated Dec. 19, 1784 [Ref: ZB-228].

WARFIELD, Sarah. See "Michael Burgess," q.v.

WARHAM, William. Took the Oath of Allegiance before the Hon. David Craufurd in 1778 [Ref: O-272].

317

WARING, Ann. See "Basil Waring, Jr." and "Basil Waring, Sr." and "Basil Waring 3rd" and "Thomas Gantt" and "Henry Waring," q.v.

WARING, Basil Sr. (1711 - Apr. 15, 1793). Youngest son of Marsham and Henrietta Waring (his first wife), Basil married (1) Henrietta Maria Digges, and had a daughter Henrietta Maria Waring, and (2) Susannah Darnall in 1753 and had these children: Marsham Waring, Elizabeth (Waring) O'Neill, Anne (Waring) (Wharton) Hall, Henry Waring, and Eleanor (Waring) Brooke [Ref: ZA-601, ZA-602]. Took the Oath of Allegiance before the Hon. Benjamin Hall in 1778 [Ref: O-276]. See "Marsham Waring" and "Henry Waring" and James "Waring," q.v.

WARING, Basil Jr. (Nov. 16, 1740? - Mar. 8, 1794?). Son of Thomas Waring and Jane Orford [Ref: ZC-196]. Ensign, 3rd Maryland Line, 1782 [Ref: D-450]. Took the Oath of Allegiance before the Hon. Joshua Beall in 1778 [Ref: O-251]. Basil Waring, Jr. married (1) Anne Gantt, and (2) Ann ---- [Ref: X-3100, which stated he was a lieutenant in the Maryland Line]. There are apparent errors in some records; therefore, it is important to see the information (or misinformation) under "Basil Waring 3rd," q.v. Additional research may be necessary before drawing any conclusions.

WARING, Basil 3rd (Nov. 16, 1740? - c1800?). Only son of Thomas Waring and Elizabeth Offutt (first wife), he married Anne Gantt and had these children: Thomas Waring, Basil Waring, Priscilla (Waring) Gantt, Anne (Waring) Duckett, Jane (Waring) Mullikin, and Edward Gantt Waring [Ref: ZA-610]. "Basil Waring, ye 3d" was a Captain in the 25th Militia Battalion on Mar. 18, 1776 [Ref: M-134, A-260]. There are apparent errors in some records; therefore, it is important to see the information (or misinformation) under "Basil Waring, Jr.," q.v. Additional research may be necessary before drawing any conclusions.

WARING, Clement. The records of the Maryland Council on Sep. 29, 1778, state that "Clement Waring of Prince George's County in the State aforesaid [Maryland] who hath been absent therefrom in parts beyond the Seas for about three years last past and hath lately that is to say within three Months now last past returned into this State, appeared before the Governor and Council and before them did severally take repeat and Subscribe the Oath of Fidelity and Support to this State contained in the Act entitled "An Act to punish Crimes and Misdemeanors & to prevent the Growth of Toryism." [Ref: E-212]. The estate of "Clement H. Waring" was probated on Apr. 7, 1795 [Ref: ZE-192]. See "Henry Waring," q.v.

WARING, Edward. See "Basil Waring 3rd," q.v.

WARING, Eleanor. See "Basil Waring" and "Henry Waring," q.v.

WARING, Elizabeth. See "Robert Bowie" and "Basil Waring" and "Henry Hilleary" and "Henry Waring," q.v.

WARING, Henrietta. See "Basil Waring" and "Henry Waring," q.v.

WARING, Henry (Apr. 19, 1762 - Oct. 11, 1835). Youngest son of Basil Waring, Sr. and Susannah Darnall, he married Henrietta Hall in 1782. She died in 1795 and "is buried with her infant at Mount Pleasant." Henry married Millicent Brooke in 1805 and had these children: Henrietta Maria Susannah (Waring) Young, Eleanor Mary (Waring) Brent, Henry Basil Waring, John Philip Waring, Mary Anne (Waring) Brooke, Elizabeth Anne Waring (became a Visitation nun known as Sister Charles), Anne Maria Waring, Susan F. Waring, Josephine Jane Waring (became a Visitation nun known as Sister Mary Samuel), Matilda Millicent (Waring) (Hill) Hardy, and Clement William Waring [Ref: ZA-603, ZA-604]. "Henry Warring" was a private in the Select Militia, Upper Battalion, on June 12, 1781 [Ref: S-6636 (Box 27, folder 82B)].

WARING, Henry Jr. See "John Waring," q.v.

WARING, James (1755 - Dec. 18, 1813). Took the Oath of Allegiance before the Hon. Thomas Williams in 1778 [Ref: O-302, R-33, which latter source spelled his name "Warring"]. He married Elizabeth Hilleary by license dated Jan. 4, 1787 [Ref: X-3100, ZB-228]. Served with his cousin Marsham Waring in the company commanded by their cousin Basil Waring 3rd during the war [Ref: ZA-602]. The estate of James Waring was probated on Jan. 10, 1814 [Ref: ZE-192].

WARING, James Haddock (1755, Maryland - 1839, Kentucky). Took the Oath of Allegiance before the Hon. Truman Skinner in 1778 [Ref: O-297, which spelled the name "Warring"]. James Haddock Waring married Anne Boone [Ref: X-3100].

WARING, Jane. See "Basil Waring 3rd," q.v.

WARING, John (c1737-1813). Fourth son of Richard Marsham Waring, he married Henrietta Maria Hall circa 1765 and had sons John Waring, Jr. and Henry Waring, Jr. [Ref: ZA-604, ZA-605]. Took the Oath of Allegiance before the Hon. William Lock Weems in 1778 [Ref: O-301]. Served on the Board of Patuxent Associators and signed a resolution at Nottingham on Apr. 21, 1781 relative to the defence of the rivers of Potomac and Patuxent and the completion of the fort at Drum Point [Ref: K-1814]. Served on a Grand Jury in 1777 [Ref: Z-23]. See "John Warren" and "Henry Waring," q.v.

WARING, John Jr. See "John Waring," q.v.

WARING, Josephine. See "Henry Waring," q.v.

WARING, Leonard (1746-1806). A son of Major Francis Waring and grandson of Basil Waring, gent., Leonard was a First Lieutenant in the 11th Militia Battalion on May 1, 1778, Capt. Jesse Hellen's Company [Ref: M-134, E-78, N-32]. He was appointed by the Council of Maryland to be the Tobacco Inspector at Nottingham Warehouse on Oct. 7, 1780 [Ref: F-318, which listed his name as "Leonard Warring"]. First Lieutenant, Militia, Capt. Jesse Hellen's Company; guarded Magruder's Warehouse in the spring of 1782 [Ref: L-19970 (Box 6, folder 21)].

Leonard Waring is buried in the Waring-Hollyday Family Cemetery on the Naylor-Baden Road in Prince George's County [Ref: Y-604, Y-615, citing MS.1616 in the Maryland Historical Society's Manuscript Division]. "Leonard Warring" took the Oath of Allegiance before the Hon. Truman Skinner in 1778 [Ref: O-297]. The estate of Leonard Waring was probated on Feb. 26, 1807 [Ref: ZE-192].

WARING, Marsham (June 4, 1754 - 1812). Only son of Basil Waring, Sr. and Susannah Darnall, he served with his cousin James Waring in the company commanded by their cousin Basil Waring 3rd in the war [Ref: ZA-602]. He also took the Oath of Allegiance before the Hon. Christopher Lowndes in 1778 [Ref: O-286]. The estate of Marsham Waring was probated on June 2, 1812 [Ref: ZE-192].

WARING, Martha. See "Richard Duckett, Jr.," q.v.

WARING, Mary. See "Henry Waring," q.v.

WARING, Matilda. See "Henry Waring," q.v.

WARING, Millicent. See "Henry Waring," q.v.

WARING, Priscilla. See "Basil Waring 3rd," q.v.

WARING, Richard. See "John Waring, Sr.," q.v.

WARING, Susan. See "Henry Waring," q.v.

WARING, Thomas. See "Basil Waring 3rd" and "Basil Waring Jr.," q.v.

WARING, William. See "William Warren," q.v.

WARMAN, Benjamin. Took the Oath of Allegiance before the Hon. Osborn Sprigg in 1778 [Ref: O-307]. One Benjamin Warman married Easter Perry by license dated Mar. 20, 1779 [Ref: ZB-229].

WARMAN, J. H. Took the Oath of Allegiance before the Hon. Osborn Sprigg in 1778 [Ref: O-306].

WARMAN, Thomas C. Took the Oath of Allegiance before the Hon. Osborn Sprigg in 1778 [Ref: O-306]. One Thomas Warman was a lieutenant in Rawlings' Regiment, Maryland Line, who was listed among the exchanged prisoners on Oct. 25, 1780 [Ref: D-616].

WARNER, Samuel. Private, enrolled by Lt. John M. Burgess, Lower Battalion, on July 20, 1776, for continental service, Maryland Line [Ref: D-35].

WARREN, Basil. Private, Select Militia, Capt. Hezekiah Wheeler's Company, July 14, 1781 [Ref: S-6636 (Box 31, folder 5)]. Rendered patriotic service by providing wheat for the military on Dec. 27, 1782 [Ref: Q-425]. See "Basil Waring," q.v.

WARREN, John. Private, enrolled by Capt. John H. Lowe on July 13, 1776, for continental service, Maryland Line [Ref: D-35, which spelled the name "John Worren"]. See "John Waring," q.v.

WARREN, William. Private, enrolled by Capt. John H. Lowe on July 13, 1776, for continental service, Maryland Line [Ref: D-34, which spelled the name "William Worren"].

WARRINGFORD, George. See "George Wallingford," q.v.

WARRIOR, Daniel. Drummer, 2nd Maryland Line, Capt. Alexander Truman's Company, 1782 [Ref: D-439].

WASHINGTON, George. See "Smallwood Acton" and "Anthony Addison" and "Thomas Naydin" and "Thomas Snowden" and "Peter Brown," q.v.

WASTENEY, John (clerk). He rendered patriotic service on Sep. 19, 1781, when the Council of Maryland directed the Western Shore Treasurer to give him money that had been appropriated for the defence of the bay to be delivered to "Stephen Steward," q.v. [Ref: G-617].

WATERS, Arnold. Took the Oath of Allegiance (affirmed) before the Hon. Benjamin Hall in 1778 [Ref: O-275]. The estate of one Arnold Waters was probated on Sep. 11, 1809 [Ref: ZE-193].

WATERS, Elizabeth. See "John Mills" and "Zachariah Mills," q.v.

WATERS, Jacob H. Took the Oath of Allegiance before the Hon. Osborn Sprigg in 1778 [Ref: O-307].

WATERS, James (Dec. 8, 1737 - 1808). Rendered patriotic service and married (1) Anne Dement, and (2) Dradin King [Ref: X-3115].

WATERS, Jane. See "Joseph Owens" and "Mordecai Waters," q.v.

WATERS, Joseph (a Dutchman). Took the Oath of Allegiance before the Hon. George Lee in 1778 [Ref: O-279]. One Joseph Waters was aged 40 in the 1776 census of Prince George's County [Ref: R-81]. One Joseph Waters married Elizabeth Mier by license dated Aug. 25, 1779 [Ref: ZB-230].

WATERS, Mary. See "Thomas Whitehead" and "George Bean," q.v.

WATERS, Mordecai (Mar. 7, 1722 - 1783). Son of Samuel and Jane Waters [Ref: ZC-196]. Took the Oath of Allegiance before the Hon. Osborn Sprigg in 1778 [Ref: O-307]. The estate of one "Mordecia Waters" was probated on Sep. 18, 1783 [Ref: ZE-193].

WATERS, Nicholas. The records of the Council of Maryland stated that on Aug. 14, 1781, "Mr. Nicholas Waters has complained to us of the manner of his being drafted for the 4th class of the Middle Battalion of Prince George's County. He asserts that William Fenly according to his apprehension and a Mr. Club were first fairly draughted, that a second draft for the same class in the manner made was improper. We suspend out opinion until we have a clear state of the facts." [Ref: G-560]. A later entry on Aug. 21, 1781, indicated the name was Walter Findley, rather than William Fenly, and the other draft was Samuel Club. The County Lieutenant also stated that "as I was informed that Waters was a young single man who had some dependance, I appointed him as the person to go, without any peique or partiallity, as I don't know that I ever saw or heard of the young man before." [Ref: H-433, H-434].

WATERS, Plummer. Took the Oath of Allegiance before the Hon. Osborn Sprigg in 1778 [Ref: O-306, which listed the name as "Plimmer Waters," but the original list (very light) at the Maryland State Archives (Box 4,

folder 29) looks like it was "Plummer Waters"]. The estate of one Plummer Waters was probated on Oct. 14, 1824 [Ref: ZE-193].
WATERS, Richard. Surgeon's Mate, 2nd Maryland Line, 1778 [Ref: D-174]. Took the Oath of Allegiance before the Hon. Benjamin Hall in 1778 [Ref: O-274]. Source X-3115 stated that Richard Waters was born 1759/60, married Margaret Hamilton Smith, and died in 1810. It should be noted that the estate of "Richard D. Waters" was probated by July 7, 1807 (date of inventory). [Ref: ZE-193].
WATERS, Richard. Took the Oath of Allegiance (affirmed) before the Hon. Benjamin Hall in 1778 [Ref: O-275]. The estate of one Richard Waters was probated on Sep. 8, 1834 [Ref: ZE-193].
WATERS, Samuel. See "Mordecai Waters," q.v.
WATERS, Susanna. See "Samuel Tyler," q.v.
WATERS, William (1733/4 - 1797). Took the Oath of Allegiance before the Hon. Thomas MacGill in 1778 [Ref: O-291, R-53]. The estate of one William Waters was probated on July 20, 1797 [Ref: ZE-194].
WATERS, William Jr. (Dec. 25, 1751 - Jan. 2, 1817). Source X-3115 stated he rendered patriotic service and married Susannah Magruder, but no such service was found in Prince George's County. Additional research may be necessary before drawing conclusions.
WATERS, York. Private, 2nd Maryland Line, 1780 [Ref: D-175].
WATHEN, Catherine. See "Joseph Edelen, Jr.," q.v.
WATKINS, Hester. See "Jeremiah Igleheart," q.v.
WATKINS, Lucy. See "John Addison," q.v.
WATKINS, Peggy. See "Joseph Wells," q.v.
WATKINS, Thomas Gassaway. Took the Oath of Allegiance before the Hon. James Beck in 1778 [Ref: O-255]. One "Thomas Watkins, Jr." married Elizabeth Sprigg by license dated Jan. 17, 1778, and a "Thomas Watkins" married Lucy Belt by license dated Dec. 6, 1779 [Ref: ZB-230]. The estate of "Thomas G. Watkins" was probated on Oct. 6, 1800 [Ref: ZE-194].
WATKINS, William. Took the Oath of Allegiance before the Hon. Thomas MacGill in 1778 [Ref: O-291].
WATSON, Abraham. Private, Rawlings' Regiment, Maryland Line, enlisted Aug. 26, 1776 [Ref: D-180]. Private, 4th Maryland Line, 1777, and reportedly "deserted" while on furlough on Feb. 1, 1778 [Ref: D-301]. The estate of one Abraham Watson was probated on Mar. 21, 1785 [Ref: ZE-194].
WATSON, Ann. See "Samuel T. Wilson," q.v.
WATSON, Benjamin. Private, Capt. Benjamin Wailes' Militia Company, Lower Battalion; on duty guarding Magruder's Warehouse in the spring of 1782 [Ref: L-19970 (Box 6, folder 21)]. The estate of one Benjamin Watson was probated on Mar. 23, 1812 [Ref: ZE-194]. See "Walter Watson," q.v.
WATSON, Elizabeth. See "Josephus Adams," q.v.

WATSON, James. Took the Oath of Allegiance before the Hon. Osborn Sprigg in 1778 [Ref: O-306]. One James Watson married Sarah Watson by license dated Jan. 17, 1780 [Ref: ZB-231]. The estate of one James Watson was probated on Dec. 8, 1789 [Ref: ZE-194].
WATSON, James Sr. Took the Oath of Allegiance (made his "I" mark) before the Hon. Alexander Howard Magruder in 1778 [Ref: O-293]. The estate of James Watson, Sr. was probated on Nov. 12, 1793 [Ref: ZE-194].
WATSON, James, of William. Private, Capt. Benjamin Wailes' Militia Company, Lower Battalion; on duty guarding Magruder's Warehouse in the spring of 1782 [Ref: L-19970 (Box 6, folder 21)]. One James Watson was a private, 6th Maryland Line, in 1778 [Ref: D-256]. The estate of one James Watson was probated on Sep. 17, 1793 [Ref: ZE-194].
WATSON, John. Private, enrolled by Capt. Alexander H. Magruder, 11th Battalion, July 25, 1776, for continental service, Maryland Line [Ref: D-38]. Took the Oath of Allegiance before the Hon. Alexander Howard Magruder in 1778 [Ref: O-293].
WATSON, Richard. Private, Capt. Jesse Hellen's Militia Company; guarded Magruder's Warehouse in the spring of 1782 [Ref: L-19970 (Box 6, folder 21)].
WATSON, Sarah. See "James Watson," q.v.
WATSON, Susanna. See "Elijah Ellis" and "Leonard King," q.v.
WATSON, Thomas. Private, Capt. Benjamin Wailes' Militia Company, Lower Battalion; on duty guarding Magruder's Warehouse in the spring of 1782 [Ref: L-19970 (Box 6, folder 21)]. One Thomas Watson married Catherine Nutwell by license dated Feb. 11, 1784 [Ref: ZB-232].
WATSON, Walter (1761, Maryland - died between Apr. 1 and Sep. 20, 1855, Virginia). Private (substitute), 1780, in continental service, Maryland Line [Ref: D-338]. Private, 2nd Maryland Line, Capt. William Murdock's Company, Mar. 15, 1781 [Ref: D-366]. Second Corporal, 2nd Guard, Capt. Henry Hill's Militia Company, Lower Battalion; on duty at Nottingham on the Patuxent, Apr. 12, 1781 [Ref: L-19970 (Box 6, folder 21)]. He applied for pension (S41301) in Albemarle County, Virginia, on July 5, 1824, aged 64, with a wife (unnamed) and an unmarried daughter (aged 30), plus a son and other married children (no names were given); his wife died before him. Also mentioned was a Benjamin W. Watson, of Albemarle County, Virginia, but no relationship was stated [Ref: P-3704, X-3120, which latter source stated that Walter Watson married Nancy Naylor]. One Walter Watson married Rachel Stone by license dated Oct. 18, 1779, and a Walter Watson married Ann Naylor by license dated Dec. 23, 1783, in Prince George's County [Ref: ZB-232]. The estate of one Walter Watson was probated on Apr. 25, 1810, in Prince George's County [Ref: ZE-194]. Additional research may be necessary befored drawing conclusions.

WATSON, William. Private, Capt. Jesse Hellen's Militia Company, before May 23, 1782; on duty guarding Magruder's Warehouse in the spring of 1782 [Ref: L-19970 (Box 6, folder 21)]. The estate of William Watson, Sr. was probated in 1802 [Ref: ZE-194].

WATSON, William, of William. Private, Capt. Benjamin Wailes' Militia Company, Lower Battalion; on duty guarding Magruder's Warehouse in the spring of 1782 [Ref: L-19970 (Box 6, folder 21)]. The estate of William Watson, Jr. was probated in 1802 [Ref: ZE-194].

WAUGH, Robert. Took the Oath of Allegiance (made his mark that looked like a pointed "R") before the Hon. Thomas Boyd in 1778 [Ref: O-261]. See "Robert Wall," q.v.

WAYPOLE, Naylor. Private, Capt. Benjamin Wailes' Militia Company, Lower Battalion; on duty guarding Magruder's Warehouse in the spring of 1782 [Ref: L-19970 (Box 6, folder 21)].

WEAKLAND, Ruth. See "John Fearall," q.v.

WEAR, James. Took the Oath of Allegiance before the Hon. Thomas Gantt, Jr. in 1778 [Ref: O-305, W-4648 (Box 4, folder 15)]. James Wear married Sarah Smith by license dated July 19, 1777 [Ref: ZB-232].

WEAVER, Jacob (1744-). Took the Oath of Allegiance before the Hon. Osborn Sprigg in 1778 [Ref: O-307, R-64].

WEBB, Asaph. See "Banks Webb," q.v.

WEBB, Banks (baptized on June 24, 1764, Prince George's County - died after 1820, Clark County, Ohio). Son of Thomas and Rebecca Webb, of King George's Parish [Ref: ZC-76, which spelled his name "Bankes"]. Private (substitute), in continental service, 1780. Private, 2nd Maryland Line, Capt. Murdock's Company, Mar. 15, 1781 [Ref: D-560, D-500, D-432, D-396, D-366, D-338, which latter source stated he was aged 16 in 1780 and born in Maryland]. He applied for pension (S40654) in Clark County, Ohio, on May 25, 1818. In 1820 he stated he was aged 60 with a wife Mary Webb (aged 45) and six children at home: Harriet Webb (aged 12), Noah Webb (aged 9), Asaph Webb (aged 7), Maria Webb (aged 6), Thomas Webb (aged 4), and Manasseh Webb (aged 3). [Ref: P-3715, which listed the name as "Barruck or Bancks or Banks Webb"]. Banks Webb married Mary Bull [Ref: X-3218].

WEBB, Harriet. See "Banks Webb," q.v.

WEBB, Henry. Constable in Nottingham Hundred, 1777-1778 [Ref: Z-3, Z-30].

WEBB, Manasseh. See "Banks Webb," q.v.

WEBB, Maria. See "Banks Webb," q.v.

WEBB, Mary. See "Banks Webb," q.v.

WEBB, Noah. See "Banks Webb," q.v.

WEBB, Priscilla. See "Samuel Downing," q.v.

WEBB, Samuel. Took the Oath of Allegiance (made his "S" mark) before the Hon. Thomas Boyd in 1778 [Ref: O-261].

WEBB, Thomas Sr. (1706-1793?). Took the Oath of Allegiance before the Hon. James Beck in 1778 [Ref: O-254, R-37]. The estate of one Thomas Webb was probated on June 2, 1793 [Ref: ZE-195]. See "Banks Webb" and "Thomas Webb, Jr.," q.v.

WEBB, Thomas Jr. (Sep. 18, 1736 -   ). Son of Thomas Webb and Elizabeth Child [Ref: ZC-196]. Took the Oath of Allegiance before the Hon. James Beck in 1778 [Ref: O-255, R-54, which latter source listed his age as 43 in 1776 census]. See "Thomas Webb, Sr.," q.v.

WEBSTER, Ann. See "John Webster," q.v.

WEBSTER, Elizabeth. See "Butler Marlow Downing" and "Butler Marlow" and "John Webster" and William Webster, Jr.," q.v.

WEBSTER, George (Sep. 29, 1752 -   ). Son of Thomas and Mary Webster [Ref: ZC-77]. Took the Oath of Allegiance before the Hon. Thomas Clagett in 1778 [Ref: O-268].

WEBSTER, James (1737 - died after 1790, Maryland). Took the Oath of Allegiance before the Hon. William Lyles, Jr. in 1778 [Ref: O-290, R-55]. James Webster married Mary Ann Phoebe [sic]. [Ref: X-3133].

WEBSTER, John (Sep. 4, 1735 - Nov. 10, 1783). Son of William and Elizabeth Webster [Ref: ZC-77]. Took the Oath of Allegiance before the Hon. Thomas Clagett in 1778 [Ref: O-266, R-39, which latter source stated he was aged 40 in 1776]. He is buried in Christ Church Cemetery at Accokeek [Ref: Y-614, which source stated he was born in 1734]. The estate of one John Webster was promoted on Dec. 9, 1783 [Ref: ZE-195].

WEBSTER, John (Nov. 7, 1759 -   ). Son of William and Ann Webster [Ref: ZC-77]. One John Webster was a private in the 4th Maryland Line, 1777, was listed as "deserted" in July, 1780, and appeared on a list of defectives in 1781 [Ref: D-178, D-415].

WEBSTER, Mary. See "George Webster," q.v.

WEBSTER, Phillip. Took the Oath of Allegiance before the Hon. William Lyles, Jr. in 1778 [Ref: O-290].

WEBSTER, Sarah. See "Thomas Dyer," q.v.

WEBSTER, Thomas (1734-   ). Private, enrolled in the Flying Camp by Lieut. William D. Beall on Aug. 4, 1776; nativity: Scotland; height: 5' 5" [Ref: D-37].

WEBSTER, Thomas (1726 - Nov. 7, 1797, Maryland). Took the Oath of Allegiance before the Hon. Thomas Clagett in 1778 [Ref: O-268, R-56]. He married Mary Guy [Ref: X-3135]. See "George Webster," q.v.

WEBSTER, William (Aug. 31, 1757 -   ). Son of Thomas and Mary Webster [Ref: ZC-77]. Took the Oath of Allegiance before the Hon. William Lyles, Jr. in 1778 [Ref: O-289]. The estate of one William Webster was probated on Feb. 23, 1832 [Ref: ZE-195].

WEBSTER, William Jr. (June 15, 1731 -   ). A son of William and Elizabeth Webster, he married Ann Turner on Sep. 12, 1756, in King George's Parish [Ref: ZC-77]. Took the Oath of Allegiance before the

Hon. Thomas Clagett in 1778 [Ref: O-268, R-55]. See "John Webster," q.v.

WEDGE, William. Private, 7th Maryland Line, enlisted Mar. 14, 1778 and still in service in November, 1780 [Ref: D-258]. The estate of "William Wedge(s)" was probated on May 29, 1793 [Ref: ZE-195].

WEEDEN, Jonathan. Private, enrolled by Ensign Alexander Truman on July 5, 1776, for continental service, Maryland Line [Ref: D-38]. Private, 4th Maryland Regiment, enlisted Apr. 3, 1782 for 3 years and sworn in Apr. 25, 1782 [Ref: D-417, which spelled his name "Weaden"].

WEEDEN, Joseph. Took the Oath of Allegiance (made his "X" mark) which was recorded on a "return of Capt. Tapley of the brig *Royal*" and filed in court by the Hon. Thomas Gantt, Jr. in 1778 [Ref: O-305, W-4648 (Box 4, folder 15)].

WEEDEN, Rebecca. See "Philip Hopkins," q.v.

WEEDEN, William. Took the Oath of Allegiance before the Hon. Truman Skinner in 1778 [Ref: O-299, which spelled his name "Weaden"].

WEEK, William. Took the Oath of Allegiance before the Hon. Osborn Sprigg in 1778 [Ref: O-306].

WEEMS, Nathaniel. Served on the Board of Patuxent Associators and signed a resolution at Nottingham on Apr. 21, 1781 relative to the defence of the rivers of Potomac and Patuxent and the completion of the fort at Drum Point [Ref: K-1814]. The estate of "Nathaniel C. Weems" was probated in May 16, 1808 [Ref: ZE-196].

WEEMS, William Lock (1735-1783). Justice of the County Court, 1777 [Ref: C-273]. Administered the Oath of Allegiance in 1778 [Ref: O-301]. He married Amelia Chapman [Ref: X-3139]. The estate of "William L. Weems" was probated on Aug. 15, 1783 [Ref: ZE-196].

WEIGHT, John. Captain, 25th Battalion, May 1, 1778 [Ref: M-135, E-62]. See "John White," q.v.

WEIGHT, Margery. See "Edward Stonestreet," q.v.

WELCH, Ann. See "Lewis Duvall," q.v.

WELCH, Nicholas. Private, 2nd Maryland Line, Capt. Alexander Truman's Company, 1782 [Ref: D-440].

WELCH, Richard. Took the Oath of Allegiance before the Hon. Christopher Lowndes in 1778 [Ref: O-283].

WELCH, Thomas (1722-1801). Took the Oath of Allegiance before the Hon. William Berry in 1778 [Ref: R-51, O-258, which spelled his name "Welsh"]. The estate of one Thomas Welch was probated in 1801 [Ref: ZE-196, whch spelled his name both as "Welch" and "Welsh"].

WELLS, Elizabeth. See "Cornelius Oliver," q.v.

WELLS, George (Jan. 11, 1728/9 - 1785). Son of Nathan Wells and Mary Duckett [Ref: ZC-197]. Took the Oath of Allegiance (made his "X" mark) before the Hon. James Mullikin in 1778 [Ref: O-296]. The estate of one George Wells was probated on Apr. 12, 1785 [Ref: ZE-196].

WELLS, George Jr. Took the Oath of Allegiance before the Hon. James Mullikin in 1778 [Ref: O-296]. The estate of "George W. Wells" was probated on Jan. 20, 1820, and the estate of "George Wells" was probated on Mar. 4, 1820 [Ref: ZE-196].

WELLS, Jacob (Sep. 21, 1735 -   ). Son of Nathan Wells and Mary Duckett [Ref: ZC-197]. Took the Oath of Allegiance before the Hon. Thomas Boyd in 1778 [Ref: O-262].

WELLS, John. Ensign, Upper Battalion, June 24, 1780, Capt. Benjamin Harwood's Company [Ref: M-135, F-203].

WELLS, John (Oct. 26, 1712 -   ). Son of Thomas Jr. and Martha Wells [Ref: ZC-197]. Took the Oath of Allegiance before the Hon. James Beck in 1778 [Ref: O-253].

WELLS, John Duckett (Jan. 2, 1733 - 1804). Son of Nathan Wells and Mary Duckett [Ref: ZC-197]. Took the Oath of Allegiance before the Hon. Benjamin Hall in 1778 [Ref: O-274]. The estate of "John D. Wells" was probated on Nov. 28, 1804 [Ref: ZE-196].

WELLS, Joseph. Took the Oath of Allegiance before the Hon. Thomas Boyd in 1778 [Ref: O-261]. Ensign, Upper Battalion, Militia, Capt. Tyler's Company, June 27, 1781 [Ref: H-320]. One Joseph Wells married Elizabeth Warfield by license dated Nov. 22, 1781, and a Joseph Wells married Peggy Watkins by license dated Feb. 1, 1787 [Ref: ZB-235]. The estate of one Joseph Wells was probated on Mar. 26, 1802, and the estate of another Joseph Wells was probated on Mar. 18, 1826 [Ref: ZE-196]. Additional research nay be necessary before drawing conclusions.

WELLS, Martha. On Mar. 20, 1840, the Treasurer of the Western Shore was directed to pay to Martha Wells, of Prince George's County, the widow of a revolutionary soldier [no name given], or to her order, quarterly, during her life, half pay of a private, commencing Jan. 1, 1840 [Ref: O-405]. See "Thomas Drane," q.v.

WELLS, Martin. Private, 2nd Maryland Line, enlisted May 24, 1778 and discharged on Apr. 3, 1779 [Ref: D-175]. The estate of one Martin Wells was probated by July 11, 1809 (date of inventory) by Mary W. Wells [Ref: ZE-196].

WELLS, Mary. See "Theodore Mitchell" and "Martin Wells," q.v.

WELLS, Nathan. See "Jacob Wells" and "John Duckett Wells" and "George Wells," q.v.

WELLS, Richard. See "William Wells," q.v.

WELLS, Samuel. Two men with this name took the Oath of Allegiance in 1778: one before the Hon. Osborn Sprigg [Ref: O-307], and the other took the Oath of Allegiance which was recorded on a "return of Capt. Tapley of the brig *Royal*" and filed in court by the Hon. Thomas Gantt, Jr. in 1778 [Ref: O-305, W-4648 (Box 4, folder 15)]. One Samuel Wells married Marth Olliver [Martha Oliver] by license dated Aug. 10, 1778 [Ref: ZB-235].

WELLS, Thomas (of Red Pond). Took the Oath of Allegiance before the Hon. Thomas Williams in 1778 [Ref: O-302].
WELLS, William. Ensign, Middle Battalion, Nov. 13, 1779, Capt. Joseph White Clagett's Company [Ref: M-135, F-13, N-35]. Took the Oath of Allegiance before the Hon. James Mullikin in 1778 [Ref: O-295]. One William Wells married Rebecca Wells by license dated Dec. 22, 1780 [Ref: ZB-236]. The estate of one William Wells was probated on Feb. 10, 1806 [Ref: ZE-197].
WELSH, George. Private, 1st Maryland Line, who was paid for his services "in cloathing" on Apr. 17, 1779 [Ref: E-351].
WELSH, John. Private, 1st Maryland Line, who was listed as a defective in July, 1780 [Ref: D-414].
WELSH, Thomas. See "Thomas Welch," q.v.
WEST, Catherine. See "James Johnson," q.v.
WEST, Christian. See "Stephen West," q.v.
WEST, Harriet. See "Stephen West," q.v.
WEST, John. Private, enrolled by Ensign Alexander Truman on July 2, 1776, for continental service, Maryland Line [Ref: D-38]. See "Stephen West," q.v.
WEST, Joseph. See "Stephen West," q.v.
WEST, Mary. See "Stephen West," q.v.
WEST, Rachel. See "Stephen West," q.v.
WEST, Richard. See "Stephen West," q.v.
WEST, Stephen (July 23, 1727 - 1790). A son of Stephen West and Martha Hall, he married Hannah Williams in 1753 and had these children: William Henry West, John Stephen West, Stephen West, Joseph West, Richard William West, Christian Hannah West, Mary West, Harriet West, and Rachel Sophia (West) Oden [Ref: U-878, U-879]. Delegate to the Maryland Convention in 1775. Appointed to collect gold and silver in Prince George's County in February, 1776, and served in House of Delegates, 1777-1778. Delegate to Continental Congress, Mar. 31, 1780 (elected but did not serve; resigned Apr. 5, 1780). Stored arms and ammunition in Marlboro in July, 1780. Executive Council, 1781 [Ref: A-5, A-132, G-4, U-70, U-78]. "A very active patriot during the Revolutionary War, who was commended by the Council for the zeal he manifested in the cause." [Ref: U-879]. The estate of Stephen West was probated on Jan. 22, 1790 [Ref: ZE-197].
WEST, William. Private, 3rd Maryland Line, enlisted Jan. 9, 1779. Capt. Horatio Clagett's Company, December, 1779 [Ref: D-295]. See "Stephen West," q.v.
WESTWOOD, William. "William Westwood" was a private, 6th Maryland Line, enlisted on June 26, 1777, and was still in service in 1780 [Ref: D-256, D-347]. The estate of "William Westward" was probated on Jan. 9, 1793 [Ref: ZE-197].
WHARTON, ----. Captain, Aug. 8, 1776 [Ref: M-135].

WHARTON, Anne. See "Basil Waring, Sr.," q.v.
WHEAT, Basil (before 1758, Maryland - died after Dec. 11, 1809, Georgia). Basil Wheat served in the Virginia Line and married Mary Ridgeway [Ref: X-3166].
WHEAT, Francis (c1738-1815). Constable, Piscataway Hundred, 1777-1778 [Ref: Z-3, Z-30]. Francis Wheat married (1) Elizabeth Ball, and (2) Sarah Upton by license dated Nov. 1, 1780 [Ref: X-3166, ZB-237]. The estate of one Francis Wheat was probated on Mar. 11, 1815 [Ref: ZE-197].
WHEAT, John (Nov. 18, 1730 -   ). Took the Oath of Allegiance before the Hon. Fielder Bowie in 1778 [Ref: R-77, and the original 1778 oath list at the Maryland State Archives (Box 4, folder 15); however, his name was inadvertently omitted from the 1778 list in Reference O-304]. "John Wheat II, the second son of John Wheate I, lived on *Friendship*, a plantation of 357 acres in 1762 in Prince George's County. He married Mary Summers, the first daughter of John Summers II of the nearby plantation *Moore's Addition*. John and Mary Wheat had a son named John Wheat. John Wheat III, son of John II, was born Nov. 30, 1733. John Wheat IV, son of John III, was born 1763." [Ref: "The Johns and Marys of the John Wheate Family," by Helen Summers Holweck, *Maryland Genealogical Society Bulletin*, Volume 35, No. 3 (Fall, 1994), p. 566]. However, it must be noted that the King George's Parish register in Prince George's County states that John Wheat, son of John, was born on Nov. 18, 1730, not Nov. 30, 1733 [Ref: ZC-78].
WHEELER, Ann. See "Tilghman Hilleary," q.v.
WHEELER, Aquilla. Took the Oath of Allegiance before the Hon. Joshua Beall in 1778 [Ref: O-251]. "Acquila Wheeler" married Elizabeth Young by license dated Feb. 26, 1778 [Ref: ZB-237]. The estate of "Aquilla Wheeler" was probated on Nov. 10, 1795 [Ref: ZE-197].
WHEELER, Clement (Mar. 13, 1737/8 - 1796). Son of Clement Wheeler and Elizabeth Edelen [Ref: ZC-79]. Took the Oath of Allegiance before the Hon. Christopher Lowndes in 1778 [Ref: O-287]. Captain, Militia, Middle Battalion, from May 1, 1778 until June 24, 1780 (succeeded). [Ref: M-135, E-53, F-203, N-36]. Rendered patriotic service by providing wheat for the military on May 20, 1783 [Ref: Q-600]. The estate of one Clement Wheeler was probated on Dec. 26, 1796 [Ref: ZE-198].
WHEELER, Eleanor. See "Samuel Wheeler" and "Ignatius Wheeler," q.v.
WHEELER, Elizabeth. See "Ignatius Wheeler," q.v.
WHEELER, George. See "Ignatius Wheeler," q.v.
WHEELER, Hezekiah (1739-1807). Captain, 11th Battalion, Mar. 15, 1776, and Captain, Select Militia, May 25 and July 14, 1781 [Ref: M-136, A-252, E-78, G-445, H-359, S-6636 (Box 31, folder 5)]. Served on a General Courts-Martial for the trial of Capt. Richard Bennett Hall, Lieut. Jeremiah Ryley, Lieut. Jonathan Wright, and Lieut. James Mullikin on July 25, 1776, at Upper Marlboro [Ref: A-553]. Captain,

11th Battalion, April, 1781, "when the British were up the Potomack River." [Ref: L-19970 (Box 6, folder 21), N-32, O-406]. Took the Oath of Allegiance before the Hon. Thomas Clagett in 1778 [Ref: O-264, R-86]. The estate of Capt. Hezekiah Wheeler was probated on Apr. 24, 1807 [Ref: ZE-198].

WHEELER, Ignatius (Jan. 23, 1731 -   ). A son of Leonard and Elizabeth Wheeler, he married Elizabeth Marbury on July 29, 1753 and had these children listed in the King George's Parish register: Luke Marbury Wheeler (born July 24 or 25, 1754), Elenor Wheeler (born Dec. 28, 1756), Elizabeth Wheeler (born Dec. 28, 1759), Ignatius Wheeler (born Sep. 9, 1763), and George Wheeler (born Aug. 1, 1768). [Ref: ZC-79, R-82]. Took the Oath of Allegiance before the Hon. Thomas Clagett in 1778 [Ref: O-268]. Second Lieutenant, Middle Battalion, May 1, 1778, Capt. Michael Lowe's Company; resigned May 15, 1779 [Ref: M-136, E-63, N-36].

WHEELER, Jacob. Two men with this name took the Oath of Allegiance in 1778: one before the Hon. Benjamin Hall and another before the Hon. James Beck [Ref: O-253, O-274]. One Jacob Wheeler married Sarah Austin by license dated Feb. 10, 1786, and one Jacob Wheeler married Susannah Igleheart by license dated June 2, 1787 [Ref: ZB-237]. See "William Igleheart," q.v.

WHEELER, Jemima. See "Thomas Bird," q.v.

WHEELER, Leonard. See "Ignatius Wheeler," q.v.

WHEELER, Luke. See "Ignatius Wheeler," q.v.

WHEELER, Richard (1747-   ). Took the Oath of Allegiance before the Hon. James Beck in 1778 [Ref: R-47, O-255, which spelled the name "Wheler"].

WHEELER, Robert. Took the Oath of Allegiance before the Hon. Benjamin Hall in 1778 [Ref: O-274]. The estate of one Robert Wheeler was probated on May 5, 1798 [Ref: ZE-198].

WHEELER, Samuel. Private, Militia; participated in capturing an enemy boat and crew on Apr. 17, 1781 [Ref: M-208]. Private, Select Militia, Upper Battalion, June 12, 1781 [Ref: S-6636 (Box 27, folder 82B)]. One Samuel Wheeler married Eleanor Wheeler by license dated Oct. 27, 1780, and a Samuel Wheeler married Ann Hilleary by license dated Dec. 4, 1782 [Ref: ZB-237].

WHEELER, Samuel Hanson. Ensign in the militia in 1779 [Ref: N-36].

WHEELER, Sarah. See "Mareen H. Duvall" and "Henry Hilleary," q.v.

WHEELER, Susannah. See "John Farrell," q.v.

WHITAKER, Robert. Took the Oath of Allegiance before the Hon. David Craufurd in 1778 [Ref: O-271]. The estate of one Robert Whitaker was probated on Sep. 3, 1790 [Ref: ZE-198].

WHITE, Abednego (1734-   ). Private, Militia, 1776 [Ref: M-208, A-325]. Took the Oath of Allegiance before the Hon. Christopher Lowndes in 1778 [Ref: O-282, R-32].

WHITE, Ann. See "John White" and "William White" and "Thomas Harwood, Jr.," q.v.

WHITE, Benjamin. Second Lieutenant, Militia, 1778 [Ref: N-35]. Second Lieutenant, Middle Battalion, Nov. 13, 1779, Capt. Joseph White Clagett's Company [Ref: M-136, F-13]. Took the Oath of Allegiance before the Hon. James Mullikin in 1778 [Ref: O-295]. The estate of one Benjamin White was probated by Oct. 11, 1803 (date of inventory) by John White [Ref: ZE-198].

WHITE, Benjamin. Took the Oath of Allegiance before the Hon. Benjamin Hall in 1778 [Ref: O-274]. He rendered patriotic service by providing wheat for the military on May 10, 1783 [Ref: Q-599]. See "John White" and "William White," q.v.

WHITE, Burgess (Mar. 20, 1758 -   ). Son of Zach. [Zachary] and Mary White [Ref: ZD-123]. Took the Oath of Allegiance before the Hon. Christopher Lowndes in 1778 [Ref: O-286].

WHITE, Cassandra. See "John Clagett, of Edward" and "Joseph White Clagett," q.v.

WHITE, Charles. There were several men with this name who served in the Maryland Line [Ref: D-51, D-342, D-355, D-442]. One Charles White married Susannah Smith by license dated July 30, 1777, in Prince George's County [Ref: ZB-238]. Addititonal will be necessary before drawing conclusions.

WHITE, Elisha. Took the Oath of Allegiance (made his "X" mark) before the Hon. Thomas Clagett in 1778 [Ref: O-269].

WHITE, Elizabeth. See "Frederick Miles," q.v.

WHITE, George. Took the Oath of Allegiance before the Hon. Osborn Sprigg in 1778 [Ref: O-306].

WHITE, James (1714-   ). Took the Oath of Allegiance before the Hon. Christopher Lowndes in 1778 [Ref: O-286, R-23].

WHITE, Jemima. See "John Connolly," q.v.

WHITE, John. There were several men with this name: (1) Private, enrolled by Capt. Alexander H. Magruder, 11th Battalion, on July 18, 1776, for the continental service in the Maryland Line [Ref: D-38]. (2) Private, enrolled by Capt. John H. Lowe on July 13, 1776, for continental service in the Maryland Line [Ref: D-35]. (3) Took the Oath of Allegiance before the Hon. David Craufurd in 1778 [Ref: O-271]. (4) Private, 3rd Maryland Line, enlisted Apr. 28, 1777; Capt. Horatio Clagett's Company, December, 1779 [Ref: D-296]. (5) Ensign, Upper Battalion, Militia, Capt. John White's Company, June 27, 1781 [Ref: H-320]. One John White married Ursula Smith by license dated Aug. 20, 1780, and one John White married Mary Brown by license dated Dec. 20, 1780 [Ref: ZB-238]. One John White, son of Benjamin and Ann, was born on Jan. 17, 1739 [Ref: ZC-197]. The estate of one John White was probated on Oct. 9, 1790 [Ref: ZE-199]. Additional research may be

331

necessary before drawing conclusions. See "Benjamin White" and "John Weight," q.v.

WHITE, Jonathan. Took the Oath of Allegiance (made his "X" mark) before the Hon. Truman Skinner in 1778 [Ref: O-298]. Private, 1st Maryland Line, under Gen. William Smallwood; wounded at the second Battle of Camden on Apr. 25, 1781; disability (invalid) pension commenced Sep. 19, 1781; resided near Upper Marlboro, Prince George's County, in 1790 [Ref: D-634, D-635, K-1814]. Jonathan White married Sarah Tarman by license dated Mar. 27, 1785 [Ref: ZB-238].

WHITE, Leonard (c1741-c1777). Private, enrolled by Capt. Alexander H. Magruder, 11th Battalion, Aug. 19, 1776, continental service, Maryland Line [Ref: D-38]. He married Mary ---- [Ref: X-3185].

WHITE, Margeary. See "Zephaniah White," q.v.

WHITE, Mary. See "Leonard White" and "Thomas Clagett" and "William Mitchell" and "Burgess White," q.v.

WHITE, Nathan Smith. Took the Oath of Allegiance before the Hon. Thomas Boyd in 1778 [Ref: O-262].

WHITE, Richard. Took the Oath of Allegiance (made his "X" mark) before the Hon. Thomas Clagett in 1778 [Ref: O-269]. Rendered patriotic service by providing wheat for the military on Apr. 18, 1783 [Ref: Q-425].

WHITE, Samuel. "Samuel White" took the Oath of Allegiance before the Hon. David Craufurd in 1778 [Ref: O-271]. "Samuel B. White" married Lethea Beall by license dated Feb. 21, 1781 [Ref: ZB-238]. The estate of one "Samuel White" was probated on Aug. 17, 1779 [Ref: ZE-199].

WHITE, Sarah. See "Thomas Clagett," q.v.

WHITE, Tabitha. See "Nicholas Farr," q.v.

WHITE, Thomas. Took the Oath of Allegiance before the Hon. Osborn Sprigg in 1778 [Ref: O-306]. The estate of one Thomas White was probated on June 10, 1801 [Ref: ZE-199].

WHITE, Thomas T. Took the Oath of Allegiance before the Hon. Fielder Bowie in 1778 [Ref: O-303, W-4648 (Box 4, folder 15)].

WHITE, William. Private, enrolled by Capt. Alexander H. Magruder, 11th Battalion, on July 18, 1776, for continental service, Maryland Line [Ref: D-38]. Took the Oath of Allegiance before the Hon. David Craufurd in 1778 [Ref: O-271]. One William White married Rebecca Blanford by license dated Oct. 11, 1783 [Ref: ZB-238]. William White, son of Benjamin and Ann, was born on July 29, 1735 [Ref: ZC-198].

WHITE, Zach. See "Burgess White," q.v.

WHITE, Zephaniah (Dec. 15, 1749 -   ). "Zephniah White" was the son of Margeary [sic] White, of Prince George's Parish [Ref: ZD-123]. "Zephaniah White" was a matross in Capt. Alexander Furnival's Company of Artillery in November, 1777 [Ref: D-573].

WHITEHEAD, Samuel. Took the Oath of Allegiance before the Hon. Benjamin Hall in 1778 [Ref: O-274].

WHITEHEAD, Thomas. Private (draft), continental service, Maryland Line, 1781 [Ref: D-382]. Took the Oath of Allegiance before the Hon. Benjamin Hall in 1778 [Ref: O-274]. Thomas Whitehead married Mary Waters by license dated Dec. 4, 1779 [Ref: ZB-238].

WHITELY, William. Private, 3rd Maryland Line, enlisted Mar. 29, 1777; Capt. Horatio Clagett's Company, December, 1779 [Ref: D-296].

WHITEMORE, Elizabeth. See "Thomas Neal," q.v.

WHITEN, Rachel. See "Richard Hunter," q.v.

WHITING, James. Took the Oath of Allegiance (made his "J" mark) before the Hon. James Mullikin in 1778 [Ref: O-296].

WHITING, Rebecca. See "John Simpson," q.v.

WHITMORE, Benjamin. On Aug. 28, 1780 the County Lieutenant wrote to the Council of Maryland to inform them that "Benjamin Whitmore thought his enrolement was returned to me, which I inclosed with the others, it seems he was an apprentice and taken away by his master, so that the class will be obliged to procure another or pay the money." [Ref: G-63].

WHITMORE, Stephen (1748 - Oct. 27, 1819). Private, 3rd Maryland Line, 1778; pension commenced on Apr. 8, 1818 [Ref: D-177, T-39]. One Stephen Whitmore married Sarah Vermillion on Dec. 23, 1790 in King George's Parish, Prince George's County [Ref: ZC-80]. The estate of Stephen Whitmore was probated on Nov. 15, 1819 [Ref: ZE-199].

WHITMORE, William. Private, 3rd Maryland Line, 1781 [Ref: D-394]. One William Whitmore married Mary Beall on May 10, 1753, in King George's Parish, Prince George's County [Ref: ZC-80].

WHITTLE, Robert. Private, 3rd Maryland Line, Capt. Horatio Clagett's Company, 1779 [Ref: D-295].

WHYTE, Ann. See "Thomas Harwood, Jr.," q.v.

WIERY, Michael. Private, 2nd Maryland Line, Capt. Alexander Truman's Company, 1782 [Ref: D-440]. On Apr. 6, 1841, the Treasurer of the Western Shore of Maryland was directed to pay to Elizabeth Wiery, widow of Michael, of York County, Pennsylvania, during life, half pay of a private, in consideration of services rendered by her husband during the Revolutionary War [Ref: O-407].

WIGFIELD, Elizabeth. See "Matthew Wigfield," q.v.

WIGFIELD, Joseph (1736-   ). Took the Oath of Allegiance before the Hon. Osborn Sprigg in 1778 [Ref: O-307, R-82].

WIGFIELD, Mary. See "Matthew Wigfield," q.v.

WIGFIELD, Matthew (c1735-1795). "Matthew Wickfield" took the Oath of Allegiance before the Hon. Joshua Beall in 1778 [Ref: O-251]. "Matthew Wigfield" married Elizabeth ---- and their children were listed in the King George's Parish register: Mary Wigfield (born June 17, 1764), Rachel Wigfield (born Jan. 19, 1766), Matthew Wigfield (born May 23, 1773), and Robert Wigfield (born Sep. 13, 1773). [Ref: ZC-80,

X-3207]. The estate of "Matthew Wigfield, Sr." was probated on Sep. 3, 1795 [Ref: ZE-199].
WIGFIELD, Rachel. See "Matthew Wigfield," q.v.
WIGFIELD, Robert. See "Matthew Wigfield," q.v.
WIGFIELD, Thomas (1743-   ). Took the Oath of Allegiance before the Hon. Osborn Sprigg in 1778 [Ref: O-306, R-83].
WIGGINTON, Jane. See "Lewin Jones," q.v.
WIGHT, John (1713-1780). "John Wight" took the Oath of Allegiance before the Hon. Christopher Lowndes in 1778 [Ref: O-284]. "John Wyght, Sr." was aged 63 in 1776 [Ref: R-27]. The estate of "John Wightt" was probated on Mar. 10, 1780, and an inventory of the estate of "John Wight" was filed by Jonathan Wight on May 29, 1780 [Ref: ZE-199].
WIGHT, John Jr. "John Wightt, Jr." took the Oath of Allegiance before the Hon. William Berry in 1778 [Ref: O-258]. "John Wight" married Rebecca Hennis by license dated Apr. 15, 1786 [Ref: ZB-239].
WIGHT, Margery. See "Edward Sprigg," q.v.
WIGHT, Thomas. Private, Capt. Hezekiah Wheeler's Company, 11th Militia Battalion, April, 1781 [Ref: L-19970 (Box 6, folder 21)].
WIGHTT, Jonathan (1749-   ). Took the Oath of Allegiance before the Hon. Richard Henderson in 1778 [Ref: O-277, R-23, which latter source spelled the name "Wyght"]. See "John Wight," q.v.
WIGHTT, Truman (of Montgomery County). Took the Oath of Allegiance before the Hon. James Beck in 1778 [Ref: O-253].
WILBORN, Robert. Took the Oath of Allegiance (made his "X" mark) before the Hon. Truman Skinner in 1778 [Ref: O-299].
WILKINSON, George. Took the Oath of Allegiance before the Hon. Osborn Sprigg in 1778 [Ref: O-307].
WILKINSON, John. Private, 4th Maryland Line, 1778 [Ref: D-179, which spelled the name "Wilkerson"].
WILKINSON, Joseph. Colonel who served on the Board of Patuxent Associators and signed a resolution at Nottingham on Apr. 21, 1781 relative to the defence of the rivers of Potomac and Patuxent and the completion of the fort at Drum Point [Ref: K-1814].
WILKINSON, William. Captain, Lower Battalion, Sep. 1, 1777 [Ref: M-137, C-356, which spelled the name "Wilkenson"].
WILLCOX, James. Private, 3rd Maryland Line, Capt. Horatio Clagett's Company, 1779 [Ref: D-295].
WILLCOXEN, Josiah or Josias. "Josiah Willcoxen" took the Oath of Allegiance before the Hon. George Lee in 1778 [Ref: O-279]. The estate of "Josias Wilcoxon" was administered by Oct. 10, 1780 (date of inventory) by Margaret Wilcoxon. The estate of "Josiah Willcoxen" was administered on Nov. 3, 1789 (account filed) by Margaret Willcoxen [Ref: ZE-200].

WILLCOXEN, Levin. Took the Oath of Allegiance before the Hon. William Berry in 1778 [Ref: O-259]. Served on a Grand Jury in 1778 [Ref: Z-90, which spelled his name "Wilcoxon"]. "Levin Wilcoxon" married Mary Brashears by license dated Feb. 11, 1780 [Ref: ZB-239].
WILLCOXEN, Margaret. See "Thomas Hardey," q.v.
WILLCOXEN, Thomas. Second Lieutenant, Company of Light Infantry, 11th Battalion, Jan. 3, 1776 [Ref: O-408]. First Lieutenant, Militia, Capt. Michael Lowe's Company, from Sep. 20, 1776 to at least May 1, 1778 [Ref: M-136, M-137, B-287, C-362, E-63, which spelled his name "Wilcoxen" and "Willcoxen" and "Wilcoxon," and Ref: N-36 which mistakenly spelled his name "Thomas Will Coxen"]. Constable, Hynson Hundred, 1777 [Ref: Z-3].
WILLCOXEN, Thomas. Private, enrolled by Ensign Horatio Clagett on July 15, 1776, for the continental service, Maryland Line [Ref: D-35]. "Thomas Wilcoxon, Jr." married Mary Hardey by license dated Apr. 23, 1781 [Ref: ZB-239].
WILLCOXEN, Thomas, of Jacob. Ensign, Middle Battalion, Nov. 13, 1779, Capt. Michael Lowe's Company [Ref: M-136, F-13].
WILLCOXEN, Thomas, of Josiah. Ensign, Militia, 1779 [Ref: N-36].
WILLCOXEN, William. Took the Oath of Allegiance before the Hon. George Lee in 1778 [Ref: O-279].
WILLETT, Christian. See "William Hutchinson," q.v.
WILLETT, Edward (1760, Maryland - July 3, 1837, Kentucky). Ensign, Middle Battalion, June 24, 1780, Capt. Samuel Hepburn's Company [Ref: M-137, F-203]. Took the Oath of Allegiance before the Hon. David Craufurd in 1778 [Ref: O-271]. He married Eleanor Fisher [Ref: X-3223, which stated he was born in 1761; however, he had to be at least aged 18 to take the Oath in 1778, so he was probably born in 1760, unless there was more than one Edward Willett]. Additional research may be necessary before drawing conclusions.
WILLETT, Mary. See "Richard Simmons" and "William Willett" and "William Marlow," q.v.
WILLETT, Ninian. Took the Oath of Allegiance before the Hon. David Craufurd in 1778 [Ref: O-272]. He rendered patriotic service by providing wheat for the military on Oct. 5, 1780 [Ref: Q-323]. The estate of one Ninian Willett was probated on Feb. 15, 1804 [Ref: ZE-200].
WILLETT, Rachel. See "Richard Price," q.v.
WILLETT, Samuel. Took the Oath of Allegiance before the Hon. David Craufurd in 1778 [Ref: O-272]. Samuel Willett married Ann Orme by license dated June 27, 1784 [Ref: ZB-240].
WILLETT, Verlinda. See "Samuel Simmons," q.v.
WILLETT, William (1743 - Apr. 5, 1785). Took the Oath of Allegiance before the Hon. James Beck in 1778 [Ref: O-254, R-46]. William Willett married Mary ---- [Ref: X-3224].

WILLEY, John. Private, 2nd Maryland Line, Capt. Patrick Sim's Company, 1776 [Ref: D-7].
WILLIAMS, Ann. See "Burch Vermillion," q.v.
WILLIAMS, Barbara. See "Thomas Owen Williams," q.v.
WILLIAMS, Benjamin 2nd. Private, 2nd Maryland Line, Capt. Alexander Truman's Company, 1782 [Ref: D-439].
WILLIAMS, Colonel. See "Zachariah Berry," q.v.
WILLIAMS, Elisha (1735, Maryland - Nov. 24, 1812, Virginia). Took the Oath of Allegiance before the Hon. Thomas Williams in 1778 in Prince George's County, Maryland [Ref: O-302]. He married Ann Swearingen [Ref: X-3227]. There was also an Elisha Williams, son of Thomas and Ellinor, of Queen Anne's Parish, who was born on May 12, 1728, in Prince George's County, Maryland [Ref: ZC-198]. The estate of one Elisha Williams was probated on Mar. 18, 1780 in Prince George's County [Ref: ZE-201]. Additional research may be necessary before drawing conclusions.
WILLIAMS, Elizabeth. See "John Boone" and "Thomas Duckett" and "Richard Duckett, Sr." and "John Williams" and "John R. Magruder," q.v.
WILLIAMS, Ellinor. See "Elisha Williams," q.v.
WILLIAMS, Hannah. See "Stephen West," q.v.
WILLIAMS, James. Private, Northern Detachment, 3rd Maryland Line, Capt. Horatio Clagett's Company, 1783 [Ref: D-501].
WILLIAMS, John. Private, enrolled by Lt. John M. Burgess, Lower Battalion, on July 20, 1776, for continental service, Maryland Line [Ref: D-35]. Private, 1st Maryland Line, who was paid for his services "in cloathing" on Apr. 17, 1779 [Ref: E-351]. "John Williams" took the Oath of Allegiance before the Hon. Benjamin Hall in 1778 [Ref: O-275]. "John Fenly Williams" was born on Jan. 1, 1756, son of Thomas and Elizabeth Williams, and married Ann Mudd by license dated Jan. 9, 1782 [Ref: ZB-241, ZC-81]. "John Williams 2nd" was a private in the Northern Detachment, 3rd Maryland Line, Capt. Horatio Clagett's Company, 1783 [Ref: D-502]. The estate of one John Williams was probated on Oct. 13, 1792, and the estate of another John Williams was probated on Mar. 3, 1807 [Ref: ZE-201]. Additional research may be necessary before drawing conclusions.
WILLIAMS, Joseph (1728-   ). Private, enrolled in the Flying Camp by Lieut. Benjamin Brooks on Aug. 20, 1776; nativity: Prince George's County; height 5' 8" [Ref: D-36]. The records of the Maryland Council on May 19, 1778, states the following in a letter to Richard Smith: "Joseph Williams has complained to us of your getting his son, a boy of 14 years old, fudled and obtaining his Mark to an Enlistment and that you have since sold him as a Substitute for Mr. Nicholas Gassaway. We are desirous of enquiring into this Matter, it is our Duty to do so and, to enable us to [do] it with Justice, we desire to see you tomorrow in the fore Part of the Day. If any Person was present at the Transaction

who will tend to prove it fair, you had better prevail on him to come with you." [Ref: E-96]. On May 20, 1778, the Council stated the following: "Richard Williams, son of Joseph, a lad of 14 years of Age enlisted as a Substitute for Richard Smith and not being an Able bodied Recruit is hereby discharged from the Service on Complaint of Joseph Williams." [Ref: E-97].

WILLIAMS, Mary. See "Zachariah Berry" and "Thomas Williams," q.v.

WILLIAMS, Osborn (c1752 - Dec. 28, 1819). He applied for and received pension S35129 in Anne Arundel County on Apr. 26, 1818. Final payment was made to his surviving children (not named) and on Apr. 22, 1854 (with payment to Dec. 28, 1819). [Ref: P-3864]. "Recruiting Warrant issued to Osborn Williams of Prince George's County for the Continental Service" on Mar. 18, 1777 [Ref: C-181]. First Lieutenant, 3rd Maryland Line, Apr. 12, 1779; resigned by December, 1779 [Ref: D-295, which spelled his name "Osburn"]. Lieutenant, Apr. 17, 1781, and Captain, Select Militia, Upper Battalion, June 12, 1781 [Ref: M-137, G-475, G-488, I-432, H-192 (which spelled his name "Osborne") and S-6636 (Box 27, folder 82B), which spelled his name "Osburn"]. Participated in capturing an enemy boat and crew on Apr. 17, 1781 [Ref: M-208]. He was paid for his services on June 17, 1783 [Ref: I-432]. "Osborn Williams" married Elizabeth Magruder by license dated Oct. 15, 1787 [Ref: X-3233, ZB-241].

WILLIAMS, Rachel. See "Thomas Williams" and "Philip Turner," q.v.

WILLIAMS, Richard. Private, 4th Maryland Line, enlisted Sep. 4, 1781 [Ref: D-404]. The estate of one Richard Williams was probated in 1794 [Ref: ZE-201]. See "Joseph Williams," q.v.

WILLIAMS, Sarah. See "Rinaldo Johnson," q.v.

WILLIAMS, Thomas (1748-1784). First Major, 25th Battalion, Mar. 18, 1776. Lieutenant Colonel, Upper Battalion, from July 9, 1776 through at least Mar. 10, 1778 [Ref: M-137, A-260, B-16, C-532]. County Court Justice, 1777-1778 [Ref: C-273, Z-90]. Justice who administered the Oath of Allegiance in 1778 [Ref: O-302]. Elected County Sheriff on Oct. 22, 1779 and still serving in September, 1781 [Ref: E-564, F-8, G-677]. Thomas Williams married Rachel Duckett [Ref: X-3235]. His estate was probated by Nov. 6, 1784 (date of inventory) by Rachel Williams and an administrative account was filed on May 15, 1799 by Rachel Turner [Ref: ZE-202]. See "John Williams" and "Elisha Williams," q.v.

WILLIAMS, Thomas. Private, Militia, Capt. Joshua Selby's Company, 1776; served in Annapolis [Ref: M-208, B-403].

WILLIAMS, Thomas Devin. The records of the Council of Maryland on Aug. 21, 1781, include a letter from the County Lieutenant of Prince George's County in which he stated that "in classing the Upper Battalion [militia], in Class No. 13, Thomas Devin Williams was drafted with a man who was an indented servant, over age and a cripple, this I knew nothing of till a few days before the drafts were to appear at

Marlbro. Williams complained that he had not an equal chance with other men unless the Class was drafted over again, as the person drafted against him was exempt by law in more instances then one; As I thought his complaint reasonable, I told him I would have the Class drawn over again for one man in the place of the person who was exempt by law, but that he must stand as one of the drafts himself. I accordingly had that Class drawn again, the lot fell on Isaac Walker, a young single man. Had the lot fallen on a marryed man Williams would have been appointed as the person to go, being the most able in the Class." [Ref: H-434].

WILLIAMS, Thomas Owen (Feb. 9, 1747/8 - Oct. 21, 1818). Son of William and Barbara Williams [Ref: ZD-123]. Ensign, Capt. Basil Waring's Company, June 9, 1777. Major, 25th Battalion, May 1, 1778 [Ref: M-138, E-63, N-33, which also spelled his name "Thomas Owens Williams"]. Took the Oath of Allegiance before the Hon. William Berry in 1778 [Ref: O-257]. Buried in Holy Trinity Churchyard at Collington. Stone moved from "Seat Pleasant" estate in 1969 at request of family members [Ref: Y-605, Y-611]. Thomas' daughter Mary married Thomas Berry [Ref: ZA-52]. The estate of Thomas Owen Williams was probated on Oct. 29, 1818 [Ref: ZE-202].

WILLIAMS, Walter. Took the Oath of Allegiance before the Hon. Thomas Williams in 1778 [Ref: O-302]. The estate of one Walter Williams was probated on July 25, 1787 [Ref: ZE-202].

WILLIAMS, Walter Jr. Took the Oath of Allegiance before the Hon. Thomas Williams in 1778 [Ref: O-302]. Private, Militia, 1781; participated in capturing an enemy boat and crew on Apr. 17, 1781 [Ref: M-208]. Private, Select Militia, Upper Battalion, June 12, 1781 [Ref: S-6636 (Box 27, folder 82B)]. Constable, Collington Hundred, 1777 [Ref: Z-3]. The estate of one Walter Williams was probated on Nov. 13, 1832 [Ref: ZE-202].

WILLIAMS, William. Private, 4th Maryland Line, enlisted May 13, 1778 and reported missing on Aug. 16, 1780 (at the Battle of Camden). [Ref: D-179]. The estate of one William Williams was probated by June 24, 1797 (administrative account) by William Williams [Ref: ZE-202]. See "Thomas Owen Williams," q.v.

WILLMAN, John. Private, Northern Detachment, 3rd Maryland Line, Capt. Horatio Clagett's Company, 1783 [Ref: D-502].

WILLMOTH, Thomas (1737-   ). Took the Oath of Allegiance before the Hon. George Lee in 1778 [Ref: O-279, R-67, which latter source spelled his name "Thomas Willmot"].

WILLS, Samuel. Private, Capt. Alexander H. Magruder's Militia Company, Lower Battalion; on duty guarding Magruder's Warehouse in the spring of 1782 [Ref: L-19970 (Box 6, folder 21)].

WILLSON, Aqualia. See "Aquila Wilson," q.v.

WILLSON, Edmond (1721-   ). Took the Oath of Allegiance before the Hon. Thomas Williams in 1778 [Ref: O-302, R-29].
WILLSON, Hilleary. Took the Oath of Allegiance before the Hon. Thomas Williams in 1778 [Ref: O-302].
WILLSON, James (1710-   ). Took the Oath of Allegiance before the Hon. William Berry in 1778 [Ref: O-259, R-22].
WILLSON, James Jr. Took the Oath of Allegiance before the Hon. Thomas Williams in 1778 [Ref: O-302]. "James Willson" was aged 31 in 1776 [Ref: R-35].
WILLSON, John (1744-   ). Private, enrolled by Capt. John H. Lowe on July 13, 1776, for continental service, Maryland Line [Ref: D-35, R-35].
WILLSON, John (1745-   ). Took the Oath of Allegiance before the Hon. William Berry in 1778 [Ref: O-259, R-24].
WILLSON, Joseph. Took the Oath of Allegiance before the Hon. William Berry in 1778 [Ref: O-259]. One Joseph Willson was aged 56 and another was aged 38 in the 1776 census [Ref: R-11, R-66].
WILLSON, Joseph Jr. (1746-   ). Took the Oath of Allegiance before the Hon. Thomas Clagett in 1778 [Ref: O-265, R-56].
WILLSON, Lancelot. See "Aquila Wilson," q.v.
WILLSON, Lingan. Took the Oath of Allegiance before the Hon. David Craufurd in 1778 [Ref: O-272].
WILLSON, Nathaniel (1718-   ). Took the Oath of Allegiance before the Hon. Fielder Bowie in 1778 [Ref: R-79, O-304, which spelled the name "Wilson"].
WILLSON, Rachel. See "Aquila Wilson," q.v.
WILLSON, William. Private, 3rd Maryland Line, Capt. Horatio Clagett's Company, December, 1779 [Ref: D-296]. See "Hannibal Lusk" and "William Wilson," q.v.
WILMOT, Dianah. See "John Dove," q.v.
WILMOT, John. Rendered patriotic service on Aug. 6, 1781 when the Council of Maryland ordered the Treasurer of the Western Shore to pay him from the bills of credit "appropriated for the present campaign" and to be delivered to John Smith Brookes, Commissary of Prince George's County, and Hezekiah Reeder, Commissary of Charles County, "and also six pounds, nineteen shillings and six pence of the same emission of the money appropriated for the defence of the state due said Wilmot." [Ref: G-545, G-556].
WILMOT, Thomas. Took the Oath of Allegiance before the Hon. David Craufurd in 1778 [Ref: O-272, which spelled his name "Wilmet"].
WILMOT, William. See "Isaac Duvall," q.v.
WILSON, Ann Dickson. See "Samuel Scott," q.v.
WILSON, Aquila (baptized July 31, 1763 -   ). "Aquilla Willson" was a son of Lancelot and Rachel Willson, and "Aqualia Wilson" married "Sarah(?) Taylor" on Nov. 26, 1791, in King George's Parish [Ref: ZC-81]. "Acquila

Wilson" was a private (substitute), Maryland Line; discharged Nov. 29, 1781 [Ref: D-412, I-6].

WILSON, Basil (1738-   ). Took the Oath of Allegiance before the Hon. Christopher Lowndes in 1778 [Ref: O-285, R-30, which spelled his name "Bazell Willson"]. Served on a Grand Jury in 1777 [Ref: Z-29]. One Basil Wilson married Ann Scott by license dated Aug. 9, 1779 [Ref: ZB-242].

WILSON (Brightwell), Mrs. ----. See "John Cecil," q.v.

WILSON, Clement. Private, Militia, 1776 [Ref: M-208, A-325]. Took the Oath of Allegiance before the Hon. James Beck in 1778 [Ref: O-254]. One Clement Wilson married Susannah Ceicel by license dated Sep. 5, 1778 [Ref: ZB-242]. The estate of Clement Wilson was probated on July 15, 1795 by Susanna Wilson [Ref: ZE-202].

WILSON, Cloe (Clour). See "John Smallwood," q.v.

WILSON, David (1743-   ). Took the Oath of Allegiance before the Hon. Christopher Lowndes in 1778 [Ref: O-288, R-35, which spelled his name "Willson"]. Private, Militia, 1776 [Ref: M-208, A-325].

WILSON, Elizabeth. See "Benjamin Burch" and "George Jones" and "Thomas L. Mitchell" and "Henry Thorn," q.v.

WILSON, George Sr. (1703-1788). Took the Oath of Allegiance before the Hon. Richard Henderson in 1778 [Ref: O-278, R-49, which latter source spelled the name "Willson"]. The estate of "George Wilson" was probated on Sep. 23, 1788 [Ref: ZE-202]. See "William Wilson" and "Benjamin Burch," q.v.

WILSON, George Jr. Took the Oath of Allegiance before the Hon. William Berry in 1778 [Ref: O-259, which spelled it "Willson"]. The estate of one "George Wilson" was probated on Mar. 4, 1793 [Ref: ZE-202].

WILSON, Ignatius (1736-   ). Took the Oath of Allegiance before the Hon. Christopher Lowndes in 1778 [Ref: O-288, R-35, which spelled his name "Ignatius Willson"]. Private, Militia, 1776 [Ref: M-208, A-325].

WILSON, James. Private, Militia, 1776 [Ref: M-208, A-325]. Private, Select Militia, Upper Battalion, June 12, 1781 [Ref: S-6636 (Box 27, folder 82B)]. Private, Militia; participated in capturing an enemy boat and crew on Apr. 17, 1781 [Ref: M-209]. Served on a Grand Jury in 1777 [Ref: Z-29]. One "James C. Wilson" married Mary A. Barnes by license dated Feb. 1, 1782 [Ref: ZB-242].

WILSON, James (1745-   ). Took the Oath of Allegiance before the Hon. Alexander Howard Magruder in 1778 [Ref: O-293, R-35, which spelled his name "James Willson"]. Served on a Grand Jury in 1778 [Ref: Z-90].

WILSON, James (1760, Scotland -   ). Private (substitute), 1780, continental service, Maryland Line [Ref: D-338].

WILSON, James, of Hugh. This name appeared twice on the lists of those who took the Oath of Allegiance in 1778: one before the Hon. William Berry and one before the Hon. Richard Henderson [Ref: O-258, O-278].

WILSON, James, of Joseph. Took the Oath of Allegiance before the Hon. Christopher Lowndes in 1778 [Ref: O-287].
WILSON, John. Ensign, 11th Battalion, Jan. 3, 1776 [Ref: M-138].
WILSON, John. "A draft, June 15th, 1778" for continental service, Maryland Line [Ref: D-328]. The records of the Council of Maryland on June 22, 1778, state that John Wilson was "a Draft from Prince George's County who had gone home again. We have sent Mr. Gordon after him and request that you [County Lieutenant] give him any necessary assistance." [Ref: E-146]. Took the Oath of Allegiance before the Hon. Thomas Williams in 1778 [Ref: O-302].
WILSON, Jonas Isgrig. Took the Oath of Allegiance before the Hon. Christopher Lowndes in 1778 [Ref: O-283].
WILSON, Joseph Sr. "Joseph Wilson, Sr." served on a Grand Jury in 1778 [Ref: Z-90]. One Joseph Wilson married Ann S. Ferguson by license dated Aug. 29, 1777, and a Joseph Wilson married Sarah Wilson by license dated Jan. 8, 1787 [Ref: ZB-243]. See "Joseph Willson," q.v.
WILSON, Joseph, of Samuel. Took the Oath of Allegiance before the Hon. Christopher Lowndes in 1778 [Ref: O-287].
WILSON, Josiah. See "George Walls," q.v.
WILSON, Josias Sollers. Private in the militia in 1776 [Ref: M-208, A-325].
WILSON, Lancelot. See "Aquila Wilson," q.v.
WILSON, Margery. See "Joseph Jenkins," q.v.
WILSON, Martha. See "William Magruder Selby," q.v.
WILSON, Mary. See "William Wilson" and "Samuel P. Wailes," q.v.
WILSON, Matthew (1741, Prince George's County, Maryland - died after Oct. 7, 1834, Highland County, Ohio). He applied for and received pension S7902 on July 23, 1834, aged 93, Highland County, Ohio, stating that he was born in Prince George's County and lived in Montgomery County at the time of his enlistment [Ref: P-3893]. Matthew Wilson married Rachel ---- [Ref: X-3248].
WILSON, Nathaniel Jr. (1753-1783?). Ensign, Middle Battalion, May 24, 1779, Capt. Edward Lanham's Company [Ref: M-138, E-414, N-36, R-11, which latter source spelled his name "Willson"]. Nathaniel Wilson married Martha Hanson by license dated June 15, 1779 [Ref: ZB-243]. The estate of one Nathaniel Wilson was probated on Sep. 13, 1783 [Ref: ZE-204].
WILSON, Rachel. See "Aquila Wilson," q.v.
WILSON, Samuel T. Corporal, Capt. Benjamin Wailes' Militia Company, Lower Battalion; on duty guarding Magruder's Warehouse in the spring of 1782 [Ref: L-19970 (Box 6, folder 21)]. "Samuel Taylor Wilson" married Ann Watson by license dated June 20, 1795, and "Samuel T. Wilson" married Sarah Hagan by license dated Apr. 10, 1805 [Ref: ZB-243].

WILSON, Sarah. See "John Ray" and "Joseph Wilson" and "Mordecai Miles Mitchell," q.v.
WILSON, Sophia. See "Samuel Perrie Wailes," q.v.
WILSON, Stephen. Took the Oath of Allegiance before the Hon. Joshua Beall in 1778 [Ref: O-251].
WILSON, Thomas. Private, Maryland Line, enlisted May 2, 1782, for the duration of the war [Ref: D-421]. One Thomas Wilson married Ann Beall by license dated Sep. 7, 1783 [Ref: ZB-244].
WILSON, William (carpenter). Took the Oath of Allegiance before the Hon. William Berry in 1778 [Ref: O-258].
WILSON, William (1746-). Second Lieutenant, 25th Battalion, May 1, 1778, Capt. Josiah Selby's Company. First Lieutenant, Upper Battalion, Capt. Selby's Company, June 27, 1781 [Ref: M-138, E-62, N-34, H-320, R-34]. Took the Oath of Allegiance before the Hon. William Berry in 1778 [Ref: O-258]. See "William Wilson," q.v.
WILSON, William. There were several men with this name who served in the Maryland Line [Ref: D-33, D-70, D-175, D-177, D-180, D-258, D-296, D-343, D-344, I-10]. One William Wilson was born in 1748 (aged 28 in the 1776). Another William Wilson, son of George and Mary Wilson, was born on Aug. 15, 1761 [Ref: R-48, ZD-124]. The estates for men named William Wilson were probated in 1793, 1804, 1807, 1815, and 1817 [Ref: ZE-204]. Additional research will be necessary before drawing any conclusions.
WILSON, Zachariah. Private (draft), continental service, 1781 [Ref: D-382]. Took the Oath of Allegiance before the Hon. Osborn Sprigg in 1778 [Ref: O-306].
WILTBERGER, Charles. See "Benjamin Burch," q.v.
WILTBERGER, Verlinda. See "Benjamin Burch," q.v.
WINBURY, George. Private, Maryland Line, by Feb. 24, 1779 when paid for his services "in cloathing." [Ref: E-308].
WINSER, Luke. See "Samuel Queen Winser," q.v.
WINSER, Martha. See "Samuel Queen Winser," q.v.
WINSER, Samuel Queen (Oct. 26, 1759 -). Son of Luke and Martha Winser, of Prince George's Parish, Prince George's County [Ref: ZD-124]. "Samuel Queen Windsor" was a private in the Flying Camp in Montgomery County in October, 1776, and "Saml. Q. Winser" served in an artillery company stationed at Annapolis in December, 1776 [Ref: D-572, D-648].
WINSTEAD, William. Private, Capt. Hezekiah Wheeler's Company, 11th Militia Battalion, April, 1781 [Ref: L-19970 (Box 6, folder 21)]. Private, Select Militia, Capt. Hezekiah Wheeler's Company, July 14, 1781 [Ref: S-6636 (Box 31, folder 5)].
WINTERSON, Joseph. See "Stephen Steward," q.v.

WIRT, Jasper (1731-1795). Took the Oath of Allegiance before the Hon. Christopher Lowndes in 1778 [Ref: O-284, R-60]. The estate of Jasper Wirt was probated on Mar. 18, 1795 [Ref: ZE-205].
WISE, Sarah. See "Thomas Wise," q.v.
WISE, Thomas (1726-   ). Took the Oath of Allegiance before the Hon. William Berry in 1778 [Ref: O-259, R-27]. This could be the Thomas Wise who was a private in the 2nd Maryland Line from May 25, 1778 until Apr. 3, 1779, when he was discharged [Ref: D-175].
WISE, Thomas (1766-   ). On Aug. 23, 1781, Sarah Wise, of Prince George's County, petitioned the Council of Maryland "that Thomas Wise, her son who was draughted in the said county to serve as a soldier 'till the 10th day of Dec. next, is not of the age of sixteen years and therefore not liable to be draughted under the law. The Council ordered that since Thomas Wise was enrolled in the militia before he was of proper age he is therefore discharged from the said draught." Also, on Aug. 23, 1781, it was recorded by William Hyde that "Sarah Wise, of Prince George's County, came before me one of the Justices of Anne Arundel County and made Oath that her son Thomas Wise was born on the 15th day of Apr., 1766." [Ref: G-576, H-443, S-6636 (Box 31, folder 43]. He might be the Thomas Wise married who Milley Robinson by license dated Dec. 1, 1787, in Prince George's County [Ref: ZB-245].
WOLSTAD, Mary. See "Joshua Beall," q.v.
WOOD, Ann. See "Thomas Gantt, Jr." and "Burch Vermillion," q.v.
WOOD, Charles. Took the Oath of Allegiance (affirmed) before the Hon. Benjamin Hall in 1778 [Ref: O-275]. The estate of one Charles Wood was probated on Apr. 7, 1812 [Ref: ZE-205].
WOOD, Elisha. Took the Oath of Allegiance before the Hon. Thomas MacGill in 1778 [Ref: O-291].
WOOD, James (1736-   ). Took the Oath of Allegiance (made his "X" mark) before the Hon. Thomas Clagett in 1778 [Ref: O-265, R-57]. See "Leonard Wood," q.v.
WOOD, James. Private (substitute), continental service, 1780, and discharged from the Maryland Line in 1781 [Ref: D-382, D-413]. Private, Militia, and participated in capturing an enemy boat and crew on Apr. 17, 1781 [Ref: M-209].
WOOD, John (Sep. 13, 1733 -   ). Son of Thomas Wood and Mary Lashly [Ref: ZC-198]. Took the Oath of Allegiance before the Hon. Osborn Sprigg in 1778 [Ref: O-307]. See "John Wood," q.v.
WOOD, John. There were several men with this name who served in the Maryland Line [Ref: D-176, D-177, D-292, D-300]. One John Wood, probably from Prince George's County, was a private, 3rd Maryland Line, Capt. Horatio Clagett's Company, 1779 [Ref: D-295]. This or perhaps another John Wood was a private, 2nd Guard, Capt. Henry Hill's Militia Company, Lower Battalion; on duty at Nottingham on the

Patuxent, Apr. 12, 1781 [Ref: L-19970 (Box 6, folder 21)]. Additional research will be necessary before drawing conclusions.

WOOD, Joseph. Private, 6th Maryland Line, 1777, and reportedly "deserted" on Nov. 13, 1779 [Ref: D-257]. The estate of one Joseph Wood was probated on Mar. 31, 1792 [Ref: ZE-205].

WOOD, Leonard. "Leonard Wood" took the Oath of Allegiance before the Hon. Christopher Lowndes in 1778 [Ref: O-287]. "Leonard Armstrong Wood" was born on Jan. 13, 1754, son of James and Mary Wood, of King George's Parish in Prince George's County [Ref: ZC-83].

WOOD, Mary. See "Leonard Wood," q.v.

WOOD, Susanna. See "Allen Burrell," q.v.

WOOD, Thomas. Private (draft), Maryland Line, continental service. Discharged from the 2nd Maryland Line in 1781 [Ref: D-413, D-175, D-382]. Two men with this name took the Oath of Allegiance in 1778: one before the Hon. Osborn Sprigg and one before the Hon. Christopher Lowndes [Ref: O-287, O-307]. See "John Wood," q.v.

WOOD, Trecy. See "Basil Lowe," q.v.

WOODWARD, Abraham. Took the Oath of Allegiance before the Hon. James Beck in 1778 [Ref: O-253]. The estate of one Abraham Woodward was probated on Mar. 26, 1781 [Ref: ZE-206].

WOODWARD, Jesse. "Jesse Woodard" was a private, 1st Maryland Line, enlisted June 6, 1778, and discharged Apr. 5, 1779 [Ref: D-173]. "Jesse Woodyard" was paid for his services "in cloathing" on Apr. 17, 1779 [Ref: E-351]. It should be noted that a "Jessee Woodward" served fron Frederick County in July, 1776, and a "Jesse Woodward" served from Charles County in September, 1778 [Ref: D-43, D-331]. Additional research may be necessary before drawing conclusions.

WOODWARD, John. "John Woodward" was a private, 2nd Maryland Line, enlisted May 20, 1778 and was reported missing on Aug. 16, 1780 (at the Battle of Camden). [Ref: D-175]. The estate of one John Woodward was probated on Apr. 27, 1810 [Ref: ZE-206, which also spelled the name "Woodard"].

WOODWARD, Margaret. See "Thomas Woodward," q.v.

WOODWARD, Thomas (Feb. 10, 1731 - 1799). "Thomas Woodard" took the Oath of Allegiance (made his "T" mark) before the Hon. Alexander Howard Magruder in 1778 [Ref: O-293]. "Thomas Woodard" married Margaret (Waters) Ijams [Ref: X-3294]. The estate of one "Thomas Woodward" was probated by Oct. 3, 1799 (date of inventory) by Margaret Woodward [Ref: ZE-206].

WOOTTON, Mary. See "Robert Bowie" and "William T. Wootton," q.v.

WOOTTON, Richard. First Lieutenant, 25th Battalion, Militia, Capt. Joshua Selby's Company, Jan. 3, 1776; served in Annapolis [Ref: M-208, B-403, O-410]. First Lieutenant, Capt. Henderson Magruder's Company, until Sep. 25, 1776 (resigned). [Ref: M-140, B-299, O-410]. Rendered

patriotic service by providing wheat for the military on Aug. 3, 1780 [Ref: Q-306, which listed the name as "Richard Woolton"].
WOOTTON, Singleton (died 1788). Second Lieutenant, 25th Battalion, Jan. 3, 1776. First Lieutenant, May 1, 1778, Capt. Hezekiah Magruder's Company. Took the Oath of Allegiance before the Hon. James Beck in 1778 [Ref: O-253, M-140, E-62, N-34, ZA-703].
WOOTTON, Turner. See "William Turner Wootton," q.v.
WOOTTON, William Turner. Quartermaster, 25th Battalion, Jan. 13, 1776 [Ref: M-140]. Appointed to collect gold and silver in Prince George's County in February, 1776 [Ref: A-132]. This appears to be "Turner Wootton" who was prominent during the war and was the son of William Turner Wootton. After the war Turner was a member of the Maryland Legislature and married Mary Mackall Bowie in 1794. They had one child, William Turner Wootton, born in 1795. Mary Wootton died in 1796 [Ref: ZA-703]. The estate of "Turner Wootton" was probated in 1760, the estate of "William Turner Wootton" was probated in 1777, the estate of "Turner Wootton" was probated in 1797, and the estate of "William T. Wootton" was probated in 1850 [Ref: ZE-206].
WORLAND, Charles (1747-   ). Took the Oath of Allegiance before the Hon. Thomas Clagett in 1778 [Ref: O-268, R-79].
WORLAND, Henry. Took the Oath of Allegiance before the Hon. Thomas Clagett in 1778 [Ref: O-268].
WORLAND, John Roby. Took the Oath of Allegiance before the Hon. William Berry in 1778 [Ref: O-259]. "Robey Worland" was aged 48 in 1776 [Ref: R-41].
WORLAND, John Sr. (1720 - died before Feb., 1790). Took the Oath of Allegiance before the Hon. Thomas Clagett in 1778 [Ref: O-266, R-11]. John Worland married Mary Brady [Ref: X-3301].
WORNALD, Ann. See "Benjamin Tucker," q.v.
WORNALL, Robey. Took the Oath of Allegiance before the Hon. Thomas Clagett in 1778 [Ref: O-268].
WORTHINGTON, Christiana. See "John Magruder," q.v.
WORTHINGTON, Jane. See "Thomas Contee," q.v.
WORTHINGTON, Margaret. See "William Lamar," q.v.
WORTHINGTON, William (1747-1820). Patriot who delivered clothing to the 6th Maryland Regiment. He is buried in the family cemetery at "The Valley" in Naylor, Maryland [Ref: Y-614, citing Revolutionary Papers (Box 3, folder 12, no. 15) at the Maryland State Archives].
WRIGHT, Absalom. Private, 2nd Maryland Line, Capt. Alexander Truman's Company, 1782 [Ref: D-439].
WRIGHT, Basil (1764, Prince George's County, Maryland - Dec. 6, 1853, Jackson County, Virginia). "Bazzell or Bazzle Right" applied for a pension (S15966) in November, 1833, in Jackson County, Virginia, stating he was born in Prince George's County, Maryland and lived in Washington County, Maryland at the time of his enlistment. After the

345

war he lived in Wood County, Virginia and married Nancy Jones, daughter of John Jones, on Feb. 13, 1804. They raised 3 boys and 4 girls (names not given). Jesse Tanner and Samuel Hines were witnesses to Basil's application in 1833. James Tanner stated he knew the widow Nancy Wright for 43 years. Nancy Tanner stated she knew the widow Nancy Wright for 50 years. James and Nancy Tanner were both of Calhoun County, Virginia [Ref: P-2889, which noted that the "widow's application too dim to read on this microcopy, see National Archives Series M804, roll #2048"].

WRIGHT, Bozely. Private, 2nd Maryland Line, Capt. Patrick Sim's Company, 1776 [Ref: D-7].

WRIGHT, John. Captain, Militia, 1778 [Ref: N-33].

WRIGHT, Jonathan. Lieutenant, 25th Battalion, June 6, 1776 [Ref: M-140, A-553]. See "John Rogers," q.v.

WRIGHT, Josias. Private, Capt. Jesse Hellen's Militia Company, before May 23, 1782; on duty guarding Magruder's Warehouse in the spring of 1782 [Ref: L-19970 (Box 6, folder 21)].

WRIGHT, Mary. See "George Adams," q.v.

WRIGHT, Nancy. See "Basil Wright," q.v.

WRIGHT, Robert. Took the Oath of Allegiance (made his "X" mark) before the Hon. James Mullikin in 1778 [Ref: O-295].

WRIGHT, Samuel. There were several men with this name who served in the Maryland Line [Ref: D-179, D-259, D-377, D-448, D-561, D-616]. One Samuel Wright married Catherine Clemmens by license dated Jan. 9, 1786 [Ref: ZB-247]. The estate of one Samuel Wright was probated on Apr. 13, 1824 [Ref: ZE-207]. Additional research will be necessary before drawing conclusions.

WRIGHT, Solomon. Private, enrolled by Lt. John M. Burgess, Lower Battalion, on July 20, 1776, for continental service, Maryland Line [Ref: D-35, which spelled his name "Solomon Write"].

WRIGHT, Thomas. Private, Militia, 1776 [Ref: M-208, A-325, R-72]. There were two men named Thomas Wright in the 1776 census of Prince George's County: one was aged 43 and one was aged 34 [Ref: R-76]. The estate of one Thomas Wright was probated on Mar. 22, 1794 [Ref: ZE-207]. Additional research will be necessary before drawing conclusions.

WYGHT, John. See "John Wight," q.v.

WYGHT, Jonathan. See "Jonathan Wight," q.v.

WYGLE, Valentine. Took the Oath of Allegiance before the Hon. Christopher Lowndes in 1778 [Ref: O-283].

WYKALL, Adam. Private, 7th Maryland Line, July 2, 1777; discharged July 2, 1780 [Ref: D-257, which listed his name as "Adam Wykell, or Vycall"]. In March, 1833, the Treasurer of the Western Shore was directed to pay to Ann Martin, of Prince George's County, widow of the late Adam Wykall, or Wycall, during her widowhood, quarterly, half pay of a private, for the services rendered by her said deceased husband, during the Revolutionary War [Ref: O-411].

WYNN, Ann. See "John Wynn" and "Thomas Blacklock" and "Robert Ogden," q.v.

WYNN, Eleanor. See "George Alder," q.v.

WYNN, Hezekiah (Oct. 22, 1759 -   ). Son of John Wynn and Sarah Robey [Ref: ZC-83]. Took the Oath of Allegiance before the Hon. Thomas Clagett in 1778 [Ref: O-265]. Hezekiah Wynn married Rebecca M. Smallwood by license dated Jan. 12, 1779 [Ref: ZB-247].

WYNN, John (Jan. 27, 1720/1 - 1782). Son of John and Ann Wynn [Ref: ZC-83]. Took the Oath of Allegiance before the Hon. Thomas Clagett in 1778 [Ref: O-269, R-87]. The estate of John Wynn was probated on Nov. 27, 1781 by Hezekiah Wynn [Ref: ZE-207]. See "Hezekiah Wynn" and "George Alder" and "William S. Wynn," q.v.

WYNN, John Jr. (July 23, 1739 -   ). Son of John Wynn and Sarah Robey [Ref: ZC-83]. "John Wynn, Jr." took the Oath of Allegiance before the Hon. Thomas Clagett in 1778 [Ref: O-268, R-87]. "John Wynn" married Ann Smallwood by license dated Dec. 12, 1778 [Ref: ZB-247].

WYNN, Lucy. See "George Alder," q.v.

WYNN, Mary. See "Bayne Smallwood," q.v.

WYNN, Priscillah. See "George Alder," q.v.

WYNN, Sarah. See "Hezekiah Wynn" and "William Smallwood Wynn" and "George Alder," q.v.

WYNN, William (1752, Maryland - died before Nov. 5, 1823, Ohio). Took the Oath of Allegiance before the Hon. Thomas Clagett in 1778 [Ref: O-267, R-87, which spelled his name "William Winn"]. William Wynn married Milicent Smallwood by license dated May 20, 1779 [Ref: ZB-247, X-3261, which latter source states it was Ann Smallwood]. See "William Smallwood Wynn," q.v.

WYNN, William Smallwood (Aug. 9, 1757, Maryland - Feb. 7, 1828, Ohio). Son of John and Sarah Wynn [Ref: ZC-83]. Took the Oath of Allegiance before the Hon. Thomas Clagett in 1778 [Ref: O-265]. Private, enrolled by Ensign Horatio Clagett on July 15, 1776, for continental service, Maryland Line [Ref: D-35]. William Smallwood Wynn married Mildred Smallwood [Ref: X-3261, which stated he was born Aug. 9, 1751]. See "William Wynn," q.v.

WYVILL, Elinor. See "William Conner," q.v.

YATES, James T. Private, Capt. Alexander H. Magruder's Militia Company, Lower Battalion; on duty guarding Magruder's Warehouse in the spring of 1782 [Ref: L-19970 (Box 6, folder 21)].

YERLING, Thomas. Took the Oath of Allegiance before the Hon. Osborn Sprigg in 1778 [Ref: O-307, and the original list (very light and faded) at the Maryland State Archives (Box 4, folder 29)].

YOUNG, Ann. See "Notley Young," q.v.

YOUNG, Benjamin. See "Notley Young," q.v.

YOUNG, David. One David Young married Henrietta Smith by license dated Dec. 17, 1784, in Prince George's County [Ref: ZB-248]. There was also a David Young who was a matross in Capt. William Brown's Artillery Company from 1777 to 1782 [Ref: S-576, S-580]. Additional research may be necessary before drawing conclusions.

YOUNG, Eleanor. See "Leonard Townshend," q.v.

YOUNG, Elizabeth. See "Aquilla Wheeler," q.v.

YOUNG, Henrietta. See "Henry Waring," q.v.

YOUNG, Henry. There were several men with this name who served in the Maryland Line [Ref: D-18, D-52, D-259, D-324, D-475, D-510]. The estate of one Henry Young was probated in Prince George's County on May 5, 1794 [Ref: ZE-208].

YOUNG, Hezekiah (Feb. 28, 1763 -   ). A son of Thomas and Eleanor Young, he married Charity Joy Ford on Jan. 6, 1789 in King George's Parish [Ref: ZC-84]. Private, Select Militia, Capt. Hezekiah Wheeler's Company, July 14, 1781 [Ref: S-6636 (Box 31, folder 5)].

YOUNG, John. Private, enrolled by Capt. Alexander H. Magruder, 11th Battalion, on July 18, 1776, for continental service, Maryland Line [Ref: D-38]. The estate of one John Young was probated on Apr. 7, 1794 [Ref: ZE-208].

YOUNG, Jonathan. See "Thomas Young," q.v.

YOUNG, Joseph. Corporal, Select Militia, Capt. Hezekiah Wheeler's Company, July 14, 1781 [Ref: S-6636 (Box 31, folder 5)]. See "Thomas Young," q.v.

YOUNG, Mary. See "Notley Young," q.v.

YOUNG, Nicholas. See "Notley Young," q.v.

YOUNG, Notley (1738-1802). Son of Benjamin and Ann Young, he was baptized in Prince George's Parish on Sep. 24, 1738. Notley married (1) Jane Digges, and (2) Mary Carroll [Ref: ZD-124, ZA-618, although Source X-3329 states he married Ellenor Digges]. His children who lived to maturity were Rev. Notley Young, Nicholas Young, Benjamin Young, Mary Young, and Ann (Young) Casanave [Ref: ZA-619]. Notley was a Court Justice in 1777 and took the Oath of Allegiance before the Hon. George Lee in 1778 [Ref: C-273, O-279]. The estate of Notley Young was probated in Prince George's County on Apr. 9, 1802 [Ref: ZE-208].

YOUNG, Ruth. See "Benjamin Jones," q.v.

YOUNG, Samuel. Private, 2nd Maryland Line, Capt. Alexander Truman's Company, 1782; promoted to corporal on Apr. 1, 1782 [Ref: D-439].

YOUNG, Thomas. Took the Oath of Allegiance before the Hon. Thomas Clagett in 1778 [Ref: O-266]. There were at least three men named Thomas Young in King George's Parish: one was born on Jan. 2, 1720 (son of Jonathan Young), one was born on Jan. 10, 1722 (son of Joseph Young), and one was born in 1733 (aged 43 in 1776 census). [Ref: ZC-84, R-40]. One Thomas Young was a private in the 7th Maryland Line from June 4, 1777 until July, 1778 (transferred to invalids corps). [Ref: D-

259]. The estate of one Thomas Young was probated in Prince George's County on Jan. 9, 1812 [Ref: ZE-208]. Additional research will be necessary before drawing conclusions. See "Hezekiah Young," q.v.

YOUNG, William (1706-1779). Took the Oath of Allegiance (made his "Y" mark) before the Hon. Truman Skinner in 1778 [Ref: R-63, O-299, which spelled his name "Yung"]. The estate of one William Young was probated on Nov. 16, 1779 [Ref: ZE-209].

YOUNG, William. Took the Oath of Allegiance before the Hon. Joshua Beall in 1778 [Ref: O-251, R-63]. The estate of one William Young was probated on Feb. 21, 1792 [Ref: ZE-209].

www.ingramcontent.com/pod-product-compliance
Lightning Source LLC
Chambersburg PA
CBHW071953220426
43662CB00009B/1116